ukuzimisela качество инновация честность обязательство kwaliteit innova
promisso kvaliteta inovacija cjelovitost obaveza kvalita ... ost o
minen 质量 创新 诚实 守信 qualité innovation intégrité enga... tät inn
ég újítás sértetlenség elkötelezés kualitas inovasi integritas komitmen qual
in sungsil chaekim kualiti inovasi integriti komitmen جودة الابداع النزاهة التعهد
kvalitet nyhet pålitelighet forpliktelse jako innowacja integralno zobowizar
jament kvalitet inovacija celovitost obaveza איכות חידוש שלמות התחייבות
miso kvalitet nyskapande ärlighet åtagande kalite yenilik doğruluk taahh
ubuHle umKhuba nbuQotho ukuzimisela качество инновация честнос
lidade inovação integridade compromisso kvaliteta inovacija cjelovitost obave
udistus kokonaisuus sitoutuminen 质量 创新 诚实 守信 qualité innovation intégr
ितет ангажимент minöség újítás sértetlenség elkötelezés kualitas inovasi integ
yakusoku pumjil hyuksin sungsil chaekim kualiti inovasi integriti komitm
kvalitet nyhet pålitelighet forpliktelse jako innowacja integralno zobow
ajament 質量 創新 誠實 守信 kvalitet inovacija celovitost obaveza kakovost inov
dad compromiso kvalitet nyskapande ärlighet åtagande kalite yenilik doğrulu
kuzimisela якість иновация честність рішучість kwaliteit innovasie integrit
aliteta inovacija cjelovitost obaveza kvalita inovace celistvost odevzdání kvali
öség újítás sértetlenség elkötelezés kualitas inovasi integritas komitmen qua

quality innovation integrity commitment ubuHle umKhuba ubuQot
tegriteit verbintenis स्तरीयता नवीनता सत्यनिष्ठा प्रतिपद्ता qualidade inovação integridade
dání kvalitet nyhed hederlighed engagement laatu uudistus kokonaisuus sito
tion integrität verpflichtung качество иновация интегритет ангажимент m
novazione onestà impegno ryo-shitsu shinkijiku seijitsu yakusoku pumjil h
量 創新 誠實 守信 kwaliteit innovatie integriteit verplichting 품질 혁신 성실
ualidade inovação integridade compromisso calitate inovatie integritate
akovost inovacija neoporecnost obveza calidad innovación integridad com
ість іновація честність рішучість quality innovation integrity commitm
обязательство kwaliteit innovasie integriteit verbintenis स्तरीयता नवीनता सत्यनिष्ठा प्रतिपद्ता
alita inovace celistvost odevzdání kvalitet nyhed hederlighed engagement laa
gagement qualität innovation integrität verpflichtung качество иновация ин
s komitmen qualità innovazione onestà impegno ryo-shitsu shinkijiku seij
النوعية الابداع النزاهة الت kwaliteit innovatie integriteit verplichting 품질 혁신
ie qualidade inovação integridade compromisso calitate inovatie integritate
neoporecnost obveza איכות חידוש שלמות התחייבות calidad innovación in
ahhüt quality innovation integrity commitment ubuHle umKhuba ubuQot
rbintenis स्तरीयता नवीनता सत्यनिष्ठा प्रतिपद्ता qualidade inovação integridade compromiss
yhed hederlighed engagement качество иннования честность обязательств

"I will never put my name on any product that
does not have in it the best that is in me."

Genuine Value is dedicated to the thousands of John Deere employees, dealers, suppliers, customers, and investors worldwide—past, present, and future.

Genuine Value: The John Deere Journey
www.genuinevalue.com

Publisher: Deere & Company
Hans W. Becherer, Chairman
Robert W. Lane, Chief Executive Officer
Curtis G. Linke, Vice President, Corporate Communications

Editor and Creative Director: John Gerstner
Production Manager: Tim Beck

Designed by: McMillan Associates
130 Washington Street
West Dundee, Illinois 60118
www.mcmillandesign.com

Art Director: Michael McMillan
Designer: Megan Kearney
Production: Anne McMillan,
Jeanne Thomson, Janice Sewell
Internet Development: Lisa Page

Contributors:
Archivist: Dr. Leslie Stegh
Copy Editor: Don Huber
Timeline History: Gene Ritzinger
Timeline Products: Roy Harrington

Copyright © 2000
Deere & Company
One John Deere Place
Moline, Illinois 61265-8098
www.johndeere.com

First Edition: July 2000

Library of Congress Catalog Number: (LCCN) 00-104019
International Standard Book Number: (ISBN) 0-86691-276-2

Printing: Graphic Arts Center
Portland, Oregon USA
www.gacnw.com

Paper: International Paper

Photography Credits: Glenn Ashby, 275; Greg Baker, 164,
266, 269; Tom Balla, 11-18, 88, 120, 154, 185; Ogy Blazevic,
174; Frank Carter, 136; Jack Cherry, 146; Tom D'Aoust, 104;
Steve Dolan, 109; John Eagles, 80; Robert Edwards, 264;
Steve Eliason, 93, 170; Christine Epperly, 60; John Gerstner,
56, 125, 126, 128, 160, 176, 255, 257, 279, 283; Richard Harcourt,
268; Iowa State University photo services, 37; Mike Kline, 158;
Michael McMillan, 1, 62; John O'Meara, 40, 68; Edwin Morgar,
270; Mike Newell, 273; Terry Rasso, 34; Thierry Righeschi, 132;
John Riley, 9, 31, 48, 66, 152, 179; Michael Schemelin, 96;
Neal Slavin, 150, 258-263; Christopher Springmann, 180;
Rand Tapscott, 54, 82, 98; Dave Thurber, 26; Larry Volbruck,
dust jacket, 44, 46, 52, 74, 86, 102, 168, 267, 276; All other
photos supplied by John Deere Archives and Photo Lab.

This book greatly benefited from the generous assistance of numerous people worldwide over the many months of its development: Michael Addington, Annette Adler, Dr. Hissam Al-Deen, Vandana Aggarwal, Samuel Allen, Linda Almanza, Rodolfo Amozurrutia, David Anderson, Dave Anderson, Steven Anderson, Ernest Arku, Cheryl Ashcraft, Jim Badger, David Banfield, Kerri Bautista, Brent Bartels, Daniel Bernhard, Catherine Blackwell, Linda Blair, Jean-Claude Blot, James Bolin, Simone Bonde, David Bradford, Hans-Georg Brandes, Richard Brennan, Jessica Brink, Thomas Budan, Brian Burghgrave, William Burgweger, Judy Burkart, Wayne Burkart, Bill Burrows, Lyle Buss, John Bustle, Mark Caffee, Tim Caldwell, Cindy Calloway, Jean Campbell, Joel Carter, Jackie Caulkins, John Cerny, Yu An Chang, Richard Charleton, Conrad Chlumsky, Young Choi, Greg Clark, James Collins, Amy Cone, John Connolly, Thomas Cordes, William Crookes, Ann Cunningham, Alyssa Cutsinger, Linda Czupka, Allen Dannenfeldt, Oscar De Jesus, Maryluz De La Puente, Ed Deener, Tom DeMay, Marty Denicus, Gregory Derrick, Tim Deutsch, Virginia Devenney, Miquel Di Stefano, Johnny Dickinson, Dennis Docherty, Darrell Donis, Dean Dort, Douglas Schenk, Jim Doyle, Olivier Dumas, Jerry Duncan, Ken Edwards, Rebecca Ehlich, Vicki Eller, Wesley Eller, Darlene Ellis, Karen Ellis, Lant Elrod, David Everitt, Eileen Falcone, Kim Feuerbach, David Fischer, Federico Fitch, Mark Ford, Scott Ford, Dennis Francis, Franz Fruechtl, Jutta Fuchs, William Fulkerson, Karen Fuller, Donald Gallagher, John Gault, Charles Gause, Marlene Gavin, Dan Gerstner, Gerald Gerstner, Lloyd Gerstner, David Gibson, Joseph Gilbert, Brian Gilmore, David Gilmore, Shane Glover, Ken Golden, Becky Gould, George Graves, Ian Gray, Jeffrey Gredvig, Scott Greene, Chuck Greif, Jayne Grissom, Dan Griswold, Ralph Grotelueschen, Gunilla Gulam, Mike Gustafson, Betty Hagberg, Rick Hagland, Steven Hamm, Kelene Hanell, Elizabeth Hardcastle, Michael Harring, Wayne Haughton, Rick Haun, Tracey Hawk, Douglas Headley, Dieter Hecht, Don Henderson, Jean Claude Hiron, Siswanto Hendryk, Allen Henning, Klaus Hermann, Jeff Herrington, James Heseman, Allen Higley, Gina Hinrichs, Kathy Hockaday, Larry Hodel, Judith Hodgerson, Philip Hodgkinson, Dr. Klaus Hoehn, Kevin Hoehn, Siegfried Hofmann, Rollie Holoubek, Dennis Holderied, Dennis Holm, Ray Hornak, Mertroe Hornbuckle, Ursula Hornung, W.R. Hubbard Jr., Jay Huber, Lonnie Huitt, Dean Hungate, Ralph Hughes, Teresa Hunt, James Israel, Bill Jacobs, J. Jeksrud, Brandon Jens, Richard Jinks, John Tse, Anne Johnson, Christine Johnson, Dale Johnson, Don Johnston, Ross Johnstone, Nate Jones, Tommy Jones, Judy Jordan, George Kalemkarian, Shari Kaplan-Thomas, Muffin Kearney, Brad Keleher, Luann Kellums, Karl Kessler, Smokey Kim, Richard Kintigh, Kim Kirschbaum, Merv Kizlyk, Dick Kleine, Michael L. Kline, Mac Klingler, Helmut Korthoeber, Ida Kramer, John Kubik, Atilla Kuecuek, David Kuhn, Hans Kunze, Dontcho Kutchoukov, John Lagemann, Deb Lamphier, Sally Lang, Phil Larsen, Lawrence Tractor Company, John Lawson, Tammy Lee, Preston J. LeMaire Jr., Mary Leonard, Katarzyna Lewicka, Lisa Li, Leong Kong Liew, Jim Lind, Jim Litton, Chris Litton, Alice Lopez, Fernando Lopez, Alvin Ma, Ed Mabry, Craig Mack, Murray Madsen, Don Macmillan, Timothy Mahan, Paul Mallon, Don Margenthaler, H.J. Markley, Wilson Mccallister, Daniel McGinn, Paul McGregor, Dean McKee, Mark McMillan, James Meenagh, David Meier, Bill Menconi, Jaime Menin, Sandy Menke, Thomas Meyer, Barbara Mickelsen, Michael Mihm, Bjarne Mikkelsen, Alton Miller, Georgia Miller, Denise Mills, James Mitchell, Steve Mitchell, Hal Moon, Mark Moore, Jack Moore, Heather Moritz, Arlindo Moura, Carol Murphy, Deborah Murphy, Susan Murphy, Lauren Murzinski, Thomas W. Myers, Christine Nagler, Noah Naidoo, Gabriele Namet, Alan Nelson, Barry Nelson, Debbie Nelson, Kathy Nelson, Randall Nelson, Dr. Oliver Neumann, Linda Newborn, Roberta Newsom, Kirk Ney, Dan Niebuhr, David Niederkorn, Nathan Nobbe, Sergio Nocedal, David O'Brien, Zack O'Brien, Steve O'Connor, Tim O'Connor, Sean O'Hanlon, Connie O'Hern, Brendan O'Mara, Teri Olson, Yvonne Ousley, Ross Patty, Lyn Paris, Callie Parrish, Dale Paschke, Robert Petersen, Clair Peterson, Joy Peterson, Ron Pettit, James Phelan, Robert Pickering, Terence Pickett, Diana Polk, Tim Polley, Bernard Poore, Alice Popescu-Gatlan, James Porter, Robert W. Porter, Terry Porter, Charles Postma, Jay Preszler, Stephen Pullin, Madhavi Pushpala, Gabriela Ragan, Lakhdar Rebahi, James Reep, Susan Reimensnyder, Ralph Reynolds, Donna Rich, Norman Riek, James Riley, John Riley, Maria Rinaldo, Patti Rippel, James Robertson, Reno Rodeghiero, John Roehrs, Theresa Rosenberg, Michael Rubino, Chuck Rubovits, Federico Ruck, Ursula Rüegsegger, Gerald Russmann, Rizwan Saeed, Carlos Salaber, Susan Salas, Cheryl Salley, Rick Saltsman, Rowan Sanderson, Gerald Saylor, Michael Scaletta, Karen Schebler, Michael Schemelin, Eugene Schick, Adrian Schuerch, Thomas Schwartz, Robert Schwieder, Jack Shallberg, Mel Short, Kim Sievers, Renata Siqueira, Haribabu Sirandas, Hendryk Siswanto, Tom Sizemore, Geoff Slade, Barrie Smith, Holly Smith, Penney Smith, Robert Smith, Wayne Smith, George Sollenberger, Olga Sparks, Deborah Stahler, Robert Stamm, Charlie Stamp, Sonja Sterling, Carol Strandlund, Erika Stranich, Anita Strickland, Mark Stroh, Susan Strub, Craig Sutton, Alan Svoboda, Nancy Swanson, Paul Swanson, Veijo Talarmo, Rand Tapscott, Byron Taylor, Christine Temperley, Renee Templet, Les Teplicky, Jacques Thiry, Rick Thompson, Frederick Thorne, Peg Tipton, Gordon Tjelmeland, Jane Tomesch, Arturo Towns, Robert Tracinski, Kathy Truster, Michael Turley, James Van Acker, Gerald Van Ravenswaay, Annette VanRycke, Angeles Villarreal, Jon Volkert, Uwe von Dolspen, Marie Von Heyl, Markwart Von Pentz, Russell Walker, Sara Wallarab, Steve Warren, Tia Watson, Will Wells, Ron Weydert, Kathy Wiegel, Mason Williams, Peter Williams, Craig Wilson, Linda Wilson, Chris Windeknecht, Tony Wise, Tom Withers, Fred Wolf, Steve Woodyard, Gene Wright, Bernd Wyrwoll, Bill Yeager, Bill York, Dave Zable, Laurie Zelnio, Ernesto Zenobi, Renate Zerngast. Wedding Photo Contributors, page 184: Wade and Lisa Bonnett, Killam, Alberta, Canada; Richard and Marian Charleton, Northumberland, England; Leslie and Jeanette Clugston, Orrstown, Pennsylvania, *King's Photography;* Mark and Sandy Dean, Sikeston, Missouri, *Tim Ludwig, Photographer;* Mark and Ann Marie Farrugia, Brownstown, Michigan; Jeffrey and Bretta Geiger, Waterloo, Iowa, *Marilyn Johnson Photography;* Robert and Kristan Hoffman, Jacksonville, Illinois; Chris and Peta Loughridge, Loch, Victoria, Australia; Markus Peter and Andrea Peter-Beck, S. Antonino, Switzerland; Paul Sinclair and Barbra Westermark, Airdrie, Alberta, Canada; Shannon and Betsy Stephens, Ravenswood, West Virginia; Frank and Klaziena Venema, Sint Johannisga, Netherlands.

Table of Contents

Genuine Value: The John Deere Journey starts with a glimpse into the life and times of the company's founder. The first four chapters focus on the values (Quality, Innovation, Integrity, Commitment) that John Deere exhibited, and remain the core values of the company today. The Timeline is a condensed history of key events and products. The People section lists current employees and retirees. The Appendix is a compendium of general information about the company.

genuine value

With the dawn of a new century and, indeed, a new millennium, it appears appropriate to pause and take stock of what has distinguished this great company throughout its 164-year history. When assessing the real bottom-line success of the company, the inescapable conclusion is that without a foundation of strong, basic values, any success would have been fleeting and would never have endured. ■ John Deere's amazing longevity and prosperity can be largely attributed to four hallowed values that were exhibited by our founder and have been long adopted by this company's employees. These four basic values are Quality, Innovation, Integrity, and Commitment. ■ At a time when basic values, or the lack thereof, are often the focal point of events on the world scene, we at John Deere believe it is important to reflect upon these core values that have

brought us through the past century and a half. Our future success hinges on how well we keep these values alive in the new millennium. ■ *Genuine Value* is the John Deere vision describing our dedication to doing things right and doing the right things for all our constituents. These include customers, dealers, employees, investors, suppliers, and the communities in which we operate around the world. *Genuine Value* encompasses the simple premise of mutual advantage. We win only if all of our constituents win. Although our core values were honed in our agricultural past, they have been the foundation of our success in each of the related businesses that have been spawned over time from our agricultural equipment origins. Based on a solid foundation of shared values, we are able to energize the adoption of operational excellence and the use of common systems, processes, and services across our varied businesses to ensure that we are greater than the sum of our parts. This creates trust and enthusiasm among all our constituents and thus delivers our promise of Genuine Value. ■ This book is all about the heritage of John Deere, but it is not a definitive history. Other great books have been written covering our history in detail. *Genuine Value: The John Deere Journey* is a collection of photos and writings that try to capture the essence of Deere & Company in terms of its values. We hope this book will serve as a source of inspiration to all who are touched by John Deere.

Hans W. Becherer, Chairman

The John Deere Story: A fictional memoir based on historical facts as interpreted by John Gerstner ————————

My Life & Times

A Fictional Memoir

IT IS SURELY A WORTHWHILE ENDEAVOR

for every human being to reflect on the meaning of

his or her life. I will attempt to do this here, although

I feel there is not much to tell. I was blessed with a

full life. I took much pleasure in simple things…

family, friends, food, laughter. I tried to live by the

golden rule. I took great pride and reward

in my work. I was a blacksmith.

I was born February 7, 1804, the third son of five children. My father, William Rinold Deere, was a tailor. My mother, Sarah Yates Deere, worked alongside him as a seamstress. Her father was a Revolutionary War soldier.

I barely remember my father. When I was eight, he set sail for England to claim a family inheritance, but sadly we never heard from him again. He wrote a letter and gave it to my older brother, William, before he left. We kept it in the bottom drawer of my father's pine desk. From time to time we would take it out and read it aloud. His words were always a lesson and comfort to us children, although they must have pained my mother because she usually left the room.

"My Dear child as I am to be absent from you many months I wish you to attend to a few kinds of instruction from one who has your welfare at heart. Be faithful to your master and to his interests, be obedient to him & Mrs. Warren, be friendly and kind to all the family. Let truth & honesty be your guide & on no pretense deviate from it, be dutiful to your mother, kind to your sister & brothers, have the fear of God before you; implore his protection & you will obtain it and likewise the good will of all mankind. May God bless you & all the family will be the constant prayer of your father & friend, W R Deere."

An early portrait of me

I remember doing all the things children did in those times, but I was no more mischievous than others. It does not befit any man to boast, but I never got into any serious trouble all through my growing up years.

I believe I can rightfully claim to being a naturally industrious child. When I was 15, without my mother's knowledge, I gained employment after day school with a tanner in our town of Middlebury, Vermont. I earned a pair of shoes and a suit of clothes. When I presented these to my mother, she smiled, but didn't have too much to say. I believe she was afraid I would leave school and not attend Middlebury College, which she had chosen for me to attend.

I did attend for a brief time, but I could see how my mother was struggling to sustain our household, and I found my interests were not in the classroom. At age 17, I signed on as an apprentice with Captain Benjamin Lawrence of Middlebury, one of the town's most prosperous blacksmiths. I had often watched him working over the forge, and I could see how important his work was to the community. He did everything from shoeing horses to repairing stagecoaches to forging farming tools. My wages were $30 for the first year; and $35, $40 and $45, respectively, for succeeding years.

After this apprenticeship in 1825, I went to work for two local blacksmiths "ironing" wagons, stagecoaches and buggies for $15 per month. The next year my mother died, and the year after that I took a bride...my school sweetheart, Damarius Lamb. We first moved to Colchester Falls (now Winooski), where Col. Ozias Buel commissioned me to do all the ironwork for the new sawmill and linseed-oil mills he was building.

Next stop was Vergennes, north of Middlebury, where I worked for a time with John McVene, a local blacksmith. Then we moved to Salisbury, where our son Francis Albert was born. Two years later, despite small resources, I purchased some land and built my first blacksmith shop at the crossroads of the main stagecoach line that started in Vergennes and ran to Boston and New York.

Things did not go smoothly. No sooner did I erect the little shop than it caught fire and burned to the ground. I rebuilt, only to have it also soon destroyed by fire. Now I was deeply in debt and was forced to sell the property only three months after I bought it.

After the birth of our second child, Jeannette, I sought and found work in Royalton, Vermont, repairing wagons and buggies. In 1832, we had another daughter, Ellen Sarah.

Still searching for better pay, our family moved again in 1833 to Hancock, Vermont. Although still in debt, I managed to borrow enough money from Dr. Josiah Brooks to buy a piece of land where I built my third blacksmith shop. Here, I made and sold tools such as shovels and hay forks. I took great pride in my work and was very meticulous and always looked for ways to improve. I started

A view of Grand Detour when I arrived

grinding and polishing the tines of the forks I fashioned, which made them slip in and out of the hay like needles. My shovels and hoes were also like no others that could be bought, and therefore were in steady demand.

But despite my perseverance and duty toward the tasks at hand, the United States was at the beginning of a national economic downturn that would eventually become known as the "Panic of 1837." It hit the New England agricultural economy especially hard by 1836. My business suffered as most farmers were so hard-pressed they did their own blacksmith work. When they did hire a smithy like me, they often paid with bartered goods rather than cash. Or they would postpone payment, and I was not one to pressure my debtors.

All along, I had been hearing about the abundance of opportunities in the West. My friend, Leonard Andrus, who was my employer in Royalton, had migrated to a place called Grand Detour, Illinois. He had told me on his last trip home that there was little manufacturing done in the county, but still a capable mechanic would have a fair field open for his enterprise. As winter approached in 1836, I could see no future in Vermont. I packed up a few things and kissed my wife and family farewell. I was bound for Illinois.

I can't begin to tell you how I felt that cold, gloomy November day in 1836 when I landed in Grand Detour, Illinois. Worn, I guess, is the best word to use. But excited, too.

I was very tired from the six-week stage and canal ride that delivered me to this little village that seemed so far from my roots back in Vermont. And I was homesick for my wife, Demarius, six months pregnant with son Charles, and the rest of our young family…eight-year-old Francis, six-year-old Jeannette, four-year-old Ellen, and two-year-old Frances.

I was also sick that I had to leave my family with only the barest means to exist. Although I worked very hard, I was seeing no better times ahead. I had no choice but to try my fortunes elsewhere. Grand Detour seemed as good as any place to start over.

I arrived in Grand Detour with just a few of my best blacksmith tools, a few household items and $73.73 in my pocket. But I was 32 years of age, strong of body, and determined to be the best at my trade. God willing, Grand Detour was where I would turn my family's fortunes for the better. Or so I prayed.

I remember some of the first evenings after I arrived; I would walk to a little bluff where I could look out over the great prairie sea that I had heard so much about back East. The sight made me think of the ocean I saw on a trip to Boston as a child, except people had huge ships to cross the sea. Even the tallest horses had great trouble getting through the sea of tall grass prairie. I heard more than one pioneer talk about the grass being so high it would go up over a horse's back with enough to spare you could tie a big knot.

My house in Grand Detour

My attention was more on the farming aspects of the prairie. From the first day I arrived, farmers told me stories of how they would "lose their religion" trying to plow the rich black gumbo prairie soil that laid so plentiful all over the Midwestern United States. The land was rich and fertile, but the task of plowing it was terrible.

The problem was that the wet gumbo soil would not slide off of the plows that the settlers brought with them from the East. They had to carry paddles with them and stop every few yards to scrape off the sticky dirt, which, after a few hours, made for some very grumpy farmers.

My first plow being demonstrated on the Crandall farm

I was too busy with work in my new blacksmith shop to give this plow problem much care. My workday would start at 5 in the morning. I would work on the broken chains and clevises, and wornout wagon tongues and odd jobs until as late as 10 at night. I could never seem to complete it all, but I was happy to be so busy, as it perfectly suited my temperament. I could never stand for idleness.

Then, one memorable day I was called to fix a pitman shaft at the sawmill owned by Mr. Andrus, who was one of the original settlers of Grand Detour. As I was walking through the mill, my eyes were struck by the sun reflecting across the polished steel of a broken saw blade. Mill saw blades, I should tell you, were about a foot wide and eight feet long with huge teeth on one side. Somehow it came to mind that this polished steel might hold an answer to the problem of wet gumbo dirt sticking to a plow moldboard.

I dwelled on this idea much of that night. The following morning I put aside some of my mechanic jobs to cut and shape a plow moldboard out of the shiny steel saw blade. I cut the teeth off with a hand chisel, and cut the moldboard and share with the help of a chisel, striker and sledge. I spent a long time trying to figure out the shape and curve of the moldboard. I wanted to arrive at the exact contour that would let the soil slide off the share without sticking. I then laid them on the fire of the forge and heated them and shaped them as best as I could with a wooden hammer so as to leave the steel smooth.

I must tell you, I thoroughly enjoyed this endeavor as it tested all my skills as a blacksmith. I heated the steel to a cherry red before shaping it into the desired form with the blows of a sizeable hammer.

I shaped the beam out of a log using an ax and draw-knife. I used the crooks of tree roots for handles. I finally succeeded in constructing a very rough plow, which I then took to Lewis Crandall, who farmed just across the Rock River. His land was on the Rock River bottom and therefore was the kind of sticky gumbo to give my plow a perfect test.

We hitched up the plow to his team, and I plowed a long, straight furrow. The plow scoured beautifully. Crandall immediately paid me for the plow, and ordered two more just like it. I was filled with pride and joy. My life was never the same after that day. 🐾

It started in 1837,

with one man's vision, rooted in the earth.

The journey continues

with the same values John Deere lived by...

Quality.

Innovation, Integrity, and Commitment.

"Since the company's early days, John Deere has been guided by quality of product and quality of relationships with customers, dealers, suppliers, and the public." —William A. Hewitt, CEO 1955–1982

JOHN DEERE

Advertised as being faster, smarter, and more comfortable than previous models, the 8000 TEN Series Tractors (and the rubber-track 8000T TENS) have the technology and leading-edge features to keep customers at the peak of productivity well into the new millennium. A new Implement Management System (IMS) allows control of up to 12 separate tractor functions at the single push of a button, greatly reducing operator fatigue and error. Another new feature, the Automatic PowerShift with its unique control system, optimizes speeds in varying conditions for maximum productivity.

Quality transcends beauty

Craftsmanship

s the humble pursuit of perfection, no matter what day it is

Dedication in work clothes…a workman at the John Deere Spreader Works in Moline, Illinois, circa 1917, painstakingly fashions wheels out of wood. The wheels were used on military ambulances the factory built under a World War I government contract.

Quality
is passion on the stage of
excellence

Machine parts—such as this big, brawny bucket-cylinder pin on a loader built in Davenport, Iowa—must meet finite tolerances before leaving any John Deere factory

anywhere in the world. John Deere uses the Baldrige Quality Award as the company's criteria for business excellence, and many John Deere units have been recognized

with state or national quality awards. These include sales branches in Dallas, Texas; Minneapolis, Minnesota; and Milan, Italy (customer satisfaction award);

and factories in Davenport, Iowa; Horicon, Wisconsin; Grimsby, Ontario; and Monterrey, Mexico. The Davenport, Iowa, factory, along with 21 other John Deere

factories worldwide, has earned the ISO 9000 quality registration.

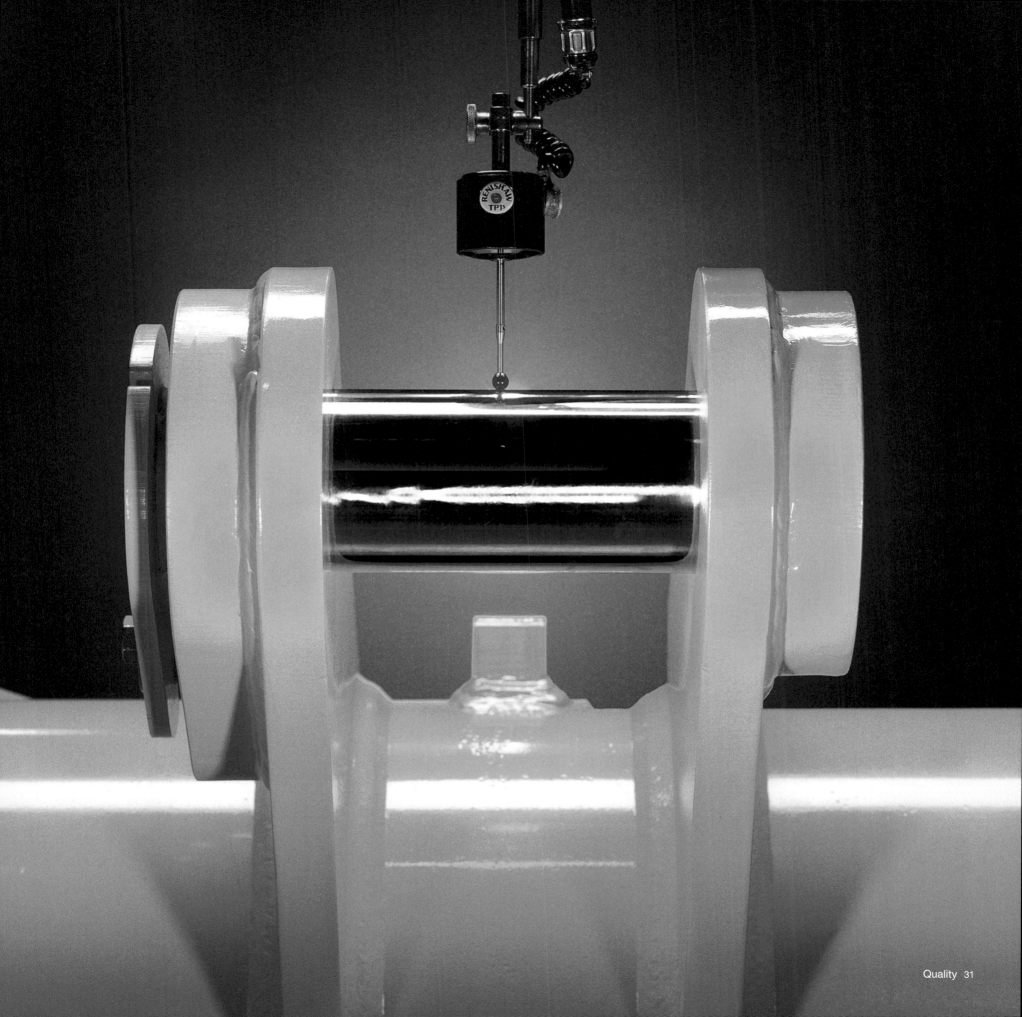

Plain and simple, dependability means delivering what you promise

The 20-drawbar-horsepower 420 Tractor built in Dubuque, Iowa, in 1955 featured such innovations as Touch-O-Matic hydraulics and push-button starting. With a 2-row rear-mounted cultivator, a determined farmer could cultivate about 20 acres of corn in a day. This compares with more than 160 acres per day with the current large 16-row cultivator— one of the reasons farm mechanization was named one of the 20th century's greatest engineering achievements by the National Academy of Engineering.

Consistency of excellence must become a habit

A row of nearly identical 40,000-pound John Deere 690C Excavators awaits final inspection before shipment to customers from the Davenport, Iowa, factory in 1980. The factory makes a wide range of construction and forestry equipment. Today's flexible manufacturing techniques and a new order-fulfillment process allow customers to place an order for a machine and have it delivered in as few as 20 working days.

QUALITY-VISUALIZED

John Deere engineers put virtual machines through real tests at Iowa State University's Virtual Reality (VR) Lab, the largest VR module in the world—funded in part by John Deere. Virtual reality allows product designers and engineers to evaluate new concepts before any prototypes are built.

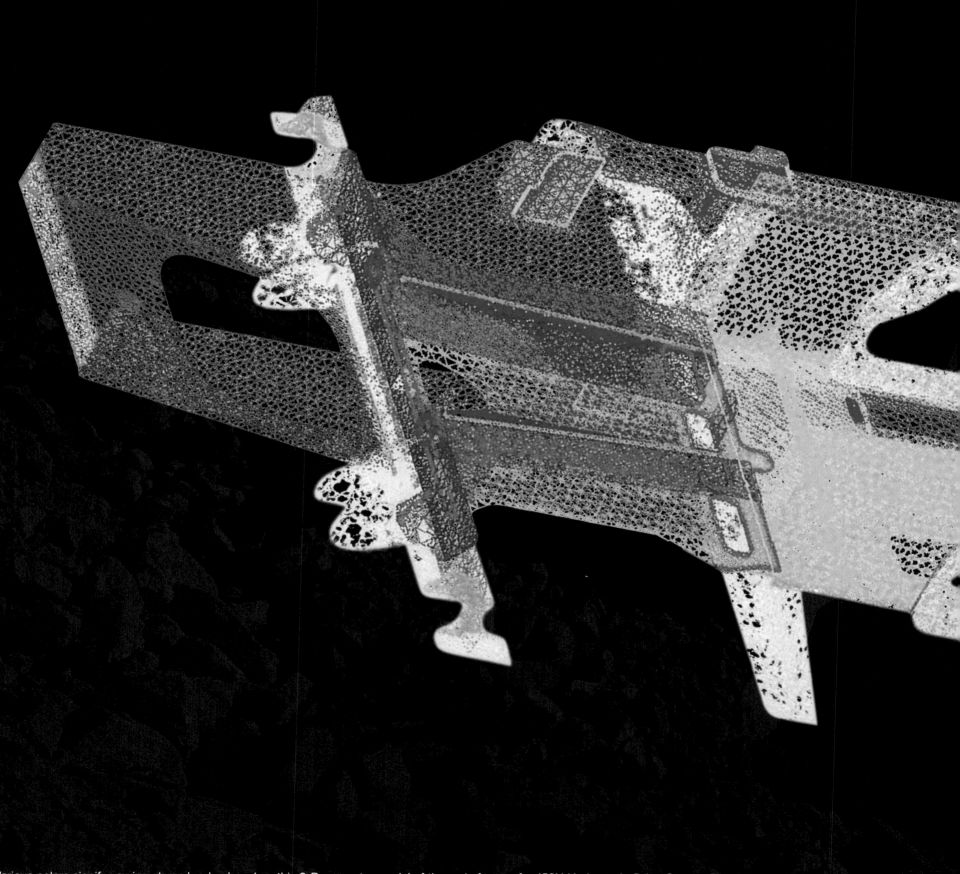

Various colors signify varying stress levels placed on this 3-D computer model of the main frame of a 450H Hydrostatic-Drive Crawler Dozer built at John Deere's Dubuque, Iowa, factory. Using computer-accelerated testing and finite-element modeling, design engineers can compress five to 10 years of customer usage into a week or two of test simulation.

The spirit of quality is sustained in the tiniest details

Business is a team sport

→ 32A → 33 → 33A

Dedicated teams like these, photographed in 1983, swiftly assemble John Deere lawn and garden tractors in Horicon, Wisconsin. The factory has a distinguished record for being a leader in innovative quality manufacturing techniques, and for building lawn tractors having the highest trade-in value. Formerly a grain drill factory, the Horicon facility started building consumer products in 1962. It manufactured its 3 millionth tractor in 1998, an LT133 Lawn Tractor.

The flexibility of the wide front end of a 3020 Tractor is demonstrated for a 1965 advertisement. Flexibility was an advantage to farmers because it provided a more stable tractor with a better ride when crossing uneven terrain. The 3020 and 4020 Tractors featured a host of operator-comfort features, including power steering, power brakes, suspended posture seat, and optional Power Shift transmission. Power Shift allowed shifting through all forward and reverse gears with just a single lever, and without clutching.

Flexibility flattens the most uneven playing fields

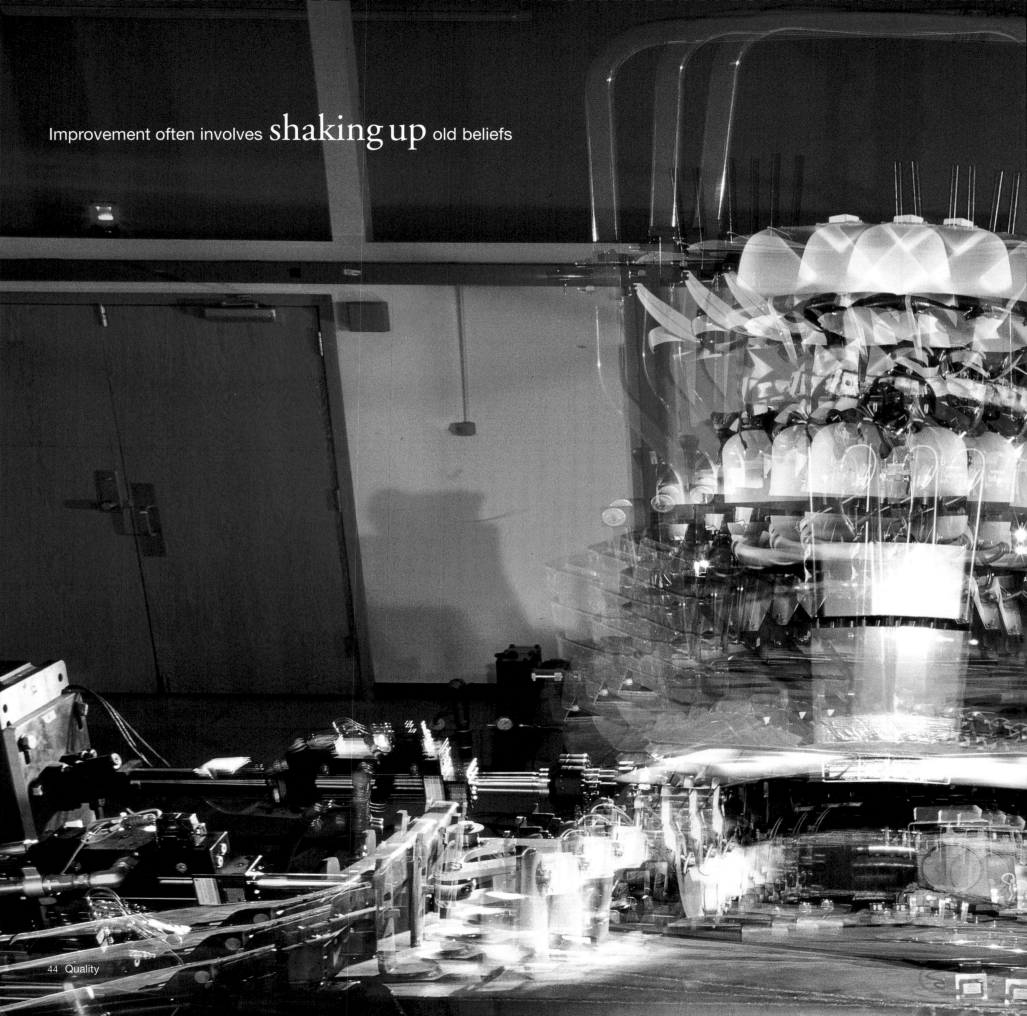

Improvement often involves **shaking up** old beliefs

Machines shake, rattle, and roll in John Deere's Accelerated Design Verification Laboratory at Moline, Illinois. Equipment such as this prototype mower is put under extreme stress, intentionally accelerated to simulate experience in the field. In just 300 to 400 hours, a piece of equipment can be subjected to all the significant load cycles encountered in 10 years of use in the field.

Leadership requires both push and pull

When ground gets hard and soil packs down, you need a tool to open it up so air, water, and nutrients can penetrate down to the turf's root zone. That's what the Aercore® 800 Walk-Behind Aerator does. It is used primarily on golf courses, but has applications for athletic turf fields and even home lawns. Fun fact: the Aercore 800 can punch as many as 582,400 high-quality holes per hour.

The Haras Rosa Negra hay and cattle farm near San Justo, Argentina, has depended on John Deere equipment and good dealer support for the entire 31 years the family farm has been in existence. Elso Antonio Ferrero, owner, became doubly interested in John Deere products and service when he bought Agronorte SRL, the John Deere dealership in San Justo in 1973. "In Argentina, John Deere is the Mercedes of farm equipment," he says. The 535 Round

Quality is valued everywhere in the world

Nationalistic pride swelled at John Deere's U.S. facilities during World Wars I and II. This employee was helping assemble the tail wheel for a P-47 fighter plane in 1942. Eleven John Deere factories had a hand in assembling 2,190 MG-1 military tractors. The company also had contracts to produce ammunition and mobile laundry units. By the end of World War II, about 4,500 employees— almost one-third of the workforce—had entered military service. There was even a John Deere ordnance battalion with 700 employee enlistees who spent 28 months in the European theater.

Pride gives work meaning

Winners stay on the *cutting edge*

John Deere has all the equipment needed to manicure any golf course. This 2500 Tri-Plex Greens Mower, photographed at Governors Club, Chapel Hill, North Carolina, is a regular on championship courses where durability, quality cutting, and amazing precision are required. The state-of-the-art 2500 Mower has an onboard self-diagnostic system and can clip a tournament green uniformly at a height of less than one-eighth inch…equal to the height of two quarters lying flat.

Success can often be found

The Human Factors Laboratory at the John Deere Technical Center in Moline, Illinois, has been shaking up preconceived notions about the human-machine interface since it was built in 1981. The "ride" of nearly any John Deere vehicle can be duplicated in the controlled laboratory environment—the farm, construction, and lawn-care

where others have not looked

industry's first. Six hydraulic cylinders can move the simulator in six directions simultaneously with enough force to make a seat belt not only recommended, but required. Audiovisual equipment adds a dynamic visual scene that lets the operator realistically perform tasks such as operating a bulldozer or harvesting a field of corn.

John Deere dealers worldwide are known for taking a keen interest in their customers. Here, on his way to deliver a new tractor in 1980, an employee of the Manuel Carrasco dealership in Campillos, Spain, stops to chat with a local sheep farmer. John Deere's operations in Spain date back to 1956.

Caring makes all the difference

Failure can be a step to success

The "Tractivator" built in 1916 is a classic example of an experimental design that missed the market but led to the development of something

of lasting importance. Twenty-five John Deere 1-row "motor cultivators" were built and sent to John Deere branches in the Midwest during 1917.

The 1-row machine received little customer interest, so another 12 months were spent modifying it into a more-efficient 2-row cultivator.

The project was finally abandoned due to a sudden and disastrous downturn in the farm economy. These early "Tractivators," however,

led to the development in the 1920s of general-purpose tricycle-type tractors, which continued to be widely popular into the mid-1960s.

There is no linear path to quality

Digital-visualization software allows John Deere engineers to design and build higher-quality products for less money. This 3-D wire-frame view of a 650H Crawler Dozer gave John Deere product engineers at Dubuque, Iowa, the great advantage of being able to evaluate service and repairability features before production started in 1999. The same digital mockup allowed manufacturing engineers to avoid any potential assembly problems, and gave dealership technicians a head start on service training.

Well-made products produce fond memories

The venerable John Deere 2-cylinder tractors that were built from 1923 to 1960 populated thousands of farms and still have a legion of fans worldwide. Affectionately named "Johnny Poppers" or "Popping Johnnies" for their distinguishable engine exhaust sound, these simple-to-repair tractors are prized by collectors. They are a common fixture at the hundreds of antique farm-machinery shows, auctions, and "swap meets" held each year. John Deere collectors have the distinct advantage of being able to purchase used

Innov

ation

"We have got to change and make an improvement or somebody else will beat us, and we will lose our trade."—John Deere, Founder, 1837

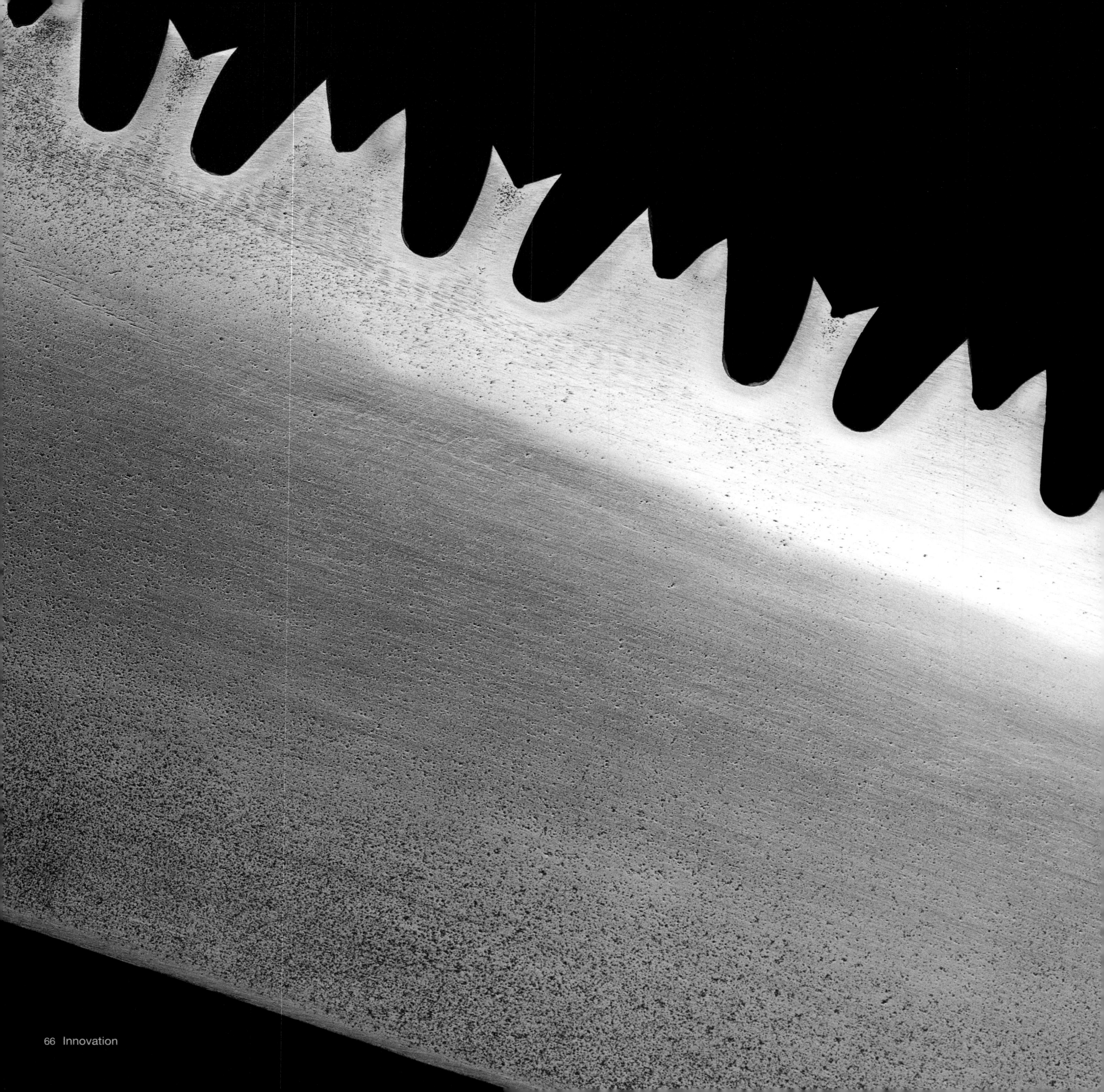

Innovation reflects beyond possibilities

The glint of sun on a discarded sawmill blade caught John Deere's eye in 1837. It was a defining moment, as it struck him that polished steel might hold an answer to the problem plaguing Midwestern farmers of wet gumbo soil sticking to their plows. The next day he fabricated a crude plow with a moldboard made from the polished sawmill blade (determined to be a reciprocating rather then a circular blade by a 1959 Smithsonian Institution study). The resulting self-scouring steel plow became one of the key innovations that sparked modern agriculture, and made settling the Midwest and the territory west of the Mississippi River possible.

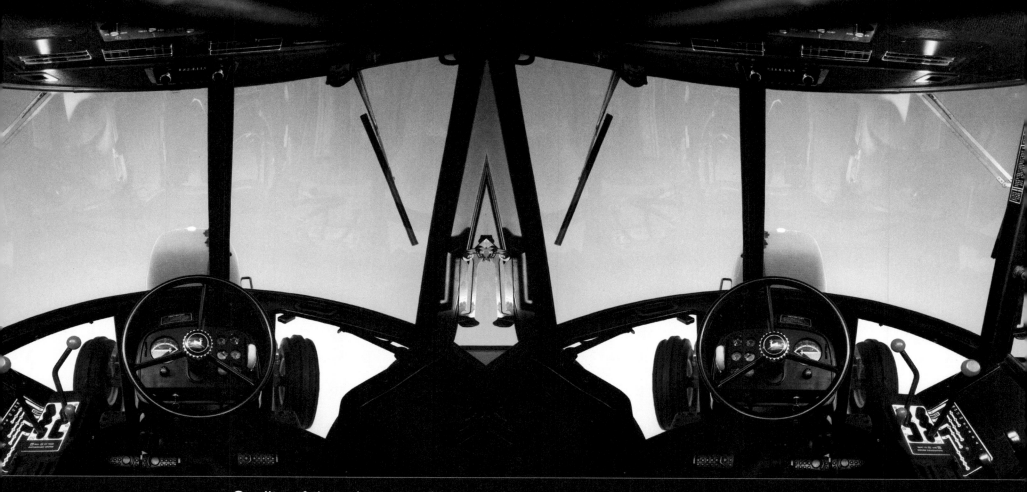

Quality of thought expands

HORIZONS

Too revolutionary to simply be called a tractor cab, the operator station introduced on John Deere tractors in 1972 was given the name "Sound-Gard.®" The Sound-Gard body combined the features needed for rapid adoption of cabs: attractive styling, easy entry, excellent visibility in all directions, noise reduction, good ride, and year-round temperature control. Almost overnight, the rest of the industry had to rethink how a tractor should look and feel to drive. The Sound-Gard body also featured emergency flashers and rollover protection, a safety innovation first offered on John Deere tractors in 1966..

Progress depends on how fast we can let go of the past

Prior to 1900, most engineering and manufacturing ideas at John Deere would have been sketched with chalk on the shop floor and then tried in steel and wood. By the 1940s, all John Deere factories had rows of drafting tables where engineers hand-figured calculations before making to-scale layouts and drawings of their latest ideas. Today, computer-aided design stations allow testing of new concepts before any metal is bent.

Imagination takes wing in cultivated minds

Perhaps the most-streamlined tractor John Deere ever built was the 3010 Grove and Orchard Tractor introduced in 1961 (shown with a 10-foot offset disk). The styling of the rear-wheel fenders was not for aerodynamic reasons but to minimize breakage of tree limbs when passing through orchard rows. The 4-cylinder 59-PTO horsepower 3010 was ideal for medium-sized farms. The 3010 Grove and Orchard Tractor has now become a highly prized collectible.

We can only achieve what we can imagine

The secret of how a cotton picker picks cotton is in the tiny, barbed spindles. There are 560 hard-chrome-plated spindles in each row unit, or 3,360 on John Deere's newest 6-row picker. Spinning at high speeds, the spindles remove cotton from the boll. For 40 years, John Deere has set the pace in cotton-harvesting innovation. John Deere was first with a 4-row machine in 1981, and first with 5-row narrow and wide models in 1990. In 1997, John Deere introduced the first production 6-row machine—the widely acclaimed 9976 Cotton Picker, capable of picking 75 acres a day.

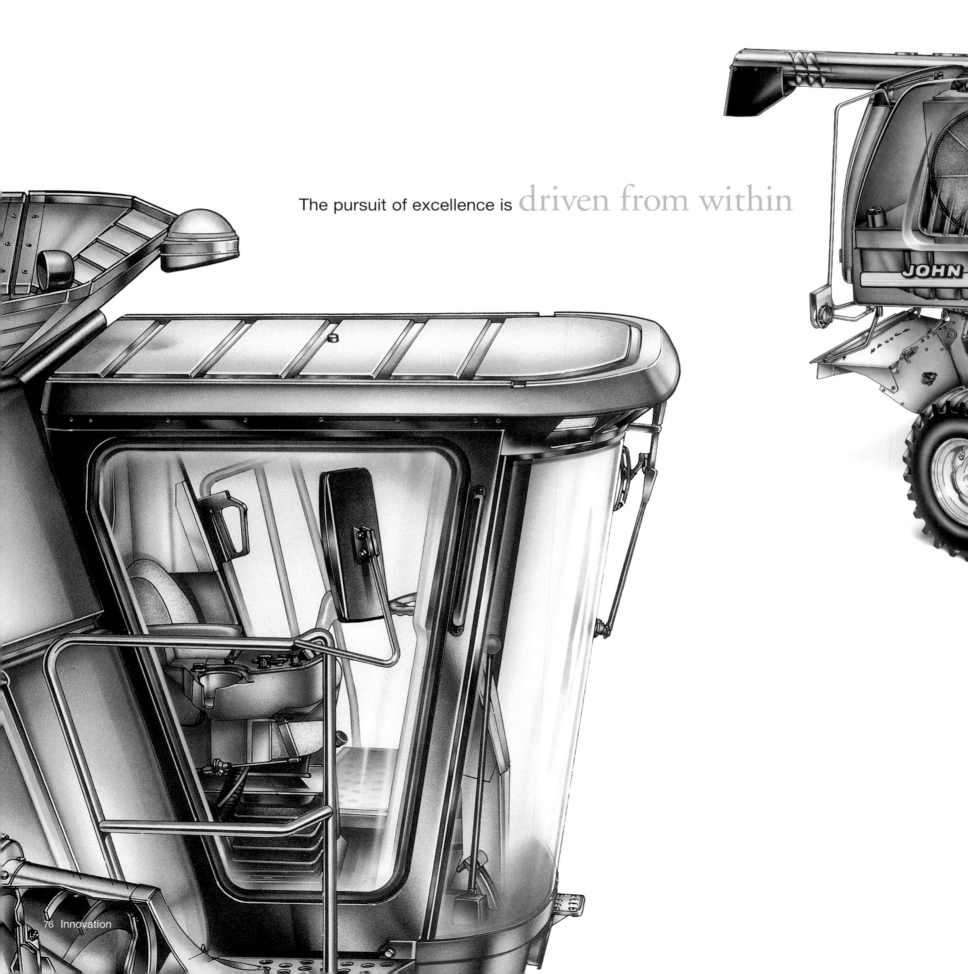

The pursuit of excellence is *driven from within*

John Deere extended its lead in the North American combine market with the introduction of the new STS Combines in 1999. Featuring revolutionary Single-Tine Separation, a patented John Deere technology, the new STS machines established benchmarks for capacity, grain quality, and all-condition harvesting.

Breakthroughs are also break withs

It may look like a funny contraption today, but in the mid-1940s, John Deere made serious attempts to offer farmers a low-cost, single-row tractor with a rear engine and excellent visibility. The small tractor never made it past the experimental stage, primarily because the unconventional design placed more emphasis on cultivating than on plowing and other important farm tasks. John Deere wound up building the much more conventional looking 1-row Model "M" Tractor at its new factory in Dubuque, Iowa.

佳 木 斯 联 合

Innovation opens many gates

John Deere is helping write the newest chapter on China, where 70 percent of the country's 1.2 billion population is engaged in farming. In the 1980s, John Deere exported 2,000 tractors, implements, and combines to China. Licenses to build John Deere tractors and combines by local manufacturers and the transfer of manufacturing technologies soon followed. In 1995, John Deere opened its Representative Office in Beijing. In 1997, John Deere Jialian Harvester Company, Ltd. (JDL), shown above, was opened in Jiamusi—John Deere's first agricultural-machinery joint-venture manufacturing plant in China. About 2,500 combines rolled away from the Jiamusi factory in 1999.

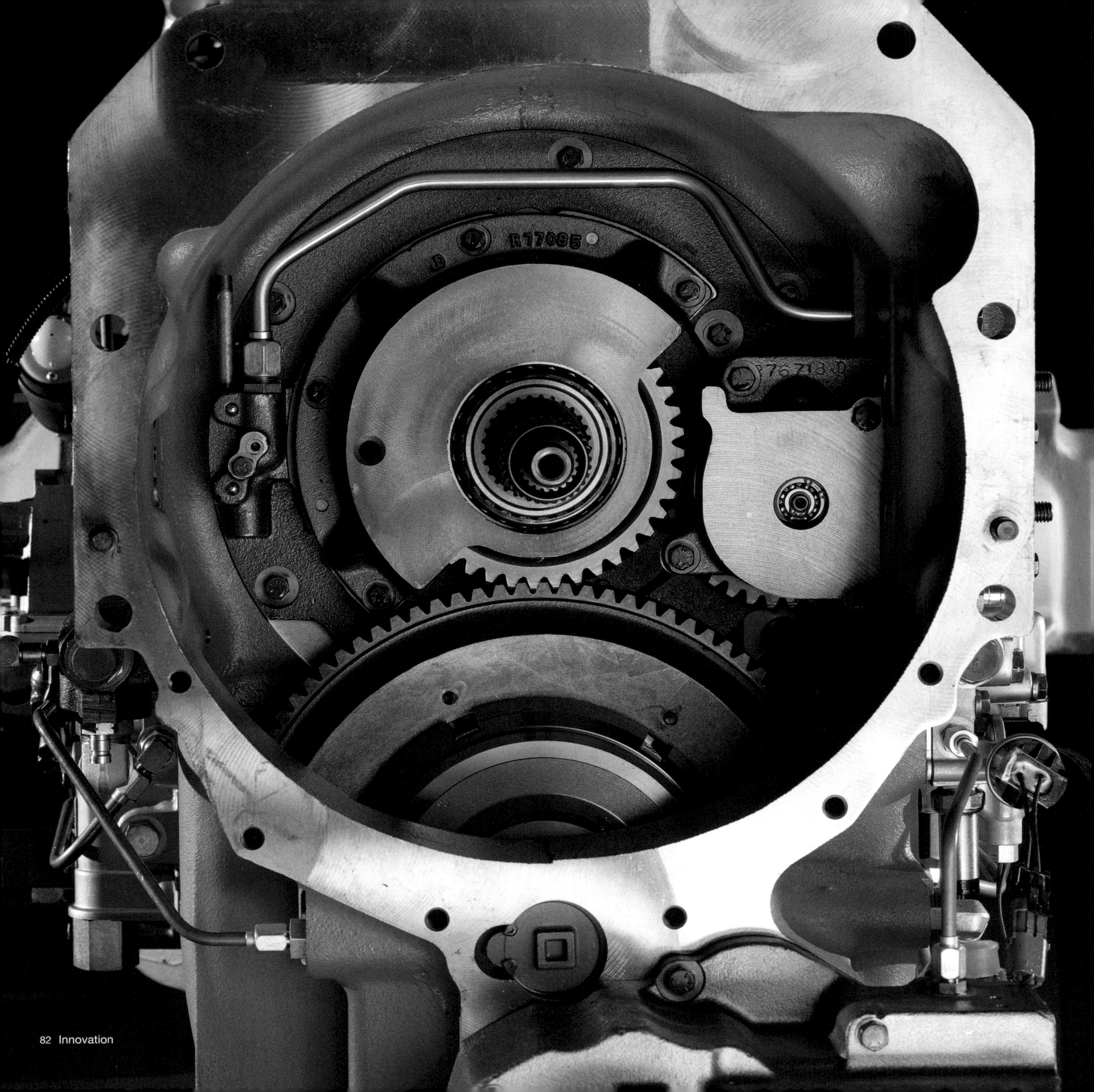

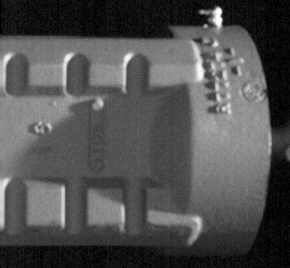

Ingenuity is engaging

Simple ideas drive evolutionary refinements of John Deere's Power Shift transmission, introduced on 3020 and 4020 Tractors in 1964. The latest smart-shift technology on John Deere Construction's 4-wheel-drive loaders evaluates ground speed and load conditions, adjusting the Power Shift transmission for smoother shifts and faster cycles. The John Deere Power Systems Group designs and manufactures transmissions and other powertrain components, as well as diesel and natural-gas engines.

Imagine replacing the sweaty hand labor of grain threshing with the speed and relative ease of operating a mechanical combine. The 12-A Pull-Type Combine, shown here behind the extremely popular Model "B" Tractor, helped thousands of farmers realize that dream. New in 1940, the 12-A became the most popular combine John Deere ever made.

Think beyond the box

Everything **looks** difficult to the unwilling

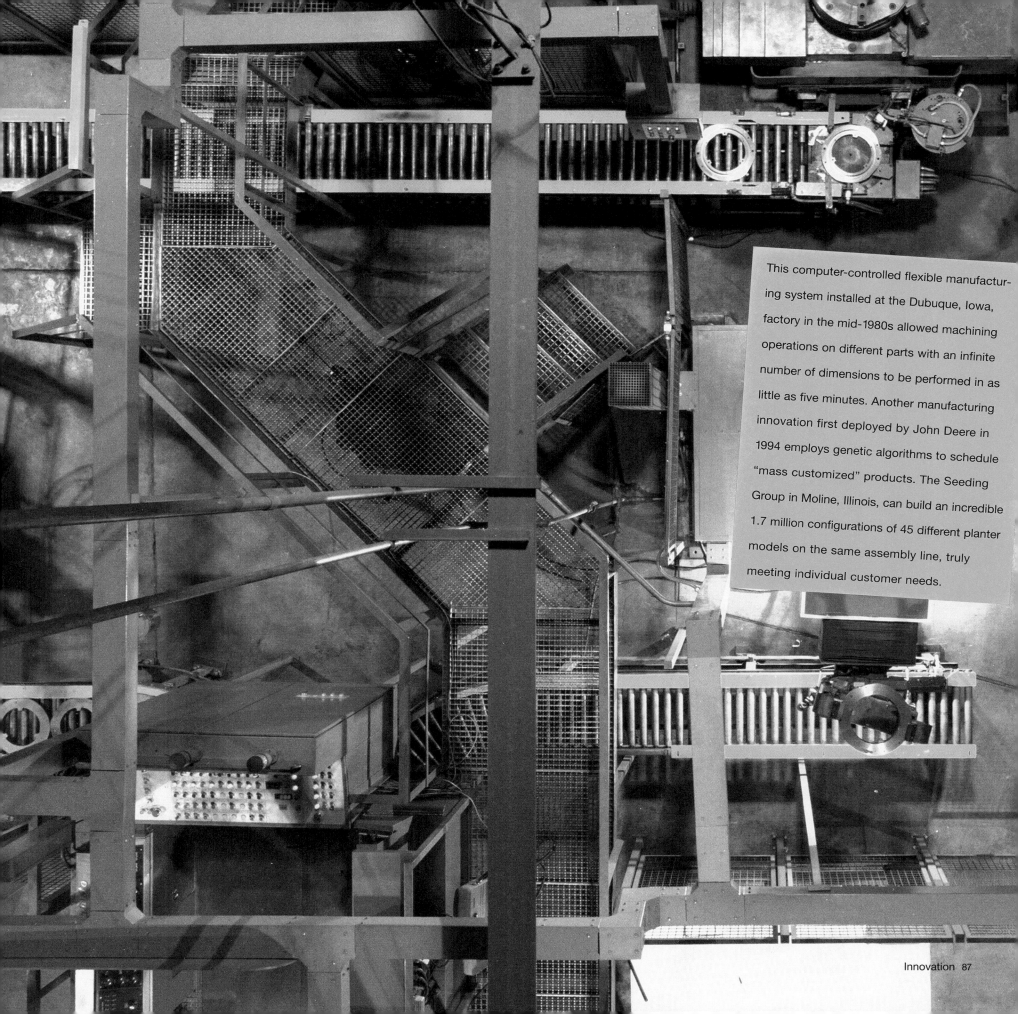

This computer-controlled flexible manufacturing system installed at the Dubuque, Iowa, factory in the mid-1980s allowed machining operations on different parts with an infinite number of dimensions to be performed in as little as five minutes. Another manufacturing innovation first deployed by John Deere in 1994 employs genetic algorithms to schedule "mass customized" products. The Seeding Group in Moline, Illinois, can build an incredible 1.7 million configurations of 45 different planter models on the same assembly line, truly meeting individual customer needs.

John Deere engineers in 1937 dreamed about building tractors that pleased the eye. The automotive industry was successfully using styling to market cars, but this was a new idea for the farm-equipment industry. A John Deere engineer traveled from Waterloo, Iowa, to New York City to try to engage the help of noted industrial designer Henry Dreyfuss. Dreyfuss was so struck with the potential of styling a tractor that he got on the train that very night and traveled to Waterloo to talk about the assignment. His successor company, Dreyfuss Associates, continues to assist in the styling of John Deere products. Henry Dreyfuss made and signed these tractor sketches in 1948.

Creativity brings life to a blank sheet of paper

Breaking new ground stems from looking at things differently

Numerous times in John Deere's history, management has changed course based on industry changes and new insights. How might the company look today if it had not decided to enter tractor manufacturing in 1918? Or branch into related fields that leveraged similar core competencies and served the same customer base? Examples include entering the construction equipment business (1947), manufacturing in other parts of the world (1956), credit (1958), lawn and grounds care equipment (1963), Original Equipment Manufacturing (1972), and providing health care (1985). Due to this diversification, about half of John Deere sales now are from divisions other than farm equipment and about one-third of equipment sales come from outside of the United States and Canada

Breaking new ground stems from looking at things differently

Numerous times in John Deere's history, management has changed course based on industry changes and new insights. How might the company look today if it had not decided to enter tractor manufacturing in 1918? Or branch into related fields that leveraged similar core competencies and served the same customer base? Examples include entering the construction equipment business (1947), manufacturing in other parts of the world (1956), credit (1958), lawn and grounds care equipment (1962), Original Equipment Manufacturing (1972), and providing health care (1985). Due to this diversification, about half of John Deere sales now are from divisions other than farm equipment and about one-third of equipment sales come from outside of the United States and Canada.

Success o v e r c o m e s obstacles

Billed as the ultimate work utility vehicles, John Deere Gator® UVs are designed to scamper over rugged terrain with hefty loads. The Gator 4x2 (pictured) has a 500-pound cargo box capacity. The heavy-duty ProGator UV carries 800 pounds and tows 1,200 pounds. The camouflage-painted M-Gator Vehicle is exclusively outfitted for use by the military and can withstand a parachute drop from a cargo plane. The quiet E-Gator Electric Utility Vehicle runs on a 48-volt battery system, enough for an average day's work.

Breaking out of the mold can be transforming

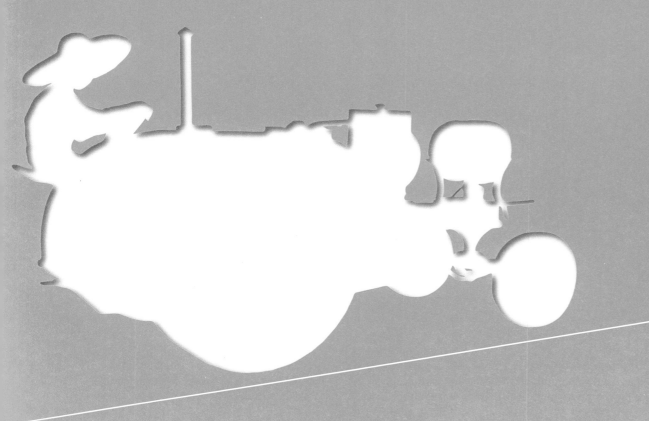

The decision to expand from horse-drawn plows and planters into tractors was painful for the board of directors in 1916. William Butterworth, then Deere & Company president, was against the idea. "I do not want to use the money of the Deere Estate or my own or that of any other stockholder in an awfully expensive enterprise which will get us nowhere in the end," he wrote. His argument was countered by fellow board member C.C. Webber who said: "I don't see how we can stay out of that business any longer. It is impairing our business." Finally, in 1918, the board voted to buy the Waterloo Gasoline Engine Company for $2.3 million. The Waterloo Boy Model "N" (shown) became the first 2-cylinder tractor made and sold by John Deere.

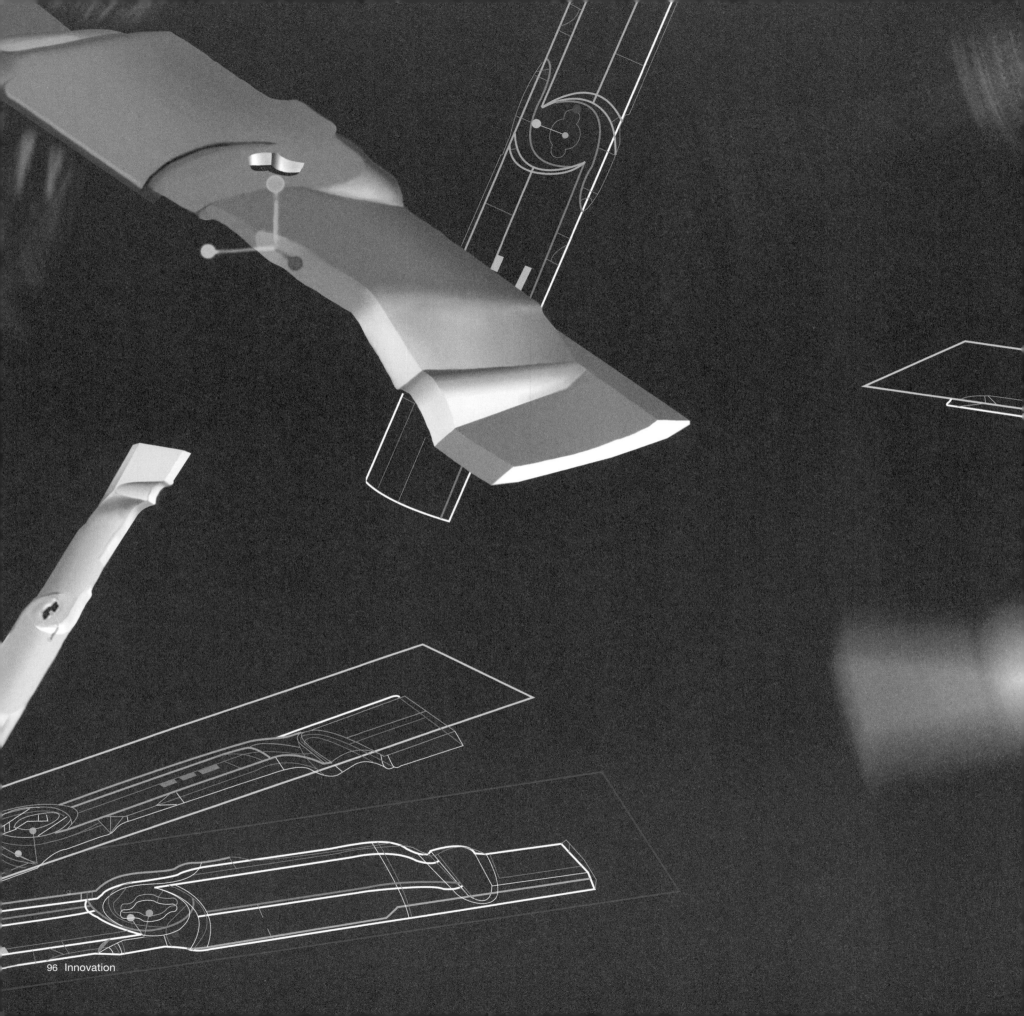

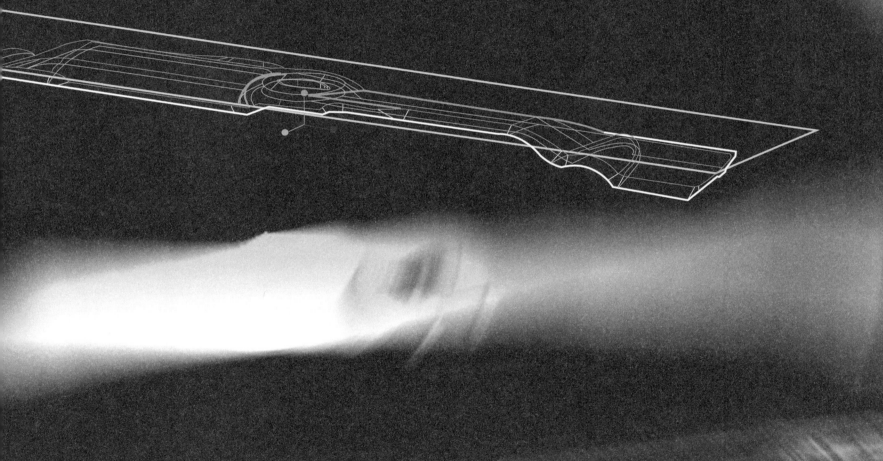

Imagination + Vision = Innovation

High-speed photography and a University of Illinois supercomputer were used to arrive at the ultimate design for the mower deck and blade of the John Deere Freedom42 Mulching Mower, introduced in 1997. The Freedom42's unique dome-deck design and counterrotating blades (shown) keep grass clippings and leaves in the mowing chamber so they're cut and recut into tiny pieces that can be left on the turf. Not only is this better for lawns, it's better for the environment. John Deere has been an industry leader in the development of effective mulching mowers and in educating homeowners and professional landscapers about the environmental and fertility benefits of mulching.

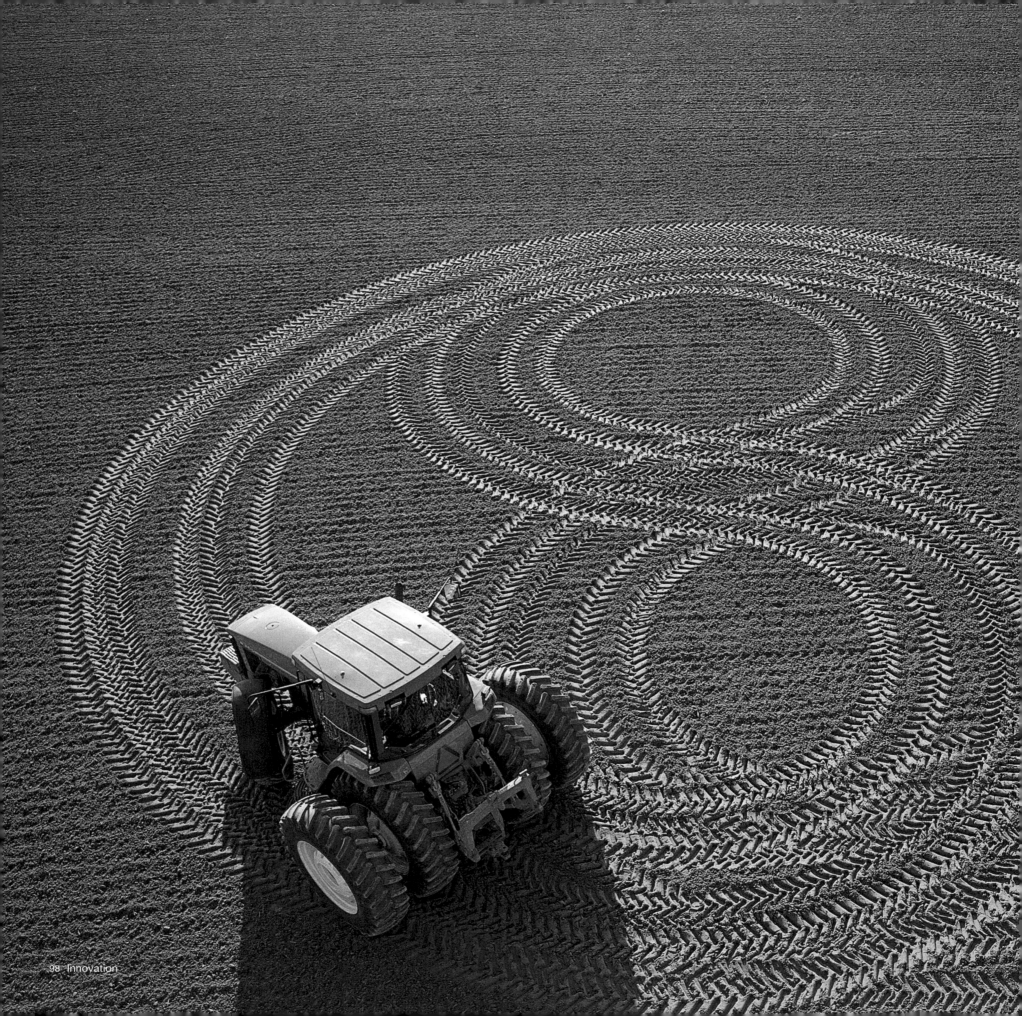

OK is never good enough

The 8000 Series Tractors, introduced in 1994, turned circles around competitive models, literally. These John Deere tractors could turn a figure eight inside the shortest turning circle (outside tire track at left) of the major competitor's tractors. This feat was achieved by moving the engine up and forward, sculpting the frame, and engineering a mechanical front-wheel drive that lets the wheels lean as much as five degrees as they turn.

Innovation finds better ways

In the 1920s, the farmer's best friend for harvesting corn (after his horse) was the corn binder. The binder cut and bundled the entire corn plants to be shocked in the field. During the winter, farmers could pick up the bundles and shuck the ears for the hogs, then feed the stalks to cattle. In a hard day, a farmer might cut and bind four acres of corn. John Deere's largest new combine, the 9750 STS with a 12-row corn head, can easily pick, shuck, and shell more than 100 acres in a day.

Visionary ideas blaze new trails

Navcom
Technolo
Inc

H1

95 - 125001   XB201014

J7

H3

U106

AD7862AR-2
9816 ▶
0F88424.1

E6

U103

John Deere's high-tech reach now extends to the heavens via the Special Technologies Group (STG). This hand-sized, round circuit board is from the StarFire™ position receiver, designed by STG's NavCom Technology Group, and manufactured by STG's Phoenix International. StarFire receivers are capable of tracking as many as 12 Global Positioning System (GPS) satellites at once, allowing the amazing position accuracy of 10 inches. Such accuracy is available in the newest GreenStar® precision-farming applications. John Deere has been pioneering precision-farming technology since 1996.

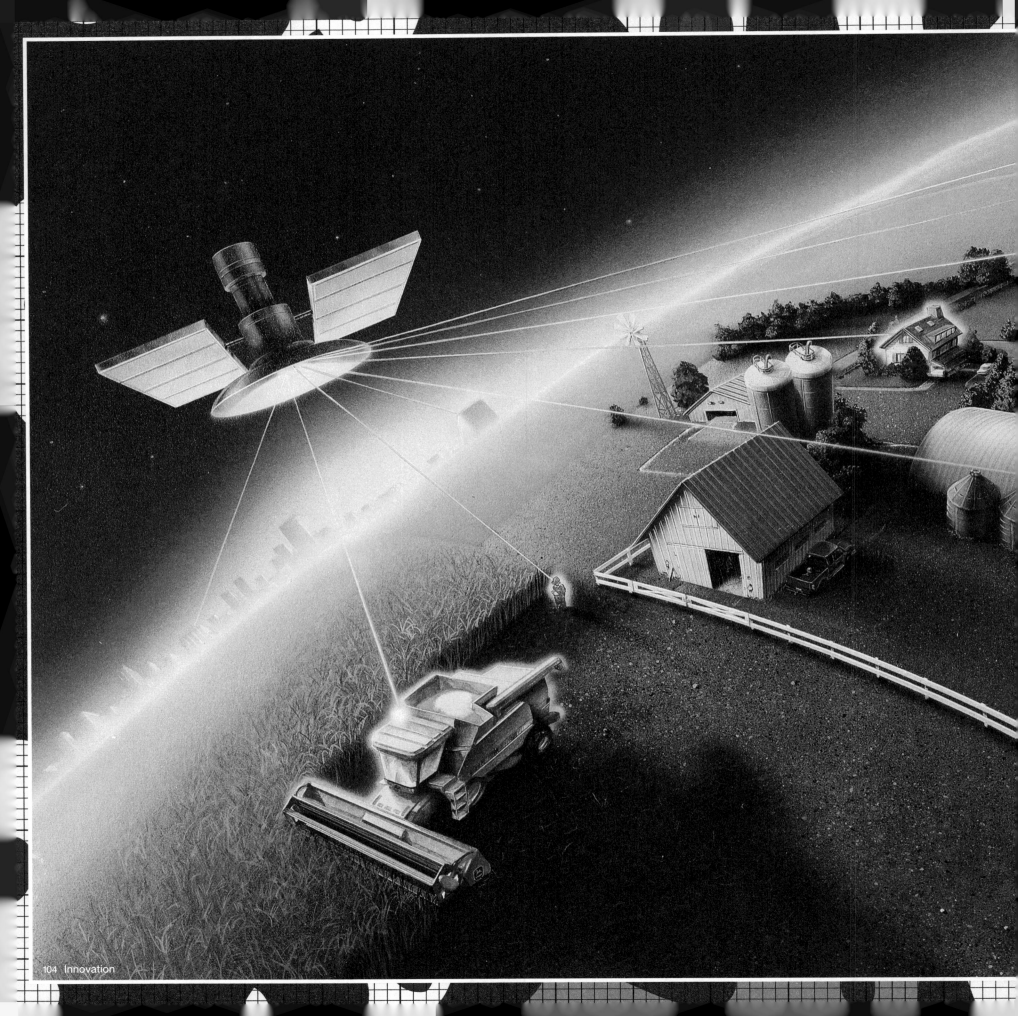

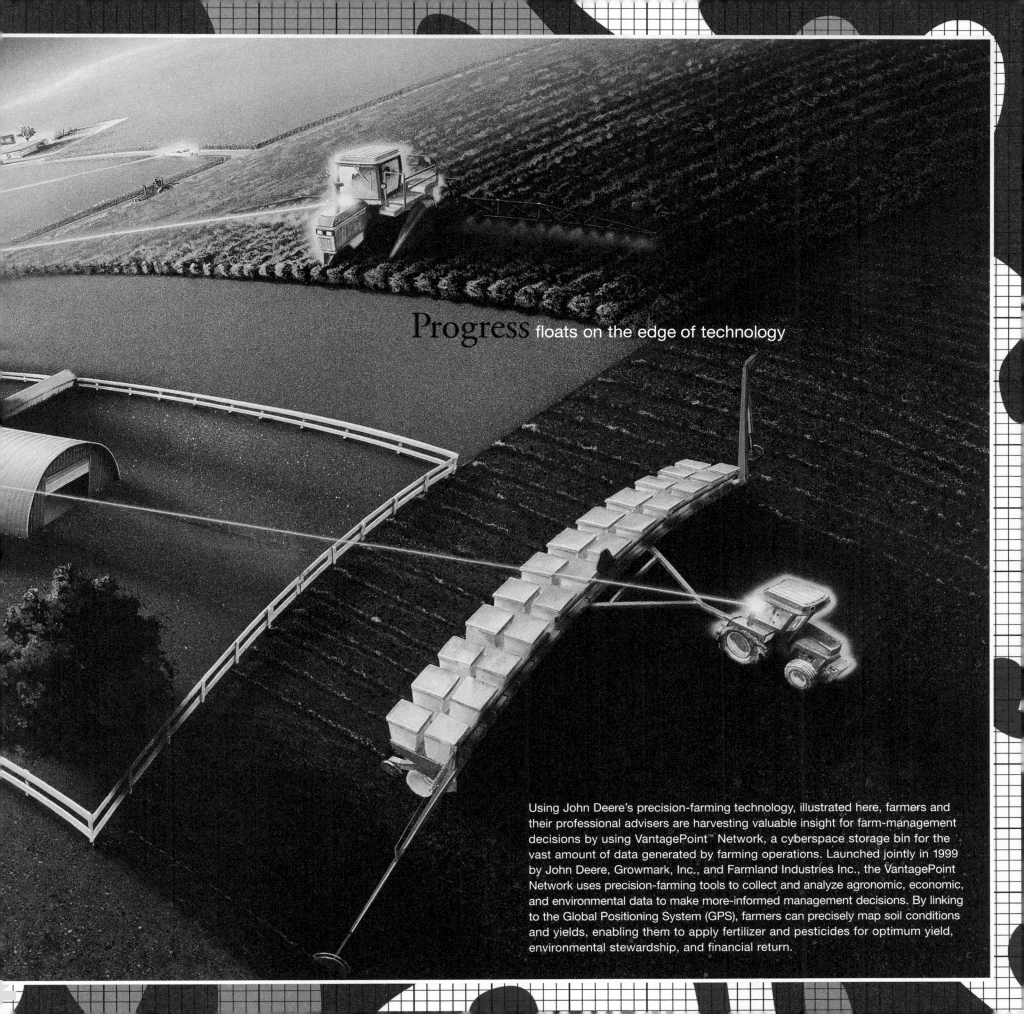

Progress floats on the edge of technology

Using John Deere's precision-farming technology, illustrated here, farmers and their professional advisers are harvesting valuable insight for farm-management decisions by using VantagePoint™ Network, a cyberspace storage bin for the vast amount of data generated by farming operations. Launched jointly in 1999 by John Deere, Growmark, Inc., and Farmland Industries Inc., the VantagePoint Network uses precision-farming tools to collect and analyze agronomic, economic, and environmental data to make more-informed management decisions. By linking to the Global Positioning System (GPS), farmers can precisely map soil conditions and yields, enabling them to apply fertilizer and pesticides for optimum yield, environmental stewardship, and financial return.

Inte

grity

"I will never from this seventh day of February, eighteen hundred sixty A.D., put my name to a paper that I do not expect to pay."
—Charles Deere, CEO 1859–1924

Integrity is doing the right thing when no one's around

Summerfallow operations run into the night on the expansive White Ranch near Shandon, California. Here, a 425-horsepower 9400 4-Wheel-Drive Tractor built in 1997 pulls a 57-foot-wide chisel plow. Depending upon the operating speed, a chisel plow this size will typically cover 30 to 40 acres per hour. The 13 high-intensity lights mounted on the tractor shine a 360-degree light pattern, letting the driver see in front, along the sides, and to the implement at the rear, as if it were daytime.

There have been huge changes in painting technology since 1986, when these combine painters were photographed at the Harvester Works in East Moline, Illinois. In the 1990s, John Deere replaced many of its dip, flowcoat, and wet-spray systems with modern electrocoating, powder painting, and robotically applied wet-spray painting processes. All of the paints used by John Deere are lead-free for a safer environment.

An honest day's work builds strength of character

Teamwork depends on the integrity of each player

The "threshing ring," a rural economic and social institution of the early 1900s, still stands as a supreme example of integrity and teamwork. At harvest time, a group of neighboring farmers agreed to work together without any transfer of money until all their crops were threshed. The annual threshing ring disappeared with the arrival of the pull-type combines. However, the same spirit of farm aid can be found today whenever a farmer is unable to plant or harvest.

We are judged by the seeds we sow

It has been said that no one on earth is as optimistic as a farmer at planting time, due to the perennial threat of insects, weeds, disease, and capricious weather. Because optimum planting days are few, field breakdowns are extremely costly, causing farmers to favor the largest and most-reliable equipment they can afford. John Deere has long prided itself on being the industry leader in parts support. Fast-moving parts are stocked at dealerships, and emergency parts orders received in regional warehouses by 5 p.m. can be processed and received at most John Deere North American and Western European dealerships the following morning.

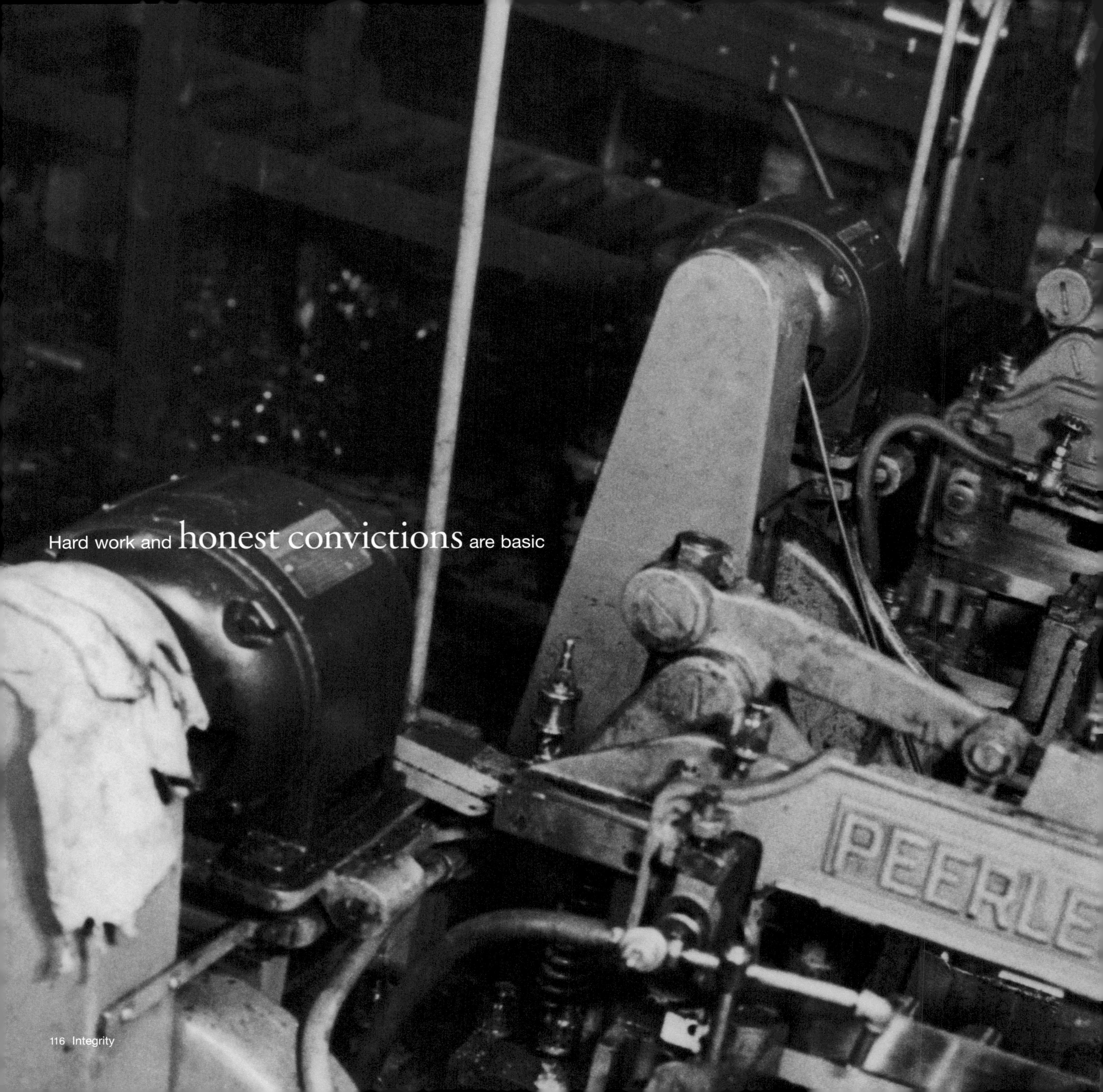

Hard work and honest convictions are basic

The industrial revolution swept through John Deere factories in the early and mid-1900s, changing working conditions for the better. Here, an employee in John Deere's Moline factory tends a power hacksaw.

Integrity is taking the high road

A John Deere 4-wheel-drive loader makes its way along a California mountain road in this 1990 photograph. John Deere's Construction Equipment Division sees a world of opportunity as global investment in roads, housing, and other infrastructure development continues to grow. The Construction Equipment Division offers more than 100 models of earthmoving and forestry equipment.

There is no more serious job than passing on values

John Deere is the subject of many unsolicited drawings, poems, and school writing assignments sent by children each year. These wonderful examples of youthful creativity prove, if nothing else, that adults are crucial role models and that kids will say—and draw—the most insightful things.

Great challenges make us stronger

This was a very impressive demonstration of raw power back in the early 1900s. Pictured is a Russell Giant kerosene-burning tractor being demonstrated with a 10-bottom John Deere plow. This plow's five 2-bottom units were lifted and dropped into the ground by the strong muscles of the two men riding the plow. Note that the farmers attending the demonstration, and even the plow lifters, were as formally dressed as they might appear in church on Sunday mornings.

High **principles** should always push us

John Deere's Commercial and Consumer Equipment Division traces its lineage back to the company's farm-equipment roots. Farmers were asking for reliable small tractor mowers they could use to groom their farmsteads. The first John Deere lawn and garden tractors were introduced in 1963, and since then John Deere has become the largest supplier of premium lawn-care equipment in the world. In addition to its extensive line of lawn and garden tractors, riding mowers, and walk-behind equipment, it now has a long line of handheld equipment. For more work capacity, John Deere provides loaders, mowers, and rotary cutters for its compact and utility tractors, along with a variety of attachments for its new skid steers—everything from buckets to backhoes. The Commercial and Consumer Equipment Division also manufactures and distributes a full-line of lawn-care products for golf and commercial turf applications. Like their bigger cousins, John Deere's lawn-and-grounds machines are painted John Deere green. This 1987 John Deere walk-behind mower, shown in front of the Lincoln Memorial in Washington, D.C., was a special silver edition that celebrated the company's 25th anniversary in the lawn-equipment industry.

Stand tall and proud

Among the thousands of *Peanuts* cartoons Charles Schulz drew in the 49 years before his death in 2000, this strip had Sally voicing a comment many other city dwellers must be thinking these days: "I've never even seen a farmer." This is not at all surprising, especially in North America where only about one percent of the population now makes a living off the land. (The number is still well over 50 percent in many developing countries.) This Kansas farmer, like farmers all over the world, is in a race to efficiently and profitably produce the food required to feed the planet's population of about 6 billion people, up from 2.5 billion in 1950.

John Deere takes extra care to make sure its toy line is faithfully scaled down and is built to last well beyond the first sandbox season. The Ertl Company of Dyersville, Iowa, has been building John Deere replicas since the 1940s, and "play-tests" new toy models for durability and safety before putting them into production. Besides replicas of most major farm, construction, and grounds-care machines—modern and historic—the line has stretched to include "role-play" and educational toys.

Every customer is crucial

The proud dignity of the staff of John Deere's sales branch in Salt Lake City, Utah, permeates this 1913 portrait. By the early 1930s, John Deere had 16 branches and more than 20 subbranches spread throughout North America. Today, due to improvements in communication, transportation, and shipping, only seven agricultural branches remain in North America.

Take pride in making the *right decisions*

Honesty in every relationship sets one apart

Chambord, the 450-year-old French Renaissance masterpiece chateau, was the inspirational backdrop for European John Deere dealers to see the latest additions to the agricultural-machinery product line in 1993. Among products given a royal send-off that year were the German-built 6000 and U.S.-built 7000 Series Tractors, and the Z Series Combines.

Walk the talk

A lone farmer walking behind a mule-drawn, single-row John Deere planter symbolizes the bleak economic picture American farmers faced during the height of the Great Depression of the 1930s. The paralyzing impact of a stock market crash, high unemployment, sagging farm prices, and two disastrous droughts forced huge numbers of farmers into bankruptcy, or to the edge. To help ease the crisis, Deere & Company's board of directors decided to carry, as long as necessary, thousands of customers who were hopelessly behind on their farm-machinery debts. It took years, but nearly 100 percent of all these past-due debts were paid back to the company. This number speaks volumes about farmers' sense of integrity and loyalty. This is the heritage on which John Deere has built its current Credit operations.

The more we **follow the right path,** the easier it becomes

The job of streamlining business processes often seems

as overwhelming and unclear as the snowbank facing this

772B Motor Grader, introduced in 1986. All John Deere

employees receive business-process training. The purpose

is to deliver operational excellence to customers by plowing

through mountains of process complexity, allowing major

savings in time and costs. The Construction Equipment

Division is reaping the rewards of a new, streamlined order-

fulfillment process that is cutting up to half the days required

from the time a customer order is received until delivery.

The best course is often long and lonely

In the late 1930s, farmers and loggers were asking for tractors with crawler tracks and a lower profile for easier and safer navigation of their orchards and logging camps. In 1940, John Deere began supplying Lindeman of Yakima, Washington, with Model "BO" Tractor chassis. Lindeman outfitted the tractors with crawler tracks and the machines became known as "John Deere Lindeman Crawlers." There was substantial demand for the crawler tractors in orchards and in logging areas. In 1946, John Deere purchased Lindeman, which proved to be the humble beginning of today's Worldwide Construction Equipment Division.

The best teams march to the same values

The Deere Cornet Band, formed by musicians among the 800 employees who worked in Moline, Illinois, in the 1880s, was one of the company's earliest cultural-support efforts. Supporting the arts continues to be an important activity of the John Deere Foundation. It helps bring arts to the communities in which John Deere has operations through grants to local symphonies, museums, and arts organizations. The company's art collection on display at the corporate headquarters in Moline and throughout other John Deere facilities worldwide includes *Hill Arches*, a bronze sculpture by Henry Moore, and paintings by Midwest regionalist painter, Grant Wood.

John Deere was the official supplier of construction equipment and snowmobiles to the 1980 Olympic Winter Games at Lake Placid, New York. Five JD672B Motor Graders lead this impressive lineup of equipment shipped to the Olympic committee. The JD672B, introduced in 1967, was the world's first all-hydraulic, articulated motor grader.

Integrity must be consistent

Cutting to the truth is the best way

Well before consolidation became a business buzzword, John Deere was growing through acquisitions of small farm-equipment companies. By 1910, John Deere was a small (by today's standards) conglomerate of 12 manufacturing entities and 25 sales organizations, most of which had been purchased. One of these early purchases was the Dain Manufacturing Company, which made hay tools like this horse-drawn mower in Ottumwa, Iowa, and Welland, Ontario.

Integrity is a lasting source of *pride*

Antique tractor collecting may be a close second behind
vintage-car collecting, judging by the number and size
of antique farm-machinery shows, "swap meets," and
auctions being staged somewhere in the U.S. almost
every summer weekend. Most shows have more than
one exquisitely restored Model "A" Tractor on exhibit,

like the one shown here. John Deere collectors are a worldwide fraternity, with serious enthusiasts known to reside in Beverly Hills, California, and London, England. With old John Deere tractors fetching ever-higher prices, many collectors seeking "green gold" have turned to implements and memorabilia such as toys, belt buckles, caps, and printed matter.

Comm

itment

"The commitment to our values has earned the respect of our customers in the past, and guarantees the success of our business in the future."
—Hans W. Becherer, CEO 1989–2000

DAWN

The sun truly never sets on John Deere customer support. Every dealer customer-support representative is continually trained to become more expert in the use of technology and total-repair-cost management. Purpose? Helping John Deere customers better manage maintenance and reduce costs for equipment such as the pictured 790D Excavator, introduced in 1987.

Commitment never quits

DUSK

Commitment is quiet and reassuring

John Deere first became a player in the golf-and-turf business in 1986, but has quickly become a championship contender due to a well-developed focus on product quality and customer support. In 1997, John Deere signed an agreement with the PGA TOUR to be the official golf course equipment supplier to the Tour's Tournament Players Club (TPC) courses located throughout the world. The PGA TOUR's new Tournament Players Club golf course in Moline, Illinois, named TPC at Deere Run, is now the home of the "John Deere Classic."

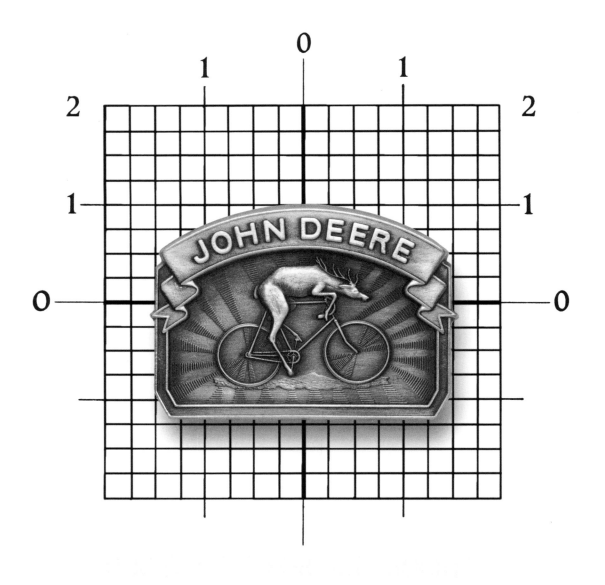

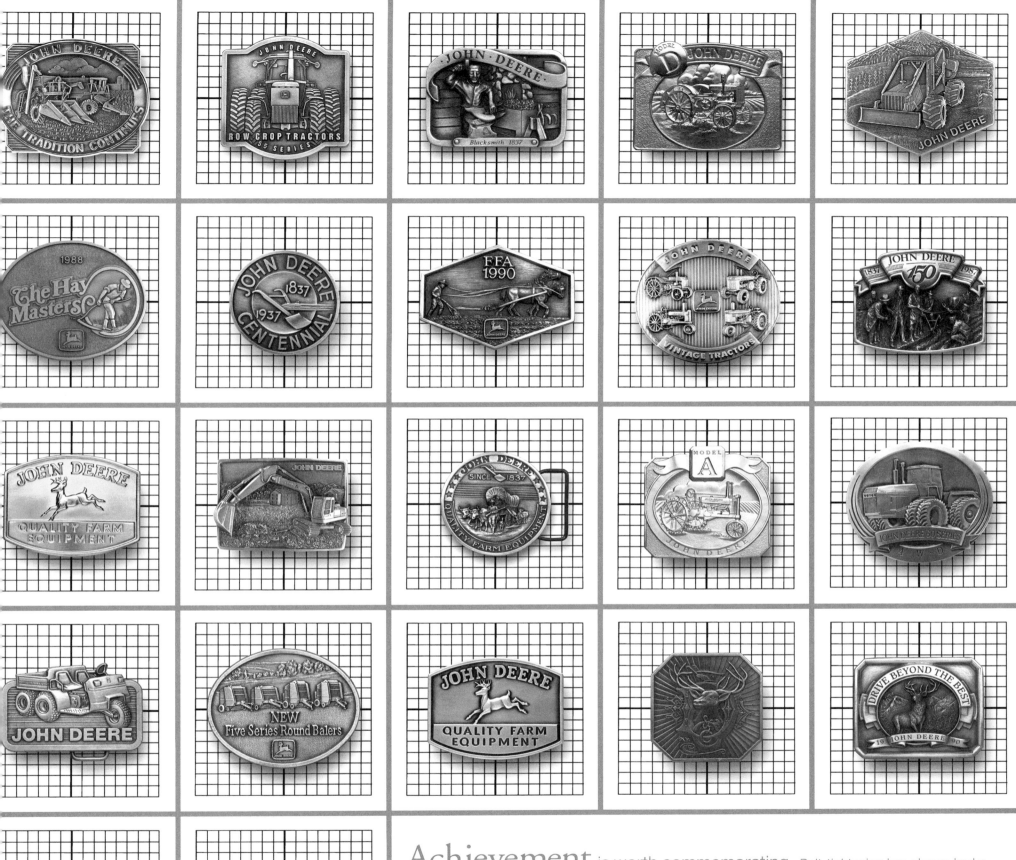

Achievement is worth commemorating.

Belt-tightening has always had a secondary meaning to John Deere manufacturing and marketing units. Over the years, hundreds of valued belt buckles have been minted to honor important new products and events such as the annual employee bicycle ride to John Deere's home in Grand Detour, Illinois, and the one-millionth lawn and garden tractor manufactured at the John Deere Horicon (Wisconsin) Works.

Persevere. Persevere. Persevere.

In an early example of focusing on customer value, the simple, versatile 2-cylinder Model "A" Tractor was extolled for being able to efficiently burn low-cost fuels such as fuel oil, furnace oil, and kerosene, as well as gasoline. This value message clearly hit home in the hard times of the 1930s. Arriving at the depth of the Great Depression, the simple and trouble-free Model "A" and Model "B" Tractors were highly successful, ranking first and second in popularity over the entire tractor history of John Deere.

Each dawn brings a new commitment

At the beginning of the 20th century, it took four farmers to feed 10 people. Today, machinery such as this 4-Wheel-Drive 9000 Series Tractor and 24-foot folding disk allows the entire Midwestern corn crop to be planted in 10 days and harvested in 20, weather permitting. One U.S. farmer can produce enough food to feed 97 Americans and 32 people in other countries. The future of farm mechanization at the dawn of the 21st century appears bright based on world population and dietary trends. About 209,000 people every day (2.4 per second) are being added to the earth's dinner tables, and diets are being continually upgraded with more meat. As a result, demand for grain is expected

Trust moves mountains

John Deere Credit's Farm Plan, "The Charge Account for Rural America™," is a revolving charge plan designed exclusively for agricultural producers. Since 1974, Farm Plan has grown to serve more than 7,000 merchants and more than 500,000 customers throughout the U.S. and Canada. John Deere Credit is one of the top 25 U.S. financial institutions, and has a managed-asset portfolio exceeding $11 billion. In addition to its revolving charge plan, John Deere Credit provides retail, wholesale, and lease financing, and offers credit financing for agricultural, construction, and commercial and consumer equipment.

ARMY OF WORKMEN AT DEERE & CO. — MOLINE.

Shared commitment is powerful

Hundreds of employees and a few family members—more than half immigrants from Sweden, Norway, and Belgium—gathered for this early group portrait, circa 1900. The occasion was the dedication of a new building at the Plow Works in Moline, Illinois. The company enjoyed strong loyalty from employees by this time through pioneering benefit programs. Reflecting the vestiges of John and Charles Deere's paternalism, health and accident benefits began in 1887. In 1907, noncontributory pensions were provided after age 65 for those with 20 or more years of service.

Commitment demands focus

Modern, high-tech products that meet customer needs for quality and value can be created only by dedicated teams committed to excellence. In this 1989 photo, assembly personnel, engineers, and employees from a myriad of departments at the Harvester Works in East Moline, Illinois, proudly pose in front of (and on) a new Maximizer™ Combine, introduced that year to enthusiastic response from farmers.

Appreciation for commitment is universal

Joseph Stalin's first Five Year Plan to build up the USSR's economic might called for extensive agricultural mechanization. Between 1929 and 1931, the Soviets bought a startling quantity of John Deere Model "D" Tractors (shown here) and other implements. In 1930 alone, more than $5.6 million of the company's $63 million in sales came from the Soviet Union. Even today, as John Deere works to develop sales in this part of the world, the quality of these

Responsibility means being a part of the community

John Deere was mayor of Moline, Illinois, in 1873 and generously contributed money and time to a wide range of local educational, religious, and charitable organizations. Dedicated in 1997, the John Deere Commons complex pays homage to the founder's civic-minded spirit. Built on 20 acres of Deere-donated land where he once worked, the Commons complex has become a major tourist attraction, drawing 300,000 visitors a year to downtown Moline, the cradle of the world's agricultural-equipment industry. The glass-enclosed John Deere Pavilion features modern and vintage equipment and interactive exhibits related to agriculture and the history of John Deere.

Stretching is an important daily exercise

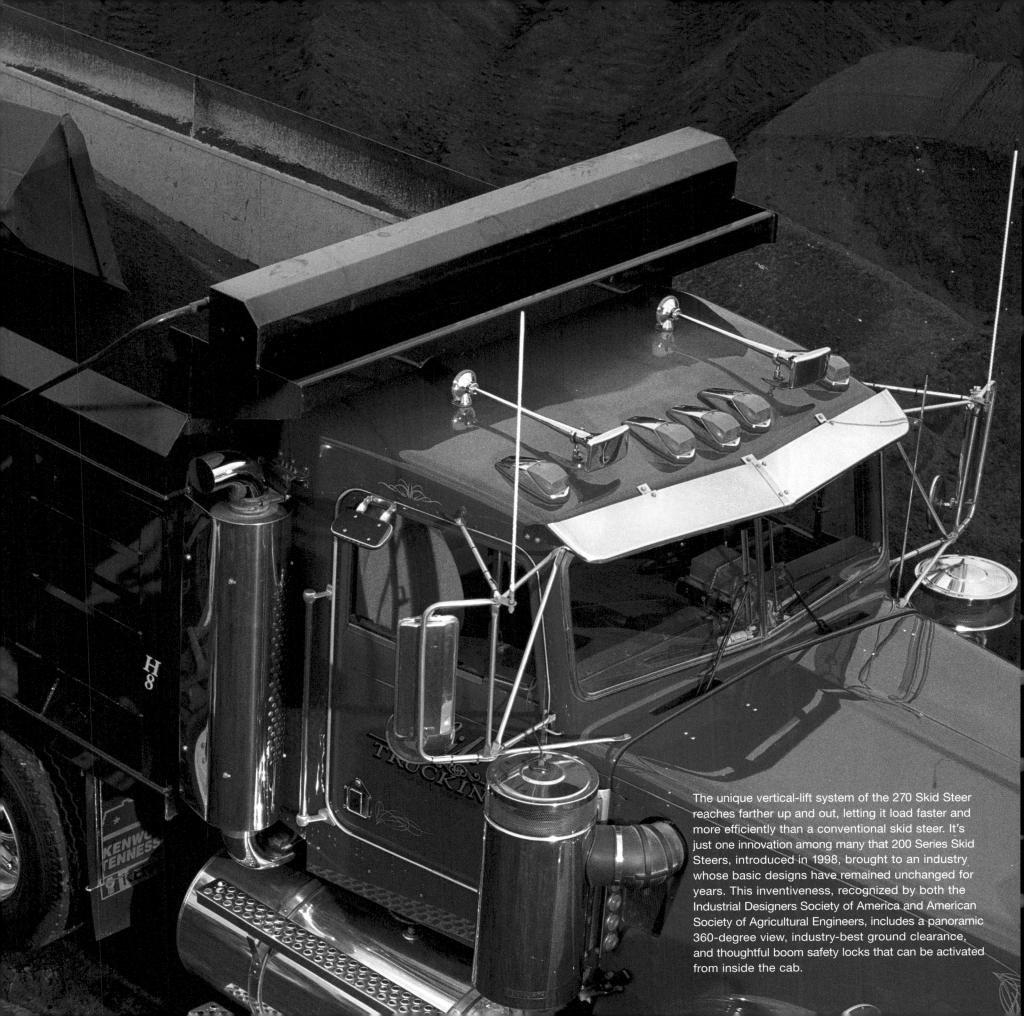

The unique vertical-lift system of the 270 Skid Steer reaches farther up and out, letting it load faster and more efficiently than a conventional skid steer. It's just one innovation among many that 200 Series Skid Steers, introduced in 1998, brought to an industry whose basic designs have remained unchanged for years. This inventiveness, recognized by both the Industrial Designers Society of America and American Society of Agricultural Engineers, includes a panoramic 360-degree view, industry-best ground clearance, and thoughtful boom safety locks that can be activated from inside the cab.

Commitment doesn't wait for the right time

Capturing some of the drama of farming, a 1960s *John Deere Day* film crew records an Iowa farmer finishing his fall plowing in the snow. *John Deere Day* is a unique dealer open-house program that has been entertaining and informing farm customers and their families annually since 1937, when film was still a novelty. Winner of many awards, *John Deere Day* is perhaps the most comprehensive and prestigious video program in agriculture today. Besides playing to live audiences of more than a half-million at John Deere dealerships annually, the videos are made available to agricultural groups, high schools, colleges, and youth organizations. Toss in some good food and fellowship and you have the reason why *John Deere Day* is still an annual high point in thousands of towns across rural North America.

Everything on earth is connected

This 1998 John Deere 1860 No-Till Air Drill allows farmers to plant a new crop in the stubble of the old, thereby reducing potential wind and water erosion of the soil. Beyond saving precious topsoil, no-till farming also saves costly trips across the field. John Deere's concern for the environment can be traced through generations of conservation-tillage and seeding products. It was in 1989, however, that John Deere introduced a seeding machine that not only made "no-till" farming possible, but made it popular. The tool was the 750 No-Till Drill and it was so successful that a larger, more-productive air-seeding version became available in 1995.

Commitment to values connects generations

Like father, like son...John Deere has long enjoyed the loyalty of multi
generations of customers. These two father-son portraits, taken about
40 years apart, are striking examples of how committed to trust and
tradition farm families can be.

Pride in work transcends time and place

Although the tools, techniques, and technology are vastly different, commitment to excellence links this circa-1900 manufacturing scene of the Plow Works in Moline, Illinois, with John Deere's newest engine factory at Torreon, Coahuila, Mexico, opened in 1997. World-class machine tools, manufacturing processes, and a very young, highly trained, and dedicated workforce have been assembled in the 500,000-square-foot facility, which manufactures 3-, 4-, and 6-cylinder engines. The assembly floor is the most computerized of any company factory. Among the plant's many advances, torques are automatically set and other adjustments made as engines travel down the line.

John Deere's global dealer organization is constantly finding new ways to provide superior customer service. In this 1989 scene, Empire Equipment Company of Sacramento, California, delivers a new 444E Loader to a customer in Empire's bustling and beautiful San Francisco Bay area sales territory. Empire has 10 sales and service locations in northern California and Nevada, and uses innovative training, rental sales, and telemarketing programs to stay customer-focused. For instant answers for hard-to-solve service problems, Empire and other construction-equipment dealers rely on electronic access to a Dealer Technical Assistance Center, a computerized bank of troubleshooting information.

Commitment means on time, every time

Without an unwavering commitment to innovation and customer satisfaction, this circa-1950 berry-planting scene might still be state-of-the-art. The driver of this John Deere Model "M" Tractor had to drive slowly enough to allow the two men on the transplanter to alternately grab a plant from a box and place it in a furrow where it could then be watered from the 55-gallon barrel. In what was surely a supreme test of teamwork, the threesome had to hold to this wearing routine for days on end.

Even if on the right track, you can't just sit still

There are weddings, and then there are John Deere weddings. For reasons perhaps impossible to comprehend without being madly in love, some loyal customers and John Deere personnel from countries as far apart as Australia and the Netherlands seem to throw ceremony to the wind and daringly dash from the church on a polished and decorated John Deere. Of course, the wedding photographers never fail to capture this unique expression of love between humans and their dear machines.

Commitment should be celebrated

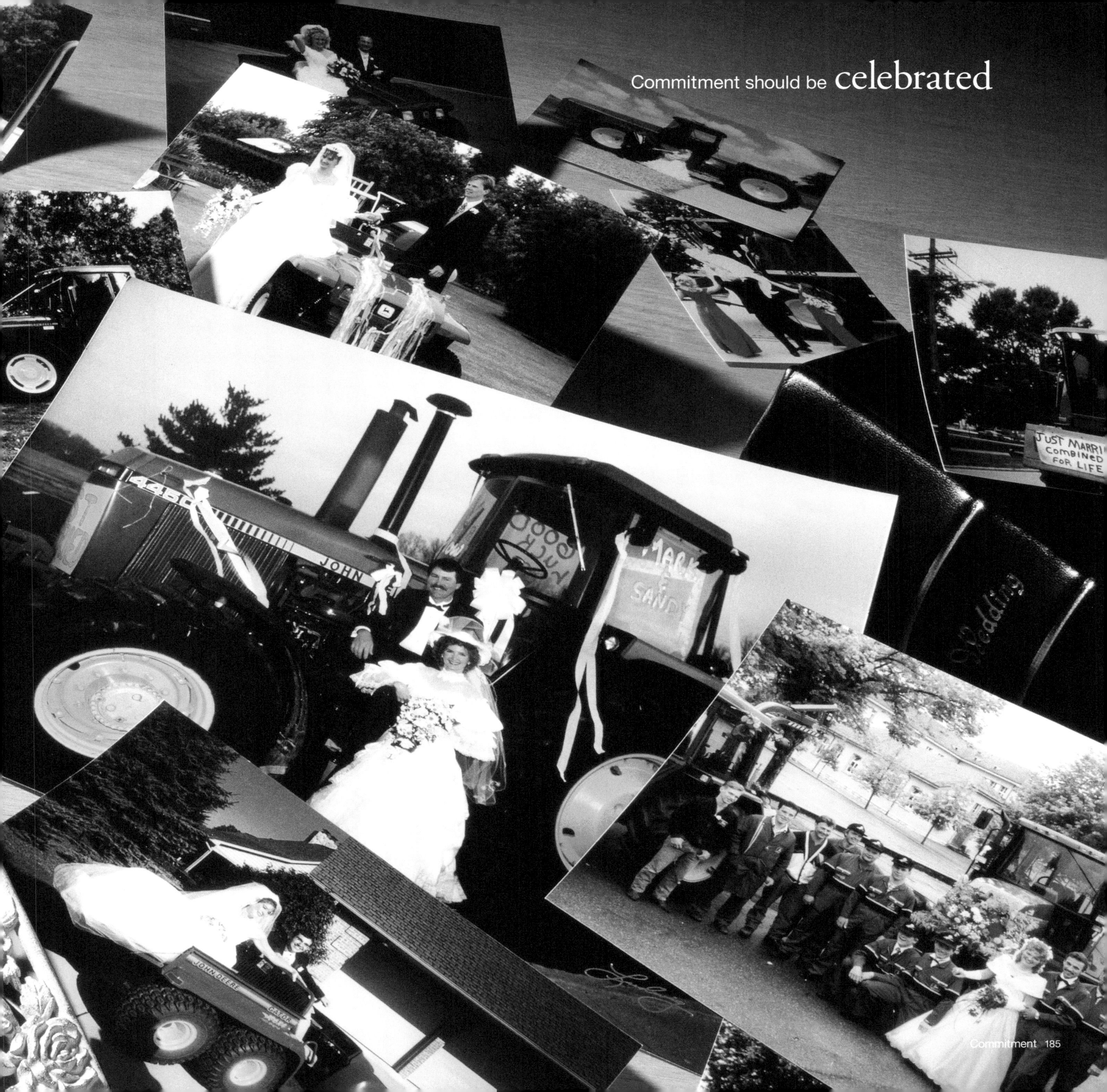

The **commitment** to quality can never stop

John Deere combines from the Zweibrücken, Germany, factory emerge from the Schlossberg Tunnel on their way to Eastern Europe. This 1990 shipment of 125 combines was a forerunner of continued strengthening in John Deere's marketing position in Eastern Europe. In 1996 and 1997, John Deere shipped 1,049 combines to the Ukraine, the single largest equipment sale ever from the Harvester Works in East Moline, Illinois.

There is an enduring strength in *togetherness*

This circa-1930 Iowa scene captures the special working relationship between a farmer and his wife that is still common on family farms worldwide. If anything, togetherness today is enhanced by advancing wireless communications and on-board computers that allow both voice and data to flow to and from vehicles and the farmstead. The farm wife's tractor in this picture is a Model "D" with a reworked horse-drawn 3-row rotary hoe. His tractor is a Model "GP" with a mounted 3-row planter. While he was planting corn, it is likely she was rotary hoeing weeds in an adjoining field.

Business relationships

must always be win-win

To the Man Delivering This New Tractor

After discussing the maintenance operations (listed on page 3) with the person receiving delivery of this new tractor and securing his signature on this new tractor delivery report, tear off and mail to your John Deere Branch House. The tractor identification stub is for the owner's billfold.

☐ Ignition System—Terminals Tight, Cleaning, Oiling, Adjusting P...
☐ Rear Wheel Brakes—Adjustment.
☐ Clutch—Adjustment, Pulley Brake.
☐ Front Wheels—Cleaning, Adjustment and Spacing.

☐ Starter and Lights—Spacing, Lights, Battery Char...
☐ Tightening Bolts and Nuts—Caution on Governor Cover...

☐ Keeping the Tractor Clean...

As this vintage front-cover company manual shows, John Deere's global marketing and dealer organization has been a source of permanent historical strength, going all the way back to the days of John and Charles Deere. The key to this historical success is the win-win, mutual advantage the company strives to maintain with its worldwide dealers, and the close relationship John Deere dealers have with their customers. Thanks to the Internet and new technology working in conjunction with John Deere Information Systems, dealers' ability to service customers and provide product support is significantly enhanced with up-to-the-minute parts and service information. The application, called JDParts, allows customers to order parts through their dealer at any time of the day or night via the Internet.

1876

1912

1936

1937

1950

1956

1968

Nothing runs like a Deere

The John Deere trademark is one of the world's most trusted and distinctive brands. The latest trademark, introduced in 2000, is the seventh evolution of the leaping deer since 1876. The new trademark resonates with the heritage of past accomplishments, and is poised for new opportunities on the horizon. Expressed another way: Nothing Runs Like A Deere.®

JOHN DEERE

Looking back and ahead:

Change is constant,

but values are enduring.

"I believe all of our present strengths have been built on the foundation of achievement, integrity, and momentum that we have inherited from our predecessors."—Robert A. Hanson, CEO 1982–1989

Timeline

John Deere mastered the ancient trade of blacksmithing as a young man in his native Vermont, turning out polished hay forks, shovels, hoes, horseshoes, and metal parts for stagecoaches, carriages, and wagons. In 1836, at 32, perhaps pulled by a sense of adventure and pushed by economic pressures, he joined the growing westward movement. His skills were in demand from the moment he arrived in Grand Detour, a northwestern-Illinois frontier settlement.

Farmers there soon impressed him with the need for a plow that would "scour," or cut cleanly through the thick, gummy prairie earth. Deere fashioned one that did just that, using a broken steel saw blade for its polished surface. It became commercially successful, winning him a permanent place in the history of American agriculture. The "steel plow" sharply increased the efficiency of pioneer farmers, and played a key role in opening the vast American prairie to agricultural development.

Deere was more than an ordinary artisan. He perceived a need and put head together with hands to devise the right product for the right time and place. He became a manufacturer, marketer, and sales manager, confident in his products, and deeply interested in quality and reliability. He advertised extensively and guaranteed what he made. This business intuition had at least as much to do with the success of his company as did his more celebrated development of a successful steel plow.

John Deere, blacksmith and businessman, died at 82 in 1886 in Moline.

1837	1838	1839

John Deere enters agricultural history. He fashions a polished-steel plow that lets pioneer farmers cut clean furrows through sticky Midwest prairie soil. Their productivity increases.

Deere's family arrives in Grand Detour, Illinois, where John has settled, from their native Vermont. Ultimately, there are nine children.

John Deere, blacksmith, evolves into John Deere, manufacturer. Later he remembers building 10 plows in this year, 40 in 1840, 75 in 1841, and 100 in 1842.

1837 John Deere develops the **steel walking plow**. Plows had evolved from biblical days and worked well in soil farmed for centuries. The high draft of plowing the Illinois prairie for the first time was compounded by soil that stuck to the plow. John Deere curved a broken steel sawmill blade that let the soil slide off the plow. Animal-drawn plows were the heart of John Deere business for the next eight decades.

Though increasingly known near Grand Detour, Deere is a tiny manufacturer compared with rivals elsewhere. In Pittsburgh, two companies make nearly 34,000 plows a year.

First practical grain drill patented. First emigrant train of covered wagons reaches California. New York, Pennsylvania, and Ohio are the chief wheat-growing states.

John Deere, blacksmith and manufacturer, adds retailing to his business repertoire. In a newspaper advertisement, he "respectfully informs his friends and customers . . . and dealers in Ploughs, that he is now prepared to fill orders" for the Patent Cary Plow.

Deere and Leonard Andrus become "co-partners in the art and trade of blacksmithing, plow-making and all things thereto . . ." Other partnerships follow in the early years.

John Gould, a partner, on Deere's work habits: "Hammering in the morning . . . at four o'clock, and at ten o'clock at night; he had such indomitable determination to . . . work out what he had in mind."

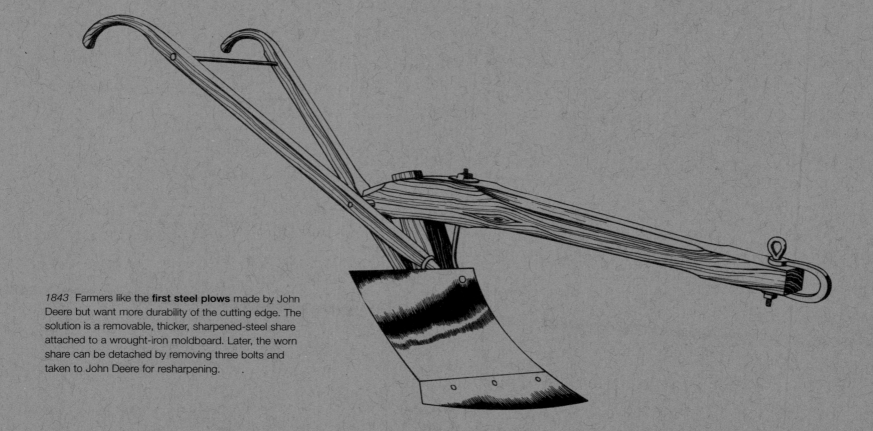

1843 Farmers like the **first steel plows** made by John Deere but want more durability of the cutting edge. The solution is a removable, thicker, sharpened-steel share attached to a wrought-iron moldboard. Later, the worn share can be detached by removing three bolts and taken to John Deere for resharpening.

CEO: John Deere

1840s

1842: Sales: $1,000
Net Income: $300
Employees: 10

H.C. Peek, a nephew, on Deere's demeanor: " . . . always well dressed, better than the average, and made a good appearance everywhere . . . a 'good liver,' 'great meat eater'—hale and hearty."

H.C. Peek on Deere as boss: "Kept everybody who worked for him busy . . . no lazy man need apply for a job with him."

An acquaintance on Deere's business style: "When a customer came into (his) shop (John Deere) would look up and ask what he wanted. Deere would listen, never saying another word, and go immediately to work on the job."

The growing plow business moves to Moline, Illinois, 75 miles southwest of Grand Detour. On the Mississippi River, Moline offers water power and transportation advantages.

Business improves. Partner Robert Tate: "Great call for breakers, breakers, breakers, and one-horse plows." A work force of about 16 builds 2,136 plows.

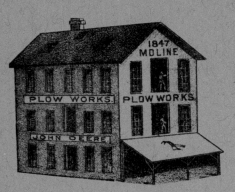

1840 A cross-section of **John Deere's blacksmith shop** as reconstructed by archaeologists. On the left, a horse walks up an inclined circular treadmill. Teeth on the tread-mill drive a bevel gear that drives a line shaft in the main building. Belts drive a bellows to keep the forge fire burning or, alternatively, for the cupola to melt cast iron. Another belt drives a large-diameter grinding wheel to polish plows. There may also have been a power hammer for forging.

1843 John Deere and Leonard Andrus become partners with the agreement that the **factory in Grand Detour** will be known as L. ANDRUS. The two-story factory builds plows until 1848, when John Deere dissolves the partnership and moves to Moline.

1848 John Deere chooses a new partner, Robert N. Tate, for his **relocation to Moline**. Tate moves to Moline first and raises the rafters on their three-story 24x60-foot blacksmith shop by July 28, 1848. Tate's diary records the finishing of 10 plows on September 26. In the first five months of 1849, this factory produces 1,200 plows.

Output statistics for Deere, Tate & Gould, as the firm is now known, show the cyclicality typical of the implement business. Inventory builds in fall and winter for "spring trade."

Most one-horse plows sell for $6 to $9. A larger "breaker" sells for $23. Product-line expansion begins; the firm sells a single grain drill for $80.

Deere buys out his partners. For the next 16 years, the company is known variously as John Deere, John Deere & Co., Deere & Co., and Moline Plow Manufactory.

Sixteen-year-old Charles, John Deere's only living son, joins the firm as a book-keeper following graduation from a Chicago commercial college.

The railroad reaches Rock Island, the town next to Moline. Six hours to Chicago, 42 to New York, boasts the railroad president.

1854 **Moline Centre-Draft Plows** claim superiority over all others for being made of the best quality of materials, lighter and easier draft, put together with bolts and nuts instead of rivets, consequently more readily repaired, and much better finish.

1855 This early **logo from Deere stationery** indicates the business has spread two ways. It now sells wholesale as well as retail. It also offers implements in addition to plows. The chain on the plow suggests it may be drawn by oxen. The plow features a front gauge wheel and a vertical knife to cut the prairie sod for a clean furrow slice.

1859 An ad for **MOLINE PLOWS** proudly boasts, "We shall be prepared at all times to fill orders for Stirring or Old Plows of every desirable style, but especially the IMPROVED CAST STEEL CLIPPER PLOW of three different styles, which is acknowledged by Farmers and others, who have seen them used, to be the very best plow in use."

CEO: John Deere

1850s

1852: Sales: $88,000
Employees: 19

Most employees earn 58 cents to $1.50 a day. A speedy piece worker paints 180 plows at a dime each—$18 for a week's work.

The first railroad bridge across the Mississippi River links Rock Island, Illinois, with Davenport, Iowa.

A John Deere advertisement: "I am putting into my plows this year a better quality of steel than is used in any other plow in this state." Output tops 13,000.

The business totters during a nation-wide financial panic. Maneuverings to avoid bankruptcy shuffle ownership and managerial arrangements. John Deere remains titular president, but managerial power passes to Charles Deere.

Only 21 when he takes over, Charles Deere will run the company for 49 years. John Deere, now in his mid-50s, returns to his first love: tinkering with products.

1857 The improved **Clipper Plow** has a rolling coulter to cut vegetation, resulting in a clean furrow slice. The basic design of the moldboard and share are still used today for tractor-drawn plows.

Charles Deere

In 1859, at the age of 21, Charles Henry Deere inherits direction of the company his famous father had founded; Charles both resembles and differs from his parent. Both have dominant and aggressive personalities. But where the charismatic John Deere expresses his in a gruff, taciturn, sometimes undiplomatic manner, the less flamboyant Charles Deere is approachable, patient, and a good listener. Where John Deere often is suspicious of colleagues and unable to delegate, Charles Deere trusts those with whom he works, and shares responsibility. Where John Deere has an intuitive, seat-of-the-pants approach to business, Charles Deere, more formally trained, understands finance and concepts such as decentralization.

Charles Deere runs Deere & Company for 49 years, more than twice as long as his father. During his tenure, annual sales increase from less than $200,000 to more than $3 million. At his death in 1907, the company is at least as strong and ready as any other in its industry for the imposing challenges of the 20th century.

1856: Sales: $140,000
Employees: 68

Operating now as the Moline Plow Manufactory, Charles Deere signs all advertising and promotional literature with his own name.

Civil War begins. Midwest farmers and their suppliers prosper during the war years as Army demand and European crop failures boost crop prices.

Large-scale Midwest farming develops during the war. Farm machinery improves, enabling expansion even by small farmers.

The company makes the Hawkeye Riding Cultivator, the first Deere implement adapted for riding.

John Deere obtains the company's first actual patent for molds used in casting steel plows. Another follows in a few months and a third the next year.

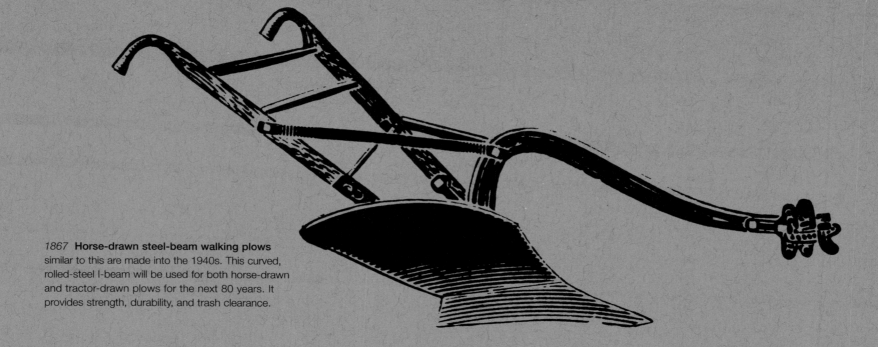

1867 **Horse-drawn steel-beam walking plows** similar to this are made into the 1940s. This curved, rolled-steel I-beam will be used for both horse-drawn and tractor-drawn plows for the next 80 years. It provides strength, durability, and trash clearance.

CEO: Charles Deere

1860s

Demarius Lamb Deere, John Deere's wife, dies at age 60. He returns to Vermont, reacquainting himself with Lucenia Lamb, Demarius' maiden sister. They marry the next year.

A Civil War legacy is an army of farmers handicapped by severe injuries. Others are hurt in farm accidents. Hawkeye Riding Cultivator advertisements note that "A one-arm or one-legged man can manage it." Another manufacturer features a sulky plow "especially adapted for small boys, old men and cripples."

Charles Deere sues Candee, Swan & Co., a competitor, for trademark infringement. The case has precedent-setting implications for trademark law. Could Deere preempt the word "Moline," which it has been using in its advertising, so that no similar product could incorporate it? The ultimate answer is no.

After 31 years as a partnership or single proprietorship, the concern is incorporated under the name Deere & Company. There are four shareholders at first, six within a year. Charles and John Deere control 65 percent of the stock.

Charles Deere and Alvah Mansur establish the first branch house, Deere, Mansur & Co., in Kansas City. A semi-independent distributor of Deere products within a certain geographic area, it is the forerunner of the company's current farm and industrial-equipment sales branches and sales regions.

1860s This **steel-beam double-shovel cultivator** is the lowest-cost way to control weeds in corn and other row crops. A single horse pulls the cultivator between the rows with the man walking behind to control both the cultivator and the horse.

1863 The John Deere **Hawkeye Riding Cultivator** permits the farmer to control the horses with his hands and the cultivator with his feet. Productivity increases with this 1-row cultivator because it is now determined by the endurance of horses instead of a man walking in soft ground.

1867 This **walking cultivator** is patented in August 1867. Although farmers might prefer riding, the lower cost of this unit makes it sell even though the man has to walk in soft ground while straddling a row of corn.

1860s This 12-inch **extra breaker plow** can be pulled by a strong team of horses to break the prairie for the first time. It has a wooden beam, a front gauge wheel to control depth, a rolling coulter to cut the sod, and a gently sloping moldboard to turn the soil over.

1860s This **rigged breaker plow** becomes available in 16- to 24-inch cutting widths, requiring three or four good horses to break the prairie. Size makes it more difficult to manhandle, so it uses a long wooden beam with adjustable-height gauge wheels up front to control the working depth of the plow.

1860s The John Deere **Michigan Double Plow** is more clever than practical. The first upper plow bottom turns the soil over into the previous furrow. The second bottom places the second slice on top in a looser condition. However, the plow costs more and requires more horses to pull it, as the soil has to be sliced twice.

1869: Sales: $646,564
Net Income: $198,237

Five basic product lines dominate the company's output through the end of the 19th century: plows, cultivators, harrows, drills and planters, and wagons and buggies.

The Order of Patrons of Husbandry—the Grange—gains strength among farmers discontented with low prices and high costs.

Virulent Grange attacks occur throughout the 1870s on the "middleman" (farm-machinery dealer) and the "monopolist" (farm-machinery manufacturer). Some Granges attempt manufacturing, unsuccessfully.

The Panic of 1873, triggered by failure of a New York banking house, begins the depression of the 1870s. John Deere is elected Moline mayor; he serves a year.

Grasshopper attacks worsen economic conditions of Midwest farmers. Still, Deere business grows. More than 50,000 plows are sold.

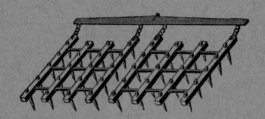

1876 The John Deere **Scotch Harrow** breaks clods, kills weeds, and levels the ground for final seedbed preparation. A wooden frame keeps its 40 steel teeth in place. This was an improvement from the earlier practice of dragging brush across the field.

1877 The **horse-drawn 2-row planter** by Deere & Mansur eliminates the tedious job of hand planting cornfields kernel by kernel. One man drives the team of horses and raises the runner openers at the end of the field for turning. A second man works a lever back and forth to drop seed into the furrows.

1879 The John Deere **1-row stalk cutter** chops corn or cotton stalks into short lengths to make plowing easier for the next crop. A pair of tines sweep the stalks parallel to the row so the rolling blades can cut them into pieces.

CEO: Charles Deere

1870s

1870: Sales: $710,640
Net Income: $104,944

1872: Sales: $646,305
Net Income: $88,469

1874: Sales: $835,769
Net Income: $93,651

Gilpin Moore develops the Gilpin Sulky Plow. It takes the farmer off his feet, puts him on a seat, and becomes one of the company's most successful 19th-century products.

Noting sagging business prospects and skyrocketing bad debts, the company institutes a 10 percent wage cut. A brief strike ends and workers return to work on the company's terms. The "leaping deer" trademark appears.

Deere & Mansur Company is formed in Moline to manufacture corn planters. A separate organization from the similarly named Kansas City branch, it will become part of Deere & Company in 1909.

An employee comments on factory lighting in this pre-electricity era: "In some parts of the shop we had gas lighting . . . In the blacksmith shop they used torches when it got dark, and everyone had a hand kerosene lamp."

A special-order railroad plow, used for track ditching, weighs 1,800 pounds. Its moldboard is 36 inches high. Rigged behind two steam locomotives, it can throw dirt 6 to 10 feet from the railroad track.

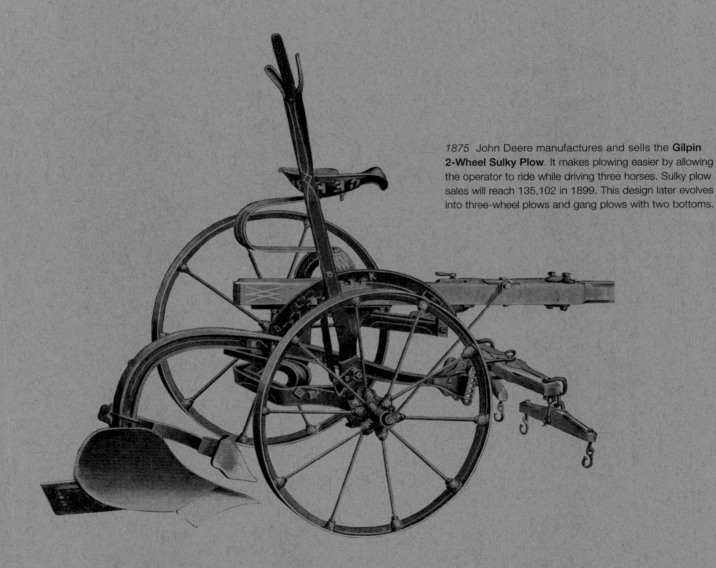

1875   John Deere manufactures and sells the **Gilpin 2-Wheel Sulky Plow**. It makes plowing easier by allowing the operator to ride while driving three horses. Sulky plow sales will reach 135,102 in 1899. This design later evolves into three-wheel plows and gang plows with two bottoms.

1876:   Sales: $1.25 million
       Net Income: $139,107

1878:   Sales: $1.08 million
       Net Income: $139,798

Wagons enter the product line early in the decade, soon followed by buggies. By century's end, company catalogs will feature Old Hickory, New Moline, and Mitchell wagons, as well as Derby, Red Star, White Elephant, Victoria, Goldsmith, and Sterling buggies.

"In the hustle for wagon trade, buggy trade and trade in general, none of us want to overlook the fact that plow trade is our principal mission," warns C.C. Webber, head of the Minneapolis branch.

Deere & Mansur Company corn planters, employing an innovative rotary planting mechanism, turn a $48,000 profit.

The five best-selling products between 1879 and 1883 are walking plows, Gilpin sulkies, cultivators, shovel plows, and harrows. Walking plows account for more unit sales (224,062) than the other four combined.

Implement prices, and prices generally, decline in the 1870s, 1880s, and 1890s. Despite this, farm implements and machines increase in efficiency, durability, workability, lightness, and strength of materials.

1885 The Deere & Mansur **sulky rake** is pulled by one horse to gather hay. When the operator lifts the rake teeth with his foot, the hay is dumped into perpendicular windrows. After drying, hay is usually loaded onto a wagon by pitchfork and hauled to the barn.

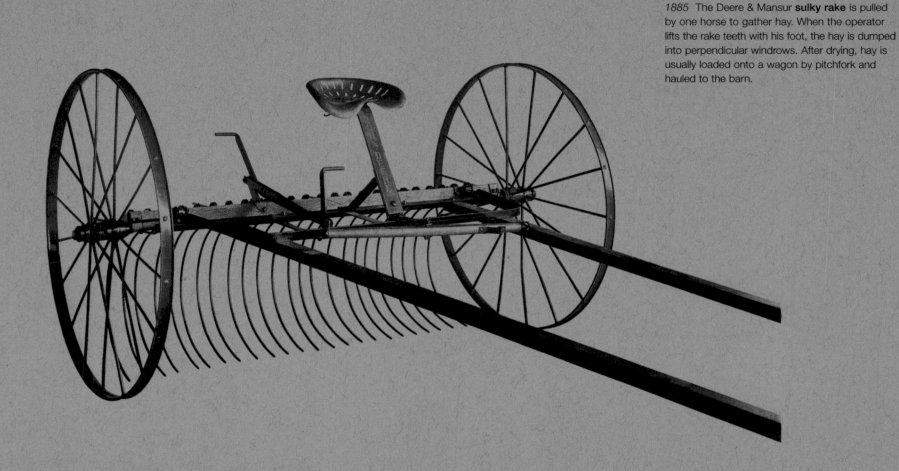

CEO: Charles Deere

1880s

1880: Sales: $1.2 million
Net Income: $150,793

1882: Sales: $1.4 million
Net Income: $221,173

1884: Sales: $1.2 million
Net Income: $162,094
Employees: 800

Manufacturing methods change radically in the 1880s and 1890s as improved machinery becomes available. Labor productivity increases.

John Deere dies in Moline at 82. "Probably no other funeral in Moline was ever attended by so many people or drew forth the public evidence of mourning," remembered one spectator. On the church altar is a sheaf of garnered grain and a large floral plow with the name John Deere on the beam.

The company begins to pay health-and-accident benefits to employees.

Steam tractors appear on American farms during the 1880s. Deere makes gang plows that tractors can pull, but not the tractors. The "Steam Age" lasts about 30 years, until the "snorting, puffing giant" is replaced by the gasoline tractor.

The company's five key branches are in place at Kansas City, St. Louis, Minneapolis, Council Bluffs/Omaha, and San Francisco.

1881 The **horse-drawn 2-row planter** by Deere & Mansur uses an innovative rotary planting mechanism. A check wire stretched across the field causes the seeds to drop at uniform intervals so plants can be cultivated with the row and across the row to root out all the weeds.

1885 The **New Deal Gang Plow** adds the rear wheel to previous designs. It helps control depth, which also can be adjusted with a lever. This 2-bottom riding plow requires four to six horses. Plows of this general design will eventually outsell walking plows and remain popular until tractors replace horses in the mid-1900s.

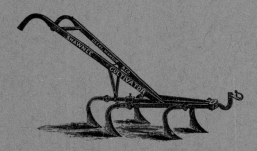

1880s The John Deere **Shawnee Cultivator** is pulled by a single horse walking between the rows of corn. Its five shovels root out more weeds than double-shovel cultivators, but the man still has to control the horse and the cultivator while walking in soft ground.

1880s The **No. 1 One-Horse Corn Planter** is a single-wheel, single-row unit. The plate-type planter drills the seed with uniform spacings, but not aligned in crossways rows. Thus, the corn cannot be cross-cultivated as if it were check-row planted. The rear drive wheel covers the seed. The man walking behind guides the horse and planter.

1880s The John Deere **Little Hoosier 5-Hoe Grain Drill** is pulled by one horse and is used to plant wheat between standing corn rows for next year's crop. The front wheel drives the seed meters, and the rear wheels gauge the seeding depth. The man walks behind, guiding the horse and the drill.

1880s The John Deere **Moline Broadcast Seeder** is a predecessor of future grain drills. Its multiple seed meters simply broadcast the seed on the surface and then depend on the shovels that follow to stir the seed into the soil. The man can ride on the seedbox or walk behind to watch seeds drop.

Deere's board recommends selling the company. A British syndicate and other suitors appear, but deals fall through and the company remains independent. The Sherman Antitrust Act passes. Among other things, it makes price-fixing through trade associations illegal.

By about this time, most farm machinery dependent upon horse power has been discovered.

Charles Deere's daughter, Katherine, marries William Butterworth, who will succeed him as the company's chief executive officer. Charles' daughter, Anna, marries William D. Wiman. Their son, Charles Deere Wiman, will succeed Butterworth.

The Panic of 1893, touched off by a New York stock-market crash, begins the worst depression of the 19th century. As business sags, competition among implement makers for declining orders turns cutthroat.

A bicycle craze grips the country. Branch catalogs push the Deere Leader, the Deere Roadster, and the Moline Special. The fad fizzles in a few years. (In the 1970s, the company returns briefly to the bicycle business.)

1890s **Disk harrows** cut weeds and the stalks from the previous crop before plowing. They are also used for the first seedbed operation after plowing. Depth can be adjusted with levers that change the angle of the disk gangs. The weight of the operator also helps penetration.

1890s The **No. 9 Horse-Drawn 2-Row Planter** features edge-drop plates for accurate planting of corn. Runner openers control seed depth and split press wheels firm the soil around the seed but leave loose soil above the seed. The planter drills corn with uniform spacing of single seeds, or hill-drops multiple seeds when check-row planting.

1893 This John Deere **New Deal 5-Bottom Gang Plow** is drawn by a steam engine (tractors haven't arrived yet). This design evolved from horse-drawn gang plows and will continue similarly for the next 50 years as tractors take over. Steam engines are slow to warm up, awkward to drive, and travel slowly. But they pull heavy loads.

1890s A **John Deere bicycle logo** is designed to promote an addition to the product line in the 1890s. The popularity of bikes rose in the 1880s when high-wheelers were being replaced by newly designed bicycles, which feature a chain drive and two equal-sized wheels with inflated tires. The masses can now master bicycle riding.

1890s The John Deere **Yazoo Sulky Lister** plants corn at the bottom of a trench used to catch limited rainfall in Nebraska and other semi-dry areas. The lister bottom is made from right- and left-hand moldboards. A shovel then opens a furrow for the seed. Two blades sweep soil back over the seed.

1890s The **disk plow** is preferred over the moldboard plow in very hard ground, in sticky soil, in rocky fields, and in newly cleared land with stumps. Disks are about two feet in diameter, but don't cover as much width as the typical 12- to 16-inch moldboards. Most horse-drawn disk plows have one or two disks.

CEO: Charles Deere

1890s

1890: Sales: $1.3 million
Net Income: $324,972

1892: Sales: $1.9 million
Net Income: $303,179

1894: Sales: $1.2 million
Net Income: $189,733

The Furrow debuts. It grows into one of the world's preeminent farmers' magazines. As the 20th century ends, it is published in 12 languages and distributed in more than 40 countries. Circulation is more than 1.5 million in 1999.

Unionization is in the air throughout the decade, but not a reality. At various times, independently of each other, grinders, molders, drillers, blacksmiths, polishers, and plow fitters walk off the job in disputes over wages, work assignments, and other matters.

The mid-1890s depression draws to an end. An era of prosperity begins for both farmers and their suppliers— a "Golden Age" that will last through World War I.

The Spanish-American War breaks out in April. When it ends in December, Spain has lost Cuba, Puerto Rico, Guam, Wake Island, and the Philippines to the U.S.

Farm crops top American exports throughout the 19th century, never dropping below 65 percent of total exports in any decade, sometimes surpassing 85 percent.

1899   The John Deere **Youngblood Driving Buggy** is being built in St. Louis. Its light weight and tall wheels make it easy to be pulled by a single horse, even at a trot. This stylish unit features an upholstered seat. The folding top protects passengers from sun and rain while providing ventilation and visibility.

1896:   Sales: $1.3 million
            Net Income: $284,147

1898:   Sales: $1.8 million
            Net Income: $412,004

Census takers confirm that while the number of implement companies has dropped by two-thirds since 1860 (to 715), many of those remaining have grown larger. Deere is one. In the 1899-1900 fiscal year, aggregate business exceeds $2 million for the first time.

Twenty implement makers, including Deere & Company and Deere & Mansur Company, announce plans to combine into the "American Plow Company." Charles Deere is the driving force, but the proposal collapses.

A giant appears: The International Harvester Company, created by consolidation of the three major harvesting-machine manufacturers.

George Mixter, plow-factory superintendent (and great-grandson of John Deere), persuades the company to install extensive environmental controls in the grinding room.

The St. Louis branch territory is split. The Dallas office becomes a full-fledged branch.

1908 The **Diamond Corn Sheller**, made by Marseilles, is sold by Deere (before it buys the company). The sheller is cranked and fed by hand. It thoroughly removes the kernels from ear corn, discharges the cobs, and delivers clean shelled corn in a bushel basket below. This is a great advancement over shelling corn by hand.

CEO: Charles Deere

1900s

1900: Sales: $2.1 million
Net Income: $495,130

1904: Sales: $2.9 million
Net Income: $35,229

For much of the decade, Deere decision-makers ponder responses to the aggressive, acquisitive International Harvester Company, whose line now includes manure spreaders, wagons, engines, and other products. Will International challenge Deere further and start making plows? Should Deere strike first and enter the harvester business?

Congress passes the Pure Food and Drug Act, and the Meat Inspection Act.

Charles Deere dies. William Butterworth, his son-in-law and heir-apparent for some years, becomes chief executive officer. The company establishes a non-contributory pension plan for employees with 20 or more years of service who have passed age 65.

George Washington Carver finds new uses for peanuts, sweet potatoes, and soybeans, thus helping diversify Southern agriculture. The Ford Model T appears, heralding the mass production of automobiles.

With affordable housing for some workers a problem, the company joins with the Deere estate to build 50 homes. By 1920, 315 homes and apartments have been built for employees in Moline and East Moline. Some are sold, some rented. After World War II, the company builds 111 more homes in Dubuque.

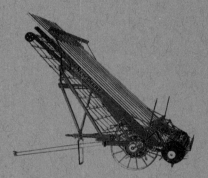

1900s The **double-cylinder hay loader** hitches to the rear of a wagon that passes over the hay. The cylinder at the rear picks up the hay and the chain conveyor carries it up and forward, dropping it onto the wagon. The man on the wagon spreads it uniformly so a full load can be carried to the storage barn.

1900s The **horse-drawn stubble digger** has an action similar to a man spading ground as the two rows of digging wheels roll along. It can be used for secondary tillage as an alternative to a disk harrow. (A similar, but shallower action is used by the rotary hoe that will be introduced a few years later. Rotary hoes still remain quite popular today.)

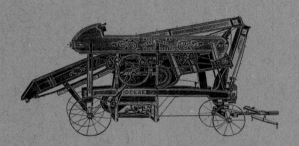

1900s The **power corn sheller** is used to shell ear corn stored after harvest. It is powered by a steam engine or an internal combustion engine. These new engines are fueled by oil, kerosene, or gasoline instead of coal or wood that a steam engine uses. The sheller is moved from farm to farm by a team of horses.

William Butterworth

Married to Katherine Deere, daughter of Charles, William Butterworth's tenure as company leader begins in 1907, just as steam engines and tractors start to replace animals as the power source on North American farms. By 1928, when he steps down to become head of the United States Chamber of Commerce, he will have supervised, albeit with some reluctance, Deere's entry into the tractor and combine businesses. Butterworth also will preside over consolidation of the company into basically its modern form.

A cautious and financially oriented lawyer, Butterworth holds conservative views on strictly business matters such as purchasing, spending, and inventory buildup. But he also has an abiding concern for employees, with a view that stresses loyalty, trust, and service. When leaving Deere, according to historian Wayne G. Broehl, Jr., "Butterworth had become the highly respected—yes, loved—father figure for the whole company." Annual sales increase during his presidency from $3 million to $64 million.

Directors launch a major reorganization. Its goal is a consolidated entity controlled by the Deere & Company board. The plan unifies factories and branches, anticipates acquisitions, and centralizes accounting and financial planning.

Experimental work in the first two decades of the 20th century increases disease-resistant plant varieties, plant yields and quality, and productivity of farm animal strains. For the first time, the company issues 400,000 shares of preferred stock. The shares are listed on the New York Stock Exchange the following year.

The modern Deere & Company emerges. It consists of 11 manufacturing entities in the United States and one in Canada, and 25 sales organizations—20 in the United States, including an export department, and five in Canada. The company also operates a sawmill and owns 41,731 acres of timberland in Arkansas and Louisiana.

International Harvester executives note that Deere has begun building a harvester factory in East Moline, Illinois, indicating it intends to compete in International's traditional market. Retaliating, they buy two plow manufacturers, thus invading Deere's traditional turf.

World War I begins. The Clayton Anti-Trust Act outlaws contracts that prohibit purchasers from buying or handling products of a seller's competitors. Full-line equipment makers like Deere have long pressed dealers not to stock competing products.

1910 **High-wheel wooden wagons** are made by the Moline Wagon Company. More than one million Moline wagons are in use when Deere buys the company. High-wheel wagons roll easily in muddy weather, hauling freight in town or grain, lumber, and other materials on farms.

1911 The **Van Brunt Grain Drill**, by John Deere, features a fertilizer box, adjustable fluted-feed seed meters, and single-disk openers. Sales reach 28,000 drills in 1912. (Still in use today, fluted-feed seed meters provide adjustable seed rates for wheat, soybeans, and other crops.)

1911 The **Light Draft Horse-Drawn Grain Binder** cuts wheat, oats, barley, and rye; ties the crop in bundles; and drops the bundles in windrows. This eliminates the backbreaking use of a scythe and cradle to cut grain, and muscle to tie the bundles.

1913 The **999 Horse-Drawn 2-Row Corn Planter** is a modern, high-quality planter and will be made for more than 30 years. It can check-row plant so the crop can be cultivated across the rows to rid weeds in the rows. Shoe openers are used for placing seed at the desired depth.

1915 The **corn binder** cuts corn or sorghum, ties it in bundles while stalks are vertical, conveys the bundles to the side, and drops them in windrows. Men then place multiple bundles in upright shocks, using twine to hold them together. Later they will be hauled in and fed to cattle, sometimes with the ears removed for feeding to hogs.

CEO: William Butterworth

1910s

1912:   Sales: $30.8 million
Net Income: $3.9 million

1914:   Sales: $31.1 million
Net Income: $2.1 million

New technology poses vexing questions to equipment makers: Is the gasoline-engine tractor a major innovation that will be adopted widely? If so, should implement makers buy them from specialist manufacturers or make them themselves?

Competitors enter the growing tractor business. Deere builds experimental and prototype models, but delays decisive action on producing what will become the most important tool of modern agriculture.

"Food Will Win the War," proclaims a popular slogan as the U.S. enters World War I. European demand pushes American farmers to unprecedented production levels for wheat and other crops.

The company buys the maker of Waterloo Boy tractors. The tractor will become its basic product. Though 5,634 Waterloo Boys are sold this year, Ford Motor Company sells 34,167 Fordson tractors. World War I ends; of 1,611 Deere employees who served, 37 died.

Labor turmoil spreads throughout the country. A bitter three-month strike over union recognition breaks out in Waterloo, the most serious employee relations strife Deere has so far experienced. The strike ends with Deere remaining non-union.

1918 The **Waterloo Boy "N" Tractor** has a kerosene-burning 25-belt-hp engine and two forward speeds of 2¼ and 3 mph. The 2-cylinder design, with belt pulley on the crankshaft, will be kept for simplicity on John Deere tractors for another four decades. This is the first tractor tested by the University of Nebraska.

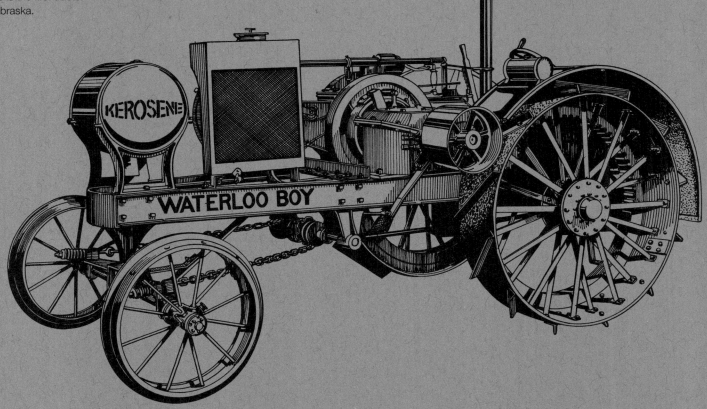

1916: Sales: $28.1 million
Net Income: $4.1 million
Employees: 6,700

1918: Sales: $42 million
Net Income: $4.8 million
Employees: 8,700

The economy nosedives. Farm bankruptcies skyrocket as the "Golden Age" of agriculture ends. Famous names, including General Motors, withdraw from the tractor field. The Federal Trade Commission accuses implement makers of price-fixing.

Bad times continue. As business shrinks, extensive layoffs follow. Waterloo Boy tractor sales plummet incredibly, to 79 from 5,045 the previous year. Wages of those still working are cut at least 10 percent.

Ford Motor Company again cuts tractor prices drastically, as it had in 1921, to attract business during hard times. This time the strategy pays off; Fordson tractor output jumps to almost 67,000 in 1922 from 35,000 in 1921.

The company launches the Model "D". A success from the start and the first two-cylinder Waterloo-built tractor to bear the John Deere name, it would stay in the product line for 30 years.

International Harvester introduces the Farmall, a breakthrough in tractor technology. Its design—rear wheels wide apart, front wheels close together—permits tractor cultivation of row crops. By decade's end, International builds almost 60 percent of farm tractors.

1924 The **Model "D"** is the first John Deere tractor designed at Waterloo, Iowa. It will completely replace horses for the western wheat farmer. It has the weight and power needed to plow, drill, mow, and thresh. This quality design will continue for 30 years with a peak of 23,806 being built in 1929.

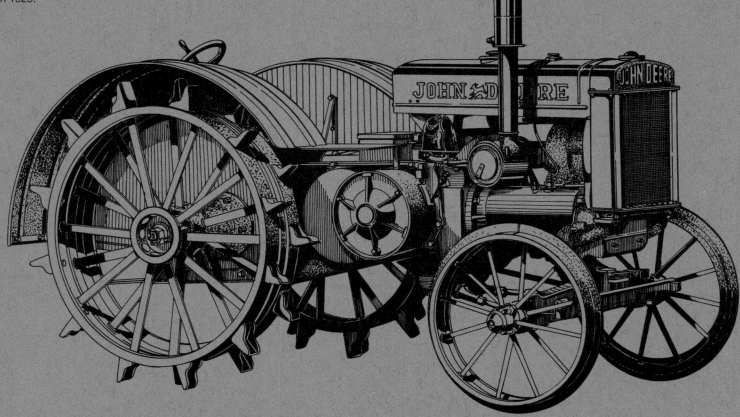

CEO: William Butterworth

1920s

1920: Sales: $61 million
Net Income: $6.1 million
Employees: 10,385

1922: Sales: $21.3 million
Net Loss: $2.5 million
Employees: 5,399

1924: Sales: $28.1 million
Net Income: $1.9 million
Employees: 5,432

Design begins on the "GP" (for General Purpose) Tractor, the John Deere answer to the Farmall.

Farm surpluses in the 1920s increasingly become an issue. In Detroit, Henry Ford institutes an eight-hour day and five-day work week at his factories.

The company produces a combine, the John Deere No. 2. A year later, catalogs advertise the John Deere No. 1, a smaller, more-popular machine. By 1929, the No. 1 and No. 2 are replaced by newer, lighter-weight versions.

William Butterworth is elected President of the United States Chamber of Commerce. Primary company managerial authority passes to Charles Deere Wiman.

The "GP" Wide-Tread, a row-crop tractor, enters the market. It is the first John Deere tractor with a tricycle front to fit between two crop rows, and a rear axle wide enough so wheels can straddle two rows.

1920s **The Model "B" Manure Spreader** has the beater-on-the-axle, a John Deere exclusive. This unique design lowers the sides to reduce the effort of loading manure by hand with a fork, a difficult job at best. The tines on the beater, which rotate opposite the wheels, tear apart and distribute the manure.

1920s The **Van Brunt "LL" Press Drill** disk openers place the seed deep to reach moist soil in low-rainfall areas. Large press wheels pack the soil firmly over the seed to get good germination.

1920s The **Dain Rake-Bar Hay Loader**, by John Deere, hitches to the rear of a wagon to pick up hay from the swath or windrow. The mechanism that picks up the hay duplicates the action of a person using a pitchfork. Additional tines lift the hay up and forward to deposit it onto the wagon.

1923 The **Model "E" Series single-cylinder stationary engines** become available in the most useful sizes of 1½, 3, and 6 hp. These engines replace muscle power on the farm for pumping water, washing clothes, sawing wood, and grinding grain.

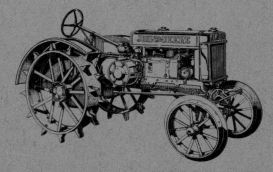

1928 The **Model "GP"** is John Deere's first row-crop tractor. It can be used to plant and cultivate three rows of corn or cotton. These tools are lifted by an industry-first mechanical power lift. The "GP" also harnesses power in three other ways: drawbar, belt pulley, and PTO.

1929 The **10-foot tractor grain binder** cuts twice as much grain as the 8-foot horse-drawn binder because the tractor does not need to rest in hot weather and can work longer days. It is driven by the tractor PTO instead of ground-driven by the bull wheel. It is built rugged for its new power source.

Charles Deere Wiman

Charles Deere Wiman, a great-grandson of the founder, becomes the fourth of his family to lead Deere & Company. His tenure, from 1928 to 1955, coincides with the Great Depression, World War II (when he will take a two-year leave of absence for government service), and a period of rapidly increasing farm mechanization. During his presidency, the size of the business increases fivefold, from $64 million to $340 million annually.

Wiman emphasizes good product design, efficient production, and engineering excellence. Engine use during his leadership tenure expands into machines other than tractors, such as self-propelled combines and cotton pickers. He exemplifies professional management, and has a unique ability to fire others to action—"the spark plug of the company," one colleague calls him. He respects the opinions of others, and recognizes the worth and integrity of the individual.

1926: Sales: $47.8 million
Net Income: $7.7 million
Employees: 7,292

1928: Sales: $64.2 million
Net Income: $11.3 million
Employees: 9,951

Consolidations leave only seven full-line farm equipment companies: John Deere, International Harvester, Case, Oliver, Allis-Chalmers, Minneapolis-Moline, and Massey-Harris. John Deere and International Harvester dominate most product categories.

A $1,200,000 embezzlement at People's Savings Bank in Moline—"Deere's bank"—threatens closure and loss of employee savings. The company writes a check to cover the loss. The bank survives.

The Great Depression hardens, forcing massive layoffs, pay and pension cuts, shortened hours, and a temporary end to paid vacations. A 1920s savings innovation, the Thrift Plan, eases the burden for some employees. John Deere continues group insurance for the unemployed, lowers rent in company housing, and starts "make work" projects.

Business is almost at a standstill. Sales plunge to $8.7 million. Though it is losing money, the company decides to carry debtor farmers as long as necessary, greatly strengthening farmer loyalty.

Despite the Depression, the company emphasizes product development. The Model "A" Tractor enters production. A similar but smaller Model "B" follows in 1935. They become the most popular tractors in the company's history, remaining in the product line until 1952.

1930 The **No. 30 Cotton Stripper** is drawn by two horses. It strips all the bolls from one row and puts them into a bin at the back.

1934 The **4-row cultivator** on an "A" Tractor features built-in hydraulic lift. Rear tractor steel wheels straddle two 40-inch rows.

1935 The **No. 5 Semi-Integral Tractor Mower** will be the best-quality mower on the market for more than two decades. It is simpler to attach than an integral mower. Because it can be fitted to many competitive tractors, the No. 5 has a large share of the market.

1936 The **Pickup Hay Baler** picks up hay directly from windrows but still requires tying of bales with wire manually. Custom operators like this baler.

1937 **Hammer mills** grind ear corn and other grains to make feed more digestible for hogs and cattle. The ground feed is blown into a cyclone tank where it is dropped into alternate sacks.

1938 The **Model "B" Tractor** becomes styled, and most farmers choose rubber tires. Electric starting and lights are an option. In 1946, Powr-Trol will offer hydraulic control of drawn implements. The Model "B" will become John Deere's most popular tractor, with 306,000 built from 1935 to 1952.

CEO: Charles Deere Wiman

1930s

1930: Sales: $67 million
Net Income: $8.2 million
Employees: 7,739

1932: Sales: $9.6 million
Net Loss: $5.2 million
Employees: 2,554

1934: Sales: $22.8 million
Net Income: $0.4 million
Employees: 7,003

John Deere, strong in wheeled tractors, and Caterpillar, dominant in tracked tractors, join forces to sell each other's products, especially in California. Strong at first, the link weakens with time, breaking finally in the mid-1960s.

The Agricultural Adjustment Act and other New Deal farm legislation helps farmers recover from Depression effects. Farm-equipment sales bounce back from their lows.

At the beginning of the decade, only 13 percent of farms have electricity. By decade's end, after passage of the Rural Electrification Act, the total rises to 33 percent. Not until the 1960s would virtually all farms have electricity.

Industrial designer Henry Dreyfuss, working with Deere engineers, streamlines the "A" and "B" Tractors. Henceforth, concern for attractive design joins traditional utilitarian values as hallmarks of John Deere products.

World War II begins. Model "L" Series Tractors, built at Wagon Works in Moline, Illinois, 1936 to 1946, enjoy an enormous boost in sales after Henry Dreyfuss' styling.

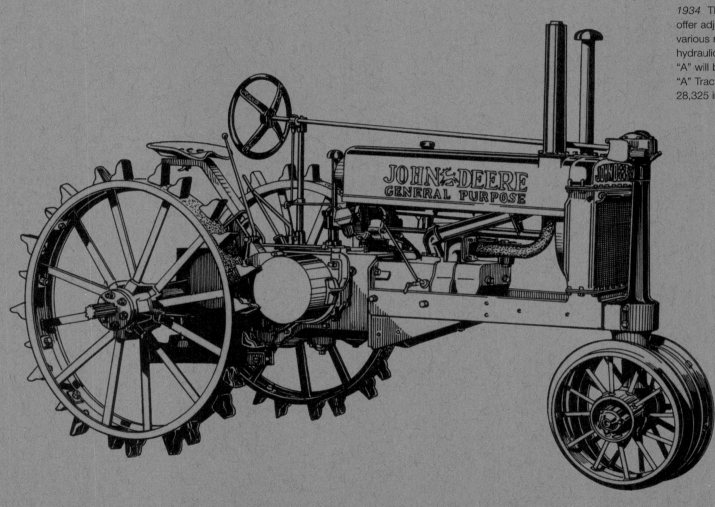

1934 The **Model "A" Tractor** is the first to offer adjustable rear wheels to fit between various row crops. Corn farmers enjoy the hydraulic lift for a 2- or 4-row cultivator. The "A" will be styled in 1938. A total of 292,000 "A" Tractors will be built, with a record of 28,325 in 1949.

1936: Sales: $71.5 million
Net Income: $11.6 million
Employees: 10,872

1938: Sales: $79.2 million
Net Income: $9.5 million
Employees: 11,821

Mechanization advances. American farms grow larger; the farm labor force shrinks. As the decade dawns, some 1.6 million farm tractors are in use, almost double the 1930 total.

The U.S. enters World War II. "Limitation orders" restrict civilian production of farm equipment, repair parts, and exports. (By 1944, with the tide of war turning toward the Allies, limitations on civilian production end.)

Charles Deere Wiman accepts a commission as an Army colonel. Burton Peek succeeds him as interim company president. Before returning to Deere in 1944, Wiman briefly directs the farm machinery and equipment division of the War Production Board.

Deere makes military tractors, ammunition, aircraft parts, and cargo and mobile laundry units during the war. About 4,500 employees serve in the military, some in the "John Deere" Battalion, a specialized ordnance group that sees service in Europe.

Price controls and food rationing affect families in the U.S. between 1942 and 1946. Frozen foods are popularized.

1940 The **12-A Drawn Combine** has a 6-foot cut with a straight-through 60-inch rasp-bar cylinder and straw rack. Grain tank holds 20 bushels. These combines soon replace grain binders and traditional threshers going from farm to farm.

CEO: Charles Deere Wiman

1940s

1940: Sales: $84 million
Net Income: $12.2 million
Employees: 13,520

1942: Sales: $133.5 million
Net Income: $12.7 million
Employees: 13,994

1944: Sales: $171.2 million
Net Income: $10.8 million
Employees: 17,245

Traditional company paternalism ebbs as John Deere factory workers endorse unions. Collective bargaining over wages and working conditions replaces a 105-year-old pattern of dealing with workers individually.

With wartime controls lifted, nationwide labor relations enter a tumultuous period. Frequent strikes ensue as management and labor test each other's strength.

The new John Deere Dubuque Works builds the Model "M" Tractor. Two years later, equipped with a tracked undercarriage, the "M" becomes available as a crawler, called the "MC". This will herald the Worldwide Construction Equipment Division. When a front blade is added, it becomes a bulldozer.

The John Deere Des Moines Works beats swords into plowshares. A former ammunition plant acquired from the government, it turns out cotton pickers and cultivating tools. Eventually it will also build plows, the company's original product.

The company's first diesel-powered unit, the Model "R" Tractor enters production.

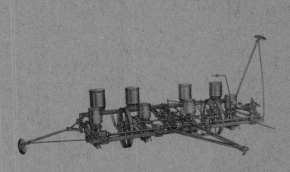

1940 The **490 4-Row Tractor-Drawn Planter** doubles the width and the speed of horse-drawn planters, greatly increasing planting rates. The 490 owner can accurately plant four times as much as his neighbor using horses. This power-lift planter can accurately check-row plant at 5 mph.

1946 The **116-W Baler** is the first on the market to automatically wire-tie. This one-man machine eliminates the dirty, sweaty jobs of two or more men on previous pickup balers. The baler is normally PTO-driven, but an engine is optional.

1947 John Deere is first with **Quik-Tatch 2- and 4-row front-mounted row-crop cultivators**. This reduces time and effort to mount the cultivator, so the farmer's only tractor can be readily switched to other uses such as mowing and raking hay.

1947 The **55 Self-Propelled Combine** features an auger platform with retracting fingers in the middle. The centered operator, grain tank, and engine give good stability and will set the industry design for many years. This combine will help start the custom-cutting business. These operators harvest grain for farmers in Texas and then work their way north to Canada as the grain ripens.

1949 The **"MC" Crawler**, manufactured at Dubuque, Iowa, is sold for use in hilly orchards, but will be used increasingly in the woods with a winch to skid logs. Its small size and weight make it easy to transport, so it also will become popular in the housing-construction industry.

1949 The **Model "R" Tractor** becomes the first diesel by John Deere. It appears to offer all the power and weight that large wheat and rice farmers can use. It provides 43 belt hp and weighs 7,400 pounds. Its 2-cylinder diesel engine is started by a 2-cylinder gasoline pony engine. It is also the first John Deere tractor to offer an optional cab.

Burton F. Peek

Burton F. Peek acts as chief executive of Deere & Company from 1942 to 1944, while his predecessor and successor, Charles Deere Wiman, performs World War II government service in Washington, D.C. Peek is distantly related to John Deere and as a boy had known him personally. Friend and adviser to three generations of John Deere men and women, Peek spends an incredible 68 years with the company, 30 as general counsel. After his stint as caretaker president, he will become chairman of the board of directors, holding that position until retirement in 1956. He will continue to serve on the board until his death at 88 in 1960.

1946: Sales: $143.9 million
Net Income: $9.6 million
Employees: 19,913

1948: Sales: $309.7 million
Net Income: $27.7 million
Employees: 26,249

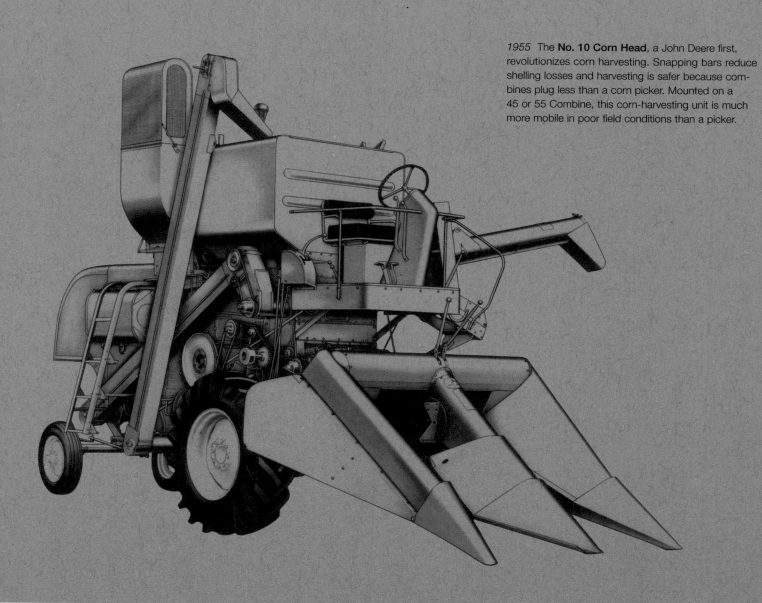

1955 The **No. 10 Corn Head**, a John Deere first, revolutionizes corn harvesting. Snapping bars reduce shelling losses and harvesting is safer because combines plug less than a corn picker. Mounted on a 45 or 55 Combine, this corn-harvesting unit is much more mobile in poor field conditions than a picker.

CEO: William A. Hewitt

1950s

Agreement with the United Auto Workers on a five-year contract ends a long period of postwar labor unrest.

The board appropriates funds for a small factory in Scotland, but in the end, terminates the project. Once before, consideration was given to manufacturing outside North America. In 1909 the board declined to act on a proposal for a Russian plow factory.

A Federal court dismisses an antitrust suit against Deere & Company. The government had charged Deere, International Harvester, and J.I. Case with illegally selling farm machinery to dealers on condition that they refuse to handle competing makes.

The Model 70 is launched as the largest row-crop tractor to date. Initially available with gasoline, all-fuel, or LP-gas engine, it will become the first diesel row-crop tractor.

Engineers develop a highly successful 2-row corn head. Attached to a new Model 45 Combine, it enables a farmer to pick, shell, and clean up to 20 acres of corn a day in a single operation.

1950 John Deere is first to sell **Safety-Trip Standards on plows** to protect the frame when a large stump or rock is encountered. The shear-pin plow trip used for years on plows is no longer adequate. Shear-pin trips require too much downtime in fields with many obstructions.

1950 The **No. 8 Cotton Picker** becomes the first 2-row self-propelled machine on the market. Its rapidly rotating barbed spindles pick only the cotton from the ripe bolls each time during two or three pickings.

1950 The **FB Grain Drill** has large-capacity seed and fertilizer boxes. Both single-disk and double-disk openers are available in 7- and 8-inch row spacings. Available in various sizes, this will be the most popular John Deere drill in the Midwest for 20 years.

1951 The **227 Tractor-Mounted Corn Picker** is a modern design with good husk removal and minimal plugging of the snapping rolls. The 2-cylinder tractor pulls a flare-box or barge-box wagon behind to collect and transport the ear corn.

1954 The **Model "N" Spreader** has PTO drive for the two beaters that break up and spread the manure, with ground drive for the conveyor chain. Its large 120-bushel capacity is now practical with a tractor doing the loading. It fills the needs of large dairy and beef farms.

William A. Hewitt

William A. Hewitt serves from 1955 until 1982 as Deere & Company's fifth chief executive officer. On his watch, manufacturing operations are rebuilt as the company diversifies beyond its traditional North American farm base into new product lines at home and into new markets abroad. During his term, annual sales will increase from $340 million to $4.6 billion. By direction and example, Hewitt encourages quality and style in all company activities, from the design of its products to the design of its buildings. In so doing, he raises the company's sights far beyond its Midwestern roots, transforming the firm into a world-class organization in both reach and image, while heightening employee morale and esprit de corps.

Hewitt, son-in-law of his predecessor, Charles Deere Wiman, is the last representative of the Deere family to head Deere & Company. He serves as Ambassador to Jamaica for three years following retirement. He dies in 1998 at 83.

1952: Sales: $383.2 million
Net Income: $35.2 million
Employees: 23,545

1954: Sales: $295.6 million
Net Income: $20.6 million
Employees: 18,538

William A. Hewitt is elected president and later chief executive officer following the death of Charles Deere Wiman, his father-in-law. He will direct the company for the next 27 years, the last representative of the Deere family to do so.

The firm steps toward becoming a multinational manufacturer. The company decides to build a small-tractor assembly plant in Mexico and buy a majority interest in a German tractor and harvester maker with a small presence in Spain. In the next few years, it will move into France, Argentina, and South Africa.

Six-row planters and cultivators, John Deere innovations, reach the market. They provide 50 percent more planting and cultivating capacity for row-crop farmers in corn- and cotton-producing areas.

The John Deere Credit Company, financier of domestic purchases of John Deere equipment, begins operations.

The company brings out the 8010, a diesel-powered, 215-horsepower, 10-ton Goliath—the largest tractor it has ever built. Only a few are sold. Soviet Premier Krushchev visits the Des Moines Works.

1955 The **No. 1 Hay Conditioner** is introduced. It is a simple PTO machine with a small, lower cast roll to pick and pass the hay between it and the upper roll. This bends and cracks forage-plant stems to cut drying time in half, helping save the valuable, nutritious leaves.

1955 The **45 Loader** features a simple, clean design with Quik-Tatch hookup so the farmer can drop the loader off and use the tractor for other work. Live hydraulics, introduced on John Deere tractors in 1952, speed loader operation. It has a mechanical-trip bucket.

1955 The **RW Wheel-Mounted Disk Harrow** is a simple medium-weight unit with rigid fixed-angle gangs. Hydraulic control provides uniform working depth at higher speeds. Widths of 7 to 14 feet are offered with 18- or 20-inch blades.

1956 The **953 Standard Wagon Gear** can carry 4 tons. More than 100,000 will be sold in its 20-year history. It meets the many varied hauling needs of farmers. It features Timken bearings, an adjustable reach tie rod protected by the front axle, and optional implement tires on its wheels.

1957 The **14T Baler** produces well-formed, twine-tied 14x18-inch bales of adjustable length. Most of these balers are PTO-driven. With the industry-first **No. 1 Bale Ejector**, short rectangular bales can be thrown into a trailing wagon, permitting one-man haying.

1958 The **440 Crawler** is John Deere's first real industrial tractor. It has five speeds, a direction reverser, and either 4- or 5-roller tracks. The T-bar on the 64 Dozer controls three functions. The integral 831 Loader will also become popular.

CEO: William A. Hewitt

1950s

1956: Sales: $313 million
Net Income: $20.1 million
Employees: 21,972

1958: Sales: $472.6 million
Net Income: $42.1 million
Employees: 30,876

1957 The **Lanz D1616 Tractor** is being built by Heinrich Lanz, A.G. when Deere purchases the German company. It has a buddy seat located on each rear fender for extra riders. Lanz Bulldog tractors use single-cylinder engines, even simpler than John Deere 2-cylinder engines. Originally, they burn crude oil but later switch to diesel-only. More than 200,000 Bulldogs are built from 1921 to 1960.

1961 The **3010 Tractor** marks the birth of the New Generation of Power. It features diesel, gas, and LP engines; an 8-speed Syncro-Range transmission; and a planetary final drive. The operator enjoys a better ride, improved controls, power steering, and power brakes. With the power of the previous 730 Tractor, it is a more-nimble, higher-speed tractor in the field.

CEO: William A. Hewitt

1960s

Four "New Generation of Power" tractor models steal the show at Deere Day in Dallas. Some 6,000 attend the sales meeting, including all U.S. and Canadian dealers.

A new tractor and implement manufacturing plant nears completion in Rosario, Argentina. In Saran, near Orléans, France, construction starts on a new engine factory. In Moline, construction begins on the Deere & Company Administrative Center.

John Deere marks 125th anniversary. Construction begins on a product engineering center at Dubuque, Iowa. Company buys a majority interest in South African Cultivators, a farm implement firm near Johannesburg.

John Deere surpasses International Harvester to become the world's largest producer and seller of farm and industrial tractors and equipment. The company ventures into the consumer market, deciding to produce and sell lawn and garden tractors plus some attachments such as mowers and snow blowers.

The Deere & Company Administrative Center opens. Designed by Eero Saarinen, it will win many architectural awards. Goals of the company and the principles behind its basic policies and procedures are outlined in the "Green Bulletins."

1961 The **16A Rotary Chopper** uses flails to chop a 6-foot width of standing forage, so pasture can be taken to the cattle. Forage is cut into even shorter lengths by three knives on the fan. The 16A will be built for more than 30 years, the record for John Deere products made since tractors replaced horses.

1962 The **600 Hi-Cycle™ Sprayer** has a low-slung 42-hp engine and 200-gallon spray tank. This self-propelled sprayer provides 60-inch crop clearance. Especially popular in cotton, it can spray, fertilize, or defoliate eight rows.

1963 The **5010 Elevating Scraper** is attached by gooseneck to a 127-hp 5010 diesel tractor with an offset operator station. Self-loading elevating scrapers do more work at less cost than regular scrapers because they require less total power.

1964 The **4020 Tractor** is the most admired tractor ever made by John Deere, with about 170,000 sold in 1964-1972. It had a 6-cylinder engine with 91 PTO hp and two new options—an 8-speed Power Shift transmission and a Power Differential Lock. The advanced features and reliability of the 4020 made it popular on large farms throughout the U.S. and Canada.

1965 The **2020 Tractor**, built in Dubuque, Iowa, offers most of the features of its bigger brothers from Waterloo, Iowa, but in a more-compact utility design. The 4-cylinder engine has two balancer shafts and supplies 54 PTO hp. One of the three PTO options includes a midpoint PTO outlet, especially useful for mowing.

1965 The **630 Combine** is designed and made in Zweibrücken, Germany, for the high-yield long-straw grain crops of Europe. It has a 100-hp Perkins diesel engine, a 41-inch cylinder, four walkers, and a 90-bushel grain tank. It uses a 10- to 14-foot grain platform.

1960: Sales: $510.3 million
Net Income: $19.8 million
Employees: 28,176

1962: Sales: $572.8 million
Net Income: $38 million
Employees: 23,586

1964: Sales: $816.6 million
Net Income: $59.4 million
Employees: 39,490

The John Deere Chemical Company, a fertilizer producer, is sold. It had been a subsidiary since 1962.

A banner year. Total sales surpass $1 billion for the first time. Earnings reach a high of $78.7 million. Farm equipment sales set a record for the fourth straight year. Industrial equipment sales notch their largest ever year-to-year increase. Lawn and garden equipment sales rise 76 percent. Worldwide employment hits a record.

The first industrial equipment sales branch opens in Baltimore, Maryland.

Color options appear for lawn and garden tractors. For a short time, traditional green and yellow are supplemented by dogwood white, and, for hood and trim, patio red, sunset orange, April yellow, and spruce blue.

Overall sales level out due primarily to a downturn in farm equipment sales. Overseas operations expand but do not produce profits. The John Deere Insurance Group is created.

1965 The **JD400 Backhoe Loaders** feature new Dubuque 300 Series engines and 8-speed transmissions. The loader is integral to the tractor for a productive working team. Popular center-mount and versatile offset-mount backhoes are optional.

1965 The **JD440 4-Wheel-Drive Log Skidder** is an immediate success as John Deere enters the forestry-equipment market. This nimble unit has a small stacking blade in front, a brush guard to protect the operator, and a winch to lift and skid logs through the forest.

1967 The **38 Forage Harvester** is all-new with exclusive rubber gathering belts for more positive, uniform feeding of row crops. It has a cylinder-type cutterhead with tungsten-carbide cutting-edge knives and a built-in sharpener. Forage is augered to a fan that blows it into a wagon or truck.

1967 The **JD570 Motor Grader** is the first in the world to offer all-hydraulic blade positioning, Power Shift transmission, and an articulated frame for a shorter turning radius. This frame design also lets the front wheels be offset from the rear wheels.

1968 The **JD544 4-Wheel-Drive Loader** uses an articulated frame to give it a tight 16-foot turning radius, a competitive advantage in maneuverability. The closed-center hydraulic system features a single lever to control the loader boom and bucket.

1969 The **JD690 Excavator** does the job of a backhoe loader but digs 21-feet deep, reaches farther, works faster, and rotates 360 degrees. It is ideal for digging basements and deep ditches. Its two-speed hydraulic-drive tracks counterrotate for easy maneuvering.

CEO: William A. Hewitt

1960s

1966: Sales: $1.1 billion
Net Income: $78.7 million
Employees: 45,978

1968: Sales: $1 billion
Net Income: $42.6 million
Employees: 42,023

1963 The **110 Lawn and Garden Tractor** has a 7-hp Kohler engine, a hand- or foot-controlled variable-speed V-belt similar to the drive on John Deere combines, and a 3-speed transmission. Most are sold with a 38-inch mower. Almost 23,000 units are sold in 1966 as people choose to ride while mowing.

1973 The **JD450C Crawler** is compact in size for easy transport and maneuverability. Its clean design, ease of operation, low downtime, and high productivity with either a dozer or a loader result in a high share of the market for the JD450C. More than 4,000 of these versatile crawlers sell in 1973, making it the best-selling Industrial Equipment product.

CEO: William A. Hewitt

1970s

The company reorganizes its management structure to reflect growing diversification. Three operating divisions emerge: Farm Equipment and Consumer Products, U.S. and Canada; Farm Equipment and Consumer Products, Overseas; and Industrial Equipment, which has worldwide responsibilities.

"Nothing Runs Like a Deere" advertises snowmobiles, a new product of the John Deere Horicon Works. The slogan lasts far longer than the snowmobile line, which is sold in 1984.

Deere and Italian conglomerate Fiat end negotiations on a joint venture that would have encompassed Deere's overseas operations. Four new "Generation II" tractor models with operator enclosures—Sound-Gard bodies—reach the market. Farm-equipment sales exceed $1 billion.

Crop failures outside North America spur massive foreign buying of American grain. Commodity prices spurt. Farmers prosper; equipment demand erupts. John Deere total sales top $2 billion for the first time. Board decides to move toward a more independent board as the first outside director is appointed.

Unprecedented demand for John Deere products, especially farm equipment, continues, but capacity and other shortages appear. Inflation increases costs. The company starts its largest expansion program. More than $1 billion will be spent on new facilities by 1979.

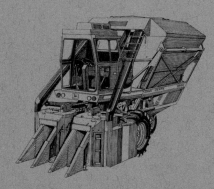

1970 John Deere **400 Series Rotary Hoes** become the first to provide spring-loaded hoe wheels. This provides good penetration while protecting the wheels from damage when hitting rocks at the fast travel speeds required for kicking out weeds effectively.

1970 The **40 Series Corn Heads** use row-unit gearcases mounted on a toolbar to permit adjusting row spacings from 36 to 40 inches. Different models accommodate harvesting two to eight rows. These corn heads are so popular that many are used on competitive combines. They are built and sold for more than 20 years.

1972 The **9900 2-Row Cotton Pickers** have all-new smaller, lighter, higher-speed drums that function better and permit higher field-travel speeds. Automatic height sensing is an industry first. Basket capacity is greater and unloading is faster to improve productivity.

1972 The **2030 Tractor** has a 4-cylinder 71-hp engine for excellent power and an 8-speed collar-shift transmission for easy shifting. The John Deere engine is made in Saran, France, and the tractor in Mannheim, Germany. More than 7,000 2030 Tractors are shipped in 1976 to farmers in Europe.

1973 The **1630 Tractor** with a 3-cylinder 57-hp engine is the best-selling of five models made in Getafe, Spain. Annual sales of the 1630 exceed 2,000 units for six years and average more than 9,000 for all 30 Series models, providing John Deere with one-fourth of the Spanish market.

1973 The **4430 Generation II Tractor** is armed with a turbocharged diesel engine and a heat-dissipating wet clutch. Three-fourths of the 4430s are equipped with the optional Sound-Gard body featuring 4-post Roll-Gard™ operator protection. A new 16-speed Quad-Range™ transmission joins the 8-speed Power Shift as an option.

1970: Sales: $1.1 billion
Net Income: $46 million
Employees: 39,868

1972: Sales: $1.5 billion
Net Income: $112.2 million
Employees: 45,063

1974: Sales: $2.5 billion
Net Income: $164.3 million
Employees: 55,962

The John Deere Davenport Works, located in Davenport, Iowa, comes on-line, manufacturing industrial-equipment components.

Equipment gets bigger, increasing farm productivity. Tractors average 40 percent more horsepower and 44 percent more weight than in 1970. Sales of both farm and industrial equipment triple and consumer-products sales soar fivefold since 1966.

Agreement with Japanese manufacturer Yanmar authorizes sale of small tractors under the John Deere name. An updated Product Engineering Center is established in Waterloo. A stock-purchase plan for salaried employees begins.

The award-winning West Office Building addition to the Administrative Center, designed by Kevin Roche, Eero Saarinen's successor, opens. Also new: Canadian headquarters in Grimsby, Ontario; John Deere Engine Works in Waterloo; and Atlanta sales branch offices.

Employment reaches an all-time high of 65,392. Sales top $5 billion, earnings $310 million, both records.

1974 The new **210 Lawn and Garden Tractor** uses a proven variable-drive 4-speed transmission. Vibration and noise are reduced by isolating the 10-hp Kohler engine and enclosing the sides. Farm-tractor styling boosts sales of these tractors, primarily used for mowing.

1975 The **7000 Max-Emerge® Planters** are all-new in 4- to 12-row sizes. Tru-Vee™ double-disk openers have depth wheels beside them for controlling seed depth, and are followed by angled closing wheels. Seed metering is by finger pickup, feedcup, or plate.

1975 The **955 Combine** is manufactured in Zweibrücken, Germany, with a John Deere 117-hp engine built in Saran, France. Its 41-inch-wide cylinder, four straw walkers, 89-bushel grain tank, 10- to 16-foot platforms, and 3- and 4-row corn heads match the needs of European farmers.

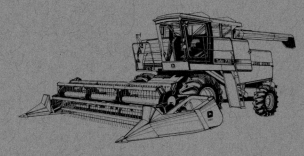

1978 The **440 Trailfire Snowmobile** provides recreation for John Deere customers. Its high-speed, 2-cylinder, 2-cycle engine is located in front for a low profile.

1979 The **4239D naturally aspirated cross-flow 300 Series diesel engine**, made in Saran, France, has been the most popular engine for many models of John Deere tractors and combines. During 1999, Saran builds its 1,300,000th 300 Series engine. These include 3-, 4-, and 6-cylinder models. In later years, many engines are turbocharged.

1979 The **7720 Combine** will become the most popular of the four sizes sold. With five walkers, a larger engine, and bigger grain tank, the 7720 provides more harvesting capacity. A 4-speed hydrostatic transmission and a Sound-Gard-style cab are standard.

CEO: William A. Hewitt

197Os

1976: Sales: $3.1 billion
Net Income: $241.6 million
Employees: 55,242

1978: Sales: $4.2 billion
Net Income: $264.8 million
Employees: 59,208

1979 The **111 Lawn Tractor** has an 11-hp vertical-crank-shaft engine and a 5-speed transaxle with an easy-to-shift control on the right fender. For fire safety, the fuel tank is at the rear. Its farm-tractor styling helps sales climb to 24,557 units in 1981. This lower-cost unit meets the needs of many customers who simply want a mowing tractor, instead of a full-fledged lawn and garden tractor.

1986 The all-new **310C Backhoe Loader** comes equipped with a torque converter, power-shift reverser, differential lock, and optional mechanical front-wheel drive that increase work output. The unitized frame isolates the engine and cab, reducing noise and vibration in the operator station and, thus, stress on the very busy operator.

CEO: Robert A. Hanson

1980s

1980	1981	1982	1983	1984
A 4-row cotton picker, an industry first, is introduced. Field tests indicate it will increase an operator's productivity by 85 to 95 percent.	The John Deere Tractor Works in Waterloo, Iowa, becomes fully operational. It wins an award for excellence in using computers in U.S. manufacturing.	Robert A. Hanson succeeds retiring Chairman William A. Hewitt.	Severe recession following rampant 1970s inflation crimps the need and ability of farmers and builders to invest in new equipment. Difficult business conditions continue through most of the decade.	With cost reduction a priority, the company looks inward. Flexible manufacturing, CAD-CAM (computer aided design and manufacturing), employee participation, cellular manufacturing, total waste elimination, group technology, and just-in-time become familiar procedures. The company acquires Farm Plan® Corporation, an agribusiness financier.

1981 The **245 Loader** features Quik-Tatch hookup and mechanical self-leveling. This rugged loader was designed jointly with and for John Deere utility tractors, including those with mechanical front-wheel drive for better traction in slippery feedlots.

1983 The **550 Round Baler,** made in Arc-les-Gray, France, produces tight twine-wrapped, weather-resistant bales four feet wide. Broad acceptance throughout the hay-growing areas of France and the U.K. result in life-time sales of more than 20,000 balers.

1983 The German-designed **2755 Tractor** and its 4-cylinder turbocharged diesel engine are made in Saltillo, Mexico, for the Mexican market. The 2755 is especially popular in the wheat-growing North, and 25,000 units are built through 1994.

1984 The **648D Skidder** has 120 hp with an 8-speed power-shift transmission. Its grapple can reach back to grab logs and then lift them forward for transport. The grapple saves the operator the time and effort of getting off the skidder to attach and detach cables.

1986 The **855 Compact Utility Tractor** has a 3-cylinder Yanmar diesel engine providing 19 PTO hp and a 2-range hydrostatic drive. Most owners choose the optional mechanical front-wheel drive. The mower, loader, and tiller can be left on while any one of the three is in use.

1986 The **F935 Front Mower** has a 22-hp Yanmar diesel engine and hydrostatic drive controlled by patented dual pedals. This highly maneuverable commercial mower can travel as fast as 10.6 mph. Triple-blade mowers are available for cutting 60 to 76 inches wide.

Robert A. Hanson

Robert A. Hanson leads Deere & Company as its chief executive officer from 1982 until 1989, a daunting period of constant challenge brought on largely by a long-lasting farm-equipment downturn following years of inflation. Through it all, Hanson guides with zest, a positive attitude, and excellent judgment. Though the company has fewer employees and facilities upon his retirement in 1989, annual sales increase from $4.6 billion to $7.2 billion. The company returns to profitability and is on solid financial footing.

Hanson, the sixth Deere & Company chief executive, is the first to be unconnected with the founding family. His appointment ends a period of Deere family leadership that lasted 145 years.

1982: Sales & Revenues: $4.8 billion
Net Income: $53 million
Employees: 48,372

1984: Sales & Revenues: $4.6 billion
Net Income: $105 million
Employees: 43,011

John Deere Health Care, Inc. is formed. Its subsidiary, Heritage National Healthplan, grows by century's end into a health-care provider for more than 700 employers and over 400,000 members in five states.

A 163-day labor strike in the U.S. severely impacts production. Employment at year's end totals 37,481, down 43 percent from the 1979 high of 65,392. For the remainder of the century, employment will remain below 40,000.

The company celebrates its 150th anniversary. Continued low farm income and lower Deere sales lead to a net loss of $99 million.

The economy rebounds after six years of recession during which weaker farmers, dealers, and equipment companies go out of business. Deere & Company sales soar 30 percent from 1987. Profit, following two years of losses, exceeds $315 million, a record. A joint venture is formed with Japanese company Hitachi to assemble excavators in the U.S.

The dividend, cut in 1982, is restored to its previous level. Funk Manufacturing Company, maker of powertrain components, is acquired.

1987 The **7200 Series Max-Emerge 2 Planters** improve on a winner. A new, simple vacuum meter permits planting faster, while providing better spacing in corn, soybeans, cotton, and sorghum. Various options enable no-till planting.

1987 The **RX75 Riding Mower** has a 9-hp Kawasaki engine and a variable-speed V-belt drive for speeds up to 5.4 mph. A rear-mounted grass collector, a front thatcher, and a lawn sweeper are optional. More than 21,000 units sell in 1988.

1988 The **1360 Mower-Conditioner** from Arc-les-Gray, France, cuts 10 feet. Its rotary disks permit high-speed mowing in wet hay and even through dirt mounds. The free-swinging tine impeller, along with the hood, scuffs the wax off grass and legume hay for faster drying.

1988 The **STX38 Lawn Tractor** has an overhead-valve 12.5-hp Kohler engine; a right-fender, in-line, 5-speed control; and a 38-inch mower. First-year sales pass those of any 100 Series Lawn Tractor, partly because it is priced almost as low as similar riding mowers.

1988 The **14SB Self-Propelled Walk-Behind Mower** has a 4.5-hp engine and a 21-inch aluminum deck. This rear-discharge mower comes with a rear bagger. This design makes the mower much more maneuverable, and clippings easier to unload.

1989 The **750 No-Till Drill** is a major contributor in the switch to drilled soybeans. Staggered openers provide consistent seed depth with good soil contact, even in no-till ground. It comes in widths of 10 and 15 feet with row spacings of 7½ or 10 inches.

CEO: Robert A. Hanson

1980s

1986: Sales & Revenues: $4.2 billion
Net Loss: $229 million
Employees: 37,793

1988: Sales & Revenues: $6.2 billion
Net Income: $315 million
Employees: 38,268

1989 The **9600 Combine** brings greater operator comfort and improved controls, a larger cylinder for better threshing, and better cleaning. Corn heads as wide as 12 rows and grain platforms as wide as 30 feet are available. The 9000 Series Combines are designed for worldwide use.

1992 The **5000 Series Tractor** line anchors the industry-leading John Deere tractor line. The highly manueverable utility machines achieve North American leadership and are established as the basic model design for use in the developing world, with production operations in the United States, Brazil, Turkey, and India.

CEO: Hans W. Becherer

1990s

1990	1991	1992	1993	1994
Hans W. Becherer, president since 1987 and chief executive officer since 1989, is elected chairman upon the retirement of Robert A. Hanson.	Lawn-and-grounds-care equipment operations in the U.S. and Canada become a separate division. Since 1970 they had been part of farm-equipment operations. The company acquires SABO, a European maker of lawn mowers.	A program is launched to encourage installation of rollover protective structures and seat belts on older tractors. In 1966, John Deere introduced the first commercially available rollover protective devices for farm tractors, later releasing the patent to the industry without charge. The company establishes eight Strategic Business Units for the first time.	New 5000, 6000, and 7000 Series Tractors drive up market shares in North America and Europe. Among 20 contenders in Germany, John Deere moves from third to first place in tractor sales. Lawn-and-garden-equipment sales top $1 billion for the first time.	The company acquires Homelite, a leading producer of handheld outdoor power equipment. It arranges with Zetor, a Czech company, to provide a simple, small tractor for developing markets. John Deere Family Healthplan centers— primary-health-care providers—open in Waterloo and Des Moines, joining one opened in Moline in 1993.

1991 The **690E Excavator** is a real dirt mover with its unique load-sensing hydraulic system powered by a high-torque-rise, 130-net-hp engine. It can dig 22 feet deep and reach 32 feet. The machine weighs 45,000 pounds. Operator controls digging by using two levers.

1992 The **Gator® 6x4 Utility Vehicle** has an 18-hp gasoline engine powering the four rear wheels with a continuously variable V-belt transmission. It can haul 800 pounds in its cargo box and tow 1,200 pounds. It's a work vehicle that makes work fun.

1992 The **6400 Tractor**, built in Mannheim, Germany, is powered by a turbocharged 4.5-liter engine delivering 85 PTO hp. A 12-speed synchronized transmission is standard, with an optional PowrQuad™ transmission available to enhance loader operation. The 6400 meets the needs of growing farms in Europe, as well as the rest of the world.

1992 The **7800 Tractor** features a 16-speed PowrQuad™ transmission. Gear selections within ranges don't require clutching. Power Shift offers 19 forward speeds, and hitch-lift capacity is increased. This All-New Breed of Power tractor represents the biggest design change since 1961.

1995 The **8300 Tractor** at 200 PTO hp uses a new approach to large row-crop tractor design. The engine is placed high enough over the front wheels to permit short turns. This powerful tractor offers the operator excellent vision and simple armrest controls.

1997 The **12.5-Liter POWERTECH® engine** is an all-new 6-cylinder engine with an overhead cam, 24 valves, and unit injection. It features electronic engine control and a 35 percent torque increase. It powers the 4-wheel-drive and track-type 9300 and 9400 Tractors.

Hans W. Becherer

Hans W. Becherer, elected in 1989 as Deere & Company's seventh chief executive officer, leads a strong and focused global company into the 21st century. He stresses "genuine value," which builds on strategies of continuous improvement and global growth to deliver superior value for stockholders, increased opportunity for employees, greater satisfaction for customers, and continuing support of the communities where John Deere operates.

Becherer helps enlarge John Deere's focus from cost reduction to include growth, renewed globalization, and new emphasis on improving quality. In addition, four separate operating divisions are created, fundamentally restructuring the company.

During his term, John Deere remains the world's premier manufacturer and seller of agricultural equipment. Annual sales and revenues increase from $7.2 billion to $13.8 billion, and earnings top $1 billion for the first time in John Deere's history.

1992: Sales & Revenues: $6.9 billion
Net Income: $37 million
Employees: 34,852

1994: Sales & Revenues: $9 billion
Net Income: $604 million
Employees: 34,252

The company's strong performance "shows that Deere & Company has become a new company in every important sense," according to the Annual Report. Among reasons cited: product technology leadership, strong emphasis on quality, and improved cost structure and asset management.

Four mid-priced lawn tractors and two walk-behind mowers branded "Sabre® by John Deere" expose company products to a broad new market. They're designed to be sold through national retailers and home centers as well as John Deere dealers.

Overseas sales top $3 billion, more than the company's entire sales total prior to the mid-1970s. The company obtains an equity position in a Chinese combine company. The John Deere Pavilion, with equipment exhibits and interactive displays, opens in downtown Moline, Illinois.

Despite late-year weakness in the farm sector, agricultural-equipment sales hit a record. Company net earnings reach $1 billion for the first time. Cameco Industries, producer of sugarcane-harvesting equipment, is acquired. Work begins on a new tractor-manufacturing facility in Pune, India.

While challenging by financial standards, 1999 is a breakthrough year for John Deere. Not only does the company record a meaningful profit in the face of a major downturn in the farm economy, but the actions of recent years to create a more-resilient world-class enterprise successfully faced their first severe test. Special Technologies Group is formed.

1997 The **310SE Backhoe Loader** features a new curved boom with a single-pin attachment for the boom and dipperstick cylinders. It is built stronger and provides more backhoe lift, crowd power, and stability. Two-lever backhoe control is standard, and MFWD is optional.

1997 The **1175 Combine** made in Horizontina, Brazil, is similar to an earlier combine made in Zweibrücken, Germany, with a 51-inch cylinder, five walkers, and a 137-bushel grain tank. Farmers growing soybeans and corn in Brazil and farmers growing wheat and corn in Argentina find the 1175 well matched to their needs.

1998 The **4600 Compact Tractor** is designed and assembled in Augusta, Georgia. The 4-cylinder engine provides 36 PTO hp. Base transmission is a 9-speed with optional PowrReverser and hydrostatic transmissions. This versatile tractor is perfect for cutting grass or moving dirt.

1998 The **240 Skid Steer** features all-new design and is made in a new factory near Knoxville, Tennessee. Its 46-hp John Deere engine powers the hydrostatic transmission. The 240 has an innovative vertical lift, good stability, and easy servicing.

1999 The **450H Crawler** features a single lever for controlling direction and steering. The dual-path hydrostatic drive senses the load and automatically adjusts speed and power. Serviceability, ride, controls, and optional cab are improved on this 70-hp crawler.

1999 The **9750 STS Combine** uses tines on a single rotor in a cage to expand the crop as it progresses to the rear for excellent crop flow, high capacity, good separation, and superb grain quality. The largest-capacity combine John Deere has ever made features a 325-hp engine and a 300-bushel grain tank.

CEO: Hans W. Becherer

1990s

1996: Sales & Revenues: $11.2 billion
Net Income: $817 million
Employees: 33,919

1998: Sales & Revenues: $13.8 billion
Net Income: $1 billion
Employees: 37,002

Hans Becherer reaches retirement, and Robert W. Lane is elected chief executive officer. The company acquires Timberjack, a world-leading producer of forestry equipment.

Using GPS satellites and wireless communication media, John Deere Special Technologies Group is developing new global vehicle communication systems. These systems can collect, process, and deliver data to manage agricultural, construction, lawn-care, and golf-course equipment and operations.

From humble beginnings as a one-man blacksmith shop in 1837, John Deere enters the millennium with more than 38,000 employees worldwide running smart and embracing new opportunities

2000 Traces of the future of machine management can be found in the **DeereTrax™ global vehicle communications system**. The service allows customers to instantly track the exact location and engine hours of every machine in their fleets using a simple Web browser. Such up-to-the-minute information allows customers to pinpoint when and where each machine will be serviced for optimum performance.

20?? Tests in the late 1990s with this **prototype driverless 8200 Tractor** open the door to an exciting new era in farming. During the demanding planting season, for example, the farmer can operate the planter while using one driverless tractor to prepare the field ahead and another to keep the planter supplied with seed and fertilizer. At harvest, the combine can be unloaded on-the-go into a grain cart pulled by a driverless tractor.

Robert W. Lane

In 2000, Robert W. Lane is elected Deere's eighth chief executive officer. Lane faces the challenging beginnings of a new millennium including accelerating global competition, worldwide industry consolidation, rapidly advancing technology, e-business transformations, and downward pressures on commodity prices. Key to the company's growth and success in the next decade, while it "e-enables" itself, will be recruiting top international talent, driving breakthrough levels of service solutions for a growing worldwide customer base, and leading the introduction of innovative technology for new and diverse customer segments globally.

People

Values come alive through people. This section recognizes the dedicated individuals who continue the John Deere legacy of quality, innovation, integrity, and commitment. The 63,676 worldwide employees and living retirees (as of January 1, 2000) are listed in order of service start date.

1919 J.A.Shipley, **1922** P.Laupp, **1923** H.B.Pence, O.J.Boxmann, **1924** E.M.Hurley, E.W.Abrahamson, T.Dhaenens, **1925** J.A.Crumley, N.S.Shinn, H.C.Hartman, **1926** A.J.Herstedt, F.G.Hileman, J.F.Stauber, **1927** O.L.Utter, L.A.Dirks, R.Marsch, H.J.Wascher, K.W.Moses, R.J.Bull, J.Kotzonel, G.W.Kroeger, R.F.Goossens, A.Waem, J.T.Findlay, F.L.Reed, **1928** H.L.Ford, W.F.Shimkus, M.F.Feliksiak, C.A.Kran, C.G.Timmerman, E.A.Wheeler, E.W.Bernard, L.W.Veys, K.L.Potter, E.Tufte, D.G.Williamson, P.V.Leaman, R.C.Detaeye, R.P.Annette, R.T.Valentine, W.F.Denolf, G.E.Eickelberg, A.J.Vandevoorde, G.M.Hummel, L.H.Briden, A.Bruyninckx, M.Tessier, C.E.Strobbe, **1929** W.F.King, C.W.Blombergson, W.H.Mee, F.Hagarty, W.S.Wood, D.C.Ainley, G.Green, H.W.Weber, J.Barret, V.J.Standaert, H.A.Thorngren, E.H.Bothun, **1930** H.J.Tadewald, C.L.Meyers, C.M.Cowell, **1932** L.H.Foxen, J.Dumontier, **1933** H.W.McCandless, L.G.Walters, W.C.Malone, M.J.Bunz, H.E.Stokes, M.J.Decoster, C.G.Hasson, R.E.Lyons, M.E.Mc Clellan, C.E.Goodrich, T.W.Faye, J.H.Cox, C.L.Depaepe, **1934** M.L.Krey, F.Struessel, J.J.Aubry, G.H.Schultz, W.J.Depoorter, B.E.Voy, L.J.Lopez, L.R.Gustafson, G.F.Scheier, P.Haegeman, C.J.Maerschalk, G.T.French, R.E.Mitchell, W.Tetmeyer, L.A.Einwalter, D.A.Campie, R.J.Olson, J.J.Hardi, F.Gage, J.D.Wormley, J.C.Carson, B.B.Johannsen, K.F.Kemp, E.H.Granholm, D.Sansone, H.R.Backerman, E.L.Conard, J.I.Cantral, G.H.Stevens, S.E.Mapes, H.F.Albert, V.F.Hein, F.B.Landuyt, H.L.Broderson, H.R.Vergane, E.R.Vanquathem, C.L.Degraeve, L.H.Hostetler, F.H.Wegner, R.C.Sheerer, **1935** H.K.Norling, M.L.Keener, R.S.Bruner, E.O.Brocka, J.J.Greshay, F.D.Webster Sr., L.B.McIntire, M.S.Churuvia, G.Hall Jr., R.W.Boehne, A.J.Pearson, A.J.Immesoete, W.R.Johnson, R.P.Schuler, G.Hillier, F.A.Gober, W.L.Nielsen, E.Ligeno, K.D.Brink, L.J.Sours, Z.W.Gapsis, G.M.Reese, W.E.Zeran, H.S.Keener, H.T.Mc Elvenny, L.H.Burk, G.A.Hoogerwerf, A.F.Talley, K.A.Baumgartner, G.W.McFadyen, R.Halvorson, C.C.Koehn, P.Uzelac, M.A.Harris, W.E.Paulson, E.G.Peterson, V.J.Tihart, A.F.Otto, A.C.Raes, A.W.Anderson, D.Kenney, E.H.Dunavin, S.F.Bright, C.B.Buckley, A.H.Hunter, L.D.Truitt, P.M.Vest, W.E.Moody, G.Marmignon, F.H.Lockard, M.E.Leach, B.G.Heber, A.A.Haegeman, J.I.Plavak, J.N.Krambeck, F.W.Harper, L.D.Decapp, G.D.Anderson, A.L.Van Raes, A.V.Taets, K.L.Satterlee, A.J.Grammens, C.Heaton, A.R.Vanoverschelde, B.W.Hollingsworth, C.A.Adams, M.M.Hayes, P.B.Holden, G.H.Eggerichs, D.D.Seefeldt, J.E.Soucinek, R.G.Nystrom, C.T.Hinman, S.D.Stang, D.E.Sholl, H.C.Jack, R.W.Hickman, F.E.Priest, D.A.Finch, H.Schlueter, A.M.Finlan, E.R.Zarling, M.M.Larson, F.E.Taylor, N.J.Sachau, L.D.Waem, H.R.Larrabee, M.I.Barron, G.J.Zuleger, W.D.Young, M.W.Faust, W.W.Acord, C.J.Babinski, C.C.Katzell, C.French, C.W.Voy, M.E.Boostrom, R.E.Morrison, O.B.Barron, W.H.Dohrmann, S.T.Glynn, R.C.Gadow, A.J.Gray, M.E.Casillas, W.P.Lyons, F.G.Decoster, H.L.Hoffman, P.J.Demarlie, H.B.Grundstrom, G.E.Stewart, R.J.Vandevoorde, T.V.Demeulenaere, F.O.Agee, K.A.Marsh, **1936** C.H.Kimbrell, J.McIntosh, A.C.Simoens, C.M.Kilgard, G.Paytash Jr., J.J.Schorpp, G.W.Le Fevre, D.E.Lynch, E.C.Lant, C.H.Rursch, L.C.Gosden, L.R.Reasoner, R.R.Paulsen, W.W.Goodrell, N.W.Lewis, F.C.Schaner, H.Plavak, C.P.Ryckaert, J.C.Veryzer, L.D.Viscioni, E.C.Greenway, L.A.Pearson, R.E.Fisher, G.L.Mullery, J.L.Montford, R.C.Case, D.O.Culbertson, R.R.Brown, R.E.Windland, E.F.Prochaska, R.F.Cox, B.T.Henderson, R.H.Peel, R.L.Carr, C.E.Neff, J.E.Manro, W.T.Nielsen, F.T.Kinney, O.Creusillet, M.D.Wilkinson, E.Powell, E.C.Pearson, W.F.Pottmeyer, D.L.Kruse, H.I.Martin, E.T.Speer, D.L.Thompson, H.E.Jensen, F.J.Lindaman, G.A.Nelson, V.L.Wegner, W.D.Harlow, J.G.Miller, H.W.Kingsley, G.V.Hanny, L.A.Mc Intee, R.N.Schmitz, R.E.Hemsath, C.L.Leeds, R.R.Garrison, W.E.Powell, J.S.Levis, J.W.Service, V.A.Dodge, M.A.Schessow Sr., G.E.Mc Donald, P.L.Barnett, J.L.Gruver, **1937** F.Lesthaeghe, K.A.Lane, G.E.Neff, H.L.Durham, O.C.Short, A.Prosen, P.J.Claeys, R.A.McNamara, H.E.Woods, F.D.Wiseman, H.J.Snavely, P.S.Koppang, H.A.Hastings, H.R.Prusia, A.B.Fox, J.S.Benak, J.F.Claeys, J.F.Mendel, L.J.Krafka, D.R.Andres, E.A.Leach, R.D.Kershaw, J.V.Rossi, E.J.Ingenthron, T.Taylor, W.M.Beard, C.M.Price, C.D.Boylan, H.J.Dekezel, R.N.Allsberry, B.H.Swanberg, D.E.Dickson, W.M.Smith, E.C.McTighe, K.W.Andrews, L.E.Granell, H.G.Henderson, A.E.Pavesic, A.L.Hubbard, D.C.Koehler, E.J.Gelande, J.Jardinet, W.H.Carmack, H.Bedek Sr., J.Bubon, R.M.Perkins, H.Sergent, C.Fentress, J.D.Shelby, C.S.Williams, R.E.Addington, R.E.Foster, R.S.Andrews, R.L.Bladel, R.P.Guetzlaff, E.F.Billhartz, H.R.Leehey, G.C.Carr, C.K.Cook, J.F.Sullivan, M.T.Paskvan, R.S.Kendall, W.G.Osthoff, M.J.Zergiebel, W.H.Nelson, F.E.Brown, E.H.Roberts, L.Aurousseau, A.L.Vandaele, E.W.Dalton, K.L.Sommers, C.A.Blomberg, R.M.Ward, 1938 R.E.Wern, W.T.Griffith, G.C.Rhea, J.E.Hildebrand, F.E.Schelstrate, R.N.Paradise, A.J.Vanauwelaer, R.N.Ickes, K.H.Elkema, A.R.McCune, M.Mitchell, T.Black, **1939** E.M.Johnson, J.B.Porter, R.M.Shassberger, L.C.Stark, J.L.Barnard, H.W.Simpson, F.C.Heitke, B.C.Probert, H.G.Kuhlman, W.W.Newsum, C.F.Plummer, P.G.Feuerbacher, V.J.Barnes, V.D.Hagelin, J.L.Reece, G.A.Martin, D.M.Williams, D.A.Oetting, J.L.Freeman, M.L.Carmack Jr., G.M.Wright, S.R.Majors, R.V.Fender, A.F.Krauel, J.Fryxell, M.Anderson, E.A.Feliksiak, G.M.Erickson, R.H.Jensen, O.G.Hoch, J.G.Shirk, J.W.Good, A.H.Degrauwe, N.E.Landry, O.J.Donath, R.E.Bell, H.R.Salmonson, C.B.Schulte, S.W.Osborne, I.D.Firch, R.E.Trunnell Jr., D.L.Haven, G.R.Hast, M.M.Alfter, B.E.Livingston, J.D.Dixon, F.E.Stewart, A.Wassenhove, **1940** L.M.Wood, J.H.Licko, B.L.Randolph, L.J.Moffatt, G.E.Sweat, G.W.Charlesworth, E.C.Congdon, D.W.Durchenwald, R.Darras, F.P.Claeys, R.Hillbert Jr., D.W.Eagle, D.R.Ferrell, C.Chambers, P.E.Struessel, H.D.Oltman, H.E.Greene, M.E.Lampman, H.L.Meyer, M.E.Dudley, J.D.Crawford, N.T.Mc Caffery, J.S.Bohmker, W.T.Haynes, J.W.Bloomquist, W.H.Owings, W.J.Gettings, C.W.Rodelius, J.W.Casteel, A.A.Senneff, J.P.Sandoval, R.L.Nelson, H.A.Close, C.J.Zwicker Jr., R.F.Vandecasteele, J.W.Thornbloom, G.Deletre, E.L.Castelein, R.L.Hoofnagle, R.U.Zollars, D.E.Gilchrist, R.F.Bailey, L.D.Youngblut, B.B.Lavine, C.A.Grundstrom, A.M.Ortman, W.A.Foutch, H.L.Troutman, F.L.Webb, P.M.Miescke, M.C.Johns, A.C.Moughler, J.F.Oldefest, L.W.Dixon, F.B.Rebholz, R.F.Fisher, A.F.Gentle, W.K.Peterson, C.O.Knight, N.A.Riffel, H.E.Emerich, R.G.Schultz, O.J.Kelling, L.H.Lind, M.L.Mc Givern, T.A.Hild Jr., W.P.Talaga, R.K.Jones, O.J.Lichty Jr., C.L.Chase, A.C.Lagaisse, H.F.Clausen, J.L.Converse, A.L.Nabb, E.M.Cunningham, T.R.Scobee, L.O.Vandyke Jr., M.J.Mc Greevy, R.Kidder, W.B.Droste, W.H.Bender, J.C.Durnan, E.Hansen, G.T.Hotzel, M.A.Clark, C.E.Maranville, J.C.Williams, L.A.Vanoteghem, L.L.Needham, P.H.Beattie, R.H.Pfetzing, W.Allison, W.E.Cook, L.H.Bock, O.G.Bengston, P.Heth Jr., R.J.Klein, E.R.Murphy, J.L.Waller, L.L.Jordan, D.E.Terhune, W.P.Banks, D.E.Snyder, A.J.Juel, **1941** S.N.Wagner, H.J.Bigham, R.D.Peterson, C.L.Stearns, A.E.Crowe, F.P.Samson, J.B.Brett, D.Durham, F.E.Eagle, A.W.Gaumer, D.M.Zvonik, J.H.Winskel, A.F.Gravitt, C.E.White, M.H.Dean, A.M.Olson, J.H.Leonard, L.E.Cornelison, W.W.Payne, A.R.Magee, P.M.Havens, O.G.Sonnack, W.J.Bowser, W.M.Taylor, R.W.Stevenson, F.Spencer, H.Lakin Jr., P.J.Paskvan, H.Thomas Jr., K.J.Mangrich, R.E.Davis, C.R.Reindl, R.E.Nilles, J.E.Andrew, R.L.Nemmers, R.P.Kronfeld, A.F.Vanerstvelde, C.R.Bloome, R.L.Pepin, W.H.Grau, L.D.Monson, F.Wassenhove, H.G.Briden, H.G.Clausen, L.G.Salter, O.W.Pysson, C.F.Troester, F.L.Anderson, R.A.Schmidt, V.Sajak, F.Lentz, H.K.Bloomfield, E.R.Marr, G.W.Miller, K.Naber, W.H.Eisele, J.W.Schneider, O.E.Mitchell, V.H.Spengler, E.S.Walter, H.H.Hoppe, J.L.Wehrle, L.F.Maenhout, D.W.Grundstrom, R.L.Bennett, H.L.Jackson, R.H.Bolt, W.J.De Maranville, J.G.Heinje, M.Votroubek, O.Adams Jr., R.D.Felkner, R.C.Sewell, C.E.Engebretson, R.E.Broshar, B.Wade, F.C.Wiklund, F.H.Sand, F.W.Ruhnow, J.C.Funk, R.C.Roba, W.T.Moseley, F.E.Hawkins, R.C.Schulte, A.T.Briggs, W.M.Conklin, W.F.Hamby, F.W.Lysell, L.H.Belman, R.L.Horton, A.Vaughn, J.H.Moughler, R.V.Weinert, B.Davidson, W.Helms Jr., B.C.Gibb, S.E.King, W.L.Sample Sr., C.L.Peterson, K.L.Larson, D.W.Anderson, J.H.Graflund, M.H.Temple, N.N.Sacks, J.M.Bailey, A.K.Norris, E.D.Ethington, L.Reles, J.S.Cummings Jr., D.J.Mihal, A.M.Buhalog, W.E.Gustin, A.J.Dejaegher, J.R.Kalvelage, A.R.Terronez, E.H.Fletcher, N.G.Doan, A.E.Cook, D.H.Armentrout, J.B.Mc Clure, L.Goldfarb, C.H.Foster, L.A.Adkisson, D.L.Johnson, A.E.Hasselbusch, W.W.Klos, A.H.White, H.W.Mason, R.C.McClung, H.D.Johnson, M.C.Willems, M.Gerry, E.T.Brunk, W.J.Silverson, R.W.Christensen, R.C.Vanoteghem, W.B.Mc Cool, M.M.Dempsey, F.J.Luchtenburg, B.R.Rudiger, R.E.Huffman, S.H.Woodward, I.R.Oddleifson, W.E.Simmons, R.O.Schultz, J.G.Vermedahl, **1942** R.Haussy, R.Mandigout, A.H.Larsen, G.W.Bateman, I.R.Walker, K.D.Olmstead, H.R.Dorman, S.B.Imsland, E.L.Hardin, T.L.Dedoncker, A.H.Wendel, J.P.Reitzel, F.J.Immesoete, D.C.Fidler, E.J.Quick, W.G.Olson, E.W.Hiatt, T.J.Windey, M.C.Swift, J.W.Parkes, A.E.Steiner, L.L.Wilson, H.W.Cobert, D.G.Brasmer, L.E.Baumeier, E.L.Marshall, C.E.Brune, J.W.Hamm, D.F.Devermann, G.H.Dame, H.M.Pulliam, E.J.Lynch, H.M.Demay, G.C.Kron, G.F.Hummel, R.H.Eastland, A.C.Rudolph, L.K.Swanson, A.W.Waterman, J.A.Simmons, W.G.Matthews, M.H.Mitchell, T.B.Adams, H.C.Smith, S.A.Grooms, D.L.Sigman, C.I.Pierce, E.J.Labond, F.J.Wagner, H.H.Reisman, R.G.Wilson, A.Donald, R.L.Howick, S.F.Tedore, R.M.Dillon, F.Doss, P.M.Mc Grane, H.D.Risser, M.W.Noltensmeier, A.L.Masters, C.G.Backerman, J.C.Folkers, R.R.Perry, M.K.Lewis, R.D.Willer, C.N.Brustkern, C.A.Kayser, C.A.Thompson, L.S.Mc Chane, E.H.Meyer Jr., G.P.Nelson, J.W.Busenbark, W.D.Mc Fadden, R.E.Westerman, G.T.Whitington, G.V.Whitney, L.E.Hewitt, L.L.Shepard, H.L.Paul, G.Bonneau, J.D.Ryan, R.G.Holzgrafe, R.C.Putz, L.H.Gienau, J.C.Stewart, S.Horni, J.T.Cole, C.R.Lake, R.A.Vollrath, S.E.Denys, G.J.Kimler, H.M.Madsen, E.Ligeno, D.M.Edwards, **1943** M.L.Ide, R.Darnell, R.M.Lee, J.W.White, W.A.Johnson, E.L.Griffin, G.L.Myers, R.K.Miller, A.P.Ligons, A.V.Heine, D.J.Frederick, G.W.Lageschulte, M.W.Akerman, R.D.Burkhart, H.H.Marti, J.W.Clarke, L.W.Harris, D.B.Jones, A.R.Defauw, J.G.Brown, J.M.Keegan, M.A.Jordan, R.F.Ladeburg, R.W.Bivens, K.R.Rusch, M.A.Malme, H.E.Carlson, G.G.Voigt, L.A.Pietan, J.Teague, M.J.Quick, H.L.Reed, V.S.Bartholomew, R.J.Moede, O.A.Houtman, M.A.Murray, H.G.Crowe, A.Mandigout, F.E.Jensen, M.L.Ashbrenner, D.G.Maulson, D.M.Hansen, R.T.Jones, E.S.Taylor, N.J.Jawoisz, H.A.David, L.J.Higginbotham, F.R.Clements, L.E.Hubbard, W.H.Campbell, C.Stojak, J.J.Porter, J.A.Janssens, V.E.Larson, E.V.Mc Donald, F.J.Vanmeenen, R.L.Gibb, J.F.Kipp, T.Dergo, D.E.Lundberg, F.Hundley, R.S.Smith, A.V.Demeyer, E.D.Gunnell, M.M.Eastman, W.C.Fletcher, L.J.Reynolds, J.B.Park, J.C.Dehner, J.E.Zollars, W.L.Johnson, F.J.Haars, M.J.Wallarab, H.R.Brahm, C.B.Lopez, E.S.Gabbard, L.M.Le Fevre, H.R.Backerman, J.J.Morris, M.J.Chiarottino, L.R.Foster, T.H.Gillman, G.W.Bunn, D.M.Johnston, E.R.Beran, W.A.Schnaderbeck, P.C.Loete Jr., A.W.Compton, S.A.Provoost, G.B.Chapman, R.L.Kline, B.A.Schaefer, A.A.Bengston, J.Gram, D.C.Gaydos, C.J.Leahy, L.A.Conway, W.C.Hawley Sr., C.C.Farren, L.W.Burt, C.W.Brittenham, A.L.Stout, G.S.Nelson, N.L.Waters, A.J.Herbsleb, M.N.Grandon, H.H.Borland, H.Nash, J.W.Dixon, V.M.Sindt, R.L.Bloodsworth, L.K.Hill, R.F.Buzynski, V.M.Rice, G.W.Hartman, M.A.Peterson, O.D.Cremeens, R.L.Verhaeghe, G.W.Bowen, J.Lloyd, A.S.Fossler, V.A.Franke, M.K.Pinks, P.G.Sassaman, R.F.Erikson, G.F.Schermerhorn, S.Ceglar, J.O.Klevan, H.L.Tucker, P.A.Braeckevelt, H.O.Perez, **1944** F.W.Denny, K.F.Beck, J.A.Berg, H.R.Larson, J.F.Nourse, L.Harrison, H.R.Mayer, H.R.Spragg, F.W.Brandt, D.W.Morris, C.D.Colburn, J.M.Johnston, C.A.Boyle, K.B.Wagner, E.J.Burke, P.I.Bivens, M.A.Petersen, R.A.Benefiel, M.C.Frank, D.D.Brown, E.L.Himes, M.L.Love, O.W.Shepard, V.N.Levendosky, R.Crawford, M.F.Skinner, J.L.Powers, J.L.Abernathy, D.L.Brown, V.K.Spence, M.E.Butler, H.D.Hickman, H.M.Nimmick, E.R.Gardner, L.S.Malier, H.E.Buck, V.G.Fairbanks, L.L.Simoens, E.M.Siebenaller, J.H.Fulton, C.R.Almquist, G.J.Kaprich, L.B.Hesse, C.C.Kintz, H.M.Mc Clain, M.A.Fick, R.I.Bradley, R.M.Sigman, E.P.Dehner, R.O.Carlson, G.N.Saur, M.W.Wiebel, R.L.Mason, C.G.Housley, W.H.Key, E.A.Gates Jr., A.Pericak, A.L.Weimer, M.S.Drobushevich, R.I.Verstraete, M.I.Hawkins, C.R.Sherk, R.Gamble, A.T.Schram, R.C.Mundt, B.A.Stephens, W.J.Tagtmeier, K.F.Schumann, D.F.Kellums, W.R.Machmer, M.L.Mc Inroy, R.G.Fisher, L.W.Untiedt, R.C.Tharp, B.D.Smith, M.Sutherland, C.J.Hurley, D.E.Gray, D.E.Eddleman, V.I.Klietz, W.W.Donahue, K.L.Mc Ahren, G.A.Parks, A.Fazio, E.M.Lohman, J.G.Schleier Sr., A.Anfinson, E.L.Baughman, R.A.Petra, A.M.Vorpahl, T.A.Wilson, W.A.Anderson, L.E.Holmstrom, J.E.Kaprich, J.Fricheteau, D.G.Konig, C.A.Musch, L.C.Heeren, L.H.Phillips, F.Bright, W.H.Graham, M.W.Croak, S.W.Franklin, R.A.Garthoff, F.Ceaser, E.F.Roggemann, L.G.Riddolls, E.Mennenga, C.L.Kirk, I.M.Staelens, G.E.Moore, K.M.Seeley, **1945** B.Otto, D.E.Lingafelter, F.L.Heckman, G.C.Emerich, M.D.Kallem, J.O.Cree, G.I.Richardson, F.A.Hanson, W.E.Mc Kay, M.R.Kloster, C.M.Glassen, E.B.Young, L.A.Rusek Jr., W.C.Pate, E.H.Lee, J.L.Weaver, J.R.Wilson, C.L.Drenner, H.C.Weaver, J.R.Terronez, E.V.Vantieghem, F.Sabo, T.H.Sandoval, C.O.Hyatt, R.M.Brooks, M.E.Oleson, A.E.Solessio, R.C.White, D.R.Ostronic, D.Rusk, R.H.Scott, A.L.Moreno, B.J.Tutinas, R.K.Crowe, E.L.Bond, F.Hoppe, E.A.Marx, L.V.Dryer, O.L.Saunders, F.E.Black, J.C.Carlo, R.I.Sinn, E.M.Meikle, C.L.Decap, C.C.Legler, E.Fuqua, W.H.Dalbey, A.J.Hemauer, T.L.Mitchell, K.G.Mosolf, P.Climenhage, T.F.Lee, C.L.Hartley, E.M.Dannaldson, S.J.Wall, M.W.Downing, R.L.Hannah, A.D.Loree, B.R.Talak, C.L.Davis, C.R.Krahn, G.O.Peterson, H.J.Roy, D.E.Gettings, J.J.Hajdu, L.D.Nass, E.M.Cross, J.M.Dickel, L.D.Schwab, V.D.King, S.B.Tarr, P.E.Hamilton, P.E.Speer, J.J.Comer, A.W.Kassel, C.L.Haughenberry, G.H.Vanhecke, R.B.Fields, R.M.Carroll, F.J.Volcko, J.W.Hilder, M.L.Miller, R.G.Berg, D.H.Turnmeyer, W.A.Cook, S.Faron, L.J.Ronnebaum, T.G.Douglass, F.J.Daley, H.M.Adams, R.S.Clifford, G.M.Brown, W.A.Dennis, W.Benge, L.Ellis, D.L.Heffelfinger, D.R.Wielage, J.H.Taylor, W.C.Mixdorf, H.G.Coopman, M.M.Navarro, G.E.Sowers, M.W.Pepples, B.Kilberg, G.F.Neiley Jr., W.J.Juergens, A.E.Solessio, E.R.Jack, P.C.Koefoed, N.Jensen, F.D.Smock, A.C.Vandhuynslager, R.F.Mizeur, J.J.Rohaly, P.H.Schilling, T.E.Donahoe, D.P.Way, E.M.Corbett, E.W.Shumaker, H.G.Carter, P.J.Smith, C.E.Essmann, L.W.Bundy, R.L.Mishler, J.A.Corso, R.F.Grau, R.W.Young, C.N.Harris, H.L.Meyer, W.F.Sims, R.L.Lines Sr., R.O.Mordhorst, C.W.Smith, D.Prochaska, E.J.Cassidy, C.M.Lusthoff Jr., D.A.Carpenter, E.B.Bandsma, E.F.Lybbert, J.L.Curtis, G.Penly, L.M.Froeliger, H.A.Byggere, R.Decker Jr., O.M.Meany, R.D.Cook, D.O.Sullivan, W.F.Nissen, C.H.Moote, F.F.Danay, J.L.Danay, B.E.Stoneking, E.W.Ziegler, J.E.Feliksiak, L.A.Loesche, L.B.Guild, A.J.Riker, L.M.Lilleg, G.C.Ellis, G.L.Kilbourn, R.F.Davison, A.M.Strandlund, L.B.Maillet, A.W.Sandberg, L.R.French, M.J.Heckart, M.J.Miller, R.Gardner, **1946** G.H.Harken, L.W.Ketels, R.E.Swanson, C.R.Brown, C.R.Tiedge, J.G.Ransdell, R.H.Ledtje, E.Sampson, C.E.Carlson, H.C.Pankow, P.Rose, H.C.Raine, J.E.Booth, D.W.Debell, W.F.Jacobs, E.W.Boldt, J.E.Heiple, A.C.Aeshliman, C.M.Rau, E.C.Eggesboe, T.R.Carroll, W.A.Lindert, W.E.Horton, J.Zaragoza, W.E.Wilson, F.W.Reagan, H.Rice, E.L.Seymour, F.G.Carruthers, L.A.Wildermuth, D.G.Carnes, R.L.Timion, H.D.Ferguson, R.F.Hall, D.J.Einck, D.L.Harbour, L.A.Shepley, J.R.Dulek, J.F.Mc Kelvey, J.L.Kota, L.M.Goddard, R.E.Ball, K.F.Backens, L.T.Meany, W.M.Reed, M.E.Durnin, C.A.Bridenbaugh, V.L.Rugen, M.L.Crossley, M.W.Stirk, W.E.Finn, D.Mc Nelly, M.Epie, B.Taillandier, E.J.Sullivan, E.W.Mc Enany, J.J.Garcia, L.G.Eddy, M.C.Knebel, W.J.Marsoun, D.M.Netolicky, F.R.Hanson, G.H.Sanford, L.K.Plaehn, O.L.Love, W.T.Hall Jr., D.L.Smith, F.W.Greenberg, A.O.Scarlett, C.D.Buffington, C.L.Reeves, E.E.Johnson, F.V.Holdiman, G.L.Dye, G.Reid Jr., J.C.Herber, L.Foulks, M.E.Ford, M.D.Fisher, E.M.Courtney, L.B.Sullivan, J.D.Buchan, M.E.Greene, D.G.Blunt, G.R.Overby, J.M.Lane, R.A.Onderbeke, J.A.Farmer, M.G.Wilkinson, V.T.Shovlain, R.L.Owens, J.D.Kent, J.Ogden, M.E.Roberts, S.A.Wisecup, A.A.Nagel, E.A.Neilson, E.C.Wyatt, G.W.Jakobsen, M.A.Cross, C.E.Hervey, F.R.Dalbey, W.J.Van Zante, B.E.Furnald, P.E.Davis, J.E.Hood, F.F.Smith, L.V.Mosier, G.V.Britt, H.W.Zimmerman, B.A.Cockrum, G.F.Weieneth, F.M.Brinkmeyer, P.W.Holder, R.J.Sloan, W.D.Roby, W.T.Mason Sr., A.Eddings, C.W.Ray, D.Hudson, E.C.Williams, H.H.Lennie, R.M.Woodrow, W.H.Happel, D.O.Smith, L.D.Anderson, W.D.Frymoyer, G.O.Skalet, H.J.Doering, L.F.Fritz, E.M.Erickson, G.D.Mattison, J.J.Sr.ail, J.L.Patterson, R.A.Kelly, W.D.Adams, W.N.Tremmel, L.E.Fenneman, R.H.Pickerell, F.N.Kopel, H.J.Daw, J.D.Johnson, R.M.Selman, A.S.Cropper, H.W.Anderson, M.A.La Salle, G.W.Morgan Jr., L.A.Schaack, M.P.Carlsten, F.Kastelic, M.L.Briggs, Z.B.Joyner, L.L.Cox, M.J.Lindblad, M.Chrisman, C.J.Wilson, E.A.Woerman, A.E.Kirklin, J.C.Olson, L.H.Hogan, M.M.Appleton, S.M.Hofstetter, W.O.Bargmann, J.S.Perez, J.T.Brennan, H.S.Krebs, D.D.Murray, C.Fairbanks, R.J.Roberts, A.E.Kapler, D.H.Johnson, L.H.Adams, V.D.Wilson, W.A.Richelieu, W.J.Jensen, W.S.Tsuchiya, H.E.Lee, J.H.Boos, J.A.Baker, G.B.Dougan, H.Roby, E.E.White, E.W.Major, D.L.Birkhead, G.Dergo, B.J.Doxsee, G.C.Watson, G.W.Reid, L.H.Durham, L.P.Wilkinson, M.J.Wilson, W.Fulbrook, D.D.Heisterkamp, L.G.Cheatum, D.L.Hall, H.R.Rice, K.B.Shover, M.M.Cox, C.G.Dorn, L.C.Tims, R.R.Barton, E.B.Walker, J.E.Mundt, L.W.Leonard, R.L.Powell, V.Svob, D.V.Boostrom, G.F.Locke, H.H.Weichbrodt, G.W.Goben, H.J.Oberhardt, T.A.Clements, E.C.Reinier, K.R.Lang, R.C.Miller, L.E.White, L.R.Cole, E.D.Devilder, H.L.Smith, D.E.Gray, G.Koop, M.W.Hanson, W.D.Roberts, W.D.Worley, D.I.Eibey, H.J.Dolson, D.F.Oltman, T.E.Henry, J.E.Goodwin, H.D.Rachford, G.Owen, E.C.Mc Donald, H.E.Johnson, P.D.Lynch, E.F.Lochte, G.L.Atkins, R.J.Burt, W.E.Crider, E.F.Evans, I.L.Myers, R.J.Mundt, R.J.Schmidt, C.E.Whitmer, D.A.Caughell, J.G.Kramer, A.D.Strauss, D.I.Boyd, M.D.Thornhill, C.L.Oberhoffer, H.D.Springer, R.E.Bahnks, A.T.Parmentier, C.E.Woodley, D.L.Dunfee, H.K.Hild, J.J.Heimermann, P.J.Gysbers, P.P.Harp, C.H.Apel, E.D.Cernetisch, K.G.Erickson, V.W.Kimm, W.E.Schram, L.C.Collis, J.T.Haferbecker, L.D.Arms, R.W.Marschke, S.E.Gilmore, A.G.Gomez, A.Hayslett III, C.L.Poyner, F.A.Strobbe, J.L.Mc Kinney, V.L.Stinson, J.A.Schulmeister, R.E.Giese, J.J.Carter, R.L.Smith, D.J.Furry, J.W.Duehr, M.J.Wordehoff, W.A.Rose, F.P.Gunnell, H.H.Hall, H.W.Coffin, A.J.Kenkel, A.Starkovich, D.A.Larson, R.L.Beldin, W.P.Petersen, M.J.Matous, R.B.Markin, H.W.Kutsch, J.Radich, P.M.Bellendier, A.R.Peterson, J.V.Larson, H.J.Richards, J.J.Kohnen, M.K.Garrison, R.V.Kellums, G.F.Gabel, L.J.Owsley, C.H.Gillooley Jr., F.W.Muller, G.M.Gloeckner, J.M.Cummings, L.K.Erickson, M.E.Wagner, E.H.Spahn, H.W.Amundsen, L.F.Alongi, W.E.Wassell, H.W.Lattner, D.A.McIntosh, H.J.Lovett, C.J.Teague, R.L.Overturf, C.A.Woerdehoff, R.E.Peterson, W.R.Welter, F.Bloodworth, R.R.Furry, H.H.Gottschalk, J.J.Woerdehoff, M.P.Lattner, G.E.Danielson, W.J.Link, B.A.Terronez, B.Wildebour, E.M.Peterson, H.H.Bash Jr., R.D.Grinstead, W.M.Mecklenburg, E.H.Long, G.W.Bolin Jr., M.J.Sefzik, R.H.Steffan, B.J.Anderson, F.C.Hardt, B.J.Uebel, E.L.Johnson, R.M.Cavallo, C.R.Trageser, N.L.Brown, R.E.Sonksen, R.G.Knapp, W.R.Blau, H.J.Kuhle, J.C.Hugill, L.M.Lynch, O.H.Gingrich, R.L.Nye, C.J.Ford Jr., J.H.Morrow, F.J.Henderson, J.J.Krizan, R.R.Schulz, R.L.Reiseck, F.Fourneret, A.R.Sines, H.L.Niece, H.J.Thomas, M.W.Jones, I.M.Peterson, B.Lamm, D.J.Grimes, E.F.Pint, G.I.Klarup, G.W.Gottschalk, H.L.Hawkins, J.Gonzales Jr., J.W.Simons, M.L.Miller, H.E.Muhs, R.E.Callaghan, V.V.Turner, F.Kasper Jr., D.Mager, G.H.Talbott, J.F.Lardner, R.G.Brooks, E.Gutierrez, E.V.Bard, J.M.Hartman, M.H.Lyon, H.C.Witter, H.D.Smock, R.R.Stanley, P.A.Gilles, R.E.Mc Daniel, E.R.Reiter, J.Phillips, L.M.Grandia, M.C.Griesinger, M.M.Matkovich, M.T.Hedquist, C.E.Smith, L.J.O Brien, J.M.Sauer, D.R.Beard, D.R.Kearns, C.L.Bates, M.A.Gordon, E.H.Heetland, D.L.Hanna, E.N.Jahn, L.W.Hagedon, O.D.Oster, R.J.Reynolds, L.Marciset, D.L.Hummel, J.L.Lyberger, W.A.Gremonprez, B.J.Weber, R.L.Newton, W.W.Weeks, A.H.Halsey, D.T.Delamore, E.A.Clapp, L.R.Davis, A.A.Schmitt, C.M.Mayfield, W.J.Wolfe, A.B.Crick, C.J.Kulish, A.W.Hufford, H.Egeley, D.M.Tuel, G.S.Francois, H.Vaughan, M.Porter, R.C.Deyoung, H.Egeley, M.O.Moulton, N.C.Mlenar, P.D.Barton, E.H.Schmidt, L.E.Premer, E.T.Mc Cool, K.E.Wand, O.F.Volker, W.M.Johnson, D.W.Oliver, R.L.Van Dyke, W.O.Truitt, J.C.Walbrun, K.E.Reints, L.A.Muntz, A.W.Thompson Jr., C.A.Bastian, G.B.Kruser, J.F.Mulligan, J.J.Gruber, D.W.Kemp, J.R.Goderis, R.W.Klawitter, J.P.Toland, M.S.Arnzen, R.C.Baker, D.G.Spieger, A.K.Harle, C.Bambrook Jr., M.C.Stufflebeem, B.P.Bruner, D.N.Ritch, G.Baker, A.A.Debruine, C.Wolf, T.A.Bridges, J.Lievin, M.E.Lehnen, D.R.Summers, B.P.Kutsch, K.I.Hillman, L.D.McBride, D.E.Crow, F.Stoffa, C.R.Schweitzer, J.G.Halliday, M.Hoffman, F.C.Nehls, I.T.Kingan, L.W.Weaver, M.C.Frost, E.L.Jones, D.C.Ford Jr., E.G.Morgan, J.E.Peterson, R.J.Schmit, **1947** K.R.Peterson, A.F.Hoffman, C.W.Wilburn, H.M.Steines, J.C.Stevens, J.J.Schiefelbein, W.D.Brallier, C.M.Bettis, E.M.Kruse, J.H.Schumacher, M.R.Weber, M.W.Dunne, W.E.Cook, W.Kudart, C.C.Adams, C.F.Clauer Jr., W.A.Garrett, R.D.Vitosh, A.D.Schilling, J.E.McCabe, P.D.Moore, V.J.Breitbach, W.E.Schwartz, R.V.Sears, W.G.Meewes, H.N.Mason, L.Bartling, M.E.Moeller, R.A.Carney, R.C.McLaughlin, M.R.Tisue, A.J.Roidl, E.C.Darby, H.J.Larsson, J.J.Kruckenberg, B.L.Murray, D.J.Meyer, W.E.Frizzell, D.E.Krueger, D.F.Stickel, H.L.Smith, R.Stephenson, T.L.Mc Kelvey, C.G.Termont, F.A.Declerck, M.A.Nordman, T.R.Thomas, W.G.Compton, L.L.Germaine, R.J.Lammer, P.H.Stemper, A.B.Voshell, F.J.Taylor, G.A.Vermeulen, J.B.Sacco, R.J.Justman, W.T.Hardin, S.B.Adams, S.R.Schilling, L.A.Baldwin, R.R.Ristau, R.I.Terronez, R.L.Krouth, R.R.Alonzo, C.E.Nelson, C.R.Mc Carty, J.J.Zahina, L.W.Fischer, T.L.Schillinger, C.Vandewalle, D.E.Shewell, R.L.Leet, R.F.Render, A.Berecz, C.T.Julson, K.B.Smith, M.G.Duke, R.E.Coughlin, L.D.Roik, C.Traxler, D.L.Callahan, F.J.Breitbach, H.D.Tisue Jr., N.P.Larkin, D.A.Dehn, M.A.Bryant, W.B.May, K.E.Starkweather, R.F.Cremer, R.H.Kohnen, A.G.Deppe, B.F.Colson, D.R.Evans, H.A.Duyvejonck, H.L.Blair, M.R.Turnmeyer, W.J.Stevens, P.E.Donnelly, W.R.Salow, E.L.Gjovig, O.F.Burgmeyer, W.J.Cunningham, E.Kinsel, J.W.Allen, R.L.Clements, J.P.Bradley, R.W.Hemphill, W.Buhr, M.Cuillerdier, A.B.Johnson, E.M.Russell, F.J.Heiderscheit, W.R.Conrad, D.J.Johnston, L.E.Bauer, S.J.Oberfoell, D.D.Derby, E.W.Rosene, L.J.King, P.L.Archibald, R.J.Weiss, S.N.Stoffel, J.H.Finks, T.Angran, J.R.Robbins, T.R.Todey, R.W.Bixby, A.R.Smeltzer, J.B.Naderman, J.D.Burechailo, J.W.Jay, R.A.Shively, R.L.Alexander, P.Bouclet, D.Delmar, R.D.Rohwedder, C.V.Lerschen, D.L.Lakin, D.P.Billington, F.X.Meehan, G.E.Stephenson, L.E.Francois, L.L.McPhail, S.J.Weismantel, G.L.Coley, G.W.Vancleve, R.F.Watkins, W.E.Praska, F.G.Beyhl, H.F.Baal, R.J.Fox, R.Marmignon, K.H.Brennan, C.L.Shaeffer, P.Jones, G.W.Blunt, A.H.Gadbois, C.A.Wood, D.E.Butts, F.C.Fairchild, H.D.Dopler, J.J.Richard, M.E.Daack, W.L.Roberts, C.W.Mattingly, R.F.Randecker, R.J.Woolf, M.Perez, C.M.Williams, R.E.Rudd, A.J.Bieber, C.A.Leeks, C.W.Toney, D.R.Johnson, J.M.Miletich, K.A.Leight, L.Jackson, R.F.Mc Dermott, W.Carr, W.L.Mc Clellan, D.C.Berghaus, F.M.Liebert, G.L.Bartscher, J.B.Morse, F.Titko, H.J.Hanshaw, J.A.Marshall, M.R.Smithart, R.W.Besch, B.J.Truitt, H.C.Ingles, W.W.Meeker, G.M.Barlow, M.Williams, C.W.Lewis, K.R.Vanopdorp,

Safety meeting at Plow Works, Moline, Illinois, 1917

P.Garr, A.E.Dethmers, D.E.Temple, L.L.Stierman, E.E.Anderson, E.L.Gustafson, M.J.Simon, A.G.Arand, F.K.Amundson, H.A.Zickuhr, E.G.Rogers, E.V.Garber, H.W.Shute, J.E.Fisher Jr., D.W.Paisley, F.G.Baker, J.A.Allen, J.A.Rush, L.J.Fitz Gerald, C.Gruver, C.V.Lingle, M.J.Blaser, P.J.Fitzgibbons, R.V.Sheldon, R.R.Stevens, J.W.Sullivan, A.M.Pedrick, A.R.Terronez, D.E.Reid, D.H.Kerr, E.R.Jones, J.C.Johnson, L.M.Powers, W.A.Rutz, J.J.Jaeger, M.A.Feller, M.J.Schell, R.E.Leibe, F.J.Ross, R.W.Heidbreder, W.P.Hagner, B.L.Arndt, C.E.Wood, C.M.Kedley, C.R.Howard, G.H.Hinke, K.H.Cameron, L.A.Clancy, C.R.Fisher, W.F.Christy, L.C.Price, T.L.Johnson, F.H.Judas, J.Huggins, W.J.Sigwarth, E.Baker, G.L.Swaim, H.F.Zey, L.D.Bellrichard, S.Rotozinski, C.S.Maas, G.A.Furry, J.J.Wasko, W.C.Wassell, J.J.Marlor, A.A.Gelande, R.J.Boleyn, L.S.Crowell, L.B.Collins, R.O.Keep, W.Thornton, G.J.Baldwin, P.L.Barton, R.A.Chavez, V.J.Neuwohner, R.D.Kennedy, E.C.Harrington, E.H.Webbeking, E.R.Blow, J.A.Kokinos, L.H.Merchie, L.M.Stenberg, M.C.Stamp, M.H.Deitrich, O.H.Suholet, O.L.Kearney, O.M.Ripperger, D.W.Spurlock, F.E.Diggins, L.D.Byrnes, A.A.Wilbricht, F.J.Loete Jr., G.C.Bloomberg, G.L.Ernst, R.A.Haupert, R.H.Thomas, D.H.Arbogast, M.A.Till, W.A.Pins, D.H.Lesch, D.L.Wingert, E.Sheehan Jr., G.F.Harmon, C.Stiles Jr., D.B.Wassell, E.A.Johnston, J.M.Resetich, J.W.Stoneburner, L.A.Fick, R.A.Degrauwe, R.H.Meier, R.Rash Jr., K.J.Meyer, L.D.Hagerman, J.P.Free, B.F.Brown, J.A.Madaffari, R.W.Fremont, D.A.Robinson, M.M.Sercu, M.W.Zejmowicz, O.E.Kamrath, R.B.Wildermuth, R.C.Pape, B.W.Nylander, F.Lee, P.R.Cummings, J.M.Edwards, P.Ferreri, E.A.Deppe, E.F.Beyer, V.H.Schrunk, G.M.Capps, J.Earl, J.Szwec, R.J.Lehnen, E.L.Frederick, J.F.Duke, R.Jones Jr., T.R.Slutts, J.Nucko, O.W.Haverland, K.W.Wildman, R.M.Climenhage, C.A.Roddick, H.C.Blasdell, R.E.Harding, R.E.Weirbach, C.J.Kaune, E.B.Stueland, H.G.Kinsinger, M.R.Vyverberg, A.H.James, C.W.Donnelly, D.C.Robison, D.M.Schmitt, G.J.Mihal, R.V.Kauzlarich, W.R.Parker, W.R.Williams, V.E.Ogle, C.J.Steines, D.C.Brown, R.J.Thilmany, E.F.Hutchins, C.Miller, H.E.Hackbarth, L.F.Tegeler, O.M.Iversen, R.L.Labare, W.E.Lundgren, W.R.Sheldon, F.S.Sproule, J.I.Navarro, J.M.Nicks, P.W.Goodwinson, R.R.Acker, R.S.Keith, C.V.Finch, D.L.Larsen, G.F.Egan, L.S.Fowler, R.L.Hibbert, E.R.Mowry, J.V.Chedister, M.D.Artus, R.J.Hennings, C.B.Westbrook, K.Dunlay, L.T.Banfield, R.J.Ford, M.M.Lange, R.A.Denning, D.E.Kammerdiner, E.G.Vierkant, E.J.Schaefer, E.Patterson, H.H.Holms, R.H.Orwig, R.Taylor, S.G.Giovenazzo, J.C.Rausch, M.A.Kuehne, C.F.Ludovissy, F.A.Wilson, P.D.Chambers, M.H.Leslein, R.J.Scherer, E.R.Lemon, H.L.Branhagen, R.A.McBride, W.H.Lord, C.A.Pilcher, E.E.Meyer, J.P.Rice, K.D.Penning, R.L.Blake, W.W.Miller, M.Karsjens, B.E.Chapman, E.P.Dowell, A.A.Cochuyt, A.W.Brase, J.L.Nauman, P.Aschbrenner, A.E.Mayne, E.J.Mueller, F.M.Friar, J.E.Probst, R.L.Schares, R.L.Sullivan, D.F.Breiner, E.J.Neyens, O.M.Mauer, T.A.Michels, G.C.Parker, H.D.Sullivan, L.D.Aten, R.E.Junker, W.W.Temby, E.J.Timmins, C.E.Herde, F.M.Simmons, L.C.Stodden, L.E.Defontaine, L.W.Dieckman, J.A.Krausman, T.J.Lynch, D.Courbat, F.J.Kappmeyer, W.H.Doland, L.E.Giebink, L.N.Hewett, L.R.Peterson, P.Zadorozny, V.E.Clark, B.J.Stone, D.E.Lloyd Sr., E.Bredhold, J.R.Ainsworth, W.N.Cheek, P.L.Gerlich, S.L.Bryson, D.J.Griffith, E.A.Williams, E.J.Pluemer, F.J.Bald, I.M.Crook, R.V.Blume, V.L.Erdman, B.Cottereau, M.L.Nelson, R.L.Brimeyer, R.Walters, C.M.Johnson, J.W.Hartman, W.M.Warring, R.L.Struss, R.R.Ruane, G.O.Haist, H.U.Fulks, K.T.Weigel, P.J.Fah, K.R.Bell, M.H.Watson, J.Wise, R.M.Lester, W.G.Sizer, W.J.Mosley, J.L.Kinney, M.Halliday, R.E.Connell, W.E.Warrick, C.Gerard, D.L.Donovan, H.J.Anderson, H.M.Hisler, J.M.Keep, R.E.Frymoyer, W.T.Uremovich, D.J.Pint, L.R.Christiansen, J.W.Beck, A.L.St Clair, C.C.Kruser, D.W.Allen, D.W.Brown, H.E.Gott, G.M.Baych, J.J.Dunn, J.O.Coney, R.E.Church, R.E.Lindquist, R.R.Gomez, T.Sacco, L.G.Buck, C.J.Mullen, F.Hodgson, H.C.Hansmeier, H.G.Dee, J.B.Modzelewski, R.E.Buckert, E.C.Welter, R.D.Mc Glumphy, H.A.McVicar, H.T.Trites, K.A.Bergdahl, M.H.Devins, P.A.Savignano, P.W.Lett, R.E.Blair, W.J.Borchardt, E.Gerbaulet, E.C.Skinner, G.Shriver, J.W.Mathes, S.R.Krofta, F.G.Steinbron, J.R.Lough, G.P.Smith, H.C.Webb, L.K.Fuhlman, D.J.Schuster, L.V.Barnes, D.Loose, J.Pulliam, C.A.Arnold, P.J.Phillips, K.A.Caldwell, L.M.Schnieder, H.V.Beitel, M.D.Strickler, M.R.Sullivan, R.M.Morgan, D.E.Kruger, D.G.Karel, D.L.Harris, R.W.Smith, L.C.Russett, R.M.Hanson, G.Agier, J.V.Hoogenakker, L.O.Behrend, D.W.Harris Jr., E.T.Lynch, L.G.Ballegeer, D.M.Heath, J.J.Meaney Jr., F.J.Oconnor, K.L.Kirkpatrick, E.L.Hansen, E.W.Clemann, F.O.Brown, I.J.Andriano, J.H.White, L.F.Cox, R.E.Fellows, R.H.Wilhelm, R.R.Holden, R.S.Hurt, D.M.Buzzell, W.W.Witt, E.D.Dorland, A.H.Welter, J.B.Reamy, E.A.Ryden, F.W.Rivey, G.L.Flouro, K.B.Amlund, N.G.Sperry, R.L.Shultz, T.D.Campbell, W.E.Stoffregen, D.E.Segebarth, H.L.Fitz, L.H.Runde, R.A.Bulen, J.W.Dennis, I.V.Dawes, P.F.Pavlovec, A.B.Clewell, J.J.Gasior, M.W.Stoffregen, O.A.Bartsch, W.H.Lloyd Jr., D.H.Smith, B.L.Seeley Jr., E.F.Harris, F.H.Ludovissy, H.W.Brandt, J.A.Hollaway, K.R.Samson, A.C.Dewulf, D.D.Moore, R.D.Mc Dougall, C.K.Harmon, H.D.Mason, J.L.Lightner, K.L.Barnes, W.E.Slavens, E.A.Bell, H.L.Bate, F.H.Harbour, L.H.Pape, M.J.Lentz, O.R.Hendricks, C.D.Adams, D.C.Elliott, J.D.Roberts, P.N.Leichtle, V.L.Dawson, V.T.Wilson, J.F.Grasso, R.J.Thomas, W.J.Chambers, H.B.Egts, M.M.Browning, A.E.Nelsen, D.R.Lanning, J.W.Miller, D.H.Plageman, E.Hodge, R.G.Kress, R.T.Nelson, V.E.Dulaney, C.L.Garrison, E.E.Strottman, J.H.Alexander, L.L.Hofner, R.L.Cox, V.A.Sabin, C.Wiersma, J.H.Dorsey, C.E.Damm, C.F.Gerhartz, G.E.Hollen, J.O.Peters, J.P.Skinner, L.McCullough Sr., R.L.Curtis, S.A.Haagenson, A.Santi, B.E.Kennedy, J.C.Barge, W.L.Kouski, C.E.Brown, D.L.Smith, F.C.Powers, J.C.Frampton, J.L.Stephens, J.W.Smith, M.F.Prochaska, M.Matthias, H.L.Lepper, W.L.Ford, A.C.Ramsey, C.Bohman, F.E.Lawson, I.Z.Maranville, J.A.Kreitinger, L.E.Atkinson, W.I.Huslig, W.J.Strosahl, L.J.Markin, M.Peterson, J.W.Weber, W.J.Hait, R.Campbell, C.F.Spoon, M.Hubbard, R.W.Jamison, W.G.Cook, C.T.Punkiewicz, L.W.Lewis, M.L.Hutt, E.F.Arnold, L.F.Franson, V.S.Grobman, W.E.Verheecke, H.C.Mc Clure, R.C.Kiesow, W.J.Davison, R.E.Johnson, W.J.Hamil, **1948** C.M.Lieder, G.J.Zimmerman, T.E.Kurtz, C.A.Lyman, F.C.Mitton, G.G.Gioffredi, L.D.Hakeman, L.E.Brown, L.G.Neuman, R.A.Thorngren, S.King Jr., T.D.Smith, A.F.Blakeslee, C.F.Knautz, E.E.Stewart, H.D.Tisue, J.L.Greco, A.H.Weir, C.T.Jacklin, H.F.Murray, L.L.Wessel, D.L.Scherbroeck, H.Nelson, J.J.Adams, A.H.Peters, C.D.Pettit, E.R.Engstrom, H.Valentine, J.B.Scott, J.G.Tamminga, R.A.Miescke, H.P.Vargas, L.W.Rhoads, C.D.Homesley, C.I.Gorman, R.V.Dahl, A.L.Freber, R.E.Ader, R.E.Allen, A.E.Breed, H.E.Birkhofer, B.R.Mohler, C.E.Jones, H.R.Huizenga, I.Dolton, R.E.Bowman, R.E.Kopp, T.L.Mason, W.G.Kimmel, D.S.Smith, G.C.Seger, S.J.Kirby, K.C.Chilton, L.H.Wiklund, W.E.Tice, R.L.De Vries, T.J.Catrone, A.J.Weber, C.W.Poe, E.A.Kamrath, R.C.Ehrig, R.H.Olson, W.F.Keith, C.Baker, E.Klein Jr., M.K.Nehls, A.R.Halbfass, P.E.Stocker, R.E.Dusing, R.E.Gillen, S.P.Kulig, A.D.Fosse, A.Turpin, F.Hanneman, J.M.Greibrok, J.D.Owens, C.C.Trice, J.A.Majcher, R.E.Groves, F.E.Davis, L.A.Turley, W.H.Newmaster, F.L.Stiles, R.E.Davis, W.E.Mc Coy, W.H.Howard, T.L.Moore, G.A.Griffin, J.A.Vicevich, J.N.Welch, C.E.Glazier, J.A.Sanders, C.E.Pirtle, L.T.Comer, A.R.Dedoncker, D.M.Johnson, E.L.Christianson, G.S.Purdy, R.H.Carruthers, M.J.Theisen, R.E.Schlotter, L.L.Mc Intyre, E.F.Roe, G.G.Unke, R.G.Mc Gee, R.L.Skillings, H.L.Clauson, L.W.Marx, E.L.Murphy, H.J.Riege, B.C.Dyke, E.A.Bathke, L.P.Smith, D.E.Gruwell, J.D.Singer, A.E.Logli, D.A.Taylor, F.S.Johnson, N.L.True, R.E.Papenhausen, E.D.Dyer, C.E.Redfern, E.L.Mc Cormick, E.L.Paxton, F.Brooks, G.W.Jensen, L.K.Crane, R.N.Cole, W.E.Ledtje, W.R.Cundiff, A.Navarro, O.R.Cloke, D.R.Frey, H.I.McCollum, R.D.Matteson, R.P.Haselhuhn, W.G.Hoffman, J.C.Garner, J.E.Corwin, D.L.Mc Intyre, J.T.Pamplin, K.A.Vaughan, M.E.Gabrielson, W.J.Taylor, W.J.West, C.J.Coker, D.Mc Carty, M.Dennis, W.D.Smith, J.J.Bagatti, M.D.Slaght, A.M.Matthews, C.R.Saner, P.W.Stogdill, G.L.Mitcham, R.H.Welk, S.J.Stellberg, B.R.Gibson, G.A.Sims, R.E.Larson, A.L.Nelson, G.L.Sharer, H.L.Johnson, J.E.Mefferd, J.W.Gragg, W.L.Baie Jr., D.A.Wilson, C.D.Wentworth, C.Knisley, E.B.Kramer, E.C.Pope, M.E.Coyne, R.R.Rambo, B.D.David, A.J.Bisignano, J.E.Ritzman, A.V.Primasing, D.A.Thomsen, D.J.Maitre, H.W.Smith, J.B.Reeves, J.L.Brock, P.J.Keileher, A.Cyrus, K.J.Essmann, C.R.Doud, C.R.Martin, J.Rankin, K.G.Talburt, M.Howard, M.W.Gross, N.G.Melrose, R.A.Wiklund, F.W.Beard, G.A.Argetsinger, H.D.Schoenberger, J.J.Romitti, L.Bullington, C.J.Oakley, G.G.Gelder, P.J.Casillas, R.A.Pagel, R.L.Houk, R.Nelson, W.H.Mundell, R.E.Smith, B.A.Burkey, G.L.Stitzell Jr., H.E.Swarthout, H.T.Beebe, N.K.Krause, R.K.Alexander, R.M.Keefover, R.V.Seaholm, F.A.Mullin, C.W.Wolf, I.F.Bartholomew, J.J.Presnell, L.H.Hawker, R.G.Peterson, E.B.Niemeier, K.L.Smith, C.F.Crysler, E.W.Krueger, F.A.Erickson, G.A.Wilson, J.N.Farnsley, W.H.McFarlin, C.R.Bergren, J.J.Hartman, K.R.Jensen, P.A.Nicholls, J.E.Hummel, K.P.Bickert, P.A.Kasel, D.H.Spicer, F.R.Burich, J.G.Chiono, J.J.Starkovich, J.R.Glenn, J.Roehr, T.Giudicessi, W.A.Baker, W.M.Duschen Jr., L.V.Hollinrake, P.S.McKnight, M.H.Horton, D.F.Renspe, H.G.Prystai, C.Frazier, C.M.Brown, D.A.Oakland, D.R.Mann, J.W.Umland, M.G.Lacher, O.R.Schoville, V.D.Rannow, A.R.Henderson, L.V.Ault, J.A.Pearson, J.R.Baird, L.A.Adkisson, O.M.Larson Jr., B.L.Cox, M.D.Samuelson, R.J.Gioffredi, R.McLean, A.R.Brickman, E.P.Carroll, H.J.Brewer, R.J.Ballard, R.W.Peachee, B.T.Klatt, J.R.Schmidt, D.V.Rosol, L.F.Fetes Jr., L.G.Doan, R.N.Eichorst, K.E.Lowe, R.M.Mc Dermott, R.N.Wills, B.J.Bruce, J.F.Polich, M.F.Ralston, R.Breithaupt, R.J.Heinrichs, R.O.Pregler, W.Feldhusen, E.F.Vannatta, E.J.Cosgrove, F.J.Behnke,

Illinois dealers and customers viewing "A" and "B" tractors, 1936

J.F.Clendenin, K.M.Johnston, C.B.Stephens, C.W.Berry, D.J.Pint, P.L.Golay, P.T.Lutgen, D.J.Vercautren, E.F.Lose, L.Merritt, R.F.Foronato, C.D.Curtis, D.M.Schroeder, F.Garcia, G.D.Cappaert, H.K.Johnson, J.Timmins, M.Best, R.E.Durbin, R.M.Peterson, D.R.Earhart, A.R.McAninch, L.J.Hansen, R.M.Chaney, R.M.Devolder, N.P.Kempf, J.A.Clark, A.E.Park, A.H.Schultz Jr., J.J.Splinter, O.D.Persons, W.M.Hickman, R.G.Puls, S.O.McReynolds, M.A.Ward, F.J.Gioffredi, R.L.Wilson, B.D.Whicker, E.C.Ryan, E.E.Taylor, M.G.Overton, S.D.Liedtke, P.J.Saveraid, C.F.Pieper, P.B.Burke, G.H.Mc Kitrick, F.L.Fazio, L.L.Jones, W.C.Amsberry, D.E.Conn, D.T.Coleman, E.E.Hale, G.D.Head, K.W.Madsen, L.M.Lose, P.A.Gorman, V.K.Yoden, F.Dabb, J.K.Jensen, B.C.Battani, B.N.Lefler, P.P.Volcko, R.E.Caldwell, R.W.Klann, W.T.Casey, F.L.Trevallee, H.J.Schneider, J.C.Doeden, M.L.Moore, W.M.Van Syoc, C.D.Volkert, D.E.Hess, H.F.Styer, J.A.Baker, J.B.Mc Cellan, T.E.King, B.B.Robbins, C.E.Kipp, D.L.Forbis, L.H.Luce, R.L.Spies, M.A.Pettis, R.O.Dunblazier, R.W.Neuenkirch, B.J.Sonderleiter, R.C.Sherrill, R.W.Page, T.H.Robson, D.M.Mace Jr., E.H.Steinbeck, K.R.Haskin, R.A.Storey, R.Toohey, R.V.Bennett, L.L.Smith, A.J.Punteney, E.P.Miller, J.W.Cornelius, M.B.Bailey, M.Stierwalt, R.W.Thomas, A.V.Maddalozzo, C.L.Lucas, D.N.Shepley, H.B.Qualls, M.Blazanin, M.H.Cornell, S.Laferrara, W.G.Wilson, A.L.Lillis, H.R.Morgan, J.G.Pelino, L.J.Hudson, N.Vasquez, A.E.Sorensen Jr., C.Jenkins Jr., H.C.Albach, B.E.Johnson, M.J.Lehman, W.L.Michael, A.F.Payne, A.P.Dyball, C.A.Patmore Jr., D.E.Overton, H.L.Terry, L.G.Schaus, E.Hutchinson, H.L.Cosper, R.W.Smith, B.E.Allen, C.C.Good, D.L.Feldman, G.A.Kline, G.Wilson, H.A.Maneman, L.A.Frye, M.V.Bahnks, H.A.Breson, J.H.Ziegler, J.M.Allen, P.E.Rash, C.A.Benning, C.A.Bradshaw, E.J.Bender, J.D.Gleeson Jr., J.O.Paxton, L.L.Dudgeon, M.B.Baarstad, M.O.Stout, M.R.Rosenberg, R.E.Lewis, R.E.Ray, E.L.White, R.E.Lester, W.A.Wengert, C.L.Potter, D.Harvey, D.L.Sharpe, D.W.Strawn, H.Mauk, J.H.Strawn, S.G.Gabel, V.M.Mathis, E.A.Wheeler, M.Cunningham Jr., J.O.Smith, L.E.Ploessl, R.L.Greif, A.Jimenez, H.E.Himanga, J.A.Kolb, J.W.Molloy, S.P.Lee, C.V.Noble, E.F.Condon, H.H.Howard, H.P.Hollister, C.W.Adamson, J.L.Thomas, V.V.Heaton, C.J.Phipps, D.Booth, A.F.Frahm, E.E.Loy, P.E.Mikles, G.E.Yamen, G.T.Walker, L.Woollums, C.E.Lalond, P.McMullin, W.S.Butcher, H.V.Montgomery, T.R.Henshaw, R.L.Mager, G.Shave, L.L.Leihsing, M.Wilson, D.F.Thompson, D.M.Stump, J.E.Evans, W.P.Dunfee, W.C.Zikuda, C.F.Monnin, D.H.Tufts, G.D.Harker, H.C.Carson Jr., J.W.Cunningham, N.E.Knox, R.V.Reed, T.B.Turner, B.J.Hauber, C.B.Mc Cready, C.R.McVey, E.E.Wagoner, G.Jennings, G.P.Miller, J.R.Maulson, L.M.Cerfogli, A.B.Shepherd, C.E.Smith, R.T.Wren, H.M.Unger, M.E.Ringgenberg, C.E.Jeglum, L.P.Larkin, L.U.Boyd, M.Wilson, W.A.Reeg, D.H.Gillman, J.C.Burich, J.A.King, J.J.Gaspar, L.M.Wixcel, R.D.Jones, T.W.Rittgers, D.R.Starnes, H.W.Treftz, J.R.Steinbach, L.H.Bartell, P.R.Hagan, W.O.Houge Jr., Z.Lanham, J.Le Coq, D.R.Denman, G.R.Sapp, J.M.Finn, W.D.Ellis, F.E.Brown, K.E.Bingham, L.E.Jolly, C.P.Smith, F.H.Rohm, J.H.Miller, M.G.Harris, M.L.Corbin, P.K.Bengs, R.L.Hackett, W.T.Attwood, A.Proust, M.K.Morehouse, V.E.Clark, J.P.Comer, K.D.Conly, M.S.Barker Jr., H.L.Portwine, M.R.Kittoe, R.H.Morris, R.O.Musgrave, E.A.Holmes, H.E.Schuster, R.E.Clark, R.E.Smith, C.Jones, E.M.Bowersox, M.A.Deer, W.E.Kirkeby, J.W.Webb, R.D.Johnson, R.E.Boatman, U.J.Ugolini, E.W.Versluys, E.G.Frederick, R.F.Devore, A.D.Sergeant, C.E.Wallin, C.Richter, H.E.Kreitzman, L.Osberg, M.L.Davis, R.J.Belluchi, R.J.Johnson, W.J.Philo, R.E.Moore, R.J.Box, R.E.Howell, R.J.Davis, W.S.Davis, A.M.Onstott, H.K.Poel, R.G.Shoafstall, R.J.Lash, H.L.Cook, C.A.Rogers, R.Saffold, F.N.Gilchrist, R.J.Thede, R.C.Stevenson, E.L.Kirkman, E.M.Carlson, F.Smith, R.Mc Kinley, C.E.O'Connor, E.L.Hidlebaugh, L.L.Kaster, M.A.Papich, R.C.Lee, L.A.Bailey, M.L.Forrester, W.F.Carson, H.E.Mason, J.Savage, R.A.Priest, S.L.Phoenix, R.D.Gietzel, O.B.Kues, B.P.Berger, D.M.Johnson, J.C.Dillon, R.G.Karn, V.H.Polaschek, C.M.McKenna, D.T.Hansen, G.H.Bickford Jr., L.C.Shelangoski, V.H.Gudehus, A.H.Den Adel, C.Weed, J.G.Cory, K.B.Williams, G.E.Erickson, H.Davis, H.A.Kopaska, A.Vandeviere, F.A.Davidson, G.Wyer, H.S.Nielsen, P.H.Mathes, H.M.Clark, R.E.Wallace, G.H.Schmidt, R.I.Du Burg, R.Madsen, R.N.Schreiber, **1949** B.L.Wilson, E.A.Duschen, J.Z.Rader, R.J.Doll, R.W.Roth, A.G.Sipe, C.E.Pratt, C.Freeman Jr., P.Rivera, R.M.Griggs, B.J.Doose, G.H.Miller, W.H.Bolster, M.R.Moon, C.H.Schroeder, J.F.Van Scoyk, W.D.Turner, W.M.Gunderson, H.Marhofer, M.K.Maloich, R.J.Vanhyfte, W.Ross, R.L.Scherer, G.D.Young, M.R.Peterson, A.J.Pavlik, F.H.Koehler, H.O.Poetter, J.J.Jaecques, R.E.Kelso, V.F.Halsey, C.Green, D.D.High, D.D.Schlomann, E.James, F.A.Thomas, N.J.Ryan, H.P.Ziegler, W.E.Meyer, G.S.Niedermair, N.R.Kenning, R.P.Cross, F.L.Bobenhouse, M.Cook, R.A.Hughes, E.P.Ulrich, A.B.Anderson, E.L.Baker, E.W.Cain, D.L.Inskeep, J.V.Hillman, P.J.Schilling, R.A.De Smet, R.L.Ulbricht, H.W.Nehls Jr., R.A.Sandberg, G.M.Scherer, L.N.Knief, R.J.Straw, R.P.Kesl, W.E.Moorehead, H.P.Cordes, D.L.Thompson, E.G.Skipton, J.A.Sharpsteen, J.H.Moore, E.F.Shepard, E.M.Ryun, C.V.Bengston, G.Sutherland, J.B.Elliott, M.M.Harden, M.F.Janzen, H.F.Jairett, W.J.Hickey, G.F.Taylor, A.R.Black, E.B.Ackley Jr., J.L.Hein, M.T.Boeder, D.Pieper, L.I.Lichty, M.F.Harms, R.D.Cool, R.H.Neels, W.A.Syverson, A.J.Bauer, L.F.Carroll, R.J.Spain, V.L.Kelly, F.Schuster, D.K.Laurie, F.D.Foster, K.W.Wickham, A.C.Mc Cune, E.L.Gray, R.B.Cronin, K.H.Lyons, F.E.Timper, H.K.Dunn, M.M.Goethals, R.M.Monson, W.O.Hall, E.H.Vanpuyvelde, H.I.Pearson, J.E.Mulvania, C.P.Sell, M.Chrasta, R.M.Waterbury, T.Anderson, W.L.Minnehan, W.Zelnio, M.J.Kuhn, D.K.Fisk, L.D.Smith, L.C.Wieser, G.B.Nelson Jr., M.H.Peters, W.L.Hamburg, J.C.Williams, B.H.Shevick, D.E.Rudig, C.E.Reighard, D.H.Dirksen, E.G.Lane, D.L.Lupardus, E.V.Graham, J.Block, E.M.Ruden, L.V.Lopez, W.G.Hofman, C.J.Sutton, R.E.Sears, H.H.Hummel, L.A.Walton, H.D.Miller, R.B.Welter, R.B.Van Zanten, D.J.Paulsen, G.W.Wolters, J.L.McMillan Jr., W.G.Wade, E.Montag, L.D.Johnson, R.B.Dolan, F.E.Wofford, T.A.Brooks, R.D.Pease, J.R.Conner, J.R.Edwards, R.I.Heidemann, S.J.Nyquist, W.R.Carroll, A.T.Meegan, J.W.Richard, G.J.Michaels, L.P.Erdman, D.G.Dolman, M.F.Van Someren, H.L.McCutchen, D.J.Heberling, J.T.Russell, R.E.Murphy, G.L.Terry, C.M.Lockwood, E.J.Klaas, M.J.Flynn, R.A.Wilmes, R.G.Ethington, D.H.Anderson, H.J.Youngblut Jr., A.K.Moeller, W.Slick, A.L.Curtis, R.H.Lohman, P.M.Kohl Jr., D.H.Pearson, L.J.De Brabander, H.G.Perschbacher, W.A.Branch, R.A.Engel, D.M.Willis, K.P.Bogue, E.Friesth, J.D.Downing, J.E.Hollowell, M.L.Niccum, M.V.Powers, R.M.Gressett, H.W.Hamrick, T.F.Bishop, T.J.Carpenter Jr., L.E.Winter, R.E.Nachtrieb, B.G.Kenney, J.A.Hintz, M.J.Mack, D.A.Polaschek, W.C.Brady, J.P.Martin, G.E.Kipp, R.F.Luehring, L.D.Tidwell, J.A.Meirhaeghe, R.J.Doherty, D.L.Voshell, H.J.Brinkman, H.K.Paulsen, R.L.Cade, D.R.Hartwig, K.W.Harrison, H.West, A.I.Albertz, G.W.Foster, M.A.Roth, G.D.Caswell, A.E.Allen, F.C.Sechovec Jr., S.Reed Jr., R.D.McCormick, J.L.Angel, P.S.Pries, R.L.Jones, R.S.Hill, G.E.Wohlwend, R.H.Mc Bride, J.L.Selchert, M.J.Decapp, M.L.Mc Daniel, R.F.Gallens, A.E.Benzel, A.J.Dahlin, W.J.Farnum Sr., L.K.Etzel, W.J.Heronimus, M.H.Miller, K.L.Meyer, H.Kolbe, D.E.Walker, E.U.Cassaidy, F.B.Spillum, H.J.Colburn, J.Degornet, G.H.Wadsworth, H.R.Lindstrom, K.C.Anderson, R.H.Rugh, W.R.Gensch, L.J.Hoffman, R.J.De Bo, J.L.Moore, G.A.Nelson, D.M.Dickerson, J.D.Vannatta, J.H.Hoeksema, P.J.Oconnor, B.J.Bognar, M.W.Dorothy, B.B.Cruse, C.L.White, E.L.Newton, L.C.Roloff, M.T.Gravitt, T.R.Slater, D.Van Galen, G.W.Smith, M.E.Davis, R.C.Westendorf, J.A.Vanspeybroeck, L.W.Chance, W.R.Henry, J.O.Carter, P.T.Quinlan, J.V.Wilson, A.R.Thomson, G.C.Moss, A.Teilloux, W.D.Behlmer, R.W.Haley, M.L.Sexauer, D.A.Nicholson, D.L.Withington, L.A.Lundquist, O.M.Ryan, B.W.Newberry, E.M.Isenberg, L.C.Scobee, M.L.Steagall, L.E.McNeill, A.C.Osburn Jr., B.E.Kent, K.J.Louck, D.B.Beckmann, D.L.Ziegler, H.W.Young, J.F.Temple, R.L.Pardee, H.H.Reynolds, W.J.Nyquist, D.E.Williams, J.P.Roelens, M.W.Spring, E.C.Barlang, A.Kollmansberger, G.Grems, J.E.Heller, J.M.Ervine, V.V.Hadley, A.U.Laurick, J.E.Maddox, W.A.Inman, W.F.Earl, L.H.Taylor, L.I.Wegner, J.W.Olson, R.E.Drewelow, E.Lucas, E.V.Holmgren, M.W.Kiekhaefer, J.L.Morrissey, E.G.Swanson, H.H.Chandler, V.A.Schaecher, E.W.Reeder, **1950** A.N.Sundvall, B.V.Lilliman, J.H.Harness, J.H.Sconyers, J.M.Brown, R.A.Hanson, V.L.McCormick, J.A.Bustos, F.A.Andreini, J.R.McKinney, L.E.Koontz, P.Blondeau, J.A.Tolmie, D.L.Allison, K.F.Ewing, R.C.Anderson, W.A.Vanoteghem, P.Ford, W.J.Bond, G.Willier, A.N.Millier, R.E.Thompson, R.W.Tobin, W.W.Aspelmeier, H.L.Galusha, R.J.O Brien, A.G.Lundberg, G.B.Cowells, V.C.Hanson, C.D.Hanson, F.Weinman Jr., V.E.Decair, G.B.Handy, J.P.Hoffman, R.L.Firth, J.D.Atkins, A.N.Mitton, R.L.Willey, J.E.Lauw, W.C.Dillon, A.V.Lupinski, H.B.Bell, R.E.Hemingway, F.J.Patton Jr., J.Votruba, A.P.Gosney, J.S.Heasley, M.A.Reiter, A.B.Skromme, G.L.Friedl, R.T.Sandoval, W.A.Galetich, R.A.Heising, R.L.Andersen, R.M.Williams, G.Hunter, S.Bruneau, D.J.Rhodes, R.W.Graves, G.Gosset, A.W.Phelps, M.A.Popelier, H.Mc Donald, K.E.Schlundt, M.G.Nolan, A.M.Vavra, W.R.Brittenham, R.L.Herman, J.M.Butler, W.Begoray, R.E.Roberts, F.P.Grant, G.H.Dolph, G.W.Olson, W.E.Hines, D.W.Amendt, J.J.Donahue, E.J.Putz, R.K.Hartman, A.E.Gronick, W.J.Kearney, L.C.Heston, A.B.Hoying, J.Darby, S.L.Null, D.C.Swanson, L.R.Beard, M.W.Lawson, R.E.Cook, D.R.Eakins, M.D.Prose, D.H.Faust, G.O.Laurie, J.K.Bright, W.R.Cochran, A.E.Monson, D.Bride, W.R.Jones, J.W.Mc Donald, L.D.Cruz, R.W.McGraw, J.W.Douglas, R.E.Harrington, W.L.Stowell, J.E.Pohlson, K.L.Boudinot, R.A.Wittren, C.E.Farrell, G.L.Medhus, L.I.McCombs, C.C.Haug, M.E.Neubauer, A.A.Hansen, G.M.Hall, P.N.Walseth, R.P.Carlson, R.W.Giertz, M.L.Lint, C.Agan, F.H.Rowe, T.C.Harrison Jr., H.R.Hedlund, R.J.Maller, C.Nelson, J.W.Smith, B.F.Lemons, E.Evans, J.H.Curry, R.F.Sackett, D.F.Lottich, D.R.Salmonson, H.D.Bunch, R.R.Reilley, E.B.Benter Jr., R.E.Henderson, W.J.Schulze, J.L.Samuelson, N.D.Mekus, W.A.Williams, W.P.Pribnow, P.H.Hutchings, H.W.Hines, M.P.Zimmer, R.A.Howell, A.T.Stolar, N.L.Shepard, D.E.Bagnall, J.D.Sutton, R.A.Tillberg, C.J.Vinyard, D.E.Collison, M.A.Kurutz, G.J.Drescher, B.G.Sneed, R.A.Stibolt, J.L.Chaney, P.D.Kuberski, I.M.Wiltsie, M.H.Demps, R.W.Carpenter, R.Melchert, A.Lamacchia, L.J.Corkery, V.A.Maxson, L.O.Bozeman, A.S.Westmayer, L.E.Beyer, C.Nizan, F.A.Kriebel, G.Zarek, W.B.Collins, A.H.Luett, E.B.Cutright, J.J.Pirotte, G.E.Bovet, L.Swartout, M.B.Karn, R.E.Carpenter, R.F.Kolinchinsky, P.Denis, J.C.Daggett, L.O.Greim, A.W.Gosney, G.B.Samuelson, M.W.Lovell, W.A.Rathbun, F.C.Lantau, J.L.Pedersen, R.D.Hill, V.M.Pittser, H.M.Duehr, J.P.Hankes, W.A.Strelow, W.A.Tobin, M.L.Opper, I.F.Williams, T.J.Anderson, W.J.Ernst, A.E.Schultz, A.G.Gasper, D.E.Cudworth, D.S.Fleming, E.L.Amfahr, L.K.Terhune, B.G.Joines, F.A.Welvaert, J.W.Finney, L.C.Schatteman, B.S.Heaton, M.R.Matson, **1951** A.L.Richards, D.T.Murphy, E.L.Schoeffel, G.R.Sovey, H.D.Burkhart, J.C.Schuldt, J.Young, K.L.Taylor, M.J.Stokes, R.F.Bard, W.A.Hying, H.W.Custer, J.E.Sinnott, J.W.Stephens, R.J.Grable, R.L.Caster, F.Staworski, H.A.Fritz, L.Thomas, M.J.Barnett, R.A.Holmes, F.J.Philipsky, G.I.Leon, J.E.Scott, J.H.Hamer, E.W.Glew, H.P.Ansel, J.E.Steffe, K.M.Cummins, M.H.Johnson, O.J.Reifsnider, G.H.Hardin, N.J.O'Dell, G.W.Gauley Jr., J.R.Lyons, J.W.Carlo, L.C.Harp, L.N.Amfahr, W.E.Johnson, R.M.Burgess, C.T.Frank, E.Brown Sr., E.L.Myers, H.V.Rath, I.B.Moffitt, M.E.Brown, V.M.Valentine, A.Nyquist, A.R.Wainwright, H.F.Breitbach, L.R.Eastman, R.J.Gusse, B.A.Marsh, C.C.Whitmore, G.L.Sallows, M.G.Hermsen, R.F.Keidel, C.A.Jenkins, G.E.O Brien, H.P.Jensen, H.Thomas, W.F.Howell, C.E.Beason, E.W.Fears, E.L.Strupp, J.H.Kress, K.E.Vickery, M.A.Miles Jr., M.C.Smolenski, R.G.Lane, A.E.Lee, E.Scott, F.Duran, F.P.Mottet, J.Parker, M.C.Laird, R.B.Dahmus, R.C.Francis, R.T.Gibson, J.E.Hunt, R.E.Denney, R.H.Webb, R.R.Schatteman, J.O.Winston, H.A.De Munbrun, H.P.Myli, J.L.Parcel, K.R.Janitzky, L.C.Besco, L.W.Karr, M.E.Nyswonger, N.L.Bride, R.L.Rechkemmer, C.D.Potter, J.B.Miller, J.F.Chickering, M.L.Peters, R.J.Schultz, F.E.White, H.R.Ross, J.A.Lawson, A.L.Hicks, D.S.Jefferson, F.H.Timmerman, T.M.Barnes, W.J.Sindt, C.L.Baker, E.W.Kinast, R.R.Troudt, A.T.Cobb, C.C.Curtis, E.C.Powers, G.H.Marshall, H.M.Rogers, T.D.Foster, C.F.Brimeyer, D.Harter, G.L.Ostrander, H.W.Brown, H.W.Powers, J.W.Kakavas, L.E.Apling, C.S.Wester, G.J.Myers, E.H.Hansen, J.K.Hanson Jr., T.C.Montgomery, B.J.Grimes, G.E.Bebout, L.Phillips Jr., M.W.Ryan Sr., J.D.Petersen, E.W.Foster, R.D.Kemmitzer, W.A.Newman Jr., A.L.Hogan, L.V.Dewulf, M.H.Schoppe, R.R.Dangel, D.J.Wilz, I.E.Cuvelier, J.D.Calloway, R.F.Ziegenhorn, T.Kalomas, D.R.Williams, M.S.Kopf, R.C.McNeil, R.D.Thomas, R.Stewart, A.W.Weiland, D.A.Hill, L.L.Ennen, R.A.McCombs, R.L.Mackie, A.Ellis Jr., E.J.Cavanaugh, H.E.Dale, D.R.Aschaker, J.Laurie, D.M.Hallas, G.L.Foushee, J.P.Leinhauser, R.G.Lindell, G.L.Gall, T.W.Hammock, A.P.Heber, K.D.Edie, L.D.Agee, R.B.Tod, W.E.Ten Pas, G.A.Cornelius, J.A.Vicevich, A.Eichstaedt, I.E.Hartman Jr., J.R.Zubke, F.C.Moreland, W.Chase, C.B.Mobley, G.H.Budworth Jr., V.L.Wenthe, L.Meewes, W.D.Stokes, W.J.Lippert, D.R.Harp, G.C.Kostas, J.V.Sample, A.G.Webbeking, E.C.Sprau, E.D.Daily Jr., F.M.Wilson, J.J.Csiacsek, C.C.Jones, C.R.Heller, J.J.Macheel, J.P.Cunningham, M.S.Schillerstrom, P.Hawkins Jr., R.D.Dixon, C.D.Fowler, M.A.Berk, R.Sawyers, J.K.Major, J.M.Speidel, W.C.Freese, D.J.McGivern, E.L.Hunt, L.A.Roberts, M.C.Roberts, D.E.Allen, D.H.Whitson, D.J.Levendusky, G.J.Birkel, G.M.Ferns, O.V.Nehls, R.S.Sprouse, H.A.Larson, H.L.Mc Dannald, R.D.Kerr, S.C.Dam, C.E.Trout, R.D.Smith,

C.Larson, R.A.Vandecasteele, T.M.Songer, C.H.Miller, I.W.Givens, M.D.Eshenko, V.E.Truman, R.J.Schuster, C.Vanhulle, G.W.Rohweder, L.L.Klug, M.M.Kane, N.M.Hostetler, J.C.Wood Jr., J.J.Rokusek Jr., J.M.Delarosa, R.L.McCune, R.E.Millard, R.J.Nicoletto, V.E.Young, R.Adler, B.Barker, D.H.Lymburner, I.A.Spady Sr., K.D.Selix, K.E.Barker, P.S.Malam, R.C.Vickroy, S.H.Hoopes, S.L.Toderick, A.R.Crawford, B.J.Ohrberg, C.W.Thornbloom, R.W.Francis, W.J.King, B.D.Jones, F.J.Whitcomb, M.L.Miller, W.B.Keegan, J.Chaumont, D.E.Shaw, E.J.McNally, G.A.Hill, G.B.Shinn, J.C.Roberts, D.F.Myers, J.T.Roseman, L.J.Schares, L.A.Skerritt, G.Elgersma, M.L.Aguirre, V.J.Miller, V.K.Page, E.E.Vandewalle, N.D.Sellers, R.D.Kircher, G.P.Artman, J.N.Golston, S.H.Ward, W.A.Wenzel, H.P.Kepner, W.L.Lester, W.E.Knox, G.F.Johnson, L.D.Westerfield, L.I.Oathout, R.Griffin, H.L.Messerschmitt, H.R.Ward, S.K.Newman, D.E.Wilford, G.Lasne, S.L.Bradfield, M.J.Francis, T.A.Williams, W.J.Goodnight, A.H.Davidson, J.R.Williams, G.E.Riley, G.N.Billmeyer, I.J.Derammelaere, T.D.Jacobson, B.F.Vogelaar, M.S.Clark, R.J.Gerstenberger, E.F.Schaefer, G.S.Soteropulos, J.E.Mobley, R.L.De Bar, T.Crees, H.L.Claeys, W.E.Benson, H.H.Voelschow, J.D.Roberts, R.A.Vander Jeugdt, R.E.Watson, W.W.Grauerholz, J.W.Curtis, M.N.Turner, C.C.Holcomb, T.R.Hawkins, W.R.Powell, N.R.Pratley, H.D.Kadavy, J.F.Arndt, R.B.Wassell, R.W.Boeke, W.D.Glendon, F.K.Weber, L.R.La Pierre, M.L.Arnold, W.L.Steuerwald, W.M.Barryhill Jr., D.D.Randolph, D.M.Pfau Jr., S.E.Anderson, E.E.Depooter, E.Smith Jr., K.C.Poling, H.Drew, F.R.Frazier, J.M.Carlson, D.L.Mitchell, E.M.McCullough, H.C.Hadley, J.A.Buckton, L.F.Rasberry, M.D.Nieman, M.J.Friedman, S.Moon Jr., V.R.Bailey, D.J.Saunders, L.E.Denny, R.L.Leasenby, M.M.Bittick, C.R.Wendell, J.C.Velon, C.M.Crandall, E.M.Noble, H.W.Brown, R.L.Boens, L.L.Clinton, D.I.Malm, J.J.Shanahan, W.E.Sampson, F.N.Taylor, A.R.Martin, D.P.Heller, J.P.Roels, M.E.Forst, M.M.Martin, B.E.Massey, H.K.Kienzle, G.K.Dice Jr., H.O.Siebke, R.C.Sproul, R.D.James, E.G.Barton, L.N.Slayden Sr., R.D.O Hara, R.D.Feaster, R.L.Heon, N.J.Border, N.Peponis, A.A.Fleege, C.White, M.Delarosa, G.R.Bishop, W.B.Mincks, G.J.Tuttle, R.J.Weaver, W.A.Shirley, E.A.Lioen, H.R.Bahls, J.E.Henkel, K.R.Hamilton, L.B.Rensberger, M.M.Poelvoorde, W.H.Hatje, E.J.Calsen, D.H.Riegel, N.E.Smith, R.E.Loomans, R.H.Weenike, W.C.Bennett, D.D.Dugan, W.D.Petersen, E.L.Whitehorn, H.L.Young, M.A.Schweitzer, W.Beebe, D.H.Wegner, M.E.Friend, R.M.Youngblood, T.J.McDowell, C.D.Spilman, D.M.Griffith, G.Wolff Jr., J.J.Link, D.J.Williams, J.A.Peterson, J.C.Hult, D.W.Phillips, R.L.Hollis, E.G.Allman, T.C.Leamon, D.Geesaman, H.J.Maring, M.J.Hood, M.M.Gislason, G.M.Housley, J.R.Williams, J.Labeau, D.F.Wolf, J.E.Munley, P.G.Hagglund, R.J.Widmar, L.C.Evans, J.C.Thomas, N.B.Chistoff, R.A.Bostrom, R.C.Pexa, S.O.Monroe, V.M.Allison, R.F.McKee, W.K.Miller, C.D.Farner, G.De Vries, H.F.Mangelsdorf, J.F.Guiter, M.E.Sneed, K.E.Gramling Jr., W.C.Thompson, K.J.Diederich, D.E.Ebbesen, D.H.Johns, E.Judkins, R.R.Gaber, W.C.Hansen, N.A.Shaffner, L.C.Larson, E.R.Moore, **1952** R.Nuffer, A.D.Aldene, C.A.Dacus, J.F.Wagner, K.R.Thomas, W.Clayton, W.H.Horn Jr., H.C.Rudd, J.E.Ashcraft, G.R.Paxton, J.W.Ackley, J.H.Hanley, R.D.Phillips, H.W.Dailey, A.I.Litterst, C.M.Mac Learn, R.J.Carlson, E.F.Waclawik, C.A.Dollar, W.K.Oliver, C.W.Bishopric, R.W.Lenser, J.T.Harlan, R.B.Ady, D.E.Foster, A.L.Witt, D.E.Ferguson, J.E.Schrage, E.T.Hartsell, W.P.Zumpf, G.E.Baliman, W.E.Gaffield, M.E.Ryerson, A.R.Webb, A.W.Krambeck Jr., A.K.Lawrence, C.W.McClintock, D.R.La Vine, H.R.Holland, R.Wedeking, W.R.Innes, J.B.Peck, K.L.Schwartz, S.A.Stevenson, R.L.Erickson, T.W.Robinson, A.Brandt, H.T.Wright, D.L.Persinger, J.R.Chebuhar, E.S.Blackburn, T.McDaniel, A.M.Brady Jr., J.E.Todey, R.J.Smith, J.D.Mitchell, R.S.Wolff, W.D.Brugman, G.Bauer, A.Lindstrom, D.Butz, R.Dube, P.Antoine, J.E.Gilchrist, K.P.Storey, B.M.Keesler, A.A.Radi, F.J.Dewaele, J.E.Patterson, K.E.Peterson, M.R.Beert, J.D.Spivey, A.A.Ong, D.L.Brooks, H.E.Heaton, M.E.Williams, R.J.Kingston, H.A.Peel, L.A.Timmerman, J.L.Van Zante, E.Turner, F.Propp, N.A.Sauter, R.D.Miller, L.Williams, C.H.Degeeter, R.A.Gongwer, R.P.Bush, R.Vallet, J.D.Mortensen, R.J.Christ, C.L.Wiese, J.H.Polacek, V.R.Whiting, W.K.Diehl, E.Browning, C.G.Northcott, H.L.Washington, E.D.Kral, R.D.Acker, R.L.Mattox, R.L.Siegel, F.J.Meyers, J.K.Hutton, R.Ciron, K.Schneider, G.W.Krumdieck, W.G.Baggett, B.C.Bartlett, R.L.Ericson, M.L.Buhrmester, C.A.James, B.J.Stephenson, B.G.Franks, V.C.Moore, J.Lambron, A.E.Dunton, D.J.Milan, F.Miner, J.G.Webb, M.J.Langenfeld, R.A.Savala, J.H.Slemaker Sr., B.A.Zmuda, F.M.Dickson, C.Casper, H.H.Hoverstad, G.K.Kost, R.P.Miller, M.Deslandes, R.L.Webb, P.D.Booker, G.Burfield, H.E.Bozeman, H.C.Warbington, D.A.Shelford, R.A.Blum, T.L.Gavin, E.J.Mackenzie Jr., O.J.Curtis, R.L.Pierce, P.Pawliw, L.D.Coop, C.C.Ludovissy, M.D.Cunningham, G.P.Jelinek, C.E.Hoppenjan, G.H.Piquett, E.L.Pagel, P.J.Luciani, S.E.Hermanson, G.D.Milligan Jr., G.E.Thompson, L.V.Cloyd, M.C.Deevers, R.D.Obadal, R.E.Douthart, R.J.Eichacker, C.Direito, K.A.Patterson, D.C.Hasken, M.V.Wolver, C.A.Nauman, M.S.Westerman, N.L.Breiner, W.E.Hemple, L.K.Hampton, G.A.Beighle, J.D.Parker, R.D.Kintzle, R.G.Buckley, V.T.Smythe, J.T.Roden, J.A.Chebuhar, C.C.Peterson, C.T.Southerland, N.E.Crooks, V.D.Hankinson, S.L.Palmer, W.N.Ashby, W.L.Thomas, S.Dorris, J.R.Velk, R.L.Tackenberg, A.R.Ponce, K.W.Reisen, R.D.McNett, **1953** D.E.Brotzman, A.Fournier, J.M.Conley, J.Puckett, M.A.Nordquist, O.H.Musgrove, P.A.Kuehl, R.L.Shipley, W.R.Judge, L.F.Obrien, F.M.Hancock, J.C.Wakeland, T.L.Loncarich, R.J.Hardy, F.M.Box, J.G.Behn, J.R.Bermel, R.M.Thomas, W.C.Gehrt, W.E.Peterson, L.F.Neels, R.E.Woodard, R.L.Carmichael, D.L.Butler, J.O.Runyan, P.S.Crouse, W.L.Fry, E.C.Watson, J.D.Robinson, E.L.Smith, L.L.Longfellow Sr., R.D.Bergman, R.E.Smith, R.F.Krayer, R.G.Beggs, R.W.Stewart, G.Grimes, J.A.Fears, R.Kudart, C.W.Kinman, J.J.Geiger, B.G.Sparks, R.A.Kelley, B.D.Brown, L.G.Tilseth, R.O.Jones, B.F.Bailey, J.W.Woudenberg, R.E.Haight, R.W.Roberson, R.C.Muntz, R.D.Leedy, J.G.Wheeler, L.K.Davis, D.A.Berns, E.W.Ivanowski, J.H.Garrett, R.W.Haney, C.J.Gosa, B.D.Halley, B.H.Kimball, C.J.Goodall, D.F.Nelson, L.F.Denaro, R.R.Olson, R.W.Lumsdon, P.D.Leamon, D.L.Nelson, F.Phillis, J.Roberts, D.M.Funk, W.M.Smith, R.A.Wilburn, S.L.Williams, R.Buffington, L.H.Mallett, C.J.Meyer, L.D.Holley, E.A.Harris, P.J.Paxton, C.W.Dailey, E.M.Lehman, E.P.Clark, A.B.Harbin, H.B.Swank, L.M.Johnson, O.C.Baker, J.E.Garrison, R.D.Mohler, R.L.Pierce, R.A.Suchy, C.W.Schreiber, M.J.Boren, J.L.Hopkins, E.N.Pence, F.W.Lyon, J.H.Cain, P.S.Schafer, C.C.Cavanaugh, B.M.Nason, E.C.Davis, H.D.Robbins, H.E.De Buhr, L.M.Rathburn, R.E.Frey, A.E.Kuefler, D.L.Ferris, L.Cherry, W.S.Mc Culloch, R.E.Crow, D.Swartz, J.R.Williams, R.C.Fry, S.M.Busby, W.A.Murray, J.G.Kester, E.B.Ely, J.A.O'Brien, N.A.Vickery, C.E.Goff, M.M.Dhaenens, L.E.Thiele, H.M.Davis, D.E.Knapp, J.H.Heischman, J.W.Henry, D.A.Essex, K.Geddes, R.E.Rogers, M.A.Lang, J.J.Hennen, F.C.Danielson, R.W.Lynn, A.W.Olson, D.D.Wara, H.M.Meinert, J.A.Graham, L.M.Helms, M.R.Olsofski, W.C.Hull, J.I.Peterson, R.H.Fairbank, G.J.Dorval, J.O.Troemner, N.B.Johnson, R.L.Pitra, W.W.Booker, R.E.Beck, R.B.Seaholm, A.Gerard, H.R.Town, H.V.Hansen, J.H.Barton, J.J.Bush, L.L.Lane, J.W.Nicholas, L.A.Arthur, R.E.Kotmair, G.J.Scott, M.R.Hoogenakker, D.F.Ireland, A.P.Delong, D.C.Bichel, D.V.Loe, E.B.Griffith, W.F.Krallman, H.P.Hanson, H.W.Van Gerpen, L.C.Sartorius, J.Cosson, G.G.Coyne, A.G.Waschek, G.L.Elbert, C.A.Hanson, J.H.Scott, L.Wheating, R.Meysenburg, C.M.Beebe, H.R.Hawkins, C.R.Halverson, K.A.Magalsky, F.P.Blanchard, L.W.Hill, E.H.Hafner, J.Ortega, A.Larcher, J.Poitrimoult, N.Tornes, E.H.Johnson, **1954** R.P.Stufflebeam, A.T.La Rew, R.C.Blake, J.D.Stover, J.D.Leggett, N.A.Schurmeier, R.Beaumont, D.T.Jones, H.W.Smith, J.B.Nichols, J.E.Horning, D.A.River, C.H.Davis, G.G.Tilp, J.L.Mumford, O.D.Hollenback, B.D.Strauss, R.C.Drefchinski, L.M.Elrod, K.K.Bowman, E.Wessel, J.E.Kinley, M.J.Clemens, R.E.Knutson, B.J.Kwiatkowski, W.F.Jeffers, R.Mangelsdorf, C.L.Seright, C.R.Eichholz, A.L.Flege, M.G.McGregor, E.H.Jordan, G.R.Sitz, R.M.Doyle, D.K.Nelson, W.H.Schwartz, J.Dumont, O.J.Kittle, H.Ball, E.E.Lambert, J.J.Beeuwsaert, B.I.Koelz, L.H.Hack, T.Draward, A.L.Slusher, G.Sannier, E.R.Lenneman, R.J.Stroh, H.L.Gullett, E.L.Schurvinske, B.Blankenship, D.Garcia R., B.L.Decker, G.L.Albright, B.L.Fox, D.R.Waldon, R.C.Hughes, R.W.Mahnke, T.T.Cook, G.Perret, W.Lewis, M.Brugman, J.R.Agan, M.B.Olson, R.C.Forsyth, R.D.Hopkins, R.Peterson, D.G.Pestotnik, L.M.Kehrer, R.K.Larsen, J.J.Cousins, R.Janvier, W.B.Gross, A.Hendricks, H.E.Guetzlaff, M.P.Kopatich, G.W.Rempel, A.I.Bowling, M.N.Tone, D.M.Stamp, D.J.Anderson, H.E.Petersen, M.F.Mirr, G.L.Marquart, R.D.Sears, R.Maliba, C.L.Hegg, G.R.Kroeger, H.M.Stone, R.Lambron, R.Chevallier, M.A.Van Zante, M.D.Johnson, R.Oger, V.J.Hasken, R.D.Nordstrom, A.D.Matheson Jr., H.Kuhnle, R.Dreux, B.L.Swales, M.J.Wilson, J.W.Goings, F.P.Maunder, L.G.Halpin, M.D.Crandall, W.G.Matthews, M.Waldron, J.R.White, H.R.Park, W.W.Waterman, W.A.Schwinke, I.W.Hayes, P.E.Wadsworth, W.Cogdill, C.W.Box, E.R.Lindquist, J.F.Fritz, G.J.Decker, J.Kulak, R.P.Doran, J.L.Culbertson, R.C.Carnahan, J.Gouot, D.M.Greim, C.W.Jameson, L.G.Beenken, P.T.Van Ee, E.E.Kollmann, L.F.Schmidt, B.J.Ffitch, B.S.Root, D.G.Strafford, D.L.Brodd, D.L.Lang, R.Ede, L.N.Clark, L.H.Van Hauen, R.W.Champ, G.L.Faulkner, H.E.Skinner, J.W.Ledbeter, W.C.Schoville, C.C.Muse, C.D.Teare Jr., C.L.Mc Enroe, K.L.Meyer, L.F.Reiss, E.Hyman, H.W.Mc Elroy, J.Walters, R.E.Reynolds, E.L.Swanson, J.M.Hernandez, R.L.Courts, J.R.Lee, L.O.Railsback, R.C.Levendusky, C.J.Lehnhardt, V.H.Hoeppner, B.Payton, R.J.Weber, W.H.Nock, L.E.Stacey, L.Tackenberg, M.J.Fulli, A.J.Herzog, D.E.Arnold, V.H.Meyer, L.H.Young, L.J.Phippen, R.G.O Connell, R.M.Mathews, M.L.Smock, D.S.Kerns, R.L.Shaffer, G.Lefort, D.R.Schurman, J.E.Warner, K.D.Courbat, T.E.Meiser, G.Riousset, C.F.Formaker, D.T.Welsh, K.J.Merkel, M.C.Enstrom, R.J.Vandewiele, W.A.Robinson, J.B.Muir, G.Epps Sr., W.R.Kauten, B.L.Michael, F.W.Barker, G.Grapp, J.W.Derr, P.K.Kuriger, R.E.Shonk, C.Schauf, F.M.Woodcock, **1955** H.J.Hartzler, C.Renault, A.A.Wortham, A.H.Frahm, C.B.Sallis, C.L.Polk, D.A.Donovan, D.E.Bolster, D.S.White, J.H.Mc Coneghey, L.R.Einck, M.E.Rodgers, M.J.Hrabovsky, M.R.Conrad, R.E.Rieks, W.W.Circus, B.Trower, F.W.Talbot, R.E.Declercq, A.H.Stessman, C.E.Hemsath, J.J.Formaro, L.H.Matthias, M.G.Mandel, R.L.Poole Jr., R.M.Cole, W.W.Hill, A.G.Debacker, C.C.Ames, D.J.Burch, F.E.Hyde, L.E.Luck, R.E.Renner, D.W.Carr, F.G.Udorvich, G.N.Schmitz, J.R.Boyer, J.R.Buckingham, J.W.McIntosh, R.L.Viers, W.W.Viers, C.L.Coder, D.D.Holmes, D.J.Weber, G.B.Lampo, K.O.Phelps, L.C.Vandewalle, L.J.Geiger, P.E.Parent, M.Stevenson, E.A.Stone, H.E.Witry, L.W.Welsh, A.C.Grafton, C.E.Blad, D.D.Danielson, D.W.Lee, H.R.Pencil, J.Vaughn, L.W.Westemeier Jr., R.H.Erickson, D.Marshall, E.F.Wilkinson, E.L.Vercautren, J.L.Welcher, J.W.Eddleman, J.W.Gooch, L.D.Acklin, L.F.Towns, R.D.Nevins, R.E.Rockhold, D.L.Derifield Jr., J.J.Youngblut, R.E.Harker Jr., R.Gomez, R.J.Smith, R.L.Miller, J.D.Magnuson, R.L.Tucker, J.Rodriguez, B.L.Rees, J.L.Jenkins, J.W.Bryant, H.L.Spragg, R.E.Stuber, F.Gomez, J.Allen, L.H.Hinkle, R.G.Kunkle, A.C.Muller, J.M.Olsen, R.W.Reuter, C.Coker, J.D.Lauer, E.A.Mc Coy, G.E.Gorby, I.I.Robinson, H.Sisk, R.C.Kiple, D.D.Jensen, G.H.Johnson Jr., J.D.Selesky, J.R.Kaufman, M.E.Todd, N.Zirbel, R.J.Grieger, W.Matlock Sr., W.W.Sangster, J.J.Goldthorn, J.L.Burnell, M.D.Young, M.Johnson, M.Ohrt, O.W.Tupper, I.H.Smuck, L.R.Smith, D.M.Edgerton, R.H.Mau, L.F.Corwin, L.W.Buls, M.J.Delarosa, S.H.Ehlers, C.W.Brown, H.A.Selk, L.H.Brooks, W.C.Panouses, D.Boger, M.D.Wilson, E.A.Wilson, H.G.Welshhons, W.D.Freel, A.P.Pfohl, J.R.Witherspoon Jr., P.A.Swarts, R.Harris, V.V.Jacobmeier, B.J.Patterson, M.W.Cook, L.W.Wilson, M.D.Rahe Jr., M.D.Rieck, R.F.Suiter, W.L.Wood, D.L.Zummak, J.R.Stanley, J.Z.McKee, K.W.Ransom, B.L.Warkins, R.W.Estel, D.P.Peterson, L.L.Thrasher, N.O.Kiesow, J.Richards, T.B.Grampp, K.J.Reveal, N.Sisk, R.E.Molstead, L.L.Zell, R.L.Robinson, T.W.Durnin, D.L.Robinson, H.W.Seales, H.W.Spooner, R.M.Gietzel, V.V.Kopecky, D.E.Coulson, J.M.Zabel, J.L.Mc Roberts, M.A.Salmonson, E.W.Bahr, W.G.Rolfes, D.D.Francis, J.S.Miller, J.V.Watts, W.D.Olsen, B.M.Keller, O.E.Oberender, P.M.Butters, R.A.Wald, R.E.Miller, J.I.Mc Collom, T.D.Swanson, L.P.Errthum, D.E.Hall, J.M.Johnson, L.F.Bechen, L.W.Niebuhr, C.M.Hochreiter, D.D.Sommerfeld, D.E.Fischer, H.M.Meaney, M.A.Miller, A.L.Frey, A.L.Terry, A.V.Earle, B.B.Roy, K.L.Ralston, M.D.Selby, A.Fernandez G., D.E.Stoffregen, R.D.Strempke, R.K.Seeley, W.K.Spears, A.A.Puhl, C.A.Duffy, D.L.Buck, F.L.Zmudka, G.C.White, H.F.Metzger, J.L.Hartzell, M.L.Heald, O.J.Stender, E.E.Gilstrap, E.L.Parker, G.A.Borsheim, A.Gonsard, E.W.Blaser, F.T.Farr, J.K.Sallinger, J.H.Cook, L.J.Foelske, P.Z.Polley, S.Day Jr., W.J.Waller Jr., R.E.Lane, D.E.Mountain, H.D.Cammack, R.L.Jasper, R.L.McLeighton, D.C.Patterson, F.H.Butters, I.J.Peterson, W.H.Butler, G.L.Nichols, J.E.Butler, D.C.Kennedy, G.D.Rutter, H.W.Beecher, C.O.Moore, F.E.Troutner, K.E.Murphy, W.W.Moore, A.Macua, C.R.Lauterbach, D.M.Brown, M.J.Wallace, V.E.Tarrell, E.M.Keener, J.C.Boardman, W.J.Smith, D.L.Schueller, R.L.Davis, C.J.Feyen, E.T.Flaten, W.Magee, D.G.Farris, E.L.Willingham, J.W.Labee, W.A.Ripplinger, W.Smith, A.H.Smith, C.A.Barneson, C.L.Kirby, G.J.Zippay, G.R.Petersen, J.W.Wanamaker, L.H.Rose, M.P.Blum, W.J.Schlichtmann, W.Treadway, W.Koehler, A.C.Blindert, D.A.Luke, L.P.Link, O.J.Nugent, R.Bishop, R.E.Allen, W.C.Schultz, W.E.Sieg, A.P.Fowlkes Jr., D.C.Johnson, G.W.Ruchti, J.W.Helgeson, L.G.Duerr, W.Tuchel, A.Ovejero, G.A.Kile, M.D.Shackleford, P.M.Smith, R.G.Barnett, J.P.Reeves, R.H.Winning, B.E.McDermott, D.E.Burge, H.L.Bellis, J.R.Rosenberg, L.E.Korte, W.E.Davis, C.H.De Long, H.D.Seidlitz, L.G.Luloff, L.Kubera, W.F.Brocka, J.C.Hines Sr., J.L.Miles, T.F.Nelson, W.F.Burdt, D.E.Jameson, R.B.Leeman, D.L.Berry, F.C.Ihm, V.W.Eck, F.H.Sanderson, J.J.Brouwer, C.H.Cheever Jr., G.H.Breitsprecker, J.G.Kidd, J.L.Soden, W.G.Van Gundy, R.D.Duneman, R.D.Weber, B.L.Boyd, D.L.White, J.K.Shepherd, K.E.Dieters, M.E.Weakly, R.W.Fowler, D.Medina, F.A.Nisius, R.C.Boardman, D.F.Popp, M.L.Flesner, W.T.Anderson, D.L.Ellis, G.D.Brunko, D.A.Mc Intyre, C.F.Miller, H.L.De Long, L.Robertson, A.P.Lindgard, D.E.Kulish, G.F.Cardy, G.N.Doering, L.J.Steffen, W.L.Laird, M.G.Lonergan, E.A.Hiber, F.M.Rauch, L.E.Vanderwerf, L.R.Frerichs, Z.F.Blizzard, M.E.Cunningham, C.C.Youngblut, C.J.Nelson, F.Henson, M.D.Harvey, N.L.Sanchez, P.W.Dickson, W.C.Eide, J.T.Foxx, M.Hoover, P.Torrejon, D.M.Danielsen, L.K.Satterlee, M.A.Stabenow, R.D.Mc Glaughlin, D.L.Westcott, H.D.Boyce, R.C.Voss Jr., W.R.Cowell, B.L.Swindle, F.H.Jacobs, J.B.Olson, J.Brockman, E.P.Sorge, G.L.Tansey, H.L.Wilson, L.D.Garland, L.Engen, R.D.Amans, C.J.Peters, C.M.Acker, D.G.Lewis, G.W.Pakala, M.J.Jennings, P.G.Claussen, R.W.Holmlund, W.Harris, W.W.Jackson, G.M.Cable, I.R.Polson, L.H.Mau, P.D.Wetrich, R.E.Bruner, R.M.Baumgartner, R.W.Ingall, R.W.Warner, H.A.Fink Jr., R.A.Woodruff, L.D.Bolton, T.D.Rich, B.C.Harpole, B.J.Carthel, C.E.Kittle, E.T.Anderson Jr., H.M.Peter, P.K.Gruys, R.E.Carlson, D.H.Polzin, J.J.Shaw, W.A.Sawyer, A.E.Price, W.J.Domer, E.J.Corkery, R.E.Buck, D.E.Lunke, D.Kelly, E.H.Kieffer, E.L.Stachovic, F.P.Goedken, G.N.Nyman, J.R.Hantelmann, W.A.Pregler, H.E.Schroeder, J.F.Haskin, L.W.Lindner, C.E.Rojohn, J.M.Wahl, R.B.Jones, R.Hopkins, E.Biegel, E.H.Wood Jr., R.E.Yates, R.J.Nelson, W.J.Jaeggi, M.C.Borchelt, C.W.Von Fumetti, D.E.Gieseman, M.Thiebaud, F.W.Lyons, D.Proctor, D.L.Hunt, S.Z.Rombakis, V.E.Rettig, W.H.Dorward, B.J.Nolan, D.R.Olson, H.A.Lentfer, J.R.Merrick Jr., N.A.Devilder, R.C.Tefft, D.L.Berggren, J.J.Butters, L.J.Robinson, O.L.Parsons, O.W.Schutte, R.D.Broell, W.O.Wagoner, J.D.Kelly, J.J.Wilberding, J.J.Kirby, R.A.Hanson, J.Gonzalez E., E.E.Dailey, J.E.Dailey, A.E.Patchin Jr., D.W.Piddington, G.E.Casteel Jr., H.R.Scranton, J.F.Kelly, J.J.Larson, G.F.Niebuhr, G.L.Ketels, V.D.Pippenger, J.D.Mc Farland, J.E.Kaufman, L.R.Wenger, R.J.Stierman, W.A.Vanderwerf, J.L.Kennicott, B.J.Rickert, D.M.Jones, G.R.Alvin, H.L.Lawrence, O.S.Ludwig, R.S.Fleming, C.E.Thurston Jr., E.P.Schneider, E.C.Greve, A.C.Hoppe, K.C.Hottenstein, F.E.Dunbar, J.F.Carrier, V.K.Soden Sr., B.Hunck, D.L.Partlow, J.M.Letchford, M.L.Harting, R.E.Szymanski, E.R.Schilling, H.W.Humphries, R.L.Nelson, H.Born, B.J.Vogel, D.G.Cone, F.E.Stevens Jr., L.H.Nickel, J.F.Carton, M.J.Leick, M.Guillemin, D.L.Smith, G.A.Peirce, K.L.Roth, K.Franck, O.W.Branch, E.J.Voltz Jr., J.P.Smith, M.H.Krouse, W.P.Hubbard, G.Lapertot, G.T.O Connor, J.Masides, C.H.Lynch Jr., J.S.Larvenz, K.H.Mac Donald, R.E.Bowman, G.M.Thornbloom, J.T.Stith, C.B.Keith, F.T.Winthurst, H.D.Yeager, K.Q.Kessler, N.A.Kipp, R.O.Taube, W.F.Miller, N.F.Martin, R.A.Berndt, L.P.Breitbach, J.B.Skiles, C.K.Stralow, L.C.Beesecker, L.G.Weber, N.J.Jingst, R.J.Payne, I.L.Koethe, R.Snyder, L.J.Forbes, M.J.Schmitz Jr., W.J.Ludovissy, L.Moreno G., J.E.Nilles, L.J.Schwartz, D.W.Welter, F.P.Coopman Jr., L.L.Salow, P.D.Klingborg, R.C.Melick, F.C.Funk, J.H.Shelton, M.D.Hosler, P.L.Sweeney, R.F.McCabe, J.B.Daniel, B.M.St Pierre, G.A.Williams, J.C.Alvin, J.D.Clark, J.J.Lehman, J.T.Givens Jr., P.L.Conway, D.R.Pierce, E.R.Cahill, R.V.Vyverberg, R.D.Schmieder, P.R.Cooprider, E.D.Oltmann, J.Rodriguez R., H.C.Wehking Jr., R.W.Smith, R.W.Engelman, B.G.Harvey, C.H.Kinyon, C.L.Bradley Jr., L.Shepherd Jr., P.L.Reeg, R.A.Young, A.P.Weber, G.R.Beck, J.R.Hohmann, M.B.Stokes, O.E.Larson, W.R.Brousseau, C.E.Eckhart, E.C.Walters, E.F.Reed, R.W.Breiner, C.Barbot, J.D.Fowler, L.D.Fivecoat, R.H.Lehms, D.W.Pont, J.W.White, P.Fedeyko, R.J.Tigges, R.L.Desmet, F.Claybaugh, T.R.Brown, A.L.White, A.W.Allison, J.A.Ringer, W.L.Byles, B.W.Martin, M.W.Dersch, B.E.Hunter, D.E.Deiter, D.L.Beechamp, D.R.Rice, L.D.Kochendorfer, R.E.Heckert, V.R.Steger, J.Garcia R., D.C.Irby, M.J.Rausch, R.L.Govier, T.R.Huberty, W.L.Welsh, B.L.Sproston, L.H.Baker, L.H.Fiedler, T.J.Amling, D.E.Hughes, G.J.Kriebs, P.M.Mies, G.Rotter, C.J.Roling, J.P.Lacke, L.E.Conrad, T.C.Taggart, J.L.Manso, B.B.Wood, J.L.Powers, S.M.Johnsrud, W.E.Bonnett, M.Kellner, D.L.Sadewasser, M.M.Clough, H.R.Walter, L.A.Gassmann, W.A.Ayres, S.Fernandez B., C.Warkins, E.J.Rauch, B.A.Everett, J.A.Jarpe, J.I.Anderson, P.E.Stemmerman, D.F.Williams, J.L.Harbaugh, D.R.Teats, E.C.Miers, F.Nemluvil, J.E.Malott, J.J.Allgaier, J.R.Seabloom, M.H.Ingersoll, R.D.Straszheim, B.C.Mills, J.E.Melloy, D.L.Filbert, F.A.Toppert, K.E.Hedger, R.K.Beemblossom, D.P.Verkruysse, V.J.Link, D.N.Medinger, K.W.Rahn, R.G.Nelson, W.E.Dixon, H.D.Stancil, G.P.Baker Jr., T.S.Boever, F.E.Schlueter, J.J.Shindelar, J.P.Steger, K.R.Hoftender, L.T.Murphy, R.D.Copley, E.Klemm, E.E.Davidson, **1956** D.L.Barton, H.D.Owens, I.C.Sanders, J.J.Wilcox, K.R.Jones, L.E.Salmonson, O.H.Croegaert, P.P.Tvarkunas, R.B.Clay, W.E.Keel, W.W.Olhausen, M.Leroy, R.G.Wharton, C.Parks, H.H.Jones, S.D.Flowers, T.E.Trotter, W.F.Turner, C.Pinsard, A.E.Mueller, D.W.Sheley, L.J.Hinderman, R.C.Hamilton, E.V.Lampe, H.J.Hokinson, M.Pruneau, F.Bohner, R.W.Emmert, I.Pantoja, F.M.Colston Jr., C.A.Miller Jr., M.Huron, R.L.Breitsprecker, R.L.Oertel, G.Eaves, D.F.Artmann, A.Pastor, D.Dicken, D.L.Jess, D.W.Dobrinske, G.L.Peterson, J.Belin, R.Pasquier, J.A.Johnson, J.W.Strange, R.D.Moore, J.F.Link, R.L.Durkin, C.R.Bennett, J.M.Jamison, R.W.Elbert, T.C.Schrader, G.W.Rastede, A.Knapp, J.A.Collins, M.S.Davis, R.L.Amundgaard, D.J.Rasmussen, J.A.Buchanan, W.W.Russell, J.Diaz M., R.Knodell, J.Valentin, R.A.Kuehl, R.D.Barnes, W.E.Smith, B.L.Stange, G.E.Corwin, G.W.Clayton, R.Luttrell Jr., L.P.Oertell, W.L.Snyder, M.I.Reno, R.F.Honzik, B.J.Strumpel, E.G.Moore, J.B.Carpenter, E.L.Mansel, B.Ribault, J.E.Wood, J.H.Johnson, H.R.Mascroft, A.E.Schell, E.N.Cermak, R.O.Frey, V.L.Wagner, W.B.Young, D.H.Morshead, D.J.Patzner, J.W.Kramer, V.A.Kramer, C.J.Lemmer, D.H.Wood, E.V.Feldman, C.E.Breihan, M.M.Garlow, R.A.Adams, E.Logan, G.N.Milligan, L.J.Elledge, M.A.Patzner, L.L.Boyer, V.G.Kramer, E.J.Heer, E.N.Freiburger, B.L.Vela, W.A.Brown, B.Fritz, C.T.Langkamp, D.L.Phillips, R.W.Brunne, W.L.Sawyer, A.L.Lose, G.P.Hampton, R.E.Heri, J.M.Lendinez, H.R.Hild, A.Perru, A.W.French, R.F.Clifford, W.E.Frazer, E.W.Howell, H.D.Breiner, R.B.Gillet, M.H.Vroman, H.H.Lovik, C.M.Lunke, P.W.Blackley, K.F.Petersen, L.E.Hancher, L.L.Clements, R.Bercher, C.A.Peterson, E.Mareske Jr., J.E.Pauletti, M.L.Klein, R.C.Spangler, R.W.Bodeen, J.O.De Bo, P.O.Shields, J.D.Bernard, R.E.Larson, R.L.White, J.Comte, J.W.Staes, A.Blumenthal, A.L.Baxter, D.D.Herron, E.I.Hingtgen, H.L.Edwards, J.A.Lyon, J.E.Hoffman Jr., J.G.McQuigg, L.R.Barquist, M.M.Fox, R.J.Morrow, T.H.Michael, C.V.Reiter, M.M.Dale, R.A.Grieve, E.C.Dettbarn, J.W.Dickerson, C.W.Guns, D.E.Nicholson, F.V.Pancrazio, R.H.Fraune, H.Fulton, R.Bergerot, C.R.Miller, C.Young, D.A.Duck, D.M.Cunningham, E.E.Ukkelberg, F.L.Pardoe, G.R.Hall, J.K.Klemmer, L.E.Miller, L.L.Mulvania, M.M.Reese, N.R.Lynn, O.E.Miller, W.Vogel, D.G.Burchett, F.Breiholz, R.J.Cirricione, R.M.Johnson, R.M.Skillings, W.Savala, A.K.Koustas, B.L.Kinkead, J.B.Young, L.A.Dalke, C.E.Holsinger, D.E.Cox, C.A.Rudkin, D.R.Dyer, G.L.Freeman, G.W.Kahle, J.D.Sanders, J.L.Colmer, J.L.Orton, J.R.Boyle, L.L.Jay, L.L.Roth, M.F.Lange, M.L.Clark, N.T.Lafollette, R.H.Wilt, R.J.Murphy, R.K.Leonard, R.L.Faidley, T.G.Menning, T.J.Manning, W.G.Stewart, W.L.Strawn, A.W.Phillips, D.Cochran, D.E.Gunnerson, D.L.Troutner, I.D.Bingham, L.A.Keil, P.M.Wingert, R.L.Ries, A.O.Calhoon, B.J.Cortez, C.J.Cousins, G.Sarauer, R.P.Mohl, V.O.Tullis, C.J.Fure, C.Pappas, G.V.Dixon, L.J.Miller, P.B.Bean, S.J.Hartung, D.H.Kyrk, D.P.Schares, H.R.De Buhr, J.Hayes, J.J.Mahon, J.R.Patton, K.J.Lowin, L.Bueter, L.W.Leisinger, M.Boger, R.E.Rote, R.L.Johnson, S.D.Allison, M.Balboa, W.Severtsgaard, A.W.Sellers, L.Smith Jr., T.J.Andrini, W.M.Hansen, R.L.Adams, B.J.Hoffman, D.L.Horn, H.L.Carlson, K.M.Olson, L.J.Kintzle, L.J.Ranard, N.H.Egan, T.G.Leavengood Jr., G.Chery, A.K.Jennes, D.W.Bolt, J.Allen, P.Gomez Jr., V.A.Splinter, W.E.Jones, C.D.Moen, D.W.Freeman, E.E.Nelson, R.C.Thomas, T.W.Campbell, J.H.Larrison, J.R.Koeneke, L.W.Clabough, J.C.Thornton, J.N.Lisby, K.A.Capehart, L.R.Bryant, D.D.Shoener, D.J.Piper, F.A.White, J.J.Hoffmann, R.L.Bristle, W.R.Bjorn, D.M.Miller, E.J.Glaser, M.L.Voshell, O.B.Hauge, C.I.Dierolf, F.M.Ward, J.L.Clingerman, V.W.Coles, J.W.Judge, A.L.Larson, E.J.Ramser, R.A.Franzen, R.H.Ohrt, R.L.Ryser, T.Hernandez, D.Meythaler, E.C.Ambs, F.L.Lane, A.J.Corsello, L.J.Theisen, A.W.Reinertson, C.J.Koerperich, H.A.Shearer, L.K.Williams, R.D.Peterson, S.J.Pazzi, F.C.Ramaker, R.S.Wilkes, W.Pearce, C.Randall, E.G.Tyler, E.H.Burke, G.G.Brimeyer, J.O.Fowlkes, M.P.Gassman, N.A.Dittmer, R.A.Medd, E.A.Staskal, V.F.Peters, W.H.York, C.D.Francis, C.F.Lange, E.J.Hasken, E.R.Schinckel, L.W.Cottrell, O.C.Mauer, R.B.Hibben Sr., B.Lopez, E.C.Byerly, F.A.Fisher, G.H.Mishler, K.P.Simon, L.F.Boehmke, P.G.Manley, W.R.Shew, D.L.Henry, E.D.Ruth, H.R.Braden, M.R.Eubank, C.A.Selensky, E.B.Pinck, F.C.Bolte, H.F.Bausch, J.A.Lilly, R.E.Devolder, R.K.Brown, W.S.Garvey, B.W.Mc Namee, G.Wilson, J.M.Goodwin, L.W.Frederiksen, E.H.Vanpelt, M.J.Rossow, V.J.Levendusky, W.E.Nerness, D.A.Talaska, E.L.Robertson, P.L.Roberts, W.H.Boltz, W.R.Wisecup, C.C.Dunnwald, J.W.Boesen, J.W.Renslow, L.J.Curry, A.F.Bert, B.L.Lee, C.J.Thomas, D.M.Rasso, D.R.Peterson, E.O.Thies, F.A.Rose, J.W.Lovell, K.K.Kelling, L.C.Pottebaum, L.E.Bergmann, L.L.Schatteman Jr., R.P.Klein, R.R.Dehnke, R.W.Jones, V.J.Maltas, C.N.Schneller, J.E.Garrett, H.D.Koppes, H.D.Schade, R.L.Rigdon, I.Garcia R., C.D.Petty, E.A.Lampo, G.D.Fillman,

Employees at Harvester Works, East Moline, Illinois, 1944

W.A.Graham, L.J.Nemmers, L.P.Diercks, L.L.Wildebour, D.M.Waddell, J.Guilbon, M.L.Deutsch, H.Plappert, K.E.Uhde, L.L.Metz, M.L.Strickler, E.A.Meyer, O.R.McMahon, R.R.Wiederholt, D.D.Stabenow, A.Rodelgo, C.C.Hanford Jr., D.E.Lorenzen, D.M.Kniss, H.C.Smith, H.J.Trefz, N.W.Legrand, R.H.Budde, W.H.Reimer, D.L.Heine, J.W.Kingsley, M.W.Raymond, R.P.Kueter, W.H.Seesland, E.W.Crewdson, M.I.Brown, W.D.Reece, G.E.Osborne, K.L.Anderson, C.A.Klocker, J.R.Linnebur, M.M.McKay, P.M.Ford, V.H.Mumma, R.H.Durley, C.C.Theodore, R.G.Miehe Jr., B.R.Cashner, J.M.Jolly, A.D.Ferguson, I.J.Averhoff, J.A.Riggs, P.F.Krambeck, V.E.Summy, W.F.Morris, C.J.Althoff, E.O.Klaas, A.D.Hoyt, A.J.Demeulemeester, D.E.Mc Vey, D.L.Leemans, F.N.Burbach, K.M.Jess, R.C.Knapp, R.L.Anderson, W.E.Berry, R.L.Davis, D.J.Bartels, F.A.Thoma, G.H.Lichty, H.C.Koppen, J.P.Boland, R.L.Gipper, R.L.Lewis, F.J.Moser, G.Mc Cully, J.R.Hochberger, W.R.Grapp, J.Melville, E.J.McFarland, H.L.Conklin, M.E.Seaman, R.H.Malmstead, S.S.Dull Jr., W.E.Hammen, W.M.Gotz, J.H.Herron, J.F.Heim, M.E.Heineman, A.Sierra, H.E.Hubbard, R.E.Swenson, C.A.Sandry, D.D.Mc Connell, L.E.Granneman, A.M.Aubry, D.L.Runde, J.Donahoe, J.R.Hansen, M.E.Fisher, B.A.Manley, G.L.Goins, J.A.Butlett, J.L.Cook, K.D.Sheppard, R.L.Kluesner, R.J.Remakel, A.G.Steger, D.J.Levins, K.D.Roof, A.K.Ingwersen, C.O.Gremore, L.J.Jerrett, J.Mondejar, D.E.Scheer, L.E.Bond, R.H.Schmidling, S.A.Stineman, T.F.Ager, O.W.Strand, R.G.Jones, D.L.Carson, G.C.Smith, J.I.Gifford, J.J.Loes, H.L.Cancho, G.Scott, C.L.Bouck, D.R.Schmid, O.L.Phillips, P.A.Waller, L.Rodriguez D., F.E.Carman, J.D.Franklin, L.F.Sanderson, R.A.Tufts, R.L.Leonard, D.Gonzalez D., H.T.Salsberry, R.H.Tranel, M.J.Schuster, E.R.Strong, K.Patton, L.J.Lentzkow, M.D.Gram, M.K.Elsberry, L.Pacheco, A.L.Savage, R.A.Gunnerson, T.Lalonde, E.G.Owens, H.G.McCaffery, J.F.Hawkins, L.E.Ricke, W.W.Bruner, J.D.Momon, J.W.Cottingham, R.A.Schneck, C.E.Holton, J.J.Koleno, K.R.Blanchard, M.H.Lawing, P.C.Regan, T.G.Olson, R.B.Hyde, L.Guadarrama, R.B.Price, D.I.Lehman, E.D.Carpenter, W.W.Sloss, D.S.Crutcher, V.E.Love, R.A.Jordan, G.C.Bassett, L.V.Staab, R.L.Holton, E.N.Suits, L.W.Titterington, J.L.Maynard, D.W.Justice, I.M.Benton, J.L.Mann, M.H.Kerckhove, N.D.Stolte, P.G.Cox, V.G.De Groote, W.C.Bell, H.R.Jones, M.J.Ugolini, K.Gengl, L.M.Dunn, W.I.Gibson, D.L.Goben, J.D.Marks, J.W.Smith Jr., **1957** C.B.Jordan, F.A.Demay, H.K.Sense, J.R.Belisle, L.S.Daman, O.E.Davis, P.M.Breckling, R.A.Plate, V.O.Ievalts, D.E.Boal, E.J.Hock, N.N.Hansen, J.F.Macdonald, A.L.Searls, C.W.Kovacevich, F.F.Barrick, L.G.Ackerlund, E.Cogollos, E.L.Smith, W.L.Rockhold, J.P.Johnson, D.E.Doye Jr., J.R.Mendoza, R.D.Oleary, V.L.Wynn, C.N.Clark, E.S.Pearson, A.L.Kabatoff, J.A.Becker, M.J.Love, R.L.Leighty, R.L.Moore, M.Sanchez M., R.C.Deporter, V.L.Devolder, J.T.Hansell, R.E.Shafer, S.J.Bonomo, J.Matalik, E.L.Wisecup, F.Garcia B., E.G.Nelson, H.J.Michel, G.Girault, J.C.Lawrence, R.T.Bogaert, V.A.Walsh, W.E.Boden, R.E.Swartout, R.F.Carter, R.P.Schwegman, D.G.Herzberg, J.L.Pridmore, R.G.Howard, S.Smith, E.Yordy Jr., C.K.Reece, E.Matalik, K.D.Hensley, R.L.Kiehna, W.A.Brown, D.W.Niedert, G.P.Frenell, R.J.Huber, R.S.Shonts, R.J.Tysma, R.L.Keith, R.P.Dedecker, W.E.Gruben, H.A.Lampe, J.A.Peterson, C.J.Graham, F.J.Poortinga, H.E.Overton, M.R.Searcy, R.T.Broderick, G.R.Finch, H.C.Dennis, G.R.Freel, J.A.Dzekunskas, J.M.Anderson, L.A.Spittel, C.J.Hauser, J.W.Beaston, M.Martin S., R.P.Cox, C.K.Wietlispach, W.D.Silver, L.R.Vollenweider, C.Huskey, G.S.Barton, H.E.Watkins, J.D.Liggett, J.J.Braden, E.M.Gaskins, L.A.Lamb, G.R.Rogers, R.A.Porter, M.Bogni, H.G.Standing, J.R.Estes, W.L.Schumacher, B.L.Terry, J.H.Dietzel, H.A.Schroeder, N.A.Ketchum, R.P.Lewis, S.P.Sharnik, R.Hubert, J.Royo, G.Freitag, P.D.Beebe, A.Gutierrez H., G.S.Landers, O.C.McBride, K.E.Gramling Sr., S.R.Creek, E.C.Dusch, J.L.Hanchett, D.R.Moens, G.C.Andrews, J.F.Calvert, D.E.Gulley, G.Lopez, M.A.York Jr., R.N.Genung, R.F.Mapes, T.H.Gannon, D.D.Wells, E.Puertas, C.C.Wilemon, D.M.Robinson, R.G.Gillespie, R.Boutrolle, G.Herrwerth, C.J.Pappaspiros, J.N.Steptoe, J.R.Seefeldt Sr., R.L.Schmidt, L.E.Carter Jr., A.Cicuendez, U.Wuttke, C.H.Millwood, C.W.Avery, S.E.Peve, R.Schaefer, M.D.Prine, A.Chassard, B.Emile, S.Colladant, P.Bouchard, M.E.Grothusen, B.J.Rowland, G.Dausmann, R.G.Hansen, F.E.Rovere, A.Bertsch, L.L.Shepherd, D.H.Linnebur, F.E.Whittemore, R.H.Kerr, C.W.Kinney, A.S.Mabis Jr., C.A.Lassey, P.M.Lillie, P.M.Pyle, G.R.Sievers, H.L.Strieder, J.A.Vande Voorde, R.V.Corton, D.B.Nelson, R.C.Zook, W.W.Funk, G.W.Gustafson, L.E.Peck, J.B.Farnam, L.G.Murdock, L.H.Sackett, M.R.Hall, R.E.Gregg Jr., R.P.Nelson, T.M.Cozad, J.K.Ronk, R.A.Michael, A.D.Klein, B.W.Grant, E.D.Duesenberg, F.H.Gardner, H.B.Kreb, H.C.Gorton, H.W.Patterson, L.H.Peterson, M.E.Schmidt, R.A.Brandt, R.A.Sohl, R.M.Steilen, W.A.Schmitt, E.H.Johnson, J.H.Shaw, J.R.Trego, O.Moreau, C.D.Isaacson, G.M.Mueller, L.H.Gay, P.J.La France, R.B.Slusarski, R.C.Lehman, R.D.Brunn, W.M.Coursey, D.G.Martin, H.W.Phillips, M.R.Leroy, N.L.Reeves, F.H.Speirs, T.A.Kowalski, G.M.Thiel, R.J.Creen, D.L.Truedson, G.F.Carlo, P.J.Classen, J.C.Lawing, R.C.Kroeger, G.R.Brinkman, S.M.Stubblefield, W.W.Weissenfluh, M.K.Todtenhaupt, A.Fraguas, C.J.Sines, E.Lewis, G.Kole, D.F.Pagel, A.E.Andersen, D.E.Heeney, R.A.Kerns, E.J.Hall, G.L.Weaver, B.P.Battin, W.D.Engstrom, D.C.Payne, B.Sandin, R.C.Flenker, S.D.Perez, R.W.Pittard, J.Diaz L., F.H.Zaderaka, J.W.Mullen, S.M.Siems, D.W.Boller, G.Kovacs, Y.Bart, M.G.Hellebuyck, R.Elhard, V.M.Anderson, J.M.Rule, E.M.Zaitz, F.D.Fowler, B.G.Sawyer, D.E.Holcomb, M.L.Miles, R.M.Sisk, C.E.Swope, D.H.Tubbs, R.W.Marr, W.F.Puttkammer, J.L.Mumma, F.P.Bonilla, G.A.Veldhoven, J.A.Braet, K.L.Settle, S.A.Helling, W.E.Smith, E.W.Hanes, J.C.Ryckaert, T.E.Crosby, N.Fuselier, O.Calle De La, A.H.Martel, F.P.Clancy, M.M.Willis, R.D.Hughes, R.W.Brittain, W.H.McCord, P.Alonso, A.E.Thrasher, D.E.Newton, E.C.Accola, F.F.Langrehr, J.M.Link, V.E.Bottorff, B.A.Brock, R.Cortizo, F.E.Jacobs, W.F.Kacprzyk, J.B.Vandermillen, F.Martin M., B.L.Mickle, E.S.Deese, G.J.Peal, J.W.Stoneking, N.A.Stuart, R.E.Webb, T.L.Thompson, W.R.Heupel, G.W.Orendorff, L.G.Schutz, R.L.Olney, W.E.Ableidinger, C.H.Daniels, G.Taylor, R.B.Sund, B.Vaughn, C.E.Bunting, D.K.Fields, J.A.Rosenthal, J.R.Miller Sr., A.O.Dhooge, C.E.Groene, C.Sandoval, D.A.Steger, D.G.Sergeant, A.Barrios, F.Prieto, L.Fernandez C., D.W.Reddick, L.J.Sizek, R.E.Shirron, T.E.Jones, D.M.Hubbard, J.L.Chinarro, N.R.Shaw, H.E.Irvine, A.W.Hoover, D.F.Dewitte, D.L.Bybee, D.R.Young, E.J.Vervaecke, F.L.Crowe, F.L.Morgan, G.D.Hunsaker, H.H.Webb, J.E.Smith, K.C.Becker, M.A.Demay, M.Mathews, R.J.Fleming, R.J.Hanson, R.L.Dailey, R.M.Shoemaker, R.R.Carlson, R.R.Manasco, V.D.Sletten, J.A.Martin G., H.E.White, H.Johnson, N.E.Wells, R.A.Dusenberry, R.A.Heaton, C.L.Hawkins, E.E.McFalls, T.L.Green, R.L.Derammelaere, A.Guy, B.C.Ott, B.H.Bradford, V.H.Wood, G.T.Carpenter, R.R.Bradley, S.Bray Jr., J.K.Saathoff, K.M.McGinnis, M.M.Miller, R.R.Morrow, C.M.Combs, D.H.Mayfield, D.L.Anderson, M.R.Johnson, H.J.Tiemann, K.K.Larson, J.H.Hiatt, A.C.Kraus, C.D.Weese, D.Z.Stout, G.R.Dejaeger, M.D.Vanacker, M.L.Marr, M.M.Stage, P.W.Carlson, R.J.Benson, V.A.Porter, C.W.Wasson, S.A.McCabe, W.J.Vandel, D.A.Defauw, K.G.Gastel, M.A.Michener, M.L.Misfeldt, V.C.Jackson, F.S.Dopler, R.E.Popp, B.O.Watkins, H.E.Rogers, L.V.Leihsing, M.C.Dorman, M.L.McShane, P.E.Thompson, R.J.Starbeck, R.W.Lopez, S.N.Black, J.L.Vaquerizas, P.Garcia C., B.M.Pasquantonio, J.Deluzet, C.J.Moseley, G.H.Abrolat, I.E.Howell, R.D.West, R.E.Leisinger, C.F.Black, J.Walters, K.E.Young, M.P.Vasquez, R.A.Beard, R.J.Nagel, D.E.Cleek, E.A.Mills, M.A.Stotmeister, R.B.Tucker, R.E.Myers, K.L.Hearson, R.L.Claeys, B.Martin Jr., J.M.Salisbury, D.M.Coil, E.C.Davis, H.Isachsen, J.A.Anthony, J.M.Lopez, R.A.Forret, W.Horn, J.N.Hudson, J.W.Kelley, G.E.Hunt, B.Jacquemard, R.D.Michels, L.Fernandez B., C.R.Winfree, M.E.Cox, J.E.Holmes, L.E.Sedwick, M.M.Hendrickx, C.R.Baird, C.R.Stokes, F.C.Simerson, G.E.Taylor, T.A.Corvaia, C.J.Pearson, D.A.Holmes, J.E.Schultz, M.J.Plager, R.A.Jones, R.W.Collins, K.E.Gulling, L.H.Mason, R.A.Clark, W.J.Duff, G.D.Frantz, H.Cuenca, C.A.Lowe, C.L.Thompson, D.W.Johnson, G.E.Fales, L.W.Mack, R.L.Harris, G.F.Smith, L.R.Wolfe, R.D.Bethards Jr., F.Beas, J.Guterrez H., A.A.Giovenazzo, B.L.Dodson, M.L.Logan, T.M.Sullivan, **1958** R.A.Beal, R.Koegler, E.Wasiluk, F.T.Faber, H.R.Schaffer, J.E.Bischoff, J.M.Dishon, L.L.Butcher, L.M.Raper, M.I.Carlson, R.K.Shields, R.Singleton, W.A.Bushkie, R.Carillon, C.Coulom, J.D.Montoto, B.S.Ford, C.R.Deiters, D.D.Allison, D.E.Martin, D.M.Miescke, D.S.Thomas, F.R.Lewis, H.M.Sarver, H.W.Kroeger, L.L.Bird, R.Carmack, R.D.Stevens, R.D.Wilson, A.W.Creek, J.E.Blair, K.W.Pickrell, P.Bois, D.R.Hatton, O.E.Hintz, R.C.Kincaid Jr., O.R.Torres, L.C.Tasinazzo, D.D.Friddle, D.D.Stanfel, E.W.Smith, G.Dunham, W.A.Naftzger, W.M.Baago, C.E.Fisher, G.L.Vandyke, J.F.Daggett, W.J.Ripperger, L.B.Gramling, F.L.McFadden, G.L.Hoff, J.E.Findley, J.W.Ryan, R.G.Holton, S.F.Cataldo, R.Salazar, A.A.Sabbe, C.R.McMurl, E.D.Hedger, J.A.Heuer, P.A.O'Meara, R.G.Huizenga, E.F.Brezavar, H.D.Glider, E.B.Wade, J.J.Murphy, M.Higuera, M.L.Terrell, R.D.Holden Jr., V.L.Wulf, R.A.Egeland, L.Douard, M.D.Baxter, M.Camino, J.J.Parker, C.D.Ingersoll Jr., R.E.Sullivan, W.J.Dell, A.L.Anderson, C.C.Staudt, D.F.Swensson, E.E.Gonzalez, J.A.Lopez, L.L.Benhart, R.D.White, R.K.McClish, V.G.Gruetzmacher, V.L.Connett, W.L.Wignall, L.A.Oliveira Jr., C.C.Wilkerson, R.C.Houghtaling, D.S.Haberman, E.V.Brown, J.T.Perry, L.R.Karns, R.L.Edwards, A.L.Kieffer, W.L.Brown, D.L.Kritz, E.A.Miller, H.A.Morgan, J.R.Doerr, R.F.Julson, W.A.Jackson, W.L.Hays, W.W.Tyler, A.A.Sapato, A.E.Rubie, D.L.Ague, G.W.Dahlquist, H.J.Segerstrom Jr., J.M.Nicks, J.W.Heffelfinger, L.J.Vonhandorf, L.W.Swemline, M.K.Ryan, R.F.Schmitt, T.H.Garvey, W.F.Schemmel, C.J.Salow, H.H.Brimeyer, J.J.Rupp, K.Pettinger, R.L.Cottrell, T.D.Swift, A.D.Mooney, A.H.Mooney, C.L.Gillies, D.L.Mickelson, E.C.Niehaus, E.C.Tigges, G.D.Anderson, J.R.Haines, L.E.Cortum, M.E.Oliver, M.K.White, N.L.Hayes, W.A.Pensel, W.L.Dolan, W.R.Templer, A.A.Obermeier, D.H.Dummer, F.B.Bennett, F.J.McClurg, J.A.Hakanson, J.E.Donahue, J.I.Pauley, J.J.Henkels, J.J.Mc Cullough, L.P.Diederichs, M.J.Hoff, R.D.Dewitte, R.L.Davis, R.O.Brimeyer, S.L.Stingley, S.W.Schleicher, T.J.Morgan, V.M.Jamieson, W.E.Julson, B.R.Kvam, F.A.Kennicker, J.C.Jones Jr., J.C.Mootz, J.W.Goodwin, K.D.Lenth, M.L.Ries, R.C.Fettgather, R.D.Esparza, H.E.Freeborn, I.W.Lammers, L.B.Huff, R.D.Rowe, R.P.James, T.B.Webb Jr., W.E.Wernimont, H.Schubert, C.J.Hochberger, G.M.Robbins, R.H.Higinbotham, T.D.Merritt, E.E.Genthe, J.K.Powers, L.N.Darden, M.Hubbard, R.J.Levens, V.P.Regan, C.J.Tigges, K.L.Chaffee, W.H.Masbruch, G.Besnou, G.Bueno, D.M.Hubanks, H.E.Klein, R.E.Bradfield, D.E.Harrison, J.J.Oneill, L.F.Homrich, P.W.Fure, S.R.Chapman, V.Thoma, C.B.Guler, G.L.Duwe, P.G.Powers, R.D.Francis, A.H.Logemann, A.R.Engling, C.A.Brock, C.E.Moser, H.R.Fischer, J.E.Christy, L.R.Stone, V.J.Vannatta, W.A.Leeks, W.F.Shaner, D.D.Noyes, D.J.Biermann, M.O.Burds, R.C.Strassmann, J.B.Fritts, J.Wignall, L.V.Hoftender, R.D.McCarty, R.G.Connett, D.E.Vatt, R.K.Rogers, C.E.Ohms, D.M.Neal, H.R.Sweeney Jr., J.F.Oeth, J.H.Dougherty, W.H.Ohms, J.L.Perez G., C.A.White, C.L.Bennett, G.H.Stephens, H.L.Brinkopf, J.L.Brown, L.L.Cronk Jr., M.J.Kilcoyne, R.J.Scharf, B.F.Hockings, G.W.Peterson, J.C.Sabers, J.L.Wachter, R.C.Bautsch, R.J.Thelen, W.W.White, C.N.Green, D.C.Kruser, G.H.Gadberry Jr., L.J.Werner, R.A.Heim, R.H.Haggard, R.S.Chapman, W.J.Donovan, G.Rioland, C.L.Dean, D.D.Milroy, G.F.Ames, J.E.Holmes, J.F.Bowden, J.R.Hess, L.L.Hansel, C.D.Meyer, J.F.Ehlers, J.J.Stumpner, L.K.Willoughby, D.J.Nauman, E.K.Everett, G.A.Chapman, J.J.Buman, J.P.Cleary, M.A.Thompson, R.E.Link, W.F.Fullerton, W.L.Gale, J.Pascual, A.L.Brown, J.D.Weydert, K.W.Patters, L.T.Davis, J.Leblanc, A.R.Reynolds, D.D.Petersen, D.J.Hocking, E.L.Airhart, R.A.Jasper, B.F.Ashmead, P.F.Massey, R.C.Adams, R.L.Bush, R.M.German, D.L.Bennett, E.J.Williams, F.G.Spielbauer, L.Willoughby, M.M.Konrardy, W.E.Reicher, A.Crawford Jr., C.S.Davis, D.R.Block, J.L.White, J.T.Cowart, P.G.Moen, R.A.Huber, R.L.Hildebrand, C.A.Hefel, J.Y.Salazar, L.Anderson Jr., R.V.Kausal, C.W.Priebe, D.D.Eilander, D.L.Otoole, E.G.Flisher, G.R.Campbell, L.H.Storey, M.R.Twedt, P.M.Smith, R.K.Simerson, V.P.Meek, W.L.Pohl, G.G.Hubbard, R.J.Wenzel, W.P.Downs, C.H.Jessen, J.H.Ploessl, A.L.Eck, B.L.Bryson, L.E.McKinley, N.W.Schreck Jr., R.F.Kunkel, C.G.Elsinger, J.Mills, W.F.Rieckens, W.J.Scharf, R.Cremier, G.Weber, H.Friedrich, T.L.Nothaft, D.Skutley, M.E.Couch, R.L.Suhl, R.V.Davis, E.E.Thompson, E.J.Hartung, J.J.Foht, A.L.Dufelmeier, C.G.Horton, D.E.Sullivan, G.M.Pitt, H.W.Mason, J.D.Sullivan, J.F.Strohmeyer, J.L.Peters, M.L.Dirkes Jr., S.R.Clark, T.Heit, T.J.Johnson, Y.Bureau, D.J.Anderson, F.R.Croegaert, L.A.Jackson, E.Peters, H.H.Hansen, L.G.Terry, M.Harkin, R.Naranjo, A.D.Fowler, J.G.Labatt, J.Nenow, L.E.Davis, B.Eastman, C.E.Pottorff Jr., F.L.Howe, K.L.Glasbrenner, L.W.Rokis, P.E.Kriener, R.J.Bimbi, V.F.Busse, W.L.Abarr, H.Kastner, K.Salewski, W.Roedel, D.F.Koschmeder, D.J.Herrmann, J.E.Stacy, W.L.Grobstick, W.L.Winegardner, B.J.Koster, E.Adams, E.L.Gansen, J.R.Lauterbach, M.D.Ripley, R.W.Austin, W.J.Stegemann, D.F.Akers Jr., E.E.Steffen, E.J.Alexander, C.R.Hinkle, J.E.Reynolds, N.R.Gustafson, D.L.Marchael, D.W.Fitzsimmons, F.J.Klein, G.R.Wright, H.E.Poese, K.R.Unangst, P.M.Vaughn, R.B.Haggin, R.J.Dinger, R.L.Farrey, T.W.Hawbaker, W.E.Delaney, W.T.Nightingale, D.J.Weber, F.B.Reinert, R.E.Hayes Jr., R.M.Offield, A.K.Engel, A.Peterson Jr., C.D.Berger, C.J.Jacobsen, L.Walters, R.E.McGee, R.J.Hayes, T.L.Feipel, W.M.Lockey, C.L.Angel, D.R.Finley, H.A.Kostka, H.W.Rhan, J.H.Eick, J.J.Haberlie, J.R.Thompson, K.D.Becker, R.J.Peterson, R.R.Parsons, R.Arcala, A.M.Wilkens, B.G.Payne, C.E.Wright, E.H.Strohecker, F.A.Hartke Jr., G.E.Sanderson, J.R.Juergens, J.W.Hooper, J.W.Mease, K.J.Crafton, D.E.Putnam, D.E.Truog, D.L.Gates, D.W.Olberding, E.B.Jones, E.F.Weber, E.L.Burkhiser, F.Camarata, G.I.Tebbutt, H.H.Goettsch, H.J.Wise, H.R.Hasart, J.D.Jackson, J.E.Jessen, J.M.Benson, L.Sisk, L.Weber, P.J.Derifield, T.F.Thomas, W.E.Nolte, W.J.Combes, W.O.Nolte, W.Stevenson Jr., B.N.Rabenberg, C.R.Love, D.L.Staley, D.M.Sorensen, F.J.Steinbach, H.D.Hanson, H.E.Doepke, H.I.Dixon, H.Johnson, H.W.Wylie, L.C.Kleinheksel, L.W.Reisner, P.A.Reinert, R.H.Gutknecht, R.L.Rider, T.J.De Long, W.A.Gross, W.D.Hawkins, A.L.Kirby, A.L.Wilharm, C.O.Lund, J.L.Derifield, J.L.Dusheck, J.W.Christoffersen, K.D.Pollock, M.F.Beener, R.H.Stodgel, R.Krutsinger, T.A.Abkes, A.A.Bandekow, D.W.Machalek, H.H.Wille, H.L.Hovey, J.F.Timmer, J.H.Mc Gee, J.K.Potter, R.D.Fowlkes, S.E.Little, T.E.Jirsa, W.A.Macomber, W.T.Hocking, S.Garcia P., A.L.Harberts, D.G.Steinbeck, H.E.Brewster, J.H.Murray, J.W.Vanostrand, M.Jenkins, N.F.Pfaltzgraff, R.J.Myers, T.H.Clark, D.N.Stevens, E.D.Wolf, J.G.Hagensten, P.L.Britzman, P.N.Valentine, R.B.Fuller, R.J.May, V.S.Putz, D.J.Engelken, G.L.Schuller, W.L.Tarter, A.L.Bennett, D.B.Carns, J.A.Dalziel, K.J.Hinkel, R.C.Paynter, R.G.Holmes, E.F.Bauer, C.B.Harker, D.D.Elson, D.L.Boxwell, F.T.Splinter, J.F.Callahan, J.I.Schwartz, M.J.Behrends, R.B.Steuck, R.L.Nichols, J.Garrido, B.F.Curry, G.O.Swisher, L.D.Hulin, R.E.Austin, A.F.Barnhart, E.T.Vogt, H.J.Kelleher Jr., L.R.Johnson, R.F.Fishnick, B.O.Martin, D.G.Brown, D.M.Noggle, G.F.Redfern, J.A.Pfohl, M.M.Callahan, R.W.Biermann, R.W.Wood, C.F.Staner, D.H.Knapp, D.J.Hall, D.M.Melton, J.McMahon, R.Weber, V.J.Ross, W.J.Sparks, E.J.Weber, F.D.Schroth, H.Burrage, J.A.Feller, L.K.Dittman, M.A.Platte, P.F.Gerhard, R.A.Reisen, R.F.Reid, W.L.Crawford, B.Frith, F.D.Webster Jr., J.O.McNeece, J.V.Tobar, R.J.Beals, T.G.Sexton, W.E.Bader, W.E.Nelson, W.F.Hinrichs, W.R.Gonnerman, D.L.Wilson, J.L.Nagel, T.H.Fouts, S.J.Kieler, T.K.Groseclose, V.F.Browne, H.L.Ellerbach, H.R.Elscott, L.D.Hanson, R.E.Higdon, T.I.Mc Kernan, C.Reed, G.F.Meier, H.F.Hayes, J.C.Andrews, J.E.Nichols, O.D.Frank Jr., F.Aviles, G.W.Lynn, L.A.Albertson, R.W.Christian, P.L.Lain, R.R.Spencer, W.L.Peterson, W.R.Wood, G.Courboillet, G.J.Eros, L.J.Earnshaw, B.L.Feeley, C.D.Walker, D.V.Trumbauer, G.A.Smith, J.Harmon, J.M.Ugolini, L.C.Johnson, R.E.Schreiber, R.L.Millbern, T.M.Thompson, R.Millbern, A.D.Jensen, G.L.Achenbach, J.M.McCabe, W.F.Paul, B.Kammarmeyer, L.A.Anklam, M.J.Diers, R.E.Debord, T.M.Lowe, D.D.Stark, H.A.Maddux, J.L.Sloan, T.J.Fangman, M.Villasevil, D.D.Beck, D.D.Smith, E.Allen, G.D.Navin, R.J.Johnson, S.E.Rebeiro, S.W.Clauson, W.E.Rudiger, J.Torrejon, N.C.Kimball, R.H.Litzkow, V.P.Hilby, D.D.Loveless, D.G.Daly, G.Jenkins, L.H.Scholtes, R.E.Towsley, E.T.Jensen, J.B.Riley, J.H.Zimmer, P.D.Jamieson, R.C.Malven, R.D.Tufte, T.L.Canada, A.P.Redman, C.T.Rief, C.Thomas, G.A.Johnson, J.D.Smart, J.K.Lawson, J.W.Hendrix Sr., L.W.Luepker, M.J.Dahlhauser, N.O.Christenson, R.C.Young, S.B.Brown, T.J.Parsons, W.J.Wagner, W.M.Wiele, D.Mc Millan, J.E.Larson, M.S.Longshore, R.D.Battani, G.D.Simpson, K.O.Allard, P.J.Lynch, A.E.Klouda, D.E.Beckman, D.L.Fairchild, M.C.Simmons Jr., R.G.Mc Coneghey, C.A.Berg, F.Huffstetler, G.E.Mitchell, J.E.Haun, J.F.Dillon, K.L.Hoer, P.L.Stephany, J.A.Gomez, L.D.Meyer, B.R.Davison, L.F.Ripka, R.C.Thompson, W.C.Lovejoy, C.O.Ransom, M.L.Klundt, E.B.Eihl, E.L.Burry, J.W.Walker, K.C.Smith, R.N.Zekoff, R.Schreiber, V.J.Hayes, M.L.Mc Cunn, N.W.Gundrum, P.R.Bolhous, D.L.Cashman, A.W.Fray, D.E.Powell, D.Lewis, G.G.Bowser, H.A.Smith, J.E.Demeyer, J.G.Petersen, K.R.Wilson, L.E.Rutter, N.N.Johnson, P.A.Gerber, R.B.Fuller, D.A.Judas, W.M.Zanders, J.T.Vrombaut, W.A.Kallenbach, E.V.Fike, H.I.Oliver, J.Dougherty, J.L.Smith, B.R.Pals, C.F.Burns, S.M.Birley, E.E.Wriedt, A.Delgado, J.G.Stratton, J.G.Simmons, T.J.Schaefer, L.G.Arnold, M.E.Hurley, P.J.Garrett, R.E.Brimeyer, R.V.Franck, S.P.Haskin, G.L.Beenken, R.R.Kirchmann, M.R.Sickels, T.D.Merrick, M.C.Topp, W.E.Wiese, F.Gonzalez T., N.G.Davis, R.A.Beringer, V.G.Jones, W.E.Ahlbrecht, H.R.Schultz, D.A.Schessow, D.J.Tigges, G.M.Coots, J.G.Tank, J.Montero, E.C.Kruel Jr., P.E.Ince, P.E.Waniorek Sr., K.G.Makinster Jr., M.E.Slininger, G.J.Niedermann, G.L.Rodden, R.J.Fisher, D.C.Stang, D.Williams, E.W.Nienkark, F.L.Teel, G.T.Earnest, H.A.Kappelman, H.D.Allen, J.H.Wagenhofer Jr., J.J.Kass, J.Kilby, J.R.Reiter, L.B.Thompson, O.L.Mc Robie, P.F.Kusy, R.C.Brenner, R.C.Konken, R.D.Wade, R.J.Roach, T.J.Helms, W.F.Shimek, W.T.Duffy, C.E.Denning, D.F.Thompson, G.D.Rowley, J.W.Zobeck, R.Creighton, R.J.Murray, D.R.Anderson, G.R.Cain, L.L.Tomlin, P.D.Schmitz, F.R.Klenzman, J.P.Mangrich, M.C.Iverson, M.F.Mades, P.G.Mc Donald, R.W.Wilson, D.F.Roe, J.W.Rich, R.D.Gebhardt, E.E.Smith, E.G.Hausch, J.C.Taylor, J.D.Forehand, K.E.Reddig, L.J.High, P.H.Overmann, R.R.Mulcahy, F.L.Collins, H.A.Weber, J.E.Griggs, P.J.Mangner, G.Bleau, B.S.Monnahan, C.R.Mills, D.D.Mc Cullough, D.M.Jaschen, V.F.Pulkrabek Jr., C.R.Cox, H.L.Patterson, J.H.Sutton, J.L.Fox, J.Peterson, L.L.Anderson, M.H.Warner, R.J.Thrasher, R.L.Blum, R.M.Cory, E.Zapata, L.Sanchez-S., A.Woodrum, B.L.Maire, C.H.Gorton, D.A.Peterson, D.A.Vogler, E.D.Smith Jr., E.R.Morris, H.G.Kohls, H.R.Steagall, J.F.Phoenix, J.R.Meana, K.D.Morehead, R.A.Farrar, R.L.Boster, R.M.Abernathy, R.R.Dinnebier, R.R.Timmons, W.G.Neuman, W.L.Dietz Jr., J.Cribbs Jr., R.L.Averill, R.R.Ragsdale, D.M.Bunce, H.J.Morgan, J.J.Boeck, R.D.Collier, F.A.Troxel, C.R.Feltes, F.C.Zimmerman Jr., G.T.Underwood, J.E.Griffin, J.E.Hagen, J.E.Matticks, J.M.Cervantes, J.S.Dudzik, L.J.Gasper, L.J.Wanie, L.R.Ludwig, M.E.Vannoy, R.E.Brink, R.J.Debaillie, V.A.Suiter, W.D.Aitken, W.H.Covault, E.M.Brown, G.O.Howell, R.Trego, C.H.Abbott, J.C.Pearson, K.Clark, M.W.Oberg, W.Tiedt, J.P.Horsman, N.F.Gliedt, R.L.Gerholdt, E.S.Schares, E.V.Cunningham Jr., J.D.Peterson Sr., J.D.Rubino, K.W.Rutherford, L.B.Troutwine, L.P.Hedrington, L.W.Kettman, R.F.Siegljff, R.L.Boney, R.L.Carpenter, V.E.Mecklenburg, W.C.Bakke, B.A.Lewis, C.J.Hopper, C.McLane Jr., D.L.Cooper, J.R.Schuler, L.O.Brown, T.A.Gloeckner, T.B.Holmes, C.A.Nelson, J.C.Potter, G.F.Moore, J.G.Edgar, W.H.Richard Jr., K.Melick, R.Gaston, D.E.Warnock, F.A.Smith, F.M.Howell, H.Taylor, J.J.Zillig, J.L.Cantrell, R.G.Crinklaw, R.Lomas Jr., R.M.Sandborg, D.L.Stinocher, G.R.Sears, J.V.Long, R.P.Doss, P.J.Hoffman, J.Montgomery Jr., T.D.Andreassen, T.V.Toemmes, W.C.Phillips, H.E.Glanz, J.L.Kappler, L.F.Heins, L.J.Weber, R.F.Pfohl, A.J.Cinkovich, D.M.Schmitt, A.R.Sulentic, B.D.Maynard, C.E.Sass, E.S.Howell Jr., P.I.Coen, D.E.Ward, A.L.Dabney, F.R.Sundberg, J.M.Schelfaut, M.D.Oldham, R.W.Edwards, R.V.Clay, H.L.Richter, J.L.Hibben, J.W.Kappelman, D.R.Page, W.C.Austin, L.R.Porter, R.L.Payne, T.Toledo, C.M.Holmgren, G.L.Smith Jr., R.A.Boens, T.B.Collins, M.Martin T., B.W.Bye, K.M.Koontz, L.G.Wagner, R.P.Hughes, C.H.Fleming, C.W.Stricker, D.F.Adams, G.G.Crivello, J.D.Deutsch, M.S.Plunkett, W.S.Thompson, G.K.Smith, J.Dzvonar Jr., L.F.Knief, M.L.Simpson, R.L.Oberle, R.P.Richardson, C.Hublard, L.Johnson, L.D.Graham, R.L.Freet, R.T.Veberg, M.L.Intermill, O.G.Evans, G.L.Johnson, J.D.Jamieson, J.K.Barnett, M.C.Lindsey, B.E.Harn, D.D.Hilger, H.M.Winfrey, J.J.Cameron, R.L.Gardner, H.L.Davis, R.F.Redig, R.L.Tullis, R.Ramirez, E.E.Clemens, E.R.Greenway, R.A.Desmet, W.E.Gabbard, C.J.Erickson, D.Brinton, D.C.James, E.W.Barnes, F.M.Anderson, G.F.Pasbrig, G.R.Cowdery Jr., H.C.Welser, H.J.Klavon, H.M.Danielson, J.C.Martin, J.J.Taffe, L.V.Lee, P.N.Gay, R.J.Gray, R.Kuhn, W.C.Lemaster, R.H.Burns, M.H.Hamil, W.E.Bravener, I.Cenalmor, E.E.Schwickerath, G.J.Cowell, S.J.Povirk, V.E.Myers, A.R.Glennie, D.C.Wilson, D.R.Stickrod, D.R.Tometich, F.H.Clement, G.D.Melear, G.L.Nicholls, I.E.Nutt, T.L.Corcoran, P.J.Benavides , C.T.Schuler, D.G.Starkey, D.L.Howard, J.F.Jefferson, D.Coburn, V.R.Van Syoc, J.Stiefvater, D.J.Powers, J.A.Bollinger, W.Odean, J.A.Sanborn, W.Maskaluk, B.G.Pratt, C.J.Kerkove, D.R.Drahos, J.C.Dopler, W.H.Porter, W.W.Shirk, D.A.Castro, M.J.Loding, K.J.Maier, T.Parks, B.J.Bowen, C.R.Almquist, C.L.Whitmarsh, L.Hyke, R.B.Chase, R.D.Mingus, V.J.Graham, D.H.Van Horn, F.J.Burke, H.C.Price, J.C.Gutknecht, J.M.Hovatter, J.Schieberl Jr., K.E.Walker, M.E.Worley, R.O.Holland Jr., R.R.Madsen, Z.Atzeni, A.Lewis, C.J.Vondracek, G.D.Olson, G.L.Washington, L.K.Moore, W.Z.Duke, A.Esteban M., E.Benito, J.L.Carson, M.L.Premoli, D.Dantzler, K.S.Mealhow, P.B.Jessen, R.E.King, D.C.Pearce, D.E.Hackwell, D.H.Platte, D.R.Hagemann, E.E.Knebel, E.L.Hart, G.B.Sullivan, G.E.Chase, G.Schatzberg, H.W.Lentsch, J.E.Rogers, J.L.Becker, J.P.Bates, L.Mc Glaun, M.H.Leisinger, N.H.Pryor, N.Roberts, P.J.Standiford, R.G.Lepsch, R.G.Mills, R.J.Baldridge, R.L.Fox, R.W.McGinnis, W.J.Bieri, W.J.Green, W.W.Romans, A.Dhuicq, E.Peña, R.Medem, B.E.Neith, G.N.Hendrickson, G.W.Chronister, K.D.Baych, M.R.Epp, O.D.Lampkin, P.J.Tory, R.A.Smith, R.J.Ortner, R.J.Tjabring, R.J.Torgerson, R.L.Hayungs, R.N.Youngblut, E.J.Hoyer, J.R.Welter, M.Hill, R.M.Insteness, T.E.Sink, D.Allen, D.L.Arbuckle, E.E.Fortsch, E.L.Geary, G.J.Ambrosy, J.J.Kipp, J.L.Anthony, L.A.Wallace, R.D.Miller, R.Ferri, R.G.Butler, W.Ravenek, H.Weir, J.E.Beasley, J.R.Finn, R.D.Damme, R.L.Blessing, H.N.Johnson, E.C.Braathen, J.H.Elliott, R.J.Theisen, R.L.Fuhrman, S.Leone, S.M.Poetzel, W.A.Olecka, W.B.Bahnks, W.E.Cook, C.K.Deaton, J.D.Lee, E.M.Russell, H.W.Allen, J.P.Kennedy, W.C.Axline, J.D.Anders, R.J.Curran, L.G.Knebel, D.L.Maddex, E.J.Pierson, J.G.Niemann, J.R.Comstock, R.A.Jackson, R.D.Kroeger, R.E.Nelson, R.J.Fritz, E.M.House, E.R.Rummans, K.G.Williams, M.J.Flaherty, M.L.Swanson, F.T.Russell, G.D.Poland, L.E.Towne, R.D.Crowl, W.G.Patten, W.W.Burkle, J.E.Seery, R.C.Miller, J.W.Rossow, F.J.Fager, R.D.Young, D.L.Jefferson, D.W.Dana, E.R.Hepler, J.B.Schwestka, L.F.Kaufman, N.G.Poppe, R.E.Flege, R.K.Hendrickson, R.Eberle, C.D.Steen,

San Francisco, California, branch personnel, 1952

R.G.Ackerman, **1959** R.M.Ross, R.T.Maynard, P.Moriceau, C.W.Schultz, D.B.Goerdt, D.W.Muehleip, E.R.Hintzman, H.R.Miller, J.D.Connor, L.E.Vorwald, L.J.Steines, L.R.Clark, R.A.Biermann, T.G.Lord, W.L.Larmore, W.S.Brogdon, J.Aguado, J.Dorado, A.R.Payne Jr., D.C.Allen, D.R.Main, D.W.Tracy, E.C.Craig, G.F.Meiers, G.R.Phillips, H.A.Anderson, H.L.Sims, J.J.Keeling, J.J.Shields, J.K.Smith, J.W.Catour, L.Q.Miles, N.D.Stickles, R.A.Fangman, R.G.Fontana, R.Knutson, R.R.Creighton, R.W.Couch, R.W.Leisure, T.Walden, V.R.Hoskins, W.Jones, D.C.Peebles, D.W.Hartwick, E.C.Hermanson, E.D.Krantz, G.E.Chouinard, G.M.Stafford, J.J.Heintz, L.D.McNair, L.H.Moore, N.A.Anderson, R.J.Hein, D.L.Verschoore, D.M.Blough, N.D.Colsch, J.W.Lumsden, K.D.Mc Dowell, R.J.Kulow, A.G.Thomas, C.F.Deeds, D.C.Gander, J.D.Patrick, J.T.Riedl, S.Johnson Jr., W.K.Reed Jr., C.E.Steinhoff, G.A.Davis, K.W.Spilde, M.G.Moschke, M.L.Fauser, R.C.Burnham, R.W.Wisco, S.L.Kieffer, R.De Biasio, A.B.Closs, A.Chapman, B.F.Sherk, C.E.Swaim, C.F.Ives, C.J.Kennicker, D.D.Siler, D.L.Wildeboer, D.R.Beaumont, E.M.Mynott, F.L.Garrett, J.H.Tank, J.R.Farley, K.J.Soppe, L.E.Sprague, L.J.Wessels, L.L.Burch, L.L.Feldman, L.L.Starckovich, L.M.Thome, L.V.Wood, M.A.Wehrspann, M.J.Pfeiler, M.L.Knollman, R.D.Bice, R.L.Thompson, R.Strawn, S.Krpan, V.Baldwin, V.D.Knief, W.F.Nixon Jr., W.H.Clark Jr., W.R.King, C.Garcia B., A.H.Bower, C.C.Branaman, D.D.Rogers, D.E.Frank Jr., D.H.Sands, G.D.Hector, G.Harting, I.E.Knipp, J.D.Marturello, J.Timmer, L.E.Hunt, M.E.Craig, P.A.Bollie, P.C.Nielsen, R.E.Remster, R.G.Thome, R.J.Wemett, R.L.Coy, R.L.Prine, T.M.Ciesielski, T.R.Kuder, T.Stirler, W.E.Dickens, A.J.Herman Jr., A.R.Rhoades, C.F.Steege, D.A.Hahn, D.G.Curran, D.G.Mc Cready, D.L.Duncan, J.F.Bolton, J.F.Schildgen, J.Howard, J.L.Greif, J.M.Mason, J.T.Freeman, L.E.Ferreter, L.G.Paradine, L.R.Marlatt, R.J.Frank, R.S.Lingard, T.E.Roush, W.A.Storey, W.R.Quibell, B.F.Meusel, C.D.Rasmusson, C.Jones, D.E.Burgus, D.E.Roeder, D.F.Renslow, D.J.Ochs, G.E.Buls, G.O.Powers, J.R.Drury, L.G.Lammers, M.E.Mulvey, P.D.Beal, P.F.Kramer, P.G.Henkels, R.L.Dunsmoor, R.L.Harris, R.L.Isabell, R.M.James, T.L.Halse, W.Odekirk, W.Reed, A.J.Merkes, A.M.Brocka, C.D.Bolsinger, C.E.Montgomery, D.D.Otto, D.L.Hoffman, E.W.Bozich, G.A.Nast, G.G.Thomas, G.S.Ronek, J.E.Eberhard, J.H.Solie, J.Rollins, K.E.Steffen, L.L.Timmerman, M.E.Wise, M.L.McCleary, R.L.Mathews, R.R.Gonzales, W.C.Poock, O.A.Spagnolo, A.Stier, B.J.Hubbert, B.L.Conger, C.A.Kruse, C.J.Shannon, C.M.Schramm, C.Williamson, E.J.Michel, F.L.Stoecken, G.Bohan, G.M.Waggoner, H.J.Friedman, I.P.Hummel, J.Elliott, J.L.Judas, J.P.McConnell, L.A.Elgin, L.E.Liedtke, L.Lister, L.R.Powers, M.E.Ehlert, M.H.Kueter, P.E.Borcherding, R.D.Feipel, R.G.Sharkey, R.W.Bohringer, R.W.Habel, W.D.Roberts, W.R.Wilkens, B.Olard, F.Juberias, B.J.Weber, C.C.Clark, C.L.Shepard, C.Larson, D.R.Miller, H.L.Carpenter, J.E.Harrison, L.M.Duckett, M.D.Derifield, P.D.Shellenberger, R.W.Fink, S.L.Damme, T.Roddy Jr., E.W.Meyer, H.J.Walitshek, J.C.Kobliska, J.F.Robinson, J.V.Manning, M.W.Miller, N.P.Averkamp, P.C.Johnson, R.L.Dunne, R.W.Malloy, A.G.Nelson, A.J.Havlik Jr., E.H.Zasada, E.M.Manley, P.A.Marts, R.A.Mather, R.E.De Neut, R.J.Hampton, R.J.Vangoethem, V.D.McColly, W.D.Dunn, W.G.Redies, L.P.Heller, M.G.Marks, P.N.Schmidt, R.V.Tigges, A.L.Hoff, D.E.Grahlman, D.J.Remakel, D.J.Wolfe, E.L.McKinney, J.A.Weber, J.A.Wright, K.H.Anderson, N.R.Legrand, P.A.Selsor, R.F.Allen, R.J.Czipar, R.L.Weygant, T.J.Dent, T.J.Ziegenfuss, V.L.Ehrig, W.C.Giesel, W.W.Webb, F.Gomez C., C.J.Wesley, D.D.Dickinson, D.J.Klinkhammer, D.J.Weydert, H.Nienoord, J.J.Joyce, R.A.Horner, R.Hynes, R.L.Andregg, S.J.Steines, A.C.Bocco, P.A.Bournissen, V.Fernandez, C.M.Johnson, D.E.Budde, D.I.Griffin, D.J.Brandt, G.E.Lestina, G.F.Burns, G.R.Pulley, H.J.Tegeler, H.T.Fisher Jr., O.L.Hennessy, P.R.Quinn, R.C.Hennings, R.C.Koppes, R.M.Brimacomb, W.H.Harvey, J.H.Hansen, L.Hakenewerd, D.K.Jewett, H.G.Kubitz, J.J.Ellison, J.L.Bogener, M.C.Nelson, P.L.Klonglan, R.J.Duffy, W.Johannsen, W.L.Revelle, A.E.Haight, C.J.Jackson, C.J.Richardson, C.M.Hinson, G.O.Bruhn, G.P.Hall, H.C.Hoffman, H.J.Roeth, I.O.Nachtman Jr., I.W.Heying, J.E.Thompson, J.H.Besler, J.L.Kopaska, J.L.Thompson, M.L.Morrow, R.C.Horton, R.D.Krabbenhoft, R.I.George, R.J.Huber, R.J.Simon, T.A.Kueper, W.G.Uhlenhopp, W.R.Ackerman, C.A.Castello, R.Penelas, B.A.Mosher, B.E.Hafner, G.W.Ellery, I.C.Hubbard, J.J.Burgess, L.B.Erdmann, L.Johnson, M.E.Meyers, V.W.Sanders, A.E.Shouse Jr., D.R.Francis, G.D.Gritton, G.J.Gruel, J.A.Winters, L.D.Kelly, M.A.Gansemer, N.G.Short, R.A.Funk, R.E.Moore, R.H.Adams, R.L.Bouska, R.M.Dennis, R.M.Paulsen, R.W.Martin, W.M.Smith, E.G.Anderson, G.F.Accola, G.F.Stappert, J.M.Williams, J.P.Wagner, M.R.Schreiber, M.Rivero, C.C.Ball, D.J.Essen, J.W.Webber, L.W.Schlotfelt, A.E.Edwards, A.J.Vonderhaar, E.E.Smith, E.H.Cliff, G.A.Perry, H.H.Lass, H.W.Hill, J.F.Elmore, P.L.King, R.A.Hartman, R.K.Griffin, W.R.Lindenberg, D.L.Ramsey, G.R.Dixon, L.C.Wubben, N.H.Pearson, R.C.Jones, R.G.Kennedy, S.Burton Jr., W.F.Bovy, W.W.Scheil, E.Plaza, A.L.Anderson, A.R.Leo, D.R.Vandermillen, G.J.Christy, J.E.Shea, L.G.Connor, L.J.Snider, R.L.Walker, R.M.Litscher, R.P.Smith, D.W.McClure, E.Williams, L.J.Gassmann, R.L.Frizell, C.L.Trevillyan, D.M.Yarges, E.W.Edwards, G.A.Welp, G.H.Reiter, L.L.Rains, R.D.Hartgrave, R.E.Hottle, T.M.Gary, D.A.Vroman, D.J.Willis, F.F.McCullough, J.J.Merkes, J.P.Masias, J.S.Meyer, R.N.Mason, R.V.Dahl, R.W.Heister, A.Arancibia, M.Boutterin, N.Merino, A.L.Droste, E.E.Liebert, J.F.Schroedermeier, J.L.Meyer, K.S.Chapman, M.D.Williams, R.L.Tone, D.M.Hoover, G.G.Becker, G.R.Frank, L.R.Heister, M.C.Box, P.M.Hayden, R.A.Caldwell, D.C.Lechtenberg, D.F.Curley, H.D.Neel, H.Tripp Jr., J.D.Regan, P.E.Brugger, R.E.Jones, R.K.Kollman, L.Otto, W.A.Kofta, W.L.Patterson, A.T.Birch, D.E.Hansen, D.E.Sommerlot, G.Rickenbrode, R.E.Webb, R.L.Warne, W.E.Carter, C.R.Strawn, G.A.Forrest, G.W.Latham, K.D.Sitler, L.D.Allen, L.L.Hagen, L.W.Crees, M.G.Kinkead, C.W.Becker, D.A.Den Adel, D.L.Deaton, D.L.Dobson, E.M.Graham, G.M.Kroeger, G.O.McConnell, M.G.Leichliter, M.P.Severtson, R.C.Klocke, A.J.Heller, D.O.Thornwall, L.G.Wilkinson, R.J.Schmitz, A.C.Ploessl, H.L.Gruel, R.L.Gerlich, G.Zapata, P.J.Bladl Jr., A.L.Samec, C.J.Haynes, C.W.Barnett, D.C.McConkey, D.W.Foust, F.R.Samec, G.N.Thomas, J.H.Mitchell, J.W.Clifford, L.W.Riegel, M.B.Harvey, M.P.Tibbetts, P.E.Bodish, P.T.Riggs, R.N.Iverson, T.E.Lorenzen, W.A.Ruthey, W.E.Sylvester, W.N.Harkins, M.Guemann, A.C.Leliefeld, B.C.Patton, D.E.Wilming, D.P.Benham, E.W.Krepfle, H.A.Reinicke, J.L.Holm, J.L.Ogburn, L.W.Simmons, M.A.Ball, D.R.Buresh, E.J.Murphy, G.J.Norte, G.L.Smith, J.J.Longnecker, J.W.Smock, L.E.Shattuck, M.Swanson, N.R.Davis, R.D.Schmitt, R.W.Granberg, W.E.Post, J.F.Stuer, L.Holmes, N.H.Boeckmann, R.W.Sickles, G.A.Wiederholt, T.J.Roberts, D.T.Heiple, G.L.Mellinger, G.R.Gwaltney, P.A.Regan, R.E.Findley, W.Severson, C.R.Townsend, G.D.Denning, G.G.Baker, G.L.Ades, K.F.Holman, L.E.Peterson, M.J.Weltruski, R.J.Jackson, V.H.Budan, W.R.Dailey, D.J.Hagen, N.W.Kirch, R.S.Allen, W.W.Mahlstedt, A.A.Dickel, D.D.Dayton, E.M.Plumley Sr., H.A.Woods, H.F.Hoepfner, J.Demartino, P.W.Croft, S.Vanveen, C.R.Gundlach, E.C.Apel, F.H.Emkes, G.J.Rambousek, J.R.Perry, J.W.Degenhardt, R.E.Smrcina, R.F.Hutschenreuter, A.Gamero, B.J.Ralfs, D.E.Baugh, D.G.Martin, D.J.Linden, E.H.Hanson, H.H.Millard, J.P.Doering, L.R.Haugeberg, L.W.Leif, R.L.Oberbroeckling, T.L.Oberhoffer, R.Bauer, B.J.Latham, F.P.Mueller, H.E.Beatty, R.C.Haskell, R.H.Mobley, R.W.Carrier, C.M.Christopherson, D.E.Nottger, F.L.Hoffman, G.D.Clark, J.B.Campbell, J.R.Vosberg, M.C.Cook, I.Martin R., D.D.Mason, D.F.Kosman, J.W.Benson, M.R.Gaber, R.E.Lee, R.F.Scoles Jr., R.H.Olsen, T.J.Tremble, D.E.Shipley, D.R.Lewis, E.V.Nolan, F.M.Leadley, J.B.Capelle, J.L.Vanderecken, R.L.Lemaster, W.Wishmeyer, J.L.Cerdan, H.J.Rensvold, J.A.Cummings, L.E.Sampson, L.G.Grady, L.J.Thompson, P.C.Beebe, P.E.Fagenbaum, P.J.Gehl, R.E.Brandel, R.L.Gillen, W.H.Riechmann, Y.A.Kramer, F.C.Soenksen, F.L.Kritz, G.G.Ambrose, J.A.Jordan, J.P.Macomber, R.D.Nichols, B.K.Highberger, M.D.Breese, R.L.Kreidler, D.A.Goebel, D.H.Milbrandt, D.J.Hadtrath, G.L.Hansen, G.S.Brandel, T.J.Dunne, B.K.Felton, G.C.Nass, G.R.Howe, P.L.Barnhart, V.O.Matthias, C.E.Casel, E.J.Wilkening, F.M.Woller, J.M.Smith, L.C.Shappell, L.E.Speck, L.M.McSween, T.W.Webb, V.C.Romeo, B.A.Kerns, E.M.Scholtes, G.Walker, J.L.Youngs, J.N.Peterson, R.E.Nank, M.Paillotte, C.C.Godsey, C.C.Isaacson, M.F.Schoneman, M.G.Giesler Jr., M.H.Sturm, M.R.Morrow, T.M.Langhofer, F.Mayer, C.H.Hesser, D.M.Stephens, F.D.Brown Jr., J.V.Logan, J.W.Eatwell Jr., M.J.Weidemann, D.F.Bark, D.G.Tripp, E.R.Heckman, G.N.Williams, L.E.Lee, R.W.Werkmeister, A.Klingenberg, K.E.Hillebrand, K.K.Eckenrod, L.H.Fulton, J.R.Stecher, R.H.Bush, E.L.Hill, F.Liverance, J.L.Towers, L.J.Templeton, T.L.Obrien, A.L.Boekhoff, J.L.Johanningmeier, M.C.Ortner, T.R.Rink, N.E.Ransford, B.F.Douglass, E.L.Creger, J.L.Provin, M.T.Donlin, W.C.Petsch, B.Engelmann, E.Niedermayer, N.Blach, P.Renz, A.C.Hyde, B.J.Harrod, H.W.Heaberlin, L.L.Haines, N.R.Mauer, R.L.Blaser, R.T.Sires, T.L.Biehn, H.L.Brock, H.L.Vandyne, J.J.Stoker, J.W.Theisen, T.E.Harvey, A.G.Britson, C.G.Minnick, J.N.Mundell, R.Loeffelholz, V.J.Deiter, V.R.Peters, C.L.Halverson, C.L.Melssen, D.F.Collins, F.A.Drouillard, H.S.Thornton, K.L.Ritenour Jr., R.W.Bailey, T.J.Rogers, V.R.Burlison, H.D.Ernst, A.M.Kemming, F.J.Erskine, J.H.Trainor, L.W.Bahls, M.J.Straker, C.J.Bresson, D.B.England, D.E.Gander, D.R.Riniker, G.E.Beenken, L.L.Lathrop, E.Ludeña, C.R.McLetchie, L.D.Bellrichard, L.Shubert, M.F.Wunderlin, N.A.Evans, W.H.Waddell, C.B.Wilberding, E.M.Manderscheid, R.M.Schute, D.F.Belloma, K.L.Smith, M.G.Tobin, R.J.Steinhoff, T.D.Curray, V.W.Welsh, M.J.Bass, M.J.Clasen, R.D.Bowers, J.J.González, J.C.Wolf, J.R.Gilliland, M.J.Dillon, R.E.Hicks, T.J.Teijen, A.J.Pavelec, A.W.Campbell, C.E.Coughlin, G.White, J.J.Grue, J.J.Jaeger, L.W.Horne, M.D.Guenther, M.M.Deckert, R.D.Cox, R.D.Finder, R.E.Norman, W.H.Miller, D.Lange, G.A.Singsank, G.W.Aurit, J.E.Hill, J.G.Butlett, J.R.Hoogenakker, J.R.Stimart, L.L.Crawford, R.E.Hall, W.R.Walkup, D.D.Folkerts, H.C.Buss, R.A.Jasper, W.R.Knudson, G.L.Urban, B.L.Lawson, B.L.McCoy, C.J.Pearson, J.N.Scruggs, L.E.Hubbard, R.A.Leibfried, T.C.McDermott, D.J.Junkins, M.D.Voss, P.F.Reiss, R.J.Meyer, R.Schroeder, W.E.Bockenstedt, C.D.Anderson, G.E.Gunderson, J.P.Duffy, K.E.Bloom, A.W.McDermott, F.E.Straka, J.D.Matthews, J.J.Steckel, J.L.Pease, K.P.Muehleip, C.E.Dunstan, R.H.Bolk, W.E.Hoffman, A.B.Ford, C.F.Koeller, C.N.Hentges, D.Averett, D.J.Fuss, E.Tolson Jr., J.D.Tracy, L.A.Bell, R.M.Johnson, A.J.Fiori, J.R.Glennon, R.H.Kramer, W.T.Brown, A.F.Lex, J.E.Spoden, J.J.Gudenkauf, M.L.Kramer, R.P.Lucas, C.A.Hethershaw, D.E.Mc Coy, E.V.Hlas, G.L.Bartling, M.L.Bigbee, N.E.Kelley, R.F.Frasher, R.L.Vosberg, F.W.Straka, M.A.Ingle, R.A.Olszewski, R.Carnevali, B.Lancho, M.Di Pangrazio, A.H.Kamphuis, C.L.Peters, E.E.Malone, G.J.Fehringer, G.M.Olson, J.B.Holder, J.R.Christopher, L.L.Hefel, R.A.Carlson, R.T.Dobbins, S.A.Johnson, V.S.Crandle, A.C.Davison, D.L.Bosworth, J.D.Marlow, T.J.Vanthournout, G.E.Stanford, H.O.Moravec, A.T.Carrasco, P.J.Whelan, S.C.Davis, D.L.Brazelton, R.L.Blair, C.A.Nielsen, C.J.Mueller, D.Knapp, E.L.Schotanus, E.W.Kaminski, G.A.Turk, G.L.Eubank, H.J.Nagel, I.L.Petrie, J.L.Draper, J.T.Omeara, M.C.Anderson, R.C.Kaiser, R.H.Gunter, R.J.Breitfelder, R.P.Kepford, R.T.Baker, W.D.Wambsgans, H.W.Rowland, R.H.Clingenpeel, G.N.Mart, J.L.McCullough, J.P.Monaco, T.Morrissey, E.Glas, B.D.Brandt, L.R.Slater, R.W.Ledbetter, B.K.Harrison, C.D.Sund, E.Miller, G.L.Rieder, J.E.Young, L.Alexander, L.J.Kerns, M.E.Turner, R.D.Bergert, R.D.Schoening, B.J.Livengood, D.P.Ryan, D.R.Nordman, D.R.Olberts, E.L.Wachs, F.Lundeen, R.E.Teale, R.W.Rydberg, J.E.Johnson, K.V.Neuwohner, R.A.Schuckert, D.E.Williams, J.J.Muehlenthaler, B.J.Mullaney, C.E.Stork, C.I.Noonan, D.L.Mueller, E.M.Hanson, J.R.McCorkle, J.V.Wagoner, R.N.Walter, T.L.Dudley, W.A.Bernatz, W.F.Davis Jr., A.A.Harris, M.Gomez, D.M.Christian, H.F.Barnett, P.Arroyo, P.Diaz, D.M.Donaldson, C.R.Higgins, G.R.White, K.E.Wood, L.G.Petersen, D.S.Tritch, A.W.Brenneis, L.Hall, N.H.Dejong, H.W.Herr, R.E.Pauletti, E.E.Warhurst, F.L.Robers, G.Clark, J.Patin, K.Call, M.E.Jorgensen, A.J.Hubbard, J.A.Hays, M.T.Holman, R.V.Digout, J.D.Deutsch, J.E.Johnson, L.B.Lewis, O.J.Walker, S.E.Graf, T.O.Rader, D.C.Griswold, L.H.Schmitt, R.L.Budden, G.N.Dellos, J.H.Dillard, L.J.Netwal, R.W.Bucholtz, T.Newquist, J.D.Penabare, B.D.Bright, F.J.Casey, J.R.Baker, J.M.Oropesa, J.Naranjo, L.Macias, B.Orgaz, M.Ruiz, A.T.Matney, A.Zelnio, C.D.Bay, C.S.Hooper, G.R.Midtbo, J.A.Price, J.S.Grams, L.B.Eberhart, L.H.Wenthe, P.R.Meier, P.S.Domingez, R.E.Reynolds, B.J.Vaughn, C.L.Vanwinkle, A.L.Bowman, L.J.Ohrberg, D.B.Moore, E.H.Harmer, G.E.Starman, H.S.Gunnerson, J.T.Meek, M.Flippo, O.P.Guyton, M.Lepers, C.C.Zook, E.A.Henningsen, H.G.Fischahs, J.H.Forest, L.G.McMullen, P.W.Wells Jr., R.C.Newnham, T.H.Crisson, W.M.Roll, A.Sanchez A., J.R.Bettinghaus, A.Del Castillo, O.E.Hutchinson, D.A.Genung, F.Cabalka, F.Sercu, G.E.Merritt, J.P.Ince, J.S.Hollowell, E.G.Munson, R.D.Stevens, T.N.Thompson, H.J.Russell, J.A.Scannell, B.M.France, B.R.Goodnight, C.E.Fowler, D.C.Kniss, J.G.Anderson, J.R.Kramer, K.Wilson, L.W.Sheraden, R.L.Shay, C.N.Fairhead, F.L.Utsinger, J.L.Martin, P.F.Ohman, P.J.Thornbloom, R.R.Anderson, T.R.Harvey, T.W.Immesoete, W.A.Rockstroh, J.Bisson, A.Villemur, C.Roche, W.D.Hill, D.A.Sickmier, D.R.Howell, E.Olsen, F.J.Ackerman, G.W.Leik, J.L.Buche, L.W.Meisner, M.F.Kunkel, N.F.Lemmon, N.J.Clous, O.Gist, R.E.Weaver, V.B.Goodman, W.E.Honshel, J.V.Kluesner, E.B.Hutchinson, D.P.Hopley, J.L.Clark, B.L.Layson, B.M.Gore, R.J.Fox, J.B.Wilson, D.A.Allison, D.C.Nimmick, M.M.Howard, P.C.Bush, F.Gonzalez M., D.D.Warfield, J.H.Eby, J.P.Wells, N.L.Carter, M.Taillon, T.Galvez, E.Taylor, M.Pommeau, P.Barazer, A.Quijano, J.E.Snavely, L.W.Melone, R.D.Spidle, D.E.Brotherton, G.Colter, R.E.Rehse, R.P.Cusick, W.L.Lofgren, W.T.Maxwell Jr., D.F.Martini, A.Martin B., C.I.Potts, J.D.Howard, R.J.Farkas, F.J.Jaramago, R.Gongora, E.G.D'Agostino, J.H.Smeltzer, A.Rodriguez G., P.Maroto, E.Konitzer, M.Moreno L., B.D.Allen, A.E.Borgonjon, C.S.Magnani, D.L.Christofferson, D.L.Swenson, H.E.Campbell, J.B.Coogan Jr., L.D.Collins, R.L.Beck, R.L.Osborn, C.M.Baldo, G.Bennett, C.W.Hilgert, J.A.Pugliese, P.Sanz, M.D.Ericson, J.Buriani, D.R.Molko, J.A.Johnson, L.Mittleider, M.J.Korey, R.J.Clark, W.R.Sturtz, O.O.Tombessi, R.G.Watson, K.C.McConnell, V.R.Reynolds, W.L.Hillmer, C.R.Hingtgen, I.G.Reiter, R.G.Kleine, D.V.Ostergaard, W.M.Smith, H.J.García, O.G.Shives, J.E.Schwartz, J.W.Miller, R.D.Hobbs, C.E.Hallin, R.L.Blair, **1960** R.E.Williams, J.L.Carius, P.J.Koob, H.W.Johnson, F.E.Hopkins, F.J.Lister, J.E.Seitzinger, L.Del Valle, V.Del Cerro, D.R.Betts, W.G.Huffman, J.Lose, R.M.Bradley, J.R.Riley, P.A.O'Connor, R.E.Lane, C.D.Slattery, C.L.Marken, C.O.Bacus, D.G.Croft, E.J.Shoemaker, G.F.Swanson, G.P.Vrban, H.E.Hoss, J.J.Fitzgerald, J.W.Vokes, M.E.Pommer, M.S.Bartell, N.P.Chiodo, O.L.Byrns, R.J.Dondlinger, T.J.Tracy, W.M.Gilchrist, A.Valdeolivas, D.D.Johnson, J.J.Weatherman, M.L.Oberlander, J.A.De París, F.Escobar, M.D.Garrison, A.Rua, L.A.Miller, E.R.Gillaspy, B.B.Alexander, C.J.Anglin, D.D.Wright, D.E.Kiefer, L.L.Nighswonger, R.C.Kershaw, T.L.Johnson, W.H.Limmer, W.D.Akers, J.Sanger, W.H.Mitschelen, H.G.Tate, C.R.Sydness, L.V.Anderson, T.Romeo, G.L.Warden, H.D.Schofield, J.V.Gale, S.Bradley Jr., V.A.Mutka, W.L.Twedt, G.Dimech, J.D.Hall, J.N.Smith, J.R.Tuttle, J.B.Mozena, D.L.Swigart, M.M.Swanander, C.J.Bunz, E.H.Roenfeld, V.Tosoni, H.L.Hudson, J.W.Herrick, T.H.Jensen, B.K.Stephenson, C.B.Harris, L.D.Williams, R.J.París, R.L.Henley, R.P.Heise, E.J.Filby, H.H.Collins, B.Black, C.E.Fitzgerald, D.M.Wetzel, M.J.Tazzioli, C.D.Williams, F.Mc Daniel, P.J.Armbrustmacher, R.S.Telfer, A.E.Griffin, H.H.Hill, J.Montero G., E.L.Schoolen, E.F.Reimers, H.A.Ramsey, J.F.McKeon, W.C.House, J.E.Glenn, W.N.Harmon, J.R.Bagley, C.E.Seiberling, K.D.Winters, W.B.Knight, H.V.Pollreisz, C.B.Reynolds, R.Ehrmann, W.F.Buxton, L.Dockins, B.L.Painter, A.Muiños, H.C.Horst, J.R.Epp, R.J.Bartusek, G.M.Hook, C.O.Hill, W.M.Swieter, E.D.Davis, R.J.Heerdink, H.Hoffmann, K.A.Fouts, A.Clement, D.Fravel, P.J.Rola', E.Schulz, G.Knerr, K.Lahm, L.Fischer, T.Hofmann, W.Kneiding, L.J.Lunde, A.Butler, C.W.Revell, J.H.Burton, A.G.Davis, T.A.Griffith, J.R.Earl, P.E.Timm, B.L.Smith, J.P.Tomich, R.D.Hink, G.L.Schweitzer, V.A.Linnum, M.Djerabi, H.F.Miller Jr., M.C.Chrisman, R.Francois, R.L.Frederick, T.A.Eidson, R.G.Bolte Jr., A.M.Sonner, S.J.Schneider, B.C.Maclennan, J.A.Foddrill, G.O.Shatzer, J.A.Jolicoeur, J.C.McNett, J.R.Patten, R.Treichel, R.D.Meinders, C.V.Jueschke Jr., J.A.Anderson, K.E.Wright, M.P.Hutton, R.E.Seusy, R.L.Day, R.L.Preston, E.M.Lichty, T.M.Wire, J.G.White, D.D.Shepard, G.L.Shepard, L.A.Cuvelier, W.G.Fox, W.K.Laylin, M.L.Siler, T.R.Baughn, J.E.Hoyt, J.E.Judge, R.C.Lance, R.H.Meier, J.D.Cherry, L.V.Anderson, D.F.Gootee, F.W.Thorne, H.L.Greenwood, K.L.Esty, A.J.Kinley, A.J.Meyer, H.E.Clue, J.A.Mangrich, J.D.Vonderheide, J.E.Morgan, T.E.Anderson, V.J.Henrikson, C.D.Wilson, L.J.Syhlman, R.L.Aschenbrenner, R.W.Briden, T.A.Elliott, U.A.Carino, G.A.Kramer, G.R.Arms, G.W.Boekhoff, L.Baker, W.P.Sedlmayr, G.M.Waltemeyer, H.W.Wittenburg, L.J.Dressel, W.J.Wilson, M.K.Heitman, W.L.Bannon, I.C.Kuennen, J.E.Giesen, R.Barton, R.D.Calvert, R.J.Richards, R.S.Buehrer, W.D.Fessler, D.E.Sutherland, H.F.Benhart, J.A.Burgin, M.Young, R.L.Schwab, V.H.Herrmann, P.J.Hayes Jr., D.G.Catchpool, H.Bear, H.F.Staack, R.D.Catchpool, C.F.Fourie, J.R.Connolly, S.E.Patton, S.R.Morse, G.R.Goodenbour, J.A.Shonka, M.D.Frericks, R.E.Thompson, R.G.Sievers, R.R.Bradley, T.W.Hamilton, V.L.Hesse, L.C.Herbst, T.H.Baish, C.C.Albrecht, C.C.Van Wey, D.C.Nefzger, D.Milbrandt, G.G.Rummens, G.Heber, G.P.Sondag, J.J.Reeves, R.B.Wilson, A.Horan, A.R.French, B.L.Stratton, C.L.Caslavka, D.A.Walgamuth, D.D.Brandt, D.F.Holub, D.L.Cousins, D.O.Blough, D.R.Johnson, E.M.Hilleshiem, G.B.Hill, G.F.Foht, G.P.Voyek, J.E.Navin, J.F.Close, J.G.Mezera, K.C.Rahe, K.H.Hudspeth, K.R.Schuler, L.C.Morse, L.E.Kiefer, L.L.Behnke, L.U.Pattee, N.W.Stoker, P.R.Standiford, R.C.Pagel, R.D.Cool, R.H.Behrens, R.J.Blocker, R.J.Kielty, R.J.Newton, R.L.Hellman, R.L.Leppert, R.P.Fager, R.R.Elliott, R.R.Simpson, R.R.Van Besien, R.W.Wadey, T.J.Fisher, T.Stone, T.W.Kayser, V.G.Sager, W.H.Kammeyer, W.W.Schons, W.W.Venenga, R.Rodriguez F., B.G.Timmerman, C.R.Stocks, D.L.Roberts, E.C.Haskin, E.W.Miller, F.A.Sharar Sr., F.A.Wieters, G.C.Thiele, G.D.Weber, G.M.Horkheimer, G.P.Burger, J.W.Quibell, L.G.Steele, L.J.Gerardy, L.M.Barton, R.J.Paynter, R.M.Martin, R.W.Rains, T.M.Mauer, A.A.Curtis, D.R.Steiert, E.L.Wagner, H.D.Haskin, H.E.Jones, J.E.Runde, J.H.Cronin, J.J.Ries, J.R.Ciesielski, J.W.Miller, L.F.Oberhauser, L.G.Miller, M.A.Cunningham, N.G.Barth, R.D.Franke, W.L.Jones, A.A.Kuennen, B.Lehmkuhl, C.E.Lawson, D.A.Bennett, D.A.Jones, D.W.Wills, F.Miller Jr., G.A.Johnson, G.T.Wagner, J.F.Hall, J.N.Sager, L.A.Michels, L.L.Bockholt, L.R.Lange, M.L.Pittman, M.W.Greek, N.L.Kleitsch, P.L.Dillon, R.L.Beckley, R.L.Niedert, R.N.Shaw, R.P.Schuster, V.G.Staebell, W.B.Montelius, W.E.Peter, E.Rodriguez M., A.C.Williams Jr., C.P.Ostdahl, D.A.Ruden, D.D.Huisman, G.D.Hiler, J.A.Conrads, J.H.Suhr, J.J.Gibson, J.N.Bingham, J.P.Dougherty, J.R.Renner, L.A.Babcock, L.D.Woods, L.G.Howell, L.W.Reeg, M.S.Voss, N.W.Lampe, R.A.Wagner, R.D.Penn, R.L.England, R.L.Marvin, W.K.Bulow, A.E.Fratini, A.E.Kaufmann, A.E.Knutson, B.Fish, C.Dobson, C.J.Adams, C.J.Weinschenk, C.N.Friedman, C.R.Haas, D.C.Ludovissy, D.C.Naber, D.H.Meyer, D.L.Gockel, D.T.Brown Jr., E.C.Shirley, E.L.Sabers, E.W.Riegler, F.H.Sabers, F.L.Edwards, F.W.Konzen, G.C.Hildreth, G.H.Strang, H.D.Douglas, H.E.Reuter Jr., H.V.Timmerman, J.J.Bauler, J.K.Juhl, J.P.Whitish, J.W.Elledge, K.F.Kutsch, L.D.Lester, L.L.Hatton, L.M.Jewett, L.R.Shaben, L.W.Baker, R.A.Palmer, R.H.Hefel, R.J.Mc Ginley, R.J.Trewartha, R.L.Cullen, R.M.Vanderah, R.R.Rieder, R.V.Blume, R.V.Huseman, S.Aasberg, W.M.White, W.R.Schult, A.J.Strang, C.J.Mowbray, C.M.Strong, D.L.Frush, E.W.Barnhart, F.C.Knoke, F.K.Koehler, J.D.Perry, J.Diers, J.J.Kelleher, J.J.McDonough Sr., J.P.Clemen, L.A.Williams, M.M.Link, P.A.Koecke, R.C.Hageman, R.E.Leach, R.E.Thoma, R.L.Wagner, S.E.Davies, T.L.Schultz, T.R.Heyberger, V.L.Dietz, W.A.Voelker, W.C.Marsh, W.G.Bartels, W.V.Beyer, M.Alonso, A.C.Sisbach, A.J.Schmitt, C.C.Pint, C.N.Kleitsch, D.E.Hull, D.F.Dougherty, D.G.O Connell, D.J.Bastian, D.J.Weber, D.Snyder, E.W.Chihak, F.E.Bentley, F.L.Smith, F.L.Thielen, G.E.Eickelberg Jr., H.C.Eiffler, K.A.Hansen, K.A.Parson, L.C.Breitbach, L.J.Haas, M.J.Ulbrich, P.E.Daugherty, P.Jamieson, R.E.Prochaska, R.J.Burke, T.M.Jackson, T.M.Mead, A.J.Behnke, A.M.Anfinson, B.R.Williams, C.V.Hoskins, D.A.Clark, D.A.Sloan, D.J.Fintel, D.L.Sexton, D.T.Noonan, G.A.Wortley Jr., G.R.Shadlow, J.F.Nissen Jr., J.W.Collins, L.H.Steffens, L.J.Pape, L.J.Schoo, L.L.Spencer, M.E.Meyer, P.Bartz, P.Thuesen, R.A.Heber, R.H.Peters, R.L.Burds, R.P.Carl, W.R.Benson, A.L.Henkle, C.G.Jochum, D.J.Ehlers, D.J.Sutter, D.W.Halbmaier, D.W.Valentis, E.N.Pfohl, F.E.Worple, G.E.Fink, J.E.Livingston, J.W.Cory, L.J.Nichols, L.J.Schlitter, M.J.Michels, W.B.Reardon, W.C.Goodrich, C.J.Biddick, C.W.Hagen, D.E.Steil, D.H.Steinle, D.K.Nesteby, D.R.Gardner, D.R.Schauer, E.C.Scherf, F.L.Schaefer, F.W.Thumser Jr., G.G.Imbus, G.N.Laprell Jr., J.A.Schmit, J.C.Hansen, J.F.Barry, J.J.Curley, K.A.Custer, L.B.Hamlett, L.E.Schiltz, L.R.Holman, L.R.Law Jr., M.A.Faley, P.J.Walsh, R.B.Wessels, R.C.Donatsch, R.C.Fitzgerald, R.E.Vaske, R.J.Iverson, R.J.Shird, R.M.Hearn, R.R.Rogan, T.G.Williams, W.C.Bown, W.D.Lee, W.G.Rombke, W.W.Launspach, A.P.Bruehahn, D.E.Ehrlich, D.F.Vonhandorf, D.W.Freet, D.W.Pearce, F.D.Staver, G.L.Albert, G.L.Blonigan, J.R.Goedken, V.D.Heins, W.M.Collins, W.West, A.F.Bemis, C.E.Lasek, C.E.Maiers, C.L.Bierman, D.A.Biermann, E.W.Appenzeller, J.E.Bush, L.F.Lewis, N.I.Millard, P.P.Fay, V.A.Hoftender, V.N.Behnke, W.R.Brown, B.J.Schockemoehl, B.R.Knipfer, C.E.Stephens, C.O.Meyer, D.J.Reardon, E.G.Schuchart, F.O.Thiese, G.G.Wild, G.L.Blake, J.D.Scherbring, J.J.Balk, J.L.Rubner, J.T.Obrien, M.A.Frank, R.F.Bechen, R.L.Kieffer, R.L.Sanders, R.M.Schmidt, W.J.Buelow, W.J.Lueken, B.J.Hoffman, D.G.Tegeler, J.W.Ryan, R.D.Drish, R.F.Steinle, S.J.Wetter, A.C.Roth, A.L.Vesperman, A.P.Barry, C.H.Chappell, C.W.Herink, E.D.Monahan, H.A.Hines, H.W.Lutes, H.W.Reichenbacker, J.E.Yoerger, L.J.Pickel Jr., N.J.Glaw, N.J.Winston, R.J.Omeara, R.L.Schaefer, T.L.Siemens, W.J.Duehr Jr., A.T.Mc Govern, C.B.Kobs, C.N.Strub, D.H.Miller, F.W.Gansen, G.A.Schroeder, H.P.Hoffman, J.F.Cook, S.R.Nauman, U.J.Mantemach, V.B.Stelpflug, D.L.Kunkle, D.P.Puhl, D.R.Clough, G.L.Evanoff, G.V.Schmitz, J.N.Friedman, J.T.Kubesheski, K.A.Rettenberger, K.C.Rang, P.E.Farrey, R.H.Koppes, V.A.Little, W.J.Christensen, C.G.Hamilton, C.J.Boyer, C.L.Lang, D.J.Rock, D.R.Harrison, J.C.Kronlage, J.R.Peacock, J.Tovar Jr., K.D.Kauffman, K.F.Jansen, L.D.Schares, R.B.Pluemer, R.D.Schoonover, R.J.McDonald, R.L.Schaal, W.J.Dougherty, W.R.Ellerman, A.N.Errthum, C.A.Feldmann, F.M.Fuerst, M.C.Wagner, D.A.Hirsch, D.D.Peters, D.E.Duncan, D.F.Gorman, D.J.Wetzsteon, D.L.Little, E.F.Rettenmeier, E.J.Zalaznik, F.E.Lane, G.C.Freymiller, G.R.Berg, H.A.Blakeman, J.C.Mc Gee, J.J.Gleason, J.R.Kean, K.J.Pickel, K.Schmerbach, L.D.Geving, L.M.Merfeld, L.R.Hardesty, L.R.Taylor, N.A.Dalsing, P.G.Scherbring, P.J.Nordhues, R.A.Burroughs, R.E.Koob, R.J.Wiest, R.L.Cottrell, T.H.Vosberg, T.L.Weber, V.A.Haberkorn, W.C.Berkley, W.C.Young, A.J.Faulhaber, C.A.Pahnke, C.G.Janssen, C.Rager, D.G.Neil, D.L.Cole,

Research engineering staff, Waterloo, Iowa, 1956

H.A.Oglesby, J.A.Fields, J.R.Ives, R.N.Legrand, S.A.Schneider, W.R.Nichols, F.Gonjar, C.J.Foley, C.U.Busch, D.C.McCartney, E.A.Bonifas, G.T.Carns, D.F.Hingtgen, D.H.Suiter, F.P.Regan, G.J.Folks, H.R.Haas, J.F.Mendez, J.H.Weber, L.A.Pope, L.E.Phelps, L.R.Mc Combs, M.V.Huberty, P.K.Mc Cormick, R.C.Rasque, R.D.Davis, R.D.Liddle, S.C.Lee, T.S.Norman Jr., V.J.Sager, C.F.Ruff, F.F.Kieler, J.L.Ragatz, T.J.Layde, A.E.Diederich, C.D.Christopher, C.G.Habel, C.Tippett, C.Vorwald, D.A.Schrobilgen, D.E.Schenck Sr., D.J.Hare, D.L.Wilberding, D.R.Duncklee, E.A.Gartner, E.F.Colin, E.Fisher Jr., G.F.Warner, H.A.Quint, H.G.Doty, J.C.Clemmensen, J.D.Crane, J.D.Swarts, J.E.Pennekamp, J.N.Stecklein, J.W.Lappin, K.W.Hanks, L.J.Meaney, M.L.Burns, O.A.Webrand Jr., P.L.Davison, R.E.Davis, R.F.Corken, R.J.Carlson, R.J.Taylor, R.L.Wirtz, R.W.McMullen Sr., T.M.Ciesielski, V.D.Soldwisch, W.C.Priebe, W.H.Wackershauser, D.C.Mueller, D.H.Thul, F.A.Libansky, F.D.Foley, J.L.McDermott, J.R.Harry, L.J.Richardson, R.L.Schilling, W.K.Ohl, A.L.Bergmann, C.W.Hite, D.R.Lewis, F.B.Udelhoven, H.F.Kemler, H.R.Mauer, J.P.Streng, N.R.Mauthe, R.D.Vanvors, R.E.Norris, T.J.Wilder, B.A.Neymeyer, H.Ridder Jr., J.F.Link, J.G.Bela, L.A.Fox, R.B.Bruns, R.C.Legrand, R.E.Sonksen, B.C.Pickel, C.E.Hansel, D.L.Jeidy, E.C.Heins, G.L.De Groote, G.L.Fleming, J.F.Huber, J.F.Tilp, J.R.Brooks, L.L.Adelmund, L.M.Smothers, R.F.Dailey, R.G.Smith, R.J.Reding, V.W.Sheehan, W.Swisher, A.E.Gobin, A.G.Haan, A.M.Boardman, D.A.Riesberg, D.J.Novak, D.M.Hertzberg, F.R.Ruetten, G.D.Shaffer Jr., G.E.Johll, G.R.Stephens, H.L.Erhardt, J.G.Ohms, K.E.Turner, L.L.Eastman, R.T.Sheldon, V.D.Ryan, G.Galeote, C.A.Bennett Jr., D.L.Koeller, D.L.Pint, D.L.Uhlenhopp, G.L.Bray, G.T.Flury, H.L.Prochaska, J.A.Lansing, J.L.Jaquith, J.P.Donlan, J.R.Sweeney, L.J.Beinborn, M.C.Loeffelholz, M.J.Stohlmeyer, R.C.Cragg, R.C.Tharp, R.D.Knox, R.G.Brewer, R.G.Richardson, R.W.Adams, W.H.Watson, W.P.Wagner, B.L.Medinger, C.D.Bouck, D.F.Lambert, D.K.Baier, E.G.Haverland, F.W.Tegtmeier, G.J.Steffen, H.J.Caughron, J.F.Farraher, J.J.Lucey, J.W.Smith, L.A.Kramer, L.L.Van Brocklin, L.P.Ruden, M.L.Dismore, N.A.Retterath, P.D.Glasson, R.A.Bertling, R.E.Quade, R.L.Davis, C.T.Hefel, D.F.Goffinet, D.H.Wubben, E.Jensen, G.L.Clements, G.W.Nosbisch, H.L.Clayton, J.A.Timm, J.C.Oberfoell, J.D.Gardiner, J.J.Banfield, J.M.Theisen, J.R.McDermott, J.R.Willis, J.W.Collins, M.H.Hefel, M.J.Kaufman, R.E.Lutes, R.L.Turner, R.S.Fowler, T.J.Hochberger, C.C.Kelley, C.T.Graham, D.W.Ehlert, G.Stoelting, J.R.Westemeier, K.Mahoney, L.F.Michael, M.L.Bolton, R.A.Labarge, R.E.Lange, R.J.Wessel, R.P.Nelson, T.J.Adams, W.B.Farrey, A.Waber, A.E.Davis, B.H.Durley, C.C.Steger, C.D.Vance Sr., C.M.Patzner, D.B.Kemming, D.F.Lemons, E.J.Feldmann, H.L.Ellis, J.J.Myers, K.C.Roschi, K.L.Spencer, L.W.Robinson, M.J.Buelow, M.Jones, R.A.Waterman, R.C.Jones, R.E.Nelson, R.Hill, R.J.Menster, R.L.Kemp, R.L.Ostert, T.M.Hall, W.E.McVay, W.L.Reinhardt, W.Westendorf, L.Ropert, M.Garcia E., B.C.Jensen, C.E.Anderson, D.E.Pagel, D.L.Friedly, G.H.Gebhard, G.J.Hingtgen, G.W.Federspiel, J.D.Clayton, J.D.Rice, J.J.Garner, J.L.Staver, L.H.Wolter, L.R.Duecker, N.D.Boyes, R.F.Becker, R.G.Fink, R.J.Medinger, W.F.Wedemeier, W.H.Bott, W.W.Wagner, D.D.Freeseman, D.P.Schilling, D.S.Brown, G.A.Sharkey, H.A.Rogers, H.D.Reyerson, K.J.Thome, K.W.Hanson, L.K.Butteris, P.P.Berntgen, R.L.Suhr, R.O.Richards, A.A.Ploessl, C.A.Menne, C.H.Seyffer, D.Strickland, E.O.Sullivan, G.J.Kunkel, G.L.Patrick, G.W.Cottrell, J.E.Selleck, J.R.Brown, J.T.Davis Sr., L.G.Amling, M.J.Goetzinger, O.L.Andrew, P.M.Pink, R.F.Pfeiler, R.G.Dix, R.L.Cigrand, S.M.Bahls, W.J.Rettenmeier, W.J.White, A.David, R.Seewald, A.H.Smith, B.J.Mills, C.D.Wendel, D.Henniges, D.L.Millard, D.R.Miller, G.R.Welbes, H.L.Toles, H.O.Martinez, J.C.Higgins, J.J.Weydert, J.L.Heiderscheit, L.D.Hagenow, L.L.Ellis, L.L.Weber, M.J.Uhlenhopp, M.L.Gibson Jr., P.A.Brunning, R.C.Fink, R.E.Johnson, R.F.Hickson, R.G.Bauer, R.J.Cartney, R.L.Moore, R.R.Blask, R.W.Morris, T.H.Davis, T.W.Cummings, W.M.Gratton, A.V.Pisarik, D.F.Higgins, D.G.Boyes, D.R.Jacobson, E.R.Kramer, G.R.Odekirk, J.Greibe, J.J.Gasper, J.K.Miller, J.L.Clarke, N.G.Oberheu, N.W.Meuer, O.J.Kringle, R.J.Jaeger, R.J.Kiefer, R.L.Demoss, R.W.Stanfley, T.Berzins, D.L.Husemann, E.J.Bowden, G.Revelle, H.G.Adams, J.A.Anderson, J.Hart, L.L.Schmidt, P.I.Cookinham, R.J.Schlamp, R.L.Avery, R.W.Frederick, V.J.Smith, W.J.Schloemer, W.L.Greene, B.V.Beau Jr., C.Dale, C.F.Funk Jr., C.R.Pierce, D.D.Milbrandt, D.E.Burrows, D.F.Becker, E.J.Kuhle, J.A.Figi, N.J.Sweeney, R.E.Jordan, R.O.Dean, W.D.Ryan, A.A.Holtz, A.E.Kerper, D.F.Cox, E.E.Luloff, R.D.Jensen, R.F.Schlueter, R.P.Clark, V.R.Trent, L.Prieto, D.A.Dalrymple, D.P.Bresnahan, J.W.Wilkinson, L.A.Clemen, R.L.Hurlburt, R.X.Noonan, W.F.Cherry, J.Ruiz, A.Rico, J.Prieto, D.J.Joyce, R.G.Dallenbach, R.K.Blume, W.Gebert, A.E.Hagen, D.E.Leslein, D.L.Heidt, G.M.Mc Inroy, G.M.Tordsen, J.G.Creighton, K.M.Taylor, L.P.Wiederholt, T.J.Welu, W.H.Frazier, D.G.Wernke, F.S.Mannina, J.A.Regan, J.L.Loveless, J.R.Schlegel, O.L.Mickens, T.E.Danielson, T.P.Anderson Jr., A.J.Pipho, C.E.Tyler, E.Biretz, G.A.Ives, H.J.Loomis, R.A.Coleman, R.J.Lampe, R.J.Schink, B.L.Knight, D.R.Slater, F.X.Gruber Jr., G.A.Kennicker, G.A.Ricke, L.N.Reisen, R.J.Jungk, R.W.Donovan, A.Calvo, A.J.Wohlert, B.P.Hanna, O.H.Leyh, P.J.Hamilton, R.D.Eckerman, R.J.Markus, T.D.Newby, T.R.Sash, D.G.Lines, D.P.Hanten, J.A.Chapman, N.L.Watson, R.A.Zrostlik, R.H.Kirschbaum, W.E.Myers, H.E.Richey, J.B.Splinter, J.D.De Vore, R.D.Lindaman, S.Gary, T.Keys, F.L.Krapfl, G.L.Webb, H.L.Meyerhoff, L.K.Grimes, R.H.Hanson, R.J.Purcell, W.A.Blanchard, W.D.Oler, J.Vita, B.G.Vanmatre, D.J.Brekke, E.F.Garthoff, M.F.Pass, P.W.Welch, R.J.Gabrenja, D.F.Wieters, E.L.Buch, R.E.McCollough, J.D.Lien, J.L.Bast, R.H.Boyd, J.Buraschi, D.H.Harman, F.L.Meyer, M.J.Hoffman, W.L.Moran, J.Bueno, B.J.Morgan, C.L.Poyner, J.C.Bruns, C.J.Meyer, D.F.Sullivan, D.J.Ennis, D.M.Depauw, D.V.Tegtmeier, G.J.Groskurth, J.Cederberg, R.G.Stejskal, S.J.Thompson, J.A.Slick, P.J.Palzkill, H.Bemis Jr., J.E.Hayes, J.M.Dolan, G.W.Kress, J.R.Kemp, L.A.Niemeyer, K.E.Justmann, R.W.Gatewood, L.H.Miller, I.L.Emil, C.K.Isbell, L.W.Sigwarth, P.A.Zumaris, T.A.Kimberlin, D.W.Smith, R.A.Sauser, R.E.Wilson, W.Dinerman, B.W.Myers, H.J.McCarron, R.J.Levis, A.D.Patakfalvi, M.Frisk, J.V.Newlin, L.Camillo, T.E.Roberts, W.L.Phillips, A.Gil, R.L.Hesse, M.R.Durham, C.E.Dekeukeleire, L.D.Taylor, M.B.Taylor, D.L.Bratton, J.A.Lumsden, E.Sarro, W.F.Willert, G.J.Voss, H.Mykolaishyn, L.B.Mumm, M.W.Kass, J.Gomez, A.Delicado, L.Lewis, R.V.Solis, R.K.Baumhover, G.Braccini, A.L.Jones, B.L.Conover, D.G.Loy, R.L.Johnson Jr., M.Terron, D.G.Ball, J.T.Yates, E.A.Oyen, P.Miche, C.B.Odell, J.A.Kuhl, J.L.McManus, J.P.McDonald, R.E.Lottes, J.Cich, G.Mora, E.J.Mickelsen, G.M.Schroeder, A.V.Fritz, D.L.Paulsen, G.J.Leifker, T.C.Keller, K.E.Bilderback, L.A.Rosin, E.L.Kretz, D.C.Willenbring, D.J.Delaney, G.J.Teasdale, J.B.Drehman, J.J.Behnke, W.E.Miller, J.E.Schmelzer, J.L.Alderson, J.J.Mansfield, N.M.Stanley, D.Pelletier, **1961** R.Lazarus, E.L.Carns Jr., G.A.Kaldenberg, K.W.Koppen, L.G.Collins, M.E.Haddad, R.E.Martin, W.G.Kelsey, W.R.Akins, J.J.Brimeyer, D.J.Hayes, G.J.Ihm, G.R.Sergeant, J.W.Thompson, R.A.Johnson, V.J.Roeder, W.A.Jackson, M.C.Anderson, R.C.Huseman, J.R.Fuglsang, J.Navarrete, H.D.Swiger, R.L.Sell, L.A.Sahilices, D.C.Delgado, A.Moreno F., W.E.Blau, A.Lanier, P.Montigny, H.Gauter, K.E.Tracy, P.E.Coates, C.H.Baldwin, D.D.Koniar, E.H.Kiefer, L.L.Ales, W.G.Muckensturm, A.A.Celotto, H.L.Randolph Jr., R.M.Maiers, A.R.Johnson, B.J.Wolfe, H.F.Jasper, P.R.Bitz, R.G.Matz, R.L.Bentley Jr., R.Peyrat, F.Garcia P., R.E.Mueller, D.D.Trautman, D.G.Stephens, J.D.Pope, L.A.Ruud, N.J.Carapella, S.A.Massey, D.R.Witwer, J.R.Mc Kain, M.L.Poese, P.J.Clemons Jr., D.W.Delgado, B.A.Chaney, T.Boisseau, K.M.McFee, F.L.Moser, K.J.Kocour, E.Seegmueller, J.Blot, D.R.Storjohann, R.P.Balzer, M.Roberts, P.Galan, F.J.Becker, H.R.Epp, J.L.Hobson, A.Corredor, L.I.Tibodeau, B.H.Cruson, F.D.Edgar, V.F.Dix, F.O.Creger, J.E.Jackson, J.L.Gonzalez S., J.M.Muñoz, J.Garnier, D.Paquis, H.J.Kaehler, J.F.Jones, C.Lebrun, H.Zimmer, M.Huether, W.Hofer, J.E.Purcell, V.Seseña, B.N.Graphenteen, D.J.Van Sky, A.Herm, E.Peukert, G.Schuhmacher, H.Berger, H.Kremkau, K.Mueller, K.Platz, M.Faul, P.Knosalla, R.Kroll, W.Katzenbaecher, D.J.Shannon, L.L.Cossairt, G.Sevin, A.Carrasco, L.Quiralte, D.E.Jackson, R.E.Grandinetti, N.W.Cooperider, B.G.Bailey, D.A.Beckius, H.A.Olsen, J.M.Pearson, B.L.Hall, E.R.Marsh, J.J.Langman, J.J.Plemone, J.Bustos, C.J.O'Gorman, W.H.Richter, W.R.Miller, C.G.Reed, A.A.Koepsell, B.D.Butler, F.D.Ferguson, G.F.Hagstrom, M.A.Hoffert, M.A.Mahr, M.A.Wikner, R.E.Mott, M.Nicholson, R.L.Kritz, G.Reibel, D.C.Freiburger, R.A.Gerhardt, R.J.Lobmeyer, R.L.Malcolm, T.J.Schmidt, T.W.Freiburger, J.Brul, J.O.Bordewick, D.A.Oberbroeckling, E.J.Beckman, F.J.Bay, J.W.Huff, O.K.Anthony, R.E.Bennett, R.H.Niedert, A.Haslam, L.O.Groom, P.C.Kester, T.O.Goodney, H.Dreiss, J.W.Jewett, R.Biot, J.Barre, W.W.Wood, F.W.Baer, M.W.Palm, G.J.Millwright, E.G.Miller, R.T.Tiller, D.F.Stewart, H.Añibarro, C.J.Pletcher, N.L.Phipps, E.J.Kruse, R.M.Digges, W.Martin III, T.Perrignon, F.Ryan, R.Lambert, A.Nepote, E.Lopez R., O.Navio, A.Guerrero, A.Marin, J.E.Mastain, J.V.Murphy, M.Gutierrez M., G.P.Driggers, G.Pean, D.Rueda, J.A.Eusebio, L.L.Smiddy, W.J.Gerlach, J.Fauchère, R.T.Harris, E.Schulze, P.K.Windeknecht, M.Poirier, J.Sanchez A., W.H.Spitznas, R.E.Reints Jr., R.J.Scheitzach, D.N.Dowsett, J.W.Marsden, L.M.Yerkey, J.D.Conner, M.E.Bender, J.L.Sproston, C.M.Corredor, M.C.Barton, T.R.Pitman, F.J.De Paul, B.F.Jenkins, C.L.Caldwell, L.N.Tertipes, B.C.Mc Kee, H.W.Scourten, F.M.Ramirez, J.E.Ferry, H.W.Powell, R.P.Salais, R.Bechtler, E.F.Standaert, W.Brown, J.Furze, P.Blazquez, D.J.Wall, E.J.Barth, F.Sekli, R.Zimmermann, A.Wittwer, M.Brea, **1962** C.Perrin, L.Vacher, G.Hee, W.Rasp, K.A.Stirm Jr., N.W.Richter, B.J.Hatchett, D.V.Anderson, R.Seprey, U.Schneider, G.W.Fagan, R.J.Vavrosky, I.M.Gober, J.J.Reihle, D.W.Montgomery, E.J.Jochim, J.R.Hall, N.F.Link, R.W.Longeville, E.Thomas, J.M.Verleye, J.C.Johnson, L.W.Jones, M.Musard, O.R.Sánchez, A.Taranne, M.L.Morgan, R.J.Lobnitz, J.A.Omilak, J.P.Russmann, E.Cintora, C.M.Doerr, J.E.Nelson, B.Chazeau, H.Quoiffy, E.R.Iñigo, B.M.Bair, C.L.Grill, H.R.Norfleet Jr., M.M.Verscheure, C.Sornique, T.C.Schwartz, G.L.Campbell, R.Leluc, J.A.Gonzalez G., D.L.Witt, S.J.Sterling, G.Gentils, Y.Perrucot, M.Perrault, A.G.Roth, P.R.Johnson, R.E.Fox, H.Lombardet, C.Leresche, L.Messaoui, M.Monot, M.A.Corella, W.W.Lobnitz, J.L.Purcell, P.E.Ossian, R.W.Sandberg, D.A.Hasenwinkel, A.F.Schwabe, S.L.Lindquist, C.J.Thiessen, D.L.Plowman, R.A.Caufield, K.Allgeier, B.L.Cashen, D.L.Berryman, L.F.McBride, L.H.Roberts, R.J.Foddrill, J.Bisson, W.R.Macgregor, A.Janke, J.M.Beeson, R.E.Mann, F.E.Turnbaugh, G.W.Cooper, H.E.Schreiber, R.G.Silliman, J.C.Gianfelice, A.Latapie, F.Doutre, J.Lemeret, E.Lorduy, A.R.Mac Pherson, E.G.Carpenter, H.W.Cufaude, J.A.Petermann, K.L.Miller, L.J.Havener, W.Miller, H.Ziehl, R.D.Frybarger, S.L.Paul, A.Eckstein, A.Molitor, F.Roth, G.Englert, H.Besau, H.Erb, H.Werner, J.Volk, K.Barnetz, K.Brandenburger, K.Korschewski, L.Fuchs, M.Staub, P.Heid, P.Rutkowski, W.Wein, J.L.Roehrs, R.F.Murphy, R.M.Gonzalez, R.P.Huston, B.W.Houseal, W.J.Worden, P.L.Henning, T.Pafundi, M.Vigneau, J.W.Rhyne, E.Zellers, F.J.Ballard, E.M.Krueger, R.M.Horine, W.W.Ballard, M.Brecheteau, O.Dolci, W.J.Teaford, L.G.Quick, H.W.Suechting Jr., J.L.Mowery, L.W.Peters, R.R.Stone, D.Otal, C.E.Blomseth, E.F.Hilbert, H.Dudek, J.E.Stump, V.V.Halverson, J.D.McCartney, C.J.Hicks, G.D.Dickson, J.O.Hayes, S.M.Gregerson, K.D.Piche, C.G.Gause, D.A.Johnson, R.M.Poterack, A.Bouin, M.A.Thompson, P.J.Farmer, R.B.Brock, J.Quemere, G.J.Huston, J.A.Hubbard, J.R.Adams, R.G.Hart, A.A.Mohr, B.J.Cline, C.R.Petrilli, D.E.Mason, D.R.Conzett, D.L.Chastain, J.L.Krafka, W.M.Anderson, M.Huchet, G.Ramos, M.N.Singbush, R.Barei, R.L.Birch, S.M.Jagodzinski, W.M.Bergstrom, J.W.Parker, D.H.Bucher, B.R.Burton, D.C.Kaukaskie, J.E.Valentine, M.Chansard, C.D.Falk, M.E.Gray III, R.A.Boney, J.P.Healy, J.Van Hille, D.J.Stange, D.J.Ward, D.R.Palmer, H.W.Becherer, R.D.Keleher, R.E.Jirsa, M.Sanz, R.N.Whitton, E.W.Meyer, J.Brochet, D.G.Peeples, C.R.Burnes, P.J.Lopez, W.H.Herold, C.François, M.Marillonnet, S.Berjonval, J.F.Souza, L.A.Tyler, P.R.Larson, K.R.Larson, G.A.Haro, D.E.Cackler, P.M.Heller, R.E.Hendricks, E.S.Schomer, J.T.Cooke, L.C.Elliott, W.D.Stuart, D.J.Longeville, G.H.Buelow, J.F.Robinson, M.C.Mitchell, S.M.Syverud, J.M.Dunn, M.Rodriguez Ll., C.E.Schultz, L.G.Moore, R.L.Lampe, A.Montes, R.N.Wilks, L.G.Mayer, L.M.Abernathy, A.R.Bagnera, D.L.Cather, F.G.Allen, M.Snook Jr., J.Delamarre, M.L.Collins, J.Tenaud, G.Laurelut, A.W.Haytcher, D.E.Curtis, J.E.Bleuer, J.K.Dunn III, M.J.Naab, O.R.Rockhold, E.E.Greif, N.D.Hobbs, D.E.Sabucco, R.A.Souers, J.W.England, L.Ilera, B.J.Sheldahl, L.D.Carson, D.A.Dobson, M.E.Davis, T.H.Dee, G.Noyers, M.Bobault, R.F.Harris, D.L.Carmack, G.A.Borden, M.Britt, M.D.Demry, C.V.Hennessey, D.A.Dilts, D.R.Louden, H.R.Gradert, J.D.Brooks, D.E.Bye, D.J.Ferneyhough, N.F.Keddy, H.G.Konig, A.J.Zandvliet, D.G.Noble, E.T.Griffin Jr., G.H.Alsop, A.Paciaga, M.P.Debel, B.R.Ledwell, E.R.Sheldrake, G.F.Fabiilli, M.J.McCarron, G.R.Hugart, G.G.Lee, V.L.Hosch, M.Wilson, D.Mery, J.R.Demay, J.R.Kassel, R.L.Johnson, G.A.Gilmore, P.Feuillet, C.J.Kane, G.E.Benner, G.E.Wynes, G.R.Fowler, K.E.Beard, T.H.Monahan, B.Seneclauze, H.C.Knox, R.D.Hotchkin, R.J.McDonald, S.L.Annette, R.Martin, E.Bailey, C.L.Maccabe, D.A.Beard, R.J.Lucke Jr., D.Thibault, J.Henrio, T.Beulin, J.L.Ruchti, N.D.Sonnenberg, A.A.Verbeke, K.W.Hakeman, J.B.Sears, J.J.Crouch, S.B.Welshhons, W.J.Marshall, W.L.Edgell, W.T.Kirby, B.Bousquin, V.L.Walker, C.R.Spittel, W.D.Emmerson, F.W.Carle, J.M.Meyers, K.T.Dorman, M.Wagner, V.F.Schneweis, P.Chene, P.Enz, F.E.Girten, C.T.Birditt, E.J.Claeys, E.V.Wortham, F.G.Tischler Jr., G.L.Mitton, J.R.Daniels, O.S.Cornejo, R.J.Hitchins, R.L.Warden, T.E.Sparrow, W.P.Stolbom, C.E.Burk, J.A.Simmons, W.P.Hutcherson, W.P.Ratliff, A.R.Walwer, D.A.Foster, G.E.Freeman, H.L.Thatcher, C.J.Petersen, W.E.Martin, D.E.Keep, D.W.Simpson, R.R.Roth, R.S.Marczi, T.A.Faoro, E.A.Gage, L.G.Brennan, L.G.Shibley, E.C.Jaquet, L.E.Passmore, D.J.Parmentier, D.R.Salmon, H.A.Bedek Jr., H.G.Ryan, M.L.York, R.C.Potts Jr., R.S.Potter, W.Freund, B.Caldwell, F.M.Johnson, R.J.Van Bell, A.E.Weaver, B.J.Hoeksema, E.L.Doss, H.Dittberner, J.A.Carson, L.R.Pufahl, R.D.Luke, R.L.Krahl, W.A.Kenyon, G.J.Cook, J.E.Huneault, E.J.Schave, W.Gore Jr., J.E.Gorman, D.A.Wilkens, D.H.Jasper, E.A.Reelfs, E.R.Steele, H.H.Stegner, J.L.Knudson, M.A.Versluis, P.E.Walker, T.J.Holcomb, R.L.Herzberg, A.L.Cook, E.Rahn Jr., L.R.Laughlin, R.L.Schwigen, T.S.Leon, M.Leguiza, R.P.Dickman, D.L.Braker, D.W.Tomlinson, H.M.Mizner, J.A.Rehse, J.J.Vanhoutte, L.M.Owens, M.E.Whitley, R.K.Sheraden, R.W.Skinner, S.Sandoval, K.L.Loving, W.L.Deadmond, C.E.Smith, D.J.Frost, D.L.Gubine, D.L.Hansen, D.L.Schnaufer, D.P.Carey, F.E.Saddoris, J.A.Buhr, J.H.Dobbs, J.L.Johnson,

Soviet Premier Nikita Khrushchev visits Des Moines, Iowa, factory, 1959

J.M.Alexander, J.M.Ciesielski, L.E.Swartz, L.L.Johnson, L.W.Keske, M.A.Crow, R.Franklin, R.J.Rundle, R.R.Mendoza, W.W.Bey, A.Jochim, D.G.Heideman, G.C.Beckman, K.F.Lichty, L.J.Youngblut, T.E.Weber, W.A.Knott, D.Clodfelter, E.R.Wentland, B.G.Relph, B.Scott Jr., C.H.Berinobis, D.E.Grafton, D.J.Kelley, D.L.Hendershot, D.L.Stufflebean, D.M.Dietz, D.Trower, E.E.Boone Jr., E.Howard, F.A.Bennett, G.D.Draper, G.L.Baish, G.L.Maitlen, G.L.Stanhope, G.R.Pietan, H.A.Hulme, H.E.Tiernan, H.G.Dill, H.V.Lichty, H.W.Nelson, J.A.Elliott, J.B.Demuth, J.E.Carver, J.G.Krop, J.P.Knebel, J.V.Johnson, J.W.Crabb, K.R.Dobbs, L.D.Reese, L.F.Barker, L.L.Myszka, L.O.Bathen, L.Schweer, M.J.Hopkins, M.L.Gillett, P.Dinnebier, P.M.Allen, R.Walker, S.Jackson, S.Sharer, T.A.Becker, T.D.Nitz, T.J.Even, U.A.Praught, W.Hayslett, W.L.Gillaspy, W.O Banion, W.R.Cunningham, W.T.Morris, G.A.May, H.Durnin, I.J.Miller, J.E.Ainley, K.J.Huber, L.M.Barron, R.A.Imel, R.A.Steinbronn, R.E.Peters, R.E.Pitsenbarger, R.W.Keith, W.R.Molstead, C.L.Fischels, D.L.Wright, H.G.Read, J.E.Deppe, J.M.Winters, J.Vandewiele, J.Wingert, A.J.Schmidt, J.F.Rochford, K.C.Wilson, K.C.Zikuda, L.L.Moore, M.Seenster, R.L.Stokes, R.R.Turner, J.H.Nissen, S.R.Curtman, A.F.Klammer Jr., C.W.Hall, D.A.Melcher, D.R.Struve, D.W.Decker, H.R.Teem, J.Hastings, J.J.Bovy, J.R.Hoffman, L.A.Wisecup, L.I.Neessen, R.J.Holmlund, R.L.Troutner, R.O.Back, R.R.Heckroth, D.D.Greenlee, D.D.Hagedorn, D.O.Gjere, E.T.Miller, F.P.Drewelow, G.W.Sankey, J.P.Mc Kenna, J.P.Schrodemier, L.J.Willett, W.F.Ziegler Jr., C.G.Jensen, C.L.Trask, J.E.Greenway, J.E.Johnson, J.H.Martin, J.T.Booth, L.F.Fitzpatrick, M.A.Ross, R.R.Knapp, T.J.Rowbotham, **1963** J.W.McFadden, C.Greslon, C.Pate, A.A.Pauwels, A.J.Nixon, A.L.Martin, A.R.Vokes, C.J.De Lange, C.W.Cullen, D.J.Finlayson, D.L.Perin, D.O.Peterson, D.Patch, D.R.Palmer, D.W.Johnson, D.W.Panoch, F.B.Bolte, G.D.Massingill, G.R.Lee, H.B.Vanroekel, H.D.Vancleave, J.F.La Crosse, J.J.Meyers, J.J.Toale, J.L.Ryan, L.C.Dooley, L.G.Cox, L.W.Wilson, M.L.Crain, P.W.Carman, R.A.Ryan, R.D.Stuber, R.F.Dale, R.H.Quade, R.L.Haines, R.L.Knosby, R.R.Verstraete, T.G.Baltisberger, T.Kespohl, T.R.Lang, W.A.Meyer Jr., W.J.Wittick Jr., A.D.Gilbert, D.G.Fender, G.S.Grgurich, J.M.Schmit, L.L.Wilkening, P.E.Armstrong, W.H.Houge, W.R.Werner, L.J.Walker, R.K.Brewster, R.R.Youmans, A.E.Hunter, D.R.Lipps, E.A.Simonson, H.L.Landrum, J.D.Lambert, J.T.Adamson, J.W.Defauw, L.D.Schrader, L.E.Gehn, L.G.Ballard, L.K.Stock, L.L.Mikkelsen, M.D.Young, M.L.Church, P.Vanderecken Jr., R.Baker, R.Fletcher, R.G.Ford, R.M.Rettig, R.P.Sumpter, R.Whipple, T.C.Thompson, T.C.Wells, W.S.Thorpe, D.J.Olson, D.R.Kloostra, R.H.Mann, W.A.O Connor, A.Mikita, D.C.Joblinske, D.F.Fisher, E.C.Leih, G.H.Verscheure, J.C.Geisler, L.L.Haskins, M.R.Fisher, J.C.Calligaro, B.H.Mumma, C.W.Lubke, D.O.Karenke, J.B.Alldredge, R.M.Stevenson, M.M.Aroza, B.L.Steel, L.R.Reinhardt, A.L.Harms, C.A.Bowman, C.W.Horner, C.W.Mullins, D.E.Beyhl, D.R.Coder, G.R.Little, H.F.Kilburn, H.K.Speckman, I.C.Rawson, J.A.Bartels, J.C.Lehr, J.L.Burgess, J.R.Schulz, J.R.Stow, J.Warren, L.D.Middleswart, L.E.Guerra, L.J.Jones, L.R.Scheff, L.T.Balmer, L.Z.Boswell, P.R.Ready, R.A.Townsend, R.E.Swanson, R.L.Miller, R.W.Jones, S.L.Carlson Sr., W.H.Despain, G.Vella, C.E.Thompson, B.J.Prince, C.L.Wright, F.T.Richardson, G.A.Stilwell, G.H.Davis, G.L.Hansen, G.L.Hodges, G.L.Koch, G.L.Noble, J.Prunty, J.R.Todd, M.Taylor, R.W.Walker, C.K.Shepard, F.D.Benson, G.G.Rupe, J.A.Schild, J.M.Murphy, J.R.Myers, L.L.Gulling, L.L.Malone, L.Proctor, R.D.Hatfield, R.E.Brooks, R.M.Ekstrand, W.H.Hall, D.A.Clark, D.D.Bengston, D.P.Cary, E.L.Garr, E.R.Twitchel, G.E.Larson, H.K.Childers, J.A.Durbin, J.D.King, J.E.Spires, J.L.Thompson, K.A.Hall, R.E.Dixon, R.J.Lehmkuhl, S.M.Hernandez, D.E.Porter, D.E.Sawyer, D.L.Karlix, D.L.Young, D.T.Smith, D.W.McQueen, H.W.Mc Clure, J.F.Karpan, K.A.Houzenga, L.B.Westemeier, L.H.Klotz, L.J.Kaalberg, M.D.Long, M.L.Yenger, S.C.Friedlein, C.W.Brandt, D.A.Crosser, E.E.Shields, G.J.Glidewell, J.A.Sanders, L.L.Johnson, M.D.Elliott, R.E.Miller, R.L.Backes, T.J.Ingold, T.M.Brobston, C.E.Wendorf, G.Boomershine, G.D.Shafer, H.W.Sellers, I.C.Jordan Jr., J.L.Greiner, J.L.Johnson, J.R.Garton Sr., L.D.Nichols, L.J.Price, L.L.Lawrence, P.L.Danielsen, R.R.Perry, T.M.Fuller, A.D.Dekeyrel, B.F.Miller, C.E.Scharer, D.A.Pedersen, D.M.Longdo, D.S.Traver, F.J.Vanoverberg, H.W.Brustkern, I.W.Koehn, J.D.Todalen, J.L.Powell, M.V.Cochran, R.C.Derifield, R.F.Plumley, R.G.Davison, R.P.Vandam, W.R.Trice, D.W.Rylander, F.J.Heskett, H.D.Boyer, H.G.Clark, L.Heckethorn, L.J.Carson, M.B.Darner, R.E.Sanders, A.J.Wirth, A.K.Walker, C.E.Mc Danel, C.L.Montgomery, C.T.Duffy, D.D.Fuerst, D.L.Snodgrass, F.E.Parker, F.M.Mc Coy, G.F.Leonard, G.V.Fisher, I.E.Lindstrom, J.D.Strader, J.P.Queener, K.S.Bunch, L.D.Detrick, L.N.Garrison, M.A.Peterson, M.W.Vavrosky, N.A.Mabeus, P.H.Boer, R.A.Swanson, R.W.Jones Sr., S.A.Thies, S.C.Dixon, V.A.Wells, W.L.Willhouse, B.W.Ethridge, D.M.Buckley, G.L.Lashbrook, K.C.Currie, L.D.Hanson, M.J.England, R.E.Morris, W.A.Frank, H.L.Roberts, H.W.Hocker, J.A.Garcia, J.G.Robb, J.V.Spooner, K.C.McIntyre, R.C.Gondocs, R.J.Vasquez, R.L.Volk, E.E.Larsen, L.M.Kirkpatrick, A.M.Wallin, D.D.Dixon, H.M.Rodell, J.G.Cooklin, J.L.White, J.W.Graham, R.E.Eckman, R.W.Harms, A.Ikeda, A.A.Sloan, A.L.Gray, C.A.Albertson, D.J.Ryan, F.D.Spaulding, G.A.Marsengill, H.A.Louden Jr., H.D.Geist, J.A.Franks, J.E.Bohnsack, J.E.Branch, J.R.Brown, K.E.Katzartones, K.R.Jones, L.A.Morris, L.D.Sloan, L.F.Thompson, L.L.Coble, L.Mincks, M.D.Atkins, M.E.Silvers, M.K.Wilson, N.V.Smith, P.D.Carruthers, R.A.Frantz, R.D.Allen, R.J.Crum, R.R.Doak, R.W.Inglis Jr., W.F.Bradshaw, W.G.Smith, W.L.Mundell, D.Barthon, D.L.Finger, F.M.Cole, G.D.Burkett, G.E.Tiemann, G.O.Ackerson, L.C.Albrecht, M.J.Eldridge, P.E.Moore, R.E.Ludin, V.E.Brown, V.E.Tidball, W.O.Ohearn, C.W.Farnam, C.W.Kinney Jr., D.H.May, D.J.Senn, D.V.Gehrke, E.E.Swanson, F.L.Verbeck, L.A.Christensen, M.G.Yelm, R.L.Lindemann, V.F.Fink, A.J.Hare, F.G.Scalf, J.N.Melton, R.H.Laxy, R.O.Johnson, S.H.Scalf, W.C.Foltz, J.Martinez, A.Carter, C.E.Franks, D.L.Demay, H.L.Armstrong, H.R.Dryoel, L.Westmorland, R.G.Dennhardt, R.L.Wisdom, A.S.Smemo, C.E.Turriff, C.L.Estes, C.M.Neely, D.A.Hayes, D.D.Nelson, D.E.Lundgren, D.E.Utterback, D.F.Dobbelare, D.H.Johnson, F.C.Barnett, G.R.Utzerath, J.E.Sampson, J.G.Blair, J.W.Caruth, K.C.Crisp, L.N.Ford, R.D.Finney, R.D.Hickenbottom, R.H.Duncan, R.L.Pettie, R.L.Vanzuyt, R.M.Sundquist, S.K.Ochsner, T.Kahley, T.R.Myers, W.B.Shreve, W.J.Kaller, A.Montenegro, J.M.Perez E., D.E.Trout, D.H.Odendahl, H.L.Adler, J.J.Beranek, J.T.Spurgeon, K.L.Noel, M.A.Mariman, R.L.Stockwell, A.T.Elas, B.L.Marcus, D.L.Anderson, L.Thomas, N.J.Yeager, R.F.Carroll, W.D.Thomson, G.L.Streitmatter, L.L.Richardson, M.L.Schriver, D.R.Peer, G.J.Stater, J.A.Corder, J.A.Linscheid, J.F.Carnahan, K.R.Johnson Jr., L.L.Lewis, L.L.Long, D.E.Anderson, G.A.Gatlin, G.N.Kern, J.H.Vanhoek, J.O.Ross, L.A.Mosher, R.A.Jones, R.C.Haesaert, R.M.Neyrinck, T.L.Reese, W.M.Coopman Jr., D.I.Patton, H.G.Gann, R.H.Raaen, R.M.Harp, V.E.Smith, W.H.Rupe, W.Harrington Jr., J.H.Holuba, W.P.Smith, F.Rodriguez, W.E.Hanna, R.E.Ohrberg, A.J.Berger, A.L.Headley, C.W.Kearse, J.E.Nelson, J.R.Kaster, L.J.Coopman, L.L.Pape, M.A.Anderson, M.D.Rigdon, M.W.Mason, R.D.Taylor, R.J.Huber, C.L.Sanders, H.C.Lenz, J.C.Joyner, J.D.Lenth, J.E.Abbott, J.H.Cassat, J.I.Hennenfent, L.F.Heyer, L.J.Dobereiner, R.L.Peeters, R.L.Westerfield, V.E.Edwards, V.H.Ramsey, W.J.Pannell, B.C.Harrison, H.P.Ware, N.D.Wright, R.L.Mc Call Jr., R.L.Riddell, F.J.Brophy, H.C.Pirtle, K.D.Schlepp, R.Fisher, A.E.Vest, B.M.Armstrong, C.F.Griffith, D.W.Lau, F.C.Toomey, F.L.Strong, G.A.Sax, I.M.Lane, J.A.Freed, J.C.Dellinger, J.R.Shadle, M.Dodson, S.R.Hiseler, W.E.Johnson, W.E.Mc Elroy, W.H.Hoffman Sr., D.McQueen, I.P.Gezel, J.F.Sullivan, P.R.Cathcart, R.R.Bartz, G.J.Prusa, G.R.Kipp, R.J.Pautvein, S.D.Lowther, P.G.Peterson, C.E.Brady, E.E.Weldon, L.W.Padavich, R.B.Gadow, R.C.Sanders, R.W.Talbot, W.R.Schultz, W.S.Lewis, N.J.Human, D.K.Shambaugh, M.Vanrycke, N.Caperchione, Q.McBride, J.L.Mattingly, D.G.Rockwood, J.D.Anderson, J.D.Waddle, J.I.Lange, W.G.Hock, D.M.Swaim, J.D.Kriskovic, J.E.Ulmer, J.W.Moore, L.J.Scieszinski, R.A.Sharp, L.D.Haufle, L.L.Eckstein, A.F.Rounds, B.N.Maring, D.L.Fink, L.W.Schatteman, R.D.Hays, R.E.Gaines, R.Police, F.Carter, G.M.Dejonghe, J.W.Wassenhove, R.D.Fuller, W.E.Kay, J.R.Sparrow, W.R.Kraklio, C.F.Neff, D.L.Helms, G.L.Pitzlin, J.A.Hudson, L.F.Schooley, R.A.Beil, R.J.Thompson, W.G.Klauck, B.F.Mace, L.J.McDonald, R.J.Rasmussen, S.R.Witt, D.L.Zippe, T.C.Watts Jr., A.L.Harter, C.E.Rowland, D.W.Smith, J.C.Britt, R.C.Worlow Jr., S.L.Watters, T.B.Sager,

W.D.Strayhorn, B.W.Wilson, C.E.White, D.C.Hampton, D.E.Lempke, E.W.Hippler, J.G.Foley, J.R.Rossie, L.D.Montgomery, L.D.Overton, L.D.Shreves, M.J.McKinney, P.C.Fransen, P.Sierra, R.K.Riley, S.Margelofsky, T.L.Lowe, B.Reichert, H.Mueller, F.W.Pettis, D.E.Smith, J.E.Scott, W.F.Lentz Jr., J.E.Magee, J.F.Oestreicher, E.E.Shewry, N.A.Rhodus, W.H.Long, E.Sandoval, J.E.Rieman, J.L.Krum, J.L.Kuehl, V.A.Wills, R.A.Marquardt, J.L.Fernandez, L.B.Stofflet, A.I.García, B.A.Landaal, A.D.Hudson, D.H.Hecht, D.J.Lee, D.L.Snyder, G.H.Clark, L.L.Traxson, L.L.York, M.Huseman, R.A.Gensch Jr., W.R.Margelofsky, W.W.Bunse, H.P.Kohler, J.E.Morney, G.Delagneau, V.Gonzalez C., C.G.Boyer, B.Huber, F.Fuehl, G.Kirchner, G.Pregizer, G.Wetz, H.Burkard, H.Eck, K.Hipp, N.Kaulbars, R.Schmitt, U.Pospisil, L.D.Haynes, R.H.Schneider, B.E.Fuller, H.W.Ehlbeck, L.E.Swindler, R.L.Noe, A.Barriopedro, B.C.Mc Donald, D.L.Freestone, D.W.Knight, F.Pierson, G.G.Krecklau, G.R.Vanthorre, I.M.Parsons, G.J.Lawyer, J.P.Mackey, L.Albone, L.J.Schrobilgen, O.J.Mc Farland, R.E.Pappas, A.Bardet, C.J.Johnson, K.E.Pauley, L.B.Spaeth, L.Lloyd, R.W.Hutchison, W.Johnson Jr., B.D.Allen, F.R.Mendoza, K.A.Gordon, W.C.Slocum, J.C.Dyer, J.H.Elliott, P.E.Wagner, S.M.Herrera, B.D.Booth, D.J.Park, G.L.Oberheu, J.B.Stainer, J.W.Stecher, L.A.Hillman, L.E.Allen, M.T.Phelan, R.D.Hansen, J.L.Archer, G.D.Heimendinger, G.F.Kelley, J.N.Winter, G.Le Jeune, M.B.Mulholland, R.M.Kitterman, L.McElrath, Y.Mercier, G.Holroyd, H.A.Ward Jr., H.D.Squires, J.D.Shipman, J.O.Bridger, J.W.Day, K.F.Weiland, L.F.Shaw, M.H.Ferretti, M.Hilton, S.E.Eli, T.R.McClure, C.Piccinato, H.A.Taylor, C.L.Chrisman, R.V.Carlson, L.Leveque, H.Piatt, D.L.Selindh, E.J.Aswegan, J.A.Brown, N.P.Kingston, S.L.Wyant, D.A.McGill, J.R.Gideon, T.S.Smith Jr., A.W.Johnson Jr., C.F.Ohnemus, D.E.Starkey, G.E.Christiansen, J.A.Larson, M.F.Smyth, R.A.Curry, R.E.Lee, S.L.Have, V.R.Janssen, W.B.Fowler, B.Alvarez , D.S.Huntrods, H.L.Burgess, R.D.Jacobsen, R.J.Lascurain, K.E.Matuseski, W.J.Graham Jr., J.D.Rolow, B.W.Wilkerson, D.E.Kline, J.M.Longval, L.W.Cofer, M.A.Allen, H.Robichet, G.P.Vetrecin, L.D.Harrison, N.N.Mtshali, K.P.Donovan, G.Andersson, L.Gauthier, C.A.Wagner, G.C.Waldon, G.E.Ruby, G.L.Nelson, H.K.Wilberding, J.A.Koch, J.A.Van Quathem, J.C.Mahnke, J.F.Baldus, L.L.Holland, M.C.Short Jr., M.R.Dhondt, R.L.Guss Sr., R.W.Eddleman, B.L.Neuendorf, D.A.Watt, R.L.Pratt, V.I.Flesher, J.Boyer, D.G.Cook, J.L.Skeel, L.A.Howlett, E.R.Algarbe, M.A.Paván, O.Waters, A.C.Korbel, E.A.Johnson, G.C.Einwalter, G.J.Williams, H.A.Rupnow, H.C.Wayson, H.F.Martens, J.J.Tuttle, J.M.Keller, J.R.Brotman, M.B.Lynch, R.J.Byrne, S.Herscovici, W.D.Fransen, W.K.Hulett, W.L.Krouse, R.A.Skromme, J.A.Sens, A.J.Kirsch Jr., D.I.Manor, E.M.Kueter, J.D.Anderson, J.E.Thompson, J.K.Ward, M.J.Gradert, O.E.Isaak, R.B.Johnson, R.H.Dahm, R.H.Strauch, R.L.Wheeler, R.N.Conzett, S.D.Thompson, W.H.Devriendt, W.J.Daack, J.L.Weber, G.L.King, T.R.Colburn, B.J.Nash, G.J.Ford, B.B.Cook, G.C.Streight, H.Von Langen, J.F.Wemhoener, L.G.Buss, M.Hoff, P.W.Keck, R.D.Weydert, R.E.Westman, B.B.West, B.A.Foster, C.E.Kainer, D.E.Wagner, D.L.Paul, E.R.Mathias, F.K.Farwell, J.D.Davis, J.T.Jansen, K.R.Burdick, L.D.Birkhead, R.R.Dirschel, R.R.Kuennen, T.L.Grooms, R.Rivera, G.Blète, J.Martin, R.Guitschula, C.Gigout, D.A.Ruch, J.F.Talak, R.L.Laird, J.Lamy, J.A.Sufficool, C.R.Penrose, A.R.Nelsen, F.P.Freese, J.H.Asmus, L.C.Gauer, L.R.Hathaway, R.J.Hennessy, G.F.Held, E.G.Trousil, G.Cavazzi, L.A.Baumhover, R.L.Van Zante, S.A.Tornes, D.Holland, E.H.Garrett, J.W.Morrison, P.L.Irwin, R.E.Hileman, V.R.Mercy, H.A.Kelly, K.M.Huffman, R.L.Henkel, L.F.Roth, D.L.Neises, F.Strosche, J.A.Flaherty, K.T.Sterwald, M.L.Wright, R.P.Noesen, G.D.Bishop, J.F.Thiede, D.H.Tesch, G.W.Franck, R.F.Billhymer, S.J.Westrom, D.Z.Russell, G.H.Millar, L.J.McNew, R.A.Clure, R.C.Ball, D.G.Bomleny, L.E.Bryant, S.Stewart, J.Nau, C.Boisot, G.Fresnel, B.K.Killion, D.D.Hanson, D.R.Blair, G.J.Fortsch, J.A.Rodgers, J.Tucker Jr., M.A.Kough, M.W.Long, R.D.Christensen, R.E.Petersen, R.Z.Whitfield, T.C.Rodgers, W.L.Brown, W.L.Shellhouse, H.E.Lammers, J.G.Mashek, J.L.Bown, J.W.Mc Namara, L.Keeling, R.P.Bruhn, R.R.Rosol, W.A.Studebaker, B.A.Carss, H.D.Happel, H.J.Eggers, H.R.Sadler, L.E.Olson, L.R.Graves, R.J.Rosol, V.A.Steva, F.Ptasnik, A.F.Wedemeier, C.P.Kelly, D.H.Semelroth, D.J.Bedard, D.L.Pope, E.H.Kaiser, E.W.Sallee, G.A.Mehl, H.L.Peters, J.E.Henderson, J.H.Anderson, J.H.Bushman, J.Mc Mahon, J.N.Wisdom, J.Nelson, L.J.Nielsen, N.L.Fernau, P.Swenumson, R.A.Giacobbe, R.D.Genz, R.L.Thompson, R.L.Ylitalo, S.Frizell, W.E.Spragg, W.H.Hilbert, W.M.Durst, W.W.Chesmore, F.C.Shattuck, H.O.Wiebel, J.W.Byam, M.H.Schraufnagel, R.V.Mangrich, S.J.Burns, R.Chamot, E.E.Nallick, J.T.Jessen, R.H.Andreasen, R.L.Jones Jr., R.L.Nelson, R.V.Quin, V.E.Parkes, C.L.Bucknell, C.L.Weitnauer, D.D.Van Ellen, F.A.Talbot, H.N.Frost Jr., M.M.Lowe, P.E.Jensen, R.D.Wake, A.H.Boglioli, R.Leraaen, A.C.Bierman, B.R.Hand, C.A.Countryman, D.M.Johannsen, D.W.Palmer, F.T.Cobb, G.Joens Jr., J.D.Price, J.K.Leach, J.L.Fillinger Jr., J.L.Shuh, O.Brown, P.M.Green, R.A.Davis, R.A.Vandello, R.D.Wason, R.E.Hopf, R.J.Davis Jr., R.S.White, T.E.Dreher, T.J.Weber, V.G.Floyd, W.E.Chandler, D.H.Bischoff, E.D.Sells, F.E.James, G.A.Even, G.E.Heuer, G.L.Hummel, J.L.Pyle, M.A.Frazier, R.E.Pierce, R.J.Clayton, D.E.Taylor, D.W.Brandt, E.L.Kite, F.L.Meyer, H.Wallican, J.A.Buerger, L.K.Hetherton, N.V.Duncan, R.C.Black, A.W.Testerman, C.E.Taylor, D.H.Gitzel, D.I.Bellmer, G.J.Kreger, H.E.Getty, J.D.Van Ree, K.E.Kanzenbach, L.E.Minks, P.C.Spencer, T.F.Weaver Jr., A.W.Hunemuller, D.L.Knittel, J.L.McCarthy, R.D.Bell, J.P.Nasello, D.D.Baker, D.E.Patterson, D.I.Kerr, G.D.Lane, H.J.Baier, J.L.Wise, P.H.Beattie Jr., R.D.Pierce, R.F.Levis, R.G.Powell, R.H.De Marce, R.H.Miller, V.A.Dietz, D.J.Albright, G.I.Harvey, L.L.Larsen, P.A.Fischer, P.J.Caperchione, R.H.Schroeder, R.J.Bender, R.J.Meier, W.D.Bogart, C.L.Walker, H.Jahnz, A.J.Cole, E.E.O'Dell, G.A.Degrande, J.A.Trunnell, J.C.Thomas, K.L.Smith, L.Berggren, R.A.Stapella, R.H.Jenney, S.A.Larsen, F.Bumpers, M.H.Lischak, M.L.Davis, A.H.Luedtke, C.L.Swank, D.Roman, E.Roeseler Jr., F.J.Gilbert, G.E.Cole, J.D.Dykes, J.D.Griffith, J.E.Hilton, J.T.Pannkuk, M.H.Baerwald, M.M.Kaye, R.A.Porter, R.G.Haigh, W.Heilmeyer, B.C.Everett, C.R.Stang, D.W.Manson, E.Reed, E.V.Needham, G.L.Lesch, J.E.Daniels, J.M.Quinones, J.Suarez, L.L.Schmidt, P.R.Quade, R.D.Eastlick, R.J.Kissel, M.Paysant, J.Wendl, U.Schmidt, J.L.Beasley, M.J.Fangman, D.L.Brown, R.D.Hauman, R.E.Keller, C.V.Anglese, H.G.Hoyt Jr., J.J.Ebert, R.D.Hartwig, R.L.Faria, R.T.Housholder, D.G.Kohl, G.A.Reif, J.L.Jones, J.P.Mc Carroll, J.Porter, M.C.Whitmire, M.F.Schultz, M.L.Snyder, G.W.Billerbeck, J.A.Kincaid, J.A.Wilberding, L.A.Woodbury, L.L.Meyer, R.J.Curry, D.L.Slininger, J.Alexander, R.R.Mc Laughlin, W.E.May, B.L.Hinkle, D.D.Seeger, D.J.Schulting, E.W.Wireman, J.D.Pabst, L.C.Becker, P.A.Gerhardt, R.C.Looper, R.E.White, R.F.Albrecht, R.G.Nelson, R.Lopez, S.A.Erickson, R.Blandin, A.L.Merritt, R.A.Creighton, W.L.Folken, D.J.Reuter, R.D.Sonnenburg, R.E.Phillips, A.Lacalle, K.A.Jensen, L.D.Tomkins, R.G.Nielsen, R.T.Kroeger, D.D.Phillips, J.R.Culver, R.E.Reveal, R.E.Wentz, S.Dwolinsky, W.Seelhammer, G.R.Walker, J.L.Sweet, W.R.Thompson, W.F.Herrmann, B.Loane Jr., C.L.Hurst, E.A.Skinner, G.L.Young, J.J.Seelhammer, J.M.Marchese, M.J.Eastman, R.E.Hasty, A.E.Ratute, D.C.Bolte, R.L.Stoffregen, A.J.Tedesco, C.C.Riley, G.E.Passig, H.W.Rolfs, J.D.Ramos, J.Goodman, J.R.Riojas, L.L.Macal, L.W.Fritz, M.B.Lawson, R.Compton, R.L.Lane, R.M.Romero, R.R.Winger, W.Thompson, D.A.Straw, D.G.Duckett, E.D.Littrell, J.E.Bolin, R.D.Jones, R.Doan, W.B.Harris, E.W.Bartz, J.I.Henderson, R.E.Stirm, S.F.Gehrke, D.Ferrari, C.R.Eveland, J.J.Majewski, J.Spear, R.E.Plung, R.J.Demuth, T.K.Held, C.E.Wolfe, E.J.Hawkes, G.R.Francis, J.J.Lund, P.Beaumont, W.Langner, B.K.Ruff, D.D.Petersen, D.L.Freese, F.E.Cambron, G.D.Shepherd, H.C.Monson, H.D.McConnell, J.L.Burch, J.M.Debord, J.P.Conicella, K.H.Westphal, K.R.Schaecher, L.D.Mishler, M.A.Forsyth, M.J.Glaudel, M.L.Gott, R.A.Stirm, R.J.Horn Jr., R.O.Finnie, S.S.Lopez Jr., T.V.Neuser, W.M.Pratt, P.Roger, C.F.Baranowski, D.C.Tisue, K.L.Carver, L.E.Shaubel, P.F.Mc Namara, W.D.Wahlberg, W.L.Gromm, A.O.Lancaster, D.L.Kepple, G.L.Larson, H.J.Penning, I.Kalinczak, L.Cross, L.D.Smith, R.D.Benhart, T.Gill, G.C.Wilson, J.J.Humble, W.K.Herrick, D.E.Eden, E.B.Hoosman, F.D.Haywood, J.H.Weisenberger, R.B.Martinez, R.H.Jaquith, V.L.Austin, W.G.Doss, A.H.Moreno, A.Metcalf Jr., D.P.Youngblut, E.A.Millen, G.L.Hansen, J.A.Napiwoski, J.R.Foltz, L.D.Mabe, L.L.Mitchell, M.J.Biederman, R.C.Fernald, R.J.Leatherman, R.M.Sprout, W.D.Borders, L.C.Colombini, J.C.Harper, J.R.Moeller, L.T.Hueitt, M.J.Searl, R.L.Baird, D.V.Patterson, F.W.Stayzer, G.L.Bisby, J.A.Plumb, R.H.Krahl, S.M.Lang, V.J.Dzekunskas, W.J.Hemminger, J.F.Nettles, L.D.Ramos, R.E.Fuller Jr., Z.H.Bowie, Z.H.Tinker, J.C.Rounds, M.Sanchez, R.A.Gomez, R.D.Steffeny, A.L.Hahn, D.D.Potter, D.J.Bovy, D.R.Margenthaler, D.W.Salisberry, G.A.Arch, G.E.Turner Jr., J.Koval, K.D.Krull, L.P.Murphy, N.S.Mott, R.A.Forrest, R.E.Helmick, R.G.Bachmann, R.Gemoll, R.J.Armstrong, R.W.Funk, T.H.Dorman, V.K.Carter, V.R.Knaack, W.M.Stanlake, B.O.Walls, D.C.Kingan, J.E.Minson, K.L.Cooper, M.L.Wexell, N.F.Paxton, R.E.Tague, R.L.Teeling, W.E.Lysell, D.E.Kuhn, E.E.Johnson, G.R.Steensgaard, L.J.Lopez Jr., P.L.Buckendahl, R.D.Nunemaker, R.J.Tholl, T.G.Dann, W.D.Holmes, E.Schares, J.R.Reading, J.T.Oliva, L.R.Anderson, M.G.Sturm, M.L.Woods, R.A.Holler, R.L.Phillips, R.M.Olmstead, S.R.Anderson, W.J.McKnight, W.L.Gentry, L.B.McCaw, C.C.Israel, J.Zuvic, N.J.Johnson, B.J.Bandelow, D.F.Jordan, D.K.Becker, E.G.Clark, G.J.Bailey, G.L.Brown, G.L.Larson, J.A.Boles, J.M.Roling, J.R.House, J.R.Jacobs, M.L.Nordholm, M.M.Lamantia, N.I.Zatorsky, R.D.Feaster, R.D.Reinier, R.G.Kell, R.L.Franke, R.P.Robinson, S.N.Knapp, V.C.Hansen, J.A.Coopman, A.J.Struss, C.H.Werner, D.A.Mc Gill, D.D.Jennings, D.D.Monteith, D.F.Pinter, D.L.Drewis, D.M.Bedard, D.R.Kruse, D.R.Lorenz, D.T.Schaefer, D.Willhite, F.Bernal, G.A.Goben, G.J.Smith, G.W.Traub, H.L.Cox, J.A.Thomas, J.D.Meester, J.Godsey, J.L.Dorn, J.L.Kroeger, J.L.Sproles, J.Lobeck, K.J.Brown, L.D.Fisher, L.E.Meirick, L.J.Delagardelle, L.L.Simmer, L.L.Stephens, L.N.Weingarten, L.R.Geiger, M.D.Sharer, M.E.Yordy, M.W.Schwickerath, N.H.Massey, R.D.Kennedy, R.Davenport, R.E.Mundt, R.E.Thurm, R.G.Struckman, R.H.Dunlap, R.K.Sandahl, R.L.Frost, R.L.Schmidt, R.O.Meinert, R.R.Bowling, R.Schroedermeier, R.T.Greene, R.Zrostlik, S.L.Snyder, T.D.Hall, T.F.Mahan, V.G.Heimbuck, V.W.Warren, W.E.Mosher, J.L.Gamez, C.Dwyer, C.H.Sundeen, E.O.Streich, G.J.Taylor, J.E.Van De Velde, J.M.Padavich, J.W.Webb, K.J.Frost, L.D.Ryckaert, M.W.Hogren, R.M.Parkhurst, A.J.Pagel, C.M.Butts, D.D.Kerner, D.E.Anderson, D.W.Trott, E.J.Kladivo, G.A.Young, H.E.Miller, J.W.Heineman, K.H.Hill, L.M.Poppe, N.H.Pryor Jr., R.D.Vandersee, R.E.Farrell, R.E.Rubendall, W.D.Gehlken, A.D.Shelton, C.J.Merrifield, C.R.Young, D.A.Creek, D.D.Degner, D.E.Webber, G.D.Titus, G.G.Gillette, H.E.Baker, H.E.Hoggard, I.L.Johnson, J.L.Ellsworth, K.W.Williams, L.Dierks, L.G.Bathen, M.E.Fisher, M.Luhring, M.V.Stout, R.A.Bowlsby, R.A.Lindner, R.F.Keim, R.W.Brown, W.L.Robinson, W.R.Lain, W.T.Hawn, D.H.Degeeter, E.F.Lawson, E.R.Miescke, G.L.Shaw, H.H.Warm, J.N.Howze, J.R.Sallee, M.R.Claus, R.C.Dean, R.F.Mellenthien, R.H.Sapp, W.A.Schneider, B.F.Pool, C.E.Leavell, C.G.Larson, C.W.Carlson, D.E.Abel, D.E.Husted, D.F.Fisher, D.G.Hutchings, E.J.Sturm, G.E.Sheldon, H.B.Brown, J.Bethurem, J.E.White, J.Mrzlak, J.S.Jordan, J.V.Levendusky, K.J.Radke, L.A.Frank, L.G.Porter, L.J.Stevens, L.T.Burke, M.L.Hofstadter, M.P.Siler, N.J.Schauls, R.A.Muenchow, R.L.Daniels, R.L.Fiebelkorn, R.L.Zimmerman, S.K.Monroe, T.R.Wendel, W.H.Walker, W.L.Kintzle, B.Scott Jr., C.J.Feggestad, D.A.Kulka, D.E.Pufahl Sr., D.G.Hansen, D.L.Hartman, G.Kienast, G.P.Pint, J.L.Gillett, J.W.Dunn, L.D.Hampton, M.E.Minikus, M.S.Ackerman, O.H.Carpenter, P.L.Snavely, R.Albertson, R.B.Glass Jr., R.J.Kruckenberg, R.L.Klomsten, R.L.Scott, W.L.Fischer Jr., W.Potter, C.L.Wilson, C.W.Duncan, D.C.Schroeder, D.Church, D.V.Breitkreutz, E.I.Kuhn, E.Merritt, F.H.Glaser, G.L.Fornero, G.R.Rickert, G.T.Anderson, H.J.Moller, J.A.Coppejans, J.N.Hunter, K.D.Campbell, K.W.Schwake, M.E.Stewart, M.J.Kurtenbach, M.M.Sloan, N.C.Shileny, R.A.Dirck, R.A.Olsson, R.G.Schuler, S.M.Spears, T.C.Dodge, T.F.Van Ee, C.C.Happel, C.D.Reed, C.S.Meyers, D.R.Kresser, G.R.Fish, K.G.Malone, L.D.Kibbee, L.E.Minikus, L.L.Brubaker, M.O.Wersinger, R.C.Hildebrand, R.J.Stuard, R.L.Smith, T.J.Wright, W.L.Hunter, W.L.Lockey, D.A.Wessels, E.E.Wehde, E.L.Seemann, E.S.Hickey, G.D.Witzel, G.Hart, J.L.Bond, L.A.Wheeler, R.G.Debuysere, R.G.Paxton, R.M.Burfield, R.W.Foss, V.L.Seedorff, C.W.Moser, D.E.Farland, D.J.Hagedorn, D.L.Drewelow, D.L.Schutte, D.M.Rumley, E.K.Johnson, F.Cantu, F.F.Sloan, J.E.Bryant, J.F.Bisbee, J.J.Melichar, J.M.Keleher, J.W.Rodts, K.Schultz, M.A.Andersen, M.A.Maddox, M.D.Rowe, M.D.Williams, P.M.Gramling, R.L.Walline, R.L.Whiteside, R.R.Engle, R.R.Helmers, S.Galvan, S.M.Hackett, A.E.Classen, C.L.Franks, C.M.Strobbe, C.Meyer, D.E.Bartels, E.E.Ersch, G.W.Hall, I.F.Hendrix, J.R.Hiatt, J.R.Holder, L.A.Brincks, L.H.Pietan, L.W.Stewart, M.E.Ballard, R.H.Douglas, R.L.Redmond, W.A.King, A.S.Hagberg, C.E.Cranston, C.L.Martin, D.M.Anderson, D.P.Genung, D.R.Lauritzen, G.C.Glass, H.A.Olson, J.A.Hupf, J.D.Lammert, J.I.Gonzalez, L.E.Newswander, L.J.Bjortomt, M.R.Kreger, R.B.Mullan, R.Bruce, R.E.Gramling, T.L.Barnhart, T.L.Snyder, D.A.Paar, D.I.Nance, D.K.Taylor, D.P.Fencl, G.D.Hatfield, J.H.Sproul, J.J.Wisely, J.P.Armbruster, K.R.Mervin, L.C.Babeu, L.D.Hartman, M.J.Unterscheidt, N.W.Braun, P.L.Klingenborg, R.L.Koontz, W.D.Zamzow, W.L.Duncan, G.A.Carstens Jr., J.L.Boomgarden, J.R.Foister, A.H.Baraks, A.M.Kreitzman, D.Crisp, D.J.Thome, D.L.Seemann, F.P.Hardy, J.A.Michael, M.E.Harris, N.C.Blanck, R.D.Rader, R.J.Flaherty, W.A.Meyer, W.C.Klavon, D.W.Stromquist, H.S.Rahn, J.M.Darling, L.E.Loeck Jr., S.R.Nelson, W.Borachok, L.L.Ferch, **1964** M.Robert, A.D.Perkins, A.L.Haars, D.F.Etringer, D.G.Coburn, D.L.Anderson, D.L.Newcom, D.W.Hixson, E.G.Heston, F.D.Johnson, F.N.Crockett, G.N.Donel, J.D.Britt, J.J.Buzzard, J.J.Surr, J.L.Millage, J.L.Sternberg, J.M.Anderson, L.A.Neyrinck, L.P.Block, L.R.Plumley, P.N.Durham, R.A.Usher, R.E.Gillman, R.F.Ashenhurst, R.J.Mensen, R.L.Kincade, S.J.Greshay Jr., V.A.Jordan, W.C.Frisby, E.Krumteich, A.Diaz-Teran, D.L.Rear, D.R.Hammond, G.L.Stephenson, J.E.Cronkleton, L.L.Schultz, R.A.Puder, R.D.Trueg, R.L.Strelow, D.A.Jenkins, D.A.Wertish, D.M.Smiddy, D.M.Wolf, E.Adams, G.A.Papish, G.J.French, I.L.Winter, J.L.Ewoldt, J.L.Gray, J.M.Stanford, L.J.McKee, L.J.Ross, L.L.Arlt, R.Booth, R.L.Albert, R.L.Gravitt, R.R.Rennick, S.L.Lovelace, W.T.Tribbett, C.Duckett, D.N.Ayres, G.G.Brooks, H.A.Kuehl, H.A.Wegman, J.Fennern, J.L.Chambers, K.M.Lane, L.Walden, R.F.Wessels, R.L.Hampton, S.W.Kleiss, T.Vandekerckhove, C.E.McCaffery, E.R.Ryan, F.H.Wille, G.E.Borchardt, G.M.Lombarczki, L.D.Plumb, P.T.Doocy, R.G.Wilburn, R.S.Lewis Jr., F.Galan, A.H.Ryder, D.D.Perry, E.C.West, E.W.Liverance, H.Babers, I.B.Ericson, L.J.Tiedt, P.H.Reiter, R.C.Humphrey, R.R.Koch, R.W.Miller, T.J.Vesey, V.R.Montgomery, A.Marcuzzi, A.C.Campagna, C.K.Holke, C.L.Newman, J.B.Galloway, J.L.Zubak Jr., M.F.Loomis, R.E.Day, A.I.Gonzalez, B.L.Carruthers, C.H.Lewis, D.H.Kueker, G.R.Gunderson, J.C.Case, J.C.Stewart, J.E.McCallan, J.H.Bennett, J.T.Smith, J.W.Frakes, K.J.Sturtewagen, L.A.Brinksneader, L.E.Hale, M.R.Byrne, N.H.Schoonover, P.E.Berger, S.G.Vallejo, V.J.Papish, M.Diaz De Mera, A.L.Mangler, D.E.Duncan, D.E.Herring, E.E.Christy, E.J.Magedanz, F.E.Giese, H.A.Peterson, H.H.Guenther, H.M.Stach, J.F.Becker, K.E.Smith, R.G.Guzman, R.J.Johnson, S.G.Hansen, A.L.Vanwinkle, D.J.Wilken, D.L.Hacker, L.N.Schares, M.H.Foster, O.E.Grimes, R.L.Lund, R.W.Kemmerer, C.C.Weber, C.F.Dulin, D.E.Pruett, I.Carter Jr., L.E.Peter, M.L.Stulir, R.D.Moller, R.J.Knobloch, R.W.Lawrence, P.Haro, A.D.Clementz, D.A.Brandt, J.D.Hanson, K.C.Roever, W.C.Kimball, W.D.Hamblin, B.J.Mills, B.L.Edwards, C.E.May Jr., C.Heidt, E.C.Pinnick, E.Dickerson, E.L.Griffin, E.W.Hollyfield, F.C.Cullor, G.H.Bahlmann, J.C.Jennings, L.J.McCauley, L.L.Minteer, P.M.Gust, R.A.Schmitz, R.J.Dano, R.L.Sage Sr., R.L.Schmitz, T.N.Nipper, O.R.Lamboglia, L.Perez, A.G.Gottfried, D.E.Ames, R.G.Frayle, R.J.Martin, F.Rivera, A.Rossell, D.E.Mullins, G.D.Rushing, G.E.Morelock, J.A.Peterson, J.M.Osborn, L.E.Hanson, R.D.Hines, A.E.Fritch, B.W.Peterson, C.A.Wubben, G.D.Lumley, J.R.Flaig, L.A.Brimeyer, L.L.Wright, M.G.Tollenaer, M.L.Dierks, P.Jimenez , A.J.Vandriessche, E.B.Pauley, G.L.Koeller, M.F.Murphy, M.Marin, C.L.Gargano, D.C.Hungate, E.C.Mayne, E.W.Telkemeyer, F.R.Bries, L.E.Edwards, M.K.Pace, R.A.Rannals, R.E.Johnson, R.M.Banks, W.P.Ruigrok, E.Garcia H., G.Quiroga, B.J.Griffith, D.L.Flaherty, J.L.Jones, J.L.Wilson, P.J.Hurley, J.Avila, V.Cambronero, E.M.Leeser, F.C.Krambeck, J.Linz, W.L.Glasgow, R.Dominguez, V.Calero, C.R.Betts, D.J.Woehl, G.K.Dittmar, J.L.Johnson, J.L.Kraus, M.D.Davis, J.Macias H., D.A.Holmes, L.M.Mc Collough, M.Torrejon, O.Boehnisch, B.A.Greer, D.A.Billmeyer, D.J.Hentges, E.J.Foss, F.J.Parker, F.T.Schulte, G.W.Simpson, J.C.Martin, J.H.Peiffer, M.J.Lahey, P.N.Exstrom, R.G.Dix, R.J.Lier, R.W.Hook, T.G.Katch, P.Menegaux, A.Perez F., C.Aguilar , J.R.Escudero, L.Garcia G., P.Dorado, J.Downer Jr., J.F.Schildgen, J.L.Hughes, J.O.Cotant, L.H.Buseman, P.E.Rettig, P.R.Klein, R.K.Schmidt, R.P.Smith, F.Ramos, D.L.Earnest, G.H.Lammers, H.A.Stubbs, J.H.Stewart, J.J.Pancrazio, J.M.Vogelsberg, J.R.Taylor, L.C.Manternach, R.E.Sprouse Jr., R.J.Arensdorf, R.L.Pickett, R.W.Leopard, W.L.Shrum, M.Sanchez V., A.Williams, D.B.Wood, G.L.Johnson, R.C.Good, R.D.Clevenger, R.Taylor, R.Martin A., J.Izquierdo, A.Martin G., A.L.Lassman, B.N.Wampler, C.B.Thiltgen, C.H.Olson Jr., D.D.Wingerter, E.A.Kurt, E.J.Stoltz, F.T.Langkamp, G.G.Steger, G.V.Ruiz, J.E.Smead Jr., J.L.Sorrell, J.P.Werner, J.R.Seefeldt Jr., J.V.Norman, L.G.Herman, L.J.Wagner, M.E.Townsend, P.A.Reuter, R.D.Burkart, R.D.Seibert, R.G.Maas, R.J.Vanderah, R.Pellock, W.D.Gillman, W.J.Tindell Jr., B.Lerasle, A.Diaz Del V., A.Hernandez B., P.Martin A., F.E.Koob, G.A.Pond, G.W.Demont, J.B.Schmitz, J.J.Lauzon, R.N.Hingtgen, F.Granados, T.Martinez D., D.B.Bullerman, E.A.Christiansen, G.F.Gindling, J.A.Charley, K.A.Biermann, K.K.Vail, A.Garcia P., A.W.Morris, D.L.Cook, E.A.Frick Jr., R.F.Vroman, J.E.Gibbs Jr., D.H.Steele, D.J.Van Cleave, D.P.Gleason, E.J.Weber, J.W.Lien, K.O.Ellison, M.Anderson, M.J.Jefford, M.Mendoza, N.Seering, O.Tronetti, P.Venditti, R.A.Volker, T.R.Johnson, V.J.Urlacher, R.Fabre, M.Bardet, C.C.Gray, D.Howard, E.E.House, J.E.Gordon Jr., K.Dietrich, D.L.Westemeier, F.V.Yost, G.F.Zweibohmer Jr., J.R.Cole, A.G.Ashpaugh Sr., H.L.Phillips, J.E.Solomon, J.H.Gallagher, J.W.Stewart, R.L.Shoemaker, I.Matas, D.E.Mather, D.I.Whitebreast, R.E.Leedy, A.J.La Fontaine, D.E.Johnson, D.H.Quillin, D.R.Crouse, E.P.Genochio, E.R.Breitsprecker, E.S.Pinck, G.C.Grutz, G.E.Strieder, H.R.Drummond, H.R.Rumbaugh, J.E.Metz, J.Springer, L.E.Bos, L.J.Kringle, L.L.Lewis, L.R.Luick, L.Vasey, M.A.Ramsey, P.L.Schroeder, R.A.Ingles, R.A.Zimmerman, R.C.Lavalley, R.D.Robinett, R.V.Rittgers, W.C.Brookens, V.Roncero, C.G.Tragord, M.F.Brimeyer, M.Gustafson, N.M.Hill, P.H.Koopmann, R.H.Nesteby, A.Gonzalez, D.I.Glider, D.L.Mefferd, E.L.Smith, J.R.Cooley, K.J.Comer, R.H.Hufford, D.E.Swearingen, E.Robinson III, R.L.Weber, A.J.Digman, E.L.Noland, F.D.Neubauer, G.D.Richmond, G.H.Larson, J.A.Mineff, J.T.Grant, J.W.Baker, K.J.Millius, L.G.Carter, L.J.Stingley, P.S.Binder, R.J.Klein, R.McCorkle, T.E.Daxon, W.L.Cousins, R.Froto, M.Henrio, A.Martin G., J.J.Downing, R.B.Williams, J.B.Neis, E.Wilson, J.E.Straetker, L.C.Mattson, A.J.Bull Jr., E.Pizano, G.R.Marty, J.E.Hanes, J.J.Schroeder, J.T.Butson, L.L.Kemp, P.V.Griffin, R.J.Wilming, W.E.Carter, W.P.Johll, D.P.Bergstrom, R.L.Westemeyer, W.F.Long, M.W.Nelson, P.J.Franks, D.T.Sorlie, M.Klocker, F.Thomas, G.R.Stauffer, J.E.Butson, A.W.Roenfeld, C.A.Rittenhouse, D.C.Iverson, D.D.Boston, D.Goodman, D.J.Hoch, J.E.Mac Holz, J.W.Nason, K.A.Hollatz, L.H.Miller, P.D.Breitbach, S.C.Victory, W.E.Hull, Y.Soehnlen, M.Magnin, J.Palomino, D.V.Garrett, E.G.Harwick, H.H.Hill, P.D.Rupp, R.E.Garner, S.Jenkins, L.E.Cuassolo, P.Maiwald, A.M.Finch, M.Williams, R.E.Lee Jr., S.R.McIntyre, L.Manzanares, A.J.Copeland, B.J.Bergren, R.A.Williams, S.Fay, G.J.Foley, L.Woods, A.Rodriguez M., A.R.Ravera, C.E.Leppert, C.J.Robey, D.E.Crawford, D.E.Johnson, F.W.Keck, G.J.Sahm, G.W.Strawhacker, H.W.Northcraft Jr., J.C.Pitzen, J.J.Riley Jr., J.W.Woodrum, K.C.Lewis, L.L.Harbarger, N.J.Hawker, R.A.Ritt, R.M.Lain, T.C.Maas, W.F.Kluesner, W.K.Kolstead, R.Dressler, C.D.Gernant, E.L.Wood, N.B.Fries, W.D.Peach, J.L.Phelps, V.Benito, G.J.Finn, C.L.Shaffer, D.A.Lueken, D.E.Dilley, D.R.Lansing, G.M.Stolley, J.P.Deaton, L.A.Doll, L.A.Ohea, M.E.Hoch, P.A.Ruh, R.D.Wernimont, R.L.Woodhouse, R.N.McClelland, R.W.Fuson, J.Suarez, A.D.Bengert, A.L.Behncke, F.G.Allen Jr., G.R.Dube, H.G.Larson, J.A.Robinson Jr., J.B.Bivens, J.Cleat, J.V.Hilby, M.T.Meaney, R.C.Rose, R.Robb, H.Magnier, J.Zefirini, S.Tedesco, M.Lemaire, A.Naeckel, B.Herfert, G.Hassinger, H.Scheid, J.Wolf, K.Gab, K.Loos, O.Becker, C.J.Haupert, D.H.Garner, D.J.Brimeyer, R.L.Dennhardt, S.R.Williams, T.W.Banfield, F.R.Rueda, L.Lamo De, B.E.Lampe, C.E.Mairet, D.G.Pestotnik, D.G.Winters, G.A.Kaiser, G.J.Driscoll, K.H.Blackwood, O.R.Bandy, R.E.Matthews, R.M.Rudolf, R.S.Loomis, R.Tiffany, S.D.Vogt, W.G.Gaber, W.H.Duenser, W.R.Deutsch, B.Kuntz, E.Montag, F.Mehrer, H.Prudlik, R.Klemm, W.Muy, B.F.Hill, F.Spurgetis, G.E.Roepsch, J.W.Wickersham, P.F.Baker, D.K.Schrobilgen, J.J.Ball, R.E.Eppler, R.L.Noppe, A.Gelineau, L.Martin P., D.J.Jerrett, H.N.Baker, W.C.Pollock, J.Esparcia, M.Urrutia, A.Triviño, D.F.Ryan, D.F.Schultz, D.G.Schueller, D.J.Jack, E.J.Johnson, J.E.Robbins, J.J.Hogue, K.M.Stclair, L.A.Aultman, L.R.Rogers, N.F.Rohlinger, R.A.Amerling, R.E.Goebel, R.F.Caldwell, R.Lindquist, T.A.Hanson, T.J.Roling, R.Loeches, C.Z.Sheldon, E.J.Konrardy, F.Leon, H.J.Stohlmeyer, J.A.Kasenberg, J.E.Jenkins, C.M.Graves, D.J.McDonnell, E.R.Moyers, L.E.Daebelliehn, R.W.Lewis, A.Donoso, C.J.Callahan, G.E.Boehm, J.W.Ross, R.R.Herrick Jr., G.Durand, F.Gonzalez S., L.D.Tisor, W.L.Wallace, H.Burgueño, A.A.Meersman, C.E.Palmer, C.J.Lee, C.M.Herburger, D.A.Doubleday, D.L.Willett, D.W.Griffin, F.F.Armstrong, H.L.Eggers, J.B.McIntosh, J.J.Vandevoorde, K.A.Bolton, K.S.Minard, P.D.Hillyer, R.R.Geiger, S.E.Bayne, Y.Baillargeaux, D.M.Briggs, F.E.Singleton, G.G.Oteri, G.L.Palmer, K.G.Roesner, R.A.Demeulenaere, W.D.Schramm Jr., A.C.Boland, C.J.Vanpelt, G.J.Breiholz, M.A.Maule, A.Notario, J.L.Romitti, J.N.Hall, J.P.Raymond, R.A.Kutsch, H.O.Garis, J.Noblot, T.J.Vosberg, C.E.Dogs, C.W.Hay, D.L.Apland, D.M.Boffeli, E.D.Engleen, G.A.Oliver, H.F.Jackson, J.H.White, J.M.Nolan, K.F.Crum, L.J.Konzen, R.D.Wing, V.R.Sheth, V.R.Soat, W.L.Stoffel, W.Peterhoff, B.Landre, G.Duval, J.Morning Jr., G.E.Brown, G.L.Henry, L.L.Hoff, R.D.Cole, C.J.Owens, T.L.Meyers, J.M.Portillo, A.Malet, A.E.Ficzere, B.H.Soat, D.R.Cummings, E.G.Turner, G.D.Eklof, G.J.Clark, H.N.Williams, L.P.Sands, R.E.Burgstrum, R.K.Hakanson, J.Gallet, R.Moulin, R.Pate, J.M.Yarza, A.W.Ward, F.J.Dillard, L.E.Melssen, A.C.Alvather, M.K.Roman, R.D.Hindbaugh, A.L.Twitty, D.F.Henson, G.L.Natwick, J.H.Hostert, L.F.Krueger, L.F.Lovell, P.R.Jackson, D.A.Freiburger, D.L.Christisen, H.G.Bennitt, J.P.Rice, K.M.Kurtz, L.J.Roth, L.L.Marcue, R.S.Chynoweth, M.Savestre, J.N.Thurston, W.L.Rettenmeier, M.Baudu, A.Herranz, E.J.Vaassen, J.E.Quail, R.Pouilly, G.Garcia G., C.A.Connolly Jr., C.S.Bourell, D.L.Raue, H.D.Edwards, J.C.Patzner, K.L.Wishmeyer, L.L.Reed, M.E.Haptonstall,

Dealers checking out new Generation II tractors at Deere Day, Dallas, 1960

R.E.Johnson, T.J.Meyer, J.E.Hine, N.A.Rogers, P.U.Birkett, R.Dumont, C.M.Meyer Willson, L.I.Nickles, G.E.Leibengood, C.D.Hosting, C.L.Loeffelholz, G.L.Brewer, J.P.Grice, L.L.Mayne, L.W.Woodard, M.G.Meyer, P.J.Droessler, R.E.Kohagen, R.J.Pink, S.J.Magnuson, T.E.Bode, W.G.Sherk, B.L.Pomrenke, J.A.Cantu, J.G.Correa, L.C.Owens, E.R.Zucca, A.Rubalcaba, A.M.Reeves, C.J.Walker, C.M.Agar, D.L.Burrough, G.K.Gellerstedt, G.P.Osterhaus, G.W.Burau, H.O.Ullrich, J.D.Spuller, J.L.Klein, L.Modlin, N.R.Lindell, P.A.Roberts, R.W.Blok, S.J.Bryan, W.E.Heller, W.L.Mochal, W.P.Whiting, G.Favache, G.Hutteau, J.Sans, D.Kiefer, J.Ochoa, A.J.Resch, D.A.Fausch, D.A.Johnson, G.T.Lopez, J.Fulbrook, R.J.Vandermeulen, R.W.Brass, A.L.Sloan, C.E.Skinner, D.G.Haegeman, G.H.Chatterton, H.P.Keller, J.E.Drury, J.P.Wolford, C.Calvillo, L.E.Brim, R.J.Phillips, E.E.Reasby, G.A.Lohmann, G.R.Schoen, I.Martinez, J.A.Driscoll, J.H.Kos, N.L.West, P.M.Nelson, R.E.Lohse, R.L.McCracken, R.R.Sovey, R.W.Curry, S.D.Schroder, T.E.Hitzhusen, T.J.Hibbs, R.Salle, C.J.Steffen, E.L.Watkins, L.M.Jackson, M.H.Scott, W.C.McCarty, R.A.Patters Jr., J.G.Valerio, J.T.Romero, J.M.Ibarra, M.Martinez , N.Revuelta, B.J.Burnett, B.W.Cottrell, C.A.Swanson, C.L.Klages, D.K.Hillery, D.L.Carolan, G.Bontems, G.M.Thorn, G.T.Frimml, G.T.Herling, J.C.Baker, J.L.Clements, L.C.Radke, L.E.Kafer, M.G.Bayer, P.M.Morris, R.A.Rymer, R.F.Laleman, R.L.Kaukaskie, R.McKinnon, W.L.Starks, R.Vignaud, G.Schulte, D.J.Michalek, G.C.Swanson, G.M.Higham Jr., L.D.Hotchkin, N.D.Malone, R.E.Mixer, V.L.Heller, W.D.Fields, R.De La Encina, G.L.Even, J.A.Meyer, L.D.Nimrick, R.L.Bieri, V.D.Haverdink, C.D.Cruz Jr., B.W.Conklin, A.E.Lundstrom, B.Coverdill, B.L.Burrows, D.H.Patterson, E.L.Wegscheid, H.J.Luth, M.L.Monson, M.V.Cunningham, W.C.Busby IV, W.M.Wilkins, A.Foussadier, A.P.Carius, G.K.Weese, S.H.Schlung, J.Bravo, L.F.Weinrich, L.P.Ambrosy, R.H.Walline, R.L.Postel, R.O.Michels, A.Esquivias, A.Garcia C., E.Del Barco, G.W.Madsen, H.E.Stiles, R.D.Thorpe, R.Klundt, A.Rodriguez M., J.D.Keil, A.Tapia, D.F.Hess, E.A.Handrow, E.Alexander, J.E.Dowler, P.V.Vantieghem, R.Greinert, D.L.Carey, W.E.Yeager, C.A.Whitmyer, D.P.Demaine, J.E.Squibb, I.Fretti, R.Henquinet, A.Chancibault, M.Rousseau, A.Merino, C.R.Detombe, D.H.Park, D.L.Ballard, G.G.Kenniker, H.W.Pollock, J.B.Hawbaker, J.C.Draper, J.L.Wright, M.G.Green, R.Burlingame, R.E.La Coste, R.L.Wood Jr., R.W.Porter, D.Martin, W.Andres, E.A.Blanco, E.Snipes, J.J.Smith, R.J.Bartels, S.G.Gulyash, G.Andre, J.A.Rodriguez G., J.E.Tomlinson, A.Perales, A.T.Buckley, D.J.Ray, D.R.Kruse, J.R.Calloway, K.A.Schikaneder, K.C.Penrod, L.P.Klein, R.E.Kottke, R.J.Kluesner, T.L.Roets, F.Barbero, G.Reder, I.Represa, L.C.Simoens, J.Aubourg, D.M.Gonzalez, I.D.Riese, J.B.Agness, J.G.Gingras, L.C.Marshall, G.Le Deist, R.Roche, G.T.Reavis, W.L.Breselow, J.Lange, V.L.Clemons, D.F.Bobholz, R.L.Lindsley, S.E.Williams, J.J.Stanton, J.R.Moede, L.L.Anderson, R.D.Hentrich Sr., R.H.Rassmann, R.L.Zuelsdorf, R.G.Litton, R.W.Kohn, G.D.Brewer, J.R.Hull, M.W.Kriebel Sr., W.L.Reifsnider, F.Voss, R.C.Dutton, R.C.Mowery, R.E.Hipkins, D.D.Hanson, B.Feldmann, B.A.Verscha Jr., D.F.Shepard, D.H.Lake, D.L.Stifel, F.C.Julian, G.T.Haas, H.L.North Jr., L.C.Ewert Jr., L.H.Trout, M.W.Anderson, N.E.Klatt, P.G.Anderson, R.C.Kurtz, R.L.Rumph, S.L.Wright, M.Bidault, G.A.Vandevoorde, J.H.Barnes, R.J.Ollerini, S.R.Shinafelt, W.L.Stabler, C.L.Schanfish, M.C.Ludwig, N.B.Scrowther, R.W.Huneke, D.R.Mengel, J.M.Coopman, M.J.Medley, R.K.Guenther, T.M.Mossage, W.E.Barry, B.F.Runyon, B.Roux, D.D.Pollesch, D.H.Sheldon Jr., D.J.Gladfelter, D.R.Waite, G.J.Marsch, G.W.Hoffman, H.L.Braker, H.R.Becker, J.L.Mosteller, K.E.Spidle, L.H.Rassmann, L.Segura, R.E.Engstrom Jr., R.F.Andreassen, R.G.Stewart, R.J.Ekin, R.R.Kahlhammer, R.W.Schultz, W.H.Kemman, W.P.Verbout, W.R.Barnes, M.Grand, B.E.Lavell, J.C.Peveler, M.J.Smedema, A.H.Schauer Jr., D.L.Versluys, J.T.Becks, R.P.Compean, J.G.Correa, W.D.Langley, C.H.Thomas, D.Dejaeger, D.M.Kochuyt, F.P.Meyer, G.G.Miller, G.N.Hingtgen, J.R.Pletkovich, J.R.Terry, L.J.Herrman, M.L.Hofstetter, M.R.Hanifen, M.R.Scarpino, R.J.Gustafson, R.M.Cousins, R.W.Ziemer, S.M.Buenzow, W.C.Johnson, W.R.Hertzer, C.Cardot, W.A.Uphold, W.E.Hawotte, O.S.Bernal, S.E.Benner, W.A.Lynn, W.T.Lee, M.Senot, L.E.Nunn, R.E.Brown, A.J.Ganem, C.Kespohl, D.W.Van Hook, E.A.Cook, E.J.Schmidt, G.W.Gunter, H.E.Rogers, J.C.Rechek, K.E.Colman, P.D.Springfield, R.D.Wade, R.L.Harris, R.W.Spencer, W.Blue, M.Lioult, K.L.Crutcher, M.J.Rankin, N.J.Green, R.G.Raymond, W.Moore, D.L.Portugue, E.J.Froberg, F.J.Frost, J.D.Mullarkey, M.E.Sales, R.L.Kraklio, J.R.Bennett, M.Smith Jr., O.B.Laufenberg, E.Ornelas, C.A.Randol, C.A.Ringle, H.J.Bowman, J.E.Shradar, J.Kompolsek, E.Roveretto, K.Fischer, D.W.Curtis, E.G.Schatzline, E.R.Whitmire, G.F.Willging, G.N.Davison, J.M.Keemle, L.E.Wheat, L.Knapp, R.L.Seim, R.R.Bull, W.F.Klier, W.R.Kemp, A.P.Isaguirre, D.Robert, M.Mathe, N.Thenault, B.Doisneau, B.Gaidot, J.Laget, W.Halm, J.A.Maffie, J.C.Bell, K.M.Hotchkin, R.E.Gordon, R.V.Gonzalez, J.Dokas, I.V.Scotta, D.Foulon, J.Lesage, A.B.McClain, C.R.Bening, D.Dee, D.E.Long, D.L.Apple, D.T.Vanarnam, E.L.Raddatz, J.E.Perry, J.H.Berns, J.J.Healy, J.R.Kerner, L.C.Engling, N.N.Manders, R.I.Sellon, R.L.Perdue, S.R.Graves, T.J.Adam, W.E.Molle, W.M.Gillespie, D.K.Litton, F.G.Pena, K.K.Clark, R.D.Powell, R.F.Mahan, R.J.Huber, R.L.Watters, D.E.Hufford, J.O.Waite, R.Liard, D.A.Shade, G.F.Weydert, L.K.Popp, R.L.Cottrell, J.Gombault, B.J.Westover, J.E.Stanley, M.G.Neitzel, R.F.Furlong, R.L.Watters, T.B.Gates, A.W.Thompson Jr., G.Cornish, J.R.Smrcina, L.C.Foltz, W.G.Coward, W.H.Miller, C.J.Frederick, H.L.Acridge, L.W.Davis, R.A.Abler, R.E.Carlson, T.D.Simpson, C.A.Clark, R.E.Farrey, C.D.Birkett, C.G.Greve, C.L.Hellmann, C.W.Kent, D.E.Havener, G.L.Jochum, J.M.Schears, J.W.Linden, L.W.Lange, P.C.Mejia, R.C.Claussen, R.C.Polakowski, R.R.Wolf, G.Lolivier, C.Lopez, J.H.Gross, L.W.Moore, M.R.Lindell, D.G.Vree, E.J.Graham, L.G.Mueller, L.L.Ziebell, N.G.Fensterman, S.E.Hornback, M.J.Martin A., A.J.Vant Hoff, B.J.Hawks, C.J.Webb, C.R.Franks, D.E.Hansell, G.W.Walker, J.J.Nenadovich, R.F.Burns, W.G.Droessler, D.A.Hofstetter, F.E.Hickman, J.E.Pearson, F.J.Gallego, M.Calvo, E.Gidoin, A.F.Grebe, A.H.Saele, A.W.Pauli, E.C.Plotts, H.Esser, J.R.Marsh, L.F.Bornhoeft, R.J.Weygandt, R.R.Schmitt, J.Lamoureux, C.Gougeon, H.Schumacher, S.Huether, G.Lemaire, C.A.Sherk, D.F.Senska, D.L.Gregory Sr., D.M.Abbott, J.B.Hutchison, J.G.Meylink, M.C.Mueller, P.Wing, R.H.Vlach, J.Foulon, V.Moreno Ll., W.E.Pahl, D.R.Clark, H.Manning, L.E.Saskowski, S.J.Rasso, B.J.Turner, H.B.Holstine, J.R.Villagomez, M.D.Smith, H.Sutter, S.Ramirez, D.E.Hoyt, G.A.Stewart, H.Failmezger, H.J.Cady, J.L.Sanford, J.W.Walton, L.F.Gravert Jr., L.L.Halbrook, R.I.Nicholson, R.J.McAllister, R.W.Owens, V.G.Loding, P.Gerbaulet, D.C.Brown, D.G.Stewart, J.H.Brown, J.Sirot, J.W.Sachau, L.D.Canfield, R.L.Dabillo, C.A.Ortiz, R.Boulet, F.C.De Wispelaere, H.E.Hamilton Jr., C.A.Nehls, H.Scott, J.L.Harper, J.Ortega, L.M.Hesse, R.P.Braeckevelt, J.Gonzalez O., C.R.Cline, J.C.Earnest, M.A.Schessow Jr., S.Y.McDanel, D.Dutauzia, G.A.Meyers, R.J.Goodhart, A.Tysma, E.J.Beyer, B.G.Alexander, D.P.Stickles, G.G.Schwartz, J.R.Schave, P.A.Navarre, P.D.Clark, R.A.Madsen, A.J.Baayen, S.D.Perkins, D.C.Yarrington, D.R.Ingersoll, G.L.Griffin, L.A.Martel, L.W.Vanlerberghe, R.L.Johnson, G.R.Sollenberger, C.G.Lundy, C.R.Watson, D.A.Keim, D.F.Akers, D.G.Wood, D.W.Crow, D.W.Glancy, G.A.Morse, G.D.Gustafson, G.H.Boyer, J.C.Wamberg, J.Grona, J.R.Tague, K.P.Simon, M.A.Noyd, M.M.Halbur, R.G.Duffrin, E.L.Smith, T.C.Desmyter, T.Figurin, V.M.Croegaert, D.M.Greene, J.H.Wixom, S.Shelton, W.J.Stokes, A.W.Ortiz, T.A.Perales, R.C.McCaw, R.G.Six, R.L.Sunbeck, W.D.Thomas, D.L.Baraks, D.L.Meggers, F.C.Stickler, G.J.Carlson, H.L.Tingle, J.A.Kaiser, K.L.Klink, M.F.Chapman, R.R.Westphal, W.J.Held Jr., M.Corredera, G.E.Kerres, H.D.Vanmeter, P.G.Alongi, B.G.Borden, B.L.Pulford, I.G.Gripp, J.H.Jebson, J.W.Gnagy, P.Esteve, M.A.Laethem, A.J.Yaucher, F.C.Collins, G.L.Swanson, H.C.Esbeck, J.R.Montegna, J.V.Neumann, L.L.Whitney, L.T.Hines, R.J.Willetts, R.W.Redden, S.L.Stephens, W.J.Green, D.Trifigny, G.E.Toppert Jr., G.L.Luckenbihl, J.C.Jones, H.J.Bianchini, R.L.Jones, D.R.Wisor, F.E.McGee, G.D.Poelvoorde, H.H.Krambeck, L.P.Granell, T.A.Matalik, J.O.Eagles, W.G.Johnson Jr., C.L.Verdick, D.L.Muhlenburg, K.W.Helmers, M.P.Saey, V.W.Saltzman, M.Moreels, A.H.Forgie, A.Johnson, D.C.Johnson, D.F.Donahue, D.W.Woodson, E.J.Esparza, E.Scarborough, F.E.Wright, G.L.Post, J.A.Bradley, J.E.Powell, J.Kocarik, K.E.Rieger, M.D.Vanderpool, P.H.Doty, P.H.Gray, R.E.Park, R.E.Pries, R.G.McConnell, R.W.Kabele, V.H.Schave, V.L.Blodgett, W.G.Rusk, W.H.Smith, L.Lenoir, E.L.Downey, J.W.Boten, L.G.Ehrhardt, L.L.Swanson, L.S.Ferreri, M.B.Winthurst, M.L.Kaesser, P.J.Felderman, R.A.Petkunas, R.N.Leader, R.S.Pehl, V.C.Pierrot, N.Ibarra, A.Vanhamme, J.L.White, K.L.Appleman, L.L.Schmidt, M.R.Franks, R.F.Rocha, R.J.Gushanas, R.P.Bartholomew, T.D.Herbert, W.E.Morgan, W.T.Christian, A.F.Declercq, D.A.Johns, H.R.Ethridge, J.D.Deneve, J.W.McDanel, K.A.Goold, K.F.Liedtke, K.L.Gustafson, N.Orourke, R.M.Nelson, R.T.Reyna, S.I.Calderon, S.L.Rotz, W.H.Joiner, M.Cobo, J.L.Cullor, E.R.Kraft, F.T.Foreman, H.G.Mc Cleary, J.E.Butler, J.L.Wilson, K.E.Muckelston, O.C.Robbins, R.A.Taylor, R.E.John, V.A.Berkemeyer, W.C.Bishop, W.R.Goethals, W.R.White, D.Roussel, K.Zahn, H.A.Flack, J.H.Kinney, K.J.Sparrowgrove, L.J.Ontiveros, H.G.Eckhardt, J.W.Pasco, L.L.Creger, C.L.Girt, D.S.Wittstock, G.J.Benson, G.L.Cooper, H.V.Humphrey, R.A.Hansen, E.D.James, E.W.Williams, L.W.Nickerson, O.E.Giles, P.Sanchez, D.C.Davis, D.E.Ewert, H.J.Hauser Jr., L.A.Bradley, L.C.Plageman, N.M.Lowery, N.M.Wehrspann, R.J.Kronfeld, R.J.Lavender, W.A.Horrell, B.Cochon, B.D.Thompson, E.P.Moser, W.E.Vermost,

Portland, Oregon, branch dealer fly-in to Deere Day, 1960

E.Rodríguez, G.Camus, D.E.Soots, D.R.Anderson, E.D.Wilson, F.G.Puentes, G.H.Smithe, J.E.Black, C.G.Grant, E.C.Goethals, J.A.Dominque, L.A.Young, R.W.Anderson, M.Wilson, A.N.Warden, J.H.Collins, R.F.Mayer, T.A.Berenyi, A.Naudin, J.Cauwenbergh, K.M.Eagan, E.G.Fothergill, G.E.Bollie, L.E.Gratton, **1965** A.Morgan, B.H.Johnson, C.J.Officer, C.P.Tady Jr., D.E.Johnson, G.C.Ewing, H.J.Martens, J.A.Muhleman, J.G.Pasturczak, J.P.Huard, J.W.Elsbury, K.E.Henthorn, R.Young, C.Guignard, M.Riou, J.Desneux, R.Thomas, J.A.Tarrero, C.Moore, R.L.Chipman, T.R.Boyd, W.C.Tate, A.M.Peiten, L.Marin, C.D.Swenson, C.K.Carey, M.G.Miller, D.L.Pierson, E.J.Graf, G.A.Pullin, J.D.Fenton, M.D.Wagner, R.A.Ashcraft, R.R.Gronowski, C.P.Schmit, I.L.Davis, R.Dix, D.E.Ovel, D.R.Hampton, F.L.Bryant, I.W.Addis, J.A.Cox, L.W.Stenger, R.E.Lothridge, R.K.Anderson, R.Schmid Jr., B.Legout, J.Vannier, M.Meunier, C.M.Van Hecke, V.A.Pobanz, W.E.Mitchell, G.E.Faris Jr., J.R.Vogel, J.W.Bell, L.L.Brumbaugh, B.L.Bankes, T.L.Thompson, J.J.Desplinter, L.R.Brandt, R.A.Forret Jr., C.J.Austin, D.A.Hallberg, D.L.Deroo, D.L.Eslinger, D.M.Davidson, F.J.Krause, G.R.Nelson, I.B.Smock, J.H.Van Klavern, K.W.Puckett, L.R.Vangelson, R.C.Johnson, R.D.Larson, R.G.Clark Jr., R.I.Stansberry, R.L.Autery, R.P.Walker, W.A.Jones, W.L.Chesney, L.A.Roberts, R.A.Bedard, R.A.Duax, R.B.Vincent, G.Gouchault, A.A.Burrage, A.W.Shaubel, D.D.Essen, D.E.Christian, D.L.Jensen, D.R.Avenarius, E.J.Frauenkron, G.H.Peal, G.K.Sager Jr., J.T.Umhoefer, W.G.Meeker, F.Lagrange, A.B.Donahue, C.W.Clifford, D.S.Jirak, E.D.Ulloa, H.L.Morrison, J.L.Wyles, J.S.Kueper, L.J.Warnke, P.L.McCormick, R.L.Kiewiet, R.W.Woerdehoff, V.F.Bockhaus, W.A.Hekel, D.E.Luck, D.F.Lyster, D.M.Siebel, F.L.Yaklin, J.C.Williams, J.G.Zapf, J.J.Wright, K.A.Clemen, M.Maynard, P.Olson, R.D.Larson, R.J.Woerdehoff, W.R.Hartman, A.R.Clemen, C.A.Lange, C.J.Pfeiffer, C.J.Schick, D.M.Smith, D.P.Heller, F.J.Vaughn, G.J.Boom, G.J.Smith, G.L.Schueller, G.M.McGrath, H.H.Gauer, H.J.Clemen, J.D.McConnell, J.Marczi, L.D.Long, L.L.Ehrig, L.L.McDermott, M.W.Couch, R.A.Tonn, R.E.Tennison, R.F.Schilling, R.J.Haupert, R.J.Ohl, R.N.Dunkel, R.R.Peacock, R.W.Hammerand, H.Goebel, D.L.Heth, D.P.Walker, G.T.Boevers, C.Harper Jr., G.J.Heitkamp, G.L.Nebel, J.H.Sauer, K.W.Boll, L.J.Lehnhoff, R.E.Duster, B.J.Postel, D.C.Nightingale, D.D.Rachuy, G.L.Coffman, J.A.Stenzel, R.M.Stenzel, W.J.Gotto, A.R.Hennings, E.N.Brahm, J.J.Lesch, J.Moore, R.R.Buol, R.W.Staudinger, T.W.Stuart, B.D.Keegan, C.A.Collins, C.A.Miller, C.E.Sadler, C.E.Smithson, C.W.Canny, D.E.Conard, D.G.Dolphin, D.J.Patters, D.Priebe, G.G.Thompson, J.A.Mueller, J.E.Versypt, J.R.Roberts, L.K.Clark, L.N.Lennie, M.J.Pauly, R.E.Olson, R.E.Salmonson, R.L.Smith, R.P.Schneider, R.R.Redington, R.W.Black, T.G.Wunder, T.L.Renfro, V.L.Ward, W.C.Brown, W.G.Comer, W.Gitch, D.Weber, L-G.Wihlborg, A.D.Frank, D.E.Oberbroeckling, J.E.Walker, L.L.Goodwin, R.A.Braswell, R.R.Richardson, R.R.Weirbach, J.De la Cruz, C.B.Lobberecht, D.F.Kastner, J.H.Griffith, J.J.Maberry, L.J.Abresch, R.J.Dreesman, D.C.Lake, D.W.Donis, D.W.Hammer, M.G.Franks, M.J.Sullivan, T.E.Van Ee, W.C.Brownell, W.J.Leibfried, L.Brockman, M.E.Welch, B.A.Kerbow, C.T.Moore, D.F.Boyle, E.F.Smith, G.A.Stater, H.D.Shemko, H.G.Crayne, J.E.Hoffman, J.E.Redman, J.M.Griffin, J.M.Lauzon, J.Polo, L.G.Sanders, L.W.Klostermann, W.J.Griffith, P.Billardon, F.D.Finch, L.C.Graham, R.C.Carnell, R.C.Jones, R.M.Kueter, A.F.Chapman, B.R.Churchill, D.R.Casper, G.D.Lloyd, J.H.Krull, L.H.Garriott, V.R.Christiansen, W.C.Burrows, W.J.Alexander, J.Nivaggioli, B.J.Hill, D.I.Mauer, J.K.Kotscher, J.R.Lindahl, M.W.Hill, R.T.Kennedy, M.C.Leihsing, R.J.Conover, A.A.Alexander, A.H.Meier, A.L.Menzel, C.A.Kress, C.W.Cooley, D.C.Young, D.H.Holtz, D.J.Farwell, D.J.Lampman, D.L.Mayo, G.F.Hildebrandt, H.S.Black, J.A.Campbell, J.D.Presnell, K.P.Thompson, L.A.Paprocki, L.P.Bistline, M.E.Alexander, P.D.Crees, R.A.Van Court, R.C.Houge, R.G.Borst, R.W.Stapes, S.E.Test, T.L.Healy, W.E.Leighty, W.H.Sonnenburg, W.S.Sachse, M.Fontaine, S.Carlot, L.Fernandez-Larrea, A.L.Thomas, F.G.Lee, T.D.Nichols, I.Couriel, K.E.Dhooge, D.E.Bilby, E.M.Johnson, A.P.Zajac, B.A.Boeckner, B.J.Vaughn, B.M.Depauw, C.A.Rowe, C.D.Herron, C.K.Thomas, D.E.Steinbach, D.F.Loney, D.L.Crawford, D.V.Johnson, E.F.Koerperich, E.V.Furry, H.C.Baker, J.W.Clement Jr., K.Hanell, N.A.Earl, N.B.Long, R.C.Paulsen, R.D.Milne, R.L.Hallmark, R.R.Anderson, S.W.Rose, T.J.Connors, W.E.Crump, W.P.Crawford, G.G.Buhrow, V.R.Marquardt, C.A.Azbill Jr., C.J.Hartl, G.L.Mumm, G.V.Pitz, H.E.Wright, J.W.Perkins, L.J.Beaudoin, R.J.Beaudoin, R.D.Ackerman, R.L.Podlashes, W.H.Meyer, D.A.Carey, D.E.Taylor, H.F.Looney, J.R.Evers, A.H.Labatt, D.E.Ruckman, D.J.Hamilton, E.J.Preszler, E.R.Wattonville, E.S.Mitchell, F.J.Kutsch, G.A.Stoeffler, J.C.Rauscher, J.S.Green, L.D.Rankin, L.W.Robinson, M.F.Schmitt, M.L.Devore, M.S.Leo, O.L.Seitz, P.A.Hoxmeier, R.A.McIntire, R.L.Pool, R.L.Teague, V.A.Houseal, J.H.Rodriguez, M.Rota, V.Romero C., C.J.Flynn, J.A.Cocayne, J.L.Marlay, J.R.Cerfogli, J.W.Besco, D.J.Dreessens, J.O.Potter, L.R.Hosford, M.C.Rostvold, M.T.Digman, A.Guerrero, D.B.Mustard, J.P.Abitz, W.H.Holliday, L.D.Reiss, R.L.Westemeier, R.W.Beckman, T.L.Larson, B.M.Stevens, C.L.Thurston, D.G.Williams, D.L.Licht, D.R.French, H.D.Avery, L.A.Polich, L.D.Daughetee, L.D.Sargent, L.F.Henry, M.E.Klonglan, O.L.Banks, P.Bailey, P.J.Hagerty, R.A.Hoveland, R.J.Esser, T.J.Manning, T.T.Lange, W.H.Gassman, M.Landers, G.Grutsch, D.L.Spielbauer, D.R.Wolf, J.E.Hinkle, L.W.Flowers, R.J.McDermott, R.S.Scholbrock, W.K.Sabers, J.Pelletier, C.W.Sivels, J.A.Myers, P.W.Ochs, T.J.Wallace, J.Bocquet, E.F.Vanblarcom, G.W.Newkirk, J.L.Johnson, S.G.Gray, B.J.Wimmer, D.J.Reilly, G.D.Miller, R.H.Kratochvill, C.D.Logli, C.J.Gunderson Jr., D.D.Imbus, D.F.Wohlers, D.L.Horstman, D.N.Welter, E.J.Neumann, E.J.Wiezorek Jr., G.G.Folks, G.J.Schockemoehl, J.H.Hying, J.L.Calvert, J.L.Johnson, J.M.Finney, K.D.Lay, K.E.Burns, L.D.Moser, L.R.McDonnell, M.C.Walter, M.G.Brown, M.M.Kennedy, R.F.Hoch, R.J.Ferguson, R.J.McLane, R.J.Robinson, R.O.Burr, R.R.Haessly Sr., S.D.Woodyard, W.R.Reynolds, P.Gorau, J.J.Thein, J.L.Felsman, M.J.Kreassig Jr., P.J.Crippes, R.W.Schoenwetter, V.R.Wilson, D.P.Wiederhold, L.D.Dickie, R.L.Basham, R.L.Heinricy, R.R.Russell, T.C.Meyer, A.De la Horra, G.Grossard, G.Gouby, G.L.Bakey, L.J.Vaassen, S.A.Weires, V.M.Crimmins, J.L.Rodriguez, T.M.Feller, A.J.Reisen, D.R.Crawford, E.R.Campbell, G.F.Penfold, L.D.Olsen, L.G.Den Hartog, M.J.Fine, M.L.Gratton, R.A.Meier-Carnithan, R.F.Eastlick, R.N.Engels, R.O.Daebelliehn, S.H.Deshler Jr., T.L.Schooley, W.J.Steil, R.Girard, C.S.Wheeling Jr., M.L.Mc Coy, P.A.Hagner, D.Clausse, F.L.Murphy Jr., J.A.Rounds, J.A.Wilhelm, M.E.Pearson, R.A.Ege, R.C.Pattinson, W.H.Thompson, D.G.Allen, F.C.Bauer, G.R.Murphy, J.D.Rose, J.W.Otoole, L.E.Vroman, R.J.Slaats, W.J.Abeln, J.T.Schwartz, R.A.Piester, C.Green, D.L.Hite, D.R.Coughennower, D.W.James, E.H.Furstenau, E.Princell, G.M.Smith, I.N.Weasner, J.L.Rukgaber, K.E.Gass, L.E.Veasman, L.R.Burton, M.J.Wadhams, M.R.Main, R.D.Britt, W.D.Wilson, L.A.Nadalutti, R.Chazeau, C.R.Paul, R.D.Toomire, R.L.Brandel, C.Pointereau, A.A.Soppe, G.L.Bodeen, H.L.Leeper, R.L.Heitz, C.L.Braun, J.J.Medina, J.M.Keating, L.D.Simons, C.Potey, A.Weber, B.Schmid, P.Veit, W.Siebert, P.Pelletier, B.L.Herrold, D.L.Timmerman, G.A.Mills, H.L.Larson, J.W.Bogart, L.T.Sandoval, M.B.Scott, M.L.Reed, R.J.Udelhofen, R.V.Sales, C.Gosme, J.F.Baker, J.Pruiett Jr., L.V.Petersen, J.E.Miles, S.A.Sefzik, J.W.Girdler, L.L.Ingerson, L.L.Smith, R.D.Vandegejuchte, R.R.Miller, T.W.Clark, D.Bolin, G.D.Green, H.G.Schuppner, J.R.Flury, L.L.Green, M.J.Stephens, M.S.Riley, R.L.Jeardeau, S.L.Brereton, C.Vellard, E.F.Plunkett, H.E.Wright, R.F.Shannon, J.Doisneau, A.L.Davis, L.D.Anderson, P.A.Brown, R.O.Griffin, R.W.Singley, A.K.Ward, C.Gaymon, D.Sutherland, E.P.Berg, G.O.Hall Jr., H.R.Peppmeier, K.E.Shepard, L.F.Schurman, M.A.Ferguson, M.D.Carr, R.L.Odle, R.W.Liddell, M.A.Alvarez, C.J.Maurer, D.R.Neubauer, M.Leterme, F.Guyot, E.Leisse, J.R.Voelzke, H.Vallet, K.D.Stokes, L.J.Garrison, B.H.Jurgensen, C.A.Ross, C.R.Rew, D.A.Nelson, L.E.Rush II, M.C.Rowe, M.T.Sinclair, N.V.Leach II, R.A.Meints, R.L.Johnson, R.T.James, F.Hermosillo, B.Crochet, L.Claud, D.Kunz, D.Mehl, E.Seibel, G.Wein, J.Kreisz, J.Leubner, R.Edelmann, R.Frech, U.Kern, W.Wendel, D.A.Schmerbach, A.Chauvineau, H.Chartier, R.D.Peterson, L.D.Littlejohn, J.Lamaury, A.Giani, A.P.Wildgrube, A.R.Gritton, D.L.Henry, D.M.Askland, F.C.Hoffman, G.L.Baskerville, L.A.Jennings, R.A.Rodeghiero, R.W.Frank, W.A.Jones, W.J.Mareck, F.Jacques, M.Moreau, R.Belluet, A.Jacqui, H.A.Kalyniuk, G.M.Roth, F.Buescher, E.W.Comstock, G.R.Westhoff, C.A.Noack, L.R.Savage, S.G.Thatcher, J.J.Fry, J.Gaber, M.Perdereau, E.R.Borth, J.A.Timmerman, J.C.Zenz, R.E.Sims, J.J.Marinas, D.A.Baker, D.G.Felderman, D.L.Breer, G.L.Rouzer, J.C.Brewer, J.F.Muntz, J.H.Wehrle, R.D.George, R.L.Crabb, R.W.Roegge, T.C.Metz, D.D.Miller, R.L.Richard, T.W.Blevins, H.Sandrock, D.J.Tietjen, L.M.Houts, B.A.Spurlock, D.W.Waite, K.M.Fischer, R.L.Anderson, J.D.Sifford, L.E.Kennicker, A.L.Kuehl, D.J.Krause, E.C.Verstraete, J.B.Noon, J.C.Hamilton, R.L.Champion, R.L.Gregory, R.R.Klein, T.J.Clemens, M.Vigneron, C.G.Porter, E.M.Hessman, K.E.Wood, D.J.Olson, L.Sajovec, R.W.Schuetz, C.G.Koecke, J.F.Gruender, R.D.Kartman, G.A.Benner, A.Joseph, P.Marzin, A.D.Thomas, B.A.Blindert, B.J.Miller, C.A.Porter, C.E.Putzier, C.F.Reimer, D.F.Kabele, D.L.Kaufman, D.M.Huyvaert, J.D.Harris, J.M.Basilio, J.V.Droessler, L.E.Holland, R.H.Casterton, R.J.Mills, R.J.Wellman, R.W.Noth, R.W.Pettit, V.E.Redfearn, W.A.Harrison, W.M.Bonnet, W.R.Lundie, W.R.Schwartz, C.R.Montgomery, D.Wielage, F.J.Healey, M.D.Bass, O.R.Mattana, D.J.Rusch, D.O.Bendixen, T.J.Hurley, D.L.Simon, D.S.Ball, C.D.Denny, D.E.Larson, R.B.Taylor, K.R.Schroeder, L.P.Diedrich, R.K.Wieben, W.Schwerdtfeger, M.A.Campanelli, L.Bourgoin, M.Labarre, J.B.Mathias, L.Lopez, R.L.Brissman, S.A.McGill, F.H.Seeman, L.N.White, C.Bailly, C.D.Smith, C.E.Penrod, D.R.Dolberg, E.J.Bell, G.B.Voy, H.F.Kuehl, H.T.Pedretti, J.A.Epplin, J.A.Ivanic, J.A.Perrenoud, J.W.Schletzbaum, L.E.Miller, R.F.Evers Jr., S.E.Brinegar, T.J.Hollander, T.A.Zelnio, A.Casteret, G.Quesnel, M.Delaire, J.W.Klimes, R.W.Decker, D.R.Johnson, H.A.Walbaum, S.Pasdach, R.J.Brooks, R.T.Thurm, D.J.Monahan, J.M.Bowman, F.Rendon, A.Lopez, D.J.Phillips, D.S.Walters, D.V.Gotzinger, D.W.Grevas, J.A.Kunkel, J.L.Palmer, K.L.Roehrs, L.A.Stottler, P.O.Larson, R.J.Hein, R.V.Parks, W.F.Chesterman, P.Fauvet, S.K.Murdock, M.F.Fonseca, M.J.Nowak, W.L.Bradley, L.R.Sangster, A.B.Chidley, A.J.La Fave, A.R.Henning, G.A.Gotto, G.F.Oelschlaeger, J.H.Currier, J.K.Hartley, J.M.Carrell, L.A.Deshane, M.R.Degenhardt, R.E.Klaas, R.Heimberger, R.N.Andriano, W.Emmert, E.J.Lynch, G.W.Maddox, O.C.Gervasoni, C.K.Stanton, D.C.Huberty, D.J.Brandt, J.C.Shaw, R.Johnson, R.L.Young, T.G.Reuther, D.W.Osborne Sr., G.H.Haugen, G.J.Stratton, J.A.Miller, K.L.Pfundstein, L.W.Kirby, M.H.Carnahan, P.W.Larsen, R.A.Fulmer, R.L.Lutz, R.W.Nelson, T.H.White, A.Dousset, M.Ody, N.Melin, Y.Debillon, J.Krizak, M.Robert, A.J.Ploessl, C.E.Kane, C.E.Rommann, D.H.Bremer, D.J.Baker, D.W.Stubben, J.A.Morrison, J.Bedard, J.H.Carton, K.De Vore, N.D.Carbiener, O.L.Fernau, R.A.Harkness, R.B.Davis, R.D.Noe, R.D.Wismer, R.E.Monroe, R.L.Zuphke, T.W.Davis, W.M.Vickery, W.R.Eick, O.P.Chiocchini, A.F.Trenary, B.Sturm, C.L.Dietz, D.H.Janssen, D.H.Miller, D.L.Gillespie, D.R.Matthias, D.T.Delamore, E.D.Seehase, E.V.Frost, J.R.Mc Clintock, L.J.West, M.J.Vosberg, P.M.Mrzlak, R.C.Burk, R.G.Jacobs, W.A.Russell, W.J.Schmidt, W.S.Hardy III, D.A.Thompson, D.G.Stamas, D.J.Price, J.E.Patterson, J.L.Ketels, L.H.Simmons, R.R.Seehase, W.J.Huch, R.D.Mokosak, W.E.Jenney, W.G.Sage, C.L.Dixon, C.N.Kimball, C.N.Kuepker, C.T.Lanigan, D.A.Hopperstad, D.D.Freet, F.R.Dillavou, F.R.Eighme, J.E.Martin, J.J.Knebel, J.L.Corbin, J.L.Wohlert, M.Adolphs, R.H.Timmer, S.G.Emberton, T.C.Mathewson, W.A.Tedore, W.C.Lowe, W.T.Roberson, A.Schwemm, D.C.Jacobsen, D.C.Michelsen, J.L.Snelling, K.C.Knebel, L.J.Duffy, L.W.Brown, M.F.Cornelius, R.E.Du Charme, R.E.Hulme, R.R.Rusch, R.Wilson, V.E.Kirchhoff, C.D.Gartin, C.R.Mc Farland, F.C.Brown, G.J.Schmitz, H.F.Blocker, J.A.Ballard, J.A.Wilbur, J.F.Gleason, K.A.Bruns, M.D.Thompson, M.L.Key, R.C.Fulcher, R.D.Gutknecht, R.L.Daggett, W.E.Carpenter, B.L.Warren, B.W.Mathews, D.D.Drilling, E.Harris Jr., H.G.Veigel, R.A.Jensen, R.A.Schellhorn, R.E.Ager, R.R.Warren, R.W.Kerns, D.L.Dixon, E.G.Kokinos, K.E.Allsup, L.A.Ehlinger, L.E.Tripp, L.J.Jones, P.M.Elliott, P.N.Thomas, R.F.Weepie, R.P.Nelson, T.A.Hagenow, W.J.Fleck, S.L.Steagall, D.R.Carlson, E.J.Smith, J.R.Mc Neal, K.L.Macomber, M.D.Grant, N.G.Obrien, R.D.Kokotan, R.J.Rice, T.R.Meeker, W.D.Day, W.F.Fratzke, A.Rabusseau, C.Senelier, H.Vorgerd, C.W.Franklin, D.D.Drenner, L.E.Picknell, J.E.Sonksen, J.L.Harp, L.J.Chase, L.J.Spencer, M.E.Fisher, N.J.Mc Namara, R.L.Pence, P.Vincent, C.B.Durham, D.R.Panas, G.W.McDanel, L.L.Patterson, T.H.Halloran, W.H.Sand, M.V.Chedister, W.L.Thomas, G.De Bodman, R.C.Fehl, R.E.Peterson, R.M.Garrette, G.Douville, R.Brissard, A.W.Riley, J.C.Adams, G.D.Kessler, J.W.Berkevich, J.A.Turchek, B.J.Williams, G.Ream, J.A.Ohrt, J.D.Neuendorf, J.R.Yungtum, J.W.Smith, L.M.Snyder, N.A.Strom, N.S.Frank, W.A.Hakemian, W.R.Hallmark, A.Rodriguez, R.Robineau, A.H.Leavitt, E.E.Clark, E.W.McElwee, R.Romiti, R.J.Taets, R.J.Silva, C.Harrison, D.C.Diehl, D.H.Pettengill, D.W.Wildermuth, F.J.Herrera, J.C.Gridley, L.Botlo, L.R.Kayser, M.K.Makinster, N.M.Buelow, R.C.Lopez, R.Phillips, T.H.Laleman, W.D.Stotts, W.F.Emary, G.Gombert, M.Louail, R.Heissler, R.Fonseca, R.L.Hickerson, A.E.Dannenfeldt, J.Akin, A.Costanzo, J.S.Payne, K.G.Henander, R.L.Collins, A.Blackford, B.A.Maurer, B.E.Crouch, C.B.Hess, C.M.Cose, C.M.Sommers, D.A.Dunfee, D.D.Hanson, D.D.Robbins, D.E.Balliu, D.G.Nichols,

F.D.Lemper Jr., G.A.Fitz, G.D.Mangrich, G.F.Murphy, G.F.Sieverding, G.L.Mosley, G.Schnurstein, G.T.Fisher, H.G.Schutterle, J.B.Demuth, J.C.Martin, J.H.Barth, J.H.Uthe, J.L.Glass, L.C.Caughron, L.Faust, L.G.Longnecker, L.J.Braniff, L.L.Blumenshine, L.N.Acheson, L.O.Bigelow, M.A.Wilson, M.G.Robinson, M.J.Herman, M.Merfeld, R.A.Norris, R.A.Osborne, R.A.Pint, R.C.Giesen, R.E.Geweke, R.E.Leigh, R.J.Leet, R.L.Ihlenfeldt, R.L.Ortiz, R.M.Davis, R.P.Immesoete, R.P.Judas, T.A.Davison, T.H.Nurre, T.M.Mc Grane, T.R.Ferguson, V.L.Hill, W.B.Walters, W.G.Scully Jr., W.J.Mc Bride Jr., W.J.Nehl, W.W.Holschlag, V.A.Cauce, C.E.Lott, C.W.Randall, G.A.Gukeisen, R.J.Wolfe, G.L.Mixdorf, J.J.Mullins, L.Myers, P.C.Stainbrook, P.J.Cady, R.L.Bloomberg, A.J.García, L.M.Lamphier, S.S.Symons, D.H.Gaffney, D.J.Hakeman, D.L.Morse, D.M.Flack, H.C.Miller, J.D.Wold, J.L.Ahlstedt, J.M.Bales, K.W.Brown, P.L.Dunne, R.L.Gibbons, R.R.Reiser, T.E.Miller, W.K.Harroun, B.Potteau, L.R.Hines, D.M.Walker, A.L.Neuhoff, D.T.Gibbs, G.C.Sweitzer, J.D.Perry, J.L.Hintzsche, L.C.Davis, L.M.Nunn, M.E.Jupe, R.F.Leibfried, T.M.Murphy, M.Maitrejean, D.Kocovic, J.Pinsault, J.E.Hecker, M.J.Kemp, W.G.Gomez, J.Gerbaulet, A.L.Testerman, B.H.Null Jr., B.W.Wienands, C.A.Back, D.Greenway, D.L.Deshane, D.L.Gordon, D.W.Fletcher, E.A.Schmit, J.A.De Clerck, J.E.Hess, J.L.Bader, J.R.Drewelow, L.R.Grunwald, M.L.Simkins, N.A.Purdy, N.J.Weber, N.L.Hoppes, P.Gregory, P.L.Shannon, R.D.Regenold, R.L.Nolta, R.L.Winegard, R.S.Ligons, R.W.Lamphier, T.Markussen, P.Jackow, R.Picard, D.J.Mc Cready, H.D.Hemmen, R.D.Harris Jr., R.E.Anderson, R.L.Ahrens, V.R.Hampton, C.L.Reiter Jr., D.D.Hayungs, D.L.Turkal, J.V.Hammar, R.E.Smith, R.J.Ward, T.W.Charley, W.F.Marlette, C.J.Langel, C.R.Thorpe, D.L.Gutknecht, J.H.Adams, J.Teague, R.E.Harting, R.E.Wasson Jr., R.F.Tribbett, R.L.Hinz, S.Saunders, T.G.Tams, T.O.Kelley, T.R.Gibbons, A.I.Redmond, B.L.Puffinbarger, C.J.Schuler Jr., D.A.Albright, D.G.Miller, E.L.Dies, G.M.Clements, J.D.Wildeboer, J.P.Miller, M.F.Shannon, P.K.Langan, R.C.Ackerman, R.Lenius, R.P.Murphy, B.D.Eveland, G.L.Dufel, L.L.Dufel, M.J.Bert, R.C.Beener, R.C.Bousselot, R.C.Burrell Jr., R.L.Devrieze, W.D.Turner, B.E.Dick, C.E.Ledingham, H.J.Ackerson, J.A.Retzlaff, J.T.Pipkin, R.D.Martin, R.L.Vande Kieft, R.M.Buelow, W.W.Jones, C.H.Cederblad, H.M.Pepperling, J.J.Dodd, N.R.Beck, N.T.Crow, T.D.Huddleston, W.C.Lawless, W.P.Rosauer, J.D.Schott, A.C.Frost, A.D.Hintz, A.R.Kruger, A.R.Wadhams, B.V.Mc Nellis, C.Cercone, C.Heise, C.L.Petersen, D.K.Kafer, D.R.Browne, E.K.Overkamp, G.H.Siefker, J.A.Collison, J.A.Tice, J.M.Wiltfang, J.R.Kuehl, L.A.Stephenson, L.C.Ottaway, L.J.Kruth, M.G.Peterson, M.L.Schreiber, M.R.Oberle, N.G.Durnil, R.V.Rhoads, C.H.Schneider, D.G.Morehouse, D.J.Plute, H.M.Fischer, L.E.Frost, M.E.Varco, M.J.Wilson, T.E.Erickson, T.R.Frost, D.W.Lindstrom, E.J.Mills, G.L.Laermans Jr., H.R.Dettmann, L.A.Millett, M.Wendling, N.A.Webb, R.D.Caldwell, R.H.Solomon, S.H.Reyes, D.E.Anderson, D.G.Carpenter, L.J.Necas Jr., M.L.Axon, O.Tennial, P.R.Castle, R.D.White, R.L.Gehrke, R.L.Taylor, E.R.Bean, J.D.Ferson, J.H.Nicholson, J.L.Pullin, L.E.Weber, R.G.Grimes, B.D.Adamson, C.S.Thorn, D.L.Mc Cully, D.R.Farrington, F.L.Lynn, G.D.Sloan, G.M.Hanks, G.W.Bauler, H.R.Robertson, L.V.Fischer, M.H.Benson, N.L.Seemann, P.A.Hickman, P.N.Wortinger, R.A.Wray, R.L.Klammer, R.S.Young, T.P.Ambrose, W.B.Mitchell, A.Depasse, C.L.Kane, E.Hedges, J.J.Mc Carthy, L.R.Bantz, M.D.Coughlin, R.K.Tague, R.P.Tharp, T.R.Herrick, D.M.Neil, H.J.Kamback, H.L.Gibson, V.T.Nunnally, W.J.Ellinger, D.R.Dallenbach, H.L.Mohler, K.L.Kraft, M.L.Weber, N.E.Chizek, M.Pelletier, C.Cohen, D.A.Norwood, J.B.Crawford, P.L.Hoey, R.A.Feggestad, F.Loesch, H.Lehner, W.Schatz, C.F.Lehman, C.O.Lau, D.L.Miller Sr., E.L.Lewis, E.M.Davidson, I.G.Knecht, J.C.Driessens, J.E.Handke, J.Rosbak, K.L.Westpfahl, L.D.Froning, L.L.Driscol, M.J.Lashbrook, M.T.Cormier, R.D.Thompson, R.J.Kuennen, R.J.Ubben, R.Y.Jenkins, T.L.Reiter, W.D.Ayers, W.D.Lynn, C.C.Clark, D.G.Henning, E.E.Van Dorn, G.D.Derifield, G.M.Stout, J.D.Payne, J.R.Weber, K.J.Voyek, M.D.Holeman, M.E.Codner, M.S.Householder, R.Cunningham, R.W.Juergens, T.L.Hetrick, F.Casella, A.M.Newberg, B.J.Bellows, C.E.Kinder, D.L.Miller, D.L.Wunder, G.E.Rasmussen, H.L.Gillette, H.L.Koehler, J.F.Sweeney, J.L.Jennes, K.C.Jarosh, L.T.Ferguson, P.V.Groen, R.H.Rahlf, R.J.Whisker, T.R.Hart, W.S.Hamilton, D.Ochssner, C.L.Meier, C.W.Burcham, H.C.Bost, J.D.Briner, J.L.Deutsch, K.E.Jenson, L.H.Dodds, M.A.Walline, O.E.Nathan, R.G.Sands, R.H.Steggall, R.W.Hellberg, T.E.Foes, T.L.Duffy, A.I.Rangel, D.E.Stumme, D.J.Jacoby, D.R.Hastings, H.F.Graves, H.Tristan, J.F.Lukes, K.L.Kehe, R.M.Fiorilla, P.Ramos, B.F.Dunlap, D.A.Weber, D.F.Starks, D.Nation, E.E.Romeo, E.J.Vierow, E.M.Gerber, H.L.Blasdell, J.A.Neuman, J.K.Sonksen, J.L.Wright, J.R.Foss, J.T.Hambelton, L.D.Voelschow, L.W.Brimmer, L.W.Fillmer, R.B.Brewer, R.F.Duster, R.G.Houlahan, R.J.Pfiffner, R.J.Pitts, R.L.Kresser, R.L.McTigue, R.T.Gohlke, S.G.Walgren, S.K.Brown, L.Champion, A.Marciset, A.Benson, C.E.Ruddell Sr., D.M.Reed, D.W.Hurry, E.T.Wester, H.B.Holtmeyer, J.A.Andrews Jr., J.A.Brubaker, J.D.Cavazos, J.L.Key, L.C.Taylor, L.D.Morris Jr., L.L.Beaton, N.L.Armstrong, P.C.Schmitz, R.L.Paisley, R.R.Higgins, R.V.Andrews, S.E.Rommel, T.E.Schueler, T.W.Parkhouse, W.A.Brandenburg, W.H.Schoonover, W.J.Culpepper, B.A.Bush, B.J.Vaughan, C.J.Kass, C.W.Shuh, C.Wright, D.J.Schares, D.J.Tjebkes, F.J.Kempf, G.C.Larson, G.H.Drewes, G.L.Warkenthien, G.R.Niemann, J.Hyde, J.L.De Long, J.M.Hoskins, J.Mayle, J.N.Austin, L.C.Powell, L.D.Spears, M.Newman, P.E.Knedler, P.G.Caldwell, R.D.Feckers, R.D.Norris, R.J.Goderis, R.W.Stefan, S.G.Karns, T.A.Maynard, T.E.Koester, E.Peifer, C.W.Gage, D.A.Mc Carville, D.C.Arthur, D.L.Wolff, E.T.Green Jr., G.L.Jackson, J.T.Burke, J.T.Morris, J.W.Price, K.C.Brandhorst, L.L.Tripp, R.C.Klotz, R.L.Bunton, R.R.Pavelec, R.R.Sierens, S.J.Spoor, S.L.Gladson, W.C.Randle, W.W.Buttgen, A.L.Trumbauer, A.Wilson, D.E.Breyfogle, D.S.Miller, E.D.Fulcher, J.A.Gerhardt, J.D.Moore, K.C.Kramer, K.W.Pittman, L.J.Sadler, M.F.Fecht, S.L.Mc Combs, S.L.Rousey, T.A.Thomason, V.D.Fulton, B.D.Morris, C.R.Rauch, D.A.Crimmins, D.E.Bullock, D.J.Stewart, D.L.Mc Millan, E.C.Jacobson, F.A.Flidr, F.C.Christenson, F.Pence, G.A.Bruns, G.A.Peverill, G.L.Krueger, G.P.Koenig, G.Schonberger, G.W.Mc Clain, H.H.Hinz, H.L.Shepard, J.E.Abram, J.E.Medina, J.F.Medd, J.R.Brady, J.R.Lee, J.W.Given, L.B.Scott, L.D.White, L.E.Clarke, M.C.Mc Geough, R.C.White, R.C.Wittmayer, R.D.Neelans, R.E.Dedor, R.E.Given, R.E.Snyder, R.G.Hockey, S.K.Lavell, T.G.White, T.L.Miller, W.N.Wiltfang, W.P.Norman, W.S.Thomas, J.Esteban, A.L.Winters, C.F.Koontz, D.L.Decrane, D.R.Carmack, E.K.Sadler, G.L.Cowger, N.R.Mc Martin, P.J.Schaefer, P.L.Hild, P.M.Naftzger, P.W.Hannah, S.F.Obadal, C.E.Walter, D.G.Orey, D.Heins, E.A.Northrup, G.R.Wainwright, J.E.Kennedy, J.L.Conrad, J.L.Osgood, K.S.Cary, L.J.Schurman, L.L.Larson, R.D.Gunderson, R.G.Dejonghe, R.L.Evans, R.L.Krueger, R.R.Dugan, R.R.Heiser, W.Brase, S.Valadares, C.A.Cook, C.G.Olson, D.L.Dana, D.L.Mumm, G.Olvera, J.J.Schaefer, K.K.Albert, M.N.Van Dyke, R.E.Mowery, R.L.Wiener, W.F.Barnett, M.J.Drewis, S.E.Delagardelle, A.J.McCool, C.F.Chrest, C.W.Starr, D.F.Duemmel, D.J.Reilmann, D.M.Phillips, D.P.Durni, E.A.Graham, G.L.Harkey, J.Aperans Jr., J.C.Townsell, J.F.Hernandez, J.L.Marks, J.M.Otte, J.R.Rice, L.A.Bowman, L.D.Peterson, L.E.Robbins, L.L.Adkins, M.C.Stewart, M.L.Haddeman, N.E.Heckmann, O.J.Morris, P.G.Stradley, R.A.Demay, R.A.Tittsworth, R.B.Frost, R.J.Messerer, R.Kolpek, T.O.Scadden, C.R.Powell, D.J.Adams, D.W.Jones, E.C.Harringa, G.J.Gleason, J.J.Casel, K.E.Creglow, T.N.Alexander, W.A.Verstraete, W.J.Lee, W.L.Betts, A.Siegner, E.R.Schmadeke, J.H.Biersner, J.J.Morf, P.J.Schaab, R.A.Hoeft, R.J.Lynch, R.L.Van Heiden, V.J.Mayberry, A.J.Erdmann, A.T.Kamp, C.C.Anders, D.F.Turner, H.W.Kern, J.W.Logan, N.V.Foster, R.E.Brown, R.Edwards, R.J.Creery, W.C.Schefsky, P.D.Beebe, W.D.Cooley, A.L.Lootens, B.B.Poore, B.D.Yeager, B.J.Snyder Jr., D.D.Finke, D.L.Pals, E.A.Thompson, G.D.De Leon, G.Kalnins, H.E.Hermann, J.C.Kohl, J.E.Hammel, L.J.Steines, L.K.Hohenmauer, M.A.Bechtol, M.G.Anderson, M.J.Kramer, M.S.Melton, M.T.Gillespie, M.Thurman, O.A.Shields, R.P.Breuer, R.W.Schieltz, M.A.Di Stefano, B.Dumont, G.Lubin, C.S.Sims, E.M.Hostens, J.A.Hancock, P.Berentz, A.C.Carlile, J.W.Christensen, R.D.Thompson, R.E.Wancket, T.L.Verstraete, D.E.Conrad, J.T.Levendusky, M.G.Ashline, P.Loudermilk, G.Le Deist, A.G.Harmon, B.R.Neal, C.F.Brockman, D.C.Vanoteghen, N.E.Gentry, R.E.Brown, R.E.Dulaney, T.L.Moon, V.T.Schoonover, N.Poupa, H.Papke, D.K.Petersen, D.M.Atchison, J.R.Buzynski, K.E.Tegeler, Q.Ross, W.W.Pierson, D.R.Baum, H.C.Scarff Sr., H.D.Swalley Jr., J.M.McWilliams, J.T.Francois, R.A.Marticoff, R.M.Costello, R.W.Yordy, B.B.Braun, C.H.Lowrance, D.P.Maring, J.A.Miller, M.J.Drewis, R.D.Klingfuss, R.H.Warner, R.L.Riley, S.D.De Temmerman, W.A.Dobereiner, D.C.Reynolds, D.E.Smith, T.E.Erickson, A.J.Henry, D.A.Frank, D.A.Roth, D.C.Cuvelier, D.D.Stahr, D.G.Folkerts, E.F.Hasken, G.A.Robb, G.B.Guyton, G.D.Beert, G.R.Wright, J.A.Burbach, J.J.Roling, J.M.Burnside, M.P.Johnson, R.E.Ayers, R.G.Harken, R.H.Carlile, R.R.Adams, R.T.McClain, R.W.Holdsworth, W.E.Taets, W.V.Ewasko, W.W.Boal, D.L.Cloves, G.J.Kotz, J.L.Knapp, J.W.Brandt, M.E.Bennett, M.J.Dancer, R.D.Poppy, R.E.Anglin, R.L.Fort, S.Thomas, V.A.Dolph, W.J.Lee, C.H.Veach, C.M.Collins, D.C.Damm, D.D.Harrington, E.L.Jones, E.P.George, E.R.Walter, J.H.Brant, L.L.Heinemann, L.W.Smith, R.J.Glanville, R.L.Hansen, R.L.Leik, A.W.Feldmann, B.D.Gilstrap, B.E.Simpson, D.E.Battin, D.E.Thomas, D.S.Bausch, F.A.Hardtke, J.L.Husemann, T.B.Benson, T.J.Runde, V.L.Staton, W.B.Blitgen, W.E.Engeman Jr., W.W.Nelson, D.Munoz, J.L.Bewley, C.W.Beauchamp, D.F.Furlong, D.G.Felderman, D.H.Simon, E.D.Klinkhammer, G.D.Moser, G.W.Danzer, H.A.Duve, J.C.Styles, J.M.Beals, J.R.Bogart, K.H.Lindecker, K.J.Timmerman, K.Kalinowski, M.B.Busch, M.K.Westemeier, N.G.Middleman, P.M.Bowers, R.B.Kelly, R.W.Hager, S.J.Pappaspiros, V.J.Martensen, W.A.Hord Jr., W.F.Vandermeulen, W.J.Hendricks, R.J.Blount, B.L.Prevett, C.L.Truitt, D.C.Vroman, D.E.Wolff, D.J.Becker, D.J.Sanders, D.L.Crawford, D.Polak, G.H.Praska, G.J.Cook, G.J.Kapetanakis, G.L.Harris, J.B.Clemmons, J.J.Steffen, J.W.Goffinet, J.W.King, L.H.Mital, L.J.Schaul, M.J.Soat, M.L.Gregory, N.W.Pierce, R.A.Edie, R.A.Gordon, R.C.Udelhoven, R.F.Collins, R.G.Campbell, R.G.Weber, R.J.Meyer, R.L.Martin, R.R.Michael, R.T.Reczynski, W.J.Busch, F.Neveu, B.Daniels, C.E.Allison, D.A.Schafer, D.J.Udelhofen, H.H.Biermann, J.E.Veasey, J.L.Bennett, K.E.Ericson, L.L.Slater, P.E.Lane, P.J.O'Brien, P.J.Schraufnagel, P.R.Kieffer, P.W.Donth, R.P.Lauer, W.D.Cook, D.L.Krier, D.L.Stonecypher, E.D.Hurr, E.R.Valentine, J.A.Howe, J.D.Cummins, J.Fickle, J.R.Morales, J.R.Scott, K.W.Strohman, M.F.Van Doren, R.Clark, R.H.Peterson, R.J.White, R.R.Fafinski, W.L.Blackburn, C.Dabauvalle, J.M.Ramos, V.Cabrerizo, B.B.Henry, L.D.Craun, R.G.Pruett, G.Gorget, B.H.Woods, A.G.Sommerfeld, A.J.Schemmel, C.D.Hurd, C.H.Baker, C.W.Goodbarne, D.A.Goepfert, D.J.Koster, D.L.Geistkemper, D.Lee, E.L.Freebern, G.L.Neisius, G.L.Wiest, G.S.Buss, J.R.Foster, K.H.Heiderscheit, L.C.Boomer, L.S.Bigelow, M.L.Schieltz, R.A.James, R.C.Kranz, R.E.Fry, R.H.Jeys, R.J.McCarthy, R.J.Murphy, R.J.Strupp, T.L.Bargman, T.L.Gaber, V.J.Hinkel, W.R.Scheckel, W.R.Thier Jr., E.Berndt, J.W.Miller, K.G.Dillon Jr., L.C.Bolsinger, L.Chapa III, M.J.Wilson, N.E.Kutsch, A.Luna, D.W.Belken, J.Anema, J.R.Mc Clellan, P.J.Bosso, R.I.Derby, A.J.Trenkamp, J.D.Burnham, R.D.Evans, R.G.Reynolds, R.P.Lievens, S.P.Delire, V.J.Abing, E.H.Mitchell, L.W.Balvanz, M.A.Bries, T.R.Newton, B.M.Rickey, C.G.Cazabon, C.W.Schlarman, D.L.McDaniel, F.L.Churchill Jr., G.C.Bries, G.W.Box, H.B.Hopp, J.D.Allbright, J.E.Dow, J.L.Schuman, J.W.Lasinski, K.J.Schmitz, K.L.Brown, L.A.Vandaele, L.E.Soyke, L.H.Brakob Jr., L.L.Kalenske, R.A.Espaniel, R.A.Wagner, R.L.Beske, R.L.Burcume, S.A.Schueller, S.P.Ryckaert, S.W.Ryckaert, T.A.Pfeiffer, D.Bourrely, B.J.Redenius, D.A.Mc Fadden, H.J.Smith, J.J.Frederick, J.J.Reuter Jr., A.Carpio, C.C.Caley, C.E.Bass Jr., C.E.Stephens, C.W.Fuller, D.E.Ward, D.R.Pickel, F.Barajas, G.E.Kirby, H.J.Kelly, J.D.Gulick, J.W.Even, M.O.Woods, W.E.Parris Jr., W.G.Roberts, A.L.Holt, A.L.Peterson, D.L.Hilkin, D.W.Droessler, G.A.Frommelt, G.W.Jones, J.E.Steiner, J.L.Ferris, P.E.Olds, P.J.Theisen, R.H.Smith, W.N.Heiar, C.B.Peeples, C.L.Gordon Sr., K.W.Miller, W.R.Leliefeld, W.Velten, A.J.Dhaenens, A.W.Coleman, C.H.Hayes, C.J.Stayzer, C.L.Dreier, D.D.Palm, E.M.Fitzpatrick, I.V.Manternach, J.H.Henkel, J.J.Balk, K.A.Price, K.L.Bahl, L.O.Kuehl, R.A.McKillip, R.E.Haugen, R.L.Hedrick, R.P.Verschoore, R.W.Simon, S.A.Ellexson, T.C.Ruchti, T.E.Franken, C.R.Mittlestadt, D.A.Schemmel, J.C.Glasbrenner, L.D.Gabel, L.D.Peterson, L.F.Konrardy, M.L.Wolff, R.D.Andrews, R.J.Kaiser, S.B.Voss, T.N.Stackis, W.F.Huber, **1966** J.Lemoine, H.Huys, A.R.Rohde, B.N.Pruett, C.L.Lawson, C.S.Uskavitch, C.T.Birditt Jr., D.A.Schlarman, D.C.Rachuy, D.F.Ricks, D.L.Abresch, D.M.Deeds, D.O.Nelson, D.R.Buell, E.A.Patton, F.Fisher Jr., G.E.Scalf, G.T.Stuchel, H.E.Carlson, H.F.Hartman, J.E.Garrison, J.F.Wyffels, J.H.Burnett, J.L.Kessler, J.P.Reilly, J.R.Piatt, J.V.Finn, L.C.Luloff, L.H.Wolfram, L.L.Klein, L.M.Huff, M.F.Schroeder, M.H.Heims, M.W.Odneal Jr., N.D.Penfield, P.J.Dehler, P.L.White, P.W.Herbst, R.A.De Young, R.L.Stevens, S.Johnson Jr., S.T.Smith, T.J.Shanahan, T.L.Logan, W.A.Mac Donald, W.F.Bauer, W.F.Wittstock, V.Cisneros, B.D.Dykeman, C.A.Bird, C.C.Casady, D.A.Alderman, D.A.Hergert, D.E.Dison, G.H.Strohbusch Sr., J.D.Cook, L.M.King, N.K.Kramer, C.A.Johns, L.Quinn, M.C.Reed Jr., M.F.Schoonover, N.W.Schap, P.J.Powley, V.M.Morris, D.J.Ruiz, O.M.Houston, R.F.Richeson, R.W.Maher, S.N.Blackwell, W.O.Wagner, J.P.Galindo, R.L.Golden, W.Bruens, C.D.Dobson, C.W.Krell, D.E.Boyd, D.J.Solis, D.M.Thoeni, E.L.Merfeld, E.Taylor, F.R.Ammerman, G.W.Schwartz, H.D.Kerkman, J.L.Stuber, J.M.Straka, J.Medema, J.P.Lucey, J.W.Austin, J.W.Barber III, L.Payne, R.C.Schiffer, R.D.La Point, R.D.Weldon, R.E.Millius, R.H.Clark, R.J.Kramer, R.L.Bausal, R.L.Greshay, R.P.Laird, R.Z.Burns, S.I.Riggle, W.J.Schaufenbuel, D.J.Sieverding, J.H.Lent, J.J.Freiburger, K.J.Kingsbury, L.E.Maxon, R.G.Mousel, R.J.Soens, R.W.Dorathy, C.T.Britton, E.M.Quinn, H.W.Newton Jr., L.L.Lincoln, R.D.Jasper, C.F.Grimes Jr., D.B.Frost, D.E.Pitzer, D.J.Koopmann, N.R.Schildgen, P.E.Brady, R.A.Stratton, R.Monk, T.Gesell, B.L.Frohling, D.M.Coates, L.Brandt, N.L.Bryan, R.C.Buckwalter, T.G.Spengler, W.C.Lodge, J.Jimenez, A.H.Le Grande, A.M.Fabiano, C.J.Hamilton Jr., D.F.Cross, D.J.Hyde, D.W.Finch, E.H.Watkins, E.L.Willkomm, G.D.Eck, G.H.Hyde, G.P.Bozzato, G.W.Kuntz, J.D.Bartlett, J.L.Sievers, L.Jolly, L.L.Bergman, L.L.Corwin, L.Luher, L.R.Jensen, L.W.Chandler, L.Welch, N.J.Gleason, O.D.Mincks, P.A.Robinson, R.G.Bechthold, R.Thomas, S.L.Callaway, S.O.Decker, T.W.Kendall, W.H.Glover, C.M.Ruden, D.R.Declercq, H.J.Ferguson Jr., K.G.Jackson, M.D.Sanders, P.H.Saul, D.L.Kenney, M.E.Klein Jr., R.A.Ruth, R.Duncan Jr., S.W.Cook, K.A.Johnston, R.D.Chuick, D.W.Heine, J.J.Bushman, J.R.Frost, R.G.De Boer, W.C.Smith, A.J.Strassman, A.L.Lind, B.M.Kremer, D.E.Zweifel, D.F.Bandy, D.F.Yuenger, D.L.Ward, D.U.Recker, G.D.Gobble, G.E.Noble, G.L.Tennis, H.F.Honey, J.A.Thomas, J.L.Synan, J.R.Dunnwald, J.R.Wright, J.R.Zweibohmer, L.J.Dubuc, M.Hill, M.J.Drummond, R.A.Blaser, R.E.Fowlkes, R.J.Reynolds, R.M.Smith, T.Mc Gowan, T.R.Lewis, V.H.Ewert, W.D.Brown, M.Escobedo, D.R.Zacharias, J.A.Schaefer, J.M.Manders, K.C.Stange, K.W.Rigdon, R.W.Brobst, V.L.Brown Jr., O.Cantú , B.D.Ryherd, D.D.Slattery, D.R.Gonzalez, L.E.Roloff, P.H.Benner, R.F.Mallon, W.G.Billingsly, W.R.Fletcher, J.J.Alvarado, J.B.Marsh, J.G.Lambert, J.O.Speckman, R.L.McGuire, G.D.Polfliet, L.J.Keuter, M.T.Bell, P.Thiebaud, A.H.Fredrick, B.J.Morton, D.D.Conradi, D.L.Blanchard, D.R.Gukeisen, D.S.Herrick, E.C.Baker, E.C.Schmitz, G.J.Johann, H.D.Nimrick, J.A.Kolker, J.H.Magee, J.P.Bivens, L.D.Baumann, L.J.Welter, L.L.Kirby, M.A.Bunch Jr., M.E.Sebastian, M.S.Triplett, P.L.McDermott, R.L.Guss Jr., R.L.Schave, S.F.Mackay, T.E.Guild, T.H.Roling, W.J.Schuckert, R.Goguet, C.C.Blackwell Jr., C.G.Berg, D.A.Kerckhove, D.E.Nelson, E.A.Carda, E.F.Dvorak, G.E.Petkunas, G.L.Smith, L.A.Lukens, L.F.Moore, M.A.Christenson, M.E.Derr, M.G.Tiede, N.W.Anderson, R.B.Dickerson, R.E.Litch, R.K.Henn, R.L.Ortberg, R.R.Fink, W.R.Shearer, W.S.Rokusek, R.Cormier, J.Courte, J.Lavidalie, V.Sanz, E.J.Schilling, J.H.Willis, M.F.Zilk, W.C.Ellison, E.D.Nelsen, R.E.Jones, R.W.Abing, W.A.Thiese, W.L.Markham, A.Israel, D.L.Aurand, G.L.Jazwick, R.L.Stoner, C.W.Moore, D.A.Gesualdo, D.L.Taylor, D.M.Geiger, D.P.McDermott, D.W.Sauer, G.E.Kelley, G.Kauffman, G.R.Butler Jr., G.R.Rogers, H.Crist, H.D.Banning, J.E.Kuehl, J.F.Scott, K.H.Irwin, O.W.Henrichs Jr., P.H.Parker, R.C.Kramer, R.H.Ferrie, R.W.Dolleslager, T.L.Sturtz, T.P.Flemming, V.D.Stewart, W.E.Fleshner, W.E.Kohrs, W.L.Houston, B.Meyer, C.A.Smith, C.W.Fisher, D.E.Kelley, G.H.Bain Jr., H.L.Cosby, J.I.Henn, J.L.Wood, M.L.Little, R.C.Reynolds, R.K.Knight, W.D.Jones, W.L.Portugue, D.E.Marriott, J.O.Dumer, J.R.Scovel, L.W.Cranston, R.E.Frasher, C.A.Knueppel, D.L.Charlton, D.L.Heideman, D.Rammelsberg, J.A.Hinders, J.C.Anderson, K.L.Wilson, K.W.Korth, O.G.Schmidt, R.A.Hoffman, R.I.Griffin, D.L.Nichols, R.E.Smith, B.H.Peters, B.Higgins, B.M.Erenberger, C.Whitaker, D.A.Cathelyn, D.D.Dolmage, D.S.Huber, F.D.Moore, G.D.Woodson, G.W.Wellnitz, H.Hodson, J.C.Schneider, J.D.Ainley, J.D.Persson, J.F.Mallon, J.S.Toppin, K.N.Poindexter, L.F.Hartman, M.G.Trapp, N.Fiscella, R.H.Pries, S.C.Scholten, W.B.Bosley, G.Muench, E.D.May, E.E.Schumacher, H.Spree, H.T.Lellig, J.C.Spring, J.E.Garrett, J.R.Clayborne, K.K.Campbell, P.L.Adrian, C.Elfritz, C.J.Hoffman, C.M.Welch, D.L.Rieck, H.J.Swehla, J.F.Gray, R.J.Boger, W.C.Kelly, W.L.Miller, W.L.Wright, C.H.Martin, E.J.Brockmeyer, R.A.Nyman, W.C.Kimes, E.J.Winstead, G.D.Leach, G.L.Titus, J.D.Deyo, J.L.Stuber, J.S.Phillips, K.P.Sanger, A.A.Frommelt, B.Diercks, C.J.Even, C.W.Lidtke, D.J.Kuhaupt, D.J.Treanor, D.W.Mennen, E.J.Lampe, G.M.Romankiw, J.D.Nelson, J.H.Skinner, J.L.Charles, J.L.Cox, J.W.Spencer, L.R.Dilley, L.R.Stanley, M.E.Voorhis, P.W.Morrow, R.E.Robillard, R.K.Eilers, R.R.Volmer, T.L.Holmes, C.J.Phillips, D.N.Brown, G.A.Sheldon, H.E.Donis, H.H.Morrill, J.C.Beal, J.C.Mote Jr., M.N.Marcussen, R.H.Fahrenkrug Jr., P.Bonnemaison, D.G.Clements, F.H.Potter, H.J.Vespestad, J.C.George, J.E.Lenius, P.A.Lindahl, E.Shook, J.M.Corsbie, P.E.Lampkin, R.L.Carter, R.L.Jaquith, R.Richard, C.R.Fleming, F.L.Genz, L.R.Paul, R.M.Wilson, W.Palmer, A.F.Horn, A.S.Larson, D.E.Albaugh, D.W.Spratt, F.R.Helm, G.L.Edwards, H.F.Nagle, H.R.Herkes, J.K.Ades, K.J.Womack, M.R.Moyer, S.T.Denger, W.G.Wallace, W.L.Quick, K.Molter, W.N.Darby, C.C.Hinrichs, C.R.Graham, D.R.Aschbrenner, E.A.Suarez, F.G.Defrancisco, L.A.Enos, L.A.Poore, L.R.Kerr, R.A.Smelser, G.Janotta, E.Hernandez S., J.Villagra, D.R.Anderson, E.C.Wadsager, G.C.Barber, J.C.Stevens, L.W.Nielsen, R.E.Barrow, W.M.Brown, W.V.White, C.E.Wyant, N.D.Houser, R.J.Otten, T.L.Rumelhart, D.R.Eighmey, P.J.Brimeyer, R.Rault, A.K.Kimball, B.D.Fishnick Jr., B.W.Garland, C.A.Shouse, C.E.Driscoll, D.A.Thomas, D.R.Odell, F.E.Cisco, H.D.Wright, H.L.Brun, H.W.Carnahan, K.G.Gaber, L.S.Davis, O.L.Anderson, P.E.Norris, P.L.Barr, R.E.Kaiser, R.H.Ohlweiler, R.J.Lane, R.M.Zenner, D.Matton, E.Kramer, G.E.Greene, H.L.Fluegel, N.B.Bakewell, V.D.Johnson, W.L.Davidson, D.L.Tharp, J.A.Soliz, J.G.Napier, J.H.Saul, R.E.Welsh, R.L.Winders, W.H.Monen, M.Dittrich, D.G.Roush, D.G.Wellmon, K.K.Hunt, R.L.Troester, W.E.Jungling, G.J.Westendorf, T.O.Torbert, D.B.Stiles, D.D.Duke, D.J.Jaeger, D.L.Hampshire, G.H.Bastian, G.L.Graveman, K.E.Norin, K.H.Johnson, L.J.Breitbach, L.R.Seery, V.A.Lampe, V.F.Weimerskirch, V.G.Hartson, W.F.Oldenburg, B.D.Dehamer, J.D.Acklin, J.D.Meyer, J.E.Avenarius, J.S.Langston, L.W.Buchanan, M.J.Riley, P.J.Smith Jr., R.A.Mc Murrin, W.G.Soncarty, D.J.Utsler, J.C.Davis, J.R.Phillips, J.W.Plog, L.Garza, L.H.Junk, N.G.Goldhorn, R.J.Rossman, R.W.Weideman Sr., A.D.Barber, D.F.Mc Kenna, G.H.Johnson, L.Mosley, M.C.Chapman, R.E.Cain, A.R.Frame, B.E.Warren, C.J.Roloff, D.L.Ellermann, G.J.Fluhr, J.B.Lang, J.L.Bright, J.M.McClure, L.Dedecker, L.R.Lietzke, M.P.Hurley, R.E.Buchan, R.E.Gustaf, R.G.Pearce, R.H.Jasper, R.J.Keag, W.G.Palmer, W.H.Shaffer Jr., P.Venon, J.D.Hare, E.Meller, J.L.Carter, L.R.Heimbuck, N.Jones, R.L.Donaldson, R.N.Hemmer, C.T.Hocking, E.Holmes, T.W.Miller, M.Cimetiere, A.H.Darragh, D.L.Rasmussen, J.Lopez, J.Martin V., V.Diaz T., B.J.Meyers, C.M.Bouldin, C.O.Handling, D.J.Hansen, D.W.Littig, D.W.Meether, G.J.Burke, G.J.Endres, J.G.Forbes, J.L.Huffman, L.L.Griffin, R.L.Miller, S.A.Mulcahy, T.R.Garton, W.J.Waterman, F.Gallardo, B.D.Vest, F.J.O Regan, G.H.Elliott, J.D.Weber, J.Sanford, L.E.Schwan, L.J.Fuhrmann, R.D.Sprague, S.C.Sternat, W.H.Head, D.A.Kohls, E.Schick, F.C.Livesay, L.F.Moneymaker, O.J.Lewis, S.Leone, D.D.Noble, D.F.Strom, E.S.Mc Dowell, K.C.Even, W.P.Marrah, M.Velasco, H.J.Blitgen, J.L.Stanton, K.L.Bass, O.M.Pychyl, P.R.McLellan, W.A.Henderson, J.Lenert, K.Hofer, N.Munzinger, J.Castellano, A.C.Fobian, C.A.Salaber, D.R.Wohlers, D.W.Feltes, E.E.Helfrich, G.Leone, L.E.Lyons, L.R.Smith, M.J.Ervin, P.L.Fisher, R.A.Heying, W.C.Buerger, W.H.Hagedorn, W.J.Fitzpatrick, A.H.Riedo, Y.Chamard, C.M.Genung, F.D.Garrett, J.R.Rodgers, R.A.Wolff, R.D.Holland, D.M.Becker, H.L.Bowles, K.J.Lechtenberg, R.J.Lechtenberg, R.R.Rieck, V.L.Ortner, B.E.Brickman, C.E.Rokes, D.C.Theisen, W.C.Burrage, L.B.Drewelow, R.Harris, R.M.Yost, D.Scott, B.P.Turner, C.E.Buckingham, E.R.Oberg, G.I.Nowack, H.J.Kobliska, H.L.Brown, H.L.Terrill, H.Nettles, J.C.Eckhoff, J.M.Sakellaris, L.L.Goodney, M.H.Keyes, P.F.Melillo, R.A.Frisk, W.C.Davis, A.Gomez, E.Cain, J.E.Cox, J.M.Flahive, L.D.Sands, M.R.Gibbs, R.E.Demink Jr., T.F.Armstrong, J.Ceton, P.Jimenez, C.Watson Jr., E.W.Buck, J.L.Schmadeke, L.W.Eick, W.Pfeiffer, C.L.Day, D.H.Elsamiller, M.L.Fischer, R.F.Dean, R.J.Richter, R.L.Caughron, W.F.Leibold, U.Dolsperg-Von, A.A.Kleppe, B.W.Kelly, C.L.Kimrey, D.E.Deiters, E.P.Ward, G.L.Nelson, G.O'Mary, G.W.Henderson, H.E.Strohecker, J.D.Hawkins, J.D.Van Brocklin, L.R.Westerfelt, M.L.Stevens, N.J.McGee, P.G.Meeden, P.H.Keller, R.D.Repp, R.M.Fritz, S.P.Farquhar, D.Frey, H.Bartl, H.Feuerstein, J.Prudlik, W.Rempp, D.Siguero, D.B.Carmichael, G.V.Soles, H.A.Hall, I.F.Gilson, D.Siems, F.L.Rowland, K.L.Squires, S.L.Starkey, W.P.Hoerstman, D.Lisciandra, D.G.Pierce, E.Farley, J.C.Stahl, J.W.Myers, R.J.Mathern, W.R.Fee, M.Chenault, A.Minaya, J.Rey, C.C.Grandberry, C.C.Mc Daniel, C.F.Carlson, E.L.Balvanz, C.C.Geyer, C.L.Fagerlind, D.J.Burton, D.L.Nolan, E.A.Kritz, E.Grandberry Jr., F.D.Johnson, F.R.Coonrad, J.A.Jungblut, J.D.Myers, L.W.Clark, N.G.Plog, P.A.Allen, P.J.Kies, R.A.Peterson Jr., R.D.Price, R.M.Murley, V.A.Zweber, W.E.Wynn Jr., W.Buchmann, D.Boxwell, D.L.Maurer, G.L.Jenson, G.O.Brocka, G.R.Thurm, I.K.Stephens, K.E.Farrier, A.J.Adams, G.J.Becker, J.Vivians, K.E.Haynie, A.B.Loding, B.L.Welcher, C.J.Monteith, D.H.Kirkhove, D.W.Frank, M.A.Wolfe, L.C.Walz, R.L.Beahr, B.J.Scanlan, B.L.Main, C.C.Wilkens, D.A.Murley, D.E.Westphal, D.J.Nimrick, D.M.Slavish, D.W.Berg, F.B.Terfruchte, F.C.Dunbar Jr., F.J.Strauss, G.L.Gruwell, H.C.Gaard, I.L.Williams, J.E.Chase, J.L.Palmer, L.J.Creath, P.E.Hartley, R.G.Moser, R.L.Perry, R.V.Orman, R.V.Strauser, S.H.McBee, T.D.Turk, V.McClellan, W.C.Foddrill, K.Bauer, A.Huertas, B.Iglesias, J.Arias, M.Antolin, P.De La Camara, J.E.Brooks, J.F.Puhl Jr., J.H.Dockman, J.L.Gatewood, L.T.Rausch, R.J.Rust, R.R.Stage,

Visitors to Des Moines, Iowa, factory, 1966

R.Stefani, C.L.Ullrick, D.E.Buck, D.V.Larsen, J.H.Mc Beth, P.E.Steele, S.C.Thomas, W.M.Dalrymple, F.R.Robinson Jr., L.L.Aswegan, R.J.Leffel, T.E.Kerr, B.T.Walker, J.L.Vrban, A.V.Kershaw, C.Matheney Jr., C.P.Davis, D.E.Laballe, D.M.Tatham, E.C.Hanson, F.S.Newsome, G.D.Morse, J.F.Loonan, L.L.Huddleston, M.J.Whitson, M.L.De Groote, R.E.Clark, T.D.Runde, V.J.Hoffman, W.J.Hesseling, W.Prinz, J.A.Ruiz, R.Plessis, J.Douvenot, A.J.Pepler, A.J.Neumann, D.I.Dowden, J.Madison Jr., J.W.Totten, R.A.Bender, R.Bell, C.Brown, D.A.Boehmer, D.L.Brennaman, E.R.Linden, J.D.Hamm, J.H.Fleming, R.D.Bennette, V.B.Crawford, M.Suck, D.J.Burke, R.Wright, D.D.Gregory, J.L.Sanders, W.H.Wilkerson III, D.H.Ingle, C.Rankin, D.E.Mc Kee, E.D.Dunne, G.Pena, J.A.Brown, J.R.Bohr, J.W.Peoples, L.D.Soyke Haake, L.G.Kok, M.E.Meyer, P.S.Lynch, R.D.Casey, R.J.Hansen, R.J.Sullivan Jr., R.L.Randolph, W.A.Kotz, G.Thomas, P.Garcia C., D.L.Bragg, K.A.Deibler, L.L.Schueller, C.J.Burke, D.L.Oberhardt, G.W.Berkenbile, H.J.Reed, J.E.Kindelsperger, J.O.Willard, J.P.Hurst, K.F.Schmitz, R.J.Jensen, R.L.Keigan, R.F.Schmid, J.R.Newcomer, B.M.Miller, C.D.Rouse, D.G.Tolles, D.M.Combs, D.W.Hild, J.F.Meek, O.D.Walters, R.A.Silva, R.P.Moseley, W.F.Hammerand, M.Watchorn, A.E.Davis, D.F.Allen, L.R.Gaffney, W.J.Vandevoorde, G.Pener, D.Sprunck, C.L.Hickman, J.A.Caradine, J.M.Legel, J.R.Mossage, M.D.Franzen, R.E.Liddle, H.A.Schick, J.P.Mohlis, T.L.Riley, C.L.Bradley, C.L.Nielsen, D.F.Meyer, D.J.Jensen, D.L.Oberlander, F.J.Lentsch, G.A.Rehn, J.W.Cook, J.W.Wilder, L.G.Mueller, L.M.Greenlee, M.E.Swygman, M.L.Frutiger, P.F.Hough, P.M.Silver, R.D.Black, R.M.Zippay, R.W.Ingwerse, V.J.Junker, V.L.Morgan, A.L.Payne, B.W.Brodie, C.A.Jenkins, D.L.Fischels, D.L.Harris, D.L.Marion, G.H.Miklis, J.C.Woodburn, J.L.Bartlett, L.L.Magee, M.R.Meyer, P.J.Strief, R.R.Smith, W.A.Prymer, A.Alves, A.Sellier, P.Budon, E.Petry, S.Bischof, A.Manso, B.Vidales, R.Frochoso, H.L.Coss, J.L.Knapp, G.F.Niemann, J.A.Jackson, J.Kerns, J.P.Davis, K.J.Kokotan, M.A.Ash, T.R.Furneaux, J.J.Mora, A.C.Shindelar, D.B.McCreight, D.E.Vandersnick, D.J.Burger, D.L.Mac Lennan, G.C.Ballard, G.E.Goodman, G.Mauritzson, G.R.Kinkade, H.F.Zimmerman Jr., H.N.Mabry, J.E.Myers, J.L.Klopf, J.L.Vogt, J.R.Fuller, L.H.Leistikow, R.A.Ernst, R.D.Peterson, R.J.Junk, S.C.Mc Farlane, S.R.Watson, W.H.Driver Jr., W.W.Wreath, J.Martinez, D.L.Vandevoorde, D.M.Galbraith, D.P.Brown, G.E.Gary, L.L.Mc Dowell, R.L.Hostens, S.K.Verbeckmoes, S.L.Bainbridge, W.D.Knight, A.L.Gary, D.C.Gibson, E.D.Brown, G.A.Higbee, H.B.Simmon III, H.J.Mawdsley, J.H.Pasquini, P.E.Mack, R.C.Thuesen, R.J.Mc Mahon, W.A.Gary, B.N.Gross, C.L.Parcell, D.I.Smith, G.W.Tindall, H.A.Earl, J.A.Schaefer, M.G.Klingler, M.K.Wyffels, T.J.Roets, D.L.Waller, G.H.Muender, J.A.Brustkern, K.A.Earl, L.J.Folchert, R.V.Neal, T.L.Lindley, M.Torrente, B.L.Warman, C.F.Fisher, C.K.Wilson, D.E.Greer, D.E.Klossner, E.N.Hansel, E.S.Smock, G.E.Smith, G.F.Bormann, G.G.Lindsay, G.L.Medd, G.R.Vanoteghem, H.F.Vieth, H.L.Kees, J.A.Forbes, J.K.Mercer II, K.B.Wedig, K.Kemming, L.G.Carmack, L.J.Winther, L.L.Feld, M.Caballero, M.J.Leone, R.A.Foley, R.B.Duncan, R.L.Collins, R.M.Mozena, W.L.Pospisil, M.Denis, A.Lazaro, E.Carretero, J.Garcia M., J.Muñoz R., M.Chamorro, M.Torres, B.A.Murphy, C.E.Whittinghill, J.E.Wilson, M.J.Cheek, R.F.Weinert, R.W.Smith, W.E.Geyer, A.D.Spencer, D.L.Pietan, D.W.Wallace, J.L.Burkard, J.R.Bagby, L.J.Nenneman, R.E.Yahnke, W.Huelsmeyer, W.R.Berndt, G.D.Pheiffer, H.L.Lively, J.A.Ocheltree, J.E.Vickery, M.B.Cleveland, M.D.Benhart, O.E.Boyd Jr., P.Badger, R.C.Oakley, R.D.Keister, S.Phillips, W.E.Gillis, J.Cuena, M.J.South, S.E.Grau, A.Lara, F.Galvez, J.Ramos V., J.Woodard, A.G.Marken, A.P.Schneider, C.G.Tyler Jr., D.G.Reese, D.J.Pollock, D.L.Evans, D.L.Riley, D.L.Soots, D.W.Ferrell, D.W.Hinrichs, E.J.Coleman, E.L.Card, G.C.Graves, J.E.Shipley, K.E.Rausch, L.L.Williams, L.M.Racine, T.L.Lamberti, T.R.Spowart, W.E.Eggleston, W.L.Montgomery, W.Moore, W.R.Hubbard Jr., M.Boré, D.Bourdeau, D.J.Goeres, R.J.Hanson, T.R.Pate, B.D.Mays, G.A.Russmann, J.M.Grover Jr., L.E.Tucker, R.D.Schipper, A.L.Spann Jr., C.M.Ford, J.L.Hart, A.W.Gruber, C.F.Werhan, R.A.Cross, F.Romo, C.C.Faust Jr., C.E.Brown, D.E.Ziegler, D.R.Stambaugh, J.W.Thomas, L.M.Ross, M.E.Barr, N.D.Kerr, P.W.Hawotte, R.D.Chase, R.D.Schauenberg, R.W.Johnson, L.Jobet, D.J.Lueck, J.A.Hostens, J.A.Milem, C.G.Burlage, D.E.Mc Ginn, H.L.Mabry, L.F.Andreatta, E.F.Brinkley Sr., H.Benz, H.Henschel, D.A.Demeyer, L.G.Amling, R.Soehnlen, C.Tello, C.B.Leonard, D.E.Simerson, F.J.Bednar, J.C.Campbell, L.L.Brooks Jr., M.Moore, N.L.Woodhouse, N.S.Novick, W.E.Chambers, A.J.Boies, D.L.Replogle, M.F.Brinkman, T.A.Digman, C.R.Berning, G.I.Henisey, J.W.Melugin, R.M.Schroeder, S.A.Sayre, W.J.Kelly Jr., G.Lorin, G.L.Bettis, L.H.Palmer, S.D.Ziegler, L.Rubio S., C.J.Kline, G.B.Ketelaar Sr., G.J.Cox Sr., J.A.Rose, K.L.Crawford, O.S.Critchfield, R.D.Glaser, T.R.Donahey, A.Pichoff, A.Valera, G.Martin C., G.P.Demay, G.W.Roberts, J.H.Burton, J.R.Kessler, A.Martinez V., K.E.Herrick, W.J.Kilburg, W.H.Harris, J.M.Sanz, D.O.Loveless, G.Buhler, A.O.Fredericks, C.Vandekeere, D.G.Archer, D.L.Whitlatch, J.L.Mac Kay, M.A.Coots, M.A.Reittinger, T.E.Hoppenworth, T.F.Kies Jr., W.A.Best, A.Digy, B.J.Johnson, D.J.Treanor, D.L.Snyder, P.Martin G., E.Nunn, J.J.Russell, J.Savicki, A.Ortega P., A.H.Bulten, A.M.Sigwalt, G.A.Priewe, G.R.Tiedt, J.H.Coleman, J.W.Kuhn, R.J.Hupf, C.D.Ronemous Jr., N.D.Olson, P.W.Waidley, B.S.Brewer, D.L.Russ, J.A.Clark, N.D.Holmes, R.H.Mock, M.Montes, E.Y.Caras, I.M.Bousson, K.T.Tomlinson, B.E.Romig, B.L.Buffington, C.A.Prose Jr., C.M.Ewalt, C.N.Toney, D.G.Davis, G.G.Kratz, G.L.Schmadeke, J.A.Robinson, J.L.Schliewe, K.L.Hewitt, L.D.Murrow, L.F.Nelson, L.R.Headington, M.A.Pretz, M.C.Saller, M.L.Alberts, P.A.Koch, R.Demott Jr., S.D.Fouts, S.O.Coulter, V.F.Franke, W.K.Wainwright, G.Mallet, B.Rodriguez J., J.L.Castillo Del, L.Villa, M.Montero R., M.Rentero, N.Gonzalez P., R.Macias J., D.A.Gienau, D.E.Bonnett, E.L.Linebaugh Jr., J.P.Stoker, L.R.Whitson, M.D.Gray, M.S.Wilson, R.M.Frueh, D.Delorme, B.D.Robertson, D.L.Lueptow, D.P.Jansen, F.B.Partlow, J.E.Baker, G.B.Vandyke, S.Saint-Martin, B.D.Bode, D.J.Mac Kenzie, D.R.Besick, D.W.Swarts, J.C.Milstead, J.E.Cable, J.E.Farquhar, J.L.Grimes, J.R.French, J.Rosauer, K.M.Frysinger, L.C.Rutherford, L.G.Walker, L.L.Fitzwater, L.L.Pickering, M.W.Tschida, R.G.Bricker, R.G.Watson, T.D.Spaur, T.J.Brown, T.J.Prevett, T.W.Myers, W.Dage, W.L.Guffey Jr., G.L.Luppen, H.W.Hudson, I.J.Waite, R.L.Davis, S.H.Nino, H.A.Devrieze, H.N.Chapman, J.Portillo, T.J.Zambrano, T.O.Ehart, R.R.Scharff, S.L.Grandberry, E.W.Beeson, G.N.Thornburg, M.E.Snyder, O.Hernandez G., A.C.Gallacher, A.Kushmer Jr., A.R.Gonzales, B.G.Brubaker, B.N.Cooley, C.J.Ryan, C.Stewart, D.E.Buell, D.Parks, E.C.Pfalzgraf, E.R.Reed, E.T.Woodyard, E.W.Kemp, F.D.Kettering Jr., G.E.Long, G.L.Stocker, J.A.Muir, J.D.Livingston, J.E.Bankson, J.F.Anderson, J.G.Verdick, J.J.Boland, J.M.Kempin, J.P.Reidy, J.R.Beldin, K.W.Ogier, L.A.Boehmer, L.G.Bosley, L.H.Ohm, L.V.Andersen, M.D.Mc Crea, O.H.Spore, R.A.Steinkraus, R.Greek, R.H.Reed, R.J.Hewitt, R.J.Mensen, R.J.Tyler, R.Jackson, R.R.Neil, R.W.Reeves, T.H.Jones, T.J.Trentz, W.H.Odefey, W.M.Kirschenman Jr., W.M.Pentecost, F.E.Meier, J.E.Clark, J.J.Sadowski, K.C.Ames, K.W.Gaugert, M.R.Raya, R.A.Schultz, R.L.Smith, F.Gil, F.Gil V., J.Ramos P., A.Tesch, D.L.Vandewalle, E.J.Vaughn, J.E.Bowling, P.D.Bandfield, R.S.Elizondo, L.Gallego, B.L.Germaine, D.T.Smith, J.A.Garrett, L.Akers, M.O.Beach, M.Reed, W.C.Baerwolf, C.L.Wright, D.E.Merrill, G.D.Beard, G.R.Myers, L.Robinson, R.A.Still, R.H.Dennis, T.B.Gray, A.M.Sheldon, C.D.Leslie, C.R.Byford, C.V.Hodgson, D.A.Tesch, D.F.Pierson, D.G.Randall, D.L.Russell, E.F.Shepard, J.A.Vincent, J.L.Downs, K.A.Miller, L.E.Eakins, L.L.Mc Clure, L.L.Schaus, L.P.Long, M.E.Breon, M.H.Hinz, O.A.Eilers, O.W.Sette, R.A.Patterson, R.C.Long, R.E.Griebel, R.E.Lee, R.E.Nelson, W.L.Walker, A.Wolf, C.Garcia M., V.Lopez R., D.E.Mc Farland, D.R.Hansen, G.D.Underwood, J.E.Sweeney, J.J.Nemitz, M.K.Tamminga, M.L.Timm, R.E.Bearbower, R.W.Long, V.H.Bishop, V.O.Dickinson, A.A.Ulrich, G.H.Clements, J.W.Harris, K.C.Roddick, N.J.Raisbeck, R.A.Zummak, D.C.Hamm, J.H.Puls, N.J.Pietan, W.B.Warren, C.Walker, L.A.Miller, L.C.Brocka, R.J.Etringer, T.P.Garthoff, B.A.McCarthy, B.R.Easley, C.D.Bauer, C.W.Miller, D.E.Zeug, D.L.Glass, D.L.Stanford, D.R.Wheeler, D.S.Charapata, G.D.Shannon, G.L.Rick, H.R.Lovelace, J.B.Przekurat, J.D.Nash Jr., K.D.King, L.A.Hester, L.G.Volbruck, M.D.Bronson, M.K.Mitchell, M.L.Hundt, M.V.Chestnut, O.A.Schildt, R.C.White, R.J.Despain, R.J.Kessler, R.L.Rieck, R.Weinmeister, S.A.Miller, T.M.Piper, T.Sinram Jr., W.C.Metzdorf, W.J.Kelly, W.J.Mayhugh, R.Boulet, F.Sanchez C., R.Guijo, D.J.Smith, J.H.Sallis Jr., J.L.Lightfoot, L.A.Ciesielski, L.D.Zeitler, M.C.Wolfgram, P.N.Beierschmitt, R.H.Peters, R.J.White, B.G.Fountain, B.R.Cook, C.L.Buyck, D.W.Carter, G.I.Mangrich, G.J.Hill, H.W.Meier, O.Lee, R.E.Olson, W.H.Millard, B.L.Davis, C.H.Rail, D.L.Remetch, F.A.Fox, J.D.Poirier, L.T.Grimm, R.B.Grant, R.D.Mills, R.K.Engstrom, S.J.White, W.J.Denning Jr., A.Grandet, B.Montant, B.Ringuede, D.Menard, G.Charpentier, B.B.Washington, J.W.Vogel, R.L.Pedersen, J.Quinot, J.Delgado D., B.R.Ballard, C.F.Ruhl, C.J.Wroten, C.L.Reese, D.G.Lamp, E.J.Minard, F.D.Hughes, F.E.Goldsberry, F.M.Garofalo, G.B.Kitelinger, G.C.Pates, G.D.Jacobs, G.L.Baasch, G.L.Bradley, G.R.Dorn, H.A.Bries, H.F.Iversen, J.Gomez, J.L.Clauson, J.R.Wilson Jr., L.A.Schwantes, L.L.Mayfield, M.A.Hendricks, M.D.Lauber, M.W.Klendworth, P.A.Miller, P.L.Greer, R.C.Schmidt, R.Desjarlais, R.E.Bohle, R.E.Bowles, R.E.Shockley, R.L.Aldridge, R.L.Johnson, R.L.Myers, R.M.Amfahr, R.N.Behrens, R.W.Horn, T.L.Carter, W.F.Bagneski, W.H.Brown Sr., C.L.Harbaugh, D.J.Kluz, F.L.Waldbusser, M.M.Beatty, T.R.Woodward, C.E.Harks, C.H.Lane, D.F.McGinnis,

Worldwide parts managers meeting, Moline, Illinois, 1969

E.Mc Cellan, E.Newman, G.C.Brandt, I.D.Lett, J.R.Bickel, L.Pacheco, R.A.Boeckmann, R.D.Johnson, R.D.Mennen, R.E.Gregory, R.L.Bruce, R.Olson, W.H.Snowden Jr., F.D.Chapman, H.L.Nelsen, M.H.Cotton, R.E.Nolta, R.L.Penning, T.M.Huegli, A.L.Weidman, B.J.Hashman, C.D.Barfels, C.E.Kanas, C.F.Treanor, D.H.Clark, D.K.Gushanas, E.G.Bickford, E.Koenigsfeld, G.K.Giese, G.T.Eng, G.V.Askew, H.A.Miles, H.J.Tank Jr., J.A.Kaiser, J.G.Parrish, L.M.Meier, L.W.Schweiger, M.A.Duncan, R.J.Boge, S.J.Steffen, W.H.King Jr., J.Beaupere, J.Hemond, D.G.Brumas, E.B.Rodriguez, G.Schares, J.E.Northness, M.C.Ahlf, M.K.Woeste, R.D.Coble, R.L.Ciesielski, S.H.Vergane, R.Forteville, D.J.Reifsteck, F.D.Carney, G.J.Novotny, H.R.Hild, H.R.Watts, J.E.Webber, R.F.Everett, S.L.Edgin, V.T.Farley, W.R.Swinton, B.G.Hough, C.C.Block, J.L.Snook, J.W.Daly, J.W.Magnuson, P.F.Craig, R.L.Peterson, R.W.Randall, S.L.Brooks, W.M.Irwin, J.Martin P., A.A.Esslinger, A.R.Grimson, D.J.Daniel, D.L.Smith, G.P.Garner, R.L.Gaston, W.P.Morehouse, E.Huguenard, B.E.Watters, B.J.Seidlitz, C.T.Cameron, D.D.Buntenbach, D.J.Brown, D.W.De Berg, G.C.Fowler, G.L.Montgomery, G.N.Ruegnitz, H.L.Epperson, J.A.Carlson, J.F.Roby, J.S.Klaren, K.K.Wieditz, K.M.McGuire, L.A.Schlueter, L.C.Hall, M.M.Kadinger, M.M.Peterson, R.D.Bellmer, R.L.Newton, T.A.Kaiser, T.W.McClure, L.Garcia R., J.A.Grizzle, J.H.Debaker, J.H.Junk, J.K.Youngbear Sr., L.D.Carter, L.R.Smith, V.B.Mc Laury Jr., W.H.Paulus, C.V.Van Horn, F.F.Moore, R.A.Mitchell, R.L.Versluis, R.N.Noel, R.R.Cate, C.A.Ryan, C.K.Hoefle, C.M.Steils, D.A.Fontenoy, G.L.Neelans, J.Smith, L.C.Weber, N.A.Mc Donald, R.H.Pennell, R.T.Doeckel, V.L.Cochran, A.J.Hansen, C.C.Vanderwerf, D.E.Coberley, D.M.Goodson, D.W.Bunger, E.F.Sebetka, G.L.Kupka, J.A.Schaefer, R.F.Stahl, W.E.McBride, W.K.Dent, A.F.Neisen, D.A.Miller, D.B.Brahm, D.J.Honn, D.W.Small, E.C.Stumme, E.J.Willhouse, F.Mettner Jr., G.A.Mitchell, G.J.Justus, G.L.Schulte, I.W.Burton, J.L.Hall, J.W.Betcher, M.J.Morley, M.R.Schmidt, P.C.McQuillen, R.J.Armstrong, R.L.Farley, R.R.Lange, W.B.Ross, W.R.Jans, A.Ladune, C.Ouannoun, R.Akbal, S.Begu, A.Santos, J.F.Garcia R., J.F.Ramos, D.L.Mc Kinney, L.E.Schueler, P.H.Ackerman, R.W.Weber, E.D.Shields, L.F.Sbiral, L.T.Pritchard, R.A.Fox, R.W.Reuter, T.Ryan, A.H.Fisher, C.J.Hines, W.C.Wilson, D.P.Mc Farlane, J.L.Niedert, M.B.Graham, R.O.Edwards, R.P.Mehlich, W.Heinzerling, A.Montoro, C.H.Schindel Jr., D.L.Jackson, D.L.Trimble, E.B.Harvey, E.G.Schaefbauer, G.C.Livingston, G.J.Miller, G.W.Ovens, J.E.Boyum, J.H.Alexander, J.S.Hendren, M.J.Lawrence Jr., N.R.Bergland, O.D.Williams, R.D.Watson, R.J.Ronek, R.M.Downing, S.R.Creek Jr., T.L.Lingafelter, P.Heraud, K.Winter, D.Diaz, V.Paton, D.H.Davis, D.W.Holm, F.Fagle, F.L.Juhl, G.O.Weber, J.R.Przekurat, L.S.Richardson, G.Gerhard, B.D.Coulter, G.L.Wunder, J.Egan, T.W.Matucha, G.A.Meier, M.J.Durham, R.R.Hantz, W.G.Winters, H.Fuentes, C.L.Harris, K.G.Livingston, L.H.Buehler, R.Grisby, W.R.Henninger II, B.A.Pfalzgraf, B.Faranda, B.H.Skatrud, B.R.Buhrow, C.M.Depooter, D.L.Davis, D.M.Anderson, E.C.Fluhr, E.K.Sims, L.M.Degenhardt, P.W.Glispie, R.M.Jones, S.R.Adams, V.L.Engh, M.Coindet, A.Bravo, C.R.Conner, D.J.Cooper, D.L.Shatzer, G.P.Dahlen, J.A.Hartman, L.A.Rodgers, L.J.Cook, D.M.Kilburg, E.E.Nordman, E.Marshall Jr., G.E.Brotman, G.J.Fisher, L.H.Sanders, L.R.Keil, C.M.Morehead, D.W.Beehner, J.F.Tix, J.Newman, R.Tena, B.K.Bohnsack, C.F.Wandro, G.G.Wyant, R.J.Schultz, R.L.Mc Calley, W.G.Brustkern, R.Guilmaille, C.A.Petersmith, C.L.Downey, C.S.Stam, D.K.Ceradsky, D.L.Watson, D.R.Emery, E.A.Krapfl, E.G.Crouch, E.P.Miller, F.E.Franks, G.L.Batterson, H.M.Kueter, H.Pruett, J.A.Streeby, J.D.Geeseka, J.J.Bustos Jr., J.P.Murguia, J.Zahn, M.M.Huggins, P.R.Lerum, R.A.Jarosh, R.D.Williams, R.J.Streger, R.L.Franklin, R.Maitland, R.P.Smith, R.Sebben, T.J.Crouch, W.W.Kizer, V.Santos, D.Winchester, J.A.Larson, J.B.Grimes, W.H.Watson Jr., D.A.Olson, D.D.Cox, D.L.Uthe, H.J.Harnisch, J.G.Kloberdanz, J.M.Crawford, L.J.Jaster, W.H.Chapman, A.D.Stevens, E.W.Miller, G.J.Navis, J.R.Sallee, K.R.Henkle, M.W.Neevel, W.D.Kampa, F.Tafolla, A.Kenehan, A.T.Luna, C.E.Franklin, C.J.Trujillo, C.R.McCarroll, D.E.Hetzel, D.W.Anderson, E.E.Becker, F.G.Steigleder, H.C.Spaulding, H.W.Findahl, J.L.Grypp, J.L.McGee, L.G.Manders, P.R.Mills, R.C.Gilkes, R.D.Mc Murrin, R.F.Burns, R.J.Knoll, W.D.Higgins, W.S.Skinner Jr., M.Velo, A.Luna, C.I.Ghere, D.P.Dedecker, E.J.Axline, E.L.Griffith, G.L.Maske, R.C.Lewis, W.V.Croegaert, F.Martinez G., C.C.Gilson, K.W.Farrell, R.B.Preslar, W.C.Vanbrunt, A.Ibañez, A.Vols, B.D.Decker, D.L.Owen, D.M.Powers, G.C.Lopez, J.D.Early, J.M.Baker, M.M.Baldwin, T.F.Rengstorf, W.A.Kappel, M.R.Bentley, B.J.Hamilton, C.F.Schoeberl, F.L.Husted, G.L.Rounds, G.R.McDonald, J.L.Adamson, J.L.Boeckman, J.W.Rettig, M.A.Lovett, M.H.Marra, R.H.Blankenship, T.J.Atkins, T.M.Cline, W.D.McCurdy, B.M.Martin, C.J.Rokusek, C.M.Wehr, C.Taylor, D.W.Benshoff, H.J.Wach, J.B.Butler, L.G.Adamzak, M.M.Lopez, M.Parsons, R.A.Zirbel, R.J.Petersen, R.L.Lingeman, R.L.Terry, T.J.Wilkinson, W.S.Eastman, Y.Mercy, W.Herschler, H.J.Kramer, J.A.Magyar Jr., J.F.Sims, J.L.Vrban, J.Mendoza, M.D.Van Buren, R.A.Goddard Jr., T.M.Fogle, C.E.Luppi, J.Pontoire, D.Dean, D.M.Hill, J.Daringer, L.M.Neubauer, W.G.Watson, C.F.Price, D.A.Funk, D.E.Timm, D.G.Fleischer, D.I.Ward, D.M.Adams, E.Andress, E.W.Hunt, G.R.Harter, H.Harreld, J.H.Patton, J.R.Smith, K.C.Dittberner, M.L.Taets, M.R.Clark, M.S.Boleen, P.P.Birdsall, R.A.Kacher, R.J.Richmond, R.J.Tangie, R.N.Rietz, R.R.Deglow, R.Taets, R.Teno, R.W.Fellner, B.J.Demont, D.L.Jordan, D.S.Sproul, J.D.Rogers, J.R.Goulette, L.N.Weber, R.D.Farr, E.Saiz, A.Rossell, D.L.Self, K.Blair Jr., L.A.Blickenderfer, L.V.Ruth, P.H.Guss Sr., R.E.Trout, T.L.Poston, W.C.Motzer, D.A.Thompson, D.L.Deeds, D.R.Lemons, E.A.Mathes, H.L.Harvey, L.C.Letchford, P.J.Schmitz, R.J.Billings, T.J.Mezera, H.R.Smith, L.E.Vroman Jr., L.Emerson, M.E.Schmitt, R.L.Fitzpatrick, C.L.Mosley, C.L.Stephens, D.E.Feight, D.E.Johnson, D.J.Clester, D.L.Baker, D.R.Axtell, D.W.Brendemuehl, E.G.Irelan, G.Aguilar, H.B.Crapp, J.C.Hamstreet, J.R.Depaepe, K.L.Nelson, L.F.Baliles, L.G.Leidig, L.R.Spurgeon, M.R.Kuipers, R.E.Dyer, R.J.Peterson, R.J.Ruhs, R.R.Gardner, S.D.Howk, W.E.Hughes, W.E.Wilson, A.Tomassini, J.Velasco, L.Diaz, M.Lopez, C.W.King, F.R.Depaepe, J.W.Martin, K.K.Shehorn, L.D.Brown, L.D.Gordon, R.Goldizen, R.L.Meyer, S.R.Garland, A.A.Herman, F.Mc Guire, J.H.Prideaux, J.W.Taylor, L.H.Whitworth, L.J.Gomez, M.L.Davis, R.D.Karel, R.Riese, E.L.Sergeant, G.E.Schmidt, J.L.Smith, W.R.Emerson, A.Dreux, D.E.Lovejoy, E.D.Leighty, J.L.Ashdown, R.L.Obryan, S.R.Payne, A.J.Borkgren, D.W.De Money, J.N.Krupicka, J.V.Hedman, L.O.Mayfield, M.E.Jones, M.R.Gerber, P.A.Swanson, P.Gust, W.M.Wright, M.Arroyo, V.Martinez G., T.W.Byrnes, D.F.Hiney, A.L.Buchmeyer, B.A.Williams, C.J.Treanor, D.L.Buchholz, D.L.Johnson, D.M.Riniker, F.I.Stiemsma, F.L.Hansel Sr., G.E.Hendren, G.J.Mannell, G.L.Dunn, H.H.Hanson Jr., J.A.Pipho, J.D.Ohlweiler, J.G.Limburg, J.L.Canfield, J.L.Chapin, R.A.Fouts, R.F.Schultz, R.J.Dedobbelaere, R.J.Pitzen, R.R.Zbleski, T.D.Fiedler, W.W.Covert, B.Mowson, A.C.Prins, D.J.Pollentier, D.L.Petsche, G.A.Graves, J.B.Tarrance, A.W.Combs, C.A.Stansberry, C.E.Foley, D.F.Mitchell, E.J.Tuttle, F.D.Franks, J.E.Meyer, L.P.Mack, R.E.Smith, S.R.Thede, L.Roman, A.R.Hayward, B.Whittle, C.D.Hickman, D.H.Ver Heul, K.R.Carlson, R.C.Wood, R.D.Brooks, R.T.Vershaw, R.W.Bronner, A.Besse, B.Wagner, A.L.Hosek, C.C.Seifert, C.E.Poncy, E.N.Garriott, E.R.Beilfuss, H.E.Martin, H.F.Sigwarth, J.A.Farrell, J.E.Jeffrey, J.E.Kuehl, J.Hockings, J.Long, J.P.Anderson, J.V.Armstrong, L.G.Anderson, L.L.Hanna, M.E.Hucks Sr., N.Higinbotham, P.W.Smith, S.W.Schneider, V.L.Streeby, G.Wuerzburger, H.Michalski, B.Whiteford, C.J.De Hart, J.C.Heinick, K.D.Nelson, C.J.Ohrt, C.L.Thomas, D.T.Mc Donald, G.A.Friday, H.L.Beenken, L.R.Headington, W.H.Wright, D.L.Wagner, J.J.Hamlett, J.M.Cervantes, J.P.Buchanan, D.R.Stenner, J.D.La Rue, R.L.Mehlert, R.P.Wiese, A.R.Sullivan, C.V.Johnson, D.E.Weydert, D.F.Goossens, J.A.Loy, J.G.Gomez, J.M.Brooks, J.W.Landmeier, R.D.Burns, R.P.Gauger, S.L.Wilkinson, T.D.Petersen, T.J.Demarlie, W.L.Owens, W.R.Bohnsack, D.F.Hartley, F.C.Peterson, F.L.Brockmeyer, G.E.Louderback, K.M.Nehl, L.D.York, L.E.Thompson, R.C.Weber, W.A.Van Eman, B.L.Dickerson, B.Sherrod, G.N.Purdy, R.W.Grams, V.E.Coudron, W.W.Wendlandt, G.G.Thornton, J.Lawless, J.M.Higgins, B.Gutierrez A., J.W.McDaniel, R.M.Feller, A.W.Van Osdel, B.M.Boland, M.L.Schmieder, L.R.Elder Jr., R.J.Piatt, S.L.Greene, A.Blazquez S., F.Velo, D.D.Tucker, **1967** F.J.Bruckbauer, E.Vogel, H.Von Rosen, K.Roesner, W.Buchloh, J.J.Linsey, M.A.Biemans, D.Poje, J.Hamoniere, L.Soudy, B.E.McCombs, D.D.Johnson, D.D.Roberts, D.G.Black, D.L.Lukehart, D.W.Littig Jr., E.Bouska, E.Johnson, F.E.Schmidt, F.F.Shemek Jr., G.J.Deloff, G.L.Beeth, H.L.Simpson, J.B.Horton, J.K.Vernon, J.R.Butler, J.R.Norris, J.W.Eklofe, K.E.Evitts, K.S.Watters, L.F.Simmons, L.O.Uhlenhopp, L.Owens, M.D.Drake, M.F.Shively, M.J.Sinnott, P.S.Erickson, R.D.Lovern, R.L.Brittain, R.Mc Coy, R.W.Marean, S.K.Strohbehn, T.D.Warner, T.L.Haberman, T.R.Butler, W.Keeton, P.Fouquet, B.L.Clark, C.R.Thomas, D.Hobkirk, D.J.Enloe, D.J.Guenterberg, G.J.Rosauer, M.M.Britz, R.G.Glasgow, R.L.Priebe, A.W.Johnson, B.E.Beebe, J.F.Cantu, J.L.Scholl, L.D.Hesse, L.L.Vande Slunt, N.D.Tuder, C.A.Dobereiner, D.C.King, D.N.Miller, J.A.Hart, J.H.Hockey, L.Barker, S.D.Hansen, A.L.Mc Niel, B.D.Abeyta, C.A.Larsen, C.K.Beckman, D.D.Solberg, D.J.Pighetti, D.Logue Jr., D.R.Covert, G.E.Gray, G.M.Smyser, J.D.Pumphrey, J.E.Davis, J.E.Peden Jr., J.F.Yenger, J.H.Hansen, J.H.Sink, J.L.Bainbridge, L.F.Parr, L.G.Welch, M.L.Renfrew, N.R.Bennett, R.A.Gibson, R.B.Griffiths, R.E.Hay, R.H.Wittke, R.R.Fremon, S.R.Block, S.W.Hill, W.L.Miller Jr., J.Thomas, C.E.Doss, J.L.Woten, J.R.Braun, L.D.Gullett, L.L.Flowers, A.B.Becker, A.H.Wise, D.E.Jarosh, E.L.Ramos, H.D.Kilby, O.J.Troester, R.T.Grovo Jr., D.A.Niedert, J.H.Haugen, L.E.Clark, R.J.Brannon, E.Akin, E.A.Simerson, R.D.Albert, W.J.Polich, A.D.Williams, B.D.Davis, C.J.Bosley Jr., D.K.Kuethe, E.G.Oberheu, H.R.Coop, J.D.Brustkern, J.E.Hopwood, J.E.Thompson, J.O.Blakely, K.P.Ricketts, L.A.Tisdale, L.A.Workman, N.R.Schmitt, R.A.Howell, T.Dragovich Jr., V.Bickel, C.N.Slaughter, C.W.Clemens, D.L.Clark, G.M.Callas, H.L.Staton, J.A.Wright, K.B.Smith, L.D.McCabe, R.C.Frazee, B.H.Staudt, C.A.McClenahan, C.Portillo, D.E.Albert, D.R.Cottrell, G.D.Schaffer, G.R.Swank, J.C.Scribner, J.E.Markussen, L.Dale, D.A.Bottema, L.J.Wienhold, R.K.Bertch, R.R.Kalkbrenner, A.M.McNeill, B.L.Shubert, C.A.Richards, C.W.Carter, D.E.Koch, D.Hernandez, D.K.Schutte, F.M.Zoz, G.F.Converse, H.W.Hofstetter, J.C.Kelley, J.D.Cloyd, J.E.Mess, J.R.Soden, J.W.Henderson, J.W.Hopkins, K.L.Pilcher, M.E.Mathews, R.D.Brown, R.D.Hopkins, R.D.Straw, R.G.Burton, R.L.Clark, R.L.Porter, R.L.Rex, R.R.Rankin, R.W.Deleon Jr., R.Wessely, T.A.Musgrove, H.Stephan, R.Castro, A.P.Miller, D.D.Hansen, D.F.Damanski, D.W.Muse, G.J.Dzekunskas, H.N.Smith, J.R.Nelson, L.E.Olson, R.A.Batchelder, R.L.Milligan, S.J.Babb, C.H.Downs, D.E.Chandler, F.G.Boyer, J.A.Baysinger, R.A.Howard, R.I.Joslin, R.L.Hendricks, R.L.Hood, S.W.Tews, T.E.Carnes, D.R.Force, K.M.Seaman, L.E.Da Billo, P.M.Whitmore, R.E.Rice, J.Painchault, D.A.Draper, D.Baker, D.C.Noyd, D.D.Randall, G.L.Otterson Jr., J.E.Booth, J.G.Boyer, K.W.Belcher, M.E.Markin, R.D.Smith, R.L.Holdridge, R.L.Schmit, W.J.Larkin, G.Watremez, K.Zimmermann, C.E.Tyrrel, D.E.Franke, E.R.Staack, V.V.Marquardt, A.Kompolsek, C.G.Gillette, G.K.Hendrickson, G.L.Juhl, G.P.Moyer, H.F.Meyer, J.F.Halverson, J.R.Burkhardt, K.F.Locke Jr., L.J.Schaffer, M.F.Deike, N.J.Zeien, R.D.Grotelueschen, R.E.Schoenauer, R.G.Muller, T.L.Flaherty, J.A.A.Kruel, R.Chevallier, A.Martin Gr., A.Perez G., G.W.Blackwell, R.A.Hoffman, S.L.Barrett, C.A.Foht, D.R.Hilbert, E.W.Roed, P.L.Atwater Jr., B.A.Conrads, D.H.Koester, E.L.Winch, G.F.Pankratz, G.J.Ives, J.H.Trainor, J.L.Watson, J.O.Hanks Sr., J.W.Van Cleve, L.E.Gooden, L.E.Stolz Jr., L.G.Birchard, L.L.Wilcox, L.T.Ferguson, M.E.Durick, M.W.Thompson, P.A.Mc Keever, R.C.Crossan, R.J.Walker, R.L.Donnelly, R.L.Poock, R.L.Salisbury, T.W.Deitch, W.M.Boehler, W.P.Coughlin, D.S.Ellis, J.L.Spaur, J.W.Chidester, R.L.Gibson, R.Williams, A.R.Kolling Jr., A.T.Woods, D.I.Heim, G.W.Buyck, J.B.Harrelson, L.A.Woodard, L.E.Mc Namee, A.J.Johnson, R.E.Gahn, T.W.Mc Coneghey, D.Clingan, D.L.Melick, M.E.Gobble, P.M.Junko, R.G.Cayouette, V.T.Pedersen, L.J.Carroll, D.D.Barfels, D.L.Schmit, E.L.Whennen, F.W.Minter, J.A.Saeugling, L.D.Percival, O.D.Gruver, R.L.Chanez, R.L.Heckart, R.W.Spurgeon, S.L.Smith, V.A.Cecak, R.Adam, B.F.Erpelding, C.E.Rauch, D.D.Niedert, D.G.Chard, D.R.Cabor, J.L.Woodward, K.G.Heriford, M.A.Gaertnier, R.C.Lantow, R.T.Mc Guire, W.T.Boas, B.G.Strath, B.J.Vanloon, D.A.Loete, D.J.Wiegmann, G.K.Wiegardt, K.R.Jones, L.J.Coulson, A.Rodriguez G., D.S.Bailey, G.D.Louder, J.J.Dyer, J.J.Schang, J.L.Aneweer, L.D.Crockett, R.N.Del Rosario, A.Gomes, P.D.Sitze, R.A.Luders, C.A.Thulin, D.C.Rokusek, D.D.Latham, D.R.Miller, E.L.Cornell, G.L.Mohr, J.A.Pruitt, J.Howe, J.P.Mousel, J.R.Palmer, L.S.Andreassen, R.L.Schofield, S.L.Forester, N.Boudart, G.Nessel, B.O.Glosser, F.A.Carpenter, H.L.Rumler, J.A.Turner, J.S.Bell, R.T.Williams, D.D.Converse, J.J.Thomas, J.W.Whitmire, L.V.Garbes, R.Crow, T.R.Conn, P.H.Pearce, R.E.Cronin, R.L.Mangrich, H.J.Rouse, J.G.Finley, J.L.Carr, J.McClelland, L.L.Almquist, M.L.Russow, R.E.McMullen, T.R.Wyllie, W.J.Freiburger, G.Garnier, E.Mueller, D.A.Allam, C.Duffie, M.A.Jesuit, B.D.Chaplin, C.G.Peters, D.E.Caputo, D.H.Bieber, D.R.Rachiele, E.C.Davis Jr., J.B.Bley, J.L.Tuttle, J.S.Robertson, L.J.Henyan, L.L.Thompson, P.J.Metz, R.A.Butters, R.A.Plemitscher, R.W.Jones, G.Recq, M.Lepage, D.J.Bierman, L.J.Anderson, R.E.Curtis, R.R.Pullin, F.P.Stoltenberg, G.L.Schelfaut, H.J.Mercurio, J.B.Ogden, J.D.Black II, J.R.Birchmier, M.Colclasure, M.D.Good,

P.J.Hurley, R.J.Schenke, R.L.La Frentz, S.L.Knoernschild, V.J.Macdonald, G.L.Taber Jr., J.H.Green, D.D.Dahlstrom, H.L.Selhost, R.Goembel, T.M.Fike, K.E.Dahlstrom, W.R.Franke, J.Champion, L.Manzanero, B.F.Morphew, L.R.Seams, A.N.Crummett, D.Tovar, F.M.Stone Jr., G.C.Douglas, J.E.Covey, M.D.Debackere, S.Johnson Jr., V.D.Grimes, V.E.Matter, V.J.Teague, J.Francisco Martins, G.Pouillot, M.T.King, J.Jacinto Fernandes, T.P.Western Jr., B.G.Bowling, C.C.Handley, D.W.Johnson, J.F.Dressel, L.L.Roethler, J.Chaveca, B.H.Vanlandegen, D.P.Christensen, J.M.Wester, K.L.Madson, L.Hoffman, L.J.Thies, R.A.Cooley, R.J.Treiber, R.P.Hammond, W.H.Steinbeck, L.Dordonnat, H.Paul, M.Dauber, E.L.Dykes, J.M.Marolf, L.E.Jeanes, N.L.Eiklenborg, S.Blanks, J.Le Bret, D.L.Smith, H.Putman, R.G.Blackstock, W.Schrepfer, M.E.Hines, R.W.Huckstadt, D.A.Clever, D.E.Horihan, J.R.Smith, L.J.Loete, L.S.Witt, T.L.Harris, W.D.Vinzant, E.Esteban, D.D.Kammerman, G.I.Franklin Jr., J.M.Bump, P.D.Whitson, R.J.Scarbrough Jr., R.Jackson, R.L.Gehrke, C.Letang, B.E.Ralston, M.J.O'Neill, A.L.Springer, B.G.Morrison, D.W.Colvin, E.D.Donelson, C.R.Hoffman, H.L.Zuck, P.C.Kell, R.Klippert, D.C.Brown, F.S.Cottrell, K.R.Silver, M.J.Ruby, R.A.Kryzanek, R.A.Young, T.D.Holverson, T.M.Holbach, F.Flaunay, J.Flouriot, J.Tissier, C.A.Barker, J.H.Pardoe, J.M.Hardy, W.H.Clark, D.A.Westberg, G.D.Dawson, L.D.Tonn, J.E.Miller, D.C.Colsch, E.L.Tate, R.E.Jackson, R.L.Bell, H.Volk, E.R.Aldrich, H.L.Faust, J.V.Diaz, L.C.Dahlhauser, D.D.Spawn, D.J.Danielsen, J.K.Priest, K.A.Stone, R.A.Schafer, R.J.Stritesky, W.D.Le Compte, M.Yepes, F.D.Hamlin, L.O.Gruis, P.A.Fuller, R.L.Bohl, M.Huelva, F.E.Bakula, M.A.Vázquez , A.Holmes, C.J.Olsen, L.D.Stillions, T.F.Fitzpatrick, C.James, J.W.Wales, R.L.Abel, R.L.Morrison, R.R.Bruening, C.D.Coughran, W.Eubanks Jr., R.R.Evans, H.M.Leguizamón, D.G.Kuchta, D.R.Austin, F.D.Cortez, F.J.Kruse, G.R.Witcombe, L.E.Ruud, L.R.Madson, P.L.Bellinger, D.Schmitt, H.Boebinger, J.H.Te Bockhorst, M.Poirier, A.Schuler, C.L.Strobbe, G.L.Martin, G.P.Weyland, J.T.Hall, L.L.Fells, M.D.Ward, N.E.Thibodeau, R.A.Jensen Meeks, R.E.Moss, T.M.Snyder, L.J.Balkan, J.C.Nelson, A.C.Erickson, G.Enderle, F.Diaz, E.J.Brown, K.D.Thorne, M.H.Staines, S.L.Irwin, R.M.Sullivan, S.V.Bernard, A.Arroyo, A.Fernandez J., C.H.Shobe, E.Lewis, G.A.Derby, A.Hernandez G., M.Sanchez G., M.L.Stiner, B.A.Hopkins, H.G.Childers, J.H.Madill, L.D.Saug, M.J.Banzhaf, R.J.Recker, C.E.Oltman, J.G.Steinbach, K.A.Enstrom, W.W.Power, D.J.Kiser, J.A.Fructus, J.Loftus, K.L.Nichols, K.R.Grenier, M.L.Prieto, R.Carr, R.G.Reimer, S.J.Petersen, S.M.Ohl, D.Wankin, F.Diaz, J.E.Barber, A.R.Miller, D.E.Tholl, D.P.Mitchell, D.R.Schwartz, J.A.Lounsberry, J.A.Weber, J.C.Lewis, J.D.Manley, J.G.Hayward, J.H.Harmon, J.M.Hammer, M.B.Siebke, M.R.Siefken, M.R.Sussex, R.D.Trask, R.G.Norton, R.K.Wright, R.L.Fisher, R.L.Schatz, R.R.Ochsner, R.V.Bartlett, J.Veziat, P.A.Bauersfeld, E.Diaz V., D.K.Ahlstrand, J.J.Jenkins, J.G.Darby Jr., D.B.Corr, D.H.Ziegler, D.O.Wippermann, G.A.Griffith, G.E.Lenhart, G.M.Seefeldt, J.A.Dickinson, J.E.Doyle, J.J.Gerstner, J.M.Van Grinsven, P.E.Beedlow, P.P.Varner, R.H.Beyer, T.E.Hegenbarth, W.J.Evans, W.W.Bickford, J.Lesceu, D.L.March, G.S.Gesme, J.L.Morgan, N.Portillo, W.C.Hankel, B.Chol, P.J.Dettmann, A.J.Gaines, E.J.Offutt Jr., R.A.Thompson, G.E.Heald, H.I.Bedney, H.V.Speer, J.E.Wier, J.H.Shuey, L.D.Porter, M.K.Schutte, R.E.Nixon, R.G.Slegl, R.L.De Witt, R.M.Fauser, S.G.Brandau, T.E.Boe, V.D.Hollman, V.R.Myles, H.Billotet, D.D.Zlabek, L.O.Bell, A.Rangel, R.C.Earl, T.R.Poock, B.J.Burke, C.M.Hawkins, C.R.Neff, D.E.Girsch, H.Grosvold, M.H.Schlichtmann, R.W.Hewlitt, S.J.Hoover Jr., T.E.Franklin, G.R.Dustin, C.W.Renkel, C.Bacrot, I.K.Wojahn, G.Otto, J.Voigt, R.Ullrich, W.Mueller, W.Utzinger, B.J.Knight, C.A.Anderson, C.Formwalt, C.J.Noecker, R.F.Parker, M.Boudin, Y.Pinguet, D.D.Guetzlaff, D.E.Paul, D.J.Barnard, J.R.Sizemore, W.F.Preston, M.Ruchet, J.M.Bridgman, S.J.Corwin, A.A.Fava, G.D.Davis, G.D.Mohling, L.E.Stone, R.C.Watson, S.W.Caughron, J.S.Mutziger, C.A.Bailey, G.H.Thomas, M.J.Causemaker, M.P.Roach, J.T.Vicevich, L.P.Nanke, M.R.Cirivello, P.Vallejo, D.D.Ludwig, L.F.Hall, P.E.Arteaga, M.V.Buck, D.L.Henderson, J.D.Avery, V.C.Manuel, W.G.Hooper, W.R.Finch, L.B.Allen, P.C.Brandt, R.H.Stampe, J.A.Kostynuk, C.K.Shover, E.M.Irelan, G.D.Nagle, J.G.Barnett, C.O.Townsley, J.F.Gruman, N.J.Miller, S.L.Olds, A.A.Peers, D.P.Sommerfelt, L.G.Bowen, J.M.Gonzalez C., E.V.Bolch, M.A.Russell, R.F.Hartwig, W.J.Rusniak, W.Deppisch, B.R.Linnenkamp, D.A.Przekurat, A.L.Berzett, J.R.Gilbert, K.A.Stephens, S.C.Sinn, R.B.Skindzelewski, C.J.Chlumsky, R.F.Habke, F.Pauvert, H.Sprau, K.Rothhaar, G.Sander, A.Eckstein, B.Striehl, G.Bauer, G.Kaulbars, H.Knorra, J.Braun, J.Prudlik, N.Becher, R.Siegert, S.Friedrich, T.Hyb, W.Bengel, W.Quick, D.J.Fonger, D.L.Mulvaney, J.A.Hutchins Jr., L.D.Schreiber, L.D.Shinn, M.B.Skowronski, W.E.Voelliger, B.W.Gentz, E.U.Koerner, J.L.Hagen, L.G.Plageman, R.F.Margelofsky, S.A.Boelter, S.S.Jones, W.O.Braemer, W.R.Brewer, F.D.Hein, N.A.La Tendresse, P.L.Karow, R.A.Friese, W.R.Braunschweig, L.Faltyn, C.D.Olson, E.L.Whisler, L.A.Zweber, L.D.Pomering, R.L.Norris, S.R.Wendorf, G.A.Grilley, W.J.Stam, A.O.Albertson Jr., D.D.Young, G.R.Koopmans, H.G.Holbach, H.W.Jaeger, J.D.Trejo, P.J.Taylor, R.L.Krueger, F.Heim, G.R.Habinck, L.G.Guenterberg, M.M.Steinman, P.L.Dittberner, W.B.Kiekhaefer, E.G.Kaiser, A.T.Hill, R.L.Glenn, D.M.Feller, S.Kusa, D.J.Straseske, D.L.Wright, J.M.Charlson, W.Henry, D.I.Watson, B.A.Nance, H.C.Swayne, M.J.Brown, R.C.Schwieder, R.F.Rogers, R.J.Grisco, R.L.Hester, R.S.Lee, P.M.Lloyd, A.S.Hufford Ney, J.A.Wiseman, Z.Rodríguez, G.Langer, D.H.Holtz, N.E.Warber, G.Kretzschmar, L.E.Buchholz, D.E.Westemeier, J.M.Jensen, K.W.Martin, L.D.Bothum, R.D.Kimball, S.T.Herringa, A.Brewer, H.Davenne, F.Bidault, G.J.Bell, M.E.Frank, L.J.Villwock, P.A.Rugloski, I.A.Mersch, D.G.Temperly, D.L.Ragon, D.M.Farnum, J.F.Quartier, L.I.Beauchamp, M.K.Smedema, R.L.Hollister, T.W.Woods, E.L.Gibbs, W.G.Humphrey, P.D.Duytschaever, L.N.Keesey, M.A.Laufenberg, D.Heycke, M.L.Hollis, R.Glas, J.Flohr, M.Morchoisne, E.Fernandez G., H.J.Davenport, H.M.Cook, S.S.Gelande, J.E.Smart, M.De Taeye, J.H.Herr, C.J.Martin, E.Stowers, C.L.Nicholson, M.J.Mitten, R.O.Burgess, R.Ferreira, G.Martinez L., J.C.Haima, R.J.Cox, A.Ortega R., R.Vasseur, J.Verbauwen, N.P.Lillybeck, H.Vila, **1968** J.C.Steinman, P.Huette, G.Boes, A.Pulido, H.D.Berns, R.D.Wetjen, L.L.Stringer, N.E.Carter, S.C.Wentler, A.L.Loecke, N.E.Hibbler, W.H.Patchin, P.Brunot, E.Lenoir, M.Pierrot, B.E.Thompson, C.N.Heape, R.L.Peyton, G.Bernwald, J.W.Crowe, C.S.Reed, D.N.Olsen, F.L.Rodgers, C.J.Wells, E.R.Melville, S.D.Loeffelholz, J.Huette, C.A.Murguia, G.A.Forret, J.E.Dedor, K.H.Paulson, L.E.Wieland, P.R.Nicholson, A.H.Voth, J.J.Vargas, R.D.Mourning, R.J.Spautz, A.Gruson, J.Poirson, G.Thiault, E.Nolte, G.L.Salley, L.M.Powless, R.E.Thomas, R.W.Jump, V.H.Sala, K.Zeiter, B.L.Rosson, J.Gil Barroca, A.K.Inman, D.L.Weathers, M.Castellano, P.Ahijado , C.A.McMichael, P.L.Pringle, A.Laies, K.D.Loete, O.L.Martin, R.F.Vanacker, W.L.Meana, M.D.Schockey, P.J.Thurman, M.A.Nolin, O.L.Hackleman, E.M.Shafer, M.L.Fouts, K.Clemens, S.Russi, R.C.Yonkers, S.M.Walker, F.Diaz, J.H.Ehlinger, L.F.Tharp, M.A.Smith, A.T.Lanser, C.P.Bonnett, J.A.Kolker, J.C.Dockerty, J.P.Bodish, J.S.Gault, T.F.Barton, W.C.Burgess, D.A.Hogan, L.J.Noack, J.Gritti, M.Patiño, D.J.Suss, G.F.Marshall, H.W.Humphrey, J.R.Fairman, R.E.Gladwin, R.J.Marshall, R.M.Brummer, R.W.Johnson, T.L.Hurst, V.Gullo, R.A.Engels, W.O.Mc Farlin, H.D.Hudson, W.D.Hist, E.H.Gracia, E.Deshayes, L.A.Pufahl, H.Riedinger, R.B.Peckler, M.W.Filson, J.Lecloux, J.F.Magner, K.E.Seitzinger, L.B.Hovenga, L.N.Chapman, R.L.Peck, W.A.Griebel, L.Boulde, S.C.Robine, D.R.Orand, J.P.Dwyer, K.H.Felsman, L.J.Hiner, R.J.Blacklock, R.P.Turgeon, S.J.Leroy, C.Thomas, D.Servoin, J.Servoin, J.Villepreux, H.Starke, M.Burckhardt, R.D.Bellamy, K.Pennington, A.Pablo De, C.R.Fuson, D.K.Newton, V.R.Learn, E.D.Ray, J.C.Marsho, V.H.Conger Jr., D.J.Nance, E.Lavalley, G.D.Forster, J.S.Rumbaugh, R.L.Mesenbrink, D.J.Humke, D.J.Wadle, G.Luens, P.Renaud, W.L.Weimer, G.Williams, H.A.Wilson Sr., J.E.Maxwell, J.J.Reiss, J.L.Culp, L.E.Hogue, L.Feye, L.J.Ripperger, M.E.Forslund, M.L.Franz, R.F.Sama, J.E.Hellmann, J.D.Wadle, M.M.Langill, C.G.Bierbrodt, C.M.Tauke, E.M.Van Acker, J.C.Mishler, L.S.Butelli, M.G.Aust, R.D.Twedt, R.G.Jones, R.W.Gibbs, S.M.Bert Hunter, H.V.Harsha, J.M.Haymaker, P.D.Wadley, R.I.Moore, V.H.Stewardson, V.S.Schmitt, J.Fraile, W.Egenberger, C.E.Sloss, B.L.Singer, D.D.Olson, E.Marshall, F.E.Olson, J.B.Boggs, J.D.Riseley, J.E.Taylor, J.L.Smithers, K.R.Burger, L.K.Williams, D.L.Nolin, K.Holden, D.J.Smith, L.E.Lovik, L.K.Rumburg, B.Carly, E.Erickson Jr., F.W.Wyrick, H.W.Ritchie, J.G.Heidebrink, J.J.Fettkether, L.S.Hoftender, P.C.Robertson, R.A.Chase, R.J.Elskamp, R.Justiniano, R.L.Rathbun, R.W.Conrad, T.E.Maynard, W.J.Nevilles, R.C.Houghtaling Jr., P.G.McGregor, D.R.Griggs, N.S.Grossmann, R.P.Fontana, O.E.Ramaglia, A.O.Sharp, B.R.Retzlaff, D.E.Strawn, D.L.Campbell, J.M.McCoy, J.W.Gehrke, W.A.Mishler, G.Litaud, A.Peon, J.L.Purves, E.Morrow, J.M.Zook, J.A.Dodson, C.S.Lundstrom, H.G.Anderson, J.A.Voelzke, J.R.Randall, M.J.Antrim, R.D.Vanderzyl, S.C.Tomich, T.E.Allen, V.Raposo, T.E.Pauzauskie, M.J.Irvin, E.J.Armbrust, H.Baier, B.A.Lovett, D.L.Carson, G.A.Bennett, G.D.Chesnut, H.A.Bushman, J.A.Bussan, J.W.Benjamin, L.H.Neumeyer, M.Conzett, P.H.Moeller, R.P.Bartlett, W.A.Winzenburg, W.D.Madara, W.E.Boston, F.J.Doser, J.Cusse, A.Dumont, G.Lemeret, J.Kitchen, M.P.Obert, D.Moizard, A.D.Yoder, B.E.Browning, J.M.Vanauwelaer, J.R.Burns, P.W.Post, R.D.Phillips, R.J.Cullen, S.E.Warren, S.R.Frankel, D.G.Budde, D.I.Miller, J.Ruet, A.C.Leinenbach, C.R.Morse, D.L.Urbatsch, G.A.Dement, G.A.Morse, J.C.Frommelt, J.L.McNamara, R.E.Arnold, J.Romero, R.Olsson, C.D.Gravitt, C.J.Brenner, R.A.Johanningmeier, R.M.Driscoll, R.P.Jarrett, R.D.Marfilius, M.J.Casas, P.N.Wooldridge, C.D.Snyder, F.J.Kukuczka Jr., J.A.Mascari, K.M.Stokeld, K.P.Kunkle, L.Westemeier, M.A.Clayton, R.E.Fox, R.H.Like, J.Patenotre, M.Haffner, W.Gehrmann, A.L.McKoon, J.L.Hall, S.L.Howe, T.C.Gibbons, W.L.Foster, C.R.Benincasa, O.Higonet, K.A.McCombs, B.S.Roper, H.A.Fisher, J.T.Smith, O.Gilbert, S.L.Lassegard, M.T.Alban, B.J.Rechek, M.I.Bowers, W.C.Wheatley, J.R.Bullock, M.Freels, S.B.Brim, S.Desmiers De Chenon, O.H.Peirano, B.F.Dekazel, M.F.Rinaldo, W.L.Holstun, A.E.Strickland Reams, L.J.Underwood, D.C.Miller, J.H.Peterson, J.R.Moore, R.R.Ludwig, S.Noland, T.L.Young, G.J.Frazier, J.G.Sawvell, O.Werner, K.L.Marshall, M.K.Cook, M.M.Roberts, R.L.Udelhofen, W.Preston, M.Riedel, J.Muller, E.M.Harmon, C.A.Ruhlmann, D.E.Siemek, F.A.Moffitt, F.D.Bush, P.J.Welbes, C.Arcos De , R.D.Stuart, W.E.Hillerich, J.M.Marques, B.C.Frazer, C.L.Becka, F.W.Mc Dougall, J.M.Cooke, L.J.Foley, L.W.Porter, R.A.Hunter, S.K.Millard, V.L.Trask, R.W.Fliss, J.Silvestri, H.Brandes, F.Benoit, H.Blietschau, H.Mueller, B.H.Peterson, H.Fredrich, R.L.Brandon, G.Oakes, B.R.Carrigan, D.R.Schultz, B.J.Hamilton, K.J.Oliver, W.A.Dey, A.Gallardo, E.M.Brustkern, J.S.Damanski, D.E.Eekhoff, E.C.Bowers, J.M.Aubry, J.R.Oaks, M.R.Strayer, A.Siguret, H.Grampp, H.Schellenberg, G.L.Philo, H.E.Aldrich, J.W.Jasper, L.M.Kannenberg, P.A.Shull, E.J.Cardona, D.A.Martin, G.D.Bisone, J.C.Bersero, W.Pietkuna, D.J.Porter, R.H.Layton, R.P.Bare, T.J.Higgins, T.N.Gust, C.Bari, J.Lozano, B.A.Kelly, E.L.Batten, J.D.Decker, L.B.Warren, J.R.Rowland, R.A.Manor, H.Hauck, T.H.Swale, J.D.Jessop, J.R.Hartman, M.E.Backstrom, R.E.Muchmore, R.L.Johnson, R.Mook Jr., T.J.Kitchen, R.D.Purdy, R.Sallis, D.J.Kessens, J.Jackson, J.S.Bell, M.L.Robbins, A.E.Carey, J.J.Hilby, J.M.Balducchi, R.B.Brennan, R.G.Timmerman, W.D.Bricker, Y.Robineau, D.J.Napel, M.S.Reeg, D.Hecht, E.Courth, G.Schnell, G.Schweickert, M.Zimmermann, O.Foerster, S.Morcillo, A.P.Lavallee, E.A.Adams, L.E.Kurt, G.E.Smith, C.M.Sandy, C.R.Gilbertson, D.J.Peters, J.F.Laures, K.C.Courage, M.L.Shaw, D.Schirmer, D.O.Smith, J.De Groote, L.S.Davis, R.D.Harpster, K.J.Mohlis, M.J.Starnes, W.L.Judas, O.Green, D.L.Thomas, L.A.Baker, G.L.Johnson, D.K.Carroll, M.E.Klaas, R.Dismer, K.Schlachter, D.R.Moody, L.R.Roberts, M.I.Murrens, T.A.Pins, R.P.Murphy, B.E.Boardman, J.T.Tibbels, M.K.Curtiss, S.T.Lester, A.E.López, D.H.Stowe Jr., M.L.Johnson, G.Bailey, D.F.Krenz, D.K.Self, M.D.Burke, R.J.Tady, J.Goffin, P.Caballero, V.Salducco, K.R.Kelley, D.K.Nielsen, D.R.Williams Sr., L.L.Cammer, N.Cohen, R.York, G.Garcia R., D.A.Washington, J.E.Paustian, S.M.Westervelt, W.C.Jenkins, W.E.Abuhl, M.Sevin, E.M.Becker, C.D.Johnson, E.H.Bogguess, B.E.Zager, C.D.Crook, F.R.Hoefle, M.L.Petersen, C.J.Jacobs, R.D.Dillon, S.J.Sorrels, M.J.Muirhead, P.Iranyi, A.R.Herrebout, B.D.McCormick, E.E.Kemnitz, J.L.Cannon, J.L.Valentine, P.E.Stevens, L.Iglesias, A.G.Pena, J.A.Addis, J.A.Trannel, R.T.Seaberg, E.Myers, P.Blancas, P.Cooper, D.R.Feliksiak, B.Aranda, E.K.Wardlow, J.C.Chan, M.D.Wesley, R.W.Farnum, W.F.Mausser, R.C.Paul, B.Hewett, **1969** J.Mercier, H.Jung, C.Fahler, D.L.Cooney, H.M.Odean, J.A.Stahl, L.J.Ehart, V.J.Brooks, G.Cuen, B.Schmidt, D.J.Arndt, D.R.Bever, E.Owen, E.T.Paprocki, J.A.Desherow, J.D.White, J.E.Skinner, J.W.Axness, L.A.Dow, L.A.Schmitt, L.L.Mitchell, N.K.Gray, R.L.Hughes, W.E.Britton, W.G.Starling, W.R.Burkart, G.D.Mize, R.E.Morrow, W.H.Huff, W.J.Elder, G.J.Ruden, J.E.Perkins, C.K.Hoste, B.L.Hill, C.R.Grother, F.J.Hardee, S.Lembre, L.Letertre, B.J.Cox, G.G.Esslinger, P.G.Merriman, L.Schneider, D.Frank, D.D.Filby, R.A.Palmer, R.F.Fisher, C.Eme, Y.Hill, W.Gnade Jr., J.D.L.C.Ruiz, T.Martinez S., C.F.Crilley, F.M.Pope, L.K.Moody, P.A.Wallace, J.E.Reavis, J.L.Cradick, R.W.Ambrose, B.J.Davis, R.R.See, A.J.Peterson, F.E.Bennett, J.K.Seifert, P.M.Reichen, J.Lorin, J.A.Rame, B.E.King, T.L.Mason, G.F.Stappert Jr., H.J.Lange, J.R.Cavanah, L.R.Carpenter, M.G.Hudson, P.F.Schwarz, Q.E.Duckett, R.E.Jester, P.Poiget, E.Iglesias, M.L.McClain, J.Bouillon, E.Czerwinski, G.R.Thorpe, G.W.Yearout, I.E.Geick, N.Watkins, R.J.Demeester, T.L.Viscioni, E.Ropert, G.Tonneau, R.Lopez M., L.W.Davidson, H.S.Robinson, S.A.Kelley, D.M.Richter, J.W.Earl, A.Martinez M., R.W.Woolfolk, A.Mahmutovic, Y.Weber, R.P.D.Moraes, J.Dominguez , C.B.W.Wojahn, L.Becker, M.Staude, E.E.Zahner, E.Gist, F.M.Adrian, W.Sims Jr., B.S.Arias Sanz, A.Carteron, S.Rodriguez, J.Pavard, J.Rousseau, P.Grioni, E.Scarborough, R.L.Smith Jr., G.Busseron, D.J.Deiss, D.L.Mentria, F.A.Marang, R.M.Phoebus, R.W.Lewis, B.Veillard, A.H.Torriglia, C.Desmazeau, J.M.Wireman, B.J.Montague, D.Y.Ash, H.Sanders, A.Beyler, D.Villepreux, E.Betz, L.E.Loveridge, R.Sanchez, D.W.Quist Jr., B.Archenault, S.Kubiak, J.C.Kruser, J.E.Richards, J.J.Veach, J.Millerschone, K.J.Oberbroeckling, R.G.McDowell, V.L.Smith, J.Poisson, T.Schoepp, D.Perdoux, J.Renner, J.E.Lake, R.Kurz, D.K.Montgomery, D.S.Hayes, E.R.Schick, M.R.Ennis, F.Dumestre, E.Leyh, L.B.Robinson, A.Hagenbucher, B.Hutzenlaub, H.Parnitzke, L.Blahowetz, N.Ehrlich, L.D.Hill, D.M.Walton, E.L.Hawkins, H.O.Schaller, J.M.Slater, L.E.Strole, L.K.Bolin, R.E.Ryan, P.Gaudefroy, H.Anderie, J.A.Hartig, M.A.Rodón, R.G.Hauschild, P.Mesland, D.D.Cottrell, D.E.Leik, G.L.Bonnet, L.A.Meier, L.G.Mormann, M.L.Fishnick, P.M.Welbes, R.A.Folk, R.I.Lange, W.J.Kaiser, E.Reichert, R.Decker, J.D.McElroy, R.M.Link, C.T.Trenholm, B.R.Montgomery, E.L.Aaberge, G.J.Hefel, J.J.Francis, J.M.Howard, J.Ladenise, J.F.Bergan, R.McEnery, A.Aboukamel, A.Fonseca, A.Hassani, A.Lyazidi, T.Lakhdar, J.J.Ibañez, D.E.Slaght, D.L.Bunyer, E.H.Schuckert, G.A.Roling, J.A.Williams, J.V.Melloy, M.Maignant, M.Chahbi, R.Hili, D.E.Kucera, D.L.Busch, D.L.Triebel, J.R.Ridley, M.C.Noonan, P.L.Kalvelage, S.R.Harris, T.Harry, T.M.Roth, T.P.Murphy, W.G.Mathers, L.D.Vaughn, T.G.Thompson, S.P.Soler, D.A.Lenstra, H.J.Hefel, D.D.Holcomb, D.L.Lansing, S.Vuicic, J.Cevaer, E.M.Gutierrez, R.E.Douglas, R.F.Caldwell, L.J.Young, A.L.Vanderheyden, F.D.Davis, G.G.Welch, H.A.Manchester, J.M.Perkins, A.Nobilet, B.Klein, J.Mehler, K.Artuna, J.C.Parks, J.W.Glassford, Z.Roskewich, B.J.White, D.L.Jaeger, G.Boyd, J.B.Harn, J.R.Thompson, L.J.Corle, P.D.Darby, R.D.Reding, W.T.Bachman, R.E.Douglas, M.Nocentini, G.A.Edwards Jr., J.Meriaud, E.Guck, S.Kieling, A.F.Holevoet, D.E.Cross, D.G.Norsworthy, D.R.Haeck, E.C.Hammett, F.E.Vail, J.J.Kubik, J.W.Hansen, L.C.Moore, L.F.Jaquay, M.Foley, N.A.Thompson, S.J.Tagtmeier, S.P.Gorzney, G.Baudoin, G.W.Phillips, D.L.Miller, F.J.Volcko Jr., D.R.Galliart, G.J.Pluemer, S.J.Raske, D.Dodson, D.K.Stricker, D.P.Jones, G.M.Perkins, J.C.Watson, J.E.Lessner, K.G.Hedgecock, R.P.Mills, W.D.Vineyard, W.Haug, J.O.Urgorri, D.Ollivier, G.Fumagalli, V.V.Wilson Jr., D.F.Sickler, B.J.Betts, J.M.Baxter, J.R.Koenig, M.A.Acherman, R.G.Rokusek, S.L.Hempel, L.A.Wheeler, M.E.Erichsen, W.E.Coop, M.A.Armstrong, F.W.Bolton, G.C.Settle, J.T.Hensley, M.L.Watts, P.H.Ballek, P.H.Williams, R.W.Ehrler, T.V.Spates, H.Seiber, C.P.Hardin, L.D.Ledbetter, D.L.Pitts, D.M.Huss, J.E.Bliss, R.C.Broessel, D.G.Beeson, G.Hamm, R.B.Wiewel, G.Boillot, G.Boulanger, A.Saindon, H.Legras, F.Paul, H.Staude, A.Moumtzis, D.D.Foley, J.T.Christiansen, C.J.Doyle, F.Cash, J.R.Heintzelman, P.R.Brimeyer, W.R.Hodge, M.C.Torres, E.C.Kent, R.L.Nash, G.R.Canfield, J.D.Piper, L.Lambert Jr., R.C.Droeszler, J.Hiron, D.J.Fehrmann, A.Castillo, M.Hidalgo, W.D.Robinson, A.Gutierrez P., E.Blanco, L.Jerez, L.Martin P., S.Espada, H.Conejo, M.Marchante, M.Millan, S.L.Brouhard, J.Ortega, D.J.Schmitt, H.Williamson, J.L.Jinks, S.A.Steele, R.J.Bilotta, J.Mousset, F.Rubio G., G.W.Nordstrom, A.Grandjean, R.Henn, R.Merker, A.Gomez O., E.Osa De La, A.Gonzalez C., C.W.Cullett, J.L.Smith, J.R.Sammon, M.E.Russell, N.S.Goodwin, J.F.Villasana, A.Gautier, K.Jordan, C.W.Caldwell, D.Gonzalez N., J.Diaz G., L.Merida, R.G.Bakula Jr., F.Cabanillas, M.Rubio M., S.S.D.Silveira, K.Horlaender, A.J.Ryden, A.R.Spivey, G.T.Hull, J.K.Hansel, L.L.Disher, M.C.De Moss, N.E.Tiedge, N.L.Davis, S.Wade, J.Paniagua, J.Solis, S.R.Pettorini, P.Bello, D.L.Polaschek, A.G.Arand Jr., B.F.Hopper, D.A.Paisley, D.A.Soppe, J.M.Vogt, K.R.Harris, L.E.Mish, M.D.Anderson, M.J.Rogers Jr., N.S.Rushin, R.G.Gerber, R.H.Avenarius, R.R.Detwiler, R.R.Kisch, T.N.Peterson, B.Royer, A.Madouri, J.Gutierrez G., R.J.Latenser, A.Carretero, C.J.Johnson, G.A.Lindquist, G.E.Orourke, J.H.Tosh, J.R.Hull, R.W.Stubbings, S.J.Hernandez, W.D.Ellis, H.Sperber, J.W.Mazibuko, C.H.Fryday, J.E.Stover, D.Floch, C.Roulet, F.Goncalves, M.Doussinault, A.Bernhard, G.Baston, M.Schwartz, R.Burgun, R.Krieger, R.Vollmar, W.Schmitt, B.O.Vickerman, H.J.Beck, J.A.Riek, J.D.Dall, J.O.Spradlin, M.A.Peters, M.M.Hennessy, P.E.Volmer, R.A.Lorenz, R.A.Montgomery, S.F.McDonald, W.J.Smith, B.L.Knockel, R.M.Setzer, D.H.Jordan, F.Tanner, W.P.Overmohle, K.L.Huntley, W.F.Wiley, B.J.Lasalle, E.L.Hines, G.A.Wagner, H.F.Glenn, J.F.Eggers, K.J.Williams, K.R.Jerrett, L.E.Clark, R.A.Larson, R.G.Pergande, J.Didelot, E.Braun, L.Zimmermann, M.Unrath, R.Ihrig, R.Krueger, G.P.Womack, M.J.Johnson, G.Galan, K.Williams, A.T.Abend, J.R.Shade, M.L.Wood, T.J.Jackoniski, D.M.Healy, D.V.Maro, F.D.Clary Jr., G.L.Stluka, H.L.Burlage, H.R.Murray, J.E.Hayes, J.R.Hankes, L.F.Bebber, M.E.Lacefield, M.N.Kilburg, R.C.Hinzman, R.H.Tigges, R.M.Wood, R.Scott, T.A.Thompson, W.E.Wallace, A.Zebboudj, A.Rodrigues, M.El Younssi, J.Svaro, M.Fayolle, R.E.Stephenson, B.R.Riegler, D.D.Waller, J.S.Borowski, A.B.Johnson, C.J.Pfeiffer, D.L.Munns, G.J.Welp, M.I.Kruser, P.A.Vanbruwaene, R.D.Strawn, R.W.McNary, D.Constantin, J.Lecoq, D.H.Morken, R.J.Heinrichs, D.A.Neyen, A.Selmani-Kerroun, M.Aloui, D.E.Reese, D.L.Peters, F.L.Brooks, J.A.Thomas, J.R.Gassen, K.J.Hager, L.Smith, M.S.Bieber, D.M.Eudaley, G.G.Bushman, K.L.Dowsett, L.D.Vanderwerf, R.C.Hinzmann, R.D.Hinzman, G.Fouassier, M.Teich, T.J.Droessler, G.R.Wachter, J.Toribio, A.M.Kean, C.N.Woodward, G.M.Elgin, K.B.Greene, L.J.Weis, L.R.Bowen, M.J.Culbertson, P.J.Hentges, P.M.Rauen, R.C.Aird, R.E.Watters, T.H.Maneman, W.G.Klein, W.Hrach, R.F.Althaus, P.T.Katsis, J.P.Oyen, R.J.Hinzmann, D.A.Brown, D.L.Frazier, D.R.Kaiser, G.J.Rojemann, G.R.Miller, G.W.Jamison, H.R.Haas, J.A.Sickler, J.B.Finkey, J.F.Hollier, R.J.Kerper, A.Bourrier, J.Lafrance, G.L.Kipper, J.J.Schriver, P.J.Habjan, R.D.Klein, T.M.Delaney, M.Acosta , N.R.Flynn, T.L.Gassman, B.C.Newell, G.C.Brewer, J.L.Eglseder, L.R.Foecking, M.M.Jones, N.M.Bowman, T.A.Brugger, T.L.Eglseder, W.H.Sheber, E.J.Wiederholt, G.T.Michels, V.Juárez, A.J.Meyers Jr., A.L.Harper, C.A.Mola, D.M.Hingtgen, G.J.Cigrand, J.C.Southard, P.E.Harrington, R.A.Moon, L.E.Johnson, P.J.Weydert, D.M.Harvell, J.A.Jenkins, G.Chevallier, D.H.Morrow, S.T.Runde, T.G.Jones, H.Giroux, M.Mountahy, B.M.Thornton, L.A.Meana, S.E.Bilderback, C.E.Burke, J.Gorman, J.J.Lyons, T.H.Beresford, E.Monniot, D.L.McLees, D.R.Parkes, D.W.Hughart, J.E.Horch, M.A.Lippert, M.J.Leppert, R.J.Hachmann, R.L.Myers Jr., W.Parkes, D.Boutterin, C.Vial, M.Morales M., G.W.Bartram, M.E.Perry, S.M.Knepper, J.Bourgeois, D.E.Ernst, J.E.Ernst, B.H.Fecht, C.B.Averett, B.J.Duncan, D.J.Timmerman, J.R.Causemaker, M.K.Kaiser, M.M.Robinson, M.W.Muir, R.Bennett, T.G.Randecker, V.T.Haywood, A.P.D.Moraes, E.G.Walker, R.Roux, B.R.Wilson, C.E.Koehn, D.J.Thiltgen, D.W.Meier, J.A.Gavin, J.Francis, J.H.Jones, J.K.Willett, L.H.Young, R.C.Overhouse, S.Benjamin, A.D.Starbuck, D.A.Markin, D.T.Caldwell, D.K.Myers, D.W.Leik, B.A.Osborn, K.M.Marshall, R.L.Johnson, B.J.Timmerman, D.C.Roquet, D.M.White, D.Neises, G.W.Vogel, H.J.Sweat, J.K.Stephens Jr., J.R.Lawler, K.F.Norpel Jr., L.Burkert Jr., L.J.Martelle, L.P.McCann, M.A.Kelley, M.N.Jaksic, M.P.Gasper Sr., N.S.Cagle, P.H.Demkier, R.Arredondo, R.D.Rapp, R.Ties, T.J.Kuhle, M.Strobel, A.Fernandez S.R., M.Romero A., D.Renou, E.E.Harmon, I.Duric, D.L.Hildebrand, J.M.Wagner, A.Alameda, J.A.Scherner, D.R.Kerkenbush, F.A.Ramler, G.H.Astgen, R.E.Till, D.Dumont, J.Soler, D.A.Bell, G.A.Benn, J.C.Heim, T.C.Walker, D.Martinez M., F.A.Townsend, H.J.Hefel, J.D.Hillary, A.Lopes-Teixera, R.K.Oberbroeckling, D.V.Ries, D.R.Kammerude, D.W.Steinhoff, D.W.Wright, F.T.Ries, J.A.Puls, J.J.Lapage, N.H.Elskamp, T.J.Brandel, R.Fontaine, J.B.Vosberg, J.W.Lamos, W.R.Smith, P.A.Tatum, T.M.Lemos, H.Erol, F.Chacon, B.Aviles, D.D.Schroeder, A.Werner, **1970** G.Hoffmann, T.L.Switzer, V.J.Schwartz, A.Martin C., B.F.Phillips, B.J.Kaiser, C.A.Storla, C.L.Kane, D.J.Krantz, D.L.Brier, D.M.Rinker, D.R.Steckel, G.Marchionda, J.Klacko, J.L.Montgomery, K.R.Marr, L.P.Manternach, M.Acord, P.N.Graham, R.E.Sweeney, R.E.Theobald, R.G.Buxton, R.Gow, R.S.Vanderhoof, R.Sines, S.K.Stokes, W.Wolverton, V.Garbrecht, R.Thiriet, D.A.Draper, R.L.Allison, J.A.Keil, M.Vukic, B.G.Monroe, D.C.Boyenga, K.W.Lester, O.L.Payton, R.E.Johnston, R.J.Wagner, S.M.Overton, T.J.Benak, J.Ruet, G.Schiffmacher, J.Blazquez, L.A.French, R.K.Perkins, R.L.Hannah, R.J.Teager, D.L.Lang, L.B.Collis, O.Rial, P.A.Trageser, M.Saeger, C.A.Hamby, D.J.Beringer, D.R.Stage, J.E.Kasemeier, J.J.Marzorati, J.L.Petrilli, N.G.Antolik, P.P.Kennedy, R.F.Hasken, S.L.Wilson, W.E.Mockmore, C.Goyer, G.Diaz M., M.Serrano, D.H.Kirk, L.P.Dowell, S.K.Michaelsen, J.Canty, L.L.Leib, M.J.Polich, T.J.Mahan, D.Ponce, W.J.Knabel, W.R.Malone, D.D.Gabrick, D.L.Joslyn, L.K.Miller, L.M.Polich, M.J.Bernhardt, M.L.Erickson, N.T.Miller, T.M.Slater, J.Fèbvre, A.Marraha, A.Younouss, F.Messina, A.Benjumea, A.Novillo, D.E.Lloyd Jr., M.Izquierdo, G.R.Reuter, L.W.Till, C.J.Robinson, C.A.Mamo, C.E.Birdsong, D.H.Biederman, D.P.Dewulf, D.W.Hemauer, E.V.Riisager, E.W.Loeffelholz, J.L.Barker, L.C.Daly, M.M.Williams, M.W.Winchell, P.M.Michel, S.A.Matz, W.K.Mills, W.P.Zorich, J.Grassot, J.Remy, G.Cordero, D.E.Knabel, D.G.Lee, R.R.Frey, B.D.Arbour, C.P.Gnatovich, D.A.Wiederholt, J.J.Lukasik, J.L.Schaeffer, J.Miller, P.E.Wiezorek, R.G.Benner, R.J.Richardson, R.Stroud, S.J.Klinge, T.J.Tigges,

Spanish employees and dealers in front of 6600 Combine, 1970

W.H.Emmelhainz, A.H.Stansberry, D.C.Carroll, M.K.Hartman, R.A.Noyes, B.R.McSparin, H.E.Sutliff, J.I.Navarro Jr., T.Medina Jr., H.Uensal, A.D.Hill, D.A.Nevling, D.C.Mills, D.L.Dusenberry, E.J.Hanfelt, J.A.Richardson, J.E.Arnold, J.V.Paulk, K.E.Irion, L.P.Despeghel, M.A.Ruth, R.C.Rettig, R.J.Kipp, W.G.Sano, R.Armbruster, E.Buzer, R.Sanchez C., D.N.Machalek, J.L.Hill, K.W.Horton, R.H.Black, J.A.Orvis, J.H.McDermott, J.J.Swanson, J.R.Haynie, R.J.Haupert, D.R.Nelson, B.R.Moore, E.M.Schumacher, J.D.Anderson, J.E.Mikkelsen, J.R.Jabben, J.Tingle, M.D.Harder, M.T.Ahern, N.L.Kilar, W.R.Miller, D.Mercier, E.Thauvin, B.Privado, M.Garcia V., R.M.Cook, S.A.Beale, B.L.Green, E.L.Schwert, J.V.Honsberger, M.R.Goyal, R.W.Bodell, E.L.Beck, M.Paty, R.Amado , A.Beaudoin, V.M.Miller, C.M.Vosberg, D.W.Beaudoin, J.R.Feehan, R.A.Baker, R.F.Bucci, R.G.Parkes, T.H.Harris Jr., W.J.Schneider Jr., B.E.Wood, G.J.House, T.C.Robinson, F.Debiez, R.Sif El Islam, B.Pillet, G.T.Marr, A.F.Loney, B.J.Goosen, D.A.Murrell, D.G.McCombs, J.F.Bailey, M.J.Trannel, R.J.Levar, R.T.Eastman, A.Cadoux, D.I.Schmidt, R.A.Henkel, D.C.Seiler, D.R.Rotchill, J.S.Payne, R.L.Haug, R.R.Sherk, T.J.Gartner, Y.Millot, A.Slimani, C.B.Donaldson, D.W.Oliver Jr., A.Niquet, G.Wagenbach, K.Reinys, K.Schmidt, L.Sfatkidis, W.Wirth, Y.Et, F.Sanz, M.Burgueño H., M.Ramallo, C.H.Hennel, I.Van Ommeren, M.K.Mueller, M.Puig, R.L.Blackbourn, W.J.Kaiser, A.Marcoux, J.Torres, V.Hernandez G., F.L.Skaife, G.C.Welp, J.B.Kaylor, N.Hammes, A.Tabib, J.Porthault, R.Pouradier, E.E.Wills, C.D.Evans, R.Wolf, C.P.Barnes, R.T.McFadden, D.Jambut, A.M.Calderon, N.Gutierrez G., H.Cizewski, C.S.Frommelt, J.Sever, V.Frankovic, D.A.Willer, D.L.Garrett, M.E.Foss Sr., P.C.Haag, G.Marcel, J.Huerga, M.Cvitkovic, P.Cafaltzis, S.P.Dempsey, P.Hampovcan, F.G.Olson, G.L.Erlandson, J.A.Van Driessche, L.B.Dahl, W.Hahner, J.A.Ames, K.E.Cruise, R.A.Hanover, R.Rae, D.Mansouri, M.L.Dowdal, L.Anderson, H.K.Silver, K.S.Pregon, R.D.Yates, W.Kedziora, Y.Romby, J.Houbert, P.J.Lerschen, R.J.Anderson, C.Bentakkouk, C.E.Essmann II, C.R.Harman, C.S.Saul, L.M.Willman, T.J.Strickland, J.M.Griff, M.Bernatovic, B.S.Murray, D.L.Bowman, T.A.Feliksiak, C.D.Hayslett, H.C.Brinkman, J.J.Dezoete, M.A.Guy, R.W.Cory, C.Martin, G.Gaufillet, B.A.Comito, C.C.Young, C.R.Trott, D.A.Brown, D.E.Schloz, F.L.Burke, H.H.Holland, H.W.Hayden, J.H.Spicher, L.Durchenwald, M.De La Fuente Jr., G.Arquez, M.Estevez, B.D.Glossop, R.M.Hilleque, V.Novak, A.C.Lehrman Jr., A.J.Morris, A.L.Curtis, B.L.Muller, C.M.Ansel, E.N.Moon, E.P.Livings, G.H.Freese, J.L.Vannorsdel, K.D.Enstrom, J.Narloch, G.F.Schenke, S.K.Kruse, S.P.Calvert, J.K.Dodge, J.R.Weller, M.D.Madsen, R.E.Moulds, R.J.Johnson Jr., R.M.Tunstall, S.C.Miller, S.J.Boushek Jr., W.H.Roffey, Y.Duponchelle, M.Kusa, U.Binroth, J.T.Orth, R.B.Towner, T.E.Hinton, D.Makhubo, H.Veld, J.O.Brautigam, J.P.Talbot, W.F.Dozier, A.Berthiot, M.Grandiere, H.L.Morgan, F.E.Rébori, G.Fenol, B.Jolyot, H.R.Fjellman, L.J.Hodel, E.S.Logemann, H.Bobertag, H.Wetzler, J.Klimmer, U.Steinbrueckner, B.M.Walker, C.M.Speights, J.B.Flaska, J.Pernoux, G.E.Smelcer, S.Ruchet, M.L.Garcia D., L.F.Shook, J.Cervantes , A.L'Heude, D.Barbereau, E.Wuerz, D.R.Miller, G.Luzin, R.Duvallet, C.A.Ford, C.E.Stewart, M.D.Wisecup, M.H.Humphrey, P.M.Murphy, C.Anderson, K.J.Mc Carty, L.A.Bingham, T.C.Blackburn, L.A.Kitchen, P.D.Calhoon, R.L.Schurman, S.Rolland, C.Thiercelin, D.T.Knapp, F.Matejicek, R.R.Hackley, J.A.Engle, B.L.Beebe, C.A.Phillips, J.Y.Dobson, R.L.Ohnstad, T.A.Schmidt, H.Bourgeois, G.Nourrisson, B.Oudry, P.Godin, A.Marcy, G.Baechtel, H.Garbe, H.Weber, I.Krieg, J.Jelacic, K.Mayer, K.Pirlich, R.Muehlum, R.Tochtermann, R.Wietstock, U.Gab, G.G.Pretorius, H.M.Carrey, R.Grain, J.Hernandez, A.B.Saunders, J.W.Petersen, M.L.Sadler, T.Mlot, E.L.Collins, A.Harami, J.Thiebaut, R.L.Hathaway, L.H.Turner, M.R.Parker, J.Porche, A.J.McKoy, J.A.Lowe, R.N.Mills, C.Charpentier, J.A.Wilson, B.R.Pennington, B.M.McAteer, E.Billard, P.D.Barker, C.K.Scott, M.G.Woodhouse, C.Garcia, R.Ferron, A.Kobinski, E.Scherer, J.Riedel, C.Sciarra, J.R.Louden Sr., K.W.Waters, L.G.Hyatt, J.Meixner, R.A.Traver, D.S.Hood, H.A.Haist, J.A.Lind, J.L.Kapuscinski, R.E.Verscha, J.W.Andrusyk, H.Riesebosch, R.L.Wilson, G.R.Winger, H.L.Climenhaga, J.M.Melloy, M.L.Lehoux, M.J.Havertape, N.Gavriilidis, D.L.Reynolds, B.R.Olmsted, C.L.Allen, D.D.Carlson, D.H.Ripperger, D.L.Anselme, K.H.Semple, K.W.Murry, R.A.Jones, S.R.Wren, W.James Jr., H.Sandikci, R.C.Lamontagne, R.E.Easterbrook, R.Hanson, D.D.Dawn, J.B.Grant, E.Kalckbrenner, E.Stefanopulos, W.Kaiser, E.A.Stori, G.M.Hamby Jr., K.E.Bower, L.M.Bain Jr., T.N.McCarthy, W.Hassert, T.A.Jenkins, T.W.Strawn, E.J.McLimans, W.E.Horton, E.A.Lane, H.L.Jagerson, L.H.Reynolds, M.L.Fording, M.T.Ready, R.Bailey, R.C.Aeschliman, S.O.Steele, T.F.McDonald, C.D.Steyn, E.M.Fowler, B.A.Bousselot, D.E.Ruby, D.W.Sr.oka, E.H.Ollie, J.D.Roff, R.S.Veach Jr., J.Gogulla, S.D.Mace, B.E.Voelker, H.P.Newton, K.A.Schebler, J.A.Phillips, B.A.Botsford, J.C.Howard, J.Huston, K.T.Brandel, L.C.Hart, L.D.Armstrong, T.H.Carpenter Sr., P.J.Spidle, D.C.Preece, A.D.Liebermann Jr., D.J.Griffin, B.A.Emerson, R.M.Guiter, S.L.Murphy, A.L.Jenkins, J.L.Davis, J.B.Myers, R.J.Crippes, **1971** P.Poiget, L.Hartmann, S.Reika, C.M.Swenson, E.J.Lentz, G.B.Steckel, J.A.Karns, J.Allick, J.Snyder, J.W.Hopkins, L.T.Pittman, S.I.Ripka, S.Y.Vanskiver, D.Lefebvre, T.L.Brantley, S.Wikstroem, J.L.Guiter, J.W.King, B.L.D Angelo, E.R.Vogel, K.A.Berkley, R.B.Bardwell, D.J.Laneser, B.D.Taswell-Miller, G.A.Dunn, W.R.Mc Quitty, M.Johnson, R.F.Thill, G.F.Wichrowski, R.B.Dupuy, R.Hirt, S.Copeland, A.Brum, D.M.Roberts, B.J.Turner, W.L.Williams, L.W.Pensel, F.D.Alexander, J.G.Bennett, P.W.Stiles, A.M.Chiappetta, B.J.McCown, D.J.Spackman, V.W.Cook, M.Gil, J.A.Wollenweber, L.V.Cox, R.T.Lundeen, E.Heldt, H.Karch, M.E.Hodges, J.Cadot, L.A.Watts, R.T.Maier, M.F.Sargent, J.Hoyle, M.L.McLemore, R.Goncalves, G.J.Satter, T.F.Robson, L.M.Sheeler, M.Turney, T.V.Simon-Harris, L.Dieter, A.L.Van Houten, M.G.Vogt, R.W.Downing, D.Thiault, B.J.Sanders, S.M.Boston, D.A.Lalonde, M.Legrand, B.E.Mauldin, P.D.Harris, L.Greulich, K.D.Thompson-Bump, J.J.Jameson, T.J.Hoeger, H.Frank, H.Ganter, M.Bucic, J.Kloster, M.D.Roling, M.R.Redmond, M.S.Thelen, B.J.Brown, H.B.Rauch, M.Tekin, V.M.Sadler, V.S.Spivey, J.Millot, D.J.Courtney, J.A.Edmunds, P.R.Riewerts, R.G.Christ, G.Kuehn, K.H.Luchtenburg, R.P.Scott, G.J.Gotzinger, J.M.Miller, J.A.Roy, A.A.Taube, J.Williams, R.F.Karnatz, B.A.Culbertson, R.Benjamin, T.L.Christian, S.D.Boeno, M.Bague, G.Robert, R.E.Chatfield, B.R.Blair, J.W.Walton, P.Halouin, W.L.Zessar, P.Lereau, B.Faron, K.Dach, D.A.Hayes, D.B.Woody, V.D.Hankins, A.M.Schreiber, C.Perez-Lopez, M.A.Neu, H.Genc, L.S.Buchanan, G.D.Prosser, K.Rabung, D.M.Whiting, J.G.Gasser, P.S.Wyatt, F.Riedinger, L.L.Baker, R.Envall, R.Chaptal, E.A.Hoffman, S.J.Jaeger, D.M.Fuerstenberg, L.Ray, J.K.Lawson, E.F.Stockel, N.J.Stroup, R.P.Miller, W.J.Fullbright, D.R.Brown, M.J.Donovan, S.Roback, J.A.Baxter, J.W.Brunskill, T.H.McLees, D.Villette, A.Ghiani, V.Grieser, C.K.Strader Jr., C.J.Lebersbach, A.Kipper, D.C.Brown, H.E.Wellman, W.Simpson, A.H.Hicks, B.J.Larson, E.V.Gruza, J.P.Fenyves, L.Young, R.F.Payne, C.Fortin, E.Bubel, E.Samstag, G.Mehne, H.Niederhauser, I.Grampp, K.Bellaire, K.Eibner, M.Haensgen, M.Lenz, W.Bayer, W.Englert, W.Schmidt, W.Schmitt, H.Heine, E.Monus, J.M.McAuliffe, W.B.Davis, J.L.Miller, A.Hirt, J.Couturier, M.E.Sowers, M.R.Patterson, S.P.Rabbass, D.M.Niedermann, T.L.Jones, D.Gauguin, D.A.Francis, M.E.Smith, W.J.Costner, W.S.Mc Swain, D.K.Pfundstein, J.Garcia, M.L.Varner, S.M.White, J.Bony, P.N.Leech, H.C.Kleynhans, R.A.Dotson, D.L.Stiffler, R.Laberheim, U.Heilig, W.Stautmeister, M.C.Rogers, B.Manenti, I.Gedik, J.C.Ferrari, W.C.Hammette, P.Vappereau, A.L.Tosset, A.A.Buentello, C.L.Rugh, E.R.Duesing, G.Smolikiewicz, T.V.Lucero, B.W.Rowland, C.F.Smith, G.L.Haas, K.B.Ploessl, G.L.Jordan, K.R.Brong, R.L.Taylor, W.C.Weems, V.Sermek, W.B.Rogers, R.B.Mohr, M.Klauder, D.L.Yoose, M.A.Mehus, M.B.O'Brien, W.Reischmann, A.Viegas-Francisco, J.Pinson, P.Rauch, R.G.White, D.F.Fecht, G.L.Thompson, R.L.Davis, T.J.Patzner, B.W.Cliff, K.J.Edwards, L.P.Lobianco, P.A.Grevas, T.L.Wright, M.C.Cahill, R.L.Belken, T.G.Friedmann, F.C.McLimans, T.G.Hitzler, S.M.Ellis, D.D.Driscoll, C.R.Tharp, D.B.Lindsey, J.L.Hansel, K.O.Haverland, P.M.Kluesner, R.M.Dempewolf, T.J.Hogan, T.J.Moore, W.P.Buckley, W.R.Bruun, R.Lambert, W.F.Morgan, R.J.Schumacher, J.C.Jones, J.P.Moore, L.T.Einsweiler, L.V.Powell, M.D.McCabe, R.A.Redfearn, S.L.Foxen, W.R.Trotter, C.J.Vogt, S.D.Firzlaff, C.E.Bossman, D.L.Powers, D.W.Apel, G.J.Pennekamp, J.M.Bellefeuille, C.Julien, A.Ferreira, M.Barthel, J.R.Rohner, R.L.Dolan, W.A.Vanhoutte, D.C.Ernzen, D.J.Rouse, L.J.Hogan, M.P.Freisinger, B.D.Thompson, B.E.Willison, B.L.Combs, D.A.Duke, D.A.Neuhaus, D.D.Hall, D.E.Gibson, D.E.Seger, D.F.Dolphin, D.R.Hefel, E.Owens, F.C.Pilcher, J.L.Nolan, J.M.Sheldahl, J.R.Michels, J.R.Nell, J.S.Shields, J.W.Baker, M.S.Hergert, N.G.Mallas, P.A.Lange, P.D.Wiklund, P.W.Standera, R.A.Harding Jr., R.B.Hornberg, R.D.Storey, R.H.Santi, R.T.Galvan, R.W.Kropp, S.F.Burich, S.J.Campero, T.Loggins, W.B.Oehlert, N.Ruspini, J.Le Tumelin, J.A.Baguley, P.D.Loy, T.J.Chantos, R.Rimlinger, D.C.Butler, G.W.Graham, C.H.Johnston, E.E.Shere, R.Ford, R.V.Combs, A.Courla, J.Hykel, G.Boureau, **1972** J.A.Stanfl, M.Korchane, A.Stenger, G.Stumpf, L.Lang, P.Rottmann, A.L.Vilmin, B.A.Cox, C.R.Garton, D.D.Finnell, D.L.Beam, D.R.Isley, E.E.Frost, F.R.Carroll, G.L.Griebel, G.P.Garza, G.Q.Birdwell, H.M.Townsend, J.Cadman, J.H.Graham, M.A.Johnson, M.K.Link, O.W.Hendricks, R.Castillo, R.F.Garrett, R.H.Meersman, R.J.Hay, R.L.Neubauer, S.W.Dickson, T.E.Maylone, T.H.Aeschliman Sr., T.H.Jenkins, T.J.Meyer, T.T.Hall, W.L.Morlan, W.R.Vogt, A.Dumery, M.Hatzenbuehler, R.J.Raabe, R.L.Caulkins, W.Ehresmann, E.C.Nutter, A.H.Riley, B.M.Husted, B.O.Cossin, C.E.Allen, D.C.Kriewald, D.H.Ehm, D.W.Herrin, F.C.Fazio, H.G.Theobald, J.R.Van Drew, J.T.Watts, L.E.Umble, M.D.Bingham, R.E.Brown, R.W.Eide, S.J.Zepeda, S.R.Goodner, W.J.Mackey, E.Laimouni, G.Manceau, L.Souville, E.Ianniello, G.Stuchly, E.P.Morrison, L.E.Davis, D.E.Summers, R.C.Johnstone, F.Tekeli, T.H.Donald, A.E.Beiderbecke, J.W.Kohls, K.L.McMillen, L.R.Ehlers, M.C.Elenz, M.Friedrich, M.Marvelli, M.R.Powell, P.W.Pfeffer, R.A.Magyar, R.B.Lake, R.D.Myers, R.E.Mellenthien, R.M.Maurer, S.W.Immerfall, T.A.Frederick, T.C.Beall, G.V.C.Maciel, A.Olives, J.R.Derby, C.J.Graham, M.E.Longnecker, S.P.Comer, W.E.Lehmer, D.L.Leibfried, R.R.White, H.Erdem, D.C.Meloy, D.P.Cook, E.J.Barry, E.R.Hooper, F.L.Morano, J.A.Randall, J.D.McCullough, J.M.Shepley, J.S.Tully, L.L.Collier, L.N.Matthias, M.S.Thom, W.D.Moravek, A.Mathon, J.L.Johnson, M.Moss, R.M.Bellon, C.A.Crump, J.R.Beckmann, R.E.Dalsing, R.L.Millar, S.Nunemaker, W.J.Aird, D.F.White, R.D.Coates, W.L.Markus, L.J.Shanahan, P.E.Stoffel, T.J.Bechen, A.Lillis, F.A.Gillen Jr., F.L.Johnson, J.F.Hantelman, K.E.Jentz, W.D.Sutton, G.Luna, C.Blot, M.Dreux, M.Nottin, Y.Soulas, C.J.Schmitt, D.A.Meier, D.D.Wilkinson, D.W.Stluka, G.A.Collins, A.P.D.Silva, S.A.Marschner, A.J.Abing, C.G.Debo, D.J.Imbus, J.H.Jones, J.J.Cushing, J.M.Fine, J.J.Gray, P.W.Murray, R.J.Errthum, W.W.Wubben, J.C.D.Abreu, C.S.O'Hern, D.F.Maahs, S.F.Skahill, J.E.Nelson, D.J.Lahey, D.L.Ament, D.M.Kress, D.R.Vannatta, H.L.Haugen, J.E.Brinker, J.M.Nicholson, J.P.Staner, J.W.Lansing, K.L.McPhail, L.J.Knockel, L.S.Hill, M.D.Chandler, M.D.Conrad, M.J.Rapp, M.R.Wilson, R.A.White, R.G.Shaw, R.J.Ginter, R.J.Weidenbacher, R.L.Smith, R.W.Luxmore, S.J.Rice, S.L.Schneider, T.F.Fah, V.J.Maegi, J.Rodrigues, V.Vintacourt, D.J.Michels, D.O.Biedermann, D.R.Robey, P.H.Heller, S.J.Schmelzer, J.R.Griswold, L.D.Flesch, L.M.Rubel, R.C.Wiegman, R.J.Ernst, S.R.Wagner, T.D.Droessler, T.J.McLimans, W.E.Carson, D.E.Delaney, E.L.Tranel, G.J.McAllister, J.P.Schmitt, M.G.Klais, P.E.Tauke, R.L.Dryer, D.A.Larson, G.G.Kirton, R.C.Lenstra, R.E.Jentz, R.M.McCarthy, R.W.Leifker, A.A.Rhoades, C.L.Seipp, D.B.Wolf, D.H.Mohrman, D.J.Glab, D.L.Queener, E.Vanni, E.W.Brown, G.G.Richardson, G.T.Robbins, H.P.Yoose, J.D.Moran, L.L.Timmerman, P.L.Birkel, R.J.Blum, R.M.Zenz, S.M.Seipp, A.Goncalves, D.A.Mann, D.J.Noel, E.C.Vanlennep, J.B.Behan, J.D.Argetsinger, J.K.Carr, M.J.Lange, M.Freudenberger, P.Schmid, C.J.Tebbe, D.C.Kingsley, D.O.Johannsen, D.R.Hoppenworth, M.J.Bowker, R.J.Wolfe, R.T.Stewart, T.V.Conlan, W.E.Branton, E.Wohlenberg, J.D.Rider, J.T.Klar, J.T.Welsh, M.E.Pfohl, R.B.Hessling, R.W.Johnson, E.Correia Da Ponte, D.J.Murphy, J.H.Hillman, D.C.Thomas Jr., D.D.Carter, D.H.Buell, E.J.Hingtgen, J.C.Sutherland, J.L.Ronek, K.J.Keller, M.D.Jackson, M.F.Allendorf, M.M.Bahr, R.A.Wentz, T.R.Harry Jr., T.W.Fleege, T.W.Paisley, V.L.Branch, V.L.Olson, J.Barrera, G.Salvatore, G.J.Lewis, A.Mursa, L.Arne Graf, B.K.Watts, C.Tingle, J.A.Hopkins, K.K.Knutson, M.H.Werner, R.R.Litscher, T.M.Miescke, V.J.Rokicki, J.Moreau, D.R.Grimes, J.W.Barth, M.T.Driscoll, A.M.Rains, C.E.Sieverding, D.Warren, G.E.Wintjen, J.M.Weidemann, R.A.Allen Jr., R.C.Kirpes, R.E.Averkamp, R.K.Engelke, R.W.Schueller, W.H.Welsh, W.J.Lester, M.Bensbaa, V.Schroeder, T.J.Anger, V.W.Kluesner, F.A.Pietan, M.D.Weltruski, W.A.Urbain, B.L.Hubbard, C.E.Knox Jr., C.E.Scott, D.A.Sink, D.E.Spaulding, D.L.Coffin, D.L.Felderman, D.M.Smith, D.R.Burbach, D.R.Fuerstenberg, D.R.Ziegenhorn, E.T.Vespestad, G.A.Wagner Jr., G.E.Hare, G.I.Ayres, G.L.Besler, G.M.Eddy, I.L.Hesse, J.A.Jacobsen, J.A.Langham, J.D.Kerr, J.L.Rhoda, J.M.Donahue, K.F.Knebel, K.J.Quist, M.J.Andera, M.R.Levins, M.W.Wisecup, P.G.Regenold, R.K.Eighme, R.L.Satterlee II, R.M.Hefel, R.W.Hibben, S.C.Barker, S.R.Bingham, T.F.Stubenrauch, V.K.Jones, W.G.Kall, W.W.Nissen, H.Schmidt, C.D.White, D.E.Pelton, D.R.Williams, D.W.Dejoode, G.E.Noel, H.Jones, J.C.Accola, J.C.Basten, J.H.Laufenberg, J.W.Schoer, K.C.Rausch, L.E.Wright, L.G.Hogue, M.P.Apling, R.E.Richmond, R.L.Moran, B.Karanfil, C.E.Bries, D.G.Carter, D.J.Loring, D.R.Funk, J.L.Kettmann, J.S.Barrett, L.J.Schwager, M.L.Ehlinger, T.L.Jensen, D.E.Miller, D.L.Reese, G.A.Kratoska, G.A.Ritland, G.W.Robinson, K.J.Thede, L.Corkery, M.A.Wright, N.E.Necker, P.J.Charley, P.M.Snyder, R.C.Harris, R.J.Schmitz, T.J.Oeschger, W.A.Broten Jr., W.B.Hoffman, W.J.Foley, Y.Karasan, A.C.Schaffer, C.E.Henricks, C.R.Wagner, D.G.Richter, D.M.Masters, M.E.Sommerfeldt, A.F.Schimming Jr., C.E.Knight, C.E.Lundy, C.H.Peyton, C.Marlow, D.A.Seegers, D.B.Gray, D.J.Laugesen, D.L.Carrington, G.D.Pratt, G.L.Kaune, G.Larson, G.M.Bonifas, G.R.Mc Intyre, G.S.Otterbeck, H.W.Forrest, J.F.Stroud, J.H.Kluz, J.P.McAskill, J.R.Wahl, K.L.White, L.C.Steiner Sr., L.W.Sievers, M.A.Milligan, M.A.Rodriguez, R.E.O'Dell, R.J.Merritt, R.W.Vogel, S.J.Walker, S.M.Harvey, W.C.Mc Danel, W.J.Vorwald, F.Aguilar, M.Stuetze, J.P.Blunt, P.D.Joyce, R.D.Hansen, R.G.Scroggins, R.J.Hill, T.A.Fink, C.S.Searl, D.E.Johnsen, D.Frederick, D.J.Devore, D.S.Bremer, G.G.Switzer, L.L.Brown, L.Peck, S.K.Dixon, S.R.Bearbower, T.J.Dillon, D.A.Kluiter, D.L.Harris, E.J.Cameron, G.C.Condon, J.N.McCarthy, K.G.Edwards, K.J.Gillespie, L.R.Frutiger, M.D.Sharitz, M.S.La Coste, R.A.Briggs, R.J.Mezera, R.M.Osterberger, S.A.Dupont, T.C.Nelson, W.G.Bohneman, G.A.Meyer, J.D.Back, L.D.Tisue, S.M.Becker, S.W.Burke, D.D.Downey, R.M.Arensdorf, B.E.Lee, B.R.Sparland, B.W.Frederick, C.D.Meyerhoff, C.F.Muenster, C.R.Fritts, C.T.Watson, D.F.Altman, D.L.Shores Jr., D.R.Giese, E.F.Parker, G.L.Nienkark, J.L.Miller, J.M.Grover III, L.J.Fischer, M.J.Johnson, M.J.Mundschenk, O.W.Robertson, P.M.Herrig, R.A.Smith, R.J.Bergfeld, R.L.Thompson, R.W.Reifsteck, S.A.Mangano, S.G.Ibeling, T.C.Porter, T.J.Kiefer, T.R.Karel, W.W.Kay, B.Drouaillet, D.R.Roberts, J.R.Hiatt, M.E.Shehan, R.D.Peterson, R.J.Moser, S.L.Lau, V.J.Oltrogge, W.Cristanello, G.L.Hyde, G.W.Petersen, J.E.Demuth, J.J.Kilcoyne, C.W.Poyner, D.L.Koehn, G.V.Cox, J.L.Saddoris, R.Ladeburg, F.A.Rubino, B.H.Sheffner, B.J.Hastings, R.H.Kern, S.L.Klinghammer, B.L.Sheppard, C.E.Wright, D.J.Johnson, D.L.McCarthy, D.L.Meade, D.Mitchem, D.W.Hahlen, E.D.Myers, E.F.Hopkins, E.J.Meissen, E.P.Pohl, F.J.Villalobos, G.J.Jerrett, J.A.Free, J.A.Griesbaum, J.Alcala Jr., J.D.Meder, J.D.Rushing, J.L.Bottomley, J.P.Massey, K.B.Murphy, L.Scott, M.C.Jay, M.F.Loy, M.J.Dietzel, M.S.Wilkening, M.V.Nelson, P.S.Nord, R.A.Youngblut, R.R.Ramaker, R.U.Timmerman, R.W.Haase, S.J.Hartl, T.E.Duccini, T.R.Avenarius, W.E.Morgan, W.W.Lindert, Z.K.Laugesen, A.Bobert, R.Le Cann, B.Jones, D.Carson, D.E.Monahan, D.R.Stoneman, G.R.Williams Jr., K.F.Davis, P.C.Dressel, P.D.Bolte, R.A.Genz, R.A.Wolf, R.C.Fletcher, R.K.Barker, R.L.Krogman, R.R.Gillen, W.D.Anfinson, J.Gomes-Eusebio, A.J.Burgess, B.D.Moran, C.Hunter, C.J.Wilson, D.J.Helmle, D.J.Lechtenberg, D.J.Schaffer, D.M.Buck, J.D.Hanna, K.R.Oelmann, P.Donnelly, P.E.Connell, R.Beckner, D.H.Howell, G.R.Robelia, R.P.Schlichting, R.W.Reeves, T.G.McDermott, T.J.Kluesner, G.Boussard, R.L.Dart Jr., W.J.Jamison, G.Herbe, K.P.Kremer, L.A.Parker, R.W.Potter, A.L.Miller, B.J.McSween, C.M.Hoffner II, C.M.Schwantes, D.A.Warrington, D.C.McElwee, D.F.Bies, D.K.Kelly, D.L.Morehead Jr., D.L.Spaulding, D.M.Johnston, D.M.Theilen, G.D.Wolfe, H.Peterman, J.A.Monahan, J.E.Berthel, J.I.Broyles, J.J.Kennedy, J.M.Knaeble, J.M.Means, J.R.Shallberg, L.A.Daros, L.E.Campbell, L.M.Braun, M.D.Millin, N.J.McCune, P.G.Colglazier, R.A.Rosetta, R.J.Schadler, R.L.Jackson, R.O.Hyde, R.R.Wrage, S.A.Roush, S.C.Bedford, S.E.Klinkhammer, S.J.Sonnenburg, S.R.Chance, T.J.Bruck, T.J.Kuhle, T.J.McDermott, T.J.Rivas, W.A.Huit, W.J.Ochse, R.Weber, D.C.Loeb, D.R.Goebel, J.P.McAuliffe, J.V.Maiers, K.L.Klemme, M.D.Burrage, R.P.Rewoldt, J.Gonsard, J.Delahaye, J.Pflugradt, C.D.Schmitt, C.L.Eggleston, G.G.Griffiths, J.F.Dausener, K.A.Bickert, K.D.Beier, L.H.Rickard, M.D.Glenz, M.J.Bovy, M.J.Luchtenburg, P.J.Wagner, C.D.Mc Intyre, D.L.Pope, J.B.Wright, J.H.Schroeder, L.B.Miller, M.J.Gibson, R.A.Barr, S.C.Bell, W.O'Neil, J.M.Vogel, P.G.Britt, W.C.Jackson, A.L.Ryden, D.L.Weidman, A.J.Fitzgibbons, C.M.Hopwood, C.R.Stewart, D.E.Mc Call, D.L.Hines, D.L.Rilling, G.A.Ryan, G.E.Jackson, G.M.Traul, J.A.Willetts, J.E.Ware, J.J.Schuler, J.L.Burke, J.S.Oneill, J.T.Wilson, L.E.Klobnak, L.F.Alger, L.N.Jones, L.W.Crumes, M.L.Conder, M.V.Neises, N.J.Fliss, R.D.Guiter, R.G.Bradshaw, R.G.Chisman, R.G.Healey, R.J.Jaeger, R.J.Meinders, R.J.Sigwarth, R.J.Winter, R.L.Mullen, R.L.Roush, R.L.Swager, R.P.Blum, R.V.Porter, S.J.Breitbach, S.J.Dickson, T.C.Foust, T.E.Courtney, T.J.Culbertson, T.R.Saner, T.W.Stewart, W.A.Petty, C.W.Ehrig, D.D.Scott, D.E.Knaeble, D.I.Pritchett, D.P.Hoyer, H.M.Barber, I.J.Peterson, J.F.Lathrop, J.J.Stern, J.W.Keefe, L.J.Feldmann, M.D.Richter, R.E.Thompson, R.J.Lynch, R.J.Martin, S.L.Christensen, S.M.Brase, T.W.Bellendier, D.G.White, D.J.Apfel, D.M.Bucknell, E.A.Lake, E.I.Massey, J.L.Ohrt, K.R.St John, L.C.Holman, M.R.Manahl, R.G.Hayungs, R.L.Moses, T.J.Westergreen, S.Maksimovic, L.Oujagir, B.C.Duehr, D.D.Ede, D.D.Schultz, D.E.Wedewer, D.L.Nelson, D.R.Hall, E.A.Pfeiffer Jr., E.L.Steffen, H.F.Stevenson, R.D.Taylor, R.L.Grote, V.I.Graveman, B.C.Digman, B.W.Williamson, J.A.Mease, J.D.Northey, L.C.Kobliska, L.V.Schaul, M.J.Anderson, M.L.Shaffer, P.J.Corken, R.N.Sturch, S.C.Smith, S.L.Adelmund, T.C.Brown, V.A.Mathias, W.R.Gautney, F.L.Kucko, G.D.Czuba, L.Murray, T.L.Sweeney, A.D.Schroeder, A.E.Smith, B.A.Gienau, B.L.Weber, B.P.Brune, C.D.Fanton, C.J.Plein, C.L.Pattee, C.M.Steger, D.C.Edmonds, D.D.Smith, D.J.Herrmann, D.J.Knaeble, D.J.Kurtz, D.J.Merfeld, D.L.Bearman, D.L.Flater, D.M.Downs, D.M.Steffen, F.M.Adams, G.D.Erner, G.English, J.B.Farmer, J.D.Haas, J.J.Murray, J.L.Scally, J.M.Brown, J.P.Mellon, J.R.Soles, J.Stallard, L.A.Wagner, L.C.Ackerson, L.E.Galliart, L.M.Carman, L.R.Gronowski, L.V.Hogelucht, L.W.Tauke, M.F.Whiteman, M.V.Castle, P.L.Meyer, R.D.Buol, R.D.Moore, R.D.Nieman, R.D.Streif, R.J.Belken, R.J.Kieler, R.L.Baker, R.L.Meyer, R.M.Dreesman, R.Nichols, R.R.Ormord, S.R.Brimeyer, T.E.Thompson, T.F.Gloden, T.H.Laufenberg, T.J.Dupont, T.R.Mc Grane, W.G.Bundy, W.J.Bowser Jr., W.J.Zubler, J.Theurier, A.Tsarouchas, H.Schwierz, P.Schwierz, D.G.Kepple, D.J.Schmitt, D.L.Ancell, D.L.Scheckel, G.R.Schissel, J.A.Schmidt, J.L.Pierce, K.M.Phillips, L.M.McQuillen, M.N.Kirsch, R.L.Miller, R.R.Ulffers, S.C.Ohms, T.E.Beau, W.B.Boyes, W.E.Bartle, W.G.Berns, A.T.Petitgout, C.A.Sturm, D.L.Osgood, E.E.Murry, E.T.McKenzie, F.L.Behr, G.C.Bries, G.F.Coyle, J.A.McAuliffe, J.F.Breitbach, J.W.Gardner, K.K.Arensdorf, M.G.Bass, P.J.Joester, R.C.Freiburger, R.N.Parsons, R.R.Hartman, S.L.Shearer, T.J.Buelow, W.J.Coney Jr., D.L.Olson, D.M.Goedken, F.J.Finnegan, G.D.Derifield, H.L.Fassbinder, I.J.Lasoya Jr., M.J.Dahl, R.J.Becker, R.R.Bartels, S.K.White, T.L.Sheldon, V.J.Steckel Jr., A.W.Link, G.F.Freeman, R.L.Schnering, R.N.Tinkham, S.L.Richmond, D.L.Goering, S.J.Bushman, A.G.Appleton, A.J.Munos, B.E.Carter, B.E.Patton, B.L.Fisher, B.W.Wunder, C.R.Breitbach, D.E.Holland, D.E.Larson, D.J.Connolly, D.L.Walton, D.W.Lauer, E.Wooldridge, G.C.Melssen, G.W.Randall, J.A.Theisen, J.D.Vanblarcom, J.G.Boyd, J.M.Powers, J.T.Clark, K.L.Caven, L.D.Martin, L.T.Holven, M.D.Howard, M.J.Edwards, M.L.Tate, R.J.Dunne, R.J.Kelley, R.M.Thompson, S.B.Whitesides, S.J.Marienau, S.J.Pitz, S.K.Martin, S.T.Kurka, T.E.Kerkenbush, T.J.Puls, T.L.Stage, T.R.Williams, W.J.Johannes, Z.P.Maiden, H.Braun, O.Adanali, D.F.Becker, D.L.Tucker, D.P.Till, E.W.Petesch, G.J.Hoeppner, J.A.Kirchmann, J.W.Mc Alpin, L.F.Steger, L.J.Mc Glaughlin, M.D.Shirley, A.Colletti, D.C.Clancy, J.F.Hughes, K.C.McDermott, L.D.Helmle Jr., R.D.Toothman, S.J.Schultz, S.L.Stern, T.L.Smith, B.W.Walters, D.F.Wiegel, G.D.Frost, J.A.Buttgen, J.L.Widner, J.V.Weathers, K.B.Zimmerman, M.A.Davis, M.A.Doeden, P.A.Curran, R.E.Wrede, R.I.McDonnell, R.L.Wilkinson, T.W.Walton Jr., V.L.Kelderman, B.L.Cousins, D.J.Apel, D.J.Reichenbacker, G.F.Brenke, J.D.Hoeppner, P.W.Melloy, R.A.Burk, S.T.Hirsch, A.A.Born, B.H.Holmes, B.J.Baugh, B.L.Scott, B.P.Whitford, C.A.Scardino, C.E.Ballard, C.L.Rizner, D.C.Pontenberg, D.G.Topping, D.J.Schuster, D.M.Cloke, D.R.Allen, D.W.Saylor, E.L.Barker, F.C.Kirby, F.I.Rachell-Bruce, G.E.Riley, G.M.Schwirtz, H.D.Bennett, J.C.Miller, J.C.Schadler, J.J.Klinge, J.J.Morgan, J.V.Munda Jr., J.W.Ashmore, L.D.Colley, L.L.Trowbridge, M.K.Arnold, M.L.Patrick, M.W.Bennett, P.E.Plowman, P.F.Wagner, R.C.Olson, R.J.Reiter, R.L.Holmes, R.W.Barrett, T.G.Winger, T.J.Gansen, T.M.Griffin, T.N.See, W.C.Broten, W.L.Frost, C.Tolen, D.L.Gilbertson, D.R.Topping, G.A.Kastli, G.J.Brummer, J.A.Kertels, J.A.Morkel, J.H.Sites, J.W.Widmann, K.J.Dallenbach, M.G.Nott, T.J.Brooks, W.E.Pichelmann, G.Athanase, G.Pommier, M.Coudray, M.Miskovic, O.Rustemovic, A.S.Holliman, A.T.Moore, D.W.Chatfield, G.A.Critchlow, J.D.Goeller, J.E.Gibbs, L.C.Homann, L.H.Ruen, R.A.Schwager, R.G.Brimeyer, R.L.Toothman, W.F.Steffen, G.Hirnet, D.M.Edminster, D.W.Miller, J.A.Sailor Jr., J.E.Lee, R.J.Sebetka, D.E.Meeker, E.Ashley, J.A.Mc Clain, R.B.Herman, R.R.Matt, R.R.Schmidt, J.A.Mc Clain, P.L.Stabenow, A.D.Garcia, A.S.Weeks Jr., B.A.Hicks, B.J.Ossian, C.W.Anderson, D.D.Berger, D.E.Johnson, D.H.Cuff, D.L.Paxton, D.W.Hubbartt, E.A.Wesson, F.M.Buller, G.J.Hirtz, G.W.Hackett, H.A.Peart, J.B.Beau, J.C.Eaves, J.L.Davis, J.N.Humphries, J.W.Royer, L.J.Timmerman, L.M.Jump, M.G.Jensen, N.L.Homb, P.R.Stemper, R.C.Schueller, R.C.Thomason, R.J.Day, R.J.Hansen, R.J.Hogan, R.L.Dabney, R.M.Arensdorf, R.R.Stratton, S.E.Kleinschmidt, S.J.Husemann, T.A.Brandt, T.A.Widmann, T.J.Etringer, T.J.Morehouse, T.L.Bergen, W.F.Blair, W.G.McGuire, R.Pagani, B.T.Kapler, J.A.Meyer, J.I.Bisbee, M.L.Molstead, M.Tagtow, R.L.Hackbarth, T.L.Schmitt, V.A.Ginter, D.E.Herbst, E.J.Dahl, J.J.Wisher, J.R.Pullin, R.L.Buttgen, T.H.Williams, A.R.Kastli, B.W.Carpenter, C.R.Mc Allister, D.J.Schluetter, F.D.Weeks, G.E.Everts,

John Deere Service Library
Product engineers, Dubuque, Iowa, 1975

J.B.Bartholomew, J.E.Rhodes, L.D.Teplicky, L.J.Joblinske, P.B.Cormeny, R.F.Vandermeulen, S.D.Tullis, S.L.Reed, D.D.Hofner, D.E.Rhoades, G.F.Lutgen, H.E.Grooms, J.W.Burgess, L.M.Buckendahl, R.D.Frey, R.W.Hilmer, A.C.Halweg, A.J.Kelly, B.L.Bardshar, B.L.Foster, B.M.Jansen, C.R.Kolthoff,
D.D.Wittenburg, D.E.Lentz, D.G.Levenhagen, D.G.Soppe, D.J.Lenz, D.L.Umbarger, D.M.Eagles, D.W.Bratt, F.W.Wolf, G.A.Hartwig, G.B.Griffith, G.J.Ernst, G.L.Hampton, G.W.Marburger, J.L.Czarneski, J.L.Merrill, J.M.Gilligan, J.M.McQuade, L.Payton, M.M.Krueger, M.R.Wolf, N.E.Dunlap, P.L.Finch,
Q.E.Williams, R.D.Hondlik, R.D.Mattingley, R.G.Klein, R.H.Gierula, R.J.Kelley, R.J.Spence, R.L.Bolsinger, R.L.Schrock, S.R.Mulcahy, T.M.Brazell, W.H.Bussan, J.Binazzi, J.Gutierrez, P.Heartsburger, A.Jourdet, C.Michalski, G.Litiere, D.L.Oldenburger, D.L.Rookaird Sr., G.K.Loonan, K.R.Smith, L.G.Heim,
R.B.Havertape, R.K.Boss, T.J.Schilling, T.R.Teal, A.E.Ginter, J.W.Kaufman Jr., M.E.Herzog, P.S.Jessen, R.L.Simmons, A.Marreiros, B.A.Bonnett, C.R.Twaites, J.A.Bries, J.P.Kemps Jr., R.D.Minard, R.L.Mootz, R.M.Hernandez, S.J.Sturm, W.G.Ball, W.K.Jochum, E.B.Masterpol, E.J.Richmond, K.J.Kerkove,
A.M.Hitzler, B.W.Mihm, D.C.Timmerman, D.J.Kowalski, D.M.Bries, D.P.Goedert, G.F.Brown, G.J.Lames, H.K.Emery, J.D.Wagner, J.E.Barnhart, J.Sanders, L.J.Churchill, M.J.O Leary, M.J.Selle, R.A.Fisher, R.E.Stanfill, R.L.Youtzy, R.M.Brautigam, S.L.Burkholder, T.J.Schmitt, B.C.Oestreich, B.P.Wofford,
D.C.Wildeboer, D.W.Miller, E.J.Webbeking, E.L.Love, H.B.Stall, J.D.Fisher, J.R.Twaites II, K.W.Schmitt, L.E.Newborn, M.J.Smith, R.J.McCallum, S.D.Schleicher, T.R.Varney Jr., W.J.Jones, A.Junior De Matos, J.Fleureau, A.M.Helbing, D.A.Bateman, D.L.Maiers, G.S.Grant, H.W.Heitman, J.C.Close,
M.C.Copeland, M.L.Cottrell, M.T.Feeley, R.S.Keenan, T.J.Blosch, T.R.Cooper, B.P.Fettkether, D.L.Dunnwald, E.C.Vierkant, J.L.Kiburz, L.M.Deves, L.R.Hoskins, M.C.Fox, R.W.Hoffman, D.H.Kramer, D.J.Pearce, D.H.Drescher, H.Schaefer, A.J.Lambe, C.W.Freisinger, D.R.Salow, F.E.Poese, J.E.Hoffman,
J.J.Weber, L.E.Havner, M.E.Roby, P.E.Dunbar, S.E.Simmons, S.T.Langas, S.W.Honshel, T.B.Pfeiffer, T.W.Vogel, W.D.English, W.E.Tesh, W.J.Rollison Jr., C.J.Doty, D.C.Elskamp, D.L.Laumeyer, D.P.Pickel, E.E.Schmidt, G.E.Felderman, J.A.Hennessey, J.D.Hager, J.W.Knutson, K.W.Larson, M.F.Pierce,
R.K.Bernard, T.J.Weidemann, W.A.Rowland, B.M.Carson-Barry, C.A.Draper, C.G.Christians, D.A.Duffey, D.French, D.J.White, D.L.Kelley, J.B.Hilger, J.L.Skaife, J.V.Manor, M.Gastello, R.M.Mc Kinsey, R.W.Elling, S.J.Elliott, T.C.Van Doren, M.Mamie, J.Prout, R.Fauconnier, R.Garbiez, P.Augustin, R.Grund,
W.R.Knipp, R.W.Baal, A.V.Hannah, B.J.Ransdell, B.M.Jones, C.E.Deppeler, C.R.Kelm, D.A.Neff, D.C.Oppermann, D.G.Krueger, D.H.Hodgson, D.J.Riedl, D.J.Tessenske, D.L.Anderson, D.M.Scott, D.W.Berg, D.W.Kerr, E.A.Ferrian, E.B.Ball, E.C.Benter, G.A.Davis, G.H.Krausman, G.M.Thul, H.H.Pelton,
H.J.Hazewinkel Jr., J.B.Mills, J.F.Rogerson, J.G.Straseskie, J.H.Cravens, J.J.Backhaus, J.R.Miller, J.T.Link, J.V.Muenchow, K.C.Clark, K.L.Kreuziger, L.F.Ruff, L.J.Holstine, L.L.Mohr, M.M.Knueppel, N.S.Sidhu, O.J.Johnson, P.E.Erickson, P.H.Ringelstetter, R.A.Buffington, R.C.Bennett, R.E.Krausman,
R.J.Beck, R.J.Scott, R.L.Cook, R.N.Mc Anally, R.S.Vollmer, T.J.Glab, W.D.Totten, W.Tagtmeier, P.Heartsburger, M.Petitbon, K.Paulus, M.Martin S., D.L.Steffen, E.F.Champ, J.J.Bockenstedt, K.M.Shippy, R.E.Hill, W.R.Owens, F.Dargent, D.H.Ross Sr., D.J.Carson, L.E.Kotz, M.D.Friedmann, R.A.Willenborg,
S.L.Thomas, T.A.Wilson, M.Bernal, F.L.Dye, L.G.Lakeman, L.J.Biedermann, L.L.Arensdorf, M.G.Collins, R.C.Welbes, V.R.Baldwin, W.J.Kelly IV, D.L.Larsen, J.M.Flenniken, K.R.Webbeking, M.J.Schoville, R.S.Ryser, S.L.Aten, W.F.Rochford, B.D.Lockwood, C.A.Toothman, C.G.Richardson,
C.M.Bloomquist, C.S.Fondell, D.A.Rinden, D.F.Kleinschrodt, D.F.Pappenfuss, D.J.Bagby, D.J.Baker, D.M.Oberfoell, D.R.Hoffman, F.J.Digmann, G.H.Peters, H.H.Jackson, J.A.Deutmeyer, J.E.McDonald, J.G.Hoffman, J.L.Oltrogge, J.Sullivan, L.A.Hefel, L.G.Czupka, M.A.Litka, M.C.Winters, M.F.Klein,
M.J.Brennan, P.A.Wolf, P.J.Kratochwill, P.T.Brown, R.E.Bensink, R.F.Bornong, R.F.Willman, R.J.Lindecker, R.J.Saylor, R.L.Compston Jr., R.W.Callen, S.H.Kremer, S.L.Armfield Penn, T.D.Jensen, V.A.Schneider, W.K.Loeffelholz, S.Bombin, D.N.Gebel, J.E.Bouska, L.E.Faylor, L.R.Hoffman, M.L.Courts,
P.L.Miculinich, R.J.Schares, R.L.Cousins, T.D.Meewes, T.J.Schaefer, E.Huether, H.Brendel, D.E.Delagardelle, J.J.Bakey, J.L.Roehr, J.L.Wittenburg, J.P.Wilkerson, L.D.Olmstead, L.D.Williams, P.J.Luensmann, A.W.Ahlquist Jr., D.A.Wach, E.W.Wray, L.C.Flooding, L.D.Anfinson, M.A.Eubank, M.H.Multer,
N.K.Bodecker, S.F.Dougherty, B.Yousfi, A.Luque-Gomez, C.W.Dyson, D.J.Luchsinger, G.Rodriguez, L.D.Johnson, L.L.Leuschen, L.S.Bright, M.G.Kelly, R.E.Lund, R.L.Sheffler, A.L.Hemphill, A.M.Shabbits, B.A.Weitz, B.Jiles, C.Munson, D.A.Slosser Jr., D.A.Westimayer, D.E.Plageman, D.L.Vanbesien,
E.Svoboda, E.W.Budzinski, G.A.Parker, G.D.Lane, G.D.Rath, G.P.Loy, J.C.Conley, J.E.Datisman, J.F.Piddington, J.J.Turner, J.K.Mrzlak, J.R.McCarthy, L.G.Anderson, M.A.Parker, M.A.Schilling, M.E.Herrera, M.G.Flouro, N.A.Nash, R.C.Heim, R.E.Brown, R.E.Ray, R.G.Nieman, R.J.Lester, R.J.Mai,
R.J.Potratz, S.W.Tullis, T.H.Lethlean, T.J.Leinhauser, T.L.Shelton, T.M.Digman, W.F.Kramer, W.R.Chase, C.Boutterin, P.Charron, C.K.Van Ee, D.G.Brooks, R.L.Jensen, R.W.Renz, T.D.Joyner Jr., C.E.Cook, C.K.Payne, D.D.Smith, D.L.Heino, J.A.Koppes, M.J.Hoffman, P.J.Frank, R.B.Schultz, S.A.Brookshire,
W.B.Butt, C.Alexander, D.E.Gates, R.L.Russell, S.L.Schirm, T.J.Noel, W.A.Speirs III, B.L.Moser, B.L.Stant, D.C.Wolter, D.D.Moser, D.J.Heller, D.J.Winter, E.F.Westfall, G.D.Coffin, G.M.Lesnick, H.J.Spitzack, J.A.Parker, J.F.Lux, J.G.Steffen, J.W.McEnery, L.B.Weisenberger, L.E.Porter, M.E.Smith,
M.J.Mulligan, M.M.Kreger, N.C.Bridwell, P.L.Aaroen, P.M.Larson, R.B.Besch, R.H.Barker, R.H.Gile, R.J.McKiernan, R.J.Peters, S.M.Bratcher, T.J.Strub, T.L.Nico, V.E.Lenzendorf, W.T.Wittmer, W.Krause, A.Sousa-Gonzales, Z.Grounis, C.J.Casteel, J.R.Kehoe, L.E.Wilson, M.E.Wrage, R.D.Brown,
A.El Garti, D.A.Kluesner, V.M.Desch, B.F.Kuenzi, D.L.Ring, L.F.Thein II, S.J.Klein, D.E.Luck, L.J.Tigges, R.A.Zappalá, P.H.Darricades, E.Halm, E.Leidenroth, L.Bauer, A.D.Engelhardt, B.J.Heim, B.J.Thompson, B.M.Witte, J.P.Hites, K.E.Hussey, M.J.Baugh, R.G.Kass, R.H.Loesche, T.W.Fiedler, G.Jeannot,
P.Lucot, P.Maillard, R.Wittenmeier, B.J.Lochner, B.J.Mickelsen, C.F.Klossner, D.D.Schumacher, D.J.Yancey, D.W.Breitkreutz, G.D.Carnahan Jr., J.H.Kuhle, K.G.Wiebelhaus, K.S.Griffith, L.O.Myers, M.E.Mrozowicz, M.Y.Seago, R.B.Hugo, R.J.Rottinghaus, R.R.Burke, R.R.Frommelt, J.Neuman,
R.D.Johnson, K.J.Barton, G.M.Schmitt, L.L.Howard, A.L.Wahl, B.C.Schaefer, B.Chavez, C.L.Schwake, D.A.Dieleman, D.C.Goetzinger, D.D.Maulson, D.H.Diebold, D.J.Cowell, D.K.Newhoff, D.L.Dorn, D.W.Duhl, E.E.Jones, G.M.Bainbridge, H.J.Bednarek, J.C.Buck, J.D.Vollenweider, J.J.Anglin,
K.E.Schroeder, L.C.Giese, L.D.Schuldt, L.E.Williams, L.F.Scally, L.J.Zimmer, M.D.Seegers, M.E.Griebel Jr., M.J.Schares, M.K.Wyant, M.L.Kelleher, M.P.Scherer, M.R.Maledy Jr., M.W.Osterkamp, P.D.Apel, R.A.Camarata, R.E.Stevenson, R.J.Berndt, R.J.Clemen, R.J.Schindel, R.L.Bille, S.C.Wood,
S.J.Delagardelle, S.M.Peters, S.P.Shippy, S.S.Jackson, S.V.Delagardelle, T.W.Scarbrough, V.L.Rans, V.M.Harp, W.M.Kreger, D.Chavaroche, S.Togan, A.M.Gillespie, B.J.Fournier, C.A.Braatz, D.D.Schemmel, D.L.Brickman, D.L.Erhardt, D.L.Hearn, D.R.Liger, J.D.Porter, J.Etten, K.Freyholtz, L.R.Naber,
R.J.Schmitz, R.L.Frost, R.W.Huber, S.L.Scoles, S.L.Weber, A.E.Rowald, C.D.Petersen, C.E.Atkins, C.G.Timmer, C.J.Cox, C.M.Riechmann, D.A.Diercks, D.J.Hemmer, D.J.Wolff, D.K.Salmond, D.R.Poland, D.W.Lennox, F.E.Lawless, G.E.Henderson, G.F.Dean, G.L.Mc Clintock, J.A.Althaus, J.C.Kobliska,
J.C.Risse, J.D.Widdel, J.E.Collins, J.M.Lynn, L.D.Mc Gowan, M.B.Irwin, M.L.Smith, P.L.Leistikow, P.N.Weber, R.A.Schweer, R.E.Funk, R.J.Betts, R.J.Fridley, R.L.Weber, R.W.Protsman, S.A.Grosse, T.A.Gray, T.C.Day, T.L.Fischels, W.F.Hildebrandt, W.Outlaw Jr., A.Martin S., A.F.Jones, A.L.Kimball,
B.K.Dunegan, B.L.Kienast, D.D.Bland, D.E.Spragg, D.H.Lalk, D.J.Doering, D.W.Mahlstedt, E.C.Burkhardt, E.J.Fowlkes, F.Levy Jr., G.A.Hansen, G.B.Huberg, G.G.Choplin, G.R.Pipho, J.A.Gillespie, J.G.Kapela, J.L.Ragsdale, J.W.Lalk, L.P.Bovy, M.Frost, M.S.Eicher, M.W.Kiley, N.E.Bruns, N.L.Bantz,
P.A.Smith, R.J.Fangman, R.K.Frackiewicz, R.Mueller, R.Smith, S.C.Scott, T.C.Turner, T.E.Hemmer, T.L.Wooldrik, W.D.Puls, W.F.Zuck, B.M.Schmitz, C.A.Stickley, C.E.Wright, D.J.Dunnwald, D.W.Dorn, H.J.Thiele, J.A.Marshall, J.F.Smith, J.H.Rooff, L.M.Miller, M.D.Grahlman, M.E.Tyler, M.G.Walther,
W.F.Marvets, A.E.Coulthard Jr., A.F.Perkins, A.W.Wendling, B.E.Wood, C.L.Glawe, C.M.Hewitt, C.R.Weber, D.A.Buhr, D.A.Frazier, D.A.Laverty, D.D.Burnell, D.D.Dana, D.D.Wubben, D.E.Zupke, D.F.Hilbert, D.J.Berggren, D.J.Friede, D.J.Gerber, D.L.Adamson, D.L.Margelofsky, D.L.Mc Graw, D.L.Nosbisch,
D.L.O Connell, D.N.Koepsell, D.P.Kuhlman, D.P.Schmitz, D.P.Werner, D.R.Jones Jr., D.V.Steinmann, D.Williams, E.E.Schmit, E.Egemo, E.F.Backens, E.J.Foust Jr., E.M.Montgomery, E.P.Jauert, E.V.Wilder, E.W.Etringer, G.A.Roll, G.A.Sheffler, G.J.Menning, G.L.Hibben, G.L.Jaehnke, G.P.Breitbach,
G.R.Albrecht, G.R.Keidel, G.R.Roths, H.D.Aldrich, J.A.Ersland, J.A.Kacher, J.C.Hester, J.D.Back, J.E.Lee, J.E.Youngblut, J.F.Hoppes, J.F.Martin, J.G.Linden, J.J.Bohlen, J.R.Kerkove, J.W.Smith, K.W.Teel, L.A.Hanus, L.Church, L.D.Luck, L.E.Leeper, L.G.Hansen, L.J.Aswegan, L.J.Lott, L.L.Even,
L.R.Gundrum, L.W.Breitbach, M.E.Jensen, M.J.McDermott, M.J.Smith, M.L.Mc Fee, M.L.Seward, M.M.Hamilton, M.P.Ebanks, M.W.Mossman, N.C.Snell, O.P.Weber Jr., P.A.Ruff, P.J.Davis, P.S.Berry, R.A.Bowman, R.B.Bloes, R.Carpenter, R.D.Miller, R.E.Donat, R.E.Weber Jr., R.F.Wieser, R.G.Frohn,
R.G.Marohl, R.H.Biretz, R.J.Beard, R.J.Schroeder, R.L.Born, R.L.Hollnagel, R.L.Kane, R.L.Youngblut, R.Pierce, R.W.Feldman, R.W.Parker, S.A.Glaspie, S.D.Van Hoozer, S.E.Richmond, S.H.Wood,
S.J.Kramer, S.J.Spence, S.L.Hambly, S.R.Brown, T.C.Ahrens, T.C.Newhouse, T.D.Noel, V.J.Johnson, V.L.Caldwell, W.Andrews, W.L.Drenner, W.S.Mitchell, Z.A.Bark, K.Nickel, A.L.Gavigan,
C.A.Schnathorst, C.L.Davis, D.Buckendahl, D.M.Bahlmann, G.J.Schauf, G.N.Crow, G.P.Kohls, J.H.Gustafson, J.J.Koeppel, J.L.Smith, J.M.Heath, J.R.Mc Kinney, M.J.Anderson, M.L.Osterhaus,
P.L.Averill, P.L.Hoppes, R.E.Foss, R.F.Nie, R.G.Moore, R.L.Kent, S.J.Bradford, S.K.Krsek, T.D.Hoath, W.S.Randall, B.P.Platte, D.F.Ohrt, D.T.Dickson, E.J.Feese, F.J.Junko, H.L.Schuhmacher,
J.L.Jarchow, M.D.Hambly Jr., M.H.Faust, M.L.Mixdorf, M.L.Taylor, T.P.Nenow, A.Bolaños, L.S.Dieguez, B.A.Starkey, C.S.Erickson, D.M.Cook, E.Riley, J.F.Lemert, J.M.Scharnweber, L.R.Fair,
N.A.Partee, R.R.Hartman, R.W.Parkhurst, S.A.Bergmann, S.S.Brallier, T.C.Rich, V.C.Benson, G.D.Eibey, G.F.Ostrem, H.M.Schares, J.E.Guetzlaff, M.D.Mc Roberts, R.C.Childs, R.J.Wilson, R.T.Kaiser,
S.J.Amsbary, R.R.Kuenstling, A.C.Webbeking, A.J.Billingsley, B.E.Schreyer, B.M.Harrington, C.A.Walton, C.B.Kelley, C.W.Heeney, D.A.Pfeiffer, D.C.Henning, D.R.O Brien, H.B.Cheeks, J.A.Horn,
J.A.Mc Enaney, J.A.Sevey, J.C.Dunn, J.E.Martin, J.L.Mc Clain, J.O.Myers, K.J.Daley, M.Blackman, M.L.Marken, M.V.Wahl, N.D.Oelstrom, N.J.Federspiel, O.L.Derifield, P.E.Johnson, R.F.Macy, R.Fink,
R.L.Schmelz, R.R.Buchholz, T.J.Barna, T.J.Brandhorst, T.J.Thyen, T.R.Lester, V.L.Marvets Jr., V.L.Sutton, C.E.Foster, D.J.Kayser, D.L.Oltrogge, E.L.Johnson, F.M.Hansen, M.D.Lenius, M.G.Gray,
M.L.Lentz, R.A.Clements, S.L.Mervin, T.L.Vollenweider, W.Nkumane, D.A.Walther, D.J.Schmelzer, I.Howard, M.Davenport, M.L.Versluis, R.C.Stumme, R.E.Kearns, T.F.Kintz, T.L.Moore, T.M.Schaefer,
A.A.Richter, A.J.Gibbs, A.L.Gray, B.M.Van Arsdale, D.G.Lee, D.J.Keith, E.C.Staveley, J.K.Underwood, J.M.Cunningham, J.P.Dierks, L.A.Boerschel, L.Watson, M.A.Sims, M.A.Wade, M.F.Dantzler,
M.J.Moss, M.S.Cronin, O.S.Grover, P.J.O Loughlin, R.E.Ackerman, R.J.Cashen, R.J.Warner, S.A.Kappel, S.B.Fisher, S.D.Cose, S.F.Pint, T.J.Caswell, W.B.Mc Coy, B.L.Perry, D.L.Walker, F.P.Washington,
P.L.Lashbrook, R.D.Peterson, R.R.See, C.B.Lyman, C.Singleton, C.W.Wade, D.E.Wilkins, D.G.Linder, D.H.White, D.L.Samuelson, D.W.Jaggers, E.C.Clouse, F.C.Chia, G.E.Ceaglske, H.C.Jennings,
J.I.Larson, J.O.Chaplin, J.S.Belthuis, K.L.Sharp, L.A.Leistikow, L.I.Stansbery, L.R.Grittmann, M.A.Burnside, M.J.Manchester, M.R.Valentine, N.J.Deering, P.J.Caffrey, R.B.Clabaugh, R.B.Terreberry,
R.D.Harbach, R.E.Corliss, R.J.Matthewson, S.B.Hamersley, S.D.Reed, T.D.Price, V.Slessor, D.Capdevilla, D.Kouznetzoff, S.Badji, A.E.Ahlhelm, A.H.Carmichael Jr., A.R.Moeller, C.L.Jensen,
C.L.Martelle, D.H.Coble, D.J.Gallagher, D.K.Carlson, D.L.Lane, E.R.Murphy, F.C.Woldan, G.D.Phillips, G.F.Koranda, G.P.Kalhorn, J.Heisterkamp, J.J.Jelinek, J.K.Loosley, J.M.Mitchell, K.O.Thompson,
L.D.Meyer, L.E.Lemke, M.H.Biedermann, M.Kouski, M.S.Rosenthal, M.W.Barker, P.R.Weber, R.A.Schmitt, R.D.Chaplin, R.E.Parker, R.E.Taylor, R.L.Tuder, R.Stumme, S.B.Hensel, S.D.Sankarsingh,
S.P.Nelson, V.N.Halbur, W.D.Sigmon, E.Schell, G.Herrmann, A.Garcia G., M.Martinez S., B.B.Jackson, B.F.Goodman, C.K.Meier, D.D.Meehan, D.H.Crow, D.L.Hunemuller, E.J.Nielsen, G.W.Hoppenjan,
H.D.Kremer, J.J.Buck, J.K.Willhite, J.M.Nielson, L.D.Smith, L.J.Heeren, L.Jackson, M.L.Sniffin, P.A.Van Arsdale, R.C.Brown, R.D.Banes, R.J.Alexander, S.Moses, S.W.Wright, A.L.Stammler,
B.J.Boeckmann, C.A.Beener, D.R.Thede, E.E.Wenger, G.J.Staff, J.R.Drury, J.W.Banks, K.J.Davis, L.E.Wood, L.Mc Fadden, M.C.Jacobsen, M.R.Rogers, V.J.Strachota, W.E.Herdahl, M.J.Masiteng,
S.J.Kirschbaum, T.A.Bohnsack, T.J.Hove, D.Miguel-Amadeu, B.A.Hayes Jr., B.E.Lehmkuhl, C.E.Backhaus Jr., C.H.Burrows, C.S.Thede, C.W.Nichols, D.E.Nelson, D.L.Carpenter, D.Q.Tool, D.R.Johnson,
D.R.Townsend, D.R.Walker, E.A.Mc Callie, E.M.Canny, E.S.Chipman, G.D.Sears, G.W.Hubbartt, J.A.Neis, J.D.Adelmund, J.J.Parker, J.M.Rousselow, J.N.Hein, J.T.Prine, L.E.Hawkins, M.L.Baker,
R.A.Moorman, R.J.Scherr, R.O.Nervig, S.E.Daugherty, S.S.Shively, W.M.Nefiodow, W.P.Denny, A.E.Huisinga, J.D.Owen, K.A.Hayes, R.C.Lewis, A.L.Gensler, L.A.Hanna, R.A.Henning, A.Rocca, R.Anop,
L.R.Dunne, R.Ramon, S.O.Crabb, T.Evans, D.R.Bradley, J.A.Jamieson, J.M.White, R.A.Miedema, B.C.Mather, B.D.Buchanan, B.J.Dowell, B.S.Hagberg, C.A.Davis, C.F.David, C.R.Young, G.M.Bode,
H.A.McClanahan, H.J.Clark, H.P.Wyatt, J.E.Banfield, J.J.Rivera, J.T.Bryant, M.A.Gaul, M.I.Moraine, P.D.Yates, R.A.Brinkman, R.C.Rueckert, R.C.Teed, R.D.Harris, R.J.Pluemer, R.Z.Speer, S.E.Haff,
W.R.Cantrell, H.Capar, C.L.Stufflebeem, G.E.Pauwels, G.P.Higham, J.W.Lord, J.W.Pruessner, R.F.Carlson, R.J.Wasko, D.D.Ayers, D.W.West, G.L.Leslie, J.F.De Biase, J.R.Medina, R.J.Llorens,
D.A.Lahmann, D.G.Benedict, R.R.Rose, S.Syhlman, W.D.Bantz, P.S.Stumphy, T.C.Eddy, M.W.Klais, A.A.Bennett, A.D.Reed, C.A.Uppena, C.W.Greely, D.J.Coulter, D.L.Troester, D.W.Francis, F.J.Baker,

Opera singer at Ottumwa Works, Ottumwa, Iowa, 1976

H.A.Webster, J.E.Hilgers, J.H.Meyers, L.D.Irwin, L.M.Haydon, N.B.Headley, P.E.Faucher, P.G.Weeks, R.D.Shaw, R.M.Maas, S.E.McNair, T.E.O Leary, W.B.Turner Jr., W.L.Jones, J.Pervin, A.W.Wimer, C.E.Humphries, D.C.Bausch, D.C.Wolfe, J.E.Derifield, J.L.Nelson, P.P.Riley, R.E.Holmes, T.C.Henninger,
W.G.Bell, D.V.Castle, E.C.Riley, G.L.Liebsch, G.L.Reiss, H.R.Curry, H.R.Holman, J.L.Christianson, K.C.Griebel, L.P.Schildgen, M.C.Diefenbach, R.G.Curler, R.L.Sawyer, R.P.Donath, T.J.Green, T.J.Lindquist, C.A.Raeder, E.J.Green, F.J.Shepherd, J.K.Whittington, J.R.Blaser, J.W.Griffin, L.Denton Jr.,
P.L.Roberts, R.L.Bridges, R.M.Kressig, S.L.Robinson, T.L.Oldfather, T.P.Hall, G.Glover, R.W.Schleusner, J.W.Scott Jr., L.A.Olds, P.A.Robinson Jr., T.L.Drilling, B.J.Handfelt, B.W.Ruehs, D.D.Koch, D.Good, D.R.Hanser, E.L.Neuburg, E.R.Shaffer Jr., F.D.Deevers, F.H.Etnier, G.A.Harrington,
G.R.Johnston Jr., G.W.Cook, H.G.Berger, J.A.Bandsma, J.A.Kirklin, J.D.Polston, J.H.Poetter, J.H.Wiese, J.K.May, J.K.Wood, J.T.Plank, J.W.Russell, L.C.Leitzke, L.D.Harding, L.J.Miller, L.O.Leitzke, L.T.Klinger, M.L.Bennett, M.R.Vonhagen, M.W.O Brien, P.A.Donovan, P.R.Henderson, P.S.Navarro,
P.T.Finn, R.L.Bartels, R.L.Fraipont, R.L.Levey, R.L.Sawyer, R.L.Schmidt, R.S.Ellestad, S.E.Kovalaske, S.M.Davis, S.W.Du Charme, W.D.Youngblut, W.V.Holter, E.Prunzel, S.Rocher, A.A.Gomez, C.C.Steiner, C.D.Niedert, C.H.Hammett Jr., C.W.Johnson, D.A.Asencio, J.J.Pasker, J.R.Gamble, J.T.Mills,
M.S.Dreessens, R.E.Steffen, R.J.Gorman, T.K.Earles, C.F.Brown, D.A.Jorgenson, D.D.Aswegen, D.D.Newton, D.E.Mc Cumber, D.M.Nelson, E.W.Brown, G.E.Yuska, J.E.Sniffin, J.L.Brooks, J.L.Swangel, P.A.Weidman, R.E.Gottschalk, R.J.Hughes, R.J.Meyer, W.C.Lambert, A.G.Spooner, D.J.Williams,
D.M.Defrieze, D.R.Becker, D.R.Hospodarsky, E.E.Young, G.S.Chamberlin, J.H.Heidemann, J.R.Luckritz, L.A.Gentle, P.J.Welsh, P.M.Dolan, R.J.Grant, R.J.Gutknecht, R.M.Smith, T.D.Koeff, W.K.Hall, B.A.Ott, B.J.Norte, D.B.Erdmann, D.G.Hawley, E.W.Meyer, E.W.Shook, F.Speidel, G.D.Diesburg,
G.L.Iverson, J.E.Worth, J.E.Yuska, K.A.Flynn, L.B.Hales, M.C.Crum, M.D.Oltmann, M.J.Donavon, M.Williams, R.G.Quail, S.A.Mc Cumber, W.F.Frost, J.Lafond, C.Hasenfratz, H.Ratsch, H.Zach, K.Groh, K.Hahnebach, L.Zimmermann, W.Schnoeder, C.Washington, G.L.Schaefer, M.J.Dunlay, P.D.Kay,
R.L.Weseman, R.R.Ebert, A.Rakea, A.Soubhi, C.Leroy, J.Chretien, J.Garcia, J.Lavrilleux, J.Mathieu, M.Dutheil, A.Bengel, H.Guenzel, H.Nowak, H.Wiederhold, J.Courbier, J.Mocan, K.Berg, M.Haupt, M.Kuppinger, P.Mueller, W.Meixner, W.Stoerzinger, W.Waschik, A.Jones, B.A.Snyder, B.I.Wagner,
C.A.Kuen, C.E.Guptill, C.M.Stitt-Oates, C.M.Swinscoe, C.R.Miller, C.W.James, D.A.Demmer, D.A.Evens, D.D.Geerdes, D.D.Tompkins, D.E.Hayes, D.L.Franks, D.M.Zimmerman, D.P.Jacobson, D.R.Woolums, D.Roby, D.W.Redl, E.A.Thrun, F.H.Vivians, G.J.Gorman, G.L.Brown, G.L.McKinley, G.L.Shepley,
G.R.Gentz, G.R.Mc Farlane, I.F.Schallau, J.A.Miller, J.D.Atkins, J.L.Dhabalt, J.P.Hawkins, J.T.Buxton, J.T.Fitch, K.C.Lehr, K.E.Freiburger, K.K.Oka, K.Kenniker, L.L.Frakes, M.E.Andorf, M.L.Etringer, M.L.Galer, M.L.Rucker, M.L.Tidwell, M.S.Oechsner, M.W.Matteson, P.M.Turner, P.S.Finger, R.A.Mc Niel,
R.A.Weissenburger, R.C.Hoffmann, R.C.Miller Jr., R.C.Pollock, R.C.Wild, R.D.Reeves, R.E.Degener, R.E.Love, R.E.Nehmer, R.F.Brown, R.F.Lindbloom, R.H.Wollenburg, R.K.Matzdorf, R.L.Gannon, R.L.Greenleaf, R.L.McNamer, R.L.Reifsnider, R.M.Scherer, R.Woodman, S.A.Bade, S.A.Newton,
S.D.Haskin, S.G.Bonifas, S.L.Etringer, S.M.Miller, T.D.Bottomley, T.E.Anfinson, T.J.Phelps, V.V.Turner Jr., W.E.Clark, W.G.Goss, J.Bouchet, A.D.Mobley, A.D.White, C.L.Schupbach, C.P.Frush, D.A.Roling, D.L.Goeke, D.M.Redenius, G.C.Denlinger, J.Buckner, J.E.Baker, J.F.Myers, J.H.Benn, J.L.Stratton,
K.J.Bauler, K.P.Adams, M.E.Kemp, M.Jenkins Jr., R.J.Weydert, R.K.Clark, R.R.Schmit, S.R.De Serano, W.Hoskins Jr., G.Renard, M.Pinho, D.A.Burgess, D.F.Rupp, D.G.Bright, D.R.McNeal, E.Pattison, F.M.Tripp, G.L.Nielsen, H.D.Riddell, H.F.Breitsprecker, J.W.Brink, J.W.Lambertson, K.A.Bries,
L.J.Wolbers, M.E.Kasemeier, R.Cook, R.J.Aswegan, R.R.Pfab, T.D.Stclair, V.E.Behlke Jr., W.C.Vognsen, B.K.Starnes, D.A.Bries, D.E.Laugesen, D.F.Schillinger, F.E.Dannatt, G.L.Gladson, J.P.Dolan, R.B.Klenzendorf, D.J.Lewis, L.A.Draeger, M.E.Adams, A.S.Kammerude, C.A.Gorter, C.P.Duyvejonck,
D.A.Haugen, D.A.Rousselow, D.C.Lawler, D.E.Rasmussen, D.J.Nelson, E.K.Smola, J.F.Deckert, J.G.Pfiester, J.H.Hinderaker, J.J.Bennett, J.J.Raes, J.O.Bell Jr., J.R.Kern, K.T.Anderson, M.C.Harris, M.K.Sanders, M.M.Giellis, R.C.Schwartz, R.D.Reilly, R.J.Buelow, R.J.Middleton, R.L.Sowers, R.P.Rupp,
R.Tenorio, S.J.Sheese, S.W.Waddell, T.M.Keenan, W.E.Linn, W.J.Hoekstra, F.Goncalves, M.Sprajcer, G.D.Hathaway, F.E.Ehlers, G.D.Kara, G.L.Kautman, J.L.Shinn, L.D.Eibey, R.F.Henry Sr., R.J.Herbst, R.L.Dake, A.Martin, A.D.Wyatt, A.M.Heath, C.A.Dunbar, D.E.Johnson, D.F.Ungs, G.L.Ersland,
J.W.Wiest, O.Jackson, P.D.Timmermann, P.E.Cox, R.Heise, R.J.Fordyce, R.Long, R.W.Harris, W.I.Harken, M.Cueff, A.J.Kress Jr., B.L.Hackbarth, D.A.Brooks, D.A.Smith, D.G.Kubitz, E.Calkins, G.J.Droessler, G.L.Weber, J.L.Evans, J.M.Waldorf, J.P.Fuerstenberg, L.B.Powers, M.J.Ehlers, M.J.Schmitt,
R.J.Heiderscheit, R.J.Wendling, R.W.Heideman, S.J.Niewoehner, T.A.Joyce, T.P.Rooff, W.A.Gale, W.H.Bunn, A.De Oliveira, B.E.Bridgman, C.A.Collins, D.E.Schmitz, D.R.Terhune, G.J.Cole, J.A.Dralle, J.R.Cagley, K.D.Love, K.R.Kauten, M.E.King, M.P.Menuey Sr., R.A.Bartz, R.A.White, R.C.Rodkey,
R.Harmon, R.L.Forbes, S.E.Gaffney, T.A.Robinson, A.C.Ireland, D.R.Meier, D.W.Loutsch, A.C.Wagner, A.E.Bunkoske Jr., A.F.Lobianco, A.J.Seeberger, A.L.Roush, A.P.Jackson, B.C.Robinson, B.P.Kalb, B.Valentine, C.H.Coulthurst, C.J.Hammer, C.J.Marks, C.M.Brakob, C.M.Conrad, C.W.Schaefer,
D.A.Kapp, D.A.Mc Vay, D.D.Harmsen, D.D.Pearce, D.D.Pepin, D.E.Dummer, D.E.Ingram, D.E.Jacobs, D.E.Milligan, D.E.Moore, D.J.Kramer, D.J.Kueter, D.J.Oster, D.J.Tedore, D.L.Hall, D.L.Sneller, D.M.Dabney, D.M.Morgan, D.R.Devore, D.W.Beukema, E.W.Gundrum, F.J.Glessner Jr., F.R.Beeler,
G.A.Fischer, G.E.Vize, G.G.Larson, G.H.Settje, G.J.Bolt Jr., G.L.Sharkey, G.R.Steger, J.B.Heiberger, J.C.Hicks, J.E.Spiegel, J.F.Fleming Jr., J.H.Mitchell, J.J.Burich, J.L.Gooden, J.M.Anderson, J.M.Driscoll, J.R.Burns, J.R.Merrill, K.E.Angell, L.D.Mast, M.A.Straseskie Sr., M.Carrell, M.N.Kass, M.R.Hickey,
M.R.Murphy, P.A.Haag, P.E.Vines, R.C.Gentosi, R.D.Biederman, R.E.Pelley, R.F.Firgard, R.H.Winterhack, R.J.Schumacher, R.L.Grasso, R.M.Pearson, R.O.Grattan, R.S.Keith, R.V.Quaintance, S.A.Graham, S.L.Wachal, T.F.Kane, T.G.Heideman, T.J.Shea, T.P.Timmerman, T.V.Zingsheim, T.W.Olson,
W.D.Abrolat, W.L.Harris, N.E.Stein, M.Kessab, A.Carrasco, C.Hoel, J.Da Silva, J.Geraud, K.Henni, G.Dahl, T.Ferreras, A.D.Johnson, A.J.Wagner, D.A.Rohle, D.L.Deppe, J.A.Raymond, J.F.Johannes, J.R.Dejonghe, M.J.Brant, M.L.Kruckenberg, P.D.Meier, R.A.Carlson, R.F.Lavenz, R.J.Eilers, R.R.Core,
S.J.Mc Kernan, O.Battistoni, D.L.Cameron, D.L.Prochaska, D.W.Schake, F.M.Pashby, G.L.Everly, G.R.Kennicker, J.D.Koch, J.O.Davies, L.A.Collingwood, M.A.King, M.D.Nash, R.C.Wright, R.J.De Moss, R.N.Beyerlein, T.G.Rose, T.R.Wilson, D.W.Perry, E.J.Banks Jr., I.Romo Jr., J.J.Dehamer, J.M.Reed,
K.R.Mattingly, L.D.Nix, M.G.Cox, M.L.Murphy, R.A.Stoneman, R.E.Quackenbush, R.J.White, R.K.Linsey, S.S.Ward, W.J.Haas, A.F.Battin, E.H.Quail, L.W.Vannatta, R.J.Miller, R.K.Huffman, B.L.Fank, D.J.Boldt, D.R.Hemmer, D.R.Swanger, K.C.Everett, R.Flickinger, V.K.Ackerman Jr., A.H.Navis, B.S.Miller,
C.F.Critchlow, C.M.Gregory, C.W.Lamb, D.C.Levenhagen, D.E.Harwick, D.J.Bellmann, D.J.Bossom, D.J.Roling, D.L.Leonard, D.W.Keller, G.Comer, G.J.Schiffer, G.P.Finzel, H.B.Heller, H.W.Flintoft, J.A.Hanson, J.D.Schulmeister, J.D.Tapia, J.H.Wroten, J.R.Bublitz, K.E.Gasper, L.A.Woods, L.Goodenbour,
L.J.Cutsforth, M.R.Deevers, M.R.Schmidt, M.W.Mc Crary, N.L.Halvorson, P.E.Fischels, P.E.Snyder, P.P.Hartzheim, R.A.Kluesner, R.C.Wolf, R.D.Knoke, R.E.Conklin, R.F.Tobin, R.J.Schwendinger, R.L.Bearbower, R.L.Buchta, R.L.Hook, R.L.Knorr, R.L.Willey, R.N.Bischoff, R.R.Ascherien, R.W.Culp,
S.D.Treanor, S.L.Watters, T.A.Newsom, T.L.Fisher, W.H.Hefel, Y.N.Bolduc, L.Samson, D.D.Hardesty, D.D.Paul, D.E.Banks, D.G.Burch, D.Sniffin, F.C.Boeckmann, J.A.Vogl, J.D.Slaughter, J.J.Appleby, J.T.Von Tersch, K.D.Wallis, K.L.Pauley, R.G.Reed, R.L.Jones, W.J.Denton, J.Schwebel, K.Blum,
A.E.Gibbs, D.A.Minard, D.L.Hall, E.F.Bruno, F.J.Wahl Jr., G.B.Stern, J.M.Niemeyer, J.R.Collins, J.R.Lowe, J.W.Meyer, M.Jones, M.L.Babinat, R.D.Nichols, R.G.Benson, R.L.Nelson, R.R.Schmerbach Jr., R.R.Siemens, R.S.Richardson, T.J.Otting, W.S.Siedschlag, Y.Barbieri, D.J.Gibbons, D.R.Headington,

J.A.Holliday, K.J.Cowell, L.J.Melton, L.J.Schulte, R.J.Gray, S.A.Nesteby, S.A.Schneider, S.D.Harberts, S.J.Comer, S.M.Lehman, W.C.Micou Jr., W.P.Leaman, W.Gab, D.Schellhase, J.M.Neuman, G.J.Geerts, J.L.O'Sullivan, R.D.Devaney Sr., T.L.Martens, T.O.Cooney, F.Barragán , A.Osel, E.Guillaumon, G.Stiefenhoefer, I.Zenger, S.Thiele, A.J.Caponigro, A.J.Roling, A.L.Davis, A.L.Steiner, C.A.Alfman, C.A.Olson, C.G.Roethle, C.J.Dolan, C.J.Truss, C.P.Valadez, C.S.Wickham, D.A.King, D.D.Thomsen, D.E.Adson, D.F.Nash, D.J.Duncan, D.L.Helmrichs, D.M.Boardman, D.M.Coleman, D.R.Simon, D.W.Jones, D.W.Vogt, F.A.Morgan-Garver, F.E.Long, F.L.Fall-Leaf Jr., G.D.Wellman, G.L.Massey, G.R.Jasper, J.C.Wiley, J.D.Weiss, J.E.Rule, J.F.Miller, J.G.Crall, J.J.Keene Jr., J.J.Walbrun, J.L.Bruce, J.L.Pearson, J.R.Gile, J.W.Vestal, K.M.Clayton, K.R.McGinnis, L.Gerstenkorn, L.J.Smith, L.L.Homan, M.A.Noonan, M.H.Okane, M.J.Zimmer, N.J.Auffhammer, P.J.Carrey, R.B.Harrison, R.B.Watts, R.C.Dooley, R.D.Herrald, R.E.Adamson, R.E.Burgess, R.H.Koehler, R.J.Christopherson, R.J.Vest, R.L.Houselog, R.L.McMain, R.M.Mc Farlane, R.R.Paul, R.W.Durham, S.L.Bevis, S.M.Foley, T.A.Brink, W.C.Shadlow, W.G.Clapp, W.H.Schesser, W.L.Wild, A.Fouillot, J.Musard, F.Cotelle, J.Chauveau, W.Fess, F.Aparicio R., J.Herrera, J.L.Garcia V., J.Oliva, M.D.Miguelez, V.Martin M., F.A.McKee, D.H.Makovec, H.L.Eiklenborg Jr., J.E.Sprague, J.F.McGehee, J.W.Blume, L.D.Geiger, P.N.Johnston, R.L.Kramer, R.W.Fluegge, S.K.Hansen, W.A.Mangan, C.Saint-Martin, B.Grumadas, D.P.Utley, G.R.Nemmers, J.D.Higginbottom, P.G.Motley, R.B.Meyer, S.F.Wand, W.M.Hurley, A.J.Kruger, D.E.Miller, G.M.Salzwedel, J.M.Lanser, M.J.Smith, M.L.Daniel, R.E.Janzig, R.J.Meyer, R.L.Hunter, R.L.Kemp, W.J.Bowdry Jr., W.W.Watson, J.C.Burlage, J.M.Leslein, M.T.Harker, R.C.Muller, R.R.Knapp, W.C.Wasmund, A.R.Monheim, C.A.Hernstrom, D.A.Raatz Jr., D.A.Theis, D.F.Henn, D.G.Whitlatch, D.H.Janssen, D.J.Brown, D.L.Walke, D.P.Gibson, D.R.McIntire, E.E.Gassner, E.J.Oliver, E.L.Coomes, G.J.Steiner, G.L.Wilkinson, H.E.Wickler, I.D.Danay, J.B.McClavy, J.D.Salscheider, J.F.Jackson, J.L.Hay, J.M.Hedrick, J.N.June, J.P.Metheny, J.R.Bell, J.W.Walker, K.E.Backman, K.J.Gratton, L.J.Foggia, L.W.Creath, M.J.Lubenau, M.J.Meier, M.J.Pluemer, M.R.Pasold, N.D.Witt, N.K.Johnson, P.P.Soppe, R.A.Brock, R.C.Beavers, R.C.Fluhr, R.C.Heine, R.D.Errthum, R.J.Gribben, R.J.Paisley, R.Miller, R.W.Argo, S.E.Porter, S.G.Kronafel, S.J.Ressler Jr., S.L.Darling, S.L.Smith, T.A.Wendt, T.E.Tingwald, T.Jared, T.M.Vandevoorde, T.R.Runde, W.C.Ousley, W.F.Smith, W.J.Benway, G.Ravat, F.Gallo, J.Balsells, E.Karabin, A.Estepa, R.Marin, D.L.Pilon, E.W.Pfab, F.J.Konig, J.J.Forkenbrock, J.R.Sherwin, J.W.Pengelly, P.W.Cunningham, R.A.Freeman, R.P.Rivet, S.L.Handshumaker, T.E.Hillebrand, W.B.Clapp, C.K.Duffy, D.A.Willford, L.Thomas, R.J.Conrad, T.Pinchback, A.Baudry, C.L.Wells, C.W.Woodward, D.P.Bussan, J.D.Lewis, J.L.Mullinax, R.A.Michels, W.C.Kramer, A.Donard, E.I.Nauman, M.C.Hubbard, R.A.Dunn, R.E.Neuendorf, T.A.Mellenberger, R.A.Bega, S.M.Ernst, W.E.Gray, A.G.Sykes, A.J.McDermott, A.M.Kiley, A.O.Henderson, B.A.Symons, B.J.Ewart, B.J.Michael, C.A.Phillips, C.D.Bounds, C.E.Dunn, C.F.Symons Jr., C.H.Heim, C.J.Sallows, C.L.Pidgen, D.D.Johnson, D.D.Rindels, D.G.Smith, D.J.Johnson, D.J.Kaumans, D.J.Koppes, D.J.Peters, D.L.Mohr, D.V.Hamilton, D.W.Augustine, E.Burnett, E.C.Jones, E.R.Kemp, E.Saner, F.R.Smith, G.A.Raes, G.B.Stewart, G.B.Tauke, G.L.Feik, G.R.Blankenheim, J.A.Middleton, J.A.Spates, J.H.Deer Jr., J.J.Cole, J.J.Heinrichs, J.K.Ruecker, J.L.Mount, J.M.Klein, J.R.Carter, J.S.Kiesow, J.Trevino, K.A.Stubbins, L.C.Stevenson, L.R.Ostrander, L.W.Winger, M.A.Weber, M.F.Fisher, M.L.Sickler, M.Lalama, M.T.Maguire, M.W.Westemeier, R.D.Brown, R.D.Fears, R.D.Williams, R.J.Rochon, R.L.Hagarty, R.L.Mayberry, S.I.Carlo, S.K.Goeller, S.L.Cook, T.A.Trenez, T.J.Devaney, T.J.Droessler, T.J.Pitts, T.J.Wessel, T.L.Davis III, T.P.Toellner, V.L.McDowell, W.C.Moffitt, W.L.Lewis, W.R.Gross, D.Chesneau, G.Doerr, D.G.Biddick, G.P.Cameron, J.L.Webb, K.N.Kintzle, N.B.Meyers, R.V.Blume Jr., S.D.Stanton, A.J.Shoemaker, E.M.McGrath, M.J.Pitzen, R.A.Jordan, R.J.Demuth, R.L.Barton, A.L.Rowell, D.J.Salow, D.O.Bartels, R.E.Duncan, S.J.Bries, S.S.Coop Finney, C.J.Butcher, L.M.Simon, S.M.Boone, R.E.Durey, A.C.Belman, A.Deich, C.F.Corbett, D.A.Blunt, D.A.Jensen, D.D.Bittner, D.E.Brown, D.E.Steffen, D.F.Danay, D.F.Rennhack, D.K.Oliver, D.L.Vande Berg, D.R.Evert, D.W.Demorest, D.W.Stewart, F.P.Lape, G.A.Timmerman, G.L.Krohmer, G.L.Parker, G.M.Marr, H.S.Dahlman Jr., J.A.Carter, J.G.Messenger, J.J.Jones, J.L.Jegerlehner, J.R.Bell, J.R.Lamere, J.R.Plowman, J.R.Puetz, K.A.Medema, K.K.Kono, K.M.Otts, K.S.White, L.C.Dodge Sr., L.K.Pollock, L.L.Richards, L.L.Webb, M.A.Scott, M.G.Martin, M.J.Lee, M.J.Smith, M.L.Keegan, M.M.Bleymeyer, R.D.Baker, R.D.Owens, R.E.Mason, R.L.Arthur, R.P.Geyer, R.R.Bussan, R.W.Schaar, S.A.Braun, S.D.Day, S.F.Delaney, S.G.Charley, S.L.Boyle, T.C.Rosenmeier, T.J.Steuer, T.W.Greiner, V.T.Eggers, W.D.Allen, W.L.Folger, W.R.Pendergast, G.Galmiche, A.Zahm, W.Decker, C.M.Dullum, D.J.Felderman, G.W.Macintosh, J.L.Moore, J.R.Schons, J.R.Whitson, L.C.Rademacker, L.M.Lasoya, M.E.Mulvehill, R.S.Turley, D.Baltasar , B.A.Riojas, B.G.Butikofer, D.A.Moline, J.L.Nash, M.R.Seavey, R.L.Gansen, S.L.Patzner, L.Bourgoin, C.J.Hefel Jr., C.T.Redfearn, D.F.Metcalf, D.J.Witter, E.J.Sanderson, K.P.Sutter, L.G.Wait, L.J.Kremer, P.J.Haverland, R.L.Peters, R.L.Wittman, S.M.McGovern, S.R.Wallace, T.L.Cottrell, J.Felgueiras, D.D.Siemers, D.E.Fleming, J.R.Ege, R.C.Einwalter, R.T.Schmitz, D.M.Arling, E.G.White, E.H.Cox, J.J.Haas, J.R.Heim Sr., K.P.Kirschbaum, R.W.Robinson, W.J.Meyer, A.J.Mills, B.J.Krausman, D.C.Peterson, D.D.Moldenhauer, D.L.Cook, D.L.Heaton, D.M.Hogan, D.M.McCarthy, D.R.Cook, F.J.Johnson, F.J.Wiggins, G.A.Kennedy, G.E.Ramler, G.L.Bircher, G.L.Govier, G.L.Vick, G.W.Fisher, H.J.Wilcox, J.J.Dalsing, J.J.Deggendorf, J.M.Ernst, J.R.Birch, K.N.Magee, K.W.Willis, L.L.Hock, M.D.Nichols, M.H.Merle Jr., R.L.Arensdorf, R.L.Campbell, R.N.Van Sickel, R.P.Schnorenberg, R.R.McDermott, R.V.Legrand, S.K.McMillin, T.L.Collins, T.L.Hinderman, W.G.Wickler, W.W.Lundy, M.Ghali, W.Guillium, A.C.Conrad, C.D.Johnson, G.H.Poller, H.R.Miehe, R.J.Bender, R.O.Reid, R.R.Lever, R.R.Schreck, V.E.Hartmann, W.T.Harkey, A.F.Lugo, C.A.Smoot, D.A.Beam, D.E.Kennedy, H.M.Volk, J.D.Robeson, J.J.Spahn, J.L.Kelly, L.F.Starr, P.H.Gray, P.W.Gardiner, R.E.Brossman, R.M.Treichel, S.J.Haverland, S.K.Dayton, S.L.Matlock, G.Biundo, K.Schlampp, D.E.Wedige, D.M.Sweerin, F.L.Alexander, G.J.Allison, J.E.Schumacher, R.A.Hinderaker, R.E.Shireman, R.J.Reddin, S.M.Murphy, H.Evenas, C.W.Sievers, D.M.Thompson, K.E.Trimble, L.M.Lobberecht, P.J.Casey, R.J.Kieffer, R.R.Van Daele, G.D.Heineman, G.J.Huffman, A.D.Carmichael, A.E.Foster, C.A.Neal, C.L.Crimmins, D.A.Schueller, D.E.Brown, D.E.Fuller, D.E.Tillou, D.F.Davis, D.G.Stowell, D.K.Moody, D.L.Child, D.L.Christianson, D.L.Wilkinson, D.R.Porter, E.R.Brasch, F.V.Apel, G.N.Oyen, G.W.Richard, H.T.Weber, J.B.Ertl, J.H.Moorman, J.J.Gartmann, J.J.Imbus, J.J.Perez, J.R.Moore, K.A.Kruse, L.L.Johnson, M.D.Miller, M.E.Hankins, M.F.Kucera, M.J.Irelan, M.W.Mullnix, P.B.Larson, P.J.McCarthy, R.A.Miner, R.J.Brimeyer, R.J.Lahmon, R.W.Devrieze, R.W.Pohle, S.L.Greenawalt, T.R.Firth, V.Domar, A.Ettaoussi, F.Vernadet, D.A.Jagger, D.J.Cuvelier, G.Lynch, J.P.Cowell, K.H.Jordan, K.M.Valentine, M.J.McClain, P.D.Horkheimer, P.E.Neitzel, R.L.Beck, S.R.Higgins, T.D.Leonard, J.H.Hollingsworth, J.J.Bahl, J.S.Ploessl, L.W.Sass, R.G.Sims, S.M.Kettmann, T.E.Wright, C.G.Beatty, D.L.Schmitz, E.M.Kerns, J.B.Ward, L.L.Vanlaningham, P.C.Beckman, R.R.Thompson, S.J.Roddick, S.Wright Jr., B.P.Keag, D.E.Juehring, D.J.Oldenburger, G.D.Clemens, J.E.King, J.R.Goderis, R.A.Hines, T.J.Hardi, W.H.Johnston, L.J.Fuller, A.G.Wernke, B.D.Hussey, B.K.Luther, C.Janas, D.G.Hodges, D.G.Ward, D.L.Bohnert, D.L.Torrey, D.P.Simon, D.W.Brown, F.A.Wilson, F.M.Hughes, G.A.Webber, G.D.Clark, G.D.Rawlings, G.G.Peterson, H.D.Smith, H.J.Huneault, J.A.Bruni, J.A.Schlueter, J.C.Tappendorf, J.M.Lammer, L.F.Edwards, L.F.Luke, L.J.Connolly, L.K.Lawrence, M.A.Corey, M.J.Boxx, M.J.McClean, M.L.Chapman, M.L.Kinnamon, M.T.Evitts, N.F.Noel, P.M.Buckley, P.M.Gustafson, R.A.Atwell, R.J.Iocca, R.J.Knight, R.N.Lamarche, R.R.Newberg, S.D.Stout, S.I.Martin, S.L.Kratzberg, S.S.Rasmussen, T.L.Plunkett, T.R.Lloyd, V.L.Williams, W.C.Rowe, W.H.Cloutier, W.L.Leibold, W.M.Kauzlarich, W.Wissner, J.E.White, E.E.Parker, F.M.St Aubin, G.L.Pitcher, P.J.Doll, P.J.Grist, P.L.Mc Combs Jr., W.R.Reed, A.P.Martinez, B.A.Marner, B.E.Nanke, C.E.Graham, C.L.Overbeck, D.E.Williams, D.R.Wassell, G.L.Gray, J.A.Ashbacher, J.D.Maxson, J.E.Wuebben Jr., J.M.Kopplin, N.T.Subh, R.A.McDonnell, R.C.Wisely, R.D.Bullock, R.G.Homan, R.R.Hammel Sr., R.S.Rumph, T.L.Thorp, W.D.Crouch, R.Joly, C.B.Hoppenjan, C.F.Schults, C.J.Lantz, D.J.Entler, G.M.Nelson, H.D.Watson, M.L.Huggins, M.N.Conley, M.W.Caulkins, P.L.Johnson, A.W.Larson, D.W.Cox, C.W.Carter, C.W.Grimm, D.D.Taets, D.G.Rowland, D.R.Lewis, D.W.Babb, E.D.Stewart, E.E.Lawrence, G.P.Gatt, H.A.Porter, J.A.Davidsaver, J.F.Reuss, J.M.Utter, J.R.Varner, J.T.Kubesheski Jr., J.W.Forrest, J.W.Mills, L.A.Wykhuis, L.C.Schakel, N.Torzsas, P.J.Ernst, P.T.Prose, R.L.Langel, R.S.Ettleman, S.L.Gassmann, S.R.Astgen, T.L.Eggerichs, V.McQueen, W.C.Forrest, W.J.Conrad, G.Feitu, C.K.Curran, J.J.Larkin, L.C.McNew, M.J.Flannery, E.Guerrero, R.Augusto, E.Cabañas, A.P.Columbia, A.R.Reynolds Jr., B.J.Vis, D.C.Hedrick, D.G.Kennon, D.H.Schmitt, D.J.Laflamme, D.R.Maricle, D.W.Harvey Jr., D.W.Puetz, E.G.Johnson, E.H.Devereux, E.R.Stutz, G.E.Tranel, J.E.Martin, J.E.Rusch, J.H.Niece, J.L.Benhart, J.L.Mc Cune, J.L.Orling, J.M.Klaas, J.M.Turner, J.R.Brust, L.T.Bigelow, M.B.Hilton, M.J.Brown, R.D.Talbott, R.E.Lindell, W.J.Fay, Y.A.Trepanier,

Australian branch personnel, 1977

G.Doney, C.Petitperrin, M.Budon, B.J.Swanson, C.L.Inman, D.R.Mitchell, E.L.Vickers, R.C.Campbell, R.J.Smith, S.C.Coleman, T.D.Salter, C.L.Kunath, G.M.Prosser, R.E.Duddeck, R.L.Dietrick, R.L.Trueg, R.L.Upman, R.Gauron, D.A.Schurman, T.P.Kearns, T.W.Schrobilgen, P.Istasse, S.Griot, H.Weis, S.Brubach, B.A.Natvig, C.A.Pierson, C.J.Bernacki, C.R.Bain, D.D.Fair, D.E.Ritz, D.F.Hackett, D.G.Ince, D.K.Sample, D.W.Rimkus, F.Hagan, J.E.Daubney, J.F.Lowrance, J.H.Glendon, J.M.Kronfeld, J.P.Cassidy, J.R.Cosby, J.S.Langston, L.C.Salzer, L.E.Bettis, M.B.Goodson, M.J.Pancrazio, M.P.Halfman, M.W.Pust, P.J.Daly, R.G.Gray, S.A.Haars, S.E.Harward, S.J.Irwin, S.J.Zalaznik, J.Poinsot, F.Woll, J.Zapp, W.Krick, C.M.Bettis Jr., E.J.Vaughn Jr., M.Jory, D.S.Miller, G.W.Lindley, L.M.Stritzke, R.E.Schueller, R.J.Kluesner, R.L.Armstrong, R.R.Wildman, D.E.Grall, J.A.Steffen, M.R.Thomas, R.E.Verly, W.Harper Jr., W.L.Potter, A.M.Rosauer, C.L.Earl, D.J.O Connor, D.O.Staton, M.R.Patterson, P.F.O Brien, R.E.Lindeland, R.R.Runyan, T.A.Neidick, T.R.Power, V.D.Smith, V.S.Downing, W.R.Mc Donald, V.L.Proctor, A.G.Fisher, C.E.Collins, D.A.Betcher, D.M.Mc Carty, D.M.Severson, D.R.Klein, D.V.Rice, D.W.Lesley, G.D.Hoffman, G.D.Williams, G.H.Glab, H.A.Timbrook Jr., J.J.Hamil, K.C.Phillips, M.S.Adams, R.A.O'Brien, S.J.Schmitt, T.A.Bump, W.I.McLaughlin, W.J.Blair, K.Kiefer, C.H.Holler Jr., C.P.Kaake, E.D.Pritchard, E.J.Kunst Jr., G.A.Puchalski, G.L.Everding, J.R.Arnold, J.W.Gunnison, B.Chateau, M.E.Fliege, R.L.Merfeld, T.J.Marckese Jr., B.L.Watson, C.D.Hilligoss, E.W.Myers, R.E.Dale, W.B.Erdman, E.L.Rios, G.E.Breckling, G.J.Zeimet, J.A.Chapman, J.P.Grimes, J.R.Carpenter, M.W.Pearson, R.D.Kime, V.L.Shaw, M.Zaghbib, C.Couvreur, J.Poullin, K.Ginder, J.Gouin, **1973** A.J.Frechette, A.Reiner, L.R.Brown, J.Pajak, D.Otto, H.Hofer, K.Lambert, A.C.Campfield, A.J.Heber, A.W.Otters Jr., B.J.Schneider, B.L.Blakeley, B.L.Landaal, C.A.Linck, C.A.Maddux, C.C.Bowers, C.E.McDaniel, C.K.Dolphin, C.L.Hartness, C.L.Mains, C.L.Stout, C.R.Rusk, C.R.Warden, D.A.Tool, D.D.Doddema, D.D.Eiklenborg, D.D.Lorenz, D.E.Moormann, D.J.Welter, D.L.Baker, D.L.Bleymeyer, D.L.Oldenburger, D.L.Patrie, D.L.Postel, D.M.Mulcahy, D.M.Paulsen, D.M.Rogers, D.N.Fischer, D.N.McElroy, D.R.Fuller, D.R.Garcia, E.J.Meredith, E.L.Schulmeister, F.F.Rocco, G.B.Robins, G.E.Wilson, G.K.Glasscock, G.L.Gallagher, G.L.Reynolds, G.L.Thompson, H.A.Gates, H.J.Kirkwood, J.A.Machu, J.A.Sallee, J.C.Muench, J.D.Dietrick, J.Doeppke, J.E.Park Jr., J.E.Wolf, J.F.Joblinske, J.Fischels, J.L.Schutte, J.M.Ritchie, K.A.Dhabalt, K.A.Paulsen, K.C.Stark, K.D.Hayter, K.L.Jessee, K.W.Hoehn, L.L.Sager, L.M.Grummitt, M.C.Allen, M.E.Carroll, M.E.Lamfers, M.G.Gibbons, M.H.Shannon, M.L.Mehmen, M.R.Kerr, M.W.Maxwell, N.E.Wright, O.J.Simpson, P.R.Bennett, R.C.Gienau, R.D.Stone, R.E.Thomm, R.G.Evans, R.J.Fingeroos, R.J.Willis, R.L.Carter, R.L.Garris, R.L.Hale, R.O.Butts, R.Olmsted, R.R.Reed, R.R.Strandgard, S.A.Knepper, S.C.Lipinski, S.E.Nimrick, S.J.Dotzler, T.A.Bailey, T.C.Koehn, T.D.Hodson, T.E.Ferry, T.J.Broell, T.J.Phillips, V.J.Mackey, V.T.Dolan, W.A.Dotzler Jr., W.A.Dunkley, W.C.Weidemann, W.W.Reddick, A.L.Mohr, C.A.Hohenberger, C.R.Weilbrenner, D.C.Manhart, D.D.Parker, D.G.Bogert, D.J.Stouthammer, E.L.Snook, F.Jackson Jr., G.A.Nyquist, G.E.Richmond, G.M.Stevens, G.R.Bragg, H.A.Lenius, H.V.Leahy, J.C.Coop, J.C.Denato, J.E.Young, J.L.Allen, J.W.Miletich, L.D.Sylvester, L.J.Watters, M.A.Snyder, M.L.Greenfield, R.C.Goodwin, R.J.Schippers, R.L.Conrad, R.L.Egert, R.L.Griffie, S.D.Barnes, T.E.Gruwell, T.W.Mc Cleary Sr., V.L.Proctor, W.D.Hamm, S.M.Cooper, J.L.Weber, A.J.Domeyer, A.W.Rosenbalm, C.D.Hopkins, C.E.Hyslope, C.J.Krause, C.M.Pfalzgraf, C.W.Jacobs, D.C.Noelting, D.H.Stroud, D.J.Polich, D.J.Weis, D.L.Larkin, D.L.Spilman, D.M.Frideres, D.P.Watters, D.R.Huddleston, E.A.Hoffmann, E.R.Menuey, F.D.Wilhelmson, F.J.Baierl, G.D.Sundquist, G.G.White, G.K.Reinier, G.L.Adamson, G.W.Heaton, H.Vander Veen, J.A.Payne, J.E.Reed, J.E.Willis, J.F.Shoelen, J.J.Owens, J.J.Slininger, J.L.Knock, K.M.Mc Bride, L.D.Brewer, L.D.Keeney, L.Pett, M.D.Conyers, M.G.Burkhart, M.H.Mc Donald, M.J.Celania, M.L.Fischels, M.R.Judge, M.T.Murphy, N.S.Cook, P.E.Isiminger, P.L.Meyer, R.D.Meyer, R.I.Bell, R.J.Wells, R.P.Schepp, R.S.Hovey, S.J.Buchanan, S.R.Vogt, T.A.Loeb, W.A.Skinner, W.M.Cummings, W.M.Sweat, W.R.Elder, A.Bohin, E.Brunazzi, G.A.Robbins, G.C.Nathaniel, J.L.Bedore, M.R.Greer Jr., R.A.Olsson, R.D.Henry, B.W.Pocock, A.L.Jungling, C.J.Fries, C.W.Linde, D.D.Heath, D.L.Caughey, D.W.Sels, G.J.Park, H.L.Kallenbach, J.D.Rickert, J.L.Voshell, J.M.Decapp, L.V.Hayes, P.W.Courtney, R.D.Stephens, R.W.Best, T.E.Tully, W.C.Morris, L.Cheval, R.Desvaux, D.A.Zeimet, D.G.Collett, G.D.Derr, G.F.Kunkle, G.V.Goedken, J.J.Wilson, R.M.Hough, S.H.Gallentine, W.G.Keister, F.E.Krantz, G.R.Eastman, J.D.Vogel, N.J.Duffy, R.E.Ackerman, R.J.Phillips, R.L.Mc Allister, S.C.Shaw, R.A.Moreno, A.J.Hoffman, B.R.Rummel, A.A.Garkow, C.A.Dalbey, C.J.Stonebraker, C.Taylor Jr., D.A.Jansen, D.D.Jahns, D.D.Kusel, D.E.Johnson, D.E.Kunce, D.J.Genac, D.P.Linke, D.R.Schmidt, D.R.Schwandt, D.R.Sparks, D.W.Scott, E.A.Schwandt, G.A.Ludolph, G.A.Miller, G.B.Claerhout, G.G.Wiesmueller, G.L.Gress, G.M.Hammel, H.R.Anciaux, J.L.Bartels, J.L.Gearheart, J.L.Vandenberg, J.R.Korte, J.R.Patrick, J.W.Leavengood, K.C.Kerr, K.D.Holley, K.J.Ferrera, K.W.Bailey, L.C.Jenkins, L.D.Garant, L.W.Kern, M.E.Maddux, M.L.Callow, P.K.Hagge, P.R.Petersen, R.E.Houdek, R.E.Rivera, R.E.Wahlstrand, R.J.Hanson, R.J.Major, R.L.Marten, R.R.Hildebrand, R.R.Wegener, R.S.Disher, R.W.Prochaska, S.K.Miller, G.Rameix, J.Fromholtz, R.Andres, B.A.Morrison, B.D.Remington, B.G.Conley, C.J.Van Dyke, D.P.Scarbrough, E.R.Doerr, G.L.Child, J.E.Peck, P.E.Urich, R.D.Peake, R.E.Price, R.J.Shaw, S.A.Hansen, S.F.Brase, S.J.McGory, W.T.Goettsch, J.R.Solis, A.Ulusoy, E.Can, D.A.Eiffler, D.L.Mutschler, F.Aitchison, J.L.Oliva, R.B.Hall, R.E.Chesterman, R.L.Jamison, B.S.Moore, G.J.Thomas, G.L.Schmidt, H.A.Vanklaveren Jr., J.C.Harness, J.F.Cecil, J.N.Farrell, J.R.Corliss, K.L.Metzdorf, L.A.Flagel, R.D.Carder, R.L.West, S.L.Gruwell, S.R.Johnson, T.C.Wehrle, W.L.Arndt Jr., W.W.McMullen, C.W.Anderson, J.M.Staton, J.N.Monat, K.J.Ledtje, L.G.Downing, M.J.Gowdy, J.A.Heiselman, R.D.Gloede, M.E.Rogers, R.D.Rokusek, A.F.Phillips, A.H.Daros, A.L.Glassel, C.A.Young, C.E.Swenson, D.A.Arndt, D.A.Chambers, D.Brown, D.D.Belzer, D.E.Brozovich, D.J.Donahue, D.J.Hecker, D.J.Schlichte, D.R.Fuiten, F.H.Nervig Jr., F.J.Reuter, G.W.Carter, H.Zabel, J.A.Groenewold, J.D.Daugherty, J.D.Voelschow, J.De La Cruz, J.E.Gilbraith, J.F.Lehman, J.H.Kuhlman, J.J.Debisschop, J.J.O'Neel, J.K.McBroom, J.L.Shullaw, L.E.Grabow, M.E.Griffis, M.L.Noonan, M.Parnell, N.D.Sticha, N.K.Baker, P.D.Sandberg, P.H.Punswick, P.J.Linnenkamp, P.R.Vershaw, R.C.Wemer, R.L.Blanchard, R.L.Celania, R.L.Dawson, R.P.Schultz, R.W.Smith, S.A.Lande, S.D.Johnson, T.E.Bobowski, T.M.Harmon, W.D.Livingston, W.H.Voss, W.J.McClure, W.J.Schmieder, H.Sandmeyer, W.Grauwickel, J.L.Mingo, A.D.Wilbanks, A.M.Sanders, D.C.Faith, D.D.Miller, F.D.Goben, F.T.Hanlon, G.A.Heying, J.R.Casillas, K.L.Williams, M.J.Sadler, M.R.Tinkham, R.C.Yeager, R.L.Spurgeon, R.W.Crawford, S.E.McCoy, S.T.Campbell, T.D.Brunko, A.E.Tegtmeier, A.F.Christensen, A.Spates, B.C.Ludwig, B.W.Beintema, C.H.Ohrt, D.J.Brinegar, D.W.Schroeder, E.K.Jones, G.J.Laclair, G.L.Collett, G.L.Sturgill, J.D.Metcalf, J.E.Kipp, J.G.Hemmer, J.Rubalcava, L.A.Gates, M.D.Erhardt, M.J.Anderson, R.D.Black, D.J.Kraus, G.L.Pashby, J.E.Duwe Jr., M.C.Meyerhoff, M.J.Potter, R.A.Mishler, C.A.Stout, C.O.Goodin, D.A.Ellis, D.E.Borwig, D.K.Keidel, J.M.Weber, K.E.Kelley, P.E.Norris, R.A.Frerich, R.L.Bennett, W.J.Sowden, E.Schmidt, D.E.Federspiel, R.L.Siebrands, A.G.Clinkinbeard, A.L.Zell, B.A.Dexter, D.B.Schuster, D.C.Mansfield, D.J.Kremer, D.W.Cornelius, G.D.Eggers, H.W.Olney, J.E.Van Eck, J.R.Hafenstein, J.R.Weber, J.W.Goode, L.F.Marshall, L.L.Jahnke, M.E.Hoss, M.J.Novak, P.J.Meyer, P.J.Raney, R.D.Michaels, R.E.Christian, R.F.Jaeck, R.H.Hoffman, R.J.Courage, R.J.Davoli, R.J.Scharff, R.L.Auxier, R.L.Groy, R.L.Johnston, R.W.Baker, S.E.Hidlebaugh, S.M.Koehn, V.D.Wygle, V.R.Jones, W.D.Bell, W.L.McCoy, R.Baudry, D.W.Kermeen, J.L.Wright, J.M.Beierschmitt, N.L.Knauss, N.R.Brown, R.Hines, T.E.Boehme, R.Krauss, A.R.Boyd, C.R.Funk, G.G.Reppe, G.M.Stevens, H.F.Armstrong, J.G.Pederson, N.P.Paschkov, R.A.Mindrup, R.A.Winger, R.D.Fauser, R.F.Bemisdarfer, R.K.Jones, S.C.Elliott, S.D.Blasberg, C.M.Hollis, C.W.Stainbrook, D.J.March, D.J.Pawlak, D.Mc Intosh, E.M.Winger, G.S.Schaefer, J.H.Schulz, L.I.Foster Jr., M.J.Headley, N.C.Green, R.A.Wildeboer, R.F.Pint, R.J.Duncan, R.P.Rauen, S.E.Cassaidy, S.S.Frazelle, W.A.Weber, S.G.C.Wilson, A.Sorce, E.Dirscherl, G.Vella, A.C.Bonwell, C.A.Tolby, J.R.Schake, L.D.Nauholz, M.E.Bruno, P.A.Estill, R.D.Lee, R.L.Manson, W.J.Thompson, V.D.Boeno, G.D.Schmidt, R.A.Fourtner, B.C.Bertrand, B.G.Peterson, C.R.Secord, D.A.Stukenberg, D.D.Haberstich, D.E.Creech, D.F.Fitzgerald, D.L.Webb, D.M.Bradley, D.P.Gilles, E.L.Milbrandt, E.R.Bauersfeld, G.D.Fitzsimmons, J.D.Egloff, J.M.Wittenburg, L.R.Ihrig, M.A.Tray, M.J.Mullihan, M.S.Marchetti, N.M.Priebe, P.C.Stohlmeyer, P.D.Wilson, P.L.Leeper, P.M.Homme, P.S.Maleck, P.W.Stadnyk, R.A.Plum, R.D.Justice, R.E.Hiatt, R.G.Nelson, R.M.Leifker, R.N.Greene, R.Ramirez, R.S.Simpson, S.D.Rowlands, T.L.Laidley, T.T.Ammons Jr., S.N.Gunther, M.Lecointe, G.Fauconnier, D.D.Werner, D.J.Thurm, K.J.Federspiel, P.R.Smith, R.D.Siebrands, R.J.Mullesch, S.C.Hickman, S.L.Hastings, W.H.Berry, F.Graci, D.L.Lechtenberg, G.R.Groom, K.L.Iverson Jr., T.J.Hartz, J.E.Bender, D.L.Mc Daniel, G.A.Brubaker, J.N.Bonfoco, J.W.Heckert, M.A.Beske, R.F.Baumgartner, W.G.Delagardelle, D.Krueger, J.C.Batla, L.N.Lewis, R.J.Shaffer, S.C.Inks, T.G.Short, R.B.Allen, A.Hulme, A.R.Wolf, B.D.Harrison, B.P.Hilborn, C.J.Martin, D.A.Petrie, D.D.Eckerman, D.E.McCurdy, D.Fisher, D.Larmour, D.W.Anderson, G.F.Berns, G.L.Miller, G.L.Robinson, G.M.Clark, H.L.Hanson, H.Mc Coy, K.R.Brown, M.A.Polito, M.D.Newton, M.D.Sampson, M.J.Schoville, P.A.Kramer, R.A.Russ, R.D.Skelton, R.J.Edminster, R.L.Marquette, R.L.Voelzke, S.Keeley, W.J.Tallman, L.Dani, J.Gauthier, A.Pie, A.Jung, A.W.Humphrey, D.J.Petty, D.R.Benge, G.A.Harris, G.L.Lau, P.M.Tray, R.R.Witt, E.Fischer, H.Reinhart, V.Mlinac, A.G.Key, D.K.Hopkins, D.L.Huffman, G.A.Ballhagen, J.W.Wilson, M.D.Grandon, R.E.Williams, R.L.Amfahr, R.T.Gray, R.W.Pommrehn, S.D.Roquet, S.M.Decker, T.J.Williams, W.M.Minard, M.R.Fink, R.D.Chidester, S.J.Pulkrabek, S.J.Russell, A.V.Block, B.Bull, G.L.Delagardelle, J.E.Burford, J.M.Gaffney, J.R.Paul, L.J.Bovy, M.G.Bond, R.J.Hedeman, R.L.Benson, B.D.Williams, B.K.Rejman, B.W.Stammer, C.R.Brewster, D.M.Winders, J.A.Cox, L.A.Kreamer, L.M.Farrell, N.J.Ward, P.D.Higgins, R.D.Walker, R.F.Bussanmas, R.F.Pladson, R.Milbourn, R.P.Alba, S.A.Eklund, V.M.Ericksen, W.D.Powell, K.Neu, G.Weis, C.Hendrix Jr., H.D.Anstey, J.E.Carter, M.Martin, N.J.Oppendike, R.L.Rice, R.R.Ragen, T.F.Van Ee, B.O.Moore, R.L.Schwake, B.L.Hilburn, B.M.Reed, C.A.Wolf, C.J.Wiley, C.S.Wolever, D.E.Wells, D.L.Roberts, D.M.Fair, E.D.Freeman, G.M.Dangelser, G.N.Birkeland, G.R.Heitman, H.G.Kanzaki, J.F.Dewitte, J.J.Larmour, J.M.Burns, J.M.Yeager, K.E.Herren, L.J.Burns Jr., L.N.Baker, L.P.Davidson, M.D.Covemaker, N.Bradley, R.E.Mc Claran, R.J.Shaubel, S.A.Papish, S.Sandoval, T.L.Stout, W.A.Primasing, W.E.Schneider, G.Mello, M.Chavigny, F.Viaud, C.Hoszkowicz, M.Aydin, J.E.Conrad, K.T.Fairchild, P.M.Killeen, A.Ribeiro, G.Dieme, R.P.Fauser Jr., D.C.Mc Cleary, D.R.Thacher, E.F.Johnston, G.D.Jeffrey, G.H.Meyer Jr., G.L.Bird, J.H.Lange, K.R.Privett, L.L.Farrell, M.D.Beck, N.H.Schold, R.E.Glasscock, R.Lampkin, V.E.Andrews, J.Felix, D.Taranne, J.Poulard, P.Aviles, C.Sorce, G.Hrube, M.Keller, S.Pilato, O.L.Scotta, O.A.Bruschini, D.S.Zuba, H.D.Shira, J.A.Bowie, J.A.Boyer, J.C.Lecleir, J.J.Strieder, J.M.Turner, J.R.Villines, K.E.Ford, L.D.Henry, L.D.Jennings, L.F.Douglass, L.L.Adamson, R.D.Rogers, R.E.Moore, R.M.Edens, T.D.Norin, W.H.Penrod II, M.Mercier, S.Cetinkaya, D.R.Thorne, S.D.Limback, T.P.Erps, C.Felix, B.A.O Brien, G.A.Heister, S.T.Alexander, C.A.McDermid, R.L.Dimke Jr., I.Breitkreitz, A.A.Johnson, D.A.Blackman, D.C.Jelinek, D.J.House, E.A.Poehlman, F.W.Nicely, G.L.Fleagle, G.L.Karenke, H.E.Schwabrow, J.Dilorenzo, J.E.Horner, J.L.Heiderscheit, J.M.Werthmann, J.O.Buck, J.R.Garbett, L.H.Rogers, M.Clemens, M.S.Sale, R.D.McFall, R.F.Eulberg, R.K.Bonner, R.L.Hatfield, S.A.Banfield, T.B.Haar, T.J.Devolder, K.Platz, R.Zimmert, M.A.Sainz, D.L.Kirk, K.L.West, L.J.Sherk, P.M.Pruett, N.P.Ernst, R.D.Lester, S.C.Gritzner, V.Reischmann, A.J.French, D.L.Wildermuth, G.S.Williams, H.E.Benford, J.R.Spear, M.A.Kelley, R.L.Hockenberry, C.A.Gengler, D.K.Hagerman, D.L.Cufaude, D.M.Cianflone, F.K.Bender, G.L.Cox, J.J.Wolbers, J.M.Bubon, K.L.Mundt, L.K.Taylor, M.E.Collopy, M.Trask, R.M.Ford, R.P.Dressler, S.F.Herbert, S.R.Webb, T.J.Culp, W.A.Larson, W.E.Long, W.H.Jones, W.I.Miller, C.Casier, J.Turmeau, G.P.Brecht, M.W.Vandewoestyne, R.K.Jones, R.P.Evans, T.B.Rathburn, J.Quievreux, C.S.Crowley, D.C.Royce Sr., D.W.Hall, M.J.Shimp, M.O.Back, A.E.Vandyke, B.A.Bowling, C.H.Hefel, C.R.Schuler, D.M.Cunningham, D.W.Mollison, F.Gaona Jr., G.A.Jackson, G.L.Boyd, H.G.Brown, H.R.Bell, J.D.Kieffer, J.F.Miner, J.L.McDowell, R.L.Carter, S.M.Cooper, T.R.Christie, V.L.Kezar, G.Weber, A.Nuñez M., D.Pardo, G.L.Dulaney, J.A.Porter, J.L.Woodard, R.J.Hamersley, A.L.Mennenga, D.K.Foster, E.Damgaard, G.M.Sines, J.C.Cufr, J.L.Wygle, L.E.Stephenson, R.U.Mohr, V.L.Sund, F.Innocente, D.A.Luloff, D.A.Peterson, G.L.Bush, K.F.Knox, M.W.Smith, P.J.Simon, T.M.Little, V.A.Boens, W.H.Aune, D.H.Hansen, N.J.Dewilfond, N.W.Oldenburger, J.D.Carlson, G.Boillot, C.Kopischke, F.Gruener, H.Kirrstetter, I.Mutter, I.Pettersch, W.Kuehnel, A.D.Singer,

B.A.Monahan, C.A.Bishop, C.M.Chestnut, D.L.Polzin, D.P.Carlson, D.R.Benedict, D.R.Larson, G.W.Nitzsche, J.C.Mausser, J.Kiers, J.M.Doser, J.N.Casillas, J.R.Kerns, L.G.Gray, L.L.Troyer, M.E.Larsen, N.C.Stahl, O.Lumpkin, R.J.Vize, R.L.Johnson, S.C.Gray, S.M.Hansen, T.L.Yelm, J.Pompon, H.Oeztuerk, H.Schwanzar, J.Preuss, K.Menzl, P.Kern, P.Risse, W.Fuerbacher, J.W.Aten, M.L.Decoster, R.N.Youngblut, S.R.Beert, S.Ghali, B.E.Vyncke, C.J.Benoodt, D.E.Daubman, D.E.Howard, D.G.Mathias, G.E.Long, G.R.Moore, J.E.Daly, J.N.Carson, L.D.Anderson, M.J.Whitney, P.Natsis, S.M.Eakins, V.Sellers, W.R.Slycord, A.V.Salvo, J.D.Morrow, S.J.Holt, D.Delaveau, M.S.Rekers, W.R.Brennand, C.L.Gruhl, D.L.Harter, E.D.Johnson, G.D.Canny, G.J.Spurgetis, G.R.Herring, H.R.Plummer III, J.A.Reamy, J.A.Schmidt, J.A.Wagner, J.F.Delaney, J.F.Husman, J.L.Day, J.L.Wyldes, J.S.Waddle, P.K.Wing, R.A.Coffin, R.E.Carlson, R.L.Disher, R.R.Reese, R.W.Graham, T.M.Vandevelde, G.Jasserin, U.Rabe, D.A.Erbst, J.Oleson, R.W.Kinney, G.Gosset, P.Karanikos, C.E.Kish, C.T.Hendrickson Jr., D.W.Anderson, G.S.Clark, J.A.Dekezel Sr., J.S.Seabloom, R.M.Owen, S.L.Splear, I.L.D.Luz, D.E.Shepherd, E.P.King, F.E.Milefchik, L.B.Verheecke, L.Hernandez, L.R.Walters, L.Westbrook, M.A.Raes, R.D.Edie, R.L.Mann, R.L.Woolums, T.D.Clark, T.W.Kittleson, W.R.Kress, C.F.Wilcox, C.L.Jones, D.R.Ashpaugh, F.G.Bries, H.W.Mercer, J.R.Andon, L.E.Anderson, L.Hampton, M.D.Polchow, M.G.Geiger, M.L.Frizell, M.O.Martinez, P.A.Paxton, R.M.Erickson, S.D.Nelson, M.Mundstock, B.W.Curtis, B.W.Davis, D.A.Harbaugh, D.D.Baer, G.L.Cox, G.T.Pinder, J.W.Burrell, M.L.Pfeiffer, N.C.Bradley, N.E.Sower, R.F.Henkes, S.P.Blackwell, T.H.Shaffer, T.P.Shehan, V.R.Mann, W.J.Domagala, W.L.Strunk, W.R.McPherson, S.Lievin, J.Cabanac, M.Da Cunha, D.Hamm, K.Wagner, C.L.Gregory, A.Suck, B.D.Davis, D.R.Boehme, G.M.Wilkinson, T.M.Mc Beth, A.E.Olson, D.E.Blackmer, J.T.Lynch, L.V.Hoskin, M.C.Brumbaugh, T.L.Young, A.R.Neamtz, D.E.Massey, D.R.Bowen, D.S.Maccabee, E.C.Collier, H.J.Mein, J.A.Carter, J.S.Waltrip, J.T.Henry, L.G.Gettler, M.S.Humphreys, N.J.Liechty, N.L.Fazio, O.D.Sample, S.G.Hansen, T.S.Becker, V.A.Jibaja, C.E.Snider, R.J.Pladson-Yetzer, T.C.McWhirt, G.Pirolley, Z.Yilmaz, J.S.Harville, T.Tasic, B.S.Freeman, C.D.Reifenstahl, W.J.Ross, S.T.Luna, C.A.Keasling, D.E.Vanzandt, J.L.Crysler, J.M.Martin, J.W.Doepping, P.J.Kirik, P.M.Minor, R.K.Jacobs, R.W.Peshek, S.C.Bradley, T.Daniel, T.M.Jones, T.N.Bowman, C.A.Hanson, J.D.Ramsay, J.E.Conklin, M.T.Foutch, R.J.Konrardy, G.Scherer, W.Dehn, D.R.Newcomb, K.M.Wilson, L.F.Richard, S.B.Barkhoff, T.J.Leohr, W.D.Winskel, J.Bourgau, H.Gaier, G.Borda, M.Senesi, E.B.Elliott, J.R.Cole, W.T.Udell, A.Anderson, A.Butera, B.D.Self, B.E.Farnan, B.Jackson, C.A.Wilt, D.W.Brott, E.Weigel, G.W.Collier, H.M.Johnson, J.A.Fay, J.W.Zbornik, L.E.Wilson, M.H.Lindaman, M.L.Callas, R.A.Jurgensen, R.J.Tabor, S.K.Hefel, V.E.Stubblefield, M.Duplan, P.Chatard, H.Kasumovic, L.Moriana, M.Hoor, M.Vazquez, A.D.Fecht, C.W.Baker, D.D.Urban, D.E.Kinard, J.E.Brown, L.D.Sheffler, M.L.Mc Combs, M.L.Wrage, J.L.Norstrom, J.O.Costansi, B.C.Evans, C.H.Klein, C.T.Buckingham, D.A.Boevers, D.J.Garza, D.W.Bush, F.H.Barnes, G.L.Osborne, H.A.Ostring, J.A.Burkett, J.A.Cochran, J.A.Plotts, J.E.Poots, L.F.Martin, L.N.Anderson, M.D.McCracken, M.L.Styve, N.T.Delagardelle, R.A.Thompson, R.E.Walker Jr., R.T.Katrynuk, E.J.Bender, R.Leblanc, J.Bildersheim, C.L.Mc Grane, D.R.Canfield, G.N.Weber, L.A.Thompson, S.R.Jones, W.E.Biedermann, D.E.Borgman, D.W.Elmore, G.G.Hirst, J.D.Holt, L.C.Goodrich, M.A.Kramer, P.G.Alexander, R.J.Splinter, W.R.Ilnitsky, J.Pascal, P.Parisien, J.C.Kinard, T.C.Mc Glaughlin, S.S.Marsau, G.Illescas, A.L.Lau, C.L.Coberly, C.L.Kinkade, C.R.Van Vooren, D.R.Pates, E.F.Rossetti Jr., G.D.Barrell, G.D.Dingbaum, J.E.Carder, J.M.Hanna, M.L.Sims, P.S.Wood, R.C.Dixon, R.H.Lees, R.J.Wells, R.S.Huslig, S.A.Christensen, S.L.Hull, T.M.Van Gerpen, V.S.Michalik, W.R.Spangler, S.Caillaud, G.Amormino, G.Stein, H.Kircheis, A.H.Jurgensen, A.Q.Taylor, B.A.Ahlschwede, B.E.Carver, D.W.Desilest, K.S.Den Hartog, M.E.Kainu, R.H.Mc Kinney, W.J.Berns, M.Berger, R.Dinkiliboerk, D.L.Elder, P.J.Labbe, H.Ibis, J.J.Schmitz II, J.Younce, K.R.Earles, L.J.Hansen, M.T.Mack, S.S.Hackett, J.A.Bell, G.Laframboise, J.C.Trudel, N.J.Chistoff, J.Archiles, J.Joseph, P.Guesdon, J.Manzano, A.C.Rolfe, C.A.Noesen, D.L.Priebe, D.R.Williams, E.L.Conway, G.C.Cayro, G.D.Rehn, J.C.Sheley, J.G.Wightman, J.L.Crosson, J.L.Fox, L.N.Hawks, M.Jones, M.V.Ashman, N.W.Hellenthal, R.D.Roberts, S.A.Toppin, T.D.Ward, J.Pereira, D.D.Stober, D.F.Schares, M.J.Young, R.L.Towns, T.Reiss, C.D.Krouse, J.F.Schoville, J.P.Youngblut, P.D.Carney, D.D.Vancleve, E.M.Carr, J.A.Miller, J.W.Dodgson, K.A.Williamson, R.W.Guetzlaff, S.Johnson, S.S.Stites, W.J.Whittington, J.Demaison, J.M.Aranda, J.Villarta, W.J.Kobliska, B.J.Sanford, D.A.Mossman, D.H.Schaubel, D.J.Mlekush, D.L.Nahnsen, D.M.Sulzer, G.A.Benson, G.J.Woerdehoff, J.A.Suhr, J.C.Casper, J.F.English, J.L.Bloom, J.M.Burkart, J.W.Maxson, K.A.Lynn, K.T.Guthrie, L.L.Decker, M.D.Beale, M.W.Porter, P.H.Johnson, P.K.Hanson, R.D.Pursley, R.E.Bachman, R.E.Nelson, R.L.Stamm, R.R.Dobbin, R.S.Thies, R.W.Grove Jr., S.L.Ellerbach, S.L.Turner, W.C.Madsen, W.C.Raeder, W.G.Robbins, W.L.Kilgore, A.Le Meau, R.Champagne, C.Lorente, G.Maqueda, D.A.Gremmels, M.L.Shepherd, R.J.Gaster, D.A.Bolte, H.F.Aurand, J.I.Lodico, J.T.Suggs, L.R.Becker, R.J.Bolduc, R.J.Mangrich, J.Marion, D.J.Kass, G.C.Carpenter, J.A.Klipping, K.F.Pittman, M.A.Schaefer, V.E.Thompson, L.Van Laer, C.J.Mullesch, D.D.Primmer, R.R.Knittle, W.R.Thode, D.M.Knipp, J.D.Buss, B.A.Duffy, B.A.Postel, B.H.Winston, B.W.Paley, D.E.Lynch, D.E.Thier, D.L.Adams, D.L.Eaton, D.L.Runkle, D.W.Kelly, E.C.Klar, G.C.Winter, G.F.Brown, G.L.Davis, G.M.Wildman, H.Williams Jr., J.M.Dougherty, L.Hill, L.R.Milner, N.J.Lessard, O.Mueller III, R.J.Lochner, S.F.Jacobi, S.J.Plager, S.P.Pedersen, V.G.Woollums, V.L.Jones, Y.A.Riggs, J.Nichols, S.A.Richards, T.E.Smithson, M.Pivot, C.Murtas, P.Wagner, L.Gomez M., S.Talavera, A.Morman, J.G.Hickman Jr., L.L.Hoyt, M.R.Wooldrik, T.R.Clark, W.H.Saxton III, N.Ince, C.L.Cary, J.P.Mason, J.W.Roloff, P.J.Colgan, P.M.Ross, P.Tovar, R.J.Vangoethem, S.M.Sadusky Jr., P.Salazar, D.L.Dufel, D.S.Feddersen, G.S.Nelson, M.H.Taylor, R.L.Kresser, D.Lambrecht, L.P.Evans, R.M.Judas, A.D.Roberts, A.L.Cochell, A.R.Hughes, A.W.Manthey, C.J.Murphy, D.A.Tyler, D.L.Adamson, F.J.Starcevic, H.E.Wisecarver, J.A.Amundsen, J.D.Webb, J.J.Van De Casteele, J.Janzen, K.C.Hawker, K.E.Mc Mullen, K.L.Miller, L.M.Delfs, M.D.Woodyard, M.R.Martsching, N.B.Kiser, P.C.Simon, P.L.Minard, R.A.Smith, R.C.Remley, R.E.Morrow, R.E.Tharp, R.L.Gienau, R.L.Jaminet, R.M.Galey, S.C.Thompson, S.E.Hoffman, S.P.Crumes, T.E.Paxton, T.J.Harriettha, T.W.Mauger, V.H.Craft, W.F.Orr, W.W.Buchholz, J.Ferreira, M.Agoyer, B.Yueksek, G.Fieger, K.Ehresmann, J.A.Bishop, D.C.Strack, G.Collier, G.L.Rizner, H.B.Wildes II, J.C.Ledesma, S.L.Overstreet, C.James Jr., D.D.Dicken, J.L.Richardson, R.R.Blaylock Jr., S.J.Elliott, J.P.Dunn, L.D.Oltrogge, M.J.Becker, R.J.Ludwig, R.M.Paulsen, S.G.Smock, S.Wagner, B.Valero, J.L.Odneal, M.R.Weber, R.D.Stufflebeam, A.F.Ross, C.M.Perschmann, D.P.Roedl, D.Sandoval, F.M.Johnson, G.A.Harmsen, G.L.Chase, J.D.Davidson, J.E.Buchan, J.H.Cain, J.H.Huddleston Jr., K.J.Mc Kenna, K.W.Minor, L.L.Muller, M.C.Kellums, M.N.Johnson Jr., P.E.Doering, P.J.Laleman, P.W.Smith, R.C.Petersen, R.E.Taylor, R.J.Smith, R.L.Rodgers, R.M.Todey, S.E.Sallows, S.G.Smith, S.L.Nord, T.D.Mc Elderry, T.L.Sutliff, W.P.Berthoud Jr., R.A.Graper, B.Herpin, M.Blazevic, B.D.Currie, D.A.Hamblin, E.Conwell, H.L.Hamre, K.D.Park, K.J.Ludemann, M.R.Neessen, R.W.Davis, S.E.Moore, D.I.Hansen, K.R.Alexander, N.J.Miller, S.W.Gotthardt, D.M.Dravis, D.M.Schatzle, J.C.Stoffregen, J.D.Cordes, P.J.Kinsel, R.D.Simons, S.A.Sheldon, R.L.Ensign, D.P.Headley, G.Grub, H.Gross, H.Hirsch, K.Becker, R.Kunze, W.Swietlik, B.W.Rogers, C.Marshall, C.R.Gillet, C.S.Henisey, C.W.Jantzi, E.A.Doyle, E.Bradshaw II, E.D.Honzik, G.A.Anderkay, G.T.Finn, J.D.Cook, J.G.Steines, J.H.Vielhauer, J.J.Lee, J.L.Beckwith, K.C.Thompson, L.E.Stephens, N.L.Swenson, P.V.Welsh, R.C.Griffin, R.H.Leider, R.J.Thorpe, R.P.Rogers, S.Y.Hawkins, T.J.Fletcher, W.A.Kelsall, W.P.Sites, W.R.Hampton Jr., P.Deguelle, G.Beauvier, J.Buchheit, A.Z.Kovacs, R.F.Boc, V.Aleksovski, C.L.King, D.A.Jones, M.P.Tilton, R.M.Trotter, C.Baudeau, D.R.Morehouse, G.D.Leyen, J.E.Abben, F.J.Pena, D.E.Sykes, M.A.Martin, B.D.Long, B.G.Kingery, D.F.Jacob, D.R.Andersen, D.T.Findlay, E.Derksen, E.J.Thome, F.W.Mc Clellan Jr., J.M.Corley, M.E.Willier, R.C.Gipson, R.Cadwallader, R.D.Fischels, R.L.Herron, W.I.Marquette, W.M.Gallagher, A.Leizour, M.Simic, R.Zimmert, G.A.Tady, H.V.Gray, K.J.Harbaugh, M.A.Wilson, S.A.Thurman, W.J.Bryant, T.L.Morehead, C.A.Wichrowski, A.D.Matthews, D.P.Payne, D.Taylor, D.W.Gray, G.W.Niedermann, J.W.Bohnsack, M.G.Klein, P.K.Mott, P.P.Viren, R.H.Tesch, R.P.Gamino, T.M.Hancks, V.D.Hare, W.H.Sager Jr., D.J.Hill, D.L.Anderson, D.M.Krause, E.Duvall, G.L.Cook, H.M.Gellerstedt, J.K.Cook, J.W.Carroll, J.W.Evitts, M.A.Deutmeyer, M.C.Juergens, M.H.Holdstock, M.L.Littrel, M.R.Olmstead, N.J.Greco, P.D.Huizenga, R.D.Lane, S.J.Harper, S.M.Rohrer, T.M.Wright, D.Millet, R.E.Vesely, A.M.Thornton, D.K.Bergmeier, G.R.Ocampo, R.E.Mosley, R.L.Garthoff, B.L.Hansen, C.E.Stohr, D.E.Mc Gowan, G.A.Brandt, K.A.Lentz, W.R.Pepperling, J.A.Kaleas, R.L.Schuety, B.N.Pierce, C.Vanmanen, D.M.Cobb, D.W.Catour, G.P.Henson, J.E.Behrens, J.P.Moore, K.D.Overturf, L.D.Anderson, L.D.Hining, L.T.Flaherty, M.M.Rucinski, M.N.Robnett, M.R.Versluis, P.J.Hillary, R.L.Higgerson, R.L.Jones, R.T.Rinell, T.L.Dennison, W.H.Overturf, W.L.Hill, G.L.Johnson, J.D.Shewell, P.S.Morford, R.E.Johnson, V.J.Lorance, E.J.Bertheau, K.M.Brashears, M.D.Clark, W.A.Gleiter, A.L.Jensen, D.A.Buckley, J.A.Coonradt, R.C.Mitchell, B.E.Trunnell, B.L.Johnson, C.E.Hessler, D.E.Locke, D.H.Gebhart, D.J.Rigsby, D.Oneal, D.P.Quinn, D.W.Deibert, E.G.Renauld, E.W.Mockmore, F.R.Utz, G.L.Clayton, G.L.Defauw, G.L.Janey, G.S.Pliska, G.W.Rigsby, H.A.Buchholz Jr., H.A.Devrieze Jr., H.G.Petty Jr., H.M.Gregory, J.D.Schafer, J.H.Herrick, J.L.Anders, J.L.Vujnovich, J.R.Phillips, J.T.Nicholson, K.E.Tigges, K.J.Valadez, K.K.Kinnan Jr., K.M.Deibert, L.J.Heimann Jr., L.R.Meadows, L.Williams, M.Johnson, M.S.Johnson, N.R.Martinez, N.R.Matuszeski, P.J.Impens, R.A.Bednarek, R.A.Schulmeister, R.D.Bird, R.D.Kokemiller, R.E.Tweed, R.G.Fox, R.J.Middleton, R.L.Rogers, R.L.Stone, R.P.Tapia, R.W.Lyon, S.L.Melton, S.W.Whan, W.H.Riske, C.Legrand, G.D.Walquist, M.A.Johnson, E.Palmont, A.E.Edwards, A.Pollard, B.E.Ritzinger, C.C.Fisher, C.L.Dewitte, D.L.Woodworth, D.R.Kring, D.W.Benter, G.L.Brogan, J.J.Smith, J.M.Florang, P.A.Tatham, R.A.Napientek, R.E.Garbett, R.J.Schons, R.L.Michael, R.S.Dixon, S.J.Ratzman, S.K.Josephson, W.A.Senchina, A.Ibanez, S.Cabrita, S.Pereira, A.Plagge, P.Klaic, R.Zelmer, D.L.Hansen, J.T.Vanherzeele Jr., A.E.Hebron, A.J.Moore, B.A.Blazek, B.J.Martinez, B.K.Giese, B.L.Higgins, C.A.Bierman, C.E.Lynch, C.L.Mennenga, D.A.Goode, D.J.Feuling, D.L.Edwards, D.M.Kurtz, D.P.Flynn, D.W.Grulke, E.I.Bowsher, F.M.Lucero, G.H.Simpson, J.D.Krueger, J.D.Staton, J.E.Rumans, J.F.Pierschbacher, J.L.Rice, J.M.Miller, J.R.Vree, K.L.Reynolds, L.B.Howell, L.E.Handling, L.F.Mark, L.L.Fischer, M.D.Kopff, M.R.Bowen, P.J.Anderson, P.T.Neff, R.A.Melchert, R.C.Davis, R.C.Sorensen, R.D.Browning, R.Dougan, R.E.Clark, R.E.Selby, R.H.Hanefeld, R.L.Hamilton, R.M.Brown, R.V.Goldizen, R.V.Hartley, S.M.Steinbach, T.A.Goeller, T.F.Baker, V.M.Meador, W.D.Wiebel, W.F.Frank, D.Fakundiny, G.Kammerl, K.Gauter, P.Eschenbaum, R.Heitmann, U.Mueller, C.R.Foster, D.A.Gerst, J.M.Burvee, W.C.Beaird, W.Bernhard, B.Dalton, D.L.Schares, L.E.Smith, R.Ritenour, T.Bruce, T.W.Nunn, V.E.Bradley, D.F.McIntire, P.L.Everson, J.Marcault, B.A.Howard, D.G.Gray, D.L.Hild, F.V.Musselman, B.A.Stokes, B.L.Hunter, C.A.Costello, C.Corby, C.E.Morgan, C.E.Rauch, C.R.McLaughlin, D.D.Biesterfelt, D.L.Aswegan, D.L.Gallenbeck, F.Dougan, F.R.Koch, G.E.Gutzwiller, G.J.Ehrig, G.L.Derby, G.L.Ritz, H.E.Steen, J.A.Giese, J.A.Mengel, J.Baierl, J.E.Richey, J.E.Sharkey, J.F.Dark, L.E.Schreurs, L.J.Burkhart, L.J.Semeniuk, L.L.Nielsen, M.A.Hoskins, N.J.Jongebloed, P.A.Morgensen, P.C.Fajardo, P.D.Richter, P.E.Heffernan III, P.T.Michl, R.A.Bauler, R.C.Declerck, R.L.Callan, R.L.Cheney, R.M.Vanopdorp, R.P.Thomsen Jr., R.W.Henry, S.P.Yu, T.A.Tamminga, T.L.Piper, T.M.Westimayer, B.Mathon, A.Mamoudou, A.Jimenez R., J.L.Reig, J.P.Salzmann, J.R.Stotts, R.A.Garrison, R.L.Johnson, R.Rickenbacker Jr., T.E.Mitchell, T.H.Thorpe, T.J.Vandewoestyne, W.E.Mc Dermott, Y.Boschel, D.Gilgert, E.G.Lee Jr., L.C.Hettinger, W.D.Kono, A.A.D.Carvalho, J.Gnatek, J.H.Green, K.M.Muldoon, L.R.Slead, R.R.Sexton, M.E.Martinez, H.Richter, A.M.Siefker, D.R.Niemeyer, G.D.Jacobsen, H.W.Corey, M.B.Morrison, R.J.Menuey, O.Kussler, A.O.Fisher, B.F.Blazeiko, B.G.Grossman Sr., C.H.Schneckloth, D.J.Blood, D.W.Leebold Jr., E.Norlen, J.A.Clark, J.C.Pearsall, J.C.Schneider, J.D.Nolan, J.E.Coyle, J.G.Hansen III, J.L.Bartlett, J.M.Madeiros-Thill, K.L.Sansale, L.L.Spittel, L.M.Gustafson, L.M.Handy, M.E.Siemers, M.E.Weirich, P.C.Sebastian, P.G.Guthrie, R.D.Hoover Jr., R.D.Masias, R.F.Atkinson Jr., R.Hopper Jr., R.J.Petras, T.H.Cagle, W.B.Brown Jr., Z.W.Reid, F.Langlois, E.Matzner, J.Bierhalter, K.Hoffarth, N.Semmet, S.Grasswill, C.D.Smith, J.E.Richey, J.K.Cook, J.P.Ducey, J.W.Gustafson, J.W.Webb Jr., R.E.Anderson, R.J.Ward, W.M.Everett, E.Baumgarten, A.N.Turner, D.A.Cain, G.D.Finin, G.R.Matzdorf, G.Webbeking, H.M.Roberts, J.F.Miller, L.C.Fulton, L.L.Werner, M.J.Overton, P.J.Hamilton, P.L.Bergloff, S.Santalucia, C.H.Bentley, H.E.Mowatt, J.A.Gibbs, J.D.Powell Jr., J.Hoskins, M.D.Lerch, P.D.Green, P.R.Engel, R.T.Streblow, S.L.Heineman, T.C.Coussens, I.L.Wilhelms, J.T.Tinney, M.D.Peck, M.J.O Connor, R.L.Troyna, P.M.Dean, A.D.Ruble, A.J.Moore, A.R.Bailey, A.R.Walker, B.A.De Vrieze, B.W.Schaffter, C.A.Hoover, C.L.Gleason, C.R.Wolfram, D.A.James, D.D.Carstens, D.E.Rigg, D.L.Hill, D.L.Roth, D.L.Schlagel, D.R.Williams, E.C.Keeney, F.B.Vallejo, G.A.Miles, G.D.Swezy, G.S.Smith III, J.R.Vaughn, K.D.Bennett, K.E.Williams, L.H.Roling, M.L.Parker, N.J.Markham, R.B.Woods, R.D.Chappell, R.D.Gast, R.L.Tackkett, R.L.Wilt, R.M.Vaughn Jr., R.R.Jensen, R.T.Brown, S.J.Bealer, S.J.Vanwynsberghe, S.R.Schoepke, T.A.Lovig, T.A.McMullen, T.A.Moore, T.I.Ahearn, T.L.Roberts, V.A.Christensen, W.C.Wilson, W.E.Gharrett, W.F.Feehan Jr., W.S.Nance, V.Savas, D.M.Schevers, L.F.Smith, E.R.Earnest, J.R.Blaser, R.J.Alvarliz, V.J.Laermans, O.H.Alaminos, R.D.Anderson, D.F.D.Nascimento, J.J.Putnam, Y.Philippe, M.Raynaud, F.Clement, H.Heller, H.Lugenbiehl, E.Ross, P.Weber, R.A.Douglas, T.F.Brady, R.Castillo, D.Bari, E.Castillo, J.Chansard, D.Delaville, D.Dudragne, R.Hatton, B.Tahedl, E.Lopez, F.Grasswill, H.Nowotny, N.Sevinc, O.Waldbuesser, R.Wacker, R.Winkler, T.Weik, V.Kern, V.Pelosi, W.Kamuf, W.Zaeh, J.Brito, J.Castillo, M.Martin G., M.Vidal, J.Taylor, A.J.Hill Jr., B.J.Hoffert, C.E.Hanser, C.K.Pierce, D.E.Francis, D.E.Sexton, D.J.Cobert, D.J.Lutz, D.K.Perkins, D.R.Morgan, G.A.Anthony, G.D.Snyder, G.G.Kloberdanz, G.L.Duggan, G.L.Jacobson, H.A.Taylor, H.L.Hyde, J.A.Bustos Jr., J.Burton, J.D.Jabben, J.J.Gardner, J.J.Mueller, J.P.Hill, K.A.Cuvelier, K.A.Vandewoestyne, K.K.Frederick, K.M.Cordes, L.D.Garretson, L.M.Lindburg, M.L.Schellhorn, M.M.Alexander, M.W.Jones, N.P.Kerns, R.A.Braley, R.E.Ford, R.F.Reed, R.L.Fike, R.Ladeburg, S.J.Ryan, T.A.Nicholson, T.E.Pepin, T.J.Cameron, T.J.Schmitt, T.K.Harper, W.D.Hartman, W.F.Toliver, W.G.Favel, W.J.Becker, W.O.Dean, B.Llaty, D.Kraft, C.H.Kresser, D.C.Annis, D.J.Pollert, D.L.Schmidt, G.J.Slick, J.L.Climenhage, M.F.Loynes, M.J.Gordon, N.Robinson, R.D.Smith, S.W.Kelly, A.L.Valentine, D.A.Holloway, D.D.Nestor, E.Gaskins, G.E.Weber, L.D.James, P.E.Versluis, P.M.Sellers, R.G.Koopmans, D.C.Weber, E.C.Johnson, L.J.Buzynski, S.H.Avera, E.Petitperrin, J.E.Bollans, M.J.Lehmann, N.E.Mangin, R.J.Siebrands, H.Cronauer, A.E.Baker, A.J.Schrader, C.E.Roate, C.L.Kelly, C.M.Stotmeister, D.A.Fortin, D.C.Schmit, D.E.Krueger, D.H.Frederick, D.L.Kelly, D.L.Sell, D.M.Sanders, G.L.Andres, H.A.Key, I.Harrington, J.C.Miller, J.D.Briggs, J.W.Reeves, M.Deleu, M.S.Dold, M.S.Middleton, M.V.Cheek, R.E.Verbout, R.J.Hippler, R.L.Hoth, S.W.Van Gundy, T.L.Scranton, A.Werner, G.Valentino, J.Walck, J.Yelamos, M.Barragan, D.M.Kopplin, J.B.Hudnall, J.H.Budworth, J.H.Ostrander, J.J.Sebetka, J.W.Gander, L.A.Westcott, L.E.Fowler, O.H.Garrett, O.J.Miller, O.L.Scott, R.Fencl, A.Legrand, B.M.Stiles, B.W.Felhouser, D.D.Bohlen, D.G.Huffman, F.F.Korndorf, G.A.Millermon, G.F.O Brien, J.C.Koch, J.L.Halupnick, L.L.Scullark, R.E.Mc Clure, S.McGarry, D.E.Edwards, D.E.Halverson, D.W.Smith, I.A.Niedert, J.R.Tinkey, K.M.Tanner, M.A.Lemon, M.E.Campbell, M.E.Schaefer, M.L.Hoffman, R.J.Fowler, R.L.Eich, S.C.Linder, D.A.Shepard, D.F.Yungtum, G.L.Boogren, H.D.Zanders, H.H.Frisch, R.Nie, S.J.Miller, T.M.Heffernen, W.H.Schwegman, R.D.Midthun, D.A.Raes, D.A.Robbins, D.J.Appelhans, D.M.Champion, D.Minck, D.R.Reed, D.W.Bernd, D.W.Dutton, E.D.Fuller, E.P.Herbst, E.Washington, F.D.Forrester, G.L.Dunn, G.R.Nosbisch, J.A.Lauer, J.A.Little, J.F.Bierl, J.L.Adams, J.L.Shook, J.P.Lob, J.R.Knipp, L.E.Ditto, L.E.Wiggins, L.G.Blocker, L.M.Doubek, M.E.Buchanan, M.J.Brustkern, M.R.Hurst, M.R.Platt, M.W.Allen, P.A.Weidman, R.J.Isert, S.A.Binns, S.L.Wordehoff, W.C.Attwood, W.R.Wurfel, W.Z.Ladwig, G.Thion, J.Borotte, J.Martinez, B.Lajci, M.Islak, V.Ekici, A.Ruiz, E.Garcia V., W.Ruiz, C.J.Eggleston, D.K.Nielsen, H.Roberson, J.P.Holland, R.A.Brown, A.A.Angela, D.A.Hugill, D.B.Bamford, F.Dixon, G.J.Earl, J.E.Brady, J.J.Delagardelle, L.R.Heacock, M.A.Atnip, M.D.Seedorff, C.Carey, C.R.Holmes, E.M.Gordon, G.H.Harkin, J.D.Nenow, K.E.Smith, O.Walker, P.K.Sommer, R.E.Franks, R.G.Buhr, T.R.Peverill, E.C.Dinneen, G.R.Estill, H.B.Isabell, J.M.Philp, M.R.Grady, R.G.Kouns, R.J.Anderson, C.Holmes, J.A.Keating, J.D.Wells, M.J.Rokes, M.J.Schmauss, B.A.Harris, B.G.Pearce, B.J.Deporter, C.L.Hestand, C.W.Wyborney, D.A.Romano, D.J.Cusmano, D.M.Bender, D.M.Graeber, D.M.Kerns, D.W.Mc Cracken, E.J.Czech Jr., G.E.Colburn, J.E.Sullivan Jr., J.F.Etling, J.J.Puhl, J.M.McKenna, J.Rivera, J.V.Fisher, L.D.Little, L.J.Leisinger, L.L.Mulligan, M.B.Lawrence, M.C.Vondracek, M.J.Lesage, M.W.O Day, N.E.Merchant, O.L.Hughart, P.A.Volcko, R.E.Smith, R.F.Rowray, R.H.Longueville, R.J.Dejaegher, R.J.Weber, R.K.Olson, R.L.Cones, R.S.Baumgartner, S.B.Bunger, S.R.Clymer, T.G.Howell, T.L.Erion, T.R.Miller, V.C.Ball Jr., I.H.Sparks, A.Reyna, A.Jessel, A.Piechaczyk, N.Lefrancois, S.Bigot, B.Gandyra, A.Calvo, C.Curto, J.M.Gutierrez G., D.A.Meyer, E.W.Mc Lean, F.G.Pine, J.W.Siemens, L.A.Gielau, M.J.Delagardelle, M.T.Barnett, M.Zobel Jr., R.R.Smith, R.W.Ebaugh, W.E.Shavers Jr., W.L.Allen, J.Genest, A.A.Barkhausen, A.J.Close, J.E.Miller, L.M.Hunter, M.G.Riley, R.A.Bergman, S.D.Lampman, S.J.Auringer, S.K.Butters, S.M.Fish, S.P.Ferguson, T.C.Lusthoff, W.A.Bowman, C.C.Hoover, C.L.Schadt, D.A.Stevens, G.C.Ward, R.Gomez, W.J.Gehrke, W.P.Serandos, E.Horbach, A.Chaires, D.Garcia, C.M.Cerra Jr., C.Mortensen, C.R.Johnson, D.E.Dahlstrom, D.L.Peterson, D.R.Dussliere, D.W.Hanson, E.B.Sandberg, H.F.Vroman Jr., J.G.De Silva, K.A.Nelson, L.J.Duquette, R.E.Cameron, R.H.Ankum, S.A.Carlson, T.C.Bechtelheimer, I.Ullmann, L.Chatillon, F.Laudenklos, F.Weber, H.Engelhardt, I.Hussong, R.Ruf, A.Tena, E.De Felipe, F.Hernandez C., J.Garcia Sanchez, J.Perez M., M.Martinez F., A.Wareing, D.M.Sears, M.D.Prater, P.J.Thompson, F.Carril, I.Perez G., L.B.Auten, R.E.Farrey, J.Marin, F.E.Wright, G.S.Marra, K.E.Lubbert, P.A.Pint, P.C.May, W.Schrepfer, B.Palomo, F.Escudero, D.G.Higdon, D.L.Ferris, D.L.Mc Coneghey, G.O.Counsell, R.Jones Jr., R.L.Forsyth, T.J.Young, T.M.Johnson Sr., A.Garcia R., D.C.Youngblut, R.D.Burton, A.R.Honn, B.F.Isley, C.E.Provin, D.A.Abbott, D.A.Ramaker, D.A.Taylor, D.J.Kauffman, D.L.Adams, D.L.Gabel, D.W.Bute, D.W.Holder, J.F.Volbruck, J.J.Hoch, J.L.Allen, J.L.Philemon, J.M.Lorenzen, J.M.Seibert, K.M.Mallon, L.J.Dvorak, L.R.Flickinger, M.A.Wilson, M.G.Quaintance, M.S.Mann, R.A.Olson, R.J.Brown, R.J.Raney, R.N.Gage, S.C.Hilton, S.C.Miller, S.J.Christiansen, T.E.Copeland, T.G.Schmitz, W.Antone, L.Bonnafoux, F.Bruno, J.Paetz, J.Hurtado G., J.M.Morillo, D.A.Wessels, D.D.Hyde, G.G.Johnson, G.S.Mayo, J.L.Schmidt, J.L.Slach, L.F.Letchford, R.A.Bulver, R.L.Hawotte, R.L.Voshell, T.J.Bengston, T.S.Post, V.A.Klacko, Z.A.McCallum, D.A.Bergmann, D.J.Fluhr, D.K.Koshatka, E.D.Lee, G.E.Becker, J.C.Hosch, J.E.Thome, J.F.Matt, K.L.Sovey, R.F.Jones, R.L.Williamson, W.C.Mc Grane, M.Grisouard, G.Heurteau, D.Spasic, M.Pesic, D.A.Wille, D.E.Meyer, D.W.Bailey, J.B.Weers Jr., S.R.Youngblut, T.Jared, L.Cruz, J.Berry, L.J.Klein, R.Crapser, R.E.Trumbauer, M.L.Bennett, C.G.Beattie, C.P.Brooks, D.J.Gonner, D.L.Rabe, D.V.Oleskiw, E.Austin, E.L.Adams, F.P.Masotti, G.P.Gibson, G.W.Runyon, J.A.Brewer, J.K.Tighe, J.L.Anderson, J.L.Murphy, J.L.Thompson, J.M.Root, L.W.Schmitt, M.A.Bahl, M.L.Morrison, M.P.Kizlyk, R.D.Blad, R.W.Skinner, W.J.Koubele, S.Adan, I.Hengy, L.Strykala, R.Blanchard, H.Wiegand, M.Ocaña, H.D.Aukes, J.I.Gunnerson, J.T.Van Ausdall, P.R.Downing, R.Arndt, R.D.Truex, R.L.Wilson, R.Stigler Jr., T.H.Egts, K.Wingert, L.G.Farley, N.R.Potter, S.C.Kapler, W.R.Dedic, F.Breña, A.Y.Burke, D.C.Latusick, G.D.Zander, H.A.Colbert, J.W.Huseman, J.W.Zenz, K.R.Everding, M.L.Schilling, P.A.Nagel, A.Justo, A.Perez, B.Vazquez-Lastra, E.Garcia, R.Fernandez, D.E.Hundley, D.M.Hemesath, L.W.Sommerfelt, R.Morais, V.Rodriguez, A.E.Dewitte, B.K.Gottselig, D.A.Banfield, E.C.Garrett, F.R.Bixby III, G.E.Kinney, G.R.Bowerman, J.E.Layton, J.G.Dragoun, J.J.Gillman, J.J.Sullivan, K.F.Keller, K.J.Conner, L.W.Ellis, M.S.Haugen, R.E.Keller, R.G.Behrens, R.J.Euchner, R.L.Heckenlively, R.L.Hughell, S.T.Tady, W.Sowell, M.J.Aragon, B.Benko, D.Roger, J.A.Cano, M.Montero, M.Vega, D.E.Wellman, F.L.Carlson, H.M.Ulfers Jr., J.S.Short, M.D.Mauderer, R.D.Ackerman, T.S.Geesaman, W.J.Berhends, M.Milic, D.J.Leeper, M.J.Martin, P.G.Luloff, H.L.Walton, P.W.Winberg, J.Gonzalez C., N.Fenandez, M.E.Dailey, A.Burrell, A.D.Todd, B.W.Larsen, C.A.Schumacher, D.A.Felton, D.W.Vickers, G.L.Severs, H.E.Foster, J.E.Arfstrom, J.R.Litch, L.M.Davis, L.R.Durr, M.H.Olvera, M.L.Gillen, M.L.Richmond, P.A.Panicucci, R.G.Gill, R.J.Spensley, T.A.Hannam, M.Rouballay, P.Zawierucha, R.Balva, A.Mahillo, A.Romero V., F.Martin M., F.Rubio P., I.Diaz, B.A.Mauney, F.C.Bunker, L.O.Ruth, E.M.Woods, A.R.Johnson, F.P.Dirks, J.C.Kave, J.D.Easter, J.F.Smith, J.S.Burich, M.W.Aldrich, P.K.Frederiksen, R.G.Lampard, S.B.Schauenberg, S.R.Coohey, J.Chevallier, A.Courtin, W.Nowak, J.T.Gredvig, H.Hamel, Q.E.Wallace, C.J.Durian, C.L.Anderson, D.C.Watkins, D.D.Stookesberry, D.F.Rice Jr., D.J.Williams, G.J.King, I.L.Griswold, J.H.Hartley, J.R.Good, J.R.Gunhus, L.B.Hayden, M.R.Cox, M.R.Johnson, M.W.Vandenbrook, N.J.Vande Voorde, R.J.Hauber, R.L.Owens, R.V.Millard, R.W.Amos, S.L.Haynes, T.Karlix, W.C.Davis Jr., Y.J.Sanders, A.Caille, C.Fournier, R.Welle, S.Maier, A.Buzon, J.Chorro, M.Jimenez P., C.M.Neuman, J.M.Medina, R.T.Starling, B.A.Datisman, G.J.Bowman, G.L.White, K.W.Engels, M.P.Campbell, P.J.King, P.J.Wilks, R.L.Clure, C.Vitabile, M.C.Valtierra, B.J.Harder, C.A.Staley, D.A.Toepfer, D.C.Lindsey, D.M.Baker, D.M.Wilson, D.T.Durian, G.R.Lahmann, J.L.Rusch, R.D.Johnson, A.Garcia H., P.Flores, G.Wolf, A.E.Hendred, A.F.Meier, A.P.Harbour, D.E.Waite, D.M.Mottet, D.M.Thomas, D.T.Drury, G.G.Bonner, G.R.Sutliff, H.Vesey, J.E.Ward, J.J.Mervin, J.L.Smith, J.M.Jacquin, J.V.Shelton Jr., L.R.Barnes, M.A.Regan, M.L.Johnston, R.D.Halverson, R.L.Cournia, S.D.Graham, S.L.Thomas, V.J.Sparacello,

Factory employees, Getafe, Spain, 1978

W.R.Garmon, J.M.Rodriguez, D.Sotteau, W.Vetterling, J.Hurtado C., J.D.Wadel, P.A.Thatcher, P.Van Dalen, A.F.Engels, C.K.Kitto, D.E.Flaherty, D.H.Ripple, E.K.Kupferschmidt, G.Gogishvili, L.D.Grimm, R.A.Rotzinger, R.A.Stanley, R.E.Chapman, S.E.Lemaster, T.H.Cord, B.S.Hoppes, C.A.Shook, C.D.Cain, D.L.Mussmann, H.Harris, J.A.Medina, M.M.Elliott, R.A.Lagaisse, R.D.Buhrow, R.J.Stout, R.L.Appleton, D.Prunier, J.A.Johnston, J.A.Mackin, L.M.Mooney, M.P.Vosberg, C.C.Knedler, C.L.Bierman, D.L.Bennett, E.R.Stromquist, G.A.Weber, J.D.Garcia, J.E.Winger, J.L.Tigges, J.P.Hamer, J.T.Foster, K.Jessome, R.D.Wilson, R.J.Hahn, R.J.Westhoff, R.T.Jinks, S.J.Holmes, S.J.Michels, S.J.Wallarab, W.E.Watts, G.Ramirez, M.Rose, B.Wedel, C.Gomes, G.Honnert, M.Hofer, A.Hernandez M., E.Jimenez, J.A.Pariente, J.M.Lopez S., P.Vicente, S.Gallardo, A.Demirci, D.Lukic, D.G.Domm, D.D.Obadal, A.D.Polzin, B.A.Siegler, D.C.Juon, D.J.Damge, D.L.Stueben, E.C.Pittenger Jr., G.B.Vandewoestyne, J.E.Juergens, J.J.Barten, J.L.Aldinger, J.L.Priske, J.T.Carpenter, J.V.Flattery, K.M.Freber, K.R.Pysson, L.L.Zuidema, M.M.Partin, M.D.Karns, M.J.Fluegel, M.K.Harkness, M.R.Hancock, N.R.Ruggles, P.A.Dudley, P.J.Hillary, P.M.Herbert, R.J.Debaillie Jr., R.J.Dotson, R.S.Walker, R.W.Miller, S.A.Lowe, S.Contreras, S.E.Chapman, S.L.Kays, S.W.Sumstine, T.J.Koenig, T.J.Willaert, T.R.Elliott, V.R.Jamieson, W.P.Ashby, A.Najera, J.Fillion, F.Vaquero, G.H.Northup, J.M.Jernigan, J.R.Pierson, L.M.Williams-Mcquieter, M.L.Anderson, P.A.Houseman, R.E.Black, R.R.Johnson, M.Uz, B.J.Hanna, L.J.Thill, M.Miskovic, D.D.Stewart, F.D.Potter, H.Wilson, J.D.Adams, R.D.Reichenbacker, T.L.Sullivan, K.Ehrenpreis, C.W.Tarr, N.A.Deen, S.A.Westergaard, D.Grand, J.Aviles, G.Lambacher, H.Leschinski, D.Lobeto, J.L.Cabezas, M.D.Sanchez C., M.J.Llorente, N.Montalvo, S.A.Allmendinger, A.F.Enes, B.J.Garr, B.L.McAninch, C.M.Cook, C.M.Plog, D.E.Beary, D.H.Kuehn, D.S.Frei, F.R.Wolf, G.D.Kopps, J.J.Campanella, L.R.Downey, P.E.Williams, P.G.Starr, P.L.Coogan, R.K.Kester, R.M.Mc Allister, R.R.Beaulieu, S.A.Thomas, S.K.Crouse, T.S.Yeatts, T.W.Smith, W.E.Sorrill, W.L.Steele, A.Cruz , M.Ruiz , R.Castillo, G.Coin, G.Picardi, J.Lecei, A.C.Moore Sr., B.A.Martin, B.S.Flack, C.Jones, D.Folkerts, G.K.Brown, H.G.Verheecke, J.A.Britton, J.D.Junker, M.A.Bogart, R.D.Spencer, R.L.Minch, T.R.Hughes, V.R.Carlson, W.L.Beardsworth, P.Rippert, J.Nuñez L., L.Simon, A.I.Molina, C.L.Hocker, C.M.Kimberley, C.R.Harp, D.F.Parker, D.G.Jolly, D.J.Blank, D.J.Kelly, D.J.Schwab, D.M.Harris, D.M.Williams, E.D.Wycoff, E.H.Golden, E.J.Mattecheck Jr., E.M.Kenney, F.C.Goodwin, G.R.Doud, H.R.Dettmann II, J.A.Horn, J.B.Highland, J.B.Hunter, J.E.Richardson, J.L.Greiner, J.P.Greenwell, L.E.Armstrong, L.M.Harrington, L.R.Ayala, M.A.Kern, M.S.Hamilton, N.G.Yeager, R.D.Pankey Jr., R.E.Elsbury, R.L.Jamieson, S.A.Birditt, S.K.Arrington, T.J.Wisecup, T.L.Shaw, T.L.Tipsword, W.N.Keck, W.R.Webb, R.Cornillier, A.Martin R., A.Serrano T., B.A.Woods, C.A.Jochim, C.L.Logue, C.M.Tatum, D.R.Walker, G.D.Snodgrass, G.L.West, J.D.Weimer, J.J.Sackfield, J.P.Vandevoorde, L.E.Stacy, M.A.Williams, R.J.Skelton, S.J.Heston, V.Turturici, R.A.Moody, R.J.Steger, J.P.Dillon, A.F.Balsdon, T.P.Miesner, F.Martinez, A.Gomes, J.Gaudin, E.Begus, H.Mueller, J.E.Martinez M., M.Darde, F.Garibaldi, **1974** C.P.Lawson, A.Wingert, E.Seiler, F.Haring, H.Tiedtke, M.Weingaertner, R.Kloet-Van-Der, U.Preiss, W.Zierath, A.H.Bliss, A.J.Hansen, B.C.Bowes, C.E.Blum, C.L.Vogt, D.D.Hudson, D.D.Schmerse, D.L.Boyers, D.M.Pauly, D.W.Drew, D.W.Meier, E.M.Carroll, G.J.Hess, J.A.Stokes III, J.D.White, J.E.Braeckevelt, J.S.Westbrook, K.D.Reilly, K.J.Waul, K.M.Brownlee, L.A.Meidam, L.D.Kelling, L.E.Stoddard, M.C.Hlavaty, M.G.Bigelow, M.J.Spurgetis, M.L.Larsen, R.A.Winter, R.Bannister, R.D.Parrish, R.J.Ronbeck, R.J.Stewart, R.L.Conley, R.P.Jay, R.Puebla, T.G.Cullen, T.L.Sheffer, S.Navarro, M.Clement, L.Le Ny, D.Dague, E.Cafaltzis, V.Riccardi, P.L.Pretorius, J.Gomez C., T.Rodelgo, B.B.Peck, B.K.Schlickman, D.F.Smith, D.L.Fogle, G.A.Swanson, G.W.Cundiff, J.S.Glosser, L.L.Johnson, M.A.Bartlett, M.L.Mayfield, M.P.Stokes, R.J.Archibald, S.T.Anderson, W.E.Clancy, E.Grasswill, F.M.Asplund, G.E.Greer, J.M.Esparza, J.M.Mac Kenzie, M.J.Johnson, S.D.Gibbs, A.J.Esparza, M.L.Coen, W.L.Gernant, A.W.Nordstrom, C.L.Olson, G.A.Weaver, G.D.Pierce, G.R.Novak, H.W.Piffer III, J.A.Battani, J.A.Brown, J.R.Buettell, J.R.Langston, L.A.Peterson, M.A.Hafner, M.A.Higley, M.B.McLaughlin, M.M.Carmody, M.W.Malmstrom, R.E.Andrus, R.E.Benjamin, R.E.Boelling, R.F.Burk, R.G.Spihlmann, R.J.Kunkel, R.L.Taylor, R.W.Abel, S.E.Cope, S.R.Powell, T.R.Fletcher, W.E.Sellers, W.L.Matheson, J.Rameau, M.Sonnet, J.Sefrin, R.Zimmer, S.Moreno J., D.J.Nunn, J.J.Johnson, M.Oliva, M.R.Schnoebelen, R.G.Norris, W.A.Peterson, F.Baroso, A.Direk, H.Kern, P.Zankl, W.Martin, D.F.Thomas, J.R.Defauw, L.E.Rasso, N.R.Maxey, T.G.Fecht, Z.Popovic, G.Coedo, C.Santoyo, R.S.Rumler, B.J.Vanklaveren, B.W.Correll, C.E.Burkett, C.E.Clark, C.J.Blackwood, D.C.Dolan, D.E.Wheeler, D.M.Griffin, D.P.Marvitz, E.L.Morgan, E.R.Akin, G.J.Burkett, G.L.Greenwood, G.R.Fichtinger, G.W.Zielke, J.A.Petrick, J.D.Coyle, J.E.Goodbar, J.J.Bowdry, J.W.Nevins, K.A.Qualls, M.A.McMillin, M.E.Crummy, M.E.Stumpf, M.R.Burns, M.R.Ghormley, N.I.McDowell, R.A.Grosse, R.C.Koontz, R.L.Mayfield, R.L.Shaw, R.P.Hefel, S.A.Wilmot, S.R.Satterthwaite, T.J.Miller, T.W.Hanks, V.L.Bein, W.E.Boysen, W.E.Counts, W.V.Frost, D.Pichard, A.Alcaniz, J.Seegmueller, K.Bentz, F.P.Schroeder, J.M.Johnson, R.J.Budden, M.Ortiz, D.Posloncec, F.Mancini, M.Botz, E.Nuñez M., B.J.Fisher, C.H.Gordon, D.L.Schupp, G.E.Ripple, J.A.Vogelgesang, J.R.King, J.W.Sickels, K.D.Bailey, M.K.Chancellor, M.L.Gallagher, M.W.Laplaunte, C.La Mattina, B.E.Halverson, J.L.Dowsett, C.Crestani, A.A.Sieverding, A.C.Van Pelt, C.K.Tedrow, D.E.McCormick, D.F.Bach, D.G.Schneck, D.J.Fontana, D.R.Briden, D.W.Hines, D.Woods, F.L.Holland, G.L.Crawford, G.T.McClure, J.C.Dayboll, J.G.Fiser, J.H.Cox, J.J.Ringgenberg, J.M.Mumma, J.S.Bustad, J.T.Lewis, K.A.Grutz, K.L.McDonald, L.F.Westmark, M.K.Luick, M.K.Wall, M.T.Flaherty, O.A.Haley Jr., P.Earney, R.C.Weed, R.D.Wheelen, R.E.Deener, R.I.Fine, R.J.Silversmet, S.J.Brannan, S.L.Hoskins, S.M.Carreon, S.N.Bowman, S.R.Burke, S.R.Davis, W.A.Macdougall, W.C.Oviatt, C.Castronovo, D.Owens, G.L.Bowdry, L.T.Rose, E.P.Thomas, K.L.Kaiser, S.D.M.Damas, G.Hengy, D.L.Weaver, M.A.Block, T.A.Hauer, D.Bandinelli, E.G.Brooks, J.C.Harper, J.J.Winters, L.J.Kurtenbach, O.G.Bilbruck, E.L.Parker, J.C.Arkland, A.Marlowe, C.G.Willard, D.A.Brace, D.L.Chapman, G.E.Hartwig, G.R.Lopp Jr., J.G.Puentes, J.K.Franklin, J.Pena, K.C.Harris, K.C.Robins, M.D.Hall, M.Tisdale, P.E.Baker, R.A.Parrish, R.D.Barbour, R.J.Huseman, R.Pierce, V.Macisaac, W.D.Labatt, C.Mallet, M.Kestek, R.Carstens, R.Yaltuk, U.Rieker, N.Garcia L., S.P.Cremer, S.P.Egermeier, W.M.Mc Clure, K.L.Rowland, L.M.Droz, B.Milicevic, C.R.Halleck, C.R.Moody, D.P.Toles, D.W.Hulme, J.S.Egts, L.H.Fugate, R.J.Rigdon, R.W.Cummins, T.Green, M.Simicevic, C.S.Hallmark, D.J.Hunt, D.R.Lolley, J.A.Bowes, K.L.Steger, L.J.Call, N.L.Filbert, P.Bargman, R.C.Darby, R.R.Ackerson, S.A.Dolan, S.C.Quist, T.J.Bulat, G.Herpin, A.Limani, D.Barkowski, E.Wirth, G.Graeff, J.M.Costa, L.A.Yuknis, B.A.Haybarger, B.H.Sparks, C.A.Moreno, C.E.Steve, C.L.Meyeraan, D.A.Morgan, D.A.Schmidt, D.J.Brown, D.K.Huffaker, D.Mayfield, D.R.Ditto, D.R.Klein, D.V.Koenig, E.R.Sarginson, F.K.Irvin, G.E.Westbrook, G.L.Versluys Sr., G.L.Willoughby, J.E.Ashcraft, J.E.Drake Jr., J.E.Saul, J.E.Schwartz, J.H.Hulse, J.H.Stanley, J.J.Sampson, J.L.Dial, J.M.Utter, J.R.Smalley, K.A.Voshell, K.E.Hill, K.S.Carlson, L.D.Boisvert, L.D.Dudgeon, L.L.Newton, M.C.Amborn, M.H.Demay, M.L.Pearson, R.A.Haslam, R.A.Hodson, R.D.Gerken Jr., R.D.Parsons, R.H.Freymann, R.L.Pigg, R.L.Tracinski, R.P.Landau, R.T.Salyers, R.W.Johnstone, S.G.Stewart, T.L.Johnson, V.E.Waggoner, W.Dauth, B.E.Cantu, G.Ringenbach, A.Rossignol, M.Simonot, P.Guyon, A.Proenca, M.Gasc, A.Winkler, B.Schnitzler, G.Zeller, H.Gleissner, H.Neuhaeuser, M.Goeksal, N.Kuerzeder, P.Pelczer, W.Kreiner, J.Perez G., J.E.Schneck, M.J.Baxter, T.D.Topping, G.Chanteloup, U.Decker, D.I.Copeland, R.E.Gustafson, M.Kessab, G.Perceval, R.Gudin, D.D.Van Loon, F.Huot, J.R.Hinke, P.Bidoire, A.A.Burns, A.D.Mc Alpin, B.J.Tangedal, B.Montgomery, C.G.Bark, C.J.Jacobsen, D.J.Alexander, D.J.Minas, D.J.Prondzinski, D.L.Mital, D.M.Halverson Sr., D.Sivertsen, G.F.Eastman, G.J.Schubert, G.M.Torgler, H.C.Hart, J.M.Burbach, J.W.Larson, K.W.Braun, K.W.Leugner, L.Jeselnik, L.Johnson, M.J.Snoddy, R.D.Sproston, R.F.Morrison, R.G.Kimpton, R.L.Schmit II, T.R.Johnson, T.V.Mc Graw, V.J.Kupka, C.Brugiere, A.Accascio, A.Bozic, A.Schlatter, J.Martin, N.Matios, J.A.Graham, T.J.Dirth, J.L.Valquiarena, J.Fernandez, D.Schliessmeyer, L.L.Ledford, P.K.Reynolds, R.L.Holmes, V.E.Curry, R.J.Kuhl, B.A.Schoellermann, A.A.Souto, B.Seitz, C.A.Kerr, V.Markwardt, D.J.Wassenhove, J.E.Debaene, K.J.Leahy, R.A.Thomas, A.E.Clark, A.E.Doggett, A.E.Rupe, A.Pauwels, A.W.Conley, C.E.Hoff, C.E.Johnson, C.J.Petersen, C.P.Lyman, D.C.Goodin, D.C.McCuddin, D.E.Colwell, D.E.McChesney, D.F.Fiser, D.L.Luke, D.M.Mc Inerney, D.R.Ross, E.D.Richards, E.M.Stenzel, F.E.Brown, F.Martinez, G.L.Cook, J.A.Droessler, J.A.Heitkotter, J.D.Harding, J.H.Hayes, J.J.Callan, J.J.Hames, J.L.Jensen, J.L.Orcutt, J.L.Stephens, J.P.Hopkins, K.D.Hayes, K.I.Wuorinen, L.D.Knock, L.M.Duncheon, L.P.Miller, M.L.Johnson, M.L.Norpel, N.E.Durns, P.J.Valentine, R.A.Capps, R.A.Williamson, R.D.May, R.E.Rohren, R.E.Showers, R.J.Smith, R.K.Young, R.L.Clausen, R.L.Shively, R.S.Keddy, T.F.Thomas, T.L.Ackerson, T.L.Newberry, T.R.Hellmann, T.W.Olsen, V.E.Blew, V.M.Gibbs, G.Constant, G.Sanchez, E.Koellner, E.May, H.Bastian, N.Muenstermann, S.Gottselig, F.Gonzalez R., J.F.Valle, J.Montaña, C.L.Nielsen, E.W.Cullinan, J.A.Andrews, J.J.Lehman, L.C.Cunningham, L.J.Amos, R.C.Riley, F.Schaefer,

Ottumwa, Iowa, employees, 1979

J.Schall, A.Gallego, F.Gomez C., I.Sanchez C., F.N.Schindler, L.J.Baker, M.A.Classen, R.D.Sebelien, T.R.Mullery, W.H.Abel, L.I.Stroher, A.Esteban M., D.N.Dirksen, L.J.Brown, T.J.Deeny, R.O.Schirm, A.G.Johnson, B.J.Sukach, B.K.Petersen, B.M.Coop, B.P.Keller, C.G.Lampson, C.K.Porter, C.L.Dundas, C.L.Scherer, D.M.Rogers, D.S.Kemmerer, E.C.Brown, G.K.Thiessen, G.M.Pint, J.A.Wilson Sr., J.J.Hark, J.L.Shue, J.R.Nelson, J.S.Childers, K.D.Eckhoff, K.P.Martin, L.A.Dean, L.E.Thompson, L.L.Woodard, M.A.Buss, M.A.Czerwinski, M.J.Bowman, M.L.Leaven, R.Carter, R.E.Boleyn, R.E.Rodda, R.L.Duvall, R.L.Huitt, R.L.Karns, R.W.Colyn, S.C.Breckenridge, T.E.Griffin, M.Medina, J.Auchere, F.Consagra, F.Koerner, F.Ridente, H.Guener, N.Babic, P.Piperni, J.Soria, C.E.Grubb, G.P.Lysenko, S.M.Berggren, D.H.Mc Nelley, G.Pittman, R.B.Galey, R.K.Burkman, R.S.Latham, S.A.Paris, C.Mueller, V.Li-Prizzi, K.W.Cantrell, B.Henderson, B.J.Budde, J.W.Townsend, S.A.Lipps, R.Desnoues, D.Coulibaly, F.Leite, J.Baccon, J.Hurst, K.Bruns, K.Kurz, K.Nau, P.Gassmann, R.Krumrey, C.J.Miller, R.L.Day, T.L.Swain, B.J.Helms, B.Miller, B.W.Pierson, C.L.Crane, C.M.Mc Nally, D.A.Johannesen, D.A.Swink, D.J.Cowley, D.L.Simmons, D.W.Porter, E.D.Mc Dade, E.E.Holland, E.S.Meyer, G.L.Vance, G.Niebergall, J.Callas Jr., J.R.Delaney, J.R.Townsend, J.W.Fowler, K.L.Carlson, L.A.Krienert, L.C.Webb, L.K.Heady, L.M.Rogers, M.A.Madole, M.D.Bleymeyer, M.D.Jensen, M.J.Venker, M.K.Kingery, M.L.Baughman, M.L.Hodges, M.M.Lindberg, M.P.Orr, O.J.Becker, R.A.Ford, R.G.Rice, R.H.Mehus, R.W.Naramore, T.E.Quinn, T.G.Taylor, T.I.Spratt, J.Vivier, E.Knapp, E.Krieg, H.Burkart, W.Bader, W.Stahl, A.Diaz V., J.Sanz, A.N.Stroup, D.D.Oflahrity, D.E.Stewart, F.W.Brandt Jr., L.E.Cain, M.J.Hootman, D.Ziemer, K.Ugurlu, B.J.Walline, D.E.Roe, D.J.Intveld, D.R.Martin, L.M.Wiebel, R.E.Richardson, T.L.Ernst, S.Yilmaz, D.E.Roberts, G.B.Schramm, P.C.Anderson, W.F.Randolph, E.Vazquez, P.Hautefeuille, K.Batton, C.David, N.J.Anderson, T.G.Shaffer, A.L.Vivians, B.N.Moore, C.D.Reed, C.H.Kastli, C.M.Gleason, C.V.Halverson, D.A.Breitbach, D.Barnhouse, D.C.Bruns, D.J.Aird, D.J.Backens, D.J.Kessens, D.K.Fox, D.L.Taylor, D.W.Devinney, D.W.Harkins, E.Aguilar, E.C.Hayes, E.L.Barnhouse, E.L.Duffee, E.T.Bean Sr., G.E.Mc Lean, G.L.Heisdorffer, G.L.Mills, J.C.Clough, J.E.Sanford, J.E.Schares, J.F.Anderson, J.R.Sullivan, L.D.Gasaway, L.E.Dempsey, L.J.Stephens, M.C.Hofstetter, M.C.Sullivan, M.K.Dolph, N.E.Johnson, P.L.Welter, P.S.Moore, R.A.Schuchart, R.E.Anderson, R.E.Sowers, R.J.Jahns, S.C.Shipley, S.J.Mittelstadt, S.J.Staskal, T.L.Gehl, T.L.Payne, W.E.Malcolm, M.I.Schuh, A.Francisco, D.Renard, M.Ruiz, P.Lapertot, G.Knapp, N.Nuhic, A.Martinez C., E.Escobar, C.S.Karlix, D.D.Sadewasser, M.A.Hansen, S.Deschamps, E.E.Gann, M.A.Reimler, R.F.Wolever, D.Milic, J.De La Rosa , G.A.Wray, J.A.Gibeau, J.H.Pickard, J.P.Jennings, P.A.Butler, C.Wachholz, R.A.Schwantes, A.E.Miller, A.P.Tank, C.L.Etjen, D.G.McManus, D.High, D.L.O Brien, D.R.Ripple, D.W.Hickey, D.W.Miller, E.Culp, F.C.Pond, G.E.Adamson, G.L.Langwith, J.J.Rhoades, J.J.Vogt, J.K.Carlyle, J.L.Heffner, J.L.McCaffrey, J.N.Champion, K.D.Van Engelenhoven, K.F.Hoffman, M.E.Krall, M.H.Miller, M.S.Sheehy, O.C.Nelson, O.E.Sanders, O.R.Timm, P.B.Reuter, P.J.Curtis, P.W.Eaves Jr., R.J.Leathers, R.J.Siebel, R.Joyce, R.K.Vanopdorp, R.L.Breitbach, R.L.Macomber, R.L.Webbeking, R.M.Howard, S.K.Sevier, S.M.Metzdorf, S.R.Benham, T.B.Stringer, T.D.Stanley, T.E.Fettkether, S.Bekhaled, D.Caprio, E.Keinz, H.Basiguezel, H.Menzl, J.Hemmer, M.Goektas, O.Manderscheid, T.Simon, D.E.Hungate, J.F.Koelker Jr., H.Demirci, C.R.Ruble, M.J.Zmuda, T.F.Bahl, R.Noel, C.A.Anderson, E.E.Whitelaw, S.Rusiti, D.E.Anderson, F.M.Graap Jr., J.E.Jones, A.D.Weston, B.L.Bekkum, B.L.Holterfield, C.M.Seefeldt, C.T.Anania, C.W.McGregor, D.G.Harris, D.L.Horton, D.M.Stackhouse, D.P.Pysson, D.R.Embrey, E.A.Price, G.L.Kirkland, H.D.Morrison, J.A.Heimburger, J.K.Prunty, J.R.Foster, J.R.Fury, L.A.Brown, L.A.Howard, L.C.Judisch, L.E.Sammons, L.K.Mohr, L.M.West, L.P.Manhart, M.D.Lambe, M.E.Carver, M.F.Schmitt, M.J.Boyd, M.J.Hoffman, M.L.Beck, M.L.Bernard, P.A.Duffy, R.C.Cook, R.D.Geneser, R.E.Boultinghouse, R.J.Stith, R.J.Wearmouth, R.L.Herrold, R.L.Miller, R.L.Nelson, R.L.Powers, R.R.Wilson, S.A.Matkovich, S.D.Fuller, S.J.Shirley, S.R.Johnson, T.J.Gooden, T.R.Leibold, U.C.Sierens, W.G.Evans, A.Aguilar, L.Quentin, J.Araujo De Deus, J.Gomez, A.D'Aquino, V.Bontempo, Z.Oeztas, D.Aragon, L.Pizarro, J.L.Kolkind, R.E.Nance, I.Oeztas, D.J.Schmitt, N.L.Cropp, M.Sarigiolis, W.Preuss, R.D.Knighton, R.J.Norpel Jr., M.Domenez, J.P.Wach, J.C.Zaratán, A.Liggins, A.Meyer, B.B.Hayes, B.J.Hoogerwerf, B.J.Spittel, B.L.Duncan, C.A.Lambert, C.B.Neubauer, C.F.Brechler, C.O.Stark, D.B.Bartch Jr., D.J.Edman, D.J.Jutson, D.L.Mathis, D.L.Morrow, D.L.Simkins, F.E.Elpers, F.J.Krause, G.N.West, J.A.Sawkins, J.B.Graham, J.C.Collis, J.F.Richter, J.F.Samuelson, J.G.Plans, J.L.Gluba, J.M.Woodard, J.Rataj, K.C.Pierce, K.R.Schneck, L.A.Baldwin, L.F.Fowler, L.G.Vancoillie, L.J.Burroughs, L.W.Gebhardt, M.E.Descastro, M.R.Nawrocki, P.C.Gillespie, P.J.Courtland, P.M.Schlimgen, R.J.Mc Dermott, R.J.Vandenberg, S.C.Defrance, S.L.Clapp, J.Lavisse, A.Mille, C.Rantien, M.Yasar, A.Molitor, E.Sauter, G.Sulz-Gropp, H.Seemuth, J.Fuchs, J.Steinheiser, J.Ulmer, K.Lohr, P.Peters, P.Ressel, R.Funk, W.Brenner, W.Groen, D.Grande, J.E.Fay, J.L.Gage, J.M.Schink, R.V.Klavitter, N.Giovanella, J.L.Sanchez, S.Busse, K.A.Leibovitz, R.C.Hahlen, R.J.Youngblut, R.W.Stuart Jr., D.D.Keeling, J.D.Jones, M.L.Spaete, R.B.Crinklaw, R.H.Delk, P.Rollin, G.W.Herum, D.D.Wilken, C.A.Madden, D.D.Gienau, D.E.Burkeybile, D.J.Bankson, D.J.Bredberg, D.L.Peters, D.L.Tarbell, D.M.Mc Cray, D.R.Elskamp, D.R.Schultz, D.S.Schumaker, E.R.Downing, G.D.Yearling, J.D.Halter, J.E.Gutierrez, J.L.Hornick, J.L.Parsons, J.R.Adams, L.C.Ogden, M.D.Leasure, N.L.Solomon, R.C.Fields, R.E.Hughes, R.H.Abbas, R.J.Miller, R.L.Bleeker, R.L.Potwin, S.Haskins, T.D.Piper, W.B.Wagner, W.J.Porter, W.M.Schoessow, J.Clement, K.Anderie, M.G.Gomez T., J.V.Wilson, K.C.Gruchow, L.D.McPherson, R.L.Abraham, C.W.Krieger, R.A.Johnson, G.Renaud, A.Badji, J.M.Ryan, M.Hurtado, D.E.Hoffmann, D.K.Hudson, D.L.Duggan, E.M.Rumler, G.A.Petersen, G.J.Pape, G.L.Baker, J.E.Brackin, J.E.Ogden, J.E.Rochester, J.L.Barber, J.L.Duncan, J.L.Kinney, J.L.Mainard, J.W.Kelbaugh, K.A.Fokken, K.A.Thomas, K.D.Tjepkes, L.J.Rieken, L.R.Propst, M.D.Scarbrough, M.H.Herron, M.P.Doherty, M.R.Nielsen, P.L.Laird, P.L.Price, R.A.Garrett, R.D.Teal, R.Moreno, R.V.Williamson, S.D.Bost, S.M.Monroe, S.N.Schiefelbein, S.R.Brown, T.W.Hoppenjan, T.W.Lower, W.G.Campbell, W.G.Radcliff, W.P.Maricle, B.F.Perales, C.M.Rusk, D.F.Overmann, D.M.Hoefer, F.J.Bennett, I.G.Baskett, J.L.Richardson, J.P.Machu, J.R.Rehmus, M.J.Wittmayer, R.M.Everett, S.A.Malone, S.E.Allen, W.R.Meier, F.Bailly, A.Lopes, B.Rouyat, D.Ljubic, M.Klinghammer, Y.Banholzer, A.R.Ferch, D.R.Fox, G.E.Rubino, G.H.Weatherspoon, H.F.Pherigo Jr., J.A.Metcalf, J.R.Gesell, L.O.Norelius, R.L.Cunningham, W.D.Morrison, W.H.Jurgensen, S.Veziat, R.M.Ferguson, W.F.Biggin, D.Machado, J.Brobst, N.Sattel, F.Conde, A.G.Cook, B.E.Green, D.A.Catour, R.L.Williamson, S.P.Kehoe, A.Meeks, A.R.Docherty, C.A.Gillen Jr., C.Conley Jr., C.J.Branning, C.L.Richards Jr., C.L.Williams, G.G.Haufek, H.D.Rapp, H.E.Dyer Jr., J.G.Hutchins, J.J.Hohnecker, J.M.Finnessy, J.T.Ball, K.D.Dexter, K.R.Wickerath, K.R.Wilson, L.D.Bumann, L.W.Averkamp, M.E.Goodman, M.J.Hansen, M.J.Norin, M.R.Van Nice, P.A.Morgan, P.J.Schaubroeck, R.A.Bishop, R.D.Foltz, R.D.Pearson, R.E.Harris, R.E.Tropf, R.N.Kulper, S.O.Haupert, W.C.Smith, M.Poisson, A.Gottwalles, D.Michel, I.Yildiz, E.T.Fakas, J.D.Reid, R.R.Bartels, S.K.Lyon, T.P.Billmeyer, B.P.Treichel, C.E.Musick, G.E.Steven, H.Teel, J.A.Berry, J.A.Kuper, J.K.Riggins, L.D.Wheelock, R.C.Carpenter, R.L.Burris, W.J.Swarts, W.R.Davis, D.J.Palmer, M.G.Troyer, M.R.Gray, R.E.Coleman, A.L.South, A.R.Weber, D.J.Hartman, E.M.Lieblein, L.R.Sherbon, R.E.Aldrich, R.G.Duffy, R.L.Bradley, S.J.Strange, T.F.Boyle, T.Hoeppner, W.L.Sykes, A.M.Hogue, B.M.Wolfe, C.A.Coates, D.A.Smith, D.C.Powers Jr., D.E.Augustine, D.G.Nelson, D.J.Carlson, D.W.Peacock, G.E.Griffin, G.J.Teed, G.V.Topping, G.W.Rhoads, J.D.Weatherman, J.K.Terry, J.L.Ennis, J.Summers, J.T.Lees, K.H.Krugler, K.J.Donaldson, L.C.Torres, L.J.Meyer, L.O.Douglas, M.A.Shaner, M.D.Miller, M.D.Spooner, M.E.Schupbach, P.A.Decker, R.A.Liberman, R.W.Bailey, S.A.Smith, S.A.Stevenson, T.C.Bruder, T.D.Sharp, T.J.Feehan, T.L.Adams, T.L.Morrison, V.L.Watters, W.L.Waterman, M.Berroubache, C.Erbas, E.Gutierrez M., C.Oliva Jr., D.J.Sodeman, D.L.Rhodes, K.M.Beckmann, L.E.Moens, M.L.Trujillo, R.L.Bettis, R.M.Fenton, R.McKay, T.R.Legel, C.B.Law, C.S.Parcel, D.C.Johnson, D.D.Snyder, D.F.Schneider, D.J.Clark, F.E.Stacy Jr., F.L.Kensinger, G.D.Hudson, H.C.Nawrocki, H.G.Dickmann, J.D.Habbena, L.R.Wilson, M.E.Smith, P.A.Lynch, P.W.Apel, R.A.Niedermann, R.H.Richter, R.L.Power, S.J.Clevenger, T.C.Stledger, M.Frenay, J.Stroh, D.C.Hilsman, J.K.Weida, T.F.Jungblut, W.L.Freiburger, J.Renouf, D.Poillerat, J.Naudin, J.De Guzman, M.Zarco, K.F.Cook, M.H.Van Wardhuizen, D.Monachino, S.Rey, D.H.Storlie, R.A.Dykes, T.L.Culley, A.L.Smothers, A.R.Retherford, C.A.Thompson, C.E.Bash, C.S.Demuth, D.C.Nystrom, D.D.Benson, D.E.Kendall, D.E.Schrock, D.J.Caudill, D.J.Ives, D.L.Manchester, D.L.Parnaby, D.R.Ball, G.R.Schutte, H.D.Payne, H.W.Tarkington, J.A.Brucher, J.A.Teske, J.E.Roberts, J.L.Smith, J.M.Craig, J.M.Schneekloth, L.L.Meredith, M.E.Westendorf, M.G.McCarthy, M.R.Sires, M.T.Gorman, R.A.Weber, R.A.Yates, R.J.Clemens, R.P.Duhl, R.R.Maiden, S.K.Jans, S.M.Ghrist, T.L.Luke, V.L.Hill, W.F.Carroll, J.Caudrelier, J.Cornu, J.Petronila, B.E.Vannatta, K.V.Hoff, L.A.Edwards, M.L.Johnson, C.Sepulveda, A.L.Tarr, C.S.Miller, G.L.Mc Gill, J.A.Knaack, K.D.Towlerton, L.D.McNeal, N.E.Barnes, N.L.Brustkern, R.V.Bomelyn, W.A.Holladay, B.Martin, J.J.Gienau, L.G.Hummel, L.G.Lapage, M.E.Shatzer, M.J.Fuller, R.R.Fiddick, R.T.Robinson, W.H.Howe, H.Kerner, W.Stauch, A.Kretschmer, D.A.Dodge, J.T.Truelsen, L.G.O Brien, A.J.Hemenway, B.A.Brustkern, B.H.Nelson, B.R.Lesniewski, C.E.Sullivan Jr., D.C.Scott, D.D.Kinkade, D.E.Dunkelberger, D.E.Ferguson, D.J.Davis, D.L.Powell, D.S.Shere, D.W.Fisher, E.M.Lombardi, G.Deanda, H.H.Jarr Jr., J.A.Drake, J.A.Driskill, J.E.Gasparovich, J.L.Burgess, J.L.Townsell, J.M.Sanger, J.M.Siems, J.P.Ellis, J.R.Brixey, J.R.Dyar, J.W.Sherrets Jr., K.E.Umland, K.H.Patterson, K.W.Rewerts, L.D.Hoofnagle, L.E.Alexander, L.J.Bredberg, L.J.Schmit, L.L.Himrich, L.M.Hoffman, M.A.Pershing, M.J.Fleck, M.J.Linneman, M.L.Martin, M.P.Pote, M.R.Schlamp, P.J.Carroll, P.M.Rottinghaus, P.W.McCarville, R.A.Knight, R.D.Krueger, R.J.Bernhard, R.J.Lasche, R.J.Rindels, R.J.Trevarthen, R.L.Mangrich, R.L.Peak, R.T.Thornburg, R.Tonn, S.M.Hotchkiss, S.R.Bennethum, S.W.Keve, T.L.Bowden, T.R.Murphy, T.T.Loftus, W.D.O'Brien, W.F.Strathman, W.J.Sikula Jr., W.M.Nash, M.Traore, K.Essert, P.Frank, F.Perez I., J.Cano, C.S.Roysden, C.W.Braatz, D.A.Lynn, G.L.Rathbone, P.C.Shahan, R.R.Junge, T.L.Terhune, C.A.Wiegel, D.C.Bausch, D.E.Round, G.E.Schoeberl, I.Appleby, J.A.Weber, J.S.Walker, M.H.Dolph, S.L.Smith, T.L.Riedl, T.L.Schares, W.L.Major, J.A.Morillo, P.Jara, A.D.Packard, D.R.Welter, D.T.Wrzesinski, E.J.Coleman, H.B.Welter, J.K.Schueller, L.K.Dubler, W.L.Jackson, M.R.Dickey, A.G.Yakish, B.D.Miller, B.L.Gott, C.L.Miller, C.S.Hansen, D.A.Weber, D.B.Davis, D.C.McCabe, D.E.Huddleston, D.J.Kloberdanz, D.L.Hoeppner, D.L.Holman, D.M.Anton, D.M.Selix, D.O.Smits, D.R.Armstrong, D.V.Nesteby, E.A.Schatteman, E.C.Begle, E.Neuendorf, E.R.Billings, E.S.Zirker, F.J.Weninger, G.L.Minikus, G.L.Wildebour, J.B.Halligan, J.D.Fausch, J.D.Johnson, J.E.Heinje, J.E.Helbing, J.F.Finical III, J.J.Tiedt, J.L.Kopplin, J.R.Lane, J.R.Stalf, J.W.Bloom, J.W.Hansen, K.L.Kent Jr., L.E.Hout Sr., L.L.Brandt, M.E.Field, M.E.Sims, M.F.Hopp, M.J.Leis, M.L.Cammack, M.L.Daggett, P.R.Mason, R.A.Cathoir, R.A.Nisius, R.J.Dessinger, R.J.Hoffmann, R.L.Crumes, R.L.Verhaeghe, R.M.Caulkins, R.O.Gonzales, R.R.Holm, S.K.Reicks, S.P.Jarnecke, S.Wolf, T.H.Hill, T.J.Deves, T.M.Kiddoo, W.G.Foss, S.D.Timmons, K.Baumann, J.E.Combs, J.L.Flattery, J.S.Vannorman, R.R.Weeks, T.J.Breidenbach, T.J.Crotty, W.N.Hubbartt, B.Saavedra, D.D.Zellmer Jr., S.R.Howard, J.Kalman, C.E.Speights, G.Perez, G.Poiget, H.Uensal, W.Appel, J.Carchano, A.M.King, B.D.Nixon, B.G.Cunningham, B.L.Lentz, C.L.Delarosa, C.S.Strasko, D.C.Meier, D.D.Peterson, D.D.Schneiderman, D.E.Gruchow, D.G.Dhabolt, D.J.Rellihan, E.K.Gordon, E.L.Beechum, G.A.Decker, G.A.Skosey, G.D.Bone, G.G.Lenius, G.L.Parvin, G.R.Knowlton, H.I.Jones, J.A.Adamson, J.A.Disch, J.A.West, J.D.Hinders, J.E.Schmidt, J.F.Fisher, J.F.Hauser, J.G.Fyfe, J.L.Lenz, J.L.Lovell, J.R.Paisley, J.R.Roedel, K.S.Keith, L.A.Ruble, L.L.Wyckoff, L.R.Roby, M.Acosta, M.C.Churchill, M.D.Wilson, M.E.Nelson, M.J.Daughenbaugh, M.Murray, M.W.Mosier, P.S.Shaver, R.Anthony, R.D.Enstrom, R.D.Stackhouse, R.J.Sanger, R.M.Burkhart, R.W.Utz, S.Arp, S.D.Grove, S.L.Crew, T.C.Lyons, T.H.Kretschmar, T.J.Knanishu, T.M.Hardy, T.R.Glessner, W.A.Glanz, W.C.Hagenstein, W.J.Mackenzie, G.A.Wunderlin, G.J.Ulman, H.D.Hancock, I.E.Landry, J.F.Hansen, K.J.Miller, P.W.Olsen, R.M.Kiddoo, M.Baran, A.A.Claeys, A.K.Campbell, J.J.Toolate, K.A.Risse, M.Savala, W.C.Robinson, V.Kraemer, R.D.Crawford, R.W.Hoffman, J.Asfir, E.Hunsicker, I.Thomas, A.J.Ayala, J.D.Moes, A.L.Abernathy, B.H.Danzy, C.E.Barrier, C.M.Shaner, D.A.Olson, D.A.Otto, D.E.Dull, D.E.Schwartz, D.F.Wiersema, D.J.Guldenpfennig, D.L.Bunker, D.M.McLaughlin, D.M.Stafford, D.R.Wolfe, E.A.Lyons, E.S.Stashi, G.E.McClean, G.L.Fassett, G.W.Davis, G.W.Wiegmann, J.E.Cabor, J.E.Lemon, J.E.Seidel, J.S.West, J.T.Wolf, K.M.Zwicker, L.G.Simpson, L.H.Schiele, L.M.Duncan, L.R.Friesth, M.A.Langner, M.D.Kniep, M.J.Hemphill, M.M.Duffy,

P.E.Zwilling, P.G.Rowe, P.L.Anderson, P.Ramirez, P.S.Clayton, R.A.Burton, R.A.McCabe, R.J.Hoffert, R.J.Smith, R.L.Lane, R.M.Edmunds, R.P.Mechtel, S.A.Hornstein, S.C.Boyd, S.F.Braun, S.J.Lake, S.R.Hendrickson, T.A.Cockrell, T.Cornelious, T.L.Huberts, T.L.Jacobson, V.L.McKnight, G.E.Harris, J.L.Richards, L.L.Crist, M.R.Graham, P.Tweed, R.B.Candee, J.Lelong, D.Gavache, G.Poil, J.Gargaud, F.Aliji, I.Bozkoyun, J.Haas, M.Pigac, B.L.Fisher, B.M.Gorman, C.A.Grey, D.D.Hasty, D.K.Mulcahy, H.A.Warren, J.R.Kutz, M.A.Porter, M.L.Loeffelholz, M.L.Wilder, R.S.Peine, T.A.Blohm, W.W.Culpepper Jr., H.Ramzi, D.A.Ackerman, D.L.Pettis, J.R.Cook, P.O.Randall, R.M.Brown, S.L.Lock, B.K.Breiby, D.R.Tink, G.L.Herbst, L.H.Poston, T.J.Kelly, A.T.Lee, B.A.Ladd, C.E.Rush, C.J.Ernst, C.M.Dufour, D.F.Stansberry, D.G.Everson, D.J.Hunstad, D.P.Francis, D.R.Manternach, D.R.Rupe, D.W.Burkeybile, D.W.Saeugling, E.J.Carroll, G.L.Quentin, J.A.Nemmers, J.D.King, J.J.Bass, J.J.Dalhoff, J.L.Damro, J.L.Whiteside, J.M.Garrett, J.P.Deiter, J.W.Murray, K.A.Woodward, K.R.Beatty, L.D.Dettbarn, L.E.Deppe, L.J.Sheakley, L.M.Aalfs, M.D.Medici, M.J.Koch, M.L.Freese, M.N.Avgenackis, M.T.Ernsdorff, R.C.Anderson, R.C.Wilson Jr., R.C.Young, R.D.Krug, R.D.Moore, R.Gould, S.A.Frahm, S.A.Ramler, S.F.Davis, S.L.Thomas, S.L.Wildes, T.A.Browne, T.J.Hruska, T.M.Moylan, T.P.Mc Bride, W.E.Brooks Jr., H.Pick, J.Giaputzis, A.F.Streicher, C.W.Mc Neer, D.P.Heisterkamp, E.P.Villafurte, J.H.Shoemaker, J.J.Koontz, J.M.Stonehouse, L.E.Leighty, M.L.Vanklaveren, N.A.Winkler, R.N.Kayser, B.L.Waddell, C.D.Shin, D.A.Gebel, D.L.Raney, J.L.Eighmey, J.Pettigrew, K.A.Rizner, L.F.Shoemaker, L.J.Foster, M.A.Starks, M.A.Wilson, R.D.Swanson, T.L.Young, W.R.Eller, J.V.Martins, J.Rodriguez M., D.R.Hanten, J.C.Roethler, J.S.Kohnen, J.Stevens, R.L.Martin, D.A.Meinheit, R.O.Martin, K.Witt, A.L.Reagan, B.A.Trask, B.P.Jamison, C.B.Smith, C.Garza, C.M.Johnson, C.S.Stevenson, D.B.Harsha, D.C.Mc Craney, D.D.Decker, D.D.Dooley, D.E.Pipho, D.E.Youngblut, D.J.Del Ponte, D.J.Drescher, D.J.Gilles, D.S.Koenig, E.A.Lee, G.E.Leete, G.L.Peyton, G.N.Gollobitz, H.E.Petersen Jr., H.L.Colvin, I.E.Krackow, J.A.Jacobsmeier, J.C.Whitehead, J.D.Adams, K.A.Loomis, K.L.Saller, K.R.Wyant, L.L.Miller, L.P.Deppe, M.Kowalske, M.R.Cook, N.O.Stefani, P.A.Marsh, P.J.Kearney, P.R.Cramer, R.A.Parker, R.G.Loney, R.G.Vanvlair, R.H.Jensen, R.J.Fencl, R.W.Frimml, R.W.Hewitt, R.W.Mc Donald, S.D.Mayberry, S.E.Pascoe, S.J.Grant, T.J.Mc Kenna, V.E.Husemann, W.D.Jones, W.J.Allen, W.L.Fowler, G.Muñoz U., J.Alejo, V.Albaladejo, V.Romero M., E.H.Jenkins, M.D.Gabbert, M.J.Corgan, P.L.Windschitl, R.T.Lindberg, A.Sow, H.Bolz, M.Polat, A.B.White, A.H.Rogers, C.R.Smith, D.A.Carr, G.A.Feldpouch, L.G.Orr, L.R.Gibbs, R.O.Gill, R.W.York, V.D.Esquivel Jr., E.G.Bassett, E.M.Butler, J.G.Jirak, K.P.Budde, M.D.King, M.L.Jackson, S.L.Arnold, D.M.Bradley, S.R.Blocker, T.E.Shea, W.Fagan Jr., A.L.Johnson, A.T.Benson, B.Bryan Jr., B.C.Luehmann, B.F.Farrey, C.C.Loeffelholz, D.H.Nagele, D.L.Mixdorf, D.W.Hanneman, G.L.Hildreth, G.N.Bradley, J.F.Zeiser, J.P.Danley, L.A.Baumhover, L.G.Dietrich, M.A.Chapman, M.D.Anderson, R.A.Hulsey, R.E.Besse, R.E.Spurlock, R.M.De La Rosa, R.M.Noring, S.B.Jones, S.E.Wurfel, S.J.Black, S.L.Scrutchfield, S.R.Anderson, W.J.Stoffregen, W.R.Hutchins Jr., J.Jacoutot, C.Lavollee, N.Vyvey, J.Garcia, R.Helfmann, M.J.Pretorius, C.Adan, J.M.Lucas, R.Jimenez L., S.Musgrove, D.E.Leonard, D.E.Miller, D.L.Vickerman, J.L.Saul, J.L.Stallman, L.G.Johnson, M.J.Ekin, M.K.Leonard, R.L.Johannes, T.E.Bueker, E.S.D.Oliveira, D.C.Davis, D.C.Nelson, D.C.Noring, D.E.Koble, D.L.Weber, E.H.Cullen, F.N.Fousek, J.C.Kemp, M.E.Ristau, S.M.Kupresin, V.J.Casper, D.L.Meyer, G.P.Bishop, H.H.Koelling, K.J.Engling, M.E.Strach, M.F.Behnke, R.A.Holt, R.J.Vannatta, D.Rocherieux, E.L.Porter, J.L.Healy, A.D.Towne, B.A.Lornson, B.B.Burnett, C.R.Doss, C.Snyder, D.L.Mann, E.J.Wagoner, F.H.Wallace, G.F.Jelinek, G.H.Cripple, G.K.Werner, H.Edmond Jr., H.M.Holst, J.A.Dondlinger, J.A.Kinnemann, J.Hong-Russell, J.J.Heinze, J.J.Zebus, J.P.Steils, J.R.Keller, J.T.Lueders, L.E.Eck, M.A.Pederson, M.J.Shinkunas, M.P.Merritt, M.Pernell, M.S.Verfaillie, N.Y.Esquivel, P.A.Gustafson, R.J.Weber, S.T.Rideout, S.W.Sexton, T.L.Shane, W.F.Mc Glumphy, P.Castillo, M.Roger, A.Zoeller, E.Mumm, G.King, G.Kohl, H.Lichti, H.Scholz, L.Gottmann, R.Basarir, W.Loesch, W.Piechotta, J.Alcaide, J.Pardo, D.D.Tracy, H.M.Sztanko, J.M.Wall, P.A.Boc, K.Hollunder, C.L.D.Alberti, M.G.Zehentner, A.Clarke, B.Hooks, C.J.Udelhofen, D.A.Bailey-Olson, D.A.Everett, D.E.Draper, D.L.Collins, H.J.Markley, J.Antrim, J.F.Hutchinson, J.L.Miller, L.C.Nosbisch, L.J.Sweet, L.L.Roberson, L.W.Marxen, M.A.Stanley, M.D.Lacher, M.E.Duffey, M.J.Coyle, M.J.Laprell, N.C.Henry, N.V.Sego, P.S.Gulling, R.D.Almendinger, R.D.Sarauer, R.J.Rapp, S.K.Poland, S.R.Thorn, S.S.Siefker, T.D.Welu, A.Tufekcic, F.Castillo, D.C.Wiederholt, D.L.Kaalberg, F.E.De Roboam, K.K.Lindquist, R.D.Wion, R.L.Austin, T.P.Burke, O.Kropp, B.J.Schwickerath, C.J.Moeller, E.J.Fink, F.W.Hofmann, H.J.Weber Jr., J.V.Girsch, M.J.Hoffman, R.A.Troutwine, R.C.Hinkle, R.De Groot, R.F.Scott, R.K.Dewitz, R.S.Monkus, J.Elegeda, B.R.Bremner, C.J.Cronan, D.L.Miller, M.J.Riley, R.F.Fangman, B.Kamkinski, C.Stavreski, G.Zorbovski, S.Stamenkovski, J.J.Viana, W.A.Jackson, A.R.Welch, B.Camp, D.A.Stover, D.D.Dingbaum, E.R.Gansemer, J.C.Taylor, J.D.Evans, J.F.Walsh, J.L.Hunt, L.C.Lindy, M.K.Gaede, P.S.Ammons, R.C.Cline, R.D.Baxter, R.E.Edwards, R.M.Jolley, R.M.Sherer, S.R.Swygman, T.J.Rosenberg, T.W.Mc Afee, W.J.Whitehead, W.L.Schneider, A.Arciba, B.Goike, B.Suder, O.Hamustafic, J.J.Olivier, J.Carretero, D.L.Hulting, J.P.Griffith, J.R.Hall, C.A.Warmuth, J.B.Warmuth, J.K.Arthun, J.Q.Flemings, L.V.Percifield, P.A.Bush, R.A.Miller, S.D.Kauten, T.R.O Connor, W.K.Wheelock, D.García, F.E.Swim, K.M.Beert, P.I.Lackey, R.A.Crisp, G.M.Gertken, D.W.Daniels, A.J.Bowe, B.J.Willett, B.P.Doland, C.V.Larson, D.M.Hahn Jr., D.W.Ferguson, F.E.Brewton, G.P.Kennelly, G.W.Meister, H.J.Nauman, J.B.Hanson, J.L.Brown, K.G.Einfelt Jr., M.G.Erickson, P.A.Ferguson, R.C.McFate, R.D.Hughes, R.E.McCurdy, R.E.Schmidt, R.G.Bies, R.H.Schmitz, R.T.Anderson, S.A.Hayes, S.F.Cavanaugh, S.R.Woods, W.Ireland, A.Yoeruek, I.Pisket, K.Wilking, C.F.Thomas, A.Lorenzzon, A.C.Loewen, A.J.Schmitt, B.C.Hoke, C.W.Barber, D.L.Hoeppner, D.M.Smiddy, E.J.Bunz, J.C.Diederich, J.R.Doy, M.D.Switzer, P.J.Livermore, T.L.Ehlenfeldt, N.Schoen, F.J.Jenkins, H.Majeri, M.J.Diederich, A.M.Rivera-Harrison, A.S.Buckner, B.D.Britt, B.J.Schieferdecker, C.L.Greif, C.S.Mueller, D.A.Ballard, D.A.Henderson, D.C.Hennel, D.L.Kalmes, D.M.Lawrence, D.Marshall, D.P.McCarthy, D.R.Folker, E.E.Ruben, E.L.Neer, G.E.Barber Jr., J.A.Killen, J.M.Patrick, J.V.Kron, K.A.McLeod, K.E.Grove, K.R.Carlson, L.J.Kluesner, L.R.Cline, M.A.Nelson, M.D.Adams, M.E.Krier, M.M.Boldy Jr., M.M.Graham, M.R.Ivey, M.W.Alexander, N.J.Jennes, R.K.Brown, R.L.Pagel, R.L.Sharpe, R.M.Barnett, R.W.Showalter Jr., S.L.Hamilton, T.G.Crawford, W.E.Grafton, W.E.Thomas, V.M.Davila, A.Moreau, H.Kiyak, H.Schneble, K.Dahl, C.A.Fortune, S.S.Morrison, J.Grand, C.H.Goehrig, C.R.Nelson, J.M.Cirricione, J.P.Bradley Sr., R.L.Henderson, R.W.Murray Jr., W.A.Loete, C.M.Christensen, D.O.Bomberry, G.O.Enderson Jr., J.A.Bales, J.R.Weber, M.D.Morrell, P.H.Schumann, P.L.Fischels, R.C.Krogh, W.G.Holscher, W.J.Abel, A.Schoenknecht, J.Ballery, P.Part, E.Silva, G.Prosswitz, G.Stillger, K.Maechtel, C.Chamorro, K.R.Foutch, B.R.Miller, C.S.Hawkins, C.W.Cook, C.W.Ware, D.E.Beemer, D.R.Christoffer, D.R.Croegaert, F.Malatesta, H.H.Roberson, H.Reed, K.M.Blitgen, K.R.Southwick, M.B.Britton, M.D.Doye, R.A.Heston, R.E.Thompson, S.C.Guldenzopf Sr., S.C.Kirik, S.J.Ballard, S.J.Birnbaum, S.P.Hermie, T.D.Kunstman, T.L.Bates, V.Jones, W.G.Tribble Jr., W.W.Graumann Jr., G.Vallet, J.Pereira, D.Linn, E.Nomine, I.Flajs, M.Mikic, R.Gab, W.Gutwein, E.P.Rodriguez, G.L.Gomez, R.A.Palmer, R.P.Peterson, S.M.Alonso, T.R.Adams, J.R.Smith, L.A.Toney, A.L.Elsamiller, D.B.Willard, D.J.Maddigan, F.E.Sprague, M.W.Russell, B.A.Bishop, B.P.Turner, C.A.Fletcher, C.A.Magee, D.A.Stumme, D.D.Polk, D.E.Mabb, D.L.Hilmer, D.L.Huck, D.L.Stock, D.R.Morrissey, F.E.Epperson, G.A.Budzine, G.G.Lalemand, H.A.Roeding II, I.J.Robinson, I.Sides, J.E.Hoffman, J.F.Martin, J.G.Couch, J.M.Goesse, J.T.Deckert, J.W.Kressin, K.S.Reed, K.W.Bunger Jr., L.A.Stumme, M.C.Brown, M.D.Bell, M.D.Wildermuth, P.K.Goodenough, R.A.Dabney, R.A.Watters, R.D.Druvenga, R.L.Dufel, R.W.Edwards, S.C.Lent, S.F.Morrison, S.J.Kuen, S.M.Nolan, W.H.Schockemoehl, W.L.Depoorter, W.T.Reynolds, M.Dukic, K.Lohr, R.Graf, L.Russell, N.A.Boyer, I.Rodriguez, D.C.Swinton, C.M.Vignes, D.M.Yuska, T.L.Stecklein, A.Garcia F., S.J.Steele, T.S.Herman, A.F.Kruger, A.J.Hoffman, A.L.Humke, A.S.Jacobs, B.J.Bashynski, C.A.Quinn, C.D.Morris, C.W.Weinheimer, D.A.Carpenter, D.A.Schaal, D.Barrett, D.C.Devries, D.G.Schaalma, D.L.Jones, D.L.Niemeyer, D.P.Weiser, E.Sandoval, G.K.Ewert, G.L.Elgersma, G.R.Van Grinsven, H.H.Schmidt, H.W.Fehling, J.Garcia, J.W.Wainwright, L.M.Hockett, L.M.Holmes, M.D.Kane, M.R.Chickering, P.M.Bowers, R.C.Ritter, R.D.Newell, R.J.Whipple, R.L.Payne, R.S.Henke, S.C.Richter, S.D.Bennett, S.Fleming, T.T.O Connor, W.C.Keller Jr., W.E.Hutchins, W.R.Williamson, K.Kiefer, A.Navio, C.J.Paul, J.R.Lerschen, R.L.Sellers, E.Holmes, J.E.Hurtado, K.C.Bonk, K.S.Casey, R.L.Varney, J.Goeritz, D.J.Krapfl, D.Mingas, K.Mai, C.F.Bedford, J.Garcia R., D.A.Montgomery, A.G.Flack, A.R.Ybarra, A.W.Musser, B.B.Burris, C.F.Temeyer Jr., C.H.Kaufman, C.L.Voss, C.Loveless, C.S.Murry, D.A.Levenhagen, D.A.Vanderlinden, D.F.Marsch, D.J.Pellouchoud, D.J.Sivertsen, D.M.Burrus, D.M.Kirby, D.W.Harrington, E.A.Betzle, E.M.Dollar, F.G.Marquez, F.L.Sutton, G.L.Heuer, G.L.Medema, G.M.Hutcheson, H.G.Peterson, J.Hawkins, J.L.Portwood, J.R.Behan, K.M.Etzel, K.R.Marvets, K.W.Beach, L.J.Nelson, M.M.Wild, M.R.Weiss, P.L.Smith, R.E.Elsamiller, R.F.Davis, R.P.Erber, S.P.Rechek, T.M.Gootee, V.L.Ramsey, W.L.Breselow, G.Redoutey, J.Boulanger, M.Mauceri, C.Matesanz, C.A.Gibson, R.L.Zumbrunnen, J.Araujo, L.Araujo, D.A.Behrens, L.C.Millman, M.K.Fisher, A.Thiault, J.Chanteau, J.Tortot, P.Durand, E.Gneuss, F.Wenzel, G.Pahl, P.Anstee, D.S.Davis, J.L.Tristan, R.L.Thorne, R.M.Mehmen, A.Soudy, J.Clément, A.Moreira, J.Bardeau, J.Bolivar, J.Da Silva, M.Hennebert, P.Fornier, A.Klein, A.Lanzinger, C.Pascual, D.Guberaj, F.Mehmeti, G.Kraemer, G.Prudlik, G.Schick, H.Weissbrodt, K.Bauer, K.Mayer, M.Gjemajlaj, M.Kaiser, M.Sertel, N.Kosumi, O.Bernhard, P.Slavik, R.Fetsch, R.Mehmeti, R.Zahn, S.Saiti, S.Spahija, U.Gleich, W.Merkel, Z.Osmic, A.Bravo, A.Velasco, F.Rodriguez-T., J.J.Garcia D., M.Molina, A.A.Stern, B.J.Philo, B.L.Knox, B.W.Gengler, C.A.Schmit, C.G.Pliska, D.G.Pushic, D.H.Patzlsberger, D.J.Hemesath, D.J.Hofman, D.J.Thompson, D.L.Brooks, D.L.Giebink, D.P.Wright, E.L.Grulke, G.E.Marshall, G.N.Skiles, H.D.Logue, J.A.Schumacher, J.Amos Jr., J.B.Geddes, J.D.Krol, J.D.McGee, J.H.Lehner, J.L.Cupery, J.L.Jackson, J.McMillan, J.W.Clough, K.D.Heidemann, K.F.Grimm, K.K.Starman, K.L.Kiesner, L.A.Guthrie, L.Goodwin, M.A.Brown, M.A.D'Almeida, M.D.Defrieze, M.E.Kienast, M.G.Scott, M.M.Fox, M.S.Ford, M.S.Sommer, N.Kelting, P.Gallagher, P.L.Young, R.C.Beckmann, R.E.Shirley, R.G.Davies, R.J.Hess, R.J.Ricke, R.L.Buhalog, R.L.Postel, R.Robertson, S.J.Jefferson, T.A.Thiede, T.G.Cook, T.L.Gillen, T.O.Butler, T.T.Carstens, W.C.Gass, W.R.Kallenberger, A.Estrada, D.Lasne, L.Poss, M.R.Pentland, R.E.Shannon, A.Abebe, A.M.Fehr, C.J.Hatton, C.L.Vanburen, D.L.Kaumans, D.L.Schrock, D.S.Adams, E.F.Wild, G.R.Westphal, L.Caldwell, L.F.Snyder, L.J.Allen, L.K.Carlson, M.J.Wielage, R.J.Burds, S.W.Taylor, G.Musard, D.L.Strang, M.J.Nagle, C.M.Herrera, L.P.Breitbach, N.G.Stamp, B.C.Bartz, C.E.Derby, C.E.McDonald, D.A.Dawson, D.C.Glessner, D.J.Lee, D.J.Stahler, D.W.Mooers, E.C.Powers, F.H.Spencer, F.J.Farr, G.E.Kron, G.J.Gabbard, G.L.Schlomann, H.D.Horstman, J.A.Metzger, J.A.Neevel, J.M.Frank, J.M.Merrick, J.R.Jackson, L.J.Jungwirth II, M.E.Lang, M.H.Ballew, M.S.Johnson, N.J.Monner, N.L.Babcock, P.K.Hildebrant, R.D.Peterson, R.R.Urbain, R.W.Ringen, S.J.Lawless, A.Garza, R.L.Michels, W.S.Hayward, A.R.Willie, C.A.Dopson, A.J.Kremer, J.C.Stanton, R.T.Werner, J.J.Kopp, W.M.Saathoff, A.J.Armetta, A.R.Voskuil, B.E.Edie, B.G.Magnusson, C.A.McAdams, C.A.Taylor, C.L.Peters Jr., D.E.Gavin, D.J.Hageman, D.J.Wright, D.R.Mellon, E.L.Chrystian, F.H.Haertjens, G.L.Gregg, G.L.Krouth, J.A.Lueken, J.L.Jackson, J.M.Devoss, K.A.Surette, K.L.Lehrman, L.D.Shollenberger, L.R.Houk, M.Bergstrom, M.E.Kirkland, M.L.Heins, O.C.Stegmaier, R.C.Vogt, R.E.Kuehl, R.P.Mayne, S.V.Nelson, T.A.Waters, W.Mosier, C.Piteira, J.Beaubras, P.Bouclet, A.Cetinkaya, D.Ostojic, A.Zahino, E.Blazquez, F.Pulido, L.A.Mateo, R.N.B.Stafford, B.J.Groves, B.J.Jacobson, B.J.Minarsich, D.C.Steines, D.D.Deutmeyer, F.L.Courbat, J.K.Bergsmith, R.D.Boleyn, R.F.Steils, S.H.Kline, W.J.Halligan, D.J.Gosa, R.H.Selk, W.E.King, O.Clemente, D.A.Slack, D.J.Chase, M.C.Miehe, R.K.Church, R.L.Schwartz, T.C.Sellon, W.McKeown, M.Garcia R., D.L.Mueller, J.C.Schueller Jr., K.E.Mayne, R.B.Gentz, T.H.Arensdorf, A.J.Bolin, A.J.Riniker, C.C.Brown, C.L.Neubauer, C.V.Montalbo Jr., C.W.Hanaway, D.E.Beske, D.E.Meyer, D.J.Barrett, D.S.Stanul, D.W.Hoefs, E.A.Hugunin, F.N.Penny, G.A.Elliott, G.A.Field, G.T.Warden, H.D.O Connell, H.W.Thielen, J.D.Hegna, J.E.Stanford, J.K.Adams, J.L.De Vries, J.P.Colley, J.R.Wolf, K.J.Kresser, L.D.Cortez, L.D.Halupnick, L.T.Hadley, M.A.Maze, M.A.Tuel, P.L.Moore, R.A.Peterson, R.A.Trepanier, R.A.Van Buren, R.F.McKeon, R.J.Nyman, R.L.Duncan, R.L.Eckes, R.L.Joachim, R.L.Kramer, R.L.Pryor, R.L.Root, R.M.Corkery, R.S.Landgraf, S.A.Hefel, S.B.Karel, S.G.Bilke, S.M.Callahan, S.M.Riedl, S.W.Boge, T.A.Neyens, T.D.Anderson, W.A.Jones, W.A.McGowan, W.E.Priewe, W.E.Satterfield, W.R.Hertensen, J.Rossignol, C.Barrau, D.Lange, J.Ladune, O.Martin, V.Winter, W.Grabler, M.Segoviano, M.A.Winn, M.J.Mc Gonegle, P.J.Wallis, R.F.Tigges, I.Kostic, B.D.Morehouse, M.L.Welch, N.J.Austin, P.R.Koob, R.D.Jordan, R.W.Nordman, S.M.Mervin, G.Fournier, G.Dick, D.C.Mc Grane, E.W.Medearis, K.K.Eckenrod, T.E.Cummings, J.Lopez, R.R.Tigges, C.Jenkins, C.L.Heister Jr., C.W.Wilson, D.E.Boge, D.J.Golden, D.P.Boyce, D.R.Wildes, E.Starks Jr., G.H.Zimmerman, J.D.Trainor, J.E.Graham, J.L.Black, J.M.Petsch, J.P.Swanson, J.W.Beers, J.W.Sorensen, K.M.Robbins, K.T.Gates, M.J.Becker, M.P.Goheen, N.L.Martin, P.M.Perry, R.J.Hodges, R.J.Miller, R.J.Strassburg, R.L.Efferding, R.M.Uelmen, R.O.Knight, S.D.Olsen, S.L.Buchholz, S.M.Collins, T.J.Schueller, W.A.Horaney, B.Tressou, P.Menigot, A.Carrozzo, G.Rittscher, F.Aparicio G., F.Merino V., H.Vaquerizo, J.Cazorla, S.Galvez, D.P.Hoeg, G.H.Massey, L.M.Deering, L.S.McLain, M.E.Link, M.L.Webber, R.E.Snyder, W.D.Russell Jr., G.Bossard, G.Thomas, G.Sommer, H.Winkelmann, K.Auer, K.Schunck, M.Goertelmeyer, P.Kohl, D.C.Wheelock, E.E.Held, G.R.Smith, L.E.Zobel, R.M.Dunn, S.C.Rollins, S.J.Hood, M.E.Spiegel, J.Nuñez T., J.J.Lampe,

Harvester Works employees, East Moline, Illinois, 1979

J.G.Gogel, K.W.Foecking, R.T.Holman, A.J.Robinson, B.J.Miller, C.D.Strien, D.A.Cirricione, D.A.Harp, D.A.Mattan, D.B.Carter, D.E.Holladay, D.J.Barry, D.J.Roelens, D.P.Reinhardt, D.W.Regenold, G.D.Zimple, G.F.Mohlenkamp, G.L.Thomas, J.A.Rausch, J.D.Lamb, J.L.Bonner, K.A.Howard, K.E.Hoeppner, K.E.Jones, L.C.Stevenson, L.W.Jones Jr., L.W.Patrick, M.C.Depauw, M.F.Heckart, M.F.Schwendinger, M.W.Lessard, P.J.Sproles, P.W.Gabriel, R.Bolduc, R.D.Smith, R.E.Zingler, R.R.Brown, S.J.Summer, T.R.Mummelthie, H.Simson, A.Mudarra, A.Perez R., E.Arriscado, B.R.Hubbard, C.J.Waller, D.L.White, E.J.Wright, J.Thomas, R.A.Abresch, S.M.Schmidt, J.Azevedo, A.Ollero, V.Ortiz, A.B.Miller, A.C.Pollreisz, A.N.Nissen, C.D.Nieland, C.I.Watson, I.L.Delagardelle, M.Justmann, R.E.Weber, R.L.Wellner, L.Jurado, M.A.Hendershot, M.J.Mostek, W.R.Plowman, M.Goodenbour, M.H.Brown, B.K.Wilson, D.F.Schilling, D.J.Eudaley, D.M.Ludovissy, D.P.De Baillie, D.R.Schricker, E.R.Van Sickle, G.E.Kanaby, G.J.Schaefer, J.A.Flack, J.M.Lashelle, J.W.Ludtke, K.G.Gebhard, K.G.Schares, K.M.Danielsen, M.A.Reed, M.C.Damaso, M.P.Hershberger, N.E.Slead, P.C.Loerzel, R.F.Nunez, R.Walters, S.P.Ellis, T.E.Mosher, T.J.O Leary, F.Juhel, J.Caillard, H.Kraemer, N.Keser, F.Gil D., L.Martinez F., M.I.Luque, D.C.Wilson, J.G.Agar, K.E.Lybarger, M.Oecal, R.Schmitt, W.Richter, M.Diaz, D.A.Eastman, D.J.Becker Jr., D.P.Haverland, D.R.Molzof, F.L.Bell, H.C.Howard, J.E.Oakes, J.H.Thurman, J.M.Heiar, L.Anderson, P.L.Schreck, P.Schroeder, R.J.Vogt, R.M.Turner, S.C.Shaw, T.J.Kastli, W.E.Wexter, M.Bergmann, A.Yugo, J.P.Galindo, K.L.Dodson, R.H.Jones, K.Beckefeld, R.D.King, R.Battocchio, T.J.O Loughlin, B.A.Christiansen, B.L.Kuhaupt, D.C.Toy, D.E.Brommerich, D.J.Hansen, D.J.Weber, D.L.Rawlins, D.M.Schoeberl, D.V.Delagardelle, D.W.Rorah, E.E.Halverson, G.E.Oberle, G.G.Welborn, G.T.Chervak, J.C.Morkel, J.H.Hayes, L.E.Foster, L.H.Blaser, M.G.Grim, M.J.Hunemiller, M.L.Brannon, P.F.Watson, P.J.Dunlay, R.D.Hotchkiss, R.E.Beau, R.E.Chickowski, R.L.Rieken, R.L.Watkins, S.T.Mc Nulty, T.V.Buchda, V.K.Herrald, W.C.Heister, R.Vivet, K.Rehberger, R.Peter, F.Bravo, J.Del Moral, J.J.Soria, L.Garcia V., D.A.Schueller, E.C.Baker, E.J.Arensdorf, W.M.Page, J.Dehlinger, A.I.Lozano, A.P.Mazza, D.R.Grass, G.C.Marshall, G.M.Olinyk, J.M.Fay, M.Feddersen, M.R.Geltz, R.C.Baldwin, R.Jacobsen, R.N.Daringer, S.J.Hansen, T.D.Sherman, D.Fuhrmann, D.A.Germain, K.R.Eberhart, L.L.Klein, L.W.Popp, M.J.Rash, R.E.Leute, R.L.Wilson, R.W.Carlson Jr., W.M.Gehrts, F.Garcia C., G.Ozanne, B.L.Johnson, C.S.Hobert, D.K.Norcross, J.D.Wessels, L.E.Ransom, L.J.Getz, L.J.Moore, M.M.Moreno, M.Nicholson Jr., M.R.Lundeen, P.A.Ballentine, P.A.Esser, P.J.Doyle, P.R.Schmidt, R.L.Hipple, S.G.White, T.L.Roberts, T.P.Swope, V.F.Brimeyer, F.Munoz, F.Fernandez B., J.Fernandez M., J.Lopez M., L.Pardo, V.Martin P., W.M.Wilming, J.Ramon, B.L.Becker, D.C.Riha, M.J.Digman, M.J.Patterson, M.J.Russell, M.S.Miller, P.Robinson, S.J.Rourke, S.J.Zarifis, T.A.Wilson, A.Sanchez P., D.B.Roberts, D.A.Wieland, D.R.Rasmussen, G.A.Simenec, S.C.Smith, S.M.Van Thorre, T.F.Mc Rae, W.L.Newman Jr., P.Mirloup, H.Ortlepp, A.V.Jorgensen, D.L.Maresh, D.W.Allen, G.T.Milton, K.L.Neumann, L.D.Meany, L.W.Fish, M.J.Primmer, R.E.Brutsche, R.Lopez, S.F.Schroeder, S.L.Smith, T.H.Smith, G.Boehles, R.Huber, R.Sebald, N.A.Tilinyane, M.Arcones, M.M.Cobo, D.J.Ackley, F.J.Salowitz, S.Richardson, T.L.Pickard, E.O.Massei, B.L.Hart, B.Smith, C.Malcom, D.K.Jewett, D.W.Roberts, L.A.Tisor, L.L.Kaster Jr., M.F.Shields, R.J.Bucknell, V.G.Buhr, Z.L.Sutherland, B.T.Nelson, L.Acosta, M.J.Almblade, S.P.Hall, M.Besada-Fernandez, A.L.Beebe, C.A.Emdy, C.J.Hartung, D.A.Snapp, D.D.Dorr, D.E.Fischer, D.G.Richmond, D.J.Hirth, D.M.Parrish, D.W.Dalton, G.D.Sigler, G.W.Garrison, H.A.Fuhr, J.A.Cox, J.D.Schlimgen, J.M.Monahan, J.T.Spurrier, M.D.Agan, M.Debooy Junge, M.R.Struve, T.C.Robine, T.E.King, T.Thorpe, W.A.Koenen, W.S.Cliff, X.N.Estebanez, D.N.Cantrell, R.E.Paxton, J.A.Calle De La, S.G.Schold, A.P.Calleja, D.D.Roesner, S.J.Clark, J.E.Rice, N.Okur, B.A.Vanhyfte, B.L.Wallace, D.F.Ptacek, D.H.Holdorf, D.K.Manchester, D.M.Walters, E.U.Templin, J.A.Splinter, J.R.Clark, L.E.Christenson, M.H.Walker, M.L.Kline, M.P.Rodriguez, R.J.Courtade, S.D.Langston, S.P.Damanski, T.Beck, A.Seibert, S.Morales O., D.C.Harkin, F.J.Mapes, J.H.Swanson, R.E.Blanchard Jr., C.Saez, B.E.Leon, D.I.Schnoor, H.J.Petersen, L.R.Grapp, M.L.Lawson, W.L.Pauley, A.Sanchez G., B.R.Jones, D.J.Eudaley, J.J.Kapalis, J.L.Christopher, J.M.Pizano, L.D.Horn, L.E.Engstrom, L.L.Schroeder, F.Baltierra, W.Habenberger, J.Olivera, L.Sanchez U., R.Lopez J., J.De Pablo, A.G.Gutgsell Jr., M.E.Langill, P.R.Dedoncker, P.R.Murray, R.Kittredge, B.Rocher, J.Mueller, A.M.Kelding, B.L.McHaney, B.Von Bobrutzki, D.E.Carlson, D.L.Smith, D.L.Westerfield, D.R.Dedoncker, D.S.Hicks, E.I.Stubblefield, F.D.Belzer, H.M.Funkhouser, J.B.Cox, J.E.Harriss, J.M.Bettis, J.P.Callaghan, K.A.Kluever, L.D.Kaiser, L.Randolph, M.A.Steger, M.S.Douglas, M.V.Ptacek, M.W.Fritz, N.A.Beatty, R.C.Cafer, R.J.Doty, R.L.Boostrom, R.M.Lee, S.A.Rockey, T.C.Willett, T.E.Zeidler, T.L.Waldmann, T.R.Schwegman, V.Goodpaster, W.B.Fetter, W.P.Stone, H.Batzler, A.Serrano G., D.G.Fink, D.P.Quinlan, P.H.Kim, R.J.Casas, D.E.Brotherton, E.M.Mink Reeves, R.R.Nale, W.E.Denman, W.Richard Jr., B.L.Dawson, C.A.Oswald, C.A.Rose, C.M.Jacobs, D.W.Luko, E.L.Stettler, F.Eubanks, L.C.Rich, L.L.Kline, M.J.Malamphy, R.D.Gibb, S.P.Hale, T.L.Mahan, A.Dominguez, J.Bautista, R.D.Secymore, B.Theveny, J.S.Neil, E.W.Kotzur, L.K.McAllister, B.J.Evans, J.D.Renihan, J.M.Wilcox, L.J.Mudd, P.P.Evans, R.E.Weber, R.L.Farrell, G.Herrera, L.L.Ranes, J.A.Aiken, G.Leggett, **1975** C.M.Geiger, J.M.Lopez, L.Renard, M.Miguel, D.Laib, E.Joensson, F.Benning, J.Bovenkamp Van De, K.Pfisterer, F.Fockel, R.Frank, R.Riedel, C.B.McIntyre, C.L.Inskeep, D.A.Bernal, D.G.Hocamp, D.H.Laudick, D.J.McIntire, D.R.Beyhl, D.R.Holderied, E.E.Cole, G.D.Richard, J.A.Hooker, J.A.Newborn, J.C.Weaver, J.E.Kuhar, J.J.Robb, J.L.Riisoe, K.D.Wicks, L.M.Fluck, M.K.Henthorn, R.J.Schroeder, R.L.Heinz, R.P.Chambers, S.B.Yakish, S.G.Henwood, S.M.Trotter, T.W.Ellicott, W.J.Hojnacki, H.Zelck, R.Flickinger, B.Masa, T.Gonzalez C., A.Capostagno, B.A.Watson, C.E.Shoup, C.L.Bjurstrom, D.A.Twigg, D.J.Martin, D.L.Hartmann, D.L.Wiebenga, D.L.Wilson, D.M.Richardson, D.R.Falkenstein, G.A.Phelps, G.C.Kemp, G.H.Malicki, G.J.Winkel, G.K.Helfert, G.L.Dellaert, G.R.Werts, H.S.Grounds, J.B.Kane Jr., J.M.Fleck, K.C.Huhn, L.A.Declerck, L.B.Ellerhoff, M.Bustos, M.J.Debaene, M.S.Vasquez, M.W.Lalan, O.L.Dunham, R.A.Bryant, R.Colvin, R.D.Buttgen, R.E.Goodnight, R.E.Mattan, R.J.Herting, R.J.Hunt, R.R.Reeves, R.R.Snyder, R.S.Grimm, R.W.Blake, R.W.Loter, S.L.Schmid, S.T.Schatteman, T.Abbas, V.L.Bauer, F.Chanteau, H.Lauer, D.R.Allbaugh, R.J.Chappell, W.M.Ferguson, H.Weber, L.Koerner, Z.Ligata, D.A.Rollins, R.L.Crider, G.W.Seffrin, L.K.Kerker, W.Fuhrmann Jr., A.Brecheisen II, B.D.Blake, C.E.Hammond, C.L.Dahl, C.Sutherlin, D.L.Swiger, G.Kimmerle, H.T.Allsup, J.A.Auxier, J.I.Orgill, J.J.Kingery, K.R.Buell, L.J.Jirak, V.R.Torres, N.Coronado, R.Freis, N.G.Bauerfeld, K.Baumgaertel, R.Philipp, J.C.Linder, J.Rodriguez, K.Noe, J.E.Summers, M.J.Katuin, R.J.Lawrence, A.D.Bell, A.N.Veloz, B.G.Engelman, C.J.Mc Cunniff, C.Pulliam, E.K.Cheek, E.M.Glass, J.J.Knox, J.L.Phillips, J.M.Allbaugh, K.J.Karlix, P.D.Regan, R.Dumoulin, R.J.Bush, R.L.Drechsel, R.P.Hawley, S.H.Campbell, T.L.Rasso, L.Jetzschmann, J.D.Robles, F.E.Graham Jr., J.T.Ponce, L.K.Holuba, T.Koch, F.J.Sutliff, J.B.Johnson, C.W.Starnes, D.H.White, D.W.Adams, G.L.Olson, J.L.Winter, L.G.Lagaisse, M.A.Gavin, M.C.Brenegan, R.J.Phillips, S.W.Speicher, W.W.Sokil, J.Berger, P.Conzelmann, D.S.Brown, T.M.Hebron, G.Barthon, J.Luche, P.Labarre, G.Decker, G.Wesch, H.Juhasz, O.Schneider, B.S.Hilligoss, C.G.Mogged Jr., D.R.Holm, D.W.Eck, G.M.Stotmeister, K.J.Smith, K.N.Chaston, M.A.Carless, N.Smith, R.A.Mowers, W.J.Kahler, A.Rathke, J.J.Jegorschki, J.A.Cavazos, R.Krieger, K.Zoeller, W.Dzemski, C.F.Stange Jr., D.R.Ernat, J.G.Feggestad, L.D.Hutcherson, N.E.Linn, P.L.Casement-Trapp, K.Wirchan, E.Kowalski, O.Sartori, R.Dickel, P.W.James Jr., O.A.Boeno, R.Bach, G.D.Tjelmeland, H.J.Hursh, R.L.Door, R.P.Seyfried, S.A.Kay, V.P.Boudeau, D.Lissek, G.Machauer, G.Venske, S.Groen, C.W.Seawel, L.V.Erlanson, R.Wentworth, L.Tusset, V.Todeschini, L.A.Canto, J.R.P.D.Oliveira, D.A.Gittens, L.L.Kuhn, W.Koenig, L.Poulard, C.M.Davis, G.A.Wiles, J.T.Baskett, K.R.Patterson, L.W.Dewitt, M.R.Bloomfield, G.Steinmann, K.Vettel, R.D.Thompson Sr., P.Decker, G.H.Sukach, O.Hartnagel, R.Weber, A.E.Blank, B.C.Little, C.K.Orth, G.F.McCormick, G.H.Johnson, G.J.Redell, G.L.Kooken, J.H.Michaelson, J.P.Higgins, R.W.Strother,

S.B.Clark, S.M.Rebro, S.R.Reineke, B.Froehlich, K.Wach, S.C.Moore, R.De la Cruz, C.S.Vannatta, L.A.Filippi, J.J.Hill, L.Sada , P.Weimann, J.E.García , T.Avila, W.Blatt, A.Carcano, J.L.Salido, C.R.Stoneman, J.B.Carboneau, C.A.Kasper, C.A.Puetz, C.Battles, E.A.Boblett, M.W.Brault, R.J.White, R.M.Willis, L.A.Izolan, H.Hiegl, J.A.Garcia D., J.B.Eagan, O.Celik, A.J.Lang, C.C.Hill, R.Fejzic, R.Fuhrmann, C.Lomo, D.M.Axsom, D.Billard, D.Neu, D.E.Soper, D.W.Tolander, E.E.Cross, J.C.Gogola, T.W.Vandenberg, F.Trinidad, M.Perez L., P.E.Myers, G.Billion, J.Galliot, A.Sponagel, G.Ries, G.Straub, H.Adelmann, H.Gassmann, J.Lindemann, N.Schaefer, G.Praehofer, H.Guenther, R.Hofer, D.H.Spoerl, G.L.Warnsholz, M.Bartlett, O.L.Boeck, E.Dott, J.A.Lorente, J.Jimenez B., V.Aliaga , D.Jimenez, F.G.Martinez, U.Krauss, A.J.Higley, J.A.Pray, J.D.Mallery, R.C.Lashbrook, R.E.Johnson, V.Saucedo Jr., W.G.Glenn Jr., G.Eberle, W.Mueller, W.Roessler, J.L.Varona, L.M.Demaio, B.C.Lundahl, D.L.Guertin, L.M.Hoppestad, G.A.Fuente De La, C.T.Mason Jr., D.M.Sullivan, H.D.Caves, R.A.Redell, R.Y.Swayne, T.J.Schaub, R.Ozuna , W.Winkler, D.Siefker, J.P.Chiapello, M.M.Mercier, M.Rodriguez, L.F.Espinoza, D.A.Katherman, S.A.Sheffler, J.M.Lewis, D.N.Dow, E.T.Kaczmarczyk, M.B.Hornbuckle, D.Matzarowits, E.Cordier, H.Beyer, L.Mueller, L.Miragoli, C.M.Fulson, D.J.Collins, J.Rose, R.W.Smith, J.Vega, O.Heinz, C.Hernando R., E.Hernandez Q., S.A.Giesemann, D.R.Stroh, J.R.Carroll, I.Martinez, C.Martin P., J.Garcia M., S.E.Davidson, N.J.Forbis, M.L.Fering, J.Jutzi, S.J.Buller, F.K.O'Toole, G.L.Kramer, J.B.Hanus, J.C.Peck, S.J.Scott, S.L.Stamp, D.Kappauf, H.Eckert, K.A.Nicholson, C.V.Salazar, M.J.Dawson, R.S.Runyan, E.M.Davis, E.Bernal, B.G.Nimrick, D.C.Everitt, G.E.Keene, W.J.Zelnio, M.Bardey, M.J.Parker, J.G.Lugo, A.H.Diaz, H.J.Serna, H.Sema, J.Eckart, L.Schwaegerl, C.G.Thompson Jr., C.R.Wilson, D.C.Winter, D.L.Schwiebert, D.R.Allison, D.T.Rodger, D.V.Hallford, E.J.Rumpza, E.L.Adams, E.W.Bodnar, G.L.Freeman, J.B.Heartt, J.D.Phelan, J.K.Vandemore, J.S.Hall, J.W.Kloet, K.F.Thompson, L.A.Avitt, L.E.Beinke, L.K.Bower, M.E.McGuire, M.J.Wegener, M.W.Musick, R.L.Gonzalez, R.R.Thomas, S.A.O'Bryan-Johnson, S.R.Allen, T.R.Roller, W.L.Davenport, W.T.Eilts, Y.I.Kerr, F.Salmoran, R.Mueller, T.Schreiber, C.Marchal, L.Moreno H., M.Garcia G., D.J.Selby, R.L.Mayfield, L.Tironi, D.L.Jeffries, K.R.Gibson, D.L.Jost, D.M.Willing, J.D.Guidry, M.A.Holste, M.R.Megraw, R.L.Basham, T.J.Lester Sr., L.Escudero, R.Lopez I., F.B.Miller, M.L.Besch, J.H.Leinart III, A.W.Andersen, D.L.Israel, D.Rainey, E.S.Dutmers, H.F.Stuart, J.L.Swanson, K.W.Baker, M.S.Cotton, R.A.Murphy, S.L.Hanson, N.Malard, A.Garcia G., A.Gonzalez A., A.Guerrero, J.Gonzalez R., V.L.Henderson, R.Salinas, R.Maillard, D.F.Horn, D.W.Staton, H.A.Brown, J.L.Kindschuh, L.Mc Coll, N.J.Algra, P.E.Avis, S.S.Zanotti, T.L.McCaw, A.Fernandez G., A.Perez R., F.Arroyo, P.Gomez F., F.Moyeda, M.J.Smith, C.Davenne, M.K.Stephens, C.J.Reschly, J.R.Smart, M.A.Beuthin, M.A.Taute, M.Heath, R.J.Bergstrom, S.M.Ivory, W.L.Haas, F.Lucena, J.Moreno V., L.Arganda, A.Rasso, D.S.Aldrich, G.E.Merrill, G.J.Wallace, J.R.Bush, P.L.Lane, R.D.Hysell, A.Vega, P.Hutinet, J.Barberon, M.Carrie, D.Schnabel, E.Gab, F.Hildenbeutel, H.Froelich, H.Quoiffy, J.Moehrer, W.Kuch, A.Del Valle, N.Vázquez , R.M.Ramirez, D.Westendorf, J.E.Michaelsen, R.M.Allen Thomas, T.L.Helmrichs, J.Novosel, J.Montero D.P., M.Baños, A.De Paiva, F.Gomez P., F.Vallejo, C.J.Ziegler, I.Binsfeld, I.Vebrath, F.L.Hoskin, L.E.De Hart, V.L.Eller, D.Hilbert, C.K.Leahy, J.L.Peterson, D.J.Sunlin, K.J.Schmitt, J.Rios, G.L.Thompson, C.Roveretto, B.Gilbert, A.Perez M., L.Rodriguez L., H.Lubin, R.T.Grafton, L.C.Thomas, S.G.Nimrick, S.F.Towlerton, E.F.De Paepe, J.A.Dawson, J.E.Stanbrough, K.J.Johnston, S.C.Dochterman, S.E.Galer, A.Cañada, A.Sanchez C., F.Rubio E., J.M.Portela, M.Rodriguez L., P.Gonzalez O., A.Dothard Jr., P.T.De Long, J.Castruita, A.L.Fletcher, B.M.Fuller, G.R.Epperly, J.S.Macvey, K.L.Blonigan, R.H.Grenier, W.F.Johnson, D.Rousseau, A.Tybl, B.Pauli, H.Langner, M.Fischer, W.Kleinsorgen, E.Gonzalez J., D.Fazilleau, C.L.Sackett, J.Desgraves, R.D.Downing, R.E.Lindstrom, R.K.Hains, I.Berger, I.Wiskow, Z.Kretschmer, U.Kramer, S.S.Dajee, A.Sevilla, F.Argumanez , G.Almarza , C.N.Spurr, J.C.Young, B.Schuppel, T.U.Thorson, A.N.Bagetti, C.Reyes, E.Gonzalez, D.A.Crandall, D.R.Shaner, F.E.Humphrey, G.G.Gernant, K.H.Mc Henry, R.A.Wallace, S.Sodaro, A.Diezma, L.Rodriguez G., M.V.Rederus, D.Gonzalez A., E.Wood, S.R.Clark, B.B.Cavender, A.R.Rinz, C.F.Gunter, D.E.Dennhardt, D.V.Mc Swain, E.M.Baucom, G.L.Wilson, M.S.Lemmon, P.J.Nyman, R.G.Sorge, A.Grimm, G.Bauer, H.Menrad, H.Mueller, J.Rohr, K.Riedel, M.Schuessler, R.Gibtner, R.Weissbrodt, S.Dagenbach, W.Schraml, V.Lever Jr., M.A.Bolton, T.M.Gould, B.S.Halstensen, G.R.Aylwin, H.E.Litchfield III, J.B.Hart, R.H.Keeler, S.C.Staats, D.L.Cheever, V.Cardoso, C.Olivares , P.Bailly, R.Stocker, B.Regnier, D.Dreux, A.Reiter-Loeffler, G.Heyde, M.Terek, C.Lorenzo, A.Chutko, A.N.Alsop, E.R.Cox, G.M.Pruette, J.L.Watt, J.M.Finnessy, K.D.Sanderson, M.S.Good, M.S.Ratchford, S.A.Zimmerman, C.S.Schroeder, M.M.Kolthoff, A.L.Escobedo, C.J.Jackson, D.H.Lindell, D.M.Jasper, E.A.Coram Jr., E.P.Yu, J.A.Decoster, J.L.Fish, P.R.Winthurst, R.C.Baechle, R.G.Miller, R.P.Banks, S.A.Ferguson, W.J.Ward, W.L.Bibbs, W.R.Holzgrafe, M.Valdez, K.Armbruester, W.Bischoff, J.Pinto, T.Sanchez F., F.Guerra, G.Salazar, C.L.Sebekow, D.A.Weber, D.L.Gilroy, E.G.Even, J.I.Fischels, J.P.Mills, J.S.Duhrkopf, R.E.Gardner, R.J.Babinat, A.D.Bass, A.J.Lamers, C.G.Boose, C.Miller, D.B.Strand, J.D.Peterson, J.L.Jensen, L.J.Thoms, L.R.Schmitz, M.A.Holtkamp, M.S.Elin, M.Vansickle, M.W.Griffin, R.A.Hanson, R.E.Wylie, R.M.Delcourt, S.W.Lawson, G.Nikelski, O.Woyke, W.Liebenwein, J.D.Steenkamp, J.A.Aparicio , E.Starks, G.N.Schmitz, K.A.Young, L.M.Thompson, L.S.Rannells, P.A.Baldwin, R.E.McCormick Jr., R.P.Carr, S.G.Heidemann, S.K.Foss, V.L.Canada, W.F.Bloes, C.Culp, D.C.Herold, D.E.Hanna, F.H.Harkness, J.W.Brown, L.Hammer, N.M.Bost, O.L.Gaston, R.J.Wilson, R.L.Boomgarden, T.R.Harkness, W.B.Butcher, L.A.Holman, L.C.Smith, R.J.Ratchford, B.A.Butters, C.D.Kilbourn, D.G.Fortin, D.N.Runyan, E.B.Pearson, G.R.Teerlinck, J.M.Erdahl, K.E.Collins, L.J.Foster, L.J.Smith, L.L.Stinson, P.A.Schreiber, P.A.Strelow, R.G.Mootz, R.Hummel, S.H.Phillips, A.D.D.S.Garcia, A.Kempfer, R.F.Myers, E.R.Miller, S.A.Dix, G.A.Carlson, P.S.Ingham, C.J.Hutchison, C.M.Schaumburg, D.H.Hartman, F.D.Niedert, M.R.Watkins, R.C.Schmitz, R.G.Uhren, R.W.Rhoads, J.L.Cedillo, M.A.Mateo, B.C.Stahler, B.L.Meighan, C.D.Gough, D.L.Clark, D.R.Petersen, J.K.Shinn, J.M.Farrell, L.V.Hughes, M.J.Weideman, M.L.Danner, S.King, S.L.Even, V.N.Hembree, F.Geubert, F.Resch, L.Ruhl, W.Bens, D.E.Young, N.Phelps, A.D.Weber, D.E.Poyner, F.J.Even, J.C.Marks, J.J.Parise, K.J.Dieken, L.Frost, P.B.Ambrose, R.E.Sickels, R.H.Carmichael, R.L.Woock, G.Duile, K.Wegerle, L.Abelshauser, L.Sturm, F.Pleite, J.F.Escribano, Q.Garcia H., C.T.Nguyen, S.C.Maury, E.C.Sullivan, M.E.Wright, K.J.Poyner, R.E.Garrison, S.K.Sheth, R.R.Haynes, J.L.Jordan, K.L.Albrecht, R.A.Dekezel, R.G.Johnson, T.L.Ladowski, M.Fernandez , D.R.Grapp, K.J.Hoffman, C.L.Riley, C.T.Weisbrook, D.Alexander, P.L.Bush, S.Thomas, G.Dupuis, M.W.Lewis, R.R.Hartman, S.A.Riddell, W.R.Payton, M.Rhoades, B.L.Whitlatch, D.C.Melton, D.V.Blanchard, E.J.Brown, E.R.Albracht, F.L.Luck, G.K.Raisbeck, G.M.Lentzkow, G.V.Pakreslis, J.E.Kirkpatrick, J.J.Fugate, K.E.Basken, L.N.Bell, L.Nguyen, M.J.Weber, M.R.Sullivan, N.J.Schrage, R.D.Sanderson, R.E.Hollenback, R.O.Rogers, S.J.Herington, N.De Leon, A.Just, L.Dominguez, M.Ballesteros, B.J.Jackson, J.E.Lange, J.J.Holverson, J.K.Johnson, R.D.Fulton, G.Beck, A.Moss, J.C.Barnes Jr., T.J.Koenigsfeld, S.M.Applonie, W.W.Barritt, W.L.Brissette, S.A.Hopkins, B.E.Dabney, C.A.Aldrich, C.A.Gibbs, D.J.Baldwin, E.L.Schneider Jr., G.Arnold, G.D.Hubbard, G.L.Riedesel, G.M.Gamble, G.W.Uchytil, J.A.Brown, K.F.Ferch Jr., L.K.Shields, L.W.Good, M.E.Prindle, M.E.Waage, M.L.Shanks, R.L.Sheedy, T.J.Garcia, T.M.Murphy, S.Saldivar, B.Baust, F.Salvador, M.Morales C., R.Cantalapiedra, D.L.Boeckmann, R.D.Bakken, S.K.Frye, A.D.Jacobson, G.F.Jones, M.Holzapfel, T.J.Hoffman, T.R.Schoenberger, M.J.Higgins, R.M.Shields, S.R.Loonan, J.W.Richards, A.Demir, B.P.Pegg, D.C.Tipple, W.P.Clarke Jr., A.Stapf, G.Fickenscher, I.Schaefer-Jonas, B.R.Simpson, C.A.Peterson, C.J.Sime, C.T.Vuk, G.P.King, K.D.Mangine, L.B.Epps, L.D.Woods, P.M.Saunders, R.A.Avila, R.F.Victor, R.J.Buzynski, R.S.Gindlesparger, S.J.Syhlman, V.A.Oldham, W.R.Morris, M.Auer, M.Glad, P.Bentzinger, P.Hochmuth, W.Lorenz, A.Buenestado, A.Donaire, F.Merino M., J.Perez S., B.M.Brustkern, D.Bumgardner, D.L.Shaner, L.M.Starks, R.G.Simons, R.J.Nissen, H.Scholl, J.L.Clendenin, M.C.King, D.M.Palmer, C.M.Wieland, D.Adelmund, E.J.Lebro Jr., H.S.Kopps, J.M.Mulder, M.C.Mauney, P.A.Lau, P.M.Gathercole, V.A.Glenn, W.T.Sorge, C.Blondeau, J.Barant, H.Cid, J.Serrano F., M.Escudero, D.T.Oswald, L.L.Larson, R.L.Stevens, W.C.Perkins, E.Wolferding, T.R.Helgeson, B.E.Harthoorn, C.L.Bienfang, C.L.Hofstadter, D.M.Bell, E.B.Caon, G.E.Trasamar, G.P.Elin, M.G.Moskowitz, M.J.Griffin, R.C.Nelson, S.D.Evans, C.Jelicic, W.Friess, A.Barquero , A.Brejano, A.Mandaloniz, C.Martin E., D.Mateo, M.Garrido, M.Ramos, M.Vallejo, D.M.Dawson, G.E.Bawek, G.F.Bush, H.D.Crain, J.R.Reindl, R.R.Engel, O.R.Vergara, R.Mueller, D.R.Chetwynd, L.F.Weiss, L.J.Toth, R.H.Harrold, F.Monreal, J.L.Navamuel, J.L.Torija, J.Novillo, P.Suela, B.A.Welu, D.L.Crimmins, J.C.Van Hook, J.F.Munn, J.L.Hungate, J.V.Vana, L.D.Newlon, M.A.Bushkie, P.A.Jaynes, V.C.Dhanens, A.J.Morris, H.Bierbauer, M.Mehler, N.Godeck, A.Ramirez, J.Piquer, M.Collado, M.Delgado, R.Parra, J.R.Heseman, H.Simonin, J.Serrano C., B.M.Dirck, J.A.Driver, T.H.Stoelk, W.C.Welzien, J.A.Scott, A.R.Toolate, C.K.Homrighausen, C.R.Stauffer, G.D.Hilton, R.J.Durkee, A.Rina, C.M.Woods, G.Theveny, C.A.Grems, V.S.Laud, **1976** A.Knerr,

Medical Claims employees, Moline, Illinois, 1979

K.Jenner, D.Gunther, A.A.Reiling, D.A.Johnson, D.E.Dawson-Ecker, D.J.Donahue, D.R.Dehn, G.D.Uherka, G.L.Sommers, J.A.Freese, J.F.Galloway, J.L.Brown, J.L.Thompson, J.M.Herring, J.Triggs, K.B.Kramer, K.L.Kashmarek, L.A.King, L.L.Ranum, M.A.Johnson, M.A.Nance, M.Ferry, M.J.Ayers, M.M.Engler, N.S.Jones-Thompson, O.T.Kinkade, P.J.Crowley, P.S.Harken, R.B.Delgado, R.D.Bullerman, R.D.Meade, R.J.Pagett, R.Tornes, R.W.Harris, S.D.Tiedt, T.Dorough, T.J.Brekke, W.C.Faust, J.Herring, A.Thoreau, H.Cochin, J.Boussion, M.Dubas, R.Marchon, A.Rutkowski, R.Brueckelmeier, A.S.Harris, C.L.Droste, D.R.Sorensen, G.G.Blank, J.M.Dygert, P.Jones, F.Santangelo, M.Gornik, P.Laun, U.Bever, V.Knapp, E.B.Everitt, J.A.Lang, J.F.Espiricueta, M.Jene, A.Ribeiro, B.W.Sorensen, E.C.Burmeister, J.P.Nyweide, R.D.Tyler, S.L.Wolf, V.E.Bisdorf, W.E.Miller, L.Sibert, A.Aleonero, G.J.Salisbury, V.K.Byers, M.F.Anderson, D.L.Mc Farland, P.A.Homolar, R.G.Jensen, B.S.Ireland, J.A.Carran Jr., M.Hicks, A.Kheireddine, J.Rothweiler, D.K.Steffen, M.E.Simbric, P.A.Peterson, R.D.Burton, T.G.Keith, V.J.Zeets, G.Renard, H.Jacquelin, P.Poignant, A.Ferati, H.Zobel, S.Fischer, W.Gutmann, A.P.Smith, M.E.Mason, R.D.Seibert Jr., V.H.Tarbox, S.Horwedel, F.A.Davidson Jr., M.Scherer, B.J.Megal, D.A.Woodhouse, D.Klunder, D.R.Gotthardt, D.T.Pham, E.D.Leonard, G.D.Mc Clain, H.W.Mullins, J.D.Fuhr, K.A.Ratliff, K.L.Hennings, K.M.Mertig, L.S.Brown, L.S.Westmorland, M.L.Corkery, P.T.Lamphier, R.N.Culp, S.E.Allen, T.E.Essex, W.A.Floyd Jr., M.E.Horst, J.L.Garcia, N.Gombault, B.Engelhardt, O.Yavuzer, R.Fabian, D.K.Newhoff, J.I.Sackett, L.R.Edgerton, D.R.Heath, I.D.Julion, M.L.Fairbanks, A.Ayaztepe, P.A.Mc Ginnis, S.Incognito, J.B.Barrett, J.S.Williams, R.A.Schoneman, R.D.Stedman, R.W.Mc Combs, S.J.Linton, I.Puschner, J.Goeppel, J.Hochlehnert, W.Ewald, A.P.Grove, B.J.McManus, C.C.Oliva, C.L.Mc Cullough, C.M.Sim, D.L.Adams, D.L.Miller, D.R.Noble Jr., E.D.Wolf Jr., E.I.Duranso, E.L.Polchow, G.A.Bush, G.R.Wadsager, J.J.Kremer, K.M.Begyn, L.C.Oliver, M.H.Johanning, M.K.Alter, M.S.Crowell, P.J.Clarke, P.K.Aring, R.A.Fisher, R.M.Vandevoorde, R.S.Hanft, S.J.Macheel, T.E.Zink, R.D.Puga, G.Marteau, G.Nourisson, M.Lantoine, V.Bozic, B.R.Glenn, G.E.Chambers, C.J.Stubenrauch, R.C.Burr, K.Rothhaar, C.I.Eckert, J.A.Kienast, S.K.Smith, C.Feuillatre, A.M.Haas, R.A.Peine, B.K.Hannigan, C.L.Mueller, J.E.Hudspeth, J.G.Appleby, J.J.Sweeney Jr., K.J.Myers, K.L.Potts, M.Gogishvili, R.W.Adams, S.A.Ganaway, T.E.Jones, T.H.Mix, M.Moualfi Aouina, E.Prismantas, G.Seewald, K.Becker, K.Christmann, M.Ayar, R.Schier, D.J.Homolar, G.L.Immich, A.J.Gianulis, B.A.Cassidy, B.W.Cook, D.J.Rodts, D.L.Brockway, D.L.Peppler, D.L.Witt, D.M.Blubaugh, D.M.Smith, J.A.Weirbach, J.L.Loonan, K.L.Swanson, M.H.Boren, P.A.Ludwig, R.D.Ahlberg, R.V.Quandt, S.B.Johnson, W.P.Beckmann, Y.J.Chartier, A.D.Santos, A.T.Pires, N.Sartori, O.S.Baumgarten, U.R.Rodrigues, A.Milic, H.Ettgen, K.Wickenhaeuser, G.H.Roach, J.F.Thompson, R.J.Wick, J.Novalic, A.R.Shaw, P.Ellett, A.D.D.Nascimento, C.M.D.Luz, D.Bender, H.Wagner, L.Kissmann, R.J.Messer, W.Wunsch, G.Throm, M.V.Alda , D.L.Wachtendorf, E.V.Thurm, A.Gil, E.Fernandez R., F.Martin G., J.Gamero, V.Rodriguez C., C.L.Johnson, D.Von Der Gathen, J.A.Jepson, L.C.Malcolm, L.M.Williams, M.L.Stowe, R.L.Bottorff, V.D.Hearn, G.Vivier, F.Spataro, M.Nemenich, D.J.Wright, D.L.Tworek, H.C.Runge Jr., M.Zeljkovic, W.Keller, N.A.Adams, C.C.Fretwell, C.S.Shaffer, D.D.Dorrance, G.K.Rewalt, J.F.Ware, L.L.Eastman, L.T.Harwood, M.A.Banks, M.A.Vickers, R.J.Hessel, T.M.Ryan, G.Turpin, A.Bourgeois, D.Depardieu, S.Marie, W.Guillemeau, Y.Giroguy, A.Kesberger, A.Xanthopulos, F.Bauer, H.Kuzmierz, H.Ripke, H.Schaefer, W.Butsch, E.Galvan, A.Benedett, C.R.Hurd, H.Krebs, O.Manteufel, A.Adell III, B.A.Meyer, D.A.Nelson, F.X.Brandi, J.C.Hostetter, J.Y.Campbell, K.P.Diehl, L.L.Bell, L.P.Begyn, M.C.Oehlerking, P.A.Dufel, R.E.Heber, R.F.Vozikis, A.Glaessner, A.Soret, P.Girault, H.Hasfeld, A.Rodriguez H., F.Martin C., J.Bellon, J.Delgado B., J.Fdz.-Maqueda, M.Goas, V.Kalkmann, J.D.Mc Vay, C.C.Immerzeel, M.D.Costa, A.L.Whitley, B.J.Ashurst, B.M.Crompton, D.M.Lawless, F.E.Ege, K.R.Chenoweth, L.J.Streif, L.M.Woods, M.A.Nelson, R.C.Petersen, S.K.Murphy, W.P.York, G.Woisard, P.Vacas, G.Klein, M.Strassner, W.Hoering, A.Criado, F.Romero S., J.A.Donaire, C.F.Watkins, D.L.Gremanis, D.R.Aslesen, J.D.Burau, H.Strauch, T.G.Zmuda, V.D.Groen, D.Betzold, M.J.Walker, A.Camacho, A.M.Vogt, B.A.Kish, R.D.Dochterman, T.J.Ryan, Y.M.Jorge, M.Duvallet, C.L'Episcopo, H.Neu, K.Goll, R.Shaqiri, S.Cendekovic, F.Ruiz, M.L.Young, C.Deschamps, G.Mace, J.L.Buck, J.L.Ehrenreich, M.L.Peyton, B.Pimic, M.F.Commodore, C.J.McComish Jr., D.A.Hoffman, J.A.Butler, J.B.Lang, L.M.Thoensen, P.J.Schmitt, W.F.Fulkerson, M.Fariney, D.M.Goodrich, M.G.Wilson, H.Stahl, G.M.Lindsay, J.E.Mullen, L.R.Duke, L.S.Enes, R.W.Lefferd, S.E.Jones, G.Oulama, D.Lessault, P.Larue, A.Bacher, A.Frick, C.Wallenstaetter, D.Ballreich, E.Herweh, G.Hassel, H.Fischer, H.Simon, H.Vogel, P.Schlechta, W.Ehrt, I.Robinson, B.L.Bowman, B.L.Jones, C.D.Campbell, C.N.Smith, G.Bayer, G.M.Hilbert, J.F.Hutchison, J.J.Wassenhove, K.D.Sievers, K.Lipiec, K.M.Moore, L.D.Swanson, S.A.Moseley, S.E.Daly, S.F.Hasken, A.Hoffmann, G.Hoffmann, H.Fritz, H.Lugenbiehl, K.Nunheim, M.Horn, U.Hesslinger, I.Garcia S., J.Rodriguez V., P.Rebollo, R.Grueso, C.K.Mathias, K.S.Dwyer, T.J.Walter, R.C.Seehase, R.L.Hamilton, B.K.Iversen, D.G.Gosden, D.R.Conklin, J.L.Smith, J.M.Bagg, K.S.Johannsen, K.W.Bolsinger, L.A.Meeske, M.D.Myers, M.E.Penne, R.A.Bjerke, R.F.Vanmeenen, M.Barbier, A.Zarans, B.Frohn, H.Moenig, R.Seberkste, T.Keller, J.N.Boyens, L.L.Lomker, L.W.Ferguson, B.Heyer, B.J.Sheley, C.F.Downey, C.G.Moneymaker, D.D.Woods, D.J.England, E.R.Fowler, E.V.Reed, J.L.Atkins, L.D.Carter, M.D.Senneff, M.E.Stover, M.H.Squires, R.L.Taylor, S.I.Fox, S.L.Bishop, S.L.Ernst, T.E.Clearman, A.Duran, G.Molina, J.Gomez P., B.K.Schultz, J.K.Powell, K.A.Hickerson, M.Gay, P.Barthon, K.Wessa, M.Wiebe, P.Nickola, W.Foerg, A.M.Quist, C.M.Simmons, L.J.Bell, D.R.Krueger, G.L.Meyers, R.A.Gordon, R.Devige, M.Huet, A.C.Carlson, C.S.Black, D.L.Packer, D.M.Ekin, D.P.Wasson, L.L.Masters, M.W.Lee, P.Seibers, R.D.Hansen, J.L.Villanueva, A.Busalt, A.Leimbeck, F.Caldarelli, H.Weik, K.Haas, A.N.Jimenez G., A.Rodriguez F., C.Torres, J.Aranda , L.Ignacio M., S.Bustos, C.I.Minteer, C.K.Moody, D.R.Dyer, R.J.Roman, V.W.Lehmkuhl, C.L.Van Wey, D.L.Carpenter, W.J.Nelson, K.E.Greenwood, W.D.Bruch, E.Dickemann, R.Oswald, A.J.Wagner, A.M.Dumolien, B.Capps, B.L.Peterson, C.E.Baker, D.J.Lee, D.R.Brummitt, E.M.Fox, H.A.Henderson, J.C.McIntosh, J.M.Church, K.D.Butler, L.A.Weston, M.D.Bealer, M.J.Festing-Smith, M.J.Parr Jr., M.Pass Jr., P.K.Northcutt, P.L.Allen, S.C.Dorbeck, T.G.Benac, T.J.Heath, W.Strosche, A.Lopes, A.Perez, J.Marcel, J.Tribot, K.Stahl, R.Unser, T.Huber, J.Zurita, D.L.Bausch, D.V.Hansen, G.D.Edwards, G.D.Martin, J.R.Hergert, J.R.Soldwisch, J.R.Wilson, R.A.Berthoud, R.H.Rech, R.O.Blain, W.M.Ebert, K.Wolf, J.Neebel, E.Mayfield, T.L.Kies, H.Sales, A.L.Fritz, D.R.Gresch, D.W.Jesse, G.L.Maring, K.A.Diehl, K.D.Kramer, K.K.Heiland, L.Davis, L.R.Burke, L.S.Miller, M.A.Mc Chane, M.D.Young, M.E.Wolf, R.J.Gilbraith, R.J.Nagelmiller, S.V.Marner, T.H.Watson, W.A.Ericson, W.L.Haynes, I.Varieux, J.Paupy, F.Groh, A.Esteban B., A.Luengo, F.Campos, J.Orgaz, R.Del Olmo, D.B.Webber, I.Fischer, B.J.Sparvier, D.A.Baele, J.E.Weber, J.H.Gilbert, J.S.Lerschen, M.L.Fraley, M.W.Keller, R.P.Spangler, S.L.Steagall, W.C.Graham, A.Blanche, A.Goncalves, S.A.Noble, A.Doukkali, J.H.Gallagher, M.F.Raymond, B.D.Morris, B.J.Mayle, C.A.Kirby, C.R.Demry, C.S.Gibson, C.S.O'Dell, D.A.Sackfield, D.C.Mitten, D.E.Habbena, D.J.Bussan, D.J.Langkamp, D.R.Elston Jr., E.H.Arku, H.P.Montez, J.A.Smith, J.H.Olson, J.J.Hartwig, J.R.Gustafson, J.S.Creen, J.T.Dowe, K.E.Allen, K.L.Kehe, M.A.Cloninger, M.T.Tull, M.W.Watkins, P.D.Ericksen, R.C.Fast, R.C.Johnson, R.C.Kuehl, R.L.Rist, R.R.Dodd, S.A.Ruhl, S.A.Wilson, S.B.Rydzik, T.F.Hayes, T.R.Waldbusser, W.C.Bartels, W.J.Dumolien, W.J.Stohlmeyer, M.Braz, P.Thorin, R.Lemosse, H.Balz, R.Klein, W.Roeckel, B.A.Huntley, L.O.Frakes, J.D.Budke, K.R.Webb, S.A.Minks, T.L.Hennel, L.Proctor, N.A.Atzen, R.Ledru, G.L.Bovee, J.P.Heister, P.M.Scherbroeck, R.F.Gorman, B.L.McCleery, B.W.Walline, C.G.Gomez, C.J.Charles, C.S.Murphy, C.T.Benson, D.A.Jones, D.A.Vanspeybroeck, D.J.Littig, D.J.Mickelson, D.J.Papish, D.K.Bradley, D.L.Bert, G.L.Littrel, J.C.Mc Dowell, J.F.Leigh, J.G.Ramos Jr., J.P.Winger, J.W.Barnes, K.L.Giesmann, L.A.Rusk, M.A.McCormick, M.L.Vanderlinden, P.L.Kulper, R.P.Dempsey, S.F.Hammer, S.J.Brennan, T.C.Rubley, T.J.Moseley, W.A.Baker, A.Da Fonseca, L.Da Fonseca, A.A.Clausman, P.M.Mc Cready, S.L.Robinson, T.K.Hall, B.Ziegler, D.N.Vancise, J.L.Williams, G.Bourgeois, M.Gonsard, M.Celik, P.Jaeger, S.Caramanna, B.K.Hartgrave, C.J.Ferguson, C.M.Hudson, D.F.Moon, D.L.Sigl, D.P.Werning, D.W.Tullis, F.A.Stewart, F.M.Ryser, G.R.Bingham, H.Rolfe, J.A.Blevins, J.D.Jenkins, J.E.Chenoweth, J.E.Temperley, J.L.Connor, J.L.Westmoreland, J.M.Hanson, J.W.Bustle, K.B.Lange, K.S.Nedoba, L.A.Chantry, L.L.Calease, M.A.Collins, M.D.Franks, M.Daugherty, M.J.McCarville, M.W.Smith, N.M.Johnson, P.A.Essmann, R.D.Ford, R.D.Stephenson, R.G.Nielsen, R.H.Hall, R.H.Skinner, R.J.Ramirez, R.L.Davis, R.P.Gloe, R.R.Miescke, R.Segura, S.C.Sonnack, T.Brooks, T.J.Brosius, T.P.Lunardi Sr., V.J.Henderson, W.H.Foster, J.Decreuze, A.Wolf, D.Kunze, E.Arnold, E.Hasic, K.Schwab, O.Wessely, W.Kasparick, A.R.Hovden, R.K.Thompson, A.Rose, D.W.Hunter, K.K.Howell, R.J.Christoffersen, R.M.Moberly, P.Penasson, N.Lamy, L.Daniel, A.F.Coppejans, B.E.Lehnen, B.H.Bland, C.D.Longeville, C.F.Norris, C.L.Cordes, D.D.Boisvert, D.L.Combites, D.L.Johnson, D.L.Ward Sr., D.Navarro, E.J.Goedken, F.J.Hunter, G.E.Price, J.C.Bradford, J.E.Galle, J.S.Dolan, K.A.Higgins, K.J.Overholt, L.E.Cain, L.G.Jessen, M.C.Leonard, M.R.Viaene, P.A.Swanson, R.A.Wach, R.J.Baker, R.W.Hemphill Jr., S.A.Gaede, S.A.Junge, S.H.McQuary, T.G.Cornmesser, T.J.Vesey, T.R.Lawrence, U.O.Rios, V.A.Rumler, W.R.Hutchison, J.B.Olivera, J.R.Hurd, A.Costanza, A.Klingler, S.Parlak, A.Calleja, B.Perez C., J.Nuñez V., J.Sandoval , M.Mencias, V.Diaz G., S.K.Mixdorf, A.D.Snyder, A.M.Guerra Jr., A.Zertuche, B.J.Mack, C.A.Southerland, C.E.Kluck, C.L.Jacquot, D.C.Seger, D.H.Bergert, D.J.Dalessandro, D.J.Dunlap, D.J.Rettenmeier, D.K.Lamphier, D.R.Hope, E.A.Sanders, E.F.Stanton Jr., G.C.Carrell, G.J.Aitchison, G.W.Steltenpohl, J.A.Herbert, J.A.Trent, J.D.Coogan, J.F.Cramer, J.K.Pitts, J.M.Gloden, J.R.Parrish, J.Y.Patrick, L.L.Jones, M.E.Twaites, M.J.Burnett, O.L.Molstre, P.E.Lee, R.A.Walas, R.J.Behncke, R.J.Desmith, R.L.Blew, R.L.Lueth, S.J.Kaesbauer, S.Lucas, T.L.Murphy, T.N.Bullock Sr., V.E.Smith, W.T.Decastecker, J.Massar, O.Serkizyan, Z.Teran, E.Fernandez T., F.Zapatero, J.Sanz, D.A.Stemp, L.E.Howard, R.E.Frederick, R.Feuerstein, D.A.Truesdell, D.L.Hinchman, D.W.Rogers, G.L.Youngblood, M.A.Reed, S.D.Felsted, W.C.Larsen, P.E.Traeger, I.Govaski, L.F.Lentz, M.L.Meeks, T.L.Steffen, A.B.Pulford, A.L.Jones, B.A.Stoneking, B.C.Gillitzer, B.K.Malloy, B.M.Dockerty, B.S.Jones, C.R.Steffen, D.A.Cordingley, D.F.Fourtner, D.R.Lund, H.M.Dierks, I.F.Hayslett, J.C.Shelton, J.L.Eilderts, J.M.Cornmesser, K.B.Dirck, L.T.Hansen, M.A.Steffen, M.K.Diericks, M.Oliva, N.E.Miller, N.H.Wistedt, R.A.Lodico, R.A.Ray, R.A.Sheppard, R.J.Laermans, R.M.Alexander, R.M.Cooley, R.M.Fliehler, S.C.Doye, S.L.Knipp, T.C.Lekar, T.M.Grimes, T.R.Slock, W.K.Lilliman, I.Villarrubia, J.Fdz.Moreno, L.Sanchez-C, M.Gonzalo, W.E.Burnett, M.R.Bright, S.P.Chamberlin, D.J.Sofranko, G.W.Neisen, J.L.Eckstein-Swift, T.L.Middleton, A.L.Hagerman, A.L.Whitmore, A.W.Hansen, B.R.Eichhorst, C.L.Jordan, D.E.Olson, D.F.Allen, D.K.Worner, D.M.Gallens, D.M.Kiddoo, E.J.Hermsen, G.J.Murphy, G.W.Neff, J.A.Facen, J.Dedobbelaere, J.H.Peters, J.K.Koontz, J.N.Mekus, J.W.Ackley, J.W.Blaser, K.G.Stelpflug, L.F.Cathelyn, L.M.Nicholson, L.Nimmers, M.D.Lincoln, M.G.Jacobson, M.L.Wittwer, M.L.Woodard, N.A.Helgerson, N.A.Warren, N.T.Spurgetis, R.C.Anderson, R.E.Norin, R.L.Carton, S.C.Engebretson, S.J.Brown, T.G.Cruz, V.L.Serres, W.E.Peterson, C.Ylan, B.Yilmaz, E.Demli, A.Rodriguez C., E.Garcia P., F.Bernabe, J.Merino, S.Crespo, E.D.Corwin, P.J.Siler, V.D.Nuebel, C.T.Wray, D.N.Rowland, G.D.Neale, K.A.Hoverstad, K.F.Werner-Deutsch, K.M.McQuillen, L.G.Gilbert, M.J.Pearson, N.V.Orlandea, T.C.Annis, M.Porcheron, A.Mueller, E.Mittmesser, F.Kowatschitsch, K.Dann, K.Schneider, W.Blatt, L.Merati, F.J.Manrique, J.F.Pulido, M.R.Iglesias, R.L.Autric , F.C.Kimber, R.S.Kussatz, E.Paquet, K.Bellaire, K.Hofer, L.Schweizer, N.Kirsch, F.Amoros, J.D.Vizuete, C.L.Schultz, D.L.Curtis, E.C.Kloft, E.D.Cooper, E.D.Funk, F.J.Corbett, G.A.Paul, G.L.Mullens, J.J.Corley, J.S.Yates, J.W.Sommer, K.D.Kuntz, K.L.Gregory, M.D.Davis, M.L.Feldpouch, R.A.Moeller, R.B.Villarreal, R.L.Cary, S.A.Layman, S.R.Rockwell, T.N.Craigmiles, W.C.Cribbs, D.C.Rexroth, H.E.Sierra, D.E.Wedeking, D.L.Schake, H.L.Willhite, J.M.Smith, K.E.Schoonover, S.J.Randall, G.Hernánez , M.Vidakovic, A.W.Parker, B.E.Luxmore, C.E.Schwendinger, C.G.Schneekloth, C.R.Zaerr, D.D.Mc Dougall, D.E.Artus, G.A.Bowles, G.A.Clearman, H.B.Rodriguez, J.D.Hanne, J.S.Henyan, K.R.Howlett, M.Barnhart, M.J.Bennett, M.P.Gentry, R.E.Hungate, R.E.McDonald, R.E.Nutt, R.J.Fluegel, R.N.Melton, R.W.Sheldon, S.A.Burleson, S.J.Till, T.J.Lovelady, V.L.Selhost, R.C.Hodgson, M.Huver, A.Carrasco, A.Montero V., A.Requena, F.Rivera, J.Muñoz M., M.Ruiz, R.Mora, F.Vanblarcom, S.P.Garrett, C.A.Girsch, G.D.Boswell, A.Hueyuek, H.Herbel, J.A.Wright, A.C.Costa, B.Keesmann, M.A.Ardell, M.P.Etringer, A.L.Johnson, C.A.Ellis, C.R.Doyle, C.S.Moon, D.C.Kies, D.J.Goetz, D.L.Britton, D.L.Cherba, D.W.Ruffcorn, E.A.Lovette, G.M.Venegas, H.L.Halsall, J.D.Edwards, J.D.Rhodes, J.G.Pollock, J.S.Dobereiner, K.S.Edmund, M.G.Boland, P.E.Leroy, R.Colvin, R.J.Wohlwend, R.L.Gamble,

R.Lucas, S.L.Sickles, T.E.White, T.M.Wehner, T.S.Early, R.F.Gerling, G.Pace, H.Catal, K.Oezzencir, K.Thorn, S.Burranchon, J.J.Steffen, N.L.Dolan, P.F.Brautigam, E.Mulder, R.Vogt, V.Freitag, H.R.Drewes, J.J.Pedersen, R.R.Canham, M.L.Robbins, L.Herdtweck, P.L.Michel, R.L.Suer, A.B.Price, B.J.Turner, D.D.McDanel, G.D.Halligan, J.D.Pirkey, J.G.Logan, J.K.Smith, L.A.Kelly, M.D.Myers, R.C.Pritchard, S.F.Klemmer, S.K.Wingler, W.D.Mugge, W.L.Petersen, T.Howald, D.Cazimi, D.Friederich, N.Cetaj, O.Yueksel, J.Rodriguez G., P.Cubero, D.A.Mullen, D.M.Kaufmann, M.J.Behnke, S.A.Cuvelier, M.A.Augustine, C.Feigenbutz, F.Glaser, J.Scherrer, A.F.Culpepper, B.J.Logue, C.A.Loding, C.J.Lievens, C.R.Boswell, C.W.Dotson, D.J.Johnson, D.K.Hanten, F.C.Bausch, G.H.Zelaya, G.Schima, H.M.Ross, J.D.Burvee, J.E.Morris, J.E.Schebler, J.K.Prohl, J.L.Kinney, J.L.Whyte, J.M.Bensing-Voyek, K.F.Hare, K.L.Nissen, L.M.Smith, M.A.Barnes, M.F.O Brien, M.J.Lusson, M.R.Vandendriessche, P.E.Stledger, P.J.Bute, P.Sapato, R.A.McMurray, R.E.Webb Jr., R.G.Karn Jr., R.M.Whittaker, S.E.Maston, S.L.Bishop, S.L.Cook, T.G.Cruz, T.J.Dixon, T.L.Anderson, W.Messerly II, J.Leroux, M.Lefevre, M.Rousseau, H.Mehl, H.Sevinc, M.Labropoulos, A.Del Cerro, A.P.Castañeda, A.Sanchez M., E.Vazquez, F.Espinosa, J.A.Bolaños, J.Gomez P., J.Gomez R., J.M.Perez M., J.Martin L., M.Aroca , M.Benito, R.Alfonso , R.De La Camara, R.Serrano C., S.Martin T., Z.Martin M., R.W.Jackson, L.L.Sickman, G.Grivotet, A.Ramtani, S.Sen, H.L.Lemon, M.J.Andersen, M.K.Backes, S.K.Chapman, I.Johnson, C.J.Bates, D.J.Briggs, D.J.Hayes, E.M.Defauw, E.M.Holman, E.M.Meincke, J.C.Girven, J.K.Jungk, L.D.Mc Coll, M.D.Sample, M.E.Nolen, N.E.Taylor, P.D.Seger, R.A.Mueller, R.C.Sehmann, R.L.Anderson, S.R.Lovell, T.B.Lockhart, F.Gouache, J.Adam, A.Krupp, F.Vella, S.Micelisopo, U.Frick, A.Felix, A.Simon, C.Arnanz, E.Serrano T., F.Rodriguez G., F.Roman, J.Lavado, J.M.Fernandez M., M.Perez M., S.Gomez G., J.M.Hartson, M.C.Coronado, D.Dirks, H.L.Plumb, K.D.Fleshner, K.R.Stallings, R.R.Rennick, S.L.Adams, R.Charlot, G.A.Cirricione, B.Bigott, M.D.Smith, C.A.Smith, C.C.Jensen, C.D.Dodd, D.D.Kipp, D.E.Jaggers, D.H.Hebbel, D.P.Harris, D.R.Schilb, F.H.Rasso, F.L.Leathers Jr., G.P.Pena, J.A.Leedle, J.C.Fletcher, J.O.Harris, K.D.Friend, K.E.Schramm, K.R.Wilson, L.K.Wilson, M.C.Hudson, M.L.Dutkowski, M.P.Stocker, M.R.Demeyer, R.B.Guse, R.G.Peters, R.Johnson, R.L.Ortiz, R.T.Kerfoot, S.E.Mc Farland, T.A.Kolls, T.C.Peterson, W.Stettler Jr., P.A.Friedrich, S.Servat, D.J.Schenk, A.Pagani, D.Constantin, E.Schikor, G.Eckert, G.Michel, H.Meyer, H.Schwenzfeier, H.Ziegler, K.Kral, P.Theis, R.Kuchenmann, R.Marker, R.Matzner, T.Jaster, L.C.Gerken, C.Thillou, S.K.Meredith, P.J.Hicks, S.A.Biretz, B.J.Hilton, B.W.Fritz, C.A.Mihm, C.A.Mylerberg, C.L.Schiebel, D.L.Gravitt, D.M.Kaukaskie, G.L.Dorhout, H.H.Esslinger, J.Chasky Jr., J.L.Walton, J.O.Reavis, J.R.Wilmoth, K.C.Long, K.P.Petersen, L.A.Tolbert Jr., L.G.Yeubanks, M.A.Schaecher, M.K.Hall, P.C.Bixby, P.R.Anderson, R.D.Brower, R.D.Lantz, R.J.Armstrong Sr., R.L.Stearns, V.A.Vandevoorde, W.R.York, M.Namyslo, M.Sitzenstuhl, J.A.Gomez, E.Basparmak, C.L.McDowell, A.A.Zakaria, D.L.Mc Caw, D.L.Polchow, G.W.Hertz Jr., K.T.Gann, L.Hart, L.L.Jarvis, P.S.Stover, S.K.Margelofsky, T.M.Whiting, T.P.Henning, A.Araujo, J.Bonneson, J.Dubus, R.Brechemier, E.Dollwett, F.Kitzmann, S.Luengo, B.J.Estes, C.A.White, E.R.Camacho, E.R.Imfeld, J.O.Nazario, K.L.Dergo, K.R.Kessler, L.L.Feldman, M.A.Slater, S.D.Gooch, S.L.Payne, S.S.Schreiber, T.E.Carpenter, W.P.Wohlford, A.J.Geuna, I.Franco, L.Freitag, H.Castro, C.Sarisoy, F.Fruechtl, G.Petzold, G.Schmidt, H.Heckmann, H.Kinder, I.Novoselac, K.Dagenbach, K.Lampe, K.Ramsauer, L.Bauer, L.Seibert, M.Bellaire, M.Mathes, P.Martus, P.Massoth, R.Hauser, R.Mitter, R.Rueck, R.Voit, W.Hoffner, B.T.Mallaney, S.J.Mahrt, D.Limet, G.Pierre, J.Domalain, U.Schuchardt, V.Salamone, B.J.Fredericks, B.J.Melahn, C.J.Collier, C.Y.Hartley, D.Debuysere, D.L.Egger, D.L.Hall, D.W.Robinson, J.A.Adams, J.L.Jones, J.M.Hoover, K.A.Christie, L.K.Miller, R.E.Sipes, R.G.Nicholson, S.E.O'Hearn, T.J.Marshall, T.R.Groves, W.G.Walker, E.M.Falls, K.Karmann, D.Ruet, D.M.Knaack, G.A.Robinett, H.Friesen, J.E.Muse, M.A.Amunrud, P.H.Plyler, G.Blin, D.Cirillo, E.Baumann, M.Eskiocak, V.Dujmovic, M.Stojakovic, G.L.Shedd, J.C.Stiltner, G.Gruenbeck, J.Fickler, B.L.Downey, B.R.Wilson, C.E.Sargent, J.E.Newcomer, J.P.Styre, J.Paris, R.V.Wells, W.F.McGovern, J.Jimenez, B.J.Biscontine, B.J.Shlaes, C.C.Caudill Jr., C.J.Hoover, D.J.Grosse, D.L.Swanson, D.R.Anderson, G.A.Callihan, K.A.Johnston, M.J.Malone, R.A.Leibfried, R.A.Raap, S.K.Depyper, S.M.Pullen, T.R.Cox, C.Paroutaud, T.Archambault, H.Rauchholz, P.Gallistl, D.Nuñez V., F.Romero A., S.Ramos , J.Merchan, A.Polat, V.A.Griffith, L.A.Dobrichan, B.J.Hall, J.A.De Meester, J.M.King, M.Charlebois, W.Wilson, A.Vaurette, J.Savigny, M.Deschamps, E.Wandsleb, F.Werner, R.Oez, M.K.Smith, A.M.Carton, C.L.Lincoln, D.F.Hanson, D.S.George, S.B.Rains, V.M.Phelps, D.Brochet, G.Turbak, J.Boivin, J.Mattern, J.Perez, A.Wendt, G.Sommer, I.Goldboom, K.Goll, K.Hufnagel, O.Ugurel, W.Kissel, W.Meyer, C.A.Blanchard, C.E.Hull, C.J.Olson, D.J.Roling, G.W.Brunette, J.T.Kreider, J.T.Tucker, L.J.Waller, M.J.Weir, M.R.Klag, R.A.Frana Guthrie, S.A.Casillas, W.L.Fountain, W.R.Butterfield, E.R.Rohde, D.Branjonneau, J.Pitou, A.Sevimli, D.Etsch, E.Herbst, H.Maurer, L.Golemac, M.Poremski, W.Lederle, W.Schweizer, R.J.Nelissen, R.Chaudeau, R.Muench, A.M.Kovacich, N.Scherer, W.L.Wiggins, C.M.Gafeney, D.C.Martens, D.J.Mueller, F.M.McKee, J.E.Paup, J.Moody, J.Watts Jr., M.L.Ray, N.C.Stover, E.Vaccaro, L.Reischmann, W.Martin, F.Garcia B., J.L.Lozano, K.R.Marr, M.L.Robins, A.Lebrun, M.Hofmann, V.Bilgic, D.K.Muller, J.L.Dalrymple, K.Stapf, J.Viaud, P.Mercier, B.P.Thompson, D.G.Turmel, D.J.Knudtson, D.P.Kelsall, D.R.Mehlert, G.D.Collins, I.L.Bland, J.M.Kemp, J.M.Rakonjac, K.S.Elster, M.G.Mootz, M.L.Goyen, N.D.Swanson, P.E.Bonstrom Jr., R.E.Ricketts, R.W.Baker, S.L.Colston, W.R.Romans, W.A.Haughton, B.Bousquet, J.Lami, B.Cejas-Palenzuele, B.Mladenovic, G.Silveira, W.Wachtel, A.Palencia, M.T.Imber, J.B.Anderson, J.P.Cravero, A.H.Hernández, C.Gonzalez, D.E.Peterson, J.F.Mitchell, C.L.Roberts, J.Alcantara, C.Gonzales-Cadierno, G.Pierrot, W.Malsac, B.Ehlers, C.A.Richardson, C.C.Rousseau, D.M.Sage, E.A.Tannreuther, J.D.Kretzman, J.R.Voelzke, L.J.Lodico, M.J.Cini, M.Kotecki, T.P.Thomson, Y.Liu, J.Lalevee, G.Gutekunst, H.Holdstein, H.Koch, J.Freuschle, K.Gruenwald, M.Lorenz, R.Schlichter, T.Drixler, U.Irmer, U.Jurack, A.J.Kellett, D.Lauer, G.Weingaertner, K.Miltner, V.Monachino, W.Werneke, J.E.Lang, M.R.Greene, R.H.Brooks, A.J.Schwarz, A.W.Koelling, B.L.Chapin, D.A.Cogdill, D.E.McGovern, D.J.Rugger, D.L.Ingham, D.M.Francis, G.Schwenk, J.R.Hinke, K.D.Baxter, M.A.Denn, M.C.Chesmore, N.Hamm, R.W.Svobodny, S.C.Anderson, D.Poisson, G.Baratin, C.Brechtel, L.Frey, P.Etzel, W.Lampert, A.Bayo, A.Rodelgo, E.Garcia D., J.M.Blazquez , A.M.Rogers, D.A.Anderson, D.A.Ford, D.A.Masteller, D.D.Debaene, D.D.Kuhens, D.E.Steere, D.Ewen, D.L.Vanerem, G.E.De Greif, G.L.Kass, J.D.Lehman, J.G.Dockendorf, J.H.Learn, J.N.Bartholomew, J.T.Moeller, K.F.Schneider, K.M.Stoner, K.N.Reiter, K.R.Bradfield, L.E.Dempster, L.Latak, M.E.Fisher, M.J.Schultz, N.W.Zier, O.L.Beitel, R.A.Mc Gee, R.J.Welte, R.K.Johnson, R.L.Heidemann, R.L.Lindell, R.L.Martin, R.L.Oldenburger, R.L.Pfiester, R.L.Stone, R.W.Wold, S.L.Babeu, T.A.Knipp, T.E.Zoelle, T.J.Short, T.P.McCann, W.J.Berry, J.F.Martin H., C.C.Schmit, K.E.Mc Allister, M.J.Carney, O.Randall Jr., S.L.Green, T.W.Quinn, A.E.Schmit, D.A.Mirs, J.A.Johnson, M.R.Holle, R.A.McCoy, R.B.Myers, R.J.Huber, R.J.Johnson, S.L.Pesek, G.H.Heying, W.A.Stevens, D.D.Vannoster, E.Carlson, E.E.Mickelsen, E.W.Hildebrandt, K.G.Lansing, P.E.Campbell, R.M.Appel, R.R.Coussens, R.S.Ramza, S.L.Rash, S.R.Lanzen, T.A.Sizemore, J.Bourgoin, K.Wolf, R.Faulhaber, R.Gross, A.Sanchez F., D.Hurtado, J.J.Jimenez G., J.L.Lopez S., J.L.Pizarro, M.Montoro, C.J.Brandel, D.W.Alexander, G.R.Fuller, L.V.Gluesing, P.E.Verschoore, R.H.De Vries, T.D.Seaman, T.J.Boyd, V.L.Ellis, K.M.Pietraszewski, A.Gauthier, P.J.Eastman, P.W.Turri III, E.D.Quasny, J.W.Lentzkow, L.E.Stephens, L.R.Dennis, R.J.Bormann, S.A.Michels, G.Humel, G.Werst, A.Antunez, I.Jimenez A., L.F.Pavon, A.J.Schmitt, B.E.Wilharm, C.L.Mc Clain, D.B.Taylor, D.C.Winston, D.D.Madsen, D.Finck, D.G.Hoskins, D.J.Fuller, J.C.Watson, J.E.Carlson, J.E.Santamour, J.L.Aguilar, J.L.Staniger, J.M.Burleson, J.W.Boruff, M.R.Long, T.F.Tock, T.W.Head, W.E.Blumhoff, W.R.McCleary, E.Sanchez A., J.Callejo, J.Zaragoza, E.S.Bergland, K.C.Mosley, D.L.Jacob, D.P.Johnston, F.D.Boots, J.D.Flaherty, J.D.Swanson, L.K.Ziegler, R.E.Fuller, R.J.Beyhl, S.M.Bromme, T.J.Arthur, F.Castaner, J.Lory, J.Marchon, R.Lagrange, A.Back, F.Danner, G.Wegner, W.Lohmann, A.Pantoja, D.J.Kubik, G.A.Hall, M.P.Heneghan, S.D.Thompson, D.L.Frost, D.P.Edsill, G.A.Handke, H.J.Brant, K.E.Lindley, C.E.Wiggins, C.J.Smith, D.A.Bush, D.E.Mueller, D.J.Lees, J.A.Northcutt, J.B.Sayles, J.D.Phillis, J.E.Moore, J.E.Volz, J.I.Anderson, J.L.Crummy, J.L.Petersen, J.M.Alstedt, J.R.Conroy, J.T.Vols, K.A.Seger, K.L.Gasser, P.J.Murphy, P.P.Schmidt, R.D.Haugen, R.E.Scott, R.W.Rogers, S.E.Misfeldt, T.M.Taylor, W.K.Meyer, A.Rubio, C.Ortiz, J.A.Diaz, J.Barroso, J.L.Maroto, J.Labrado, L.Ahijado, P.Almodovar, V.Moreno F., A.R.Hepler, D.S.Suby, J.L.Henley, D.D.Tyer, J.M.Gleason, M.G.Miller, M.G.Nelsen Jr., P.E.Frisch, R.C.Rhode, T.C.Woods, B.C.Melton, B.L.Perez, C.Barajas, C.Fuller, D.L.Clevenger, G.H.Becker, G.L.Wonser, J.A.Martinez, J.F.Herbert, J.W.Hargrave, M.D.Koppen, S.A.Freeman, S.L.Voss, W.D.Bainbridge, W.L.Dowell, B.Zahm, C.L.Hungate, T.G.Kotrogiannis, H.Duratovic, O.Kamin, G.R.Bean, L.J.Klendworth, L.M.Meyer, R.F.Emanuel, T.D.Scheidel, C.A.Neuendorf, D.A.Rogers, J.F.Benson, R.A.Handke, R.K.Vanderbilt, G.E.Hicok, J.E.Barnes, J.Barbosa, M.Jackson, P.Fritz, **1977** J.C.Walters, M.J.Verhulst, J.Beguinot, C.Guillard, M.Noel, B.Rabe, E.Buehler, F.Grueb, G.Hohler, J.Herrmann, N.Seiler, R.Kirsch, W.Wetz, D.S.White, A.L.Lopez, A.M.Nimmer, B.J.Stone, C.L.Pieper, C.T.Sherrill, D.J.Duffey, D.J.Ghrist, D.J.Skantz, D.L.Gramenz, D.L.Kramer, D.L.Malm, D.M.Bigham, D.M.Foley, D.Popp, D.R.Baker, D.R.Hess, D.R.Lemke, D.W.Paschke, E.G.Wethington, J.A.Ries, J.A.Stacey, J.E.Cochran, J.O.Nieting, J.R.Degreve, J.R.Henkels, J.R.McCarthy, J.R.Rasmussen, J.S.Virnig, K.A.Bonnen, K.E.Cramer, K.H.Friesen, K.S.Rogers, L.B.Fields, L.E.Nourse, L.R.Thomason, M.A.Bailey, M.C.Mc Kinney, M.D.Bragg, M.E.Ellis, M.K.Block, M.K.Pulford, P.F.McGill, P.J.Pensyl, P.L.Carter, P.L.Mallett, R.A.Boge, R.A.Graham, R.A.Hatch-Mc Gohan, R.A.Vandenberghe, R.G.Saylor, R.S.Early, R.S.Etten, R.W.Swim, S.C.Van Earwage, T.L.Davis, T.N.Litton, W.C.Rehn, W.L.Sutton, M.Malherbe, D.Wilhelm, H.Schulze, H.Thoni, S.Torner, U.Kurz, V.Steinmetz, H.L.Johnston, K.D.Iverson, L.D.Kleckner, R.J.Frazier, T.L.Erbst, L.Tesch, D.R.Clow, E.R.Keay, M.D.Noel, M.S.Sottos, R.A.Wollin, R.C.Wells, D.A.Hill, D.W.Price, J.P.Burkey, V.M.Weber, D.C.Payne, L.R.Eastman, R.E.Mc Daniel Jr., A.L.Wichrowski, A.R.Graham, A.W.Carmack, B.R.Beadle, C.A.Benhart, C.A.Ortiz, C.M.Vandyke, C.P.Bleuer, D.A.Davis, D.A.Packer, D.A.Sheldon, D.E.Lewis, D.E.Riddell, D.K.Breiby, D.M.Johnson, F.E.Cashman, F.V.Wright, G.D.Wheeler, G.P.Garnica, H.A.Hohensee, H.D.Samuels, H.H.Crook, J.A.Mesmer, J.M.Christensen, J.M.Jones, J.S.Foster, K.D.Power, K.F.Dewater, K.J.Timmerman, K.L.Johnson, K.L.Schmitz, L.K.Mathews, M.A.Johnson, M.E.Addington, M.E.Deer, M.E.Osborn, M.M.Selhost, M.V.Klinkner, R.D.White, R.J.George, R.J.O'Dell, R.L.Eichelberger, R.S.Downing, R.W.Dorathy, S.W.Reilley, W.J.Brown, W.S.Murray, W.T.Long, R.Communeau, Y.Petitpas, B.Goecmen, K.Goebel, K.Loesch, M.Hartmann, P.Erlewein, P.Mollet, V.Freitag, W.Froehlich, W.Kondrusas, A.Blazquez M., A.Cedillo, A.Illana, A.J.Soldevilla, A.Saavedra, C.Sanchez M., D.J.Soler, E.Torrejon, F.Fernandez M., F.Pascual, G.Godoy, J.A.Ahijado, J.Bejar, J.Botonero, J.Castañeda, J.J.Llorente, J.L.Conde, J.Macias M., J.Orgaz, L.Arroyo, L.Jerez, L.Sanchez S., M.Gil, M.Jimenez M., M.Martin-F., P.Magan, S.Diaz, S.Patiño, J.C.Vermeulen, F.Groeger, L.A.Gray, L.Madlock, R.L.Lundberg, R.R.Krucker, M.Fournier, V.L.Martin, A.G.Almanza, A.L.Carr, B.C.Holstlaw, C.Dreon, C.L.Engholm, C.L.Olson, C.R.Tisdale, D.E.Adams, D.E.Feeney, D.G.Walls, D.L.Elliott, D.M.Curry, E.H.Lutz, E.J.Simon, G.A.Declerck, G.B.Wainwright, G.H.Klavohn, G.Y.Hunt, H.L.Baker, J.A.Bell, J.C.Rastede, J.D.Swanson, J.J.Headley, J.M.Betzle, J.M.Haynes, J.R.Davis, J.R.Radosevich, J.S.Devolder, K.A.Griffin, K.R.Cassatt Jr., M.D.Officer, M.E.Neels, M.L.Castro, M.W.Jenkins, P.A.Vogel, P.D.Quinn, P.H.Bishop, P.M.Retterath, R.A.Martin, R.L.Shaffer, R.P.Hensley, R.W.Moore, S.J.Heinz, S.L.Schultz, S.M.Cullison, S.S.Corwin, T.Quinn, J.Fernandes, H.Atik, M.Djuric, P.Nedic, R.Metzner, U.Bojchev, F.Sojo, J.Garcia S., M.Mayo, B.J.Bennett, D.R.Utech, D.I.Lowrey, H.K.Bowman, J.L.Ihlenfeldt, J.M.Delarosa, L.L.Portz, B.J.Johnson, K.F.Hill, A.A.Taylor, B.J.Kelso, C.M.Johnston, C.S.Griffin, D.M.Starks, E.J.Conroy, E.W.Petersen, F.L.Black, J.E.Harsh, K.H.Stegman, L.D.Sigler, L.L.Link, L.Thurmond Jr., L.W.Martin, M.E.Anderson, M.J.Wheeler, N.E.McEniry, N.R.Smith, P.A.Fleming, P.A.Geddes, P.K.Ryser, P.S.Huey, R.C.Thome, R.J.Wiedner, S.K.Billings, T.J.Collis, T.R.Smith, V.A.Brown, C.Montemitro, J.D.Sass, L.L.Busch, V.M.Hopkins, F.Schmitt, D.A.Felderman, D.D.Bach, D.P.Johnson, J.Turmeau, M.E.Parker, P.Sacher, K.A.Howard, A.Da Costa, C.J.Hanten, D.C.Snider, D.E.Hutcherson, D.J.Dorr, D.R.Brimeyer, J.C.Kinney, K.J.Enright, K.R.Peterson, T.M.Gordon, V.A.Dolter, W.M.Scheppele, W.S.Gehner, Y.Chang, A.Le Roy, J.Remy, A.Montemitro, U.Persch, B.A.Borne, E.A.Mason, F.H.Koch, G.W.Nicholson, J.W.Ough, M.S.Sims, P.R.Davis, R.A.Sinclair, R.A.Young, R.F.Jordan, R.Fuller, R.J.Bond, S.M.Lamberti, V.L.Thorson, J.Thiry, B.Nolleau, G.Dackermann, G.Poetzsch, D.W.Evans, L.R.Ames, P.C.Elphinstone, R.A.Falcioni, K.L.Anderson, J.D.Lamos, P.G.Espeland Jr., A.Duggan, D.A.Carter, D.G.Robinson, E.L.Van Fleet, E.P.Stolley, F.A.Swicegood, G.Vandergroef, J.A.Jensen, J.C.Driscoll, J.K.Van Nest, J.R.Andon, K.L.Hilk-Brokken, L.D.Crane, L.R.Reiss, M.C.Mason, M.J.Brodell, R.A.Green, R.E.Wells, S.A.Sims, S.E.Baldwin, Y.J.Lessard, Z.S.Hawley, D.Constantin, C.Wald, P.Feuerstein, R.Pfeifer, M.Hernandez A., R.D.Stracener, H.Kemler, L.M.Carey-Grant, R.J.Carey, P.Lesage, C.J.Eckhoff-Knock, T.E.Bonwell, M.Sanli, A.C.Antony, A.E.Logan, B.D.Evans, B.E.Johnson, C.D.Jorgensen, C.E.Hurt, D.L.Shearer, G.L.Schuler, J.J.Fuller, J.L.Krizek, J.R.Burke, J.S.Cook, M.L.Ruhter, N.D.Gosa, S.M.Mac Call, T.L.Mc Clellan, V.M.Dharia, W.R.Williams, K.Tadic, P.Kunzmann, A.Puerta, J.M.Gomez V., C.A.White, D.L.Hill Sr., G.S.Hartson, J.A.Schram, R.D.Bisson, R.L.Sergeant, R.M.Peeples, S.P.Carter, C.D.Sackfield, E.W.Thackeray, M.A.Lough, M.R.Weichers, B.Nadot, M.Roth, W.Gehrig, A.W.Scharff, D.L.Stambaugh, B.L.Hesse, C.A.Brown, C.E.Kastler, D.F.Fuller, D.J.Cook, D.L.Banford, D.L.Wirtz, D.M.Harmon, D.R.Kraemer, G.Cherry, G.F.Nickol, G.R.Kircher, J.B.Weatherson, L.D.Hatcher, R.D.Fauser, S.J.Hutchinson, T.J.Casper, T.L.Loper, W.C.Robinson, D.Thierry, M.Lasne, M.Gonzalez T., B.C.Wedeking, D.A.Smith, J.W.Horn, N.H.Wilson, P.R.Miltenberger, J.S.Jackson, L.F.Fox, C.I.Cornelis, C.L.Buchner, D.G.Smysor, E.Bily, J.A.Lemon, J.W.Bowes Jr., P.W.Hischke, R.J.Godden, R.L.Wetta, S.K.Schultz, G.Gerboin, B.Schifferdecker, H.Brendel, K.Zimmermann, M.Dolic, W.Zorn, M.Carbonell, M.Olmo, D.L.Madole Jr., G.D.Cameron, G.L.Brown, J.L.Engelstad, L.E.Guldenpfennig, L.L.Grespan, M.B.Watkins, M.D.Schilb, R.C.Hogan, R.G.Lanzen, R.R.Majors, V.Rauber, A.Duflon, J.Lanson, C.Saric, H.Kraemer, I.Schiegel, M.Fiederlein, P.Hohmann, P.Spiess, R.Voegele, J.L.Rodriguez A., S.S.Donnelly, H.R.Bensing, M.L.Adamson, J.Martinaud, E.Lehmann, F.Sigmann, S.K.Fox, B.L.Antisdel, D.R.Ball, E.K.Delagardelle, H.P.Chapline, J.C.Tessier, L.M.Baze, M.E.Hyba, M.Ruzylo, P.P.Lang, R.E.Jones, R.O.Long, T.A.Katch, E.Fischer, J.P.Lorenzzon, V.M.Wentz, V.R.Reghelin, K.Heiler, Z.Kaschel, Z.Qetaj, F.Guillen, B.E.Askeland, C.S.Klein, J.M.Potter, L.D.Reed, T.C.Davis Jr., N.Zimmermann, A.C.Anderson, J.V.Coin, L.L.Wallace, R.L.Miller, J.C.Frost, A.Villafranca, D.J.Hemberger, D.J.Sergesketter, D.T.Neher, G.D.Bakeris, G.L.Coulson, J.Bealer, J.D'Amico, J.K.Stanley, J.L.Lees, L.L.Lenker, M.A.Milburn, M.E.Levy, M.T.Meersman, P.A.Brucker, S.C.Dedecker, T.M.Pritz, W.P.Franti, M.Duhem, C.Gaujard, B.Papion, C.Dhardivillers, J.Fleureau, A.Ruiz, D.A.O'Neill, L.E.Bartholdy, B.A.Wainwright, B.J.Fouts, C.Avolio, C.J.Sackman, N.Kohagen, R.A.Neasi, R.E.Pinard, S.C.Cunningham, A.De Sousa II, R.L.Mc Inroy, M.L.Payne, A.Digout, B.A.Sowers, D.J.Rowan, F.J.Esparza, G.Brown, J.C.Allen, J.E.Hughes, J.E.Sandler, J.R.Rizner, L.A.Sullivan, L.J.Main, L.L.Burkholder, M.A.Dibernardo, M.M.Cahill, N.L.Blackwell, P.S.Kepner, R.A.Wallace, R.D.Harvey, R.L.Beam, R.L.Burton, S.D.James, S.W.Carthey, W.A.Heitzman, W.L.Waters, N.Soumare, A.Engelhardt, R.Bianga, W.Freidel, R.L.Blanchard, S.J.Nieman, T.E.Fleshman, T.R.Hall, B.A.Blumhoff, N.L.Larsen, R.A.Strausse, S.D.Vanwatermeulen, T.R.Miller, J.M.Saldaña, C.A.Scala, A.T.Noel, C.E.Stewart, C.F.Hahn, C.J.Haynes, C.J.McDonald, D.A.Moffitt, D.C.Taylor, D.L.Frere, D.R.Crosby, D.R.Laird, F.B.Kernan, G.A.Stanger, G.G.Gooch, I.B.Bragg, J.B.Noack, J.Hollenback, J.J.Witt, J.L.Claus, J.L.Crosby Mcintire, J.M.Smith, J.P.Morrissey, M.J.Luebbers, M.M.Schlapia, M.P.Roelens, M.Parson, P.A.Gomez, P.D.Davis, P.F.King, R.H.Sutton, R.L.Black, R.L.Faith, S.D.Anderson, S.J.Bennett, T.W.Paxton, V.D.Fisher, W.Bolz, A.Rodriguez M., J.L.Espada, M.Perez G., D.E.Brentise, B.G.Gordon, S.J.Brucher, T.L.Dallenbach, E.Clarkson, E.P.Hazelfeldt, F.Rolighed, H.Spurgetis, L.J.Bowman-Eastman, M.H.Watt, T.L.Wuestenberg, W.E.Nybeck, P.C.Hernández, G.Baudoin, A.Tannenberg, C.Domianello, E.Hery, F.Gaenzler, F.Neumayer, G.Opp, H.Wachtel, J.Domsitz, K.Cnyrim, R.Pokorny, U.Bell, W.Huber, W.Kumpf, W.Liebig, L.Martinez T., J.M.Aguilar-Ramirez, C.A.Beach, C.A.Benson, C.A.Reis, C.M.O'Leary, D.A.Vancleve, D.A.Voltz, D.B.Johnson, D.D.McLaughlin, D.M.Pettifer, D.R.Schmidt, E.A.Thompson, E.J.Rowenhorst, E.M.Mejia, F.L.Kraklow, H.E.Walker, J.E.Pauletti Jr., J.G.Perdew, J.J.Brady, J.M.Herrick, J.M.Schmitt, J.R.White Jr., J.S.Heiser, J.W.Bergheger, K.J.Nickerson, K.L.Rennison, K.M.Ireland, L.W.Jackson, M.J.Guyton, M.L.Thompson, P.E.Mack, R.D.Blasdell, R.D.Gravitt, R.J.Stawicki, S.A.Legrand, S.B.Polka, S.M.Davenport, T.E.Huntley, T.V.Rizk, A.Vock, H.Reinert, H.Willmann, M.Evisen, M.Schneider, R.Wendland, G.R.Hill, A.G.Wilson, J.G.Howerton, J.P.Schroeder, A.Braun, R.C.Walton, M.Mace, F.D.Willett, C.M.Perkins, D.D.Coburn, D.F.Cain, D.H.Schumaker, E.J.Loveridge, J.A.Bearbower, J.Brand, J.F.Golz, J.W.Reinhardt, K.R.Baker, K.S.Hilgendorf, L.M.Markey, M.G.Hall, R.A.Ohland Jr., R.P.Davis, R.W.Meyer, S.R.Thuesen, T.A.Trasamar, T.M.Heiar, T.W.Sellers, A.Moreno R., P.Gonzalez B., M.Groisillier, P.Verdicchio, M.Klingmann, P.Kelava, C.M.Smart, M.J.Kislia, M.T.Petersen, S.J.Ward, S.P.Long, C.W.Nice, J.R.Turkal, R.H.Doggett, B.L.Vanoteghem, M.Schuetze, C.A.Mc Elderry, D.A.Ramirez, D.B.Winkler, D.F.Reynolds, D.J.Bergheger, D.J.Farkas, J.A.Teijido, J.J.Kessel, J.K.Anderson, J.M.Jones, J.R.McGinnis, J.T.Gordon, K.A.Marinangeli Jr., L.C.Parker, L.Carter Jr., L.F.Ballegeer, L.M.Nitzel, N.J.Moeller, O.Iversen, P.J.Sausedo, P.T.Harvey, R.E.Brown, R.L.McBee, R.L.Ruth, R.M.Janssen, S.B.Murphy, T.E.Finch, W.A.White, W.C.Folks, W.C.Sheldon, W.M.Willett, Y.J.Gratton, M.A.Flores, B.Guenderoth, H.Gebauer, P.Hejl, W.Kern, N.Brown, J.Gomez D.C., B.J.Seaman, G.L.Combs, J.A.Fullmer, M.D.Porter, B.Schneider, C.A.Rathsack, D.R.Roach, F.Powell, G.Mandel, R.P.Crowley, S.E.Owens, D.M.Wethington, D.R.Speller, F.D.Griswold Jr., G.L.Cramer, G.L.Grebner, G.Nicholson, J.F.Hill, K.E.Coulter, L.A.Smarr, M.E.Jones, M.J.Myers, M.L.Drew, R.G.Miller, R.J.Michels, R.W.Hood, S.L.Hickman, T.L.Albers, T.S.Martin, J.L.Morales, A.Coutout, G.Hasska, R.Alcantara, E.Benes, S.Dobrotka, W.Umhey, J.J.Auzmendi , N.Manzano, B.A.Lyman, H.L.Brasher, R.E.Gobin, M.Chabaud, B.E.Shimkus, D.J.Weiland, G.L.Brocka, R.D.Neuendorf, R.W.Westeren, B.J.Lee, B.M.Boehm, J.C.Giehm, K.M.Saffell, D.M.Massa, F.J.Bennemeer, G.Wittmann, C.Van Der Slik, A.W.Rowe Jr., B.W.Lough, C.E.Campbell, C.L.Burris Jr., C.R.Foster, D.A.Schrimsher, D.F.Dodge, D.J.Melloy, D.P.Cortez, D.S.Betts, D.W.Doland, F.F.Plumb, G.E.O'Neill, H.C.Gilliam, J.A.Theisen, J.C.Carey, J.Coronado, J.M.Van Weele, J.O.Wright, J.Paricka, K.F.Ney, K.L.Caldwell, K.M.Franklin, K.M.Lyle, M.J.Riney, M.L.Fincher, N.J.Colwell, P.M.McCarthy, R.L.Tapscott, R.M.Buenzow, R.P.Martinez, S.I.Duffey, S.J.Eubank, T.M.Mayfield, W.L.Meyerhoff, E.R.Janón, M.Foliard, G.Casenave, J.Thibault, C.Guastaferro, P.Michel, S.Ciaola, D.J.Porter, F.Kajdacsi, B.W.Dahl, J.Peterson, E.J.Styles, J.R.Smith, E.W.Anderson, B.A.Burns, C.S.Engnell, D.A.Eckert, D.E.Ecker, D.F.Meehan, D.I.Blake, D.J.Demling, D.L.Boone, D.R.Anderson, D.Stierwalt, E.A.Champion, E.C.Pulliam, G.A.Miller, G.F.Fox, G.L.Olson, G.W.Newman, J.E.Smith, J.E.Tanner, J.K.Carlson, J.L.Bainbridge, J.L.Clark, L.A.Lewis, L.C.Cale, M.L.Johnson, M.R.Burton, N.F.Exley, N.J.Erickson, P.L.Cater, P.M.Tapscott, P.Turner, R.L.D'Hooge, R.L.Lester, R.S.Denys, R.T.Horsfield, R.W.Phillips, S.C.Fosdick, S.L.Sabers, S.M.Parker, T.N.Taylor, W.Dixon Jr., F.Ficarra, G.Costanzo, H.Erny, J.Gund, J.Stauter, M.Lautenschlager, R.Fessler, A.F.Donnelly, M.O.Moore, Z.Andrijevic, J.Guenon, R.K.Ingamells, S.M.Sawyer, D.Maupin, C.L.Pipho, C.S.Everhart, B.L.Forsberg, C.A.Bybee, C.Amann, D.B.Keleher, D.E.Carothers, D.E.Morse, D.H.Killen, D.J.Chaney, D.L.Christensen, E.A.Hogbin, E.E.Lewis, E.J.Macik, G.C.Baxter, I.E.Boden, J.A.Darin, J.C.Goossen Jr., J.R.Francescon Groene, J.S.Grissom, J.W.Eastland, K.E.Evans-Dahms, K.L.Kreinbring, K.L.Ricke, L.L.Breiby, M.L.Wilkinson, M.Z.Ziegler, R.A.Kriebel, R.A.Sloan, R.E.Hall, R.K.Popp, R.L.Parker, R.M.Passmore, R.W.Parish Sr., S.C.Howe, T.A.Roman, T.R.Pancratz, V.A.Johnson, R.Ruet, G.Wolperth, J.Staebe, P.Benker, R.Freund, R.Wieloch, W.Metz, A.Perez D., D.Corrochano, D.Manzano, I.Ruiz, J.Cortes, M.Ocaña, M.Sanchez M., M.Torres, T.Martin A., H.Herberger, B.B.Messer, C.L.Sproul, E.M.Burt, R.J.Cerchi, G.Q.Gilbert, J.E.Rottinghaus, J.H.Wedeking, R.J.Loch, R.L.Schoeberl, C.F.Conover, M.Shimp, W.A.Williams, A.W.Mohling, B.N.Stover, C.L.Brock, C.L.Schramm, D.A.Schafer, D.D.Kelley, D.F.Ware, D.L.Hendershot, D.L.Maeltzer, E.J.Kennedy Jr., F.H.Staton, F.J.Walker, J.M.Scullin, J.R.Burke, J.W.Wright, L.L.Hampton, M.A.Mauger, M.A.Thompson, M.M.Courbat, N.Long Jr., P.H.Quigley, P.M.Hathaway, R.W.Griffin, S.A.Wohlwend, S.K.Elliott, T.C.Speaker, T.J.Siegel, V.M.Gorecki, W.A.Brett, W.E.Allen, W.E.Ehlers Jr., J.Holy, P.Wieczorek, S.Guerinaud, D.J.Gothard, P.Kunz, D.V.Metzger, S.A.Jesus, J.Flury, C.A.Ostrom, C.W.Simpson, D.Clark-Harris, D.E.Higgins, D.J.Francis Jr., F.L.Partlow, G.A.Kight, J.A.West, J.H.Wells, J.J.Cavanaugh, J.K.Ochsner, J.T.Ahern, L.A.Turner, L.D.Mc Greevey, L.E.Johnson, L.G.Lyle, M.A.Temple, M.J.Eckhardt, M.J.Sandler, M.N.Mayfield, N.J.Emery, P.W.Webber, R.C.Mc Dougall, R.I.Kramme, S.J.Clark, S.R.Case, B.C.Newendorp, C.Watkins, D.A.Reuter, D.B.Bush, D.M.Hirsch, D.M.Youldon, F.A.Joshua, J.A.Vermost, J.D.Ferris, J.L.Bocksnick, J.R.Howell, K.E.Shields, L.N.Smith, M.A.Bergene, M.A.Snowden, M.L.Coffman, M.L.Grems, N.A.Wigant, P.A.Coopman, R.D.Thompson, R.H.Rannfeldt, R.K.Hegg, S.A.Holmes, S.E.Frels, S.E.Wolfe, S.P.Wellman, S.W.Wood, T.K.Withers, P.Breney, M.Kervarrec, P.Grespier, W.Heinzmann, P.Toledano, J.F.Wood, J.G.Mc Cubbin, U.Nguyen, D.L.McElhiney, P.J.George, M.Glaessner,

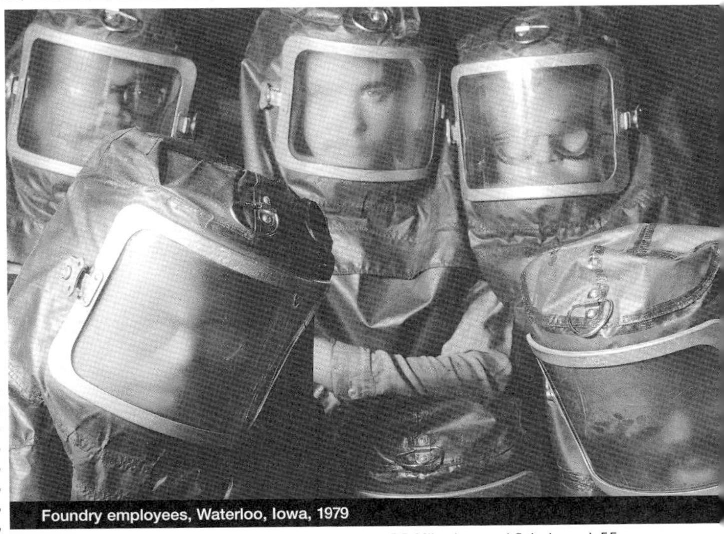

Foundry employees, Waterloo, Iowa, 1979

B.E.Sullivan, B.G.Blanchard, B.J.Carr, C.A.Studer, C.R.Scannell, C.W.Alexander, D.D.Bloom, D.Deloose, D.F.Fox, D.G.Boychuk, D.H.Kopp, D.M.Bland, E.W.Adams, G.E.Sparks, G.L.Frazier, G.W.Bower, J.E.Ballard, J.K.Schupbach, J.M.Sutter, J.R.Rather, K.D.Schiess, K.E.Schaecher, K.J.Einsweiler,
K.J.Smith, K.L.Troyer, K.L.Wesenberg, K.M.Peiffer, L.L.Holmes, L.T.Tull, M.J.Harrod, N.K.Marinangeli, N.L.Dilenbeck-Dedecker, R.A.Wiederholt, R.E.Peterson, R.F.Brownlee, R.P.Schwertner, R.W.Bergfeld, S.A.Curry, S.A.Gerhardt, S.E.O Brien, S.G.Kean, S.J.Windisch, S.L.Baethke, S.P.Vandervinne,
S.R.Tokle, T.D.Bebernes, T.Smith, W.L.Husmann, Y.Boisset, J.Valette, N.Bourgoin, J.Chatillon, A.Urbina, M.Viñuelas, B.L.Grebner, N.J.Roland, J.E.Finley, J.H.Kieffer, J.O.Hurd, L.A.Corbett, L.G.Brandt, S.R.Loveless, D.L.Marshall, E.W.Hamilton, S.K.Vance Nottger, W.R.Ernst, B.L.Johnson,
A.E.Walker Jr., C.C.Patel, C.J.Mills, D.A.Hagge, D.E.Claus, D.G.Hungerford, E.H.Barr, E.J.Reiser III, E.R.Kreis, G.B.Wessel, G.L.Aversing, G.W.Turner, H.S.Hsu, H.T.Uehle, L.A.Luepker, M.J.Anderson, M.L.Parpart, M.S.Weinert, P.E.Pinkston, R.C.Machholz, R.D.Bremner, R.M.Deer, R.R.Crow, R.R.Piatt,
S.G.Dolph, S.G.Korrect, S.M.Nicks, T.M.Wensel, W.M.Martin, A.Ferreira, K.Hofbauer, E.Guzman , M.Huecas, M.Moscatel, J.Guerra, E.M.Hertzer, J.M.Gille, A.L.Paris, D.C.Murphy, D.J.Wolak, M.A.Hau, M.E.Baumgarten, R.Boom, S.A.Just, M.G.Fitzgerald, L.Arsac, H.Kunt, R.Marceaux, A.M.Young,
A.W.Phillips, B.R.Kenney, B.W.Warhurst, C.E.Hamer, D.D.Eller, D.J.Turner, D.M.Carr, D.W.Chinlund, E.K.Blanshan, F.J.Krone, J.A.Metz, J.A.Peterson, J.A.Weime, J.D.Dodge, J.E.Rotsaert, J.L.Yearling, J.M.Mewes, J.N.Berreth, L.J.Anderson, M.D.Kirkpatrick, P.M.Dalessandro, R.D.Hess, R.D.Johnson,
R.E.Thompson, R.L.Groves, R.W.Fones, S.A.Koltookian, S.T.Lyon, T.S.Olson, T.W.Bruck, W.J.Merritt, J.Gaujard, A.Lamberti, D.G.Medina, F.F.Gallagher, H.E.Vorberg, M.Robinson, R.D.Wilkening, C.Ortega, C.S.Sr.iver, D.W.Brock, D.W.Nordquist, E.G.Baumann, G.E.Van Damme, H.A.Welke, J.A.Brickson,
L.S.Shadle, M.J.Greenwood, M.J.Hoogerwerf, M.M.Desmet, M.T.Gacioch Jr., P.M.Pettit, R.D.Tognetti, R.L.Hanson, R.W.Kintigh, R.W.Thode, S.A.Cady, S.E.Stevens, S.M.Greiner, T.M.Allbritton, T.R.Laity, V.J.Depoorter, V.J.Houts, V.J.Ziegler, M.Derrien, R.Leroy, G.Riedl, H.Ludwig, J.Muñoz A., M.Merino,
J.A.Wulf, M.R.Heard, L.J.Gross, J.Nogrette, B.Foerster, E.Klein, E.Kretschmer, E.Paaris, G.Radszuweit, O.Wildberger, S.Lang, W.Schalk, P.L.Overholt, N.Feix, V.Peric, D.Masson, F.Sauer, G.Thron, J.A.Mingo, C.E.Carlson, D.R.Larson, E.J.Gentry, F.R.Midkiff Jr., G.P.Baker, G.R.Cooper, J.E.Huckstadt,
K.K.Van Lengen, M.E.Kennedy, M.J.Harrington, S.M.Vanthournout, T.L.Carlson, W.K.Christofel, P.A.Harden, N.Milicevic, D.D.Rhodes, D.Whitlock, R.P.Pauwels, E.Kohl, D.W.Ange, T.M.Dukes Jr., B.J.Verner, B.R.Thornberry, D.A.Brimeyer, D.D.Sterk, D.M.Thompson, I.L.Gladfelter, J.J.Guilliams,
J.W.Drews, M.L.Moeller, N.J.Versluis, P.C.Wood, P.G.Darrah, R.C.Esterlein, R.E.Nelson, S.G.Bridge-Chase, S.J.French, T.J.Baird, T.L.O Conner, T.L.Wood, V.J.Warneke, E.Gilmour, J.Rigoulot, J.Robinot, G.Rotunno, A.W.Whitehair, R.Hill, R.R.Proctor, M.A.Mc Donald, K.D.Krutsinger, S.J.Drew,
W.Wandel, B.P.Volfson, D.A.Declercq, D.J.Swehla, L.J.Fox, M.A.Heiderscheit, M.A.Natsis, M.E.Dillavou, M.P.Hennebry, P.Boyd, R.D.Perkins, R.E.Humphrey, R.E.Kelley, R.K.McCalester, R.S.Weaver III, S.B.Hazard, S.B.Ilax, S.R.Foster, T.J.Christian Jr., T.J.Claus, W.J.Rosenbaum, J.Chevanne, B.Dodeski,
E.Tickle, T.A.Weber, W.G.May, E.Montero L., J.Moreno F., P.Muñiz, A.T.Griffiths, S.A.Powers, S.M.Meiser, D.Maire, A.L.Mills, C.A.Williams, C.D.Brown, C.M.Fisher, D.A.Goldensoph, D.J.Mirs, D.L.Rusk, D.M.Clark, G.Blunck, K.S.Dechert, L.M.Ker, S.A.Davis, T.E.Gasser, T.McMillan, C.P.Barbaro,
C.Robinson Jr., D.G.Schramm, D.J.Grattan, D.L.Coleman, D.R.Dedobbelaere, D.R.McConaghy, H.D.Coons, H.R.Akers, J.B.Lampasona, J.R.Byrd, L.P.Smith, L.T.Scura Jr., P.J.Schmitz, R.A.Hill, R.A.Lebrun, S.L.Weeks, T.M.Smith, V.Chari, J.G.Gonzalez, J.Pierre, F.Ruiz, J.Le Provost, P.Chastel, P.Venet,
S.Escartin, E.Bindner, G.Hambsch, G.Luder, H.Buerner, H.Martin, H.Oppermann, H.Thiede, K.Luber, M.Braun, M.Ofer, R.Maurer, R.Schwab, T.Montag, W.Beier, W.Rosinus, P.W.Selby, C.L.Peterson, J.O.Culver, S.M.De Graeve, H.L.Bridle, R.M.Kopps, B.F.Bartholomew, F.Harris, F.L.Peters, G.C.Halverson,
G.W.Striegel, I.E.Dilley, J.A.Marshall, J.F.Henderson, J.M.Graham, K.A.Hackbarth, K.P.Wilson, L.M.Enders, M.J.Behnken, S.L.Jones, T.R.Moothart, H.Ayala, J.L.Palomares, M.Dutertre, E.E.Steinhauser, J.R.Eipper, J.M.Dalmolin, H.Y.Williams, A.L.Murry, B.J.Feuchtwanger, C.A.Clendenen, C.J.Hinz,
D.K.Chaudhari, D.R.Flattem, E.K.Hovenga, J.F.Peacock, J.J.O Connor, J.R.Stevenson, K.C.Sastry, K.K.Widdel, L.C.Tyler, L.E.Beechamp, M.C.Patel, N.J.Barsic, R.A.Thompson, R.L.Johnson, S.L.McMillan, T.A.Parrott, T.A.Sorenson, T.E.Osenberg, D.D.Danay Jr., J.N.Johnson, K.E.Willems, M.L.Earhart,
A.R.Anderson, J.W.Bullock, J.W.O Neal, R.Castillo, R.G.Martensen, R.M.O'Brien, S.A.Handy, T.P.Sanchez, W.A.Heller, W.P.Thompson, J.F.Espinoza, K.E.Brumpton, J.H.Armstrong, B.E.Blaser, L.F.Owens, L.W.Jellison, P.E.Kernan Jr., T.J.Longman, T.N.Laird, G.G.Prather, J.L.Diaz, K.E.Anderson,
A.S.Farber, B.J.Roby, C.J.Vargas, C.L.Rommel, C.S.Gladden, D.E.Carman, D.L.Melcher, L.Rash, M.A.Leisure, M.L.Shellberg, M.T.Senatra, N.A.Venter, P.G.Thornburg, P.R.Shah, R.A.Zerngast, R.E.Witte, R.L.Meredith, R.V.Lybarger, S.E.Meyer, T.D.Pickett, W.R.Sharpe, C.M.Cornwell, W.E.Peterson Jr.,
W.Weston, L.Patel, M.R.Murphy, P.L.Egel, R.S.Green, W.A.Marzolph, L.A.Hernandez, C.Georget, J.Breton, A.Witti, B.Sawierucha, F.Malik, H.Schmidt, J.Scheuermann, L.Baermann, N.Strasser, V.Talarmo, F.Senft, H.Ebel, R.A.Clarke, C.E.Feeney, D.D.Jorth, G.A.Maitlen, G.B.Tappan, J.A.Veloz,
J.E.Mentel Jr., J.R.Orr, J.S.Quick, K.D.Vyncke, M.E.Stevens, S.C.Thode, T.J.Dix, V.J.Collins, R.Degrave, M.Bastian, L.R.Toraason, R.O.Rangen, R.F.Predmore, P.Marcoux, W.Eustachi, B.J.Moffatt, D.A.Ohms, D.E.Stewardson, D.M.Matkowski, J.A.Lehman, J.D.Schrunk, J.W.Heflin, J.W.Terry, K.A.Carlson,
K.L.Fuller, R.E.Hoeppner, R.J.Dolleslager, S.J.Jungwirth, S.L.Dickson, S.L.Neels, W.J.Vorva, L.Vivier, A.Jonietz, R.A.Martin, C.Staiger, F.Abel, H.Berberich, E.P.Weathers, G.C.Carpenter, H.W.Shallean, M.R.Behnkendorf, B.E.Guthrie, C.M.Dibble, C.S.Tunwall, D.S.Conklin, H.E.Mucci, I.E.Armenta,
J.F.Reimler, J.L.Maritt, L.J.Stegh, L.J.Stensland, M.E.Althaus, R.H.Hanson, T.A.Swallow, T.J.Lyman, M.Chapet, E.Schwarz, W.Betzwieser, J.A.Bates, E.A.Hutchins, P.Simon, A.Jain, A.W.Hargett, B.J.Lineberger, C.S.Conrad, C.T.Simenson, E.M.Albertson, J.G.Pena, N.J.Klemmer, R.A.Paar, Y.Liao, P.Galliot,
D.Jacquin, P.B.Sharp, K.Noerenberg, S.J.Davis, G.Koch, H.Luetzel, H.Trapp, W.Gromes, C.W.Taylor, D.G.Strickland, D.L.Kuhn, D.Oney, G.D.Robeson, H.Parker Jr., J.D.Andreassen, K.R.Clifton, L.J.Chiarelli, L.J.Roseman, P.S.Junginger, R.A.Saucedo, S.R.Heraly, S.S.Ross, T.C.Hodges, V.E.Byrd, P.Cortez,
D.Guichard, F.Pancucci, J.K.Kalishek, R.L.Meier, C.Torres, J.F.Junker, C.D.Kinkade, D.C.Christensen, G.B.Johnson, K.A.Graff, L.C.Zaputil, R.L.Forest, T.E.Angel, T.L.Simbric, A.Rojas, F.Armendariz, C.L.Pletcher, R.M.Ellingsen Jr., D.L.Tyler, G.Walton Jr., L.B.Fisher, J.A.Treviño, D.P.Ferguson, D.S.Collin,
E.J.Batt, G.C.Cavazos, J.L.Taber, M.C.Monson, T.C.Schwake, H.Sosgornik, K.Klippel, K.Suhleder, F.Baena, P.J.Machu, A.L.Kornegay, D.K.Herrick, D.R.Coomes, G.Annis, J.A.Backstrom, J.C.Robinson, P.Carter, K.N.Beatson, J.I.Toledo, C.J.Poremba, D.R.Rebouche, G.J.Hird, M.A.Henning, M.J.Davis,
O.L.Love, R.L.Thompson, S.L.Smith, T.A.Matzen, R.Herzberger, A.A.Gauger, D.R.Hardy, J.A.Hoffman, J.C.Craig, R.L.Narum, T.O.Moore, G.Bullwinkel, H.Schaefer, M.Haase, S.Messmer, P.Kraus, M.Ritter, B.J.Goebert, E.O.Alber, G.F.Holmes, J.Minson, K.R.Smith, M.V.Nelson, S.L.Beardsley,
J.Redondo R., D.Montez, G.L.Sylvester, J.C.Danielson, A.A.Larson, E.H.Gifford, J.H.Anderson, R.D.Hillyer, J.P.Aguilar, J.Piña , P.Notario, J.A.Marshall, M.A.Kemple, R.Fennelly, C.Montero, C.H.Kimrey, J.Robinson, R.K.Hawkins, W.R.Phillips, M.Rippberger, R.Villanueva, A.V.Duncan, B.J.Lang,
D.H.Stack, E.K.Eubank, G.R.Kottman, P.A.Curry, S.D.Hanna, A.Sanz , A.Tellez, J.Alcala , J.Espada, M.Nuñez S., S.Borrego, M.L.Pearson, J.Jamet, J.A.Hutchison, M.L.McNeal, R.L.Wilson, J.Eugene, F.Albarran-Araujo, H.Huntemann, H.Kirschner, H.Stratmann, M.Hellmann, W.Fichtner, O.C.Greer,
R.C.Imbt, R.M.Poneleit, M.K.Smith, J.D.Salas, D.C.Smith, L.V.Albanese, R.M.Darin, F.Galland, J.Simon, K.R.Kessler, A.Moreno R., J.Flores, J.Martinez D.L.C., J.Muelas, J.Paramo, M.Vidal, P.Benitez, S.Martin J., A.Lobato, E.Diaz R., J.J.Diego De, J.L.Rodriguez R., M.Burgueño M., **1978** G.Wagner,
M.Heinemann, W.Hoffmann, C.Maniurka, G.Malik, E.Merlo, L.Mateo, S.Bolaños, T.Rivera, C.L.Hoppestad, C.S.Eilers, D.A.Blum, D.A.Coordes, D.E.Olsen, D.H.Baker, D.M.Birkhofer, E.C.Nielsen, J.L.Hinton, M.C.Chaney, M.D.Hallauer, M.L.Nelson, P.R.Brown, P.W.Brooks, R.J.Moron, R.W.Sellers, T.Wiest,
M.Lee, B.M.Keys, S.Montgomery, M.Taki, I.N.Franck, G.A.Stinson, G.G.Fagersten, J.W.Francis, L.M.Reich, M.B.Runde, R.J.Saelens, S.J.Lotz, T.E.Jones, E.Rodriguez M., F.Gonzalez P., A.L.Seeba, B.L.Bennett, B.M.Morales, C.K.Harding, C.L.Prosise, D.A.Skinner, D.L.Cashman, D.L.Kastler, J.Woida,
L.M.Cappaert, M.A.Sanborn, P.A.Hansen, P.E.Honan, P.J.Orourke, S.W.Ahlers, T.E.Wiles, W.H.Cave, R.Jimenez C., M.Cuevas, J.A.Roseberry, S.A.Nelson, E.E.Urrutia , D.J.Rylander, M.K.Kar, V.P.Bergstrand, G.Campos, J.Nocete, L.Fernandez, N.Pariente, O.Carriches, D.L.Santee, A.S.Benn, G.R.Howe,
J.S.Deiters, L.P.Groulx, T.L.Peters, J.Oropesa, J.S.Bonfoco, M.D.Farmer, W.S.Walters, B.B.Brock, D.L.Hawkins, J.A.Schraeder, J.R.Duncan, K.L.Sommers, M.M.Bancroft, R.D.Rauh, R.Metler, R.E.Amozurrutia , B.Kempf, H.Jaeger, H.Raiser, J.Rojas, M.Scheib, E.M.Pellon, M.Cortes, A.Pirrus,

Welders, Ottumwa, Iowa, 1979

A.R.Mc Grath, D.J.Jamieson, G.L.Angles, M.A.Friedman, M.C.Fitzgerald, M.M.McCune, R.L.Neal, S.P.Quinn, W.M.Mosher, A.Clement, A.Serrano A., J.Estepa, M.Garcia R., D.H.Brown, I.A.Bamberg,
M.E.Nicewanner, C.M.Jett, G.D.Forster, J.C.Logan, J.Hernandez, J.R.Behrends, M.Winger, T.L.Batten, W.J.Olujic, L.Luckemeyer, M.M.Whitney, R.R.Foss, J.L.Jones, K.M.Knobloch, M.P.White,
R.K.Reynolds, V.S.Weaver, W.R.James, G.Mure, E.Loehr, W.Schleppi, A.Mingo, F.Barragan , K.Engel, P.J.Devault, A.E.Swanson, A.Leslie, E.L.Harris, J.D.Stewart, J.M.Berkeley, S.J.Mosqueda, E.Bea,
H.E.Moon, R.D.Rulifson, S.G.Hayes, S.W.Jost, A.I.Eckert, J.L.Cantu, C.Collins, J.Schubert, L.Mueller, R.D.Griffin, G.Troutier, C.L.Herbst, H.E.Collins Jr., J.M.Beardsley, K.J.Robison, S.J.Walsh,
S.P.Masotti, N.Chapa , C.W.Holtz, J.R.Hernandez, J.A.Robinson, J.R.Dehmer, M.D.Gill, M.J.Catoe, R.L.Taylor, R.M.Frere, E.Sartori, R.F.Schneider, T.G.Milbrandt, B.Py, F.Cepeda, J.L.Herranz , N.Galvez,
G.Elm, M.A.Harris-Lawhorn, M.A.Melton, R.D.Madson, S.A.Pratt, J.M.Dixon, D.P.Sims, D.P.Willaert, J.R.Martelle Jr., N.H.Ola, S.C.Schippers, E.L.Holmes, C.S.Lay, D.W.Johnson, N.M.Haynie,
R.F.Stevenson, P.R.Rohde, Y.Lepinay, A.Brandenburg, A.Heller, A.Strandes, S.Sonntag, N.Weiand, G.G.Neal, T.R.Richards, F.Sanchez, P.Jeanblanc, J.Morel, J.Klein, M.Kurz, A.Forcelius, E.Haller,
C.B.Zerull, K.A.Benson, P.A.Johnson, R.B.Gatton, G.Lenormand, U.Reischmann, J.M.Gorski-Johnson, P.A.Cotton, K.M.Laleman, A.Jandt, I.M.Denton, K.P.Mahlow, K.R.Curtis, R.R.Johnson,
S.J.Ferguson, J.Sai, B.Schwarz, T.A.Aplin, C.K.Tibbits, J.A.Hartley, K.A.Kirschbaum, M.S.Seibert, R.C.Southwick, P.R.Bell, R.Allmang, C.D.Turner, C.L.Klein, A.M.Storm, D.C.Chard, D.J.Black, J.F.Green,
L.L.Lewis, M.A.Munson, M.R.Lute, R.A.Baldwin, R.L.Glover, T.L.Worthington, W.L.Mottl, D.Melchiori, B.L.Stookesberry, J.Tovar , A.Ventre, J.M.Hancock, M.Catel, R.Wood, D.L.Dewitt, J.R.Tickle Sr.,
S.K.Campbell, H.Buendia, G.Weber, R.J.Malbeuf, R.C.Vande Walle, D.D.Matthews, P.A.Ortiz, R.S.McKee, S.A.Andrews, T.M.Hartog, W.E.Klotz, A.Orona, J.von Stegmann, D.L.Brooks, L.M.Cothron,
M.S.Cook, M.S.Linn, N.J.Jones, P.J.Flynn, W.H.Lipkea, D.J.Goering, P.M.Zulik, J.A.Flores, C.A.Ehlers, D.B.Stickney, D.D.Barkema, D.R.Yoder, J.S.Milligan, M.Guereca, W.A.Ardueser, J.L.Wigand,
B.J.Newberg, D.R.Edmiston, J.F.Wilson, J.H.Dreier, K.A.Ritter, R.H.Clark, R.W.Hinton, S.L.Wildemuth, W.T.Young, B.Alanis, J.Reyes , A.Liesy, A.Noe, E.Hohmann, W.Seebald, B.Katz, B.R.Hamlyn,
D.L.Koehler, G.L.Groulx, H.E.Werling, J.E.Hardzinski, J.T.Bell, K.L.Ehrecke, K.W.Thayer, L.M.Wells, M.A.Chmelar, M.J.Finnegan, M.P.Zimmer, P.G.Beal, S.D.Huhman, S.J.De Braal, S.K.Smoldt,
T.D.Doyle, U.H.Kugler, H.Wagner, D.R.Disher, B.D.Hendricks, J.A.Dale, M.C.Meyer, O.G.Combs Jr., T.E.Hughes, J.R.Lord Jr., K.A.O'Brien, G.Fuentes, M.H.Chapman, E.Guerinaud, C.A.Myers,
C.L.Johnson, D.W.Hendricks, F.Jursik, J.A.Laird, J.J.Koster, M.J.Thayne, R.E.Vonnahme, R.Hickey, J.Mary, W.Donnerstag, M.G.Gilpin, B.C.Satterfield, J.F.Herring, D.M.Gage, G.W.Lichti, J.M.Crow,
L.S.Wolf, M.Bedis, M.J.King, R.A.Bishop, S.L.Rossell, L.W.Sereda, R.Flores , D.H.Campagna, M.J.Denicus, B.Steller, E.Karcher, F.Hohl, G.Freund, H.Al-Deen, H.Buchholz, H.Dannigkeit, O.Hipp,
P.Schlaefer, I.Esquivel, G.Legrom, G.M.Maceachern, E.A.Arreaga, D.R.Van Nest, F.S.Martin, J.P.Kulis, K.E.Anderson, R.J.Janoski, C.B.Allison, D.J.Easton, F.M.Vitorino, F.Mattei, J.M.Conrad, L.J.Brizgis,
M.J.Scharf, R.S.Lesso, S.A.Stewart, G.L.Molina, J.F.Surber, M.J.Mortz, M.Rascon, K.Fischer, A.C.Kirchoff, A.E.Nico, A.J.Gallenbeck Jr., D.C.Vogt, D.P.Hauk, F.J.Feucht, J.A.Katsma, J.E.Giedd,
J.L.Koerner, K.J.Navin, O.C.Gietzel, R.F.Gubin, J.A.Gamez, H.Jennewein, B.K.Knutson, C.M.Fiers, F.L.Degraaf, F.S.Cruse, K.J.Stoss, K.M.Wilt, M.W.Mendoza, P.R.Axtell, R.D.Beachler, R.D.Hamm,
R.D.Smith, R.E.Kimmel, R.J.Kooken, S.R.Chesser, V.M.Seitzinger, W.Dixon, J.Bertail, R.De la Fuente, J.A.Gonzalez, C.R.Zogg, D.A.Burton, I.Maceachern, R.A.Rodriguez, T.S.Cordes, T.W.Giese,
J.Muller, M.D.Kinrade, M.L.Johnson, R.D.Donatsch, R.G.Peterson, R.J.Lunardi, W.B.Goings, M.L.Tarrant, I.Woitaschik, E.C.Dixon, G.A.Kittel, J.E.Mason, J.K.Clark, L.Z.Boswell Jr., S.C.Bowman,
C.L.Kramer, D.L.Colgan, H.M.Saunders, R.Rankin, H.Montag, H.Schuetz, J.Kwiotek, J.Reinig, L.Magin, M.Lurg, P.Wieczorek, R.Kaufmann, S.Lindner, T.Metzger, W.Boxheimer, W.Hald, W.Rausch,
W.Wolf, A.J.Kimmerle, D.J.Aubry, J.M.Brems, J.Altmann, R.A.Demeyer, R.W.Duehr, A.Almanza, B.J.Smith, C.A.Beckley, D.L.Schueller, G.L.Wells, J.V.Atwell, K.D.Schrader, L.A.Bartels, M.A.Martin,
M.D.Gladden, R.Cabreda, R.Latham, S.M.Lagrange, T.A.Isaacson, T.J.Portz, B.Sheedy, J.Zinn, E.A.Rector, M.G.Rasmussen, R.J.Zeimet, T.J.Byard, A.G.Snow, K.Ernst, L.J.Garrett, M.L.King,
M.T.Cowser, E.Jeffries, T.G.Tribble, V.Greer, C.R.De Decker, C.S.Wignall, J.A.Emmons, J.J.Gisel, K.B.Fagan, K.M.Smith, M.L.Robison, N.P.Wagner, R.A.Hanson, R.L.Hesler, R.R.Schadey,
R.W.Schellenberg, T.Nguyen, Z.S.Fitzgerald, J.Gamez, R.Bolies, G.Palmer, G.S.Kalemkarian, G.W.Gottman, G.B.McCumber, J.E.Nordstrom, L.H.Hermann, R.A.Seemann, T.J.Roberts, B.A.Harris,
P.J.Schmitt, C.L.Mooney, C.M.Martz, D.C.Maupin, E.J.Jesko Jr., G.D.Margelofsky, J.Gray, K.C.Blusher, K.F.Beenken, K.J.Klomsten, K.L.Briggs, L.M.Wagner, R.A.Kok, R.A.Tesch, R.J.Coffey, R.L.Eckermann, R.L.Love, T.J.Netzer, C.Guerinaud, D.C.Wells, D.L.Schmidt, G.T.Ginter, J.J.Severance,
M.L.Ullrich, P.J.Cooley, R.L.Reeg, W.A.Saner, C.C.Rose, L.M.Truong, J.A.Middleton, D.A.Paulson, A.A.Marthaler, A.R.Gorter, B.J.Mc Millan, D.A.Baumann, D.C.Ralston, D.E.Brandon, D.F.Darby, D.G.Nichols, D.W.Maguire, D.W.Wood, E.J.Jeglum, K.James, L.A.Riches, M.J.Hamann, M.J.Hayes,
M.R.Youngblood, P.J.Dehn, R.J.Boynton, R.J.Briggs, R.L.Howerton, S.L.Pender, T.L.O'Brien, T.M.Gipple, A.Hofmann, G.J.McGarry, M.A.Helderman, R.J.Walters, R.L.Wyant, S.J.Johnson, R.H.Fletcher, H.L.Grapengeter, R.K.Bauer, S.H.Meguffy, S.L.Bradley, C.Gaboreau, A.Mende, B.Krippleben, B.Lange,
E.Hauck, E.Scherer-Kube, E.Wilhelm, F.Elsasser, H.Wiefels, K.Singer, M.Gauter, M.Potztave, H.C.Turnbull, J.C.Portillo, P.Moreau, B.J.Dunbar, B.L.McClellan, E.A.Lesch, E.B.Jones, E.P.Donovan, G.L.Holcomb, J.H.Moenck, J.J.Taber, K.L.Cordingley, L.L.Armstrong, L.M.Nimmers, M.J.Coyle, R.L.Nelson,
S.A.Regan, S.D.Franks, T.Ramirez, G.J.Weegink, L.Angeles, G.Acker, G.Moeckl, G.Ziegler, A.Morales R., A.E.Braun, C.A.Porter, C.C.Rash, C.P.Windeknecht, C.V.Henry, D.D.Mueller, D.J.Tressel, D.M.Weets, D.R.Sheley, F.P.Smith, G.A.Ouart, G.W.Rumph, I.S.Sherrod, I.W.Hawkins, J.A.Morris, J.P.Gregory,
J.S.Schroeder, K.C.Ketelsen, K.K.Lesh, K.M.Maher, L.K.Boots, M.A.Begyn, M.A.Yusko, M.D.Ragona, M.E.Mellon, M.G.Maring, P.A.Cremer, P.F.Nell, R.E.Miller, R.J.Melliere, R.L.Chase, R.L.Lee, R.M.Nehls, S.E.Steffeney, S.H.Stoltenberg, S.J.Galaviz, S.R.Downing, S.W.Lantz, T.A.Rose, T.G.Dunakey,
W.L.Carter, C.I.Mabaso, B.D.Adams, C.L.Jahns, D.D.Wassenhove, F.Ruiz, J.A.Ehlers, J.A.Hecht, K.E.De Silva, K.Kelly, P.S.Seidel, R.M.Sherman, R.M.Thielen, J.D.Michels, J.E.Zelhart, S.L.Goke, T.R.Brown, D.A.Mergen, A.I.Johnson, B.J.Daye, B.M.Nichols, C.J.Kuiper, C.R.Etheridge, D.A.Klann,
D.C.Braun, D.D.Grubb, D.J.Bilgrien, D.K.Wells, G.L.Albertson, G.L.Collins, J.Aguilar, J.D.Dehn, J.D.Groves, J.E.Landenberger, J.L.Hartley, J.M.Yero, J.R.Seyller, J.W.Callas, L.D.Ryckaert, M.D.Denkhoff, M.D.Parkins, M.E.Feiertag, M.J.Lilienthal, M.L.Davis, M.M.Willis, R.H.Louderback, R.M.Kaster,
S.M.Anderson, S.R.Bell, W.A.Mc Carns Jr., W.P.Rusch, W.R.Sutt, P.Leclerc, D.Feiler, G.Hemmer, W.Wieczorek, A.Cumplido, F.Hernandez C., J.M.Gonzalez S., R.Talavera, C.T.Lanham, D.J.Givens, M.R.Donatsch, R.J.Devriendt, G.Salazar, C.H.Wille, P.K.Schueller, R.G.Richard, D.P.Hopkins, C.W.Bean,
G.D.Cantrell, J.R.Medinger, J.Tubler, C.L.Kennedy, C.P.Rubley, D.L.Merten, E.A.White, F.O.Covert, G.D.Disher, G.J.Dalcourt, J.D.Knisley, J.D.Olah, J.F.Theisen Jr., J.P.Garczynski, J.V.Long Jr., K.R.Weaver, M.E.Lund, M.M.Follmer, P.R.Simon, R.A.Slavens, R.A.Wucherer, R.D.Volkstorf, R.E.Bennett,
R.M.Gratton, S.C.Gibson, S.J.Thode, T.K.Watters, Y.D.Faucher, D.Lupi, C.K.Nalley, W.M.Loch, D.E.Collier, D.J.Garibaldi, R.P.Nelson, T.J.Strein, T.M.Fier, C.H.Baker, K.D.Bybee, K.L.Mc Ginn, D.L.Morman, L.P.Bredesky Jr., B.Lefèvre, G.Laufer, H.Walter, M.Becker, S.Grabietz, A.Garcia, A.J.Virag,
A.S.Timbo, C.A.Gravatt, C.D.Shrum, D.A.Bowman, D.L.Bogenschneider, E.R.Hess, G.L.Forster, G.L.Muntz, J.Bartelt, J.E.Hopper, J.G.Leppo Sr., J.J.Wilgosh, J.M.Semprini, J.R.Lewis, M.D.Dolash, M.E.Thompson, M.P.Connell, M.S.Larvenz, M.S.Mitchell, R.E.Cherrington, R.K.Ehmen, S.L.Rieser,
T.J.Marinelli, T.J.May, T.M.McMahon, V.M.Gress, W.D.Frank, A.L.Paltridge, G.Bitsch, H.Haag, J.Mueller, M.Weigelt, P.Scheliga, R.Ludwig, W.Kulessa, W.Rill, G.F.Scott, C.H.Wesenberg, L.P.Brozovich, D.E.McStockard, H.R.Lobberecht, L.A.Jacobi, B.L.Ash, J.Duarte, M.Pretet, M.J.Ehlers, B.T.Tovar,
C.E.Leisinger, C.G.Farmer, D.D.Bahr, D.E.Lauersdorf, D.L.Lerum, D.M.Durant, D.M.Kilmer, E.L.Crowley Jr., F.J.Pepper, G.E.Suiter, H.V.Allison, J.C.Johns, J.E.Mabeus, J.S.Etten, K.L.Chhoun, M.A.Nelson, M.A.Vande Berg, M.D.See, M.M.Berry Jr., M.P.Christians, M.W.Thompson, N.M.McCarville,
N.Moran, P.G.Peters, R.F.Cuchra, R.H.Hill, R.P.Rosenow, R.R.Madden, S.C.Del Ponte, S.J.Hofman, S.R.Price, T.J.Stone Jr., W.R.Beske, J.Motzko, C.L.Doucet, G.Fauvain, D.Lopez D.L.T., D.D.Stack, R.E.Giordani, A.L.Williamson, B.A.Mc Govern, B.M.Stone, C.A.Martins, C.B.Robb, D.H.Brewer,
D.K.Mc Elroy, D.L.Baber, D.W.Trees, G.E.Spettel, J.A.Schrempf, J.A.Vockroth, J.L.Fowler, J.L.Nitzschke, L.A.Fischer, L.F.Isenberger, M.A.Aubry, M.D.Tentinger, M.T.Olsen, N.S.Beaver, N.S.Woodin, P.E.Petrick, P.R.Bakalar, P.S.Gorman, R.D.Devaney Jr., R.N.Wonase, R.P.Bailey, T.M.Cornally, W.J.Evans,
A.L.Rojo, A.Zafra, Fco.Jimenez G., S.Igualador, A.T.Williams, G.A.Corelis, M.L.Freeman, T.M.Wagner, W.Olbrich, D.A.Wineberg, D.J.Greenawalt, D.W.Durst, J.L.Moriarity, R.D.Jenkins, K.Wendel, T.R.Bailey, C.W.Dwyer, D.Gonzalez, D.R.White, G.L.Marchand, G.W.Wynn, J.P.Centeno, J.W.Rasch,
K.H.Christoff, L.A.Lisko, M.A.Nefstead, N.Prathammanon, P.B.Otte, R.D.Gold, R.E.Davidson, R.L.Nelson, R.W.Lange, R.W.Samplawski, S.M.Lisko, S.S.Kopff, T.A.Deutsch, V.E.Lansing, A.Mueller, E.Moser, A.Haro, B.Diaz, E.Orgaz, M.Carretero, S.Garcia D., C.Vidrine, F.J.Trobaugh, F.W.Cernetisch,
N.L.Goss, E.L.Swenson, J.B.Cummins, J.P.Frederick, M.G.Peirce, K.West, A.D.Kreiner, D.J.Douglass, D.L.Howk, D.M.Cason, D.R.Peck, D.W.Snyder, E.D.Ambort, G.L.Burrows, J.D.Hutter, L.Wilder, R.P.North, R.S.Kruczynski, R.W.Hawkins, S.J.Maaske, S.L.Odson, T.R.Sorak, G.Sander, N.Ruiz,
P.J.Romero S., D.J.Whitworth, D.F.Ott, J.L.Talley, M.E.Thompson, S.J.Flagel, M.Destrez, A.E.Olsson, A.F.Elliott, C.H.Winston, C.S.Thorman, J.E.Uchytil, J.J.Coughlin, K.M.Dabney, K.M.Sertich, M.M.Swehla, R.A.Barrow, R.C.Halweg, R.L.McCarthy, S.J.Lang, C.De la Garza, R.E.De la Garza, G.Armbruster,
K.Stopfer, L.Ordelt, T.Assenheimer, D.W.Brown, P.E.Stanley, A.L.Samplawski, A.M.Raya, B.J.Lange, B.L.Roate, C.R.Wolter, D.E.Woods, D.M.Giese, D.R.Aschaker, D.S.Meyer, D.W.Gensch, J.A.Jordan, J.A.Lynch, J.J.Czarneski, J.M.Kiebel, L.A.Bierl, L.A.Kruel, R.J.Walsh, R.L.Burris, R.M.Durfee,
S.A.Covert, S.K.Kline, S.L.Cady, T.D.Farley, T.J.Yaroch, R.Bouton, P.Meckler, B.J.Merritt, M.J.Kelly, V.F.Leihsing, W.J.Oeth, E.P.Tosoni, G.Ziegler, T.L.Thompson, R.A.Gronoski, B.G.Hayden, B.G.Held, B.J.Schultz, B.K.Bamke, B.M.Sievers, C.M.Oppermann, D.A.Bahr, D.C.Beske, D.E.Herrick, D.J.Headon,
D.L.Winter, D.R.Jaques, E.H.Jahns, F.M.Simpson, J.A.Dresen, J.Hoffman, J.W.Tadych, L.A.Thurston, L.Parks, M.E.Frick, R.E.Franke, R.R.Schrab, R.W.Poetter, S.A.Kieliszewski, S.H.Anderson, T.J.Anfinson, T.J.Thompson, T.L.Weeks, P.Flores, J.A.Silversmet, L.C.Lambert, R.J.O'Meara Sr., R.B.Beebout,
W.G.Korpela, B.A.Foust, C.D.Schroeder, C.E.Mabry III, C.R.Schrodt, D.B.Waldorf, K.W.Hammer, L.S.Sharp, P.J.Michaelides, R.D.Knar, R.J.Babcock, S.A.Moore, A.E.Sergeant, C.Johnson, C.M.Kruger, D.M.Mottet, J.D.Brunet, J.H.Hansen, J.L.Watson, M.W.Losee, R.C.Marchand, R.D.Moore, N.Sanzano,
A.H.Fyfe, A.L.Champine, A.Mortale, B.A.Miller, B.E.Walker, C.A.Tjaden, C.L.Dillion, D.A.Kremer, D.G.Buser, D.J.Nehmer, D.K.Gainey, D.M.Jenkins, D.N.Schlaefer, D.S.Jauert, G.M.Marshall, J.E.Dewilde, J.H.Carson, J.M.Bahls, K.M.Ryan, L.A.Zuhlke, L.M.Sniffin, M.F.Mc Millan, M.M.Wilson, M.Madsen,
N.D.Tittle, P.Harbin, R.D.Kuehl, R.H.Henkel, R.R.Lange, S.J.Harper, T.R.Napper, V.L.Hicks, W.E.Gensch, D.López , F.Jimenez G., D.G.Helm, J.W.Payton Jr., G.M.Luterek, J.Ramirez, D.L.Yarbrough, E.H.Williams, J.K.Koranda, R.D.Strunk, T.J.Otting, E.Chasseur, F.Oster, H.Greving, K.Umbs, W.Heinz,
C.F.Marks, C.M.Hansen, C.P.Davis, C.S.Dickinson, D.E.Sheldon, D.L.Brown, F.P.Douglas, G.L.Williams, I.R.Koch, J.Denger, J.Entz, J.L.Clime, J.R.Butler, K.J.Schmidt, M.E.Petersen, P.R.Moore, R.E.Burton, R.E.Nelson, R.K.Ostrem, R.L.Sweet, T.J.Gloviak, P.Linger, J.M.Martinez R., D.J.Sathmary,
K.R.Smith, M.Hinrichs, R.G.Greenlee, S.Minor, K.C.Twardawa, G.Kolodziej, J.L.Hesprich, D.A.Decker, D.A.Moline, E.J.Neibauer, J.A.Kegler, L.R.Roof, M.E.Gorski, W.Strand, R.Krebs, B.A.Munger, C.A.Ashcraft, J.M.Green, K.R.Young, M.L.García , B.Philardeau, L.Perruchini, C.D.Fakin, **1979** C.Joensson,
F.Hauck, G.Bofinger, H.Schwab, I.Kretzschmar, K.Hermann, M.Engel, P.Fischer, R.Gross, R.Schreck, R.Wick, D.Schneider, E.Moll, G.C.Williams, K.I.Clayphan, P.Powell, A.W.Lumby, B.G.Martin, B.R.Mize, B.W.Mueller, C.D.Snowbarger, C.L.Schneider, D.A.Payne, D.Alexander, D.C.Truex, D.D.Gundacker,
D.E.Holmes, D.J.Giesinger, D.L.Sturm, E.J.Harding, E.O.Bradford, E.W.Reem, F.J.Young, G.A.Jameson, H.White, J.A.Glosser, J.A.Israel, J.A.Sears, J.K.Cozad, J.L.Kimberley, J.M.Wyffels, J.P.Buller, K.A.Hein, K.G.Faes, K.M.Higgins, K.M.Wiebel, K.V.Winner, L.A.Mowers, M.A.Illingworth, M.E.Dabney,

M.G.Ackley, M.H.Larsen, M.J.Mareck, M.L.Krueger, P.V.Downing, R.Aukee, R.D.Mc Inroy, R.M.Harycki, S.C.Pounds, S.F.Eldrenkamp, S.W.Post, T.S.Derrick, V.R.Williams, W.E.Solveson, C.R.Garcia, D.Le Mette, A.D.Sheidler, D.C.Donohue, D.F.Wulfekuhle, F.G.Becker, K.Bachman, S.H.Brown, T.D.Stinocher, W.M.Duggleby, C.A.Capritta, D.J.Harken, G.S.Doescher, J.A.Erickson, J.C.Boyer, K.A.Lykam, K.B.Heise, K.L.Biederman, K.T.Bailey, L.Koepsell, M.L.Landon, M.L.Wilson, P.K.Erickson, R.E.Schmidt, R.L.Buby, R.R.Patterson, S.Ostring, B.Schneble, E.Klatt, M.Pfeiffer, D.J.Westfall, D.L.Dixon, P.J.Marohl, R.J.Tetzlaff, R.L.O'Dell, K.Ziegler, M.J.Morrison, A.M.Lee, B.J.Davis, B.L.Hardiek, D.A.Rhadans, D.D.Bolstad, D.E.Meyer, D.F.Reynolds, D.H.Hafenstein, D.L.Abeyta, D.L.Hammerstrom, D.M.Zimmerman, D.R.Johnson, E.H.Kok, G.J.Forcier, G.L.Dostal, G.L.Gassner, G.V.Jaeger, H.R.Nitschke, J.C.Wachter, J.F.Lee, J.J.Jongebloed, J.L.Geving, K.B.Ganser, K.W.Lindert, L.A.Ryan, L.D.Fjelstul, M.A.Schultz, M.F.Frederick, M.J.Herrick, M.W.Laugesen, N.E.Muzzy, O.F.Hawes, P.E.Duffy, R.A.Kurtz, R.C.Storlie, R.D.Paar, R.R.Winter, S.P.Peery Jr., T.J.Nehls, T.L.Larson, V.L.Braun, V.R.Dufour, B.Jungkind, H.Schmitt, H.Schwab, K.Reindl, S.Hornstein, C.L.Noel Jr., C.V.Dotseth, D.J.Warren, E.Skulj, L.B.Pettijohn, P.H.Rabbass, P.L.Empie, S.E.Meinzen, S.J.Earl, T.E.Guess, T.L.Huth, W.M.Christofferson, A.J.Zock, B.B.Estes, G.F.Finch, L.R.Huitt, E.F.Mc Kenna, L.M.Hirst, R.Garcia, A.D.De Joode, A.K.Swindler, A.Perez, B.D.Burnett, C.J.Kadinger, D.G.Stogdill, D.J.Smith, D.M.Bohneman, D.M.Forsberg, G.P.Johnson, J.G.Selkirk, J.P.Fritz, J.S.Mack, J.T.Gilbert, K.H.Bruckner, K.L.Weynand, L.W.Rauser, M.Caro-Rios, M.W.Meyer, N.K.Hammock, P.J.Thilges, R.A.Hoffmann, R.L.Pufahl, R.Nelson, S.M.Roedl, S.N.Moss, A.Bittner, G.Carpintieri, G.Gehlbach, H.Loeher, L.Tuscher, U.Berg, S.G.Minter, D.E.Boone, L.C.Hensley, M.Salazar, J.A.Hanshaw, S.A.Boss, B.A.Coers, B.A.Halverson, C.E.Pensyl, C.L.Arms, D.A.Thomas, D.E.Wuenne, D.H.Hagen, D.L.Daniels, E.E.Shore, G.R.Hansen, J.A.Hinz, J.A.Kalb, L.M.Long, L.R.Andrew, M.D.Schwartz, M.D.Scott, R.D.Wyant Jr., R.E.Bradley, R.R.Schmidt, V.O.Dickinson Jr., W.E.Schneiter, B.Olbrich, G.Scheliga, H.Dorn, R.Schnoeder, D.J.Sachse, G.A.Buhalog, K.L.Van Buren, B.G.Koepke, J.L.Beckham, K.R.Kebler, R.J.Lorenz, A.Blair, C.A.Blanchard, D.C.Henriksen, D.E.Merkel, D.M.Matthews, G.R.Noth, M.Brent, M.M.Gans, T.J.Clark, T.L.Wylie, A.R.Rodrigues, G.R.Pohl, J.Pereau, J.Veron, S.Pivet, A.Schneider, B.Haetty, B.Lang, F.Butz, G.Hrdina, H.Huether, J.Reitemeyer, O.Hofmann, R.Kranzbuehler, W.Kuehnle, W.Reck, B.A.O'Neel, C.L.Schonher, D.E.Carver, D.F.Murphy, D.J.Stillmunkes, K.L.Newman, S.F.Clark, S.K.Stroup, W.C.Little, A.Leonard, C.Moczko, E.Zieger, K.Halicki, N.Werling, R.Damek, V.Heilmann, W.Veit, S.J.Hayden, J.C.Huntley, W.L.Quinlan, J.Horvat, P.J.Smith, J.D.Feehan, L.M.Hibben, J.V.Martinez, N.Kolettis, A.J.Voight, A.M.Watts, B.Mattina, D.L.Toellner, D.R.Jones, E.A.Larson, E.R.Pauley, E.Torres, G.L.Freeman, J.A.De Vries, J.A.Fischer, J.D.Smith, J.M.Raether, M.A.Rader, M.M.Rose, N.J.Dewey, P.J.Thonn, R.E.Bauch, R.S.Witte, R.T.Lange, L.R.Mello, M.Delfosse, R.Escartin, B.Podkowik, G.Foegle, J.Rech, R.Schneider, B.J.Ernst, R.K.Templeton, P.A.Deleon, R.A.Holoubek, B.R.Wadhwa, R.Huegel, D.R.Reifsteck, G.W.Smith, K.S.Marsh, P.J.Burge, S.A.Gebhardt, S.R.Cooney, A.R.Handrow, B.J.Terrell, C.A.Lesley, C.B.Belisle, C.M.Smart, D.T.Deloy, G.J.Blum, G.L.Miner, G.R.Douglas, J.F.Zabloudil, J.J.Jenkins, J.L.Bagenstos, J.R.Cewe, K.A.Megna, K.E.Pancratz, L.D.Nienkark, M.J.Willcox Jr., R.K.Welch, R.M.Amundson, R.M.Jarrett, W.J.Jarrard, C.F.Perryman, S.Djouad, E.Talaska, P.Sarantis, R.Goehring, T.Anacker, H.C.Cierreck, J.Barillon, M.Anceaux, K.Sammel, A.J.Westimayer, M.Makedonski, N.M.Martin, D.C.Weitz, K.H.Hendrix, M.P.Meenan, M.W.Lombardi, D.D.McClintic, G.E.Stone, J.R.Grigg, J.S.Conway, R.D.Bailey, R.D.Heinje, R.D.Huston, R.E.Brammer, R.L.Sigmund, R.P.Finnessy, S.K.Imfeld, S.L.Erber, S.R.Ephraim, D.Leclere, H.Kraemer, J.Leiner, L.M.Todd, B.L.Schroeder, C.K.Lasell, C.S.Rabe, D.L.Wickham, J.A.Weydert, K.E.Bratcher, L.J.Combs, N.G.Stoeckel, P.T.Kennedy, R.A.Genge, R.W.Derudder, S.J.Custer, A.Froncek, A.V.Neto, D.D.Godoy, G.Schubert, I.Rusinek, J.O.D.Silva, J.Tormes, M.A.Rodrigues, V.C.Fruhling, F.Villarreal , J.Madrigal , M.Gouillon, B.Trieb, G.Lutz, H.Rimbacher, H.Sonntag, J.Scholtes, J.Weiss, K.Zahn, W.Rinsche, G.Kurz, B.L.Marco, B.W.Hawkins, D.D.Braun, D.D.Reiners, D.M.Corkery, D.O.Petersen, D.R.Hendershot, D.S.Parrish, D.W.Hansen, J.F.Williamson, J.P.Clark, K.H.Phillips, M.F.Ponik, M.P.Kress, R.B.Sharp, R.E.Sorrell, S.K.Thiede, S.L.Wolfram, C.Bourdin, J.Prudent, H.Fuetterer, W.Schwarz, M.Gunther, P.M.Beachler, S.L.Mc Allister, D.D.Morgan, M.J.Barnes, T.P.Cottrell, A.Garcia, A.R.Brownstone, B.L.Soldner, C.J.Jarvis, C.L.Maddox, C.R.Drews, D.D.Sandley, D.E.Lynn, G.T.Kiser, J.A.Coonradt, J.A.Tucker, J.H.Meany, J.R.Erickson, K.E.Kreitzman, K.M.Sawyer, R.W.Bridgland, S.J.Jensen, S.R.Iyengar, S.R.Mason, S.W.Mealey, T.K.Fellmer, T.L.Mosher, D.Jaquet, H.Kmiecinski, J.Lazar, L.Morper, P.Petri, K.J.Arensdorf, D.Meyer, P.Kraus, D.L.Declerck, D.E.García, R.Zion, P.P.Tigges, B.A.True, B.H.Porth, C.R.Stickles, D.A.Kehret, D.E.Carothers, D.G.Criddle, D.S.Crowl, D.W.Rodts, K.M.Ponciano, K.O.Budde, L.J.Elrod, M.A.Bliss, M.L.Borseth, P.B.Davis, P.K.Schilling, R.A.Felland, R.D.Salsman, R.E.Walker, R.F.Howe, R.R.Stolze, S.J.Hurst, T.F.Christensen, T.J.Hocking, V.D.Beninga, H.Bour, C.P.Peterson, J.Galland, F.L.Sanchez M., L.Moreno D.C., M.Mata, W.A.Volz, F.Delaplanche, A.Beem, C.M.Gardner, D.W.Barham, D.W.Dethorne, G.E.Currie, J.L.Preston, J.R.Bishop, K.A.Christie, M.A.Kemmer, R.A.Bahr, R.L.Carlson, R.L.Grady, R.R.Johnston, T.A.Burleson, K.R.Hawk, L.L.Almanza, R.D.Frields, D.Breitenreicher, E.Butz, E.Saiko, G.Hofmann, H.Bauer, H.Steiger, M.Schell, R.Aefelein, R.Ascherl, R.Hein, R.Lenski, R.Rothermel, R.Sextroh, R.Weis, S.Mehlhorn, A.D.Hoy, A.G.Piasecki, A.J.Maurer, A.V.Wood, C.A.Kimpton, C.A.Liebscher, C.E.Blong, H.T.Long Sr., J.L.Hugaert, J.O.Engen, K.E.Hagemeier, K.L.Seward, L.G.Bohnert, P.M.Gedye, R.J.Maes, R.Morris Jr., R.R.Walker, R.W.Lewis, S.B.Lawrence, S.K.Iaccarino, S.W.Collier, T.C.Keating, T.L.Gallagher, H.M.Lago, B.F.Allport, C.Evezard, L.Porthault, P.Merlu, R.Duquesne, E.Felix, H.Harjung, H.Lampe, J.Moch, M.Geier, M.Limanoski, S.Bauer, W.Hahnebach, W.Neureither, W.Schlachter, E.Ayllon, E.Rodriguez V., J.Gach, W.Maurer, J.H.Draeger, B.Poiget, P.Gautier, G.H.Euchner, J.L.Richardson, B.Pecastay, B.H.Frank, B.J.Eads, B.S.Dudley, C.L.Brockmann, D.D.Boyer, D.E.Lockwood, D.J.Rocker, G.C.Weekes, G.R.Comer, G.R.Hudson, H.E.Thomas, H.L.Barnes, H.T.Long, J.E.Laermans, J.F.Vermeulen, J.H.Varner, J.R.Mack, K.J.Vosekuil, P.A.Wood, R.E.Defauw, T.L.Park Jr., W.M.Dalbey, D.Linke, F.Edinger, H.Dressler, L.Lanno, M.Pergegaj, W.Weber, X.Pascaire, R.L.Gilcrest, A.F.Hartung III, B.J.Groleau, B.J.Gustafson, C.A.Starr, C.L.Mitchell, D.A.Huntley, D.C.Boller, D.C.Johnson, D.Hennessey, D.L.Bristol, D.M.Cullinan, E.O.Shaw, H.E.Pockelwald, J.A.Veach, J.C.Ritchart, J.L.Schmidt, J.R.Hesser, K.L.Richmond, K.L.Wedan, L.A.Quanstrom, L.L.Holste, M.S.Collentine, M.T.Clairmont, P.A.Hillery, P.A.Parrick, P.D.Boyle, R.A.Juel, R.A.Meirhaeghe, R.D.Davis, R.E.Puckett, R.P.Bray, R.P.Shah, R.S.Stewart, R.W.Landsinger, S.L.Morris, S.L.Neuman, S.W.Falline, T.G.Cook, T.L.Wachter, T.R.Hodge, V.Wentz, G.R.Ellis, S.H.Vareberg, A.Gaillard, H.Antonoglou, J.Andres, R.Drexler, R.Schmitt, T.Horlaender, W.Madeja, G.M.Hill, S.L.Neagle, S.Pandza, B.J.Steege, J.M.Steinhauser, H.Schumacher, A.R.Propst, B.F.Gunia, C.A.Corgan, C.E.Sustman, C.L.Elliott, D.B.Miller, D.R.Meiresonne, G.C.Poquet, G.M.Compton, G.R.Pitman Jr., H.L.Gentz, J.C.Glover, J.C.Spence, J.L.Schwartz, J.T.Taylor, K.Core, K.R.Holt, L.F.Wages, L.Ulrey, M.B.Kopp, M.L.Ploessl, M.M.Alderden Jr., M.S.Rashid, P.D.Prybil, R.F.Inskeep, R.K.Taylor, S.M.Strub, T.L.Hartley, T.L.Hilbert, T.L.Jacks, T.R.Hendricks, W.D.Tucker, A.J.Iglesias, L.Guichard, B.Vossion, D.Aguesseau, L.Marois, B.Heyde-Von-Der, K.Stegner, P.Schmidt, R.Wiens, U.Peter, D.Kirschner, E.Schaff, T.J.Renner, I.Marinkovic, R.M.Karsjens, B.A.Lanzen, B.E.Presti, D.C.Timm, D.H.Nguyen, D.M.Weiskopf, D.M.Zorns, E.E.Bartosh, J.A.Knuckey, J.J.Demmer, J.L.Broadwater, J.L.Williams, J.W.Selby, L.J.Tucker, L.L.Lund, M.A.Trumbley, M.C.Anderson, M.L.Miller, M.L.Pietz, M.L.Trent, M.R.Moffitt, P.A.Prouty, R.H.Auliff Jr., R.J.Batten, R.J.Cherrier, R.V.Ramirez, S.B.Bean, S.J.Kincaid, S.K.Mills, S.M.Lujan, T.C.Galarowic, T.J.Brzezinski, V.D.Bandelow, W.C.Luthy, W.H.Barr, M.Robin, S.Svrga, A.Fucci, A.M.Holmgren, B.L.Kertai, C.M.Beek, H.J.Norman Jr., J.A.Kalina, J.D.Podein, J.M.Gimmy Sr., K.A.Culbertson, L.L.Hirsch, L.M.Young, R.K.Blocker, R.L.Young, S.I.Emilio, C.Fleury, H.Seyer, V.Brill, M.E.Nice, M.P.Schmitz, C.Goujon, J.Fauvet, J.Hennebick, B.Siebert, G.Andres, H.Marschall, P.Schang, R.Franke, R.Gorini, R.Irlbeck, R.Runkel, S.Kendyk, W.Bettinger, C.W.Lafollette, H.W.Letcher, R.B.Benefiel, R.E.Young, R.L.Young, S.B.Marsden, A.F.Salaber, C.G.Neal, D.A.Morey, D.J.Burkert, E.B.Toole Jr., F.J.Dobbins, G.A.Tapprich, G.J.Frerichs, G.R.Campbell, H.A.Bullen, J.A.Daley, J.L.Cruce, J.M.Tolliver, K.G.McLaughlin, K.L.Kaalberg, K.M.Johnson, L.E.Nice, L.K.Offutt, M.J.Kieffer, M.L.Entler, M.L.Krueger, N.C.Zbornik, O.Tristan, R.L.Cady, R.L.Smith, S.A.Albright, T.J.Hahn, T.J.Olson, T.L.Eckman, T.L.Johnson, T.W.Nelson, W.S.Aring, G.Schnoeder, H.Ham, J.Kuznik, K.Buchheit, O.Demirtas, W.Marek, J.T.Giordana, L.B.Schroeder, S.C.Karney, Y.Auvray, J.D.Lambdin, L.K.Hall, W.Chochol, T.J.Wunderlin, C.A.Kovalcik, C.E.Donaldson, D.L.Gillette, D.M.Ramsey, F.S.Lacroix, J.A.Hitz, J.D.Gildersleeve, J.D.Steele, J.G.Brown, J.L.Lee, K.E.Hilderbrand, K.G.Kiser, L.B.Babers, L.R.Thompson, M.C.Dooley, N.Forrest, N.I.Reiland, N.M.Johnson, P.A.Hernandez, P.S.Newman, P.W.Devlin, R.F.Pursley, R.L.Edwards, R.L.Johnson, R.Sanders, S.C.Mehuys, T.A.Sorensen, T.A.Vogt, T.B.Wiseman, C.Bouclet, D.Tezard, J.Quetard, M.Sarr, B.Bath, E.Pohl, M.Pljevljak, M.Vogel, A.Grande, A.Hernandez F., J.L.Pajares, P.Gonzalez G., J.R.Cerny Jr., W.H.Agee, M.A.Velasco , A.A.Laporte, D.J.Nicholson, D.L.Cavanaugh, D.M.Harrington, D.M.Payne, G.J.Mc Cabe, J.T.Hamrock, K.L.Kriebs, L.M.Wyckoff, M.A.Herrick, M.A.Sterling, M.D.Blonski, P.A.Seams, R.G.Sutter, S.E.Kennedy, T.C.Hoyt, K.Maurer, A.R.Pender, B.C.Iversen, C.D.Horhn, C.J.Curry, C.J.Ehlert, C.J.Gillies, C.Milton, D.A.Stack, D.B.Tayloe, D.F.Cappaert, D.K.Dewey, D.L.Spencer, D.R.Morrow, D.R.Niska, D.R.Wood Sr., E.R.McKenzie, F.J.Lorenzi, G.E.Lovested, G.L.Kendall, G.S.Revankar, J.A.Lorenz, J.A.Noble, J.D.McKinley, J.G.Hollett, J.M.Tobias, J.W.Wienkes, K.A.Ackerman, K.S.Roberts, L.L.Kriener, M.A.Caufield, M.L.Gabelmann, M.T.Ngo, P.A.Watson, P.L.Bergheger, P.R.Murken, R.B.Bila, R.C.Mendoza, R.D.Armbrester, R.D.Carter, R.J.Johnston, R.L.Hoyt, R.L.Tiffany, R.M.Lewison, S.A.Vandenbos, S.L.Nicholson, S.M.Larson, T.A.Breheny, V.P.Huhmann, W.G.Cameron, B.Brochet, P.Condolf, A.Acar, H.Kurz, P.Huver, C.A.Zuhlke, R.Hopkins, I.Wackershauser, B.M.Staver, J.A.Redman, R.J.Gonzalez, M.Schricker, J.Ayala, J.Gasulla, J.Louchati, B.Halajda, J.Sawczuk, S.Sope, B.G.Tyson, B.S.Wallarab, C.A.Brown, D.D.Rock, D.J.Guenther, D.L.Hoffman, D.M.Roe, F.H.McCleery III, G.D.Bergquist, J.A.Benson, J.D.Anderson, J.K.Hancock, J.K.Hanson III, J.L.Ehlers, J.L.Veys, J.S.Rule, K.L.Foreman, K.R.Pierce, L.D.Blankenship, L.J.Letts, L.K.Vickerman, M.B.Wagner, M.E.Bodwell, M.F.Stickler, M.J.Bredesky, M.J.Hilby, M.W.Steen, N.D.Skjerseth, N.J.Morehead, P.J.Murray, R.A.Salter, R.Finch, R.G.McEllhiney, R.M.Andes Jr., R.R.Boeding, S.A.Heine, S.K.Shirley, T.B.Hunsaker, T.C.Thor, T.L.Irwin, W.C.Hunt, B.R.Shields, J.Mele, M.J.Rubie, W.J.Culbertson, W.L.Hutchinson, G.Donatien, C.Miller, D.M.Freund, J.D.Johannsen, K.J.Harmon, K.L.Towns, L.A.Timmerman, M.J.Fuller, M.J.Sellers, N.C.O'Brien, O.Jung, P.Sagers, R.K.Olvera, R.L.Langford, R.M.O Neill, W.S.Schnathorst, A.Puyrenier, E.Gehres, E.Schmitt, J.Dannhaeuser, M.Neuhof, S.Vitello, W.Wingert, B.J.Foster, B.L.Rippentrop, B.T.Cote, C.D.Temperley, C.M.Klaren, C.P.Logan, D.A.Lemke, D.A.Michaluk, D.D.Mundhenke, D.D.Pittman, D.F.Peterson, D.R.Teel, E.D.Kasemodel, G.J.Kedley, G.R.Suppes, G.W.Green, J.A.Marshall, J.F.Roach, J.G.Iwanski, J.L.Tieskotter, J.L.Tribbey, J.S.Bisbee, J.W.Berg, K.J.Bennett, K.J.Bultsma Sr., K.S.Metternick, K.S.Reed, L.D.Blair, L.E.Bull, M.A.Holder, M.C.Chamley, M.J.Mueller, M.L.Hartson, R.D.Eakman, R.D.Thier, R.E.Sirota, R.F.Konopka, R.G.Rohret, R.R.Arnold, R.R.Timmons, S.A.Jones, S.Brunette, S.C.Anciaux, S.E.Haley, S.H.Johnson, S.J.Johnson, S.K.Nienkark, T.A.Carlson, T.L.Elliott, T.M.Oftedal, W.R.Saelens, J.G.Ontiveros, J.L.Vargas, D.A.Orona, M.W.Kandis, P.D.Zierke, R.L.Nickerson, T.K.Roller, C.Leplatre, M.Chardin, C.Zigolanis, F.Schroeter, G.Carnarius, B.Bystrom, C.L.Zimanek, D.J.McCleary, A.Vazquez, M.D.Hopson, E.L.Stokes Reed, A.T.Chan, B.A.Morgart, B.A.Westerdale, B.M.Rodgers, B.S.Matsumoto, C.A.Benson, C.L.Burnett, C.L.Rubley, C.S.Weatherington, D.A.Boyce, D.A.Larson, D.E.Brems, D.E.Speed, D.J.Hocking, D.P.Hartson, D.Sykes, E.B.Jackson, E.Hing, F.O.St Clair, F.W.Starr, G.A.Reid, G.D.Currie, G.N.Cusovich, J.G.Curlott, J.H.Cox, J.L.Specht, J.M.Blaser, J.T.Torres, K.R.Olson, L.G.Hanson, M.E.Anderson, P.L.Dahl, R.D.Smith, R.D.Sweat, R.J.Smola, R.J.Westerdale, R.L.Fisher, R.L.Jurek, T.E.Parker, T.J.Love, T.L.Johnson, V.K.Ryan, W.T.Kranz, M.T.Blanco, P.Tabuteau, S.Bongibault, A.Gross, T.Taylor, J.A.Klaassen, M.A.Carr, P.M.Wiles, J.A.Farias, J.D.McChurch, R.W.Sanders, W.E.Thomas, A.A.Castro, B.B.Rudner, B.M.Dalfonso, B.W.Blaser, C.A.Lisius, C.Williamson, D.E.Shadley, D.F.Meyer, D.J.Catour, D.L.Peters, D.R.Bender, D.W.Hoadley, F.A.Kerulis, G.T.Zeppuhar, J.A.Morningstar, J.A.Newhouse, J.A.Swartzendruber, J.C.Ziebarth, J.J.Postal, J.K.Neighbours, K.J.Schumacher, K.L.Newman, K.W.Williams, L.D.Roome, L.K.Rickert, L.P.Williams, M.D.Ducey, M.L.Skinner, P.A.Janssen, P.Augie, P.M.Meeker, R.A.Gauthier, R.A.Hirtz, R.E.Whitney, R.H.Hunsinger Jr., R.J.Pieper, R.M.Hind, R.S.Finkler, S.J.Kautz, S.W.Leech, T.Wilson, V.L.Meyer, R.Girard, C.Kioussis, E.Leiner, M.Golubov, J.Legrand, P.L.Bristol, R.C.Hove, S.Shaw, T.A.Shambeau, G.M.Kraus, C.B.Snyder, C.M.Schultz, D.A.Gipp, D.Kirk, D.L.Foster, F.W.Weston, G.A.Morett, G.D.Jones, G.E.Spaans, G.F.Hoard, J.E.Borro Jr., J.E.Harl, K.A.Kopp, M.B.Ruger, M.H.Evans, P.M.Jennings, R.R.Welch, S.B.Detrick, T.C.Spitzfaden, V.Vogt, P.Guerault, P.Plisson, E.Terzis, G.Morawietz, H.Sevim, A.Rojo-Canseco, A.M.Langdon, J.L.Kerr, K.W.Garrison, L.L.Hopp, J.Carret, J.M.Schreiner, R.M.Young, E.Eder, E.Holtkotte, H.Bauer, H.Mueller, H.Weiss, J.Dittmann, K.Linz, R.Van, V.Kapoor, D.J.Dies, J.F.Demmer, M.A.Cook, M.C.Harrison, M.S.Egert, R.D.Russell, R.L.Vyncke, R.R.Beach, T.M.Grasmick, W.A.Bork, C.Leconte, D.Giroux, J.Estelle, P.Bracquemond, X.Pinault, Y.Gojon, A.Rapisarda, B.Rudzki, C.Mai, J.Ceri, M.Pohl, P.Schady, W.Hartmann, A.J.Jostman, R.A.Martin, D.W.Hasenmiller, G.Cruz, M.Lobato, D.C.Van Lauwe, D.J.Hoefer, D.R.Hummel, J.E.Campbell, J.R.Saner, K.J.Kearney, R.L.Duncan, D.C.Smart, D.J.Vantieghem, D.L.Shields, D.Nagovan, D.T.Park, E.W.Dany, H.Sandoval, H.W.Wilkens, J.K.Falcone, J.W.Beebe, K.D.Beiner, K.M.Kuebler, N.R.Meggers, R.H.George, R.J.Reichenberger, R.K.Rowland, S.D.Waage, T.H.Carlson, V.L.Mosenfelder, J.Bruneau, N.Roock, N.Schlichting, W.Zimmermann, P.L.Stanhope, V.R.Ballard, W.S.Bloom, R.J.Quinlan, C.B.White, B.A.Schroeder, B.R.Rognstad, C.J.Nielsen, D.D.Brooks, D.P.Levengood, E.M.Kinney, G.W.Locke, G.Zeller, H.L.Mikkelsen, H.Tuchel, K.M.Koenig, K.P.Scharpf, L.M.Zach, M.A.Mueller, M.J.McGuire, M.L.Duncombe, P.A.Mitchell, P.D.Bounds, P.T.Cheng, R.G.Hoyer, R.G.Quetschke, R.J.Estrada, R.L.Murphy, R.T.Swope, S.J.Royes, S.L.Prebyl, S.M.Kirkpatrick, T.A.Murphy, T.J.Ludwig, T.J.Parshall, T.Jones, W.H.McQuiston, J.L.Tse, J.Louppe, A.Kalinski, D.Langer, H.Abele, J.Loehr, M.Gerhardt, Q.Lokaj, R.Moskwiak, C.J.Greenleaf, P.Satabin, R.L.Steckelberg, E.Rodrigues, O.Muller, A.Kerst, B.G.Pinson, K.J.Hagarty, L.A.Atwater, L.E.Kappeler-De Braal, M.N.Meister, M.W.Parsons, P.P.Knoell, R.M.Jarnecke, S.A.Sizer, T.W.Moris, P.Belpalme, A.Essig, A.Kosch, H.Hutzelmann, K.Maddox, T.C.Hampton, A.M.Sinner, F.H.Burroughs, G.R.Kinkead, J.B.Kuhn, K.A.Hubbard, L.R.Hartquist, M.J.Talbert, R.E.Kasten, V.L.Winter, W.B.Kaufman, D.Alix, H.Tuczykont, S.Bisson, W.Schuele, C.A.Hampton, C.M.Chapman, C.W.Strandlund, D.K.Davis, F.J.Kamish, M.L.Stoneking, M.M.Buhr, S.L.Mc Dowell, W.E.Ellis, C.R.Dinon, J.Barton, J.Paquet, M.Candelon, G.Bichard, G.Sery, S.Houze, T.Foucher, T.Le Marchand, Y.Curiel, A.Bauer, D.Hartmann, F.Obenauer, J.Mayer, L.Allegra, M.Serr, C.L.Vannatta, D.L.Martin, G.D.Arney, J.J.Etienne, K.D.Dollar, M.H.Buescher, M.J.Girsch, P.C.Lagatta, T.E.Meier, B.Maillary, C.Renou, S.Jefimic, W.Ritter, D.M.Darnell, R.Contreras, C.S.Vickroy, D.B.Werkheiser, G.P.Fowler, H.D.Helsel, J.P.Vanthorre, K.B.Melton Jr., M.J.Simosky, R.G.Hand, V.D.Heusinkveld, W.A.Eshelman, W.M.Mohn, D.J.Mallmann, G.Haberkorn, H.Przybilla, M.Atay, Y.Latz, C.S.Mack, B.Kraiter, D.K.Sabin, P.L.Berthoud, E.Kaiser, B.J.Squire, D.W.Moon, L.W.McLaughlin, N.N.Lanzen, R.C.Meerstein, S.M.Boyer, T.L.Gustafson, C.J.Morris, D.R.Rebhuhn, J.L.Collins, J.M.Mausser, L.M.Sawyer, M.G.Gould, T.K.Hein, C.Dziura, J.Maillot, T.Walz, B.Bischof, C.Winternheimer, F.Eigenmann, G.Hochlehnert, H.Friess, J.Buscher, J.Gund, J.Schneider, M.Gross, R.Herrmann, R.Oster, T.Mueller, R.Zehnder, F.Sulger, G.Strauss-Wenz, U.Teschner, B.A.Nelson, C.A.Bowers, D.M.Schafer, D.S.Paxton, J.D.Kemp, K.L.McLain, L.G.Lanning, M.A.Ehlert, M.H.Shea, M.W.Snyder, R.L.Reichen, R.L.Shahan, R.W.Bixby, T.J.Britt, T.J.Seegers, N.Rapine, W.Wilhelm, J.Niemiro, C.T.Avery, J.M.Bartholomew, D.L.Mattson, J.J.Phelan, M.A.G.D.Santos, R.Korkmaz, B.E.Klintworth, M.Goujon, E.Stoeckle, H.Huber, H.Sandmeyer, H.Steinbach, I.Ben-Ameur, J.Mateiczuk, K.Bachmann, L.Filsinger, O.Lehner, P.Rickl, R.Braun, T.Weis, W.Gab, R.P.Johann, F.Brunet, M.Lambert, P.Girard, A.Broedel, A.Geschwill, G.Duda, G.Gilge, G.Woelk, H.Laxy, H.Oehl, J.Kirch, L.Varga, V.Kahrimanovic, B.J.Budde, B.J.Paasch, C.A.Bryson, D.L.Moon, D.R.Lukasik, D.W.Workman, G.H.Beecher, G.Martinez, J.F.Mathia, J.Smith, J.W.Carruthers, K.C.McKee, K.L.Condari, K.L.Higgins, L.A.Carlson, M.M.Wade, N.L.Butler, R.C.Bell, S.M.Strassburger, W.C.Sellers, C.V.Loweth, G.Kopp, A.R.Mitchem, C.P.Spyrow, D.R.Dopler, J.M.Nelson, L.A.Ochs, L.A.Wieneke, L.J.Norman, M.J.Sandoval, P.D.Gage, P.L.Falck, R.F.Johnston, R.J.Carruthers, R.J.Exman, R.U.Sumpter, R.W.Ceurvorst, T.Chokkalingam, N.A.D.Carvalho, V.Lipke, C.Ulrich, D.Popovic, E.Lottas, F.Di-Carlo, F.Heindler, F.Mainka, K.Kouratzidis, W.Letsch, Y.Bacaksiz, J.H.Becht, F.Marciniak, A.Ali, K.Berni, A.C.Shaw, B.F.Kacer, B.L.Rugh, C.S.Calloway, D.A.Boyles, E.S.Wright, H.J.Reisen, J.A.Hayden, J.K.Drake, M.Collison, S.M.Dyer, S.P.McCann, V.L.Ball, C.Keller, I.P.Bender, M.P.Torres, P.C.D.Silva, M.Augendre, S.Schrobiltgen, M.Toupance, B.Koenigsmann, D.Leonard, H.Rudolphi, J.Cieslik, P.Gulowaty, V.Kovacevic, W.Fuerguth, G.M.Bauwens, P.T.Shaw, R.A.Rondeau, E.D.A.Rodrigues, A.H.Escobedo, C.A.Fitzpatrick, S.Lo Giudice, B.L.Ault, D.J.Berezinski, D.L.Primo, D.L.Scrutchfield, D.M.Broghammer, D.M.Deering, D.P.Gantz, E.R.Theis, J.A.Gries, J.D.Switala, J.R.Merrill, L.J.O'Brien, M.E.Hall, P.L.Olmstead, R.A.Lund, R.D.Shirk, R.J.Hicks, S.P.Lang, B.Jousserand, C.Courte, A.Gruenfelder, A.Spitalny, G.Borowka, P.Pfeiffer, P.Simicic, R.Maciej, W.Kinzig, K.E.Hunt, R.W.Hillis, S.E.Hamilton, B.A.Pix, C.A.Clay, L.E.Smith, R.M.Oestreich, B.K.Fryk, C.J.Talik, C.M.Congdon, D.J.English, D.L.Corbitt Jr., D.M.Lestor, G.L.Watt, G.S.Webb, G.T.Dold, I.R.Brown, J.Overbeeke, K.E.Haydon, K.L.Zitterich, L.L.Sheley, N.W.Riek, P.L.Gravitt, R.V.Landrum, S.A.Yoder, S.C.Guns, J.Guerin, A.Eren, A.Guenes, A.Jasici, E.Iseler, E.Rudy, F.Fuehl, H.Frankfurter, H.Reis, H.Schlachter, H.Schurin, J.Kuppelmeier, K.Fessler, M.Klee, P.Georgel, R.Mattausch, S.Gueven, T.Eiffler, U.Schmid, V.Gemmiti, V.Sciandrone, W.Baumgart, W.Luber, J.A.Calvente, K.M.Jansen, H.Schynol, J.Hollstein, D.Schmitt, L.Weiss, C.Basroger, S.Mat, L.W.Lange, M.A.Brooks, M.G.Dobson, F.C.Sturmer, D.Girault, J.Barre, J.Goueffon, P.Lange, A.Dietz, F.Katt, H.Greil, L.Ibarzabal, L.Ihrig, P.Lopez, T.Sananikone, W.Buehler, S.A.Anguiano, P.B.Reed, A.H.Kajewski, A.M.Allen, E.J.Buehler, E.M.Brazell, F.M.Sandoval, G.J.Ackley, J.A.Williams, M.Gelman, R.A.Simon, L.Monget, L.Perthuis, E.Linke, H.Jaeger, H.Miosga, J.Chmielewski, M.Pino, P.Plewik, W.Knauer, P.Murga, B.Jordy, J.G.De Ruiter, J.Livingstone, M.Lindsay, P.Pastor, R.Herold, M.Terzi, C.V.Lohf, F.Rios, H.R.Mickley, J.E.Howell, L.A.Kellums, W.H.Disney, G.Gaveriaux, A.Lecei, H.Braun, J.Delejan, M.Bicer, A.Entzi, J.A.Mayberry, W.E.Buhr, P.G.Jackson, A.Zetovic, B.J.Reynolds-Hogan, C.R.Ramsey, G.L.White, J.Rodrigues-Vicente, W.T.Vittori, C.J.Phillips, D.J.Macdonald, J.L.McKee, R.W.Nelson, V.J.Hiatt, D.Pelle, J.Taillemitte, M.Hylaire, P.Baltazar, G.Brucculeri, H.Redweik, S.Livatino, S.Pusch, S.Senyildiz, P.Ianniello, S.Bajrami, D.V.Detloff Jr., D.J.Cowan, J.L.Niehaus, K.L.Duvall, L.S.Ganz, S.M.Pye, T.A.Peterson, T.M.Reynolds, T.W.Holder, W.D.Bishop, G.Heim, G.Hirsch, H.Herr, H.Vogel, M.Herr, M.Mattner, R.Schelling, S.A.Bodenhamer, E.Fischer, M.Tokat, E.D.Dorris, G.A.Doherty, J.D.Avery, J.S.Gillette, K.D.Howard, K.L.Fobert, R.S.Rangel, W.L.Stalter, D.Thiercelin, G.Hatton, J.Bonnin, J.Mirault, B.Cetin, D.Hiegl, M.Smiciklas, P.Otto, S.Dominquez, T.L.Ball, B.Patriarche, E.F.Rhyne, B.J.Benson, D.J.Brubaker, D.W.Kmoch, J.C.Walter, J.Ernat, L.D.Albansoder, M.S.Hubbard, P.C.Burke, R.G.Stowe, S.J.Haywood, W.H.Mortier, Y.M.Rapp, D.Descharmes, J.Tuilard, P.Nicaud, A.Fortmeier, E.R.Henning, V.A.Zaroda, J.J.Cepeda, W.C.Fierce, R.Rodriguez, B.A.Hansen, C.A.Lane, J.A.Mc Donald, J.C.Moreno, I.J.Martins, E.G.Hatfield, J.G.Eli, J.W.Rosenthal, G.Clément, A.Boulay, P.Pedel, J.Skaletz, M.Berwanger, M.Oeztuerk, T.Oeztuerk, Z.Stosic, B.A.Dirck, B.W.Griggs, D.D.Reeves, D.G.Newman, K.J.Jensen, K.L.Cox, M.C.Rubino, M.H.Erickson, M.S.Larson, P.J.Correa, R.T.Schmerbach, S.A.Felton, W.P.Santy, A.Oenal, G.Neskudla, M.Dominkovic, D.C.Hopkins, E.E.Engelhardt, M.J.Boyle, R.R.Castillo, D.Ludwig, D.Rosenzweig, E.Krieger, G.Geissler, K.Seeberger, R.Gaertner, S.Halabiya, C.D.Weaver, D.C.Gill, J.K.Munts, J.L.Clevenger, J.L.Obermiller, K.M.Syverson, L.L.Zelnio, M.J.Beaudoin, R.J.Steinbach, R.L.Black, S.D.Corcoran, S.D.Hanson, S.D.Sharp, S.M.Berg, V.E.Hardy, C.Nagler, R.Banspach, B.M.Paulsen, A.E.Tucker, S.A.Bargo, B.Moisson, R.E.Anderson, C.B.Fickenscher, D.A.Wymore, M.E.Abbey, M.I.Elkin, R.A.Petersmith, R.J.Esser, S.K.Hodson, W.E.Marze, N.Hardy, T.Passaniti, J.R.Goff, R.R.Zeidler, W.F.Briggs, R.Huang, **1980** F.G.Mildner, A.Radmacher, E.Draga, F.Erbach, H.Gelb, H.Hirschpek, H.Wawra, J.Montag, K.Eustachi, K.Muench, K.Templin, N.Ehrhardt, O.Lorenz, P.Odermatt, P.Patzke, R.Brechtel, R.Kohl, R.Moch, W.Brod, W.Schneider, W.Trinkl, W.Ziegler, B.D.Campbell, B.S.Randall, C.L.Brody, D.A.Richards, D.E.Meek, D.H.Budelier, D.R.Lindenfelser, E.K.Paasch, G.A.Jackson, J.A.Clouw, J.E.Sandberg, K.A.Rensvold, L.E.Redinbaugh, M.C.Allgaier, M.J.Adams, R.D.Moehlis, R.L.Bebout, S.S.Meyer, T.E.Williams, T.H.Moeller, B.Blanc, E.Cassegrain, J.Gourcilleau, P.Duverger, R.Chauvelin, H.Schwartz, S.Fumagalli, D.L.Collier, D.S.Ennen, F.R.Dunlop Sr., M.E.Senechal, J.M.Farro, E.N.Manhabosco, A.Lavender, B.A.Kammer, C.S.Bundschuh, D.A.Skriba, D.K.Larder, D.V.Lackey, D.W.Mitton, E.M.Simmonds, G.E.Hart, H.J.Schaab, A.Dobelek, J.H.Hoffmann, J.J.Albano, J.W.Crone, J.W.Hankins, K.Dykas, K.E.Hurning, K.G.Dejaeger, K.J.Suiter, L.L.Junis, L.M.Arthur, M.J.Verstraete, P.M.Bleymeyer,

Horicon, Wisconsin, factory employees celebrating one-millionth tractor, 1984

R.D.Robinson, R.J.Renze, T.J.Hatalsky, C.Delgado, A.Vosges, B.Girard, A.Titze, B.Goulon, H.Gansert, H.Kansy, H.Sroka, J.Bryla, L.Kraft, M.Didone, M.Huhnke, M.Zipse, R.Burkhardt, T.Mrozek, V.Heydecke, W.Bialas, W.Keller, W.Marsolek, B.J.Rolfs, K.K.Keeler, M.L.Deboer, R.D.Dinnes Jr., F.Gast, T.D.Ziegler, T.E.Lamar, A.M.Jones, B.J.Runde, D.A.Dahlby, D.E.Johnston, D.J.Caughron, D.L.Jones, E.G.Hayes, G.O.Scheer, H.B.Williams III, J.D.Schultz, J.E.Humphrey, J.L.Westmorland, J.M.Cahill, J.S.Gehrke, J.T.Pierce, K.A.Thompson, L.C.Preete, M.J.Jackson, M.O.Youngblood, P.D.Parker, P.J.Fisher, R.A.Martin, S.J.Schmidt, A.Schuppe, J.Le Bourdonnec, E.Wunder, F.Pechloch, J.Wittek, P.Chwalek, U.Schwoebel, R.E.Crosbie, M.J.Brown, A.Franck, C.Heimann, J.Franz, C.A.White, E.P.Stephenson, F.A.Clark, J.A.Ryckaert, J.L.Eagan, J.W.Henningsen, L.S.Doyle, W.D.Burns, M.A.Schmidt, A.L.Klein, C.A.Sass, C.J.Forlines, C.J.Murphy, J.A.Angel, J.L.Carr, L.J.Cowart, N.A.Flaherty, R.E.Fobair, R.J.Scheetz, S.L.Dudzinski, W.I.Leach, W.O.Ellis, H.Rivera, M.Pluchon, P.Bomberault, G.Bachmann, B.R.Stephens, C.E.Senatra, A.K.Bazzocco, D.A.Broeker, D.A.De Clerck, D.A.Kernan, D.D.Mc Kain, D.J.Dabler, D.K.Carter, D.M.Turner, D.R.Butt, G.L.Anderson, J.E.Roach, K.E.Erickson, M.A.Eckard, M.K.Bell, M.R.Goswami, R.A.Roels, R.L.Pilger, R.P.Schmidt, S.J.Lonsdale, T.J.Meyer, V.E.Wiley, D.Soubret, G.Bonk, S.Stagno, V.Musso, G.A.Williams, D.P.Michalek, B.E.Nelson, B.L.Boivin, C.J.Peters, D.D.Jones, G.E.Luster, G.M.Roberts, K.G.Van Roekel, M.C.Tipton, M.D.McCollum, A.A.D.Reis, A.Arenhardt, A.L.Scherer, A.P.Johann, A.Schweig, A.V.D.Silva, F.J.D.L.Silveira, F.J.Fritzen, I.Borgmann, I.V.Maron, L.J.Kraemer, M.L.S.D.Santos, M.Vintacourt, O.Duarte, O.Patias, R.Leonhardt, V.M.Vogt, A.Lautensack, C.Deuschel, E.Heck, E.Hoefle, F.Stief, G.Gropp, H.Fischer, H.Kuhn, I.Pettinger, K.Eckert, U.Berger, Z.Malki, A.L.Johnson, A.M.Quayle, A.R.Mc Gee, B.T.Brown, C.A.Jungling, J.M.Schaeffer, K.J.Bernt, L.K.Luster, L.S.Wheelen, M.C.Videbeck, M.D.Anderson, M.J.Cowell, P.M.Heun, R.M.Newsom, T.H.Griswold, V.J.Lowery, W.A.Powers, W.L.Anderson, D.ROBINOT, D.Lissonnet, D.Poher, P.Broutin, T.Billard, A.Chabounia, C.Cibis, C.Schneider, E.Schneider, M.Karkilla, B.L.Plunkett, R.A.Righi, N.A.Bower, B.M.Hough, S.Friess, C.L.Gramling, G.A.Hepker, J.A.Atkins, K.A.Moran, L.M.Craig, L.W.Rounds, M.J.Ontiveros, P.R.Gibson, R.A.Abbott, S.D.Klarkowski, A.V.Steffens, M.Laengle, L.Grossl, A.Weis, S.K.Allen, A.L.McBride, B.J.Hare, C.J.Weirbach, D.T.Easterlund, E.J.Pongres, J.A.Dollar, J.B.Aubin, J.Wignall, K.E.Ginter, T.R.Rettenmeier, O.B.Schlemmer, J.Bazin, D.Valencia, J.Gladis, B.S.Huffstetler, R.E.Roggendorf, H.Steiner, B.M.Siddall, D.L.Doss, L.J.Livesay, L.L.Skinner, L.S.Peterson, M.A.Hayner, O.R.Greene, R.J.Miller, T.K.Schooley, M.Gillot, R.Leal, F.T.Solis, L.N.Nichols, Y.A.Mascari, J.S.Carter, D.R.Dort, J.A.Gilliland, A.Hankammer, J.Nauertz, A.Elliott Jr., E.L.Kloida, J.C.Jensen, J.J.Gordon III, K.A.Rowland, K.E.Giese, K.H.Werning, K.J.Hudders, R.E.Nederbrock, R.T.Williams, S.L.Mettee, T.A.Cooney, T.M.Bruce, T.P.Townsend, V.L.Ackerman, H.Fusiger, J.C.L.Gomes, J.V.M.Alves, O.Kotz, R.Saraiva, M.Quentin, P.Eliot, M.Beauhaire, H.Mueller, W.Reischmann, B.A.Clark, N.E.Roberts, J.Shipp, D.E.Linnebur, E.A.Lomelino, G.B.Hallas, J.F.Brozovich, L.L.Brown, M.A.Driskell, M.B.Skahill, M.P.Zinnel, R.J.Wagner, D.Schlemmer, J.A.Leal, J.E.D.Silva, R.E.Beilke, A.Psardelis, H.Andres, P.M.Kowolik, S.V.Tullos, G.Carbon, D.H.Bryant, V.N.Schmidt, W.Tatomir, A.A.Hollings, C.E.Henning, C.K.Beerling, D.E.Armstrong, J.A.Koenig, J.B.Schmidt, J.R.Reitz, K.D.Musgrove, L.D.Bickford, M.G.Wayne, M.L.Lewis, R.F.O'Malley III, R.J.Whitford, R.K.Barnes, R.P.Flamm, S.J.Benda, V.L.Teas, W.E.Postma, H.Speiser, B.J.Haussmann, B.K.Taylor, D.L.Helms, D.O.Doss, J.A.Seals, J.E.Fetes, J.E.Maltby, M.H.Bowers, M.J.Hellige, M.J.Jones, R.A.Dreiling, R.W.Butikofer, S.N.Watson, T.A.Ragon, P.D.Scheibelhut, K.E.Burke, B.K.Starkell, D.J.Finzel, D.R.Penny, J.W.Shay, M.H.Doyle, R.A.Roselle Jr., D.Martin, C.L.Filbrandt, D.L.Harrison, J.K.Hale Jr., K.E.Taylor, M.L.McClenahan MD, R.A.Seres, M.A.Treviño, A.Nowack, B.Maemecke, D.Kuehnreich, E.Barth, E.Geissler, F.Gaertner, G.Woerner, H.Fassott, H.Gernsheimer, J.Fiedler, J.Stahlmecke, K.Wottke, L.Wolf, M.Jedinger, R.Rehm, T.Weber, B.L.Lutz, G.T.Jones, K.M.Fraher, P.D.Mohr, R.S.Smith, L.T.Silver, W.J.Stoker, D.Gizeria, M.A.Fensterseifer, H.Stephan, A.E.Zander, B.A.Thomas, C.D.Trentham, D.A.Ludwick, D.W.Hallas, K.D.Kleeman, P.V.Savignano, M.Guenot, K.Schewes, P.Ehrmann, D.A.Lathrop, K.L.Huggins, R.K.Blanshan, R.M.Mally, S.M.Crete, T.I.Nakedi, J.A.Rodríguez, D.L.Wethington, S.L.Wadsager, W.J.Gabriel, H.Nagao, N.Casteret, A.Poulin, D.D.Erdy, J.R.Poell, S.E.Shoger, T.A.Gildehaus, W.R.Anderson, L.Huver, R.R.Yado, I.L.Hedstrom, J.O.Veltri, E.Kitzmann, J.Hilsheimer, K.Konopka, P.Driemel, P.Seiboth, S.Licht, J.Adolf, D.J.Loewen, F.W.Nelson, I.A.Lenz, T.L.Nissen, F.H.Wales, A.Seib, A.Zimmermann, C.A.Guerra, A.M.Impens, D.L.McManus, J.E.Reeves, L.J.Cappelli, R.J.Schebler, W.J.Cauthen Jr., X.E.Wilson, Y.E.Robinson, M.J.Makgabutlane, M.J.Sobende, L.S.Bullard, T.A.Bering, E.L.Bender, M.G.Gotcher, R.A.Sergesketter, R.D.Dunkin, R.D.Lair, R.M.Kramer, S.R.Anderson, S.Pfisterer, D.A.Harrison, J.A.Roversi, M.L.Whiteman, E.Zenobi, C.R.Busch, G.D.Clark, G.Detrick, K.J.Ford, M.A.Guinn, M.E.Bader, M.L.Adamson, M.T.Wire, G.M.Sawvell, M.T.Robbins, G.W.Griffiths, L.J.Adams, J.G.Morales, A.Schmelzinger, E.Reulecke, R.Aulmich, B.A.Arntson, B.E.Bauer, C.H.Koehn, C.R.Jones, C.S.Erickson, D.F.Wells, D.J.Strempke, D.J.Zack, F.K.Sanders, G.D.Armstrong, G.D.Luxon, G.H.Wiezorek, G.J.Laudick, J.D.Sundberg, J.E.Garbin, J.K.Borseth, J.M.Behrendt, J.R.Read Jr., K.L.Vaughters, M.A.Bishop, M.A.Brockman, M.D.Snyder, M.L.Ford, P.S.Nitka, R.H.Eichhorst, R.J.Curtis, R.L.Ehrlich, R.R.Barton, S.A.Jensen, S.P.Maller, T.E.Sharp, Y.H.Everton, R.Koopmans, R.J.Jensen, S.C.Olson, A.J.Woodcock, B.C.Borcherding, J.M.Plathe, K.R.Moder, L.D.Haidsiak, P.A.Fisher, R.D.Shirk, S.M.Gray, T.L.Snipes, T.W.Schwartz, W.L.Smith Jr., J.J.Roell, J.M.Smarr Sr., D.L.Kaus, G.W.Hardy, G.W.Lemert, M.A.Andresen, M.A.Beckman, M.W.Schramm, P.A.Meyer, P.S.Wilczynski, R.J.Zipse, R.M.Laveau, T.M.Scott, T.O.Norton, T.P.Smith, W.A.Griese, D.Primaz, A.Zumaran, J.K.Mc Donald, L.L.Lovich, M.C.Lee, P.G.Trainor, W.D.Neunsinger, E.D.Kunzler, A.Garcia, J.L.Venzor, G.B.Dumser, C.W.Gouws, B.L.Carlson, F.F.Bratton, L.A.Dunn, P.M.Van Dyke, R.H.Stoedter, W.M.Taylor, S.K.Bedis, E.Auer, E.Graef, G.Hoerrmann, K.Graber, K.Harnisch, K.Mueller, N.Mattern, H.D.Basso, E.Grimaldo, D.A.Sebben, M.T.Bergeron, Y.M.Carter, J.Belton, J.Ramos, V.L.Villalon, J.A.Sandau, R.Arevalo, H.J.Hirt, B.Silva, J.R.Jabanoski, M.L.Lentz, C.A.Ritter, L.J.Sartor, S.F.Ramirez, R.Campos, H.Lundeen, M.S.Manala, O.Bliard, J.R.Patton, M.S.Cook, R.D.Manfull, A.Merkel, D.Mueller, H.Paschaloglu, H.Schmitt, H.Steffan, I.Ban, J.Alter, J.Parthenschlager, K.Binder, K.Kuerschner, M.Kern, P.Waber, R.Gaa, R.Lemme, S.Pfeiffer, W.Hrach, J.W.Rauber, A.Schlachter, K.Dickgiesser, K.Weick, L.Schlachter, R.Schlachter, R.Werner, D.W.Jeffers, E.B.Kochhann, B.C.Barnett, L.C.Kirkland, J.Ludwig, C.Vera, I.Strapasson, A.Pasket, D.M.Beck, S.E.Karlix, J.M.Chayé, D.Wunsch, P.R.Johnston, E.Burger, G.Kistner, J.Kennel, J.Rohr, K.Maurer, R.Kamuf, C.Legeay, A.C.Townsend, B.A.Hill, J.M.Adams, W.W.Pulliam, J.N.M.Camargo, H.Yueceer, E.D.Simpson, S.Hernandez, H.Calderón, S.J.Mokone, K.E.Mason, A.M.Pearson, M.Soto, S.R.Cruz, V.De la Cruz, F.Morales, A.Sehy, P.M.Chance, P.Kgobisa, D.S.Morris, D.K.McCarthy-Golz, J.K.Hodgerson, K.A.Ligeno, P.P.Johnston, A.F.Widz, V.C.Kiefer, D.Striegel, L.Saunders, S.D.Kos, T.E.Knoll, H.Carbon, H.Karstaedt, H.Neitzel, P.Schuster, J.P.Vazquez, T.R.Buchanan, **1981** R.D.Spangenberg, C.A.True, C.S.Lehman, D.E.Macleod, E.J.Hanson, G.M.Beuse, K.L.Shirley, L.B.Glantz, V.M.McVietty, J.C.Villarreal, D.B.Nimmo, P.E.Woollard, K.Hertel, P.A.Phillips, J.C.Foiles, J.K.Gregersen, A.Rotter, H.N.Mack Jr., S.E.Pigg, J.H.Quinn, E.C.Barichello, E.M.Pebane, S.L.Vandemore, J.B.Hourigan, A.Spacke, E.Ebert, E.Rausch, C.A.Greenway, C.J.Qualls, K.R.Garvey, P.A.Kosmicki, C.E.Schwingel, I.J.Glienke, J.M.Franco, L.Konig, V.Felten, A.O.Rodrigues, D.R.Devooght, J.S.Laing Jr., R.J.Bettis, R.T.Evans, F.J.Saucedo, S.D.Schaffer, M.M.Johns, M.P.Haselhuhn, R.Foster, A.Stec, E.A.Ullmann, F.L.Pasch, G.Sackser, J.L.Wachholz, L.Reisner, M.A.Ackermann, O.C.Roglin, J.M.Lundahl, T.L.K.Carpes, R.B.Kipf, L.K.Lundquist, E.Heil, I.Schimmel, K.Loose, D.G.Bernier, D.M.Goodwin, E.A.Johnston, R.M.Comp, S.S.McCalmon, T.J.Christensen, S.Lozano, V.L.Canada, A.V.Grellmann, J.Kelley, T.M.Bethune, O.Dockhorn, I.Kalkbrenner, J.Manrique, P.Martinez, R.Portillo, F.S.Ward, J.McCallister, N.G.Lane, P.G.Hammell, C.Abeling, L.Dezelus, A.Gaess, A.Hoffmann, E.Baumgartl, H.Egert, H.Mietner, K.Baumann, M.Jaeger, D.M.Meier, L.Orendorff, P.O.Barnes, J.De la Cruz, D.J.Patel, R.Silva, R.S.Lau, I.A.Peiter, R.Knoebl, E.Wolf, H.Fleig, L.Stegner, A.M.Arkebauer, W.G.Leon, S.Lesniak, E.L.Bauer, J.H.Walters, K.J.Fuhr, S.J.Boney, J.C.Kaed, C.B.Whitehead, G.T.Ghere, L.A.Foulk, R.A.Depauw, R.D.Gaskins, V.Goering, M.D.Testerman, M.W.Heckenkamp, R.E.Dold, E.L.Phahlane, J.Fulbrook, G.H.Morris, J.D.Griffith, J.E.Maller, M.D.Angel, P.I.Brandt, T.A.James, J.E.Hill, B.K.Vermeer, D.E.Young, D.R.Fuzzen, G.A.Sportel, J.R.Hill, K.J.Lekowski, L.D.Green, M.A.Larson, P.A.Soucy, P.C.Freiburger, T.A.Zehner, T.J.Carr, W.T.Yingling, F.Sanchez, J.Bardin, B.Sroka, E.Dohr, D.A.Lambert, F.J.March, K.A.Magalsky, M.A.Maddox, R.D.Stahlhut, R.J.Louis, T.H.Prall, N.Van Rooyen, J.L.Caulkins, M.P.Cavanagh, C.A.Munier, J.M.Speckerman, J.T.Kron, R.A.Valenzuela, L.J.Dhabalt, S.Favache, G.P.Geiger, J.L.Parrott, S.J.Lawless, S.L.Moulton, F.Castañeda, J.C.Schoeman, F.I.Green, R.Newbery, M.Maldonado, M.D.Tope, A.Eisenhut, A.Lenik, B.Fichtenmeier, J.Micheli, J.Thornton, W.Tacke, D.E.Antle, D.F.Diljak, D.M.Breidinger, R.A.Wilson, R.L.Webber, F.G.De Leon, S.Titz, D.E.Wilson, R.J.Hutchins, S.J.Hebert, P.Finamore, G.R.Broderick, L.Leipold, J.Steinhoff, A.F.Steinbeck, V.L.Ruff, D.W.Murphy, G.Passon, H.Weinmann, K.E.Clark, L.G.Winter, A.Wanger, J.Binder, L.Hoffmann, M.Konieczny, P.Gross, R.Lennert, W.Garimort, W.Huebner, C.E.Davis, D.D.Casper, M.W.Stroh, T.A.Vermeulen, B.Wilhelm, E.Hillenbrand, F.Volf, J.Mulatz, K.Hillenbrand, W.Jakob, C.J.Bowen, D.A.Dicker, M.J.Dow, M.M.Butticé, D.R.Gerse, J.McNeal, J.A.Martinez, J.Buransky, V.Staudt, R.B.Mashilo, J.D.Smith, J.M.Knudsen, M.L.Reed, H.Paul, A.Zimmer, C.Koch, D.Will, M.Kaltenegger, S.Kammerer, T.Will, T.Zeidler, U.Wacker, W.Reichelt, D.E.Stickle, C.J.Pearson, T.A.Miller, T.B.Pyle, P.A.Fortune, J.L.Fleming, M.I.Frederiksen, R.Ullmann, M.Morin, J.Maerz, W.Herzog, B.J.Gitch, E.M.Donahue, S.E.Buechler, E.Holzer, G.Tilse, G.Weber, J.Klensch, K.Heilig, M.Baumann, M.Hausner, P.Weber, R.Bluegel, V.Corso, G.Gonzalez, P.Romang, C.A.Salley, U.Zimmermann, C.L.Abbott, D.L.Lewis, D.W.Nelson, T.E.Randerson, V.H.March, G.Bleier, G.Toffel, K.Schwarz, M.Sutter, W.Loritz, T.L.Brown, R.Rothhaar, B.A.Law, C.Rachiele, D.K.Landphair, J.L.Maddox, J.M.Hagman, B.Stassen, D.Huver, H.Unser, M.Kuna, M.V.Nightingale, T.M.Leonard, B.L.Spittel, B.P.Ryan, T.Ferris, A.Frei, A.Kabtni, B.Kelly, E.Balikci, E.Haag, G.Dammert, M.Haubrich, M.Klenk, M.Koppenhoefer, W.Weiss, A.H.Van Hooydonk, K.E.Truster, M.M.Shay, S.J.Farrell, D.Heim, N.Torner, S.Radulovic, E.Batzler, D.A.Talley, E.Solis, J.A.Hechimovich, R.E.Reyes, A.Kern, B.Neu, D.J.Kassulke, M.Bohrer, L.A.Aucoin, J.M.Cantu, B.P.Burghgrave, D.J.Mac Donald, N.Korndorf, R.S.Seal, A.Herzog, E.Acikkol, H.Guth, I.Lepp, N.Krokanz, R.Stalyga, U.Fuchs, F.Meszner, L.Lukic, O.Gruenberger, M.G.Gartland, B.Kristensen, P.Iglesias-Solier, D.R.Thornton, J.M.Hiatt, K.A.Gault, R.D.Reed, A.Fischer, A.Wuest, E.Pasternak, F.Jelic, I.Lovrincic, M.Gisy, P.Lostetter, P.Muenkel, V.Seifert, W.Loerz, A.Browning, G.E.Anderson, P.J.Hoerner, T.W.Fowles, E.Kolb, K.Glaesner, U.Kirchner, R.Outen, E.F.Anders, J.C.Scott, M.Raflik, D.Nomine, S.Soumpholphakdy, W.Bader, V.Lo, W.H.Laforte, A.Schwartz, F.Ley, P.Frentzel, M.G.Ramos, M.J.Garity, R.L.Corder, R.S.Goddard, R.Ernstberger, W.C.Burgweger, G.Knebel, J.Arl, O.Thuerer, S.Hamzic, J.W.Henchy, M.Klein, G.B.Rankin, **1982** R.W.Lane, C.Pyro, E.Bosak, E.Minder, K.Kaemmer, K.Willeke, R.Dalbert, W.Stach, B.D.Eich, J.P.Caldwell, J.P.Elbert, L.L.Graflund, R.H.Wright Jr., C.Guerrero, B.Herberger, P.Rebmann, S.Huether, V.Hunsicker, E.Schuetz, H.Belz, R.Goebel, M.K.Mkwanazi, L.M.Lundgren, V.M.Bowman, G.Baumgaertel, G.Woll, H.Dinges, J.Fabing, S.Hernandez, F.Ponce, M.Lux, J.D.Lagemann, W.J.Heska, G.Livingstone, R.Whitehead, A.Hudson, F.Valenza, K.Bauer, N.Heyd, K.Hesse, G.L.Margelofsky, A.Fechner, A.Schweitzer, E.Brumm, G.Humburg, G.Ziegler, K.Notheis, M.Fischer, M.Lejeune, R.R.Clark, A.Compagnon, D.A.Rex, E.Klaus, E.Richter, J.A.Butzke, J.R.D.Santos, J.Richter, M.L.Ziegler, S.L.Tischler, A.Ivezic, C.Wagner, J.Mesaros, V.Mehner, E.Haase, F.Schommer, R.E.Tato, S.H.Wujcik, F.Machleb, H.Pillong, I.Engl, K.Weiss, M.Yueksel, W.Seyler, H.L.Sistar, A.Rodriguez, D.J.Bennett, E.L.Drescher, K.A.Van Echaute, N.L.Orlich, T.L.Van Herzeele, D.C.Ruefer, C.R.Hereid, D.K.Moldenhauer, D.M.Vanderhei, J.A.Gonzalez, S.K.Dose, J.Gonzalez, A.Amrioui, E.Goelzer, F.Fuchs, F.Gumbel, J.Hoffmann, K.Gaertner, K.Klatt, T.Schmidt, W.Hirsch, W.Wenzke, J.A.Van Loggerenberg, C.A.Richards, J.A.McAllister, M.Dimitrijevic, K.M.Martin, M.G.Pedelty, W.Jonda, T.L.Johnson, E.J.Kappaun, H.Kraft, K.Langmaier, J.C.Kleynhans, C.W.Cokeley, C.M.Ullmann, M.Tor, B.E.Smith, C.R.Demuth-Kresser, C.B.Ohnysty, P.Walter, A.Friedt, E.Moetschl, G.Schauder, M.Brakhan, J.A.Homolar, J.B.Niemann, R.A.Downing, T.E.Hays, A.M.Gordon, K.Metzger, J.A.Miller, J.J.Vandecasteele, J.A.Soto, J.Guevara, A.Eberle, B.Wolf, D.Collins, H.Baumann, H.Rutkowski, O.Brune, W.Klein, R.A.Marx, A.Roth, B.Lembach, B.Stahl, D.Spielvogel, E.Schober, H.Braun-Leva, H.Huebner, K.Gaertner, P.Clabault, P.Mattern, T.Brenneisen, S.E.Laughlin, E.Schwarz, G.J.Ames, B.A.Larsen, J.R.Cobb, J.Salas, C.Rivierre, A.Roedel, C.Embach, G.Schmitt, G.Weiser, H.Oberfeld, J.Eifler, J.Mast, J.Schoenholz, K.Herrmann, L.Weser, M.Berger, M.Fischer, M.Kaercher, M.Kohl, M.Konradt, M.Sander, M.Seufert, O.Pfister, P.Benke, P.Seibert, S.Volz, V.Daub, W.Schindler, C.L.Berglund, D.Becker, E.Muranyi, G.Fox, W.Hilpp, C.Frean, H.Stark, A.Klug, E.Geiger, K.Kraemer, K.Quaty, M.Hunsicker, T.Selinger, A.Mantione, B.Fellbermeier, H.Jochim, R.O.Maier, G.Boehm, M.Lutz, A.Hoffmann, F.Skrelja, H.Niesporek, H.Weick, H.Wuest, O.Skupinski, R.Kilian, R.Luickhardt, U.Fox, U.Hillenbrand, E.Conzelmann, E.Felkel, H.Waesch, R.Hoehnle, B.C.Ross Jr., F.Schroen, B.L.McCready, R.Humphries, H.J.Payne, A.Wild, G.Ritter, M.Hrubyj, M.Baudry, M.Goncalves, R.Hernandez, M.Istiquam, M.Naji, E.Simon, T.Mueller, H.E.Sisk, A.A.Marcelli, M.Brocard, K.A.Thomas, C.Lange, R.Grassel, T.Hirsch, T.K.Atkins, A.Sanchez-Garcia, E.Christ, J.Reich, L.Heilmann, W.Hempel, P.L.Matalik, G.Novak, H.Kuenstler, H.A.Deluca, C.A.Bianco, **1983** J.B.Velázquez, A.Babylon, C.Moedersheim, E.Brinkmann, J.Faure, J.Hoffmann, C.Belton, R.M.Ludwig, M.Casella, G.Aufrand, F.Merle, H.Nourrisson, J.M.Becker, T.D.Mohorne, L.L.Barnard, R.N.M.Walker, T.Baillet, R.Jeannot, J.Marcel, G.Simonis, H.Gottfried, J.Galert, L.Bernt, R.Holler, N.Kraljic, L.C.Bolico, D.Demoly, S.A.Mersch, A.Decker, A.Wipprich, C.L.Diehl, P.R.D.Costa, R.Andre, J.Baillet, B.Demontfaucon, D.Jacquey, G.C.Day, E.Reiss, J.Gonzales, J.Limbeck, J.Wintrich, K.Korber, O.Burger, R.Winkler, E.Stoll, J.Bornert, G.Guenon, S.Guerreiro, L.Baugey, J.Cusse, G.Ullrich, G.L.Foxx, Y.Wittner, M.Hauk, M.Bulteau, B.Sprengard, D.Hartmann, E.Breitwieser, H.Wenzel, J.Gyoergy, M.Puetz, J.Grisot, D.Hornig, F.Stadtmueller, R.Kircheis, T.Heath, L.P.Brye, P.Barz, R.Zimmermann, S.K.Stender, A.Martin, L.Fleureau, D.Bigey, U.Fernau, M.J.McGuire, K.P.Platz, J.G.Ortiz, M.T.Ledford, D.E.Carter, M.Bucher, P.Bucher, F.Duchene, M.Stumpf, E.Buehrer, E.Lluch-Riera, H.Conradi, H.Fluhrer, H.Zakrzewski, I.Bloch, J.Frerich, K.Sturm, V.Hildebrandt, G.W.Goddard, D.E.Bianco, J.A.Geary, J.Fermaud, J.Grossaulle, J.H.Plyler, S.Cartier, P.Ducret, M.Mendes De Oliveiro, M.Schwarz, J.Eusebio, D.Jeannot, J.A.Mata, E.Steiner, H.Kochanek, K.Braunhardt, K.Heller, K.Klug, K.Stollwerk, M.Heim, S.Porcari, W.Schneider, M.Bardey, C.Gouerand, H.Ulupinar, M.Dauskardt, S.R.Puhl, Z.J.Wright, T.Weber, J.J.Rodriguez, E.H.Ciuro, S.Medina, S.Kipper, M.A.Kastenmeier, P.C.Lauer, A.Haeusler, A.Hillebrandt, E.Doebler, E.Schmidt, H.Baumann, H.Rosenheinrich, R.Andress, E.Chateigner, N.E.Bergmann, O.M.Waechter, F.H.Smith Jr., G.H.Pittman, L.D.Wilson, T.L.Smith, A.Ehrhardt, A.Schmetzer, B.Giebfried, E.Roldan, F.Mueller, J.Mandel, M.Biedermann, M.Englert, P.Haitz, R.Becker, R.Wernz, T.Gaa, T.Grunert, U.Schmitt, U.Weidner, B.Freyer, D.Weihrauch, F.Mangol, F.Seifert, G.Cruz, J.Garza, D.A.Thomson, A.Brochard, C.B.Hampton, J.P.Vanvooren, W.C.Buckingham, C.D.Felten, B.A.Rubincan, J.Martin, A.Walter, B.Dauenhauer, W.Neumann, W.Sefrin, C.L.Stahler, M.E.Melville, D.Pretet, P.Mundry, V.Medeiros, J.Party, J.Menin, L.K.Kenevan, L.Castillo, A.Rauland, G.Clauer, M.Rimkus, P.J.Hunt, N.B.Teixeira, U.Fleck, W.Roemmler-Walz, W.Milne, S.Caballero, S.A.Seidel, C.D.Rosa, J.R.García, A.Wanger, E.Kabas, H.E.Kruger, J.Bacrot, B.Thiebaut, C.J.Ulatowski, D.M.Morgan, G.D.Moldenhauer, G.R.Lange, J.A.Kulka, S.Strappe, R.Ramos, C.A.Hutter, C.A.Pritchard, D.H.Stegner, J.J.Collins Sr., K.D.Fuller, K.J.Baumann, L.M.Navis, S.G.Shananaquet, J.Tristan, R.Vela, R.Gonzalez, R.Reyna, J.Guichardan, C.L.Piccolo, J.J.Castillo, H.Breiner, J.Hoefle, K.Horlaender, W.Leutnecker, A.B.Aschaker, D.D.Herbst, D.J.Otto, E.E.Zuhlke, J.E.Voskuil, K.F.Nickel, L.L.Krueger, L.P.Priesgen, N.J.Hermann, R.A.Priewe, R.L.Mc Farlane, R.L.Wendt, R.T.Cangson, R.W.Giese, S.A.Cears, S.M.Cruz, T.F.Gillich, T.W.Strub, J.A.Martinez, M.Juarez, J.Crevoisier, **1984** E.Zeissler, G.Beck, H.Metz, M.Weidig, R.Klein, W.Berger, J.Baumann, B.Buhler, P.Dirand, P.Manenti, L.Maret, D.Poissenot, A.R.Mc Lean, B.Barman, D.B.Backhaus, D.B.Flouro, D.E.Shadley, D.G.Muenchow, E.Castle, E.L.Matthews, G.A.Keller, G.C.Boldt, G.E.Lake, G.E.Lueder, G.G.Ritchart, G.R.Sitzman, G.W.Reddie, J.A.Kuenzi, J.E.Mc Cormick, J.J.McLaughlin, J.P.Faris, J.R.Rechek, K.H.Lodahl, M.E.Gustafson, R.D.Schutte, R.H.Cears, R.W.Tesch, W.J.De Maa, C.M.Forbes, A.Garcia, A.J.Griepentrog, C.D.Polzin, C.R.Rake, D.A.Williams, D.C.Kuen, D.E.Schumacher, D.L.Flesch, D.L.Schroeder, D.L.Walters, F.A.Neuman, G.A.Kenning, J.A.Hoffmann, J.E.Tobak, J.H.Helmeke, J.L.Klawitter, J.R.Vree, K.E.Kaiser, K.R.Whipple, L.J.Moore, L.L.Moede, M.E.Blankenheim, M.W.Patzer, P.C.Buechel, R.A.Klodowski, R.A.Rux, S.L.Krause, T.G.Daniels, W.A.Wendt, W.R.Woerth, J.Rumayor, A.N.Petenon, I.P.Turra, R.Escamilla, Z.V.Dalcin, D.L.Brandau, J.Gayola, M.Hofer, M.Mueller, S.A.Hofeldt, T.M.Pettis, A.Fuchs, N.Robles, C.Jones, D.S.Way, E.J.Blum, R.J.Bazaz, R.M.Gigon, W.T.Figart, R.Pedo, A.Megagianis, A.Schneider, E.Alles, F.Bosslet, G.Russhardt, H.Breitscheidel, H.Doerzenbach, H.Frey, H.Weis, H.Werner, O.Ludwig, P.Zinck, R.Stark, W.Schmidt, J.J.Checolinski, J.Soto, I.Garcia, L.P.Soulsby-King, A.J.Walter, A.V.Gross, C.D.Nascimento, C.N.Konopka, C.Rauber, J.L.Correa, O.D.Silva, P.R.Bohrer, R.V.Jacobi, V.Silva, F.Decugniet, P.Lomberger, R.Maret, J.A.Cardenas, I.Friedrich, K.Woopen, R.W.Wolf, J.Obregon, A.Zimmermann, J.S.Tock, M.L.Vogel, G.Fillion, G.Fischbach, M.Jacoutot, B.E.Culp, D.Beyeler, J.J.Carucci, J.L.Webb, J.T.Hansen, E.Obregon, J.Beltran, J.Leos, J.Ramos, A.Kurczecky, E.Ruffing, F.Bleiholder, H.Freitag, J.Medert, M.Speicher, R.Lorenz, W.Baumann, R.J.Findlay, S.S.Voelliger, C.Martinez, E.Carranza, G.Crucet, F.Jacquin, D.Funke, E.Druet, D.Prudent, S.L.Harwood, M.L.Gunther, K.D.Tharp, S.Soto, J.M.Felten, I.Samstag, P.R.Vesey, D.M.Myers, M.R.Kulina, W.L.Long, L.Ramos, E.Dueck, G.Ilbuga, G.Uhl, H.Epting, H.Oster, H.Wamser, J.Kirchner, K.Koenig, K.Lanzer, M.Hoffmann, M.Paulshofen, R.Schaefer, U.Berth, W.Klein, K.K.Pryor, P.Martin, A.J.Sharpe, R.Fuhro, J.L.Smith, G.Hulin, P.Mercier, E.Stolle, W.Cook, R.Guzman, A.Kuehn, C.A.Durand, D.J.Ledley, J.D.Lowrey, R.F.O'Brien, R.W.O'Brien, R.W.White, P.Albrecht, I.Kobal, M.Mert, S.J.Kirkland, M.Philippon, D.N.Sonenberg, K.R.Shire, M.R.Vail, J.A.Ibarra, A.Torres, R.Gomez, S.Cabello, J.E.McVay, D.R.Carrell, S.R.Tharp, A.A.Graham, E.C.Johnson, A.Gaa, B.Kuenstler, C.Riedel, D.Sickmueller, H.Celik, H.Huber, J.Perez, F.Berger, B.M.Sastre, G.Arassus, D.Cizel, I.Turan, P.Denizot, C.Kaya, S.Robouam, D.U.Vogt, S.R.Clancy, T.P.Smith, H.Reyes, J.Lett, P.Glaessner, C.Hutinet, W.Fuchs, C.C.McDonald, J.L.Keown, K.L.Lay, C.S.Beason, D.M.Brockway, J.L.Head, J.S.Mathews, T.R.Jones, G.Blietschau, R.Blasytko, U.Herrmann, S.Flores, C.Fischbach, P.Sebbah, F.Chaumette, A.Kolar, G.Prus, W.Weissbrodt, M.J.Rhodes, J.Cook, L.E.Mason, R.Sjolander, D.J.Thelen, D.R.Plumley, J.F.Roche, V.Altissimo, P.Adame, M.Wagner, J.L.Thompson, A.M.Williams, M.L.Wassell, F.J.Rodriguez, D.L.Stegemann, J.L.Kimrey, U.G.Perez, D.A.D.Silveira, D.Schemeit, E.Jonas, F.Wuerz, H.Aldorf, H.Gehrhardt, I.Pruefer, K.Eberle, K.Jaeger, L.Kuhlmann, L.Ogric, M.Daechert, M.Rackwitz, R.Mache, C.B.Schneider, J.J.Longoria, N.Bonvalot, P.Jous, D.A.Harvey, J.D.Kuehn, D.Brendel, R.Raepple, M.Balderas, F.Paez, K.K.Sloan, B.Hotz, P.Sosgornik, P.Wenz, R.Krieger, A.Huttmann, J.D.Holt, A.Sander, S.Niemietz, U.Roeschner, E.Albrecht, H.Macarty, O.F.Hines, P.B.Ray, P.F.Thomas, J.Boucher, A.Wrobel, C.E.Irion, C.E.O'Brien, D.B.Hartley, D.P.Niederkorn, E.F.Wolkenmuth, E.Fecanin, E.W.Whitcher, G.A.Veidel, J.A.Petruzates, K.A.Gontarek, K.M.Kearney, M.W.Hopp, R.A.Kaufmann, W.S.Patterson, J.L.Vallejo, J.Campenet, B.Wiesner, D.Schlierf, E.Gmeiner, E.Renner, G.Paulshofen, K.Pajurek, K.Schmidt, M.Schober, W.Baier, A.Piscitelli, R.A.Hoffman, V.Vongpraseut, F.Rode, A.Cibura, S.Durak, E.Saras, U.Otten, L.B.Reed, R.V.Myers, V.P.Bloomfield, A.Kurz, A.Riedel, A.Weiland-Rheindorf, B.Misch, C.Gund, G.Novak, H.Bastel, H.Hoehnle, J.Seitz, M.Grossmann, M.Riehl, M.Roeckl, P.Ries, S.Pfister, S.Spahn, U.Haas, D.W.Coates, A.Hunsicker, F.Goth, G.Emig, K.Hoffmann, J.L.Servat, L.Butzke, V.J.Lucas, J.Albrecht, J.Robin, A.Vollmar, G.Knobloch, H.Burkhardt, H.Reischmann, R.Heim, T.Hilsendegen, T.Roesler, D.D.Golden, J.A.Benge, P.P.Kruger, M.Jimenez, E.D.Sills, M.A.Harring, R.O.Engler, L.R.Kimrey, P.L.Starrett, T.J.McKee Sr., J.Roets, E.E.Jiménez, G.L.Curtis, Y.Demaison, G.Huether, J.L.Nunu, A.J.Townsend, P.S.Vercautren, C.Pardo-Bouzas, E.Striegel, K.Haubelt, M.Zieger, P.Thorn-Issa, T.Dembowski, A.J.Petermann, J.L.Henn, J.Soto, M.Rauber, J.S.Thompson, S.P.Knutson, T.A.Widstrand, I.Guengoer, J.Bolot, B.K.Posey, M.A.Salinas, M.R.Villarreal, V.J.Graves, B.Dervin, P.Dahl, J.A.Bustos, R.Goetz, A.Renteria, D.K.Luchman, K.Kremer, A.Alvarado, G.Feest, G.Marker, G.Nabinger, H.Fell, J.Bagley, M.Kipper, W.Gaa, H.Uhlemeier, C.G.Rubio, S.M.Nielsen, D.C.Goslowsky, S.Chevigny, P.Teron, S.Wodarz, N.Rodríguez, A.A.D.Motta, R.Dittrich, W.Essig, A.Torres, S.Mendoza, W.Aberspach, J.E.Landeros, D.J.Morrison, E.M.Rodriguez, V.Trautmann, A.Klingel, F.Werner, J.Kupper, K.Baumgaertner, K.Kurde, R.Ritter, W.Duemas, M.Z.Bastian, A.Flores, G.Bischoff, H.Franz, N.Zoz, V.M.Ortiz, K.A.Clark, H.A.Gonzalez, J.A.Sanchez, J.Cuellar, J.F.Gómez, J.Gonzalez, U.Kolb, J.B.Martinez, E.Eguia, **1985** D.Mahr, F.Zachmann, G.Fernandez-Delgado, G.Haas, H.Scheffel, I.Hack, K.Bitsch, K.Halbgewachs, M.Kehrer, O.Singer, P.Greif, P.Thompson, P.Unger, S.Zimostrat, W.Zahn, T.Bateson, C.A.Kimberley, L.E.Spencer, S.L.Cooley, M.C.Fensterseifer, J.Godon, G.Bischoff, R.Haller, J.Hutinet, J.Weyrauch, J.R.Pastryk, L.G.Turner, S.A.Kern, C.Loesel, A.Feix, A.L.Casagranda, E.L.Kappaun, V.Franco, V.Kunz,

Augusta, Georgia, employees celebrating 10,000th tractor, 1993

A.Vásquez , B.Ibarra, C.G.Garza , G.Mueller, K.Pilz, C.D.Pizarro, A.Leal, D.M.Kalmes, R.F.Baldenegro, J.M.Morales, J.S.Orozco, N.Gabriel, J.C.Niño, J.Suárez , A.M.Hernandez, D.J.Messer-Mc Farlane, N.L.Reid, T.F.Lebar, J.Millot, J.Eckert, L.R.Hanke, A.A.Rodriguez, J.A.Salazar, E.Brass, G.Pohl, H.Polke,
K.Wilhelm, O.Pfeiffer, L.A.Ciuro, E.Villela, A.Bernhard, M.Blatt, E.Salas, N.Ledezma, B.A.Parshall, D.V.Curlis, L.S.Paarman, A.Slowinski, L.Flink, R.J.Woodruff, H.Wrodarczyk, R.Peter, M.J.Brenneis, N.D.Hedrick, A.V.Zappe, H.Storey, D.F.Borges, D.Rosch, G.Rajczuk, J.T.Kamphorst, L.M.Marques,
P.Hartmann, V.D.J.Alves, S.Blautzik, L.K.Ladwig, P.A.Corsello, F.Zamora, H.Zielinski, A.Strenger, D.G.Fenley, G.Nielsen, H.Haberzettl, H.Klaer, H.Schweitzer, K.Fauer, K.Haupt, L.K.Ripple, J.V.Garcia, A.Celebi, G.Galazka, H.Wiora, J.E.Bingham, J.M.Lauer, L.E.Gekas, M.M.Hoffstetter, S.Glenn, G.Balz,
J.Gawlitza, M.Kubatzki, M.Mercan, S.S.Schneider, J.A.Duran, H.Gil, J.M.Monjaras, P.Almaguer, R.Walck, J.Heim, R.F.Watling, J.A.Vega, B.Kilian, D.Martsch, H.Strobel, W.Roessler, S.J.Hogg, C.Silva, S.S.Geary, D.E.Zendejas, R.J.Ortiz, B.Reischmann, J.Resnik, D.De Oliveira, A.P.Tokheim, E.Troc,
G.A.Westbrook, G.M.Summers, K.C.Hicks, R.A.Melone, R.M.O'Brien, C.E.Jorge, B.J.Verástegui , D.Caraty, B.Villhauer, G.Mueller, H.Grossjohann, H.Klevenz, P.Schweizer, P.Wolnitz, R.Bentzinger, S.Hofmann, W.Roessler, Z.Grimm, J.D.Phillips, M.Ernst, S.K.Luker, J.Rosales, R.Schmidt, J.L.Rosso,
R.Buchheit, E.K.Anklin, F.G.Francis, J.C.Killian, J.C.Riley, M.A.Seeley, M.Luchtel, P.C.Glenister, T.M.Franco, L.M.Owen, N.Drescher, S.Topalli, P.A.Mathias, R.M.Bierbrodt, F.J.Ramirez, P.A.Zul, M.Ernst, M.Harrer, R.Fleig, R.Scholler, C.J.Evans, J.D.Curry, D.Klosek, E.Binek, J.Buhl, W.Leusch,
A.B.Ferrer Jr., E.Schmidt, H.Ksionsek, J.Tschischka, K.Bauer, K.Fitterling, K.Triebskorn, R.Pfann, L.L.Caslavka, M.Pape, B.Sauer, H.Wagner, A.Iwczok, G.F.Spellman, A.Drexler, E.Orlik, D.H.Switzer, M.Rubio, A.Krause, R.Sluzalek, R.Ulitzka, T.Altas, J.W.Kneedler, A.Shields, H.J.Moreno, J.M.Swayze,
F.L.Dunn, H.Helisch, J.Zemella, W.Matte, P.J.Bejarno, J.H.Meinert, W.Q.Walker, A.Rohrbacher, G.Bolleyer, H.Dasdemir, J.Schmitt, K.Forgbert, M.Zivkovic, K.L.Engbrecht, M.S.Wylie, P.J.Neal, T.A.Pharo, T.J.Graff, D.Maechtel, J.Ewald, S.G.Relf, V.M.Moran, C.L.Sipes, F.J.Louw, D.J.Comer, J.A.Cousins,
J.K.Kannenberg, M.E.Wilder, R.D.Wilcox, G.Garza , C.A.Reuter, J.S.Vines, A.Schultzek, U.Frank, K.Zimmer, I.Roth, A.A.Gliosci, D.Allgeier, M.L.Wooten, T.F.Jones, J.A.Zachert, L.E.Heiselman, W.B.Silvestri, D.Mayer, H.Hensing, H.Kraft, H.Tahedl, J.Gaertner, J.Neumann, K.Buck, M.Cudyk, M.Kaziow,
W.Gall, W.Griesbaum, W.Lochbrunner, W.Neser, S.W.Crenshaw, A.N.D.Almeida, S.Nocedal , G.Wystrach, L.Rebolledo-Gonzalez, S.Haas, V.Gomolla, L.M.Tekippe, C.J.Johann, E.Fronza, R.Leal, P.Morales, G.R.Hendrickson, Y.Wakefield, D.J.Price, J.S.Acosta, C.R.Rider, F.J.Esser, M.J.Perez, A.Baierle,
D.Wetzel, L.C.Kremer, H.Boeh, S.Mello, S.R.Bivins, C.A.García , F.Arellano, A.Brabanski, J.Bernard, R.Schwind, S.Halupczok, C.A.Rosales, E.Treviño, C.Tayanc, H.Lutz, M.Erol, J.Kosilek, N.Blietschau, S.Pedersen, G.M.Barnes, M.G.Peragine, A.Guerra , D.Moussard, A.Kinda, A.Piontek, A.Vollbrecht,
A.Wolf, E.Moos, G.Piontek, H.Haehnel, R.Emmert, R.Gabriel, B.A.Skramstad, C.L.Dywiak, D.L.Tolford, H.Giel, J.Kowol, J.Rettig, S.B.Block, W.A.Hedgepeth, H.Biefel, T.Serr, W.Lubonski, K.Duemmler, L.Rudolph Jr., L.Kolodziej, P.J.Nagel, S.L.Siddle, S.S.Erwin, K.Bittner, D.J.Henderson, A.Eberle,
E.Reisig, J.Hofbauer, J.Jaersch, L.Bethke, M.Berlinghof, M.Brec, M.Schaden, P.Weinsheimer, R.Gund, S.Montag, U.Rammhold, R.Born, A.Wellhausen, E.Lapp, H.Muenkel, J.Bode, M.Lang, R.Krauss, B.Senger, J.Bachmann, J.Sauer, K.Kiefer, L.Schopf, M.Baesel, R.Kneis, T.Knoblauch, U.Wagner,
W.Sefrin, W.Stobbe, D.E.Talbot, J.Young, E.Frisch, M.Borek, R.Janitzki, M.A.Pasculli, J.M.Mata, J.A.Lahaie, J.E.Brown, J.R.Saltsman, M.A.Carpino, M.E.Sandon, B.Zorn, J.Dreher, R.Schmitt, W.J.Kotze, A.Hernandez, D.L.Barrett, M.S.Hemenway, W.M.Banks, H.Schreiber, N.Schymos, M.Garcia,
W.Jaeger, E.A.Bavazzano, R.A.Belger, A.Doenmez, P.Bless, D.L.Posey, T.D.Hayes, M.N.Lange, A.Ok, E.Eckel, H.Zorn, J.Baehr, J.Pucko, J.Wagner, R.Schmidt, R.Seitz, S.Bauer, T.Mueller, W.Gaa, W.Prieschl, W.Warzecha, D.D.Metke, D.M.Seering, D.O.Semrau, J.K.Knoll, J.V.Marquez, L.M.Peterson,
M.A.Hofmaier, M.E.Williams, M.J.Rieman, R.R.Davison, R.Simpson, S.A.Brown, B.Spagnolo, G.Makowski, M.Lang, S.Terron, C.J.Frank, C.L.Vogel, J.L.Mac Donald, J.W.Nitschke, J.W.Warnkey, L.E.Herfel, L.K.Rohr, M.E.Adams, P.R.Sanford, S.C.Ziehme, T.A.Brady, T.M.Lyon, W.J.Flury, B.Weik,
J.M.Garza, A.A.Kohls, A.B.Rodewald, B.W.Ferstl, C.L.Sigl, C.R.Haselow, D.F.Knoll, D.L.Maleck, E.A.Gerth, G.A.Henderson, G.J.Broome, G.L.Zuehlke, J.A.Amos, J.C.De Vries, J.G.Hanson, J.K.Tillou, J.L.Linde, J.W.Hemling, L.A.Riese, L.Douglas, L.L.Frank, L.W.Ulrich, M.D.Roedl Jr., N.L.Hahn, P.J.Gerth,
R.A.Brooks, R.F.Neuman, R.S.Stutz, S.L.Schuppel, T.L.Samplawski, J.Escobar , H.Hambsch, M.Laabs, V.Nielsen, A.Leto, C.J.Slane, E.F.Drewniany, J.H.Barrett, J.V.De Angelis, K.D.Roberts, A.H.Beltran, A.Weinkoetz, B.Khim, F.Lauer, K.Seiler, S.Sander, B.M.Beaudry, D.M.Kahle, J.Maechtel, R.Eichler,
J.Sanchez, B.J.Sheldon, G.G.Stange, J.J.Wasmund, M.Hoque, C.R.Marx, W.E.Rice, K.E.Gerendas, J.R.Wichrowski, M.J.Hurst, W.G.Reichard, H.Stockenberger, H.Wiedehage, S.Gaier, O.Lecuona, V.L.Todeschini, T.Fenucciu, M.Schoenl, S.Marggrander, D.M.Townsend, W.J.Bratton III, S.Cansi,
C.A.Kolwey, F.Kiel, D.L.Harter, **1986** A.Dalgauer, A.Hanf, F.Hintennach, F.Knapp, H.Kieling, H.Schroeter, H.Wolf, H.Zeh, K.Scharfenberger, L.De Bisschop, O.Kemmner, R.Decraecker, T.Wendt, U.Boeser, W.Hollstein, B.J.Owens, C.R.Voight, D.G.Miller, D.L.Chapman, M.A.Westhuis, T.L.Kohl, W.C.Stair,
A.D.Keels, C.R.Fraley, D.B.Tatham, D.L.Fryhling, J.N.Vangeest, T.J.Budan, X.Terrier, G.Weick, M.Appel, M.Kampa, J.C.Hawkinson, L.A.Gonzalez, P.P.Mundstock, L.López , G.Rheinheimer, C.A.Meierotto, M.M.Garlet, D.Barth, A.Rossler, I.Schoninger, L.L.N.D.Souza, I.Helisch, E.E.Subutzki, A.Jung,
G.Bleichner, H.Lehmann, K.Theobald, K.Wiegand, L.Held, R.Schott, B.D.Payne, M.Buchignani, R.L.Middleton, R.D.Prough, P.Castro, D.Groschopp, C.Vogelgesang, B.C.Porter, R.S.Brubaker, S.D.Godfrey, E.C.Boeck, H.Erbach, J.Berner, J.E.Garza , I.A.Benatti, D.A.D.Rocha, E.A.Nagel, E.L.M.Quoss,
G.Peiter, J.L.Fagundes, L.M.Oppermann, V.D.Rosa, V.J.Henke, G.Hilzendegen, J.L.Kerns, J.L.Barrera, A.Link, I.Azaroglu, K.Dauskardt, M.Jackowski, T.Kamuf, R.Nissen, A.R.Caratenuto, P.Kapferer, R.Schmitteckert, I.C.Miller, J.B.Endres, C.Tamez , H.Glasstetter, R.Urbina, N.Dias, B.A.Wagner,
G.Thompson, C.Zimpel, J.F.Caballero, J.Henriques, A.Hoping, A.Meitzner, B.Blum, E.Magin, E.Mueller, G.Namet, G.Schleppi, G.Stahl, H.Loderer, K.Rommel, M.Klee, T.Wuest, D.F.Easley, J.B.Pattison, I.A.Eckert, J.J.Beltramino, G.Slotta, S.J.Osgood, B.J.Mickelson, A.Heinrich, P.Schimmel, R.Rotter,
R.B.Gross, T.Fischer, H.M.Schuth, J.Kulczyk, M.B.Arndt, F.A.Van Schepen, K.E.Becker, M.A.Vicario , B.Haas, C.Schneider, F.Delgado-Nunez, G.Olbrecht, H.De Muer, K.Hartstirn, P.Kotliba, W.Bruemmer, N.S.Newbery-Eddy, J.A.E.Pasquali, R.Bechtold, A.Ribeiro, E.Rosch, N.J.Diesel, M.K.Ballweg,
R.T.Hurban, C.L.Hundt, E.Mueller, A.Altherr, H.Jost, I.Schelinski, J.Stefan, P.Doeringer, P.Pirro, R.Studenic, S.Schraml, J.P.Gartner, R.W.Porter, R.W.Van Der Westhuizen, D.Di Marco, A.E.Greer, B.K.Stephenson, L.J.Bodenmann, R.M.Jahnke, S.J.Palmer, A.A.Peres, D.A.Nicoletti, H.N.Correa,
I.G.Kahlbaum, J.Tormes, V.J.D.S.Salgadinho, S.Schneider, A.L.Timmerman, C.M.Cook, D.D.Harken, G.D.Meier, H.J.Novelli, K.J.Frommelt, P.C.Chappell, P.W.Craft, R.A.Lange, S.L.Kooker, V.L.Paustian, L.A.Pundrich, C.C.Hampton, J.I.Millard, Y.S.Ousley, A.M.Warden, C.A.Myers, D.L.Robison,
J.A.Robbins, L.J.Dalrymple, L.L.McManus, M.A.Struble, M.J.Mack Jr., R.C.Terronez, V.A.Gleason, A.M.Miles, C.B.Gress, D.A.Yergler, J.E.Messerly, J.H.Doyle, K.A.Belk, S.B.Allen, W.E.Lunke, H.Franco, E.Geissler, F.Kutscherauer, G.Gazmilo, K.Juch, K.Neidig, K.Wurst, M.Koschig, M.Schuler, R.Bartl,
R.Heizenroether, T.Huelshoff, T.Windisch, W.Hauck, J.L.S.Venites, B.W.Houge, H.E.Hundley, A.Lautenchleger, K.E.Manning, M.A.Parks, R.Betz, S.Maesel, L.T.Ackermann, D.R.Nagle, E.A.Bratz, C.J.Mc Leran, D.A.Jerauld, D.F.Ravenscraft, D.H.Schilling, H.B.Ballweg, L.M.Korndorf, V.Manteufel,
A.Simonis, D.Gawlick, E.Jarosch, F.Rheindorf, H.Conzelmann, H.Sommer, J.Habenberger, R.Hernecker, S.Jenssen, W.Schmidt, C.B.Cooper, D.Lovell, M.L.Laverrenz, D.S.D.Campos, E.Haeberlin, O.P.Johann, D.L.Loding, J.N.Schneider, K.D.McCarty, W.Kirchheim, A.Heil, A.Weis, C.Glad, D.Mueller,
G.Jakob, G.Zabe, J.Lang, M.Heidenreich, P.Klagyivik-Dalheimer, P.Merkel, R.Kamuf, T.Sonntag, W.D.Hausch, J.L.Vervaecke, L.C.Wilson, S.D.Pettit, S.W.Rhodes, I.Fuchs, I.J.Bender, R.Hammer, C.J.Hendges, H.H.Housman, B.A.Pliner, D.M.Caldwell, I.C.Carter, J.E.Smith, L.A.Long, R.G.Ketron,
S.J.Turner, C.M.Clawson, K.J.Freidel, D.L.Phillips, V.O.Peiter, B.Buchheit, B.Kovacs, H.Wieschalla, K.Enkler, M.Neu, M.Weber, P.Schmidt, V.Benedek, M.K.Jones, M.Rech, J.McFalls, K.R.Zobel, R.L.Gust, I.J.Bonmann, P.R.Kowalski, C.S.Kopacek, S.K.Schmidt, D.A.D.Carvalho, A.Koetz, O.Halmann,
S.D.Stuckey, A.J.Franco, J.A.D.Motta, J.A.Perinazzo, M.H.Devore, R.B.Edenborg, W.E.Reeves, A.Jimenez-Espejo, B.Paetow, C.Marhoefer, H.Jung, H.Schmetzer, H.Schwegler, H.Stephan, J.Moench, M.Schuepferling, R.Schwarz, T.R.Shannon, S.J.Sartor, R.Ehlich, E.Wunsch, J.L.Ramirez, J.E.Nolin,
M.Just, J.F.F.Neto, C.A.Cain, C.J.Bertrand, G.F.Byrd, R.Massei, R.D.Anderson, W.L.Browder, C.A.Ribeiro, V.Webler, T.S.Spors, D.L.Le Rette, M.Appelt, H.A.Lynaugh, R.N.Bailey, A.Keuter, H.Scholl, J.Helfrich, K.Helbig, M.Pirrung, M.Reda, D.D.Gromalak, M.K.Morrow, R.G.Karnatz, R.L.Quick, M.E.Stori,
H.P.Lafranchi, C.B.Johnson, I.J.Brotherson, K.E.Lenhart, K.J.Moriarty, M.E.Reiland, M.J.Epperly, P.Tate, T.C.Whelan, C.Kelley, N.E.Foster, D.J.Sheehy, J.B.Bingham, L.E.Stratton, P.M.Whelan,
E.O.Catzin, F.Soppelsa, C.H.Nitschke, T.J.Owen, B.Koehler, H.Braun, H.Langlotz, K.Knerr, O.Menzel, U.Hansen, G.R.Johnson, C.M.Nance, R.M.Ramírez, R.A.Tahan, M.S.Isler, R.Lima, B.A.Fortune,
B.L.Canney, D.S.Swift, J.M.Gerovac, L.J.Ballew, M.F.Ford, J.H.Addison, M.A.Fletcher, **1987** A.Georgiadis, A.Schmitt, A.Zimmer, G.Benda, G.Gradmann, G.Oehlbach, H.Trummheller, K.Schneider,
P.Hettinger, P.Pluto, S.Rollert, D.L.Reaves, G.A.Howell, M.A.Hermsen, M.V.Rosenstiel, R.D.Coble, Y.Chang, H.A.Sendoya, Y.A.Chang, E.Alvarez, B.L.Schellin, L.A.Lackas, L.H.Spencer, M.A.Bursik,
M.J.Dollarhide, R.A.Clark, J.B.P.Quedi, P.G.Tong, J.A.Benedetti, I.F.Trein, J.J.L.Spohr, D.Dial, H.A.Payne, L.A.Caldwell, L.D.Wallace, L.K.Tandy, R.A.Olson, D.M.Lam, A.Jahnes, E.Reis, S.D.S.Viana,
D.J.Eckert, E.P.Rodrigues, H.A.Zolin, J.E.D.S.Vieira, N.Ribeiro, P.P.Hendges, A.Black, D.A.Wilson, P.A.Engelberth, D.W.Petersen, R.Jaramillo, R.Lecomte, H.Boehm, H.Myatt, H.Ratsch, K.Kafaltzis,
L.Schmitt, R.Seiler, W.Scherer, A.S.Quayle, K.L.Hiatt, L.L.Plathe, M.L.Prindiville, A.Schulz, D.L.Wening, J.Borges, L.Nunes, N.Kahlbann, B.J.Brewster, V.L.Smith, W.S.Grund, G.A.Ceniceros, V.Bieger,
C.J.Testroet, R.W.Reid Jr., S.J.Gomez, W.G.Grant Jr., C.A.Mattjie, C.D.Nascimento, C.R.Haas, E.J.Conrad, J.A.D.Santos, J.L.Duarte, J.Patias, J.S.Heberle, J.V.Felten, L.D.Hilgert, M.L.D.Brito,
M.O.Baisch, M.R.Stamm, P.A.Gubert, P.O.N.D.Souza, R.Richter, R.Silveira, I.Schubert, A.M.Blunk, L.W.Killough, I.Decker, A.Haeuser, J.Spiller, K.Graf, W.Berlinghoff, W.Jung, C.P.Parsons, D.E.Roy,
D.S.Bush, J.C.Oakley, S.C.Pugh, V.Grutka, J.Puhl, B.F.Shires, M.E.Stallsmith, A.J.Zappe, E.S.Jones, T.K.Larson, A.V.Reder, J.M.Teter, P.A.Yocum, R.L.Snedeger, O.Belarmino, A.Neuhaus, D.G.Terra,
G.Rensch, I.A.S.D.Lima, M.Turra, P.R.Filho, J.Rodríguez , G.Nadeau, J.D.Klauck, J.M.Gee, V.L.Richardson, A.A.D.Carvalho, D.L.Wallace, K.S.Schmidt, M.A.Giblin, R.Sahlberg, A.Gaertner, A.Tasasiz,
E.Friess, L.Spatz, P.Glatting, U.Von Prittwitz, V.Klingel, W.Dittler, W.Hoenig, D.E.Minor, M.F.Perkins, M.R.Smith, T.M.Pahowski, V.G.Sims, L.L.Watkins, F.L.Vanwylick, J.D.Marion, P.W.Miller, W.R.Kyle,
B.L.Claus, G.D.Butler, G.D.Moody, J.W.Venditti, L.M.Toth, W.R.Mathias, H.Roveretto, A.Veldhuizen, D.L.Hubbard, G.E.Dalcourt, J.E.Meenagh, K.L.Jones, L.A.Butt, M.D.Haberkorn, R.G.Vachon,
R.P.Paille, S.Riddell, T.A.Lacy, T.J.Rapier, E.Schleyer, F.Soutschek, H.Kneip, H.Martin, K.Altmann, L.Altrock, M.Lindner, C.M.Deschenes, D.D.Lombarczki, H.J.Bedard, J.A.Hermoza, J.R.Laurence,
R.A.Eaton, T.Pietrelli, T.S.McSween, G.B.Horton, G.F.Edwards, K.K.Roland, L.A.Sherk, M.A.Ford, M.M.McCauley, P.D.Gibson, R.D.Klauck, R.L.Bisson, S.J.Tamminga, S.McClain, S.R.Beaudoin,
S.W.Mullins, W.P.Campbell, T.A.Maccabe, D.Colquhoun, J.S.Turner, K.M.Ellestad, M.C.Reed, N.M.J.Fensterseifer, S.O.Stewens, A.Fabiano, E.Goertzen, G.L.Labbe, J.B.Robertson, J.Vant Sant,
P.C.Lessard, R.R.Deveney, S.D.McCaffery, B.E.Smith, D.P.Menard, J.L.Shaubel, M.A.Parsons, M.D.Nalley, L.J.Duffee, R.G.Walter, L.Rossi, F.E.Vales , A.Konieczny, H.Donnerstag, H.Ernst, H.Gaertner,
H.Gericke, H.Hug, M.Hehn, W.Seebald, W.Sickmueller, V.Warken, A.M.Abasto, A.K.Chastain, D.J.Klyn, W.A.Meyerer, S.Roy-Muniak, M.M.Howard, P.A.Vanderbeck, I.Ataseven, G.E.Warr, A.Baltatzidis,
E.Hummig, G.Szczepaniak, H.Ebeling, H.Eisenmann, L.Hauenstein, R.Kett, R.Kopp, R.Yildirim, W.Hofer, E.A.Duvenage, E.T.Z.Peiter, S.Hernandez, T.A.Buchmeyer, A.C.Evans, C.J.Fehn, H.Zieger,
M.Colak, J.L.Haberman, J.D.Parkin, M.A.Vermeulen, C.A.Zaczina, M.Emekci, E.Wellings, F.M.Gregory, F.Young, K.K.Sonvichit, M.D.Barber, R.E.Wolfe, P.D.Mullinax, V.D.Wright, M.Butz, D.Jaeger,
H.Oster, K.Belz, M.Hochlehnert, P.Pierrot, P.S.Granell, S.A.Doster, E.Duratovic, U.Schuessler, A.F.Gingles, A.J.Lee, B.T.Clauson, D.L.Bryant, K.Y.Barnes, L.Carter, M.A.Nitz, A.Leist, A.Weiss, A.Zimmer,
B.Schlindwein, H.Berger, H.Heck, H.Oess, J.Munz, K.Gomes, M.Blank, M.Buehler, M.Dreier, M.Koenen, M.Stadler, R.Hartmann, S.Henn, S.Kuegler, Z.Erdogan, L.Calvillo, J.Kirchknopf, J.S.Sears,
M.A.Jennings, M.F.Searcy, M.W.Sand, E.Boissenot, C.M.Evans, D.D.Weigel, J.M.Hermiston, V.C.Williams, J.Engler, A.Ogasa, F.Erk, A.M.Philson, R.D.Lavallee, D.A.Bloch, M.M.Markum, A.L.Rohde,
A.Baermann, A.Kromer, B.Ernst, D.Hindenlang, H.Grillenberger, K.Buehler, M.Schmidt, W.Moos, J.A.Macarthur, A.Jendritza, T.Baron, A.D.Pritchard, B.E.Gilbey, J.S.Griffiths, N.A.Lind,
S.A.D.Nascimento, A.Noworzyn, P.Barcik, L.I.Fisher, J.M.Tessneer, Y.Tetrault, H.Schnabel, K.Luanglath, B.R.Atkins, C.A.Tolles Jr., J.B.Mistry, U.Battaglini, A.D.Pettis, C.L.Esparza, D.K.Olsen,
F.D.García, L.M.Galera, C.Seubert, D.Peters, G.Mahlmann, L.Weltscheck, R.Rivinius, R.Schmidt, S.Gria Spinelli, J.Mouchel, B.M.Vanhyfte, C.L.Spieker, M.D.Taplin, R.Perry, T.T.Sass, A.Bohn, K.Heger,

Monterrey, Mexico, employees at Gente Deere 10K race, 1993

K.Sakar, T.Baumann, B.B.Bosso, C.D.Nordell, N.Winders, P.A.Duncan, P.E.Lynch, T.E.McBride, H.Chavarria, M.G.Castillo, J.R.Meersman, D.L.Doran, S.E.Mahieu, G.Delgado, R.Santillana, N.Vazquez,
C.A.Dean, T.R.Knickmeier, M.T.Hupfer, Z.M.Laidens, J.S.Hatlevig, S.M.Frost, A.O.Carvalho, A.O.D.Mattos, M.M.Riddle, J.I.Torres, P.Suarez, M.C.Skilondz, R.L.Novotny, G.A.Cepeda, G.Torres, K.Baus, R.Kusicka, H.J.Bezaury, J.R.Aitken, R.Vazquez, N.Breunig, W.Heim, P.Fouillot, B.R.Andreassen,
J.O.McReynolds, M.H.Willis Jr., R.D.Allen, H.Heiler, G.L.Wood, J.M.Duguay, L.L.Skaife, T.L.Dagnon, P.Escobedo, J.Kleine-Lamping, D.L.Forret, R.S.King, W.Kendrick, M.Heissler, M.Seitz, F.J.Garza, R.Castillo, R.Urbano, F.J.Flores, H.Mondragón , C.D.Prather, M.J.Kiester, S.T.Carl, T.L.Dick,
E.R.Fernandes, R.M.Morrow, E.Koblenzer, J.Mathes, P.Seufert, D.L.Noe, R.Shorts, C.E.Ríos , S.Carter, A.D.Dick, B.Clemmer, J.C.Currence, U.Veith, J.A.Matthias, R.L.Sanford, T.O.Meister, V.R.Sieben, J.G.Ramirez, J.Robles, A.S.Kane, J.Curless, K.M.Simmons, G.W.Henderson, M.L.Herfel, **1988**
E.Grund, H.Riemschneider, I.Werdan, R.Ernst, R.Harloff, A.S.Stoelk, C.Richardson, D.A.Murphy, D.M.Bryant, J.D.Compston, J.R.Gray, L.S.Bentall, M.A.Beedlow, R.A.Riggs, T.L.Hawkins, W.P.McManus, G.Valdameri, C.Lohse, B.K.Rodgers, C.E.Hilderbrand, D.J.Steel, L.Flynn, R.Kratzmeier, W.Militzer,
J.Tyler, Y.M.Boucher, D.L.Krauspenhar, A.R.Martinez, F.Bonilla, A.Marcel, G.Rotter, M.Frank, N.Chapuis, F.E.Tousaw, K.F.Anderson, M.A.Delgado, O.Almaguer , J.A.Morales, J.M.Ruiz, P.Lopez, B.D.Maynard, D.J.Lloyd, H.L.Wright, J.Kirkpatrick, M.E.Claeys, M.W.Wise, T.L.Kozma, B.A.Colunga, B.Geiss,
G.Pieper, H.Martin, M.Maurer, R.Hochlehnert, B.J.Swain, K.L.Hessler, S.J.Leonard, T.R.Chewning III, H.L.Arellano, V.Stanek, J.J.Sanchez, L.J.Grimes, L.S.Swanson, M.C.Herrold, S.M.Armando, J.M.Gonzalez, M.E.Long, W.Rottmann, B.L.Kinderman, D.Tedder, E.J.Barr, J.C.Riley, T.R.Mickelson,
M.V.Redzko, A.Stadtlober, A.Stec, A.Vianna, D.Sartori, E.C.Coitinho, F.Marschner, G.Q.D.Silva, J.A.Bagetti, J.C.Martins, J.S.Heberle, L.O.Wouters, M.Fischer, M.R.Krause, P.C.Martens, R.Kohl, A.Hellmann, V.M.Galindo, M.Urbanczyk, D.E.Johnson, D.Herrera, J.Gauna, A.H.Folden, E.H.Bell, J.W.Howard,
C.A.Lamas, D.L.Hall, G.T.Biederman, A.Ratzel, H.Haass, M.Munoz-Lopez, N.Butzig, T.Erman, V.Richter, W.Engelhorn, F.J.Cepeda, B.B.Loredo, D.J.Wilson, F.R.Mack, M.A.Hardin, P.A.Davis, P.A.Verdouw, R.B.Russell, J.P.Martinez, O.Dumas, S.M.Daley, C.L.Mattjie, S.Munier, L.A.Crawford, L.M.Kincaid,
V.F.Sakellarios, J.L.Ibarra, P.M.Bemus, G.H.Taborda, J.G.Craddock, K.Frick, R.Egri, F.T.Rivas, M.A.Lorenzoni, M.J.Ruiz, A.O.Zunkel, K.L.Cook, I.A.Fry, R.R.De los Santos, P.R.Laverdiere, A.Gil Barroca, A.Halbgewachs, B.Leibowitz, E.Fuchs, H.Fischer, H.Sonderschaefer, K.Gressel, K.Schlichter, O.Czech,
P.Haecker, E.Maloney, G.A.Hoover, J.A.Irons, J.A.Shader, K.E.Kell, M.J.Allen, A.Klinger, J.M.Baumann, L.L.Schoninger, M.L.Pohl, R.R.Schuster, V.R.Schacht, A.Guerel, R.L.Niedenthal, D.L.Witt, G.L.Woodard, J.O.Richter, N.L.Johnson, S.K.Adams, S.M.Dew, J.Gonzalez, J.L.Carretero , M.Ayala,
R.A.Esparza, H.Kessler, H.Surauf, I.Ratajczak, I.Weiss, J.L.Irby, P.Lau-Loskill, A.Jess, B.J.Schwarz, B.S.Sisario, L.R.Cribb, P.A.Hitchcock, S.J.Davis, T.J.Engman, J.M.Montemayor, J.Gatzka, K.M.Reep, A.D.Jones, C.M.Monroe, K.S.Richardson, T.L.Huston, H.Cantu, D.M.Mackedanz, A.Anicio, F.Helbig,
G.Wyss, H.Jandt, I.Freiler, O.Yalcin, B.T.Hurley, D.C.Schmidt, D.E.Spearman, D.R.Young, J.A.Collison, J.A.Snyder, R.Boyce, R.D.Polk, R.H.Hoang, A.Aguillon, J.Garcia, E.Cal, U.Palaz, V.Gallo, J.A.McDonnell, J.D.Lawes, T.A.Miller, M.L.Serrato, B.D.Dailey, B.L.Conrad, C.P.Franklin, D.L.Gunhus, R.L.Haun,
H.M.Gil, J.J.Mendoza, E.Perez, E.Jous, E.P.Hansotia, J.A.Ficzere, J.D.Pinnow, J.E.Martinson, J.K.Roberts, K.F.Kolda, K.J.Granatier, K.S.Thomas, P.J.Nelson, P.R.Ingalls, T.D.Thelen, T.R.Macdonald, F.L.Kuntz, H.Gaeng, S.Domisse, G.J.Remaly, J.Quintanilla, J.J.Reyes, C.A.Christopher, C.A.Schafer,
C.M.McCall, D.L.Willet Jr., J.P.Romanick III, L.I.Tollison, R.A.Jongerius, J.A.Pais, V.D.S.Viana, R.F.Golightly, W.L.Mills, B.Jauneau, C.D'Heylly, L.Lemaire, J.E.Butts, B.Menetrier, P.Martinez, C.Chaton, B.J.Dolesh, S.E.Parker, G.L.Slovak, J.C.Oncken, L.A.Whitaker, M.Woo, P.J.Blomgren, R.J.Lynn,
S.N.Machado, A.G.Ortiz, R.Alvarez, E.Kruhl, G.Cotaris, G.Trcak, W.Koelz, W.Mitsch, W.Wunsch, A.I.G.Holmner, A.P.Potthoff, D.A.Cameron, D.K.Church, L.K.Scholz, M.A.Smith, T.L.Armstrong, A.Heinzmann, H.Kampert, J.Kutschera, J.Liszka, L.Poterek, M.Napierala, S.Zimnicki, T.Koese, D.E.Gaugert,
M.L.Coffey, R.Rodriguez, H.Brosch, E.E.Banks, F.Cruz, J.M.Zimmer, K.R.Donahey, L.A.Meredith, L.J.Zweber, L.L.Masengarb, S.B.Egan, S.L.Lisk, J.L.Garza, G.Wardenga, J.A.Gonzalez, R.Hartmann, K.W.Dold, L.M.Peterschmidt, M.Renner, S.E.Arellano, R.H.King, S.S.Martens, T.S.Menke, L.Guillemin,
P.Giroux, H.Kizil, O.Cervantes, J.L.Gamez, K.L.Stewart, M.A.Arancibia, A.Belter, E.Preis, L.A.Tudino, M.A.Deangeli, F.Linares, P.A.Ryan, K.D.Currier, K.L.Cunningham, K.M.Russell, P.A.Graham, G.Garza , G.Porras, F.Eheim, H.Andres, H.Richter, J.Reckinger, P.Dulisch, W.Vomend, A.Roveretto, T.L.Drake,
R.Espino, R.Salgado, S.Lopez, H.Zimmermann, M.Wetterich, S.Esser, C.S.Pope, J.J.Sams, M.A.Reed, T.J.Jennings, G.A.Fiorilla, M.Vazquez, M.W.Germain, T.A.Vershaw, T.Worthington, G.Balaj, M.A.Di Pangrazio, S.R.Pereyra, E.A.Muñoz, R.F.Rivera, C.G.Murray, J.G.Hoff, M.S.Mallas, N.M.Cicao,
L.M.Riseley, J.Pikos, F.Filippi, A.Hernandez, D.C.Hapner, G.A.Breningmeyer, K.A.Pittz, R.A.Munsch, K.G.Hall, M.E.Flaherty, R.E.Nevius, R.J.Walker, T.L.Porter, E.A.Castello, F.J.Zamora, A.Gajdera, A.Wojtalla, E.Gaida, H.Emmerling, P.Kuehn, M.A.Ramos, C.M.Johnson, K.D.Benge, R.Johnson, B.A.Heine,
B.M.Heddy, J.K.Light, M.J.Sharp, A.Halter, B.Vogelbacher, E.Jung, F.Gersdorf, G.Villhauer, H.Roecke, J.Meyer, K.Kreimes, R.Baumann, S.Kern, P.L.Winstanley, F.Sandoval, G.R.Foot, S.Bryan, J.A.Martinez, A.Szczodrek, J.Gabor, M.Sobel, T.Schmitt, A.Auer, A.Danilov, A.Kempf, C.Boehm, C.Russo,
D.Dreyer, D.Kerbl, O.Wagner, P.Kauf, S.Guerleyen, S.L.Hatleberg, M.Schaden, A.L.Bolton, A.R.Gosnell, A.S.Moyers, B.M.Gillum, C.G.Cobble, C.J.Dentlinger, C.Williamson, D.A.Bowman, D.E.Myers, D.J.Melton, D.L.Jones, E.C.Peters Jr., E.I.Gillespie, J.K.Hicks, L.A.Clewell, M.A.Davis, M.A.Galle,
M.B.Farris, M.W.Malone, R.D.Kimery, R.Irelan, R.L.Britton, R.S.Cash, S.G.Peters, S.J.Barham, T.D.Parman, T.R.Reed, M.Maltzahn, C.Gandyra, J.Kotzot, R.Hick, S.Kropidlo, J.J.Berkley, W.A.Grassie, A.Bender, F.A.S.Massuda, E.Bordier, N.Roskosch, J.D.D.R.Mattos, W.Richter, J.M.Martinez, L.A.Salinas,
M.A.Velazquez, D.L.Guaschino, D.D.Craig, D.K.Anderson, L.D.Ogden, L.E.Miller, F.J.Alvarado, L.F.Walker, C.Chambellant, W.Vives, M.J.Eyre-Maly, W.M.Behan, A.A.Ziegler, L.F.Hinojosa , R.Di Luise, A.Blaschke, A.Jaeger, A.Kaupp, E.Buehler, E.Roth, H.Knebel, J.Bugla, J.Rehberger, K.Diesler, K.Heinlein,
P.Schramm, S.Falk, S.Woll, T.Hofstetter, J.C.Aguado , A.Bernhard, A.Michalski, J.Glaser, J.Reinholz, J.Rewak, M.Erbay, M.Heil, M.Wiench, R.Labisch, S.Novalic, S.Oechler, U.Beigel, W.Szyszka, Z.Simson, A.Crippa, A.J.Richardson, T.L.Schroeder, J.A.Peña, G.Barghioni, A.Henriques, S.Sainty,
S.K.Wollett, A.Schmidt, C.Piazza, I.Goekce, I.Laber, M.Oez, R.Stabel, S.Yazgan, F.J.Lara, M.Stojakovic, J.Siegwald, J.Tkocz, M.Wojtalla, G.R.McCluskey, E.L.Rea, J.M.Campanella, D.Muller, G.A.Schultz, L.A.Fretwell, E.Ruiz, F.Villasana, H.Vogel, M.Buehler, C.Neal, H.Franiak, A.M.Muche, D.A.Everding,
G.J.Francis, J.S.Ulrich, K.E.Young, P.J.Kuhlman, R.G.Palmateer, R.Garcia-Sequeira, W.W.Eck, A.D.Rosa, J.L.Cano , E.Brandt-Schorpp, D.L.Juehring-Thomson, R.Vazquez, B.Hemmer, E.Goerlitz, G.Horst, H.Jordis, H.Weber, H.Wirth, O.Bodirsky, O.Mueller, V.Heiler, W.Reber, W.Zimmermann, B.A.Curtis,
L.A.Rice, T.E.Tabaska, K.A.Pereira, C.Morales, A.Schwindt, D.Heidenreich, R.Herrmann, M.L.Kahl, J.Aguayo, E.Kaminski, S.Riley, A.M.Packer-Boagard, J.A.Searcy, L.C.Miller, L.G.Palmer, L.J.Reed, S.L.Karzin, T.A.Cox, A.Hemmer, H.Schaaf, S.Slawik, T.Kleinschmidt, B.Garza, N.A.Ragsdale, B.K.Bresser,
R.Vanderbeck Jr., G.Escobedo, D.Stypa, F.Kabacs, H.Malcher, J.Hrusovsky, W.Kloepfer, C.Ortiz, N.B.Naidoo, J.L.Lesh, J.M.Adams, E.Vazquez, B.W.Cochran, M.M.Kenyon, G.Lang, H.Trapp, F.Martinez, J.A.Davidson, J.F.Waas, J.T.Moehn, K.K.Martinez, O.A.Erichsen, S.M.Bennett, G.M.Savard, A.Pickert,
E.Sonns, F.Gundacker, G.Jaeth, J.Beckerle, K.Ewald, L.Schaefer, T.Jilg, T.Ruprecht, C.Nivert, A.Strobel, A.Yaman, B.Bodmer, C.Chaslin, G.Huver, J.Kessler, K.Krick, T.Cebulla, W.Brauch, D.A.Wiebbelling, R.N.Henke, J.Stolz, G.E.McCord, R.A.Kirkwood, E.G.Kahlbaum, U.Bachstein, J.D.Curington III,
J.M.Allred, L.D.Campbell, T.R.Cameron, J.H.Martinez, P.Reyes, P.Knapp, R.Gajdera, M.T.Gaytan, A.M.Nichols, P.E.Watson Jr., W.Zutter, I.Navarro, U.Glaesner, J.A.Phillips, J.R.Gimpel, L.D.Guyer, M.J.Duffy, K.J.Young, R.Leal, A.Hofmann, A.Schumilas, B.Hein, H.Trapp, K.Knuettel, K.Tuerk, M.Spiske,

R.Mueller, V.Seker, W.Bodinka, Z.Chruslicki, B.K.Bergemann, G.L.Thacker Jr., J.D.Voss, J.S.Grant, M.T.Gardner, T.K.Jarrett, C.T.Adamson, D.Luickx, J.Megel, W.Lurka, C.J.Bender, A.Rojas, J.Montoya, L.A.Salazar, M.A.Cepeda, A.S.Weber, D.L.Holtz, E.S.Schmitz, R.E.Rutledge Jr., S.D.Wosepka, E.Duran, B.Cordier, C.D.Moore, J.M.Moser, N.A.Aimi, B.Geisel, J.E.Burke, P.L.Foy, T.J.Theofilis, H.D.Grant, **1989** A.Gauch, C.Zschiebsch, D.Esau, F.Kurtz, H.Klamm, J.Faller, J.Wuerzburger, K.Saemann, G.Martinez S.T., J.J.Smith, R.Madsen, J.Party, A.Klein, A.Spitzbart, D.Bauer, M.Baumann, M.Schopp, M.Schrepfer, M.Vogel, S.Korhuesinaz, W.Knobloch, C.R.Jones Jr., J.L.Freeborn, P.Broaden, D.Busschots, M.C.Brown, M.L.Chapin, P.J.Hill, A.J.Grebner, K.A.Leafgreen, T.G.Adams, W.Goeritz, J.H.Miller, H.Gutierrez, J.Pirnay, A.P.Wilczynski, D.D.Jurmu, D.W.Hankins, M.J.Tanguay, M.L.Woods, S.F.Gietzel, S.R.Kraft, T.A.Jacklin, J.M.Arredondo, R.Reynoso, B.Wos, H.Wallner, I.Fix, K.Beinsen, L.Polok, A.J.Van Den Berg, K.J.Schmid, L.J.Riggs, N.P.Robbins, S.G.Anderson, L.D.Reu, A.B.Schulte, D.Makue, D.J.Mc Guire, K.A.Cord-Rausch, L.D.Earwood, M.L.Ngo, P.A.Reed, R.G.Riddle, J.L.Sanchez, M.Singler, G.A.Mehl, M.A.Myers, C.J.De Baillie, D.J.Poston, G.J.Hudson, P.A.Mc Leish, P.K.Olson, R.C.Sathmary, R.H.Church, T.R.Turner, C.F.Evans, D.M.Quinn-Lindsey, J.M.Vickroy, K.K.Kovacevich, J.O.M.Vieira, M.E.Fritsch, M.Ferreira, O.Muller, P.R.Teixeira, F.Gutzler, F.Wartenpfuhl, G.Zahn, H.Rembert, K.Baus, K.Kohlhepp, N.Kumm, C.Schafer, G.Brumpton, J.Slater, V.R.Connor, G.J.Kobow, J.K.Vorlander, L.Neely-Mcduffy, S.E.Osterhaus, T.Gillani, I.Hernandez, A.Fenucciu, R.Kremer, J.H.Maartens, G.Haag, H.G.Graham, J.L.Joens, R.B.Needham, S.K.Swafford, S.L.Diaz, S.M.French, W.E.Harper, S.Scherer, J.Cannelle, S.Hmamou, H.Jendrzej, R.Stutzmann, E.F.Torres, S.K.Hill, E.Ferrari, N.Staffen, A.Radszuweit, T.L.Trevillyan, N.P.Araujo, M.B.Tuomy, A.Leonhardt, C.D.Halmann, C.J.Robe, C.R.Petermann, D.L.Gomes, E.C.A.Correa, E.M.Bialas, F.O.Fagundes, J.P.P.D.Santos, J.V.Wiskow, L.D.Santos, M.A.D.L.Silveira, M.A.Person, M.Hartmann, P.S.D.Souza, R.L.Hermes, V.L.Marx, V.Weiss, J.N.Juarez, J.Dedole, G.Barlian, M.Bauer, D.M.Kimberley, R.S.Villarreal, R.M.Hanson, K.Dintinger, J.V.Lamb, S.K.Montgomery, S.S.Vardell, T.M.Ross, C.U.T.D.Oliveira, J.J.Torres, P.Gonzalez, A.Baluk, B.Perali, H.Hallwachs, K.Baehr, M.Seberkste, P.M.Nelson, R.H.Sullivan, J.M.Parga, T.Descollonges, J.Hulin, G.Virot, A.Schmid, J.Andres, W.Brnabic, J.A.Garcia, R.Castillo, R.Garza, B.J.Sands, B.W.Peterson, D.M.Laufenberg, L.D.Gotthardt, L.J.Cates, S.J.Tate, T.L.Gallagher, A.Kourtessis, E.Panek, J.Kosilek, J.Lozano, J.Schneider, S.Pytel, R.J.Bowers, J.Sanchez, C.A.Serroul, C.A.Stefani, A.R.Alt, J.J.Johnson, J.P.Dreier, M.E.Mattis, P.J.Blacher, R.L.Sterken, T.A.Snell, A.Klos, A.Wachtel, G.Nowak, G.Wolf, J.Prusko, J.Seifer, M.G.Gerlach, C.Guerra, J.S.Franke, R.C.Morey, E.A.D.Carvalho, J.B.Randolph, A.M.Kramme, W.A.Graves, A.M.Hyde, E.Fraser, G.Biondi, K.Kiefer, M.Huber, P.Karabasch, W.Hasenfratz, P.Nel, J.J.Cravero, O.R.Delgado, A.Gutzler, D.Quoiffy, P.Sibla, W.Schmitt, S.Estrada, J.Fournier, A.N.Thomas, M.C.Husak, E.Gillner, C.Aguilar , P.Hall, D.E.Revels, D.S.Desherow, L.N.Corrado, N.L.Leader, T.J.Epperson, T.S.Stahl, W.A.Redeker, G.Denizot, F.Marcel, D.Marcel, J.Drescher, F.D.R.Ernst, J.D.Hasty, R.J.Bakken, A.M.Scott, C.L.Easter, F.N.Seth, J.C.Wistehuff, K.M.Kleywegt, P.A.Dyar, R.K.Wright, S.E.Wilson, P.Bas, P.Maret, P.Moreau, D.L.Danz, G.J.Vannoni, K.K.Kleman, D.J.Wink, S.K.Pearce, V.L.Albrecht, J.R.Echeverría, M.J.Winters, E.Bonnin, J.Goncalves, M.Menetrier, E.Loughlan, G.Beck, H.Hofmann, M.Magin, R.Kryscyk, S.Hecht, C.V.De Pol, A.M.Cockayne, D.R.Barloon, C.Roche, A.Senger, D.Karst, E.Sobotta, R.Russillo, S.Veres, J.K.Kronlage, H.Sprunck, L.Wollbrecht, I.Leeck, J.D.Lopez, J.E.Frederick, J.M.Murdock, J.S.Logan, K.R.Knight, L.M.Cournoyer, L.M.Heath, S.C.Hayes, T.J.Huegel, W.A.Floyd III, C.J.Meacock, O.Rodriguez, L.Y.Vanderheyden, A.L.Wetzel, G.A.Marten, J.J.O Brien, K.M.Hatlevig, L.D.Less, M.E.Matter, O.L.Bultsma, J.M.Velazco, M.Saavedra , H.Cousson, M.Mueller, P.Schlicht, M.M.Daoust, C.P.Wehner, J.R.Cortez, P.J.Needham, A.C.Anderson, B.K.Clouse, B.L.Bailey, C.A.Brown, L.W.Fortner, N.R.Tinker, O.R.Hickman, S.D.Hopson, S.M.Hall, T.R.Brown, I.Conde, B.E.Dalton, C.L.Morgan, J.D.Behan, J.J.Steppuhn Henderson, J.L.Elsey, L.D.Trager, M.A.Renner, M.J.Haxmeier, R.D.Wood, R.H.Wineland, T.J.Kilworth, T.J.Trelstad, T.M.Schildroth, T.R.Burress, D.B.Althaus, J.J.Ringwald, M.V.Hindrichs, N.A.Mathis, J.L.Martinez, A.Kartal, B.Pastuszka, H.Renner, J.Altmann, M.Dusza, P.Sarchossis, S.Becker, T.Link, W.Rothenbusch, A.M.Castro, G.D.Hohnl, L.K.Palm, L.L.Labrie, M.J.Beedlow, B.S.Deiters, D.E.Wolf, L.M.Anding, P.L.Dowling, P.S.Walton, R.L.Dennis, S.W.Bardwell, J.Guerrero, E.Gola, I.Gruber, J.Janta, M.Mehl, J.A.Rasgado, M.A.Christenson, W.C.Holstun, D.G.Niebuhr, J.M.Raatz, K.M.Skinner, R.A.Fritz, R.E.Smalley, T.O.Attleson, C.Stephan, D.Ceyhan, J.Nickles, A.P.Kotze, T.D.Koch, J.F.Saenz, E.Becker, P.Menara, G.M.Johnson, S.Rodriguez, B.G.Schmitz, G.D.Dupre, J.A.Brindle, A.Atamer, H.Becher, H.Fahning, J.Huebner, M.Christner, R.Coombs, R.Dauber, R.Gaa, R.Gantner, S.Oeztuerk, W.Weigold, C.D.Vinzant, M.M.B.D.Silva, J.Garcia, J.M.Villarreal, J.Regino, G.Lesiak, H.Yedigoel, I.Loeser, C.L.Johnson, J.Alvarado, J.A.Duesing, J.L.Meixelsperger, J.Snyder, S.J.Appell, J.A.Peña, I.C.Wray, M.L.Poehlman, T.E.Havens, W.S.Merritt, A.Eychenne, E.Wieczorek, H.Czech, M.Wrobel, B.L.Roberts, G.B.Kidd, F.Gonzalez, J.G.Mata, P.Smith, A.L.Till, C.A.Motiff, L.J.Yager, M.P.Hogan, T.R.Caldwell, M.A.Cera, W.Widera, J.Zarate, B.A.Cunningham, B.J.Beals, C.J.Butts, M.J.King, M.J.White, T.F.Crow, D.J.Purdy, E.Davila, K.S.Wanless, M.S.Christians, T.L.Wise, W.J.Marshall, C.Rodriguez, P.S.Berndt, F.V.Peiter, J.F.Marsh, J.Grimault, E.Tuerke, F.Hess, G.Haesner, H.Lackner, H.Schweickert, K.Brenner, K.Heilmann, L.Noe, R.Lang, R.Schwierz, T.Brien, L.J.Rodts, M.W.Mihm, J.Braunagel, P.Nieto, D.Condruz, R.Olvera, D.K.Wink, G.M.Sime, J.P.Nolin, J.S.Markussen, S.M.Holznagel, P.Kucharczyk, J.Morley, D.K.Franz, G.A.Dewulf, H.Valimont, A.Rusakiewicz, B.Rennholz, B.Ringhof, H.Pudack, M.Geiler, M.Sebastian, R.Merkel, J.L.Livingston, R.M.Morrow, A.L.Carnes, B.W.Luecke, D.L.Schares, R.J.Gotto, D.Duck, M.Tischbierek, M.G.Toscano, C.Clement, K.G.Nies, R.E.Bair, S.K.Parsons, F.A.Cerda, F.J.Reyes, J.Villarreal , R.Barrera, M.Palacios, R.F.Zey, T.M.Thompson, B.Kraemer, H.Freyer, H.Schmiemann, H.Spiess, J.Lang, L.Szopa, P.Gegusch, R.Ploesser, W.Rempp, G.Boillon, J.Baptist, U.Frenzel, D.R.Trisler, E.H.Albright, J.Chavez, P.A.Valdez, Y.Caner, A.L.Lee, L.E.Harris, M.A.Ferris, R.Piechotta, Z.Kirs, A.Hernandez, S.M.Campos, M.Weiss, R.D.Zaun, D.J.Fox, J.H.Woolford, R.Hernández , G.S.Clark, E.Salazar, C.L.Rosseter, M.S.El-Zein, R.L.Garland, B.E.Cerretti, L.I.Perlo, F.D.Livramento, E.Stoeckle, H.Hembd, H.Hering, H.Rapke, H.Smolik, J.Bastian, L.Camus, L.Hochlehnert, W.Kroll, W.Walter, B.A.Sehmann, L.J.Gomez, C.A.Chitolina, J.L.Molina, C.Baudin, J.Clausse, A.Futterer, A.Zinn, C.Hatzler, G.Dagenbach, J.Wander, M.Spaenle, R.Hoffmann, J.H.Suarez, J.A.Calderon, E.J.Schneiders, J.Hughes, R.J.Stanton, T.W.Battersby, S.L.Cook, J.J.Contreras, C.A.Lewis, D.L.Neumayer, J.G.Blaker, M.A.Sackett, A.Ibarra, H.Krumbacher, N.Zahm, J.Martinez, J.Martinez, M.Paul, R.J.Schoutteet, J.M.Slater, L.R.Reisner, L.Sires, V.J.Pint, A.Stryjak, S.J.Paskvan, C.Pagliari, M.E.Spiers, T.L.Bolt, D.Swann, E.Rottmann, F.Weissgerber, H.Armbrust, J.Sellner, L.Hess, M.Arnold, M.Lang, N.Piechotta, O.Venske, T.Welsch, F.Koch, R.Boeser, R.Keller, B.S.Wasson, D.S.Longnecker, S.D.Bolt, A.Tyrogalas, F.Boeser, U.Mauk, C.S.Plumley, B.A.Bartels, D.J.Dunek, J.E.Sheldon, J.H.Jones, J.L.Buck, J.P.Kane, A.Seelinger, M.Temel, L.A.Manzanares, T.L.Morrison, D.R.Guinn, M.M.Mc Cullough, R.J.Czarnecki, T.A.Reasby, D.C.Larsen, T.Buczynski, C.A.Santana, D.W.Mairet, G.L.Burris, J.T.Keemle, A.Lara, D.Lorre, R.J.Roseby, D.P.Jones, C.R.Alberti, E.Dauenhauer, H.Beyer, H.Niemiec, J.Strauss, P.Kirschniok, P.Wojtalla, W.Schaumburger, C.J.Mottet, P.K.Buchholz, M.Reich, S.Misterek, G.A.Cloyd, J.K.Malec, R.Espinoza, W.K.Wood, E.W.Rocha Rivarola, L.E.Comer, R.S.Ratcliff, J.Amy, L.F.Kane, R.Ramos, **1990** H.Christiansen, K.S.Shipley, M.L.Hill, T.A.Hicks, A.Guendel, B.Holzmann, B.Polzer, B.Schenkenberger, D.Pieper, E.Kulessa, E.Thoennes, H.Lieb, J.Romero-Rentero, L.Bickelmann, M.Trinler, M.Witczak, N.Drabas, O.Streckfuss, R.Bielfeld, U.Sauter, W.Treiber, D.Chapa, K.E.Johnson, L.S.Padgett, R.A.Pickering, G.C.Hirt, O.Luckemeyer, P.D.N.D.Menezes, J.Maier, G.C.Coetzee, B.Miller, D.E.Walahoski Jr., H.N.Hoover, J.L.Crawford, J.W.Stratton, K.L.Brouwer Jr., M.D.Cadby, P.J.Lacy, R.E.Hanes, S.A.Hickok, S.J.Cripple, S.P.Robisky, T.J.Ridout, T.T.Lanier, D.Chapa, J.G.Gallegos, L.Jacquinot, M.A.Budan, R.J.Koppen, H.Resouloglu, T.Haag, P.M.Richards, J.A.Huedo, S.M.Carr, D.H.Killian, D.C.Behney, E.E.Fox, J.A.Anderson, P.Y.Stapleton, R.K.Taylor, R.L.Guinn, R.L.Spain, L.A.Martinez, F.Blanchard, R.Mludek, J.A.Claussen, J.K.Carroll, T.J.Hayes, M.V.Padilla, E.Wandra, M.M.Long, B.J.Busch, D.A.Carr, J.A.Weihs, J.D.Wattonville, J.R.Barrows, K.K.Surface, K.L.Lundak, N.S.Falls, A.Aniol, J.Zimmermann, F.Agundez, D.Gladin, J.A.Tenorio, A.M.Ellis, D.O.Powell, F.D.Williams, J.A.Radke, M.T.Mullins Jr., P.G.Burns, P.J.Merfeld, T.L.Archer, M.A.Leonard, J.L.Cardona, J.E.Goodney, J.J.Menard, M.J.Simon, C.P.Gutierrez, C.Lavezard, B.Thomas, D.Ibanez-Ramirez, E.Hoeh, H.Korbus, H.Lissek, K.Knerr, L.Pierschalik, O.Wilhelm, P.Dreier, R.Goebel, U.Hunze, W.Deller, W.Pfeil, A.Ostroski, C.Muller, L.L.D.S.Brum, N.Kempf, P.A.Sieben, R.Barbosa, M.A.Villarreal, M.Almaguer, A.J.Olney, D.E.Swartslander, D.R.Lynch, H.M.Tometich, N.T.Gruver, S.E.Lundeen, W.H.Snowdon, A.Gizeria, A.M.Jurach, D.Brandalise, D.Dreifke, E.A.Pilz, E.C.Marostega, E.Dressel, E.R.D.D.Souza, F.J.Rehbein, G.L.Kristensen, J.Mantelli, M.A.Soares, M.R.Beck, O.D.Moura, P.C.Fritzen, P.R.Stamm, W.Rissling, S.B.Phillips, C.A.Staniek, S.Renard, L.M.Bjorlin, C.V.Hensley, J.C.Sawiak, L.J.Paustian, M.R.Ready, P.A.Cox, V.A.Judge, C.Reiche, K.Bowers, K.Schewe, P.Eustachi, I.D.S.D.Santos, D.R.Blancett, C.G.Echavarri, J.Luecke, W.Baumann, G.Malik, C.Naranjo , J.L.McGill, N.Cameron, P.A.McCreery, W.A.Rotzien, A.I.Wiprich, A.Roberti, A.Wiprich, C.C.Schmitt, C.L.Ebert, C.Schweigert, J.Pilz, L.D.D.Vargas, L.Ribeiro, L.Schoninger, O.R.Valencio, V.Radieske, D.J.Hart, F.Gaytán , L.V.Zimmermann, D.S.Frese, J.O.Bromley, T.D.Hollerud, P.Y.Ooi, D.Rueckert, E.Rehm, J.Wolf, K.Gabriel, M.Ayan, M.Mertes, S.Stegmann Von, V.Lueders, J.M.Campo, R.Franet, D.H.Hecht, D.R.Howland, M.J.Minteer, P.J.Diefenthaler Jr., S.E.Pehowski, T.A.Currier, O.Harrass, R.J.Doncon, P.A.Hodgkinson, C.N.Tungblut, E.L.Michelsen, I.Schoninger, R.N.Luchterhand, T.E.Davies, H.Muñiz, G.Langer, G.Mildenberger, C.Muller, D.P.Ramp, L.Coronado, S.Dubiel, G.D.Johnson, M.Mikkelsen, C.M.Davis, M.A.Maiwald, R.Wood, C.Gotowski, N.Kaya, C.Herrera, H.Flores, D.J.Rebhuhn, F.E.Clark, A.F.Saueressig, J.Quiroz, E.S.Buchholz, B.G.Defrates, J.F.Mata, D.M.Williamson, A.Jakubik, A.Narloch, E.Kessler, E.Schoepf, G.Jung, G.Kube, H.Bischoff, L.Ritter, M.Popovic, W.Hergeth, W.Morsch, B.J.Sanders, G.O.Jung, J.H.Alexander, K.B.Golden, R.M.Preacher, S.P.St Ledger, M.A.Marmolejo, R.Hildebrand, W.Eisleb, J.E.Humphries, J.G.Limon, M.Sieron, V.J.Williams, C.A.Jahn, C.P.Cline, L.J.Kiser, S.E.Davison, S.Chandra, O.Treviño, A.K.Parkinson, D.I.Bishop, D.L.Enyeart, L.E.Kingsbury, M.L.Bouma, R.G.Williams, T.M.Johnston, V.L.Lowe, J.Hernandez, A.Kedracki, G.Przadka, B.B.Stockton, E.M.Tysma, M.Spaniol-Metzler, M.Avila, C.A.Phillips, D.J.Riessen, D.S.Wright, J.W.Webb, K.L.Henn, M.Smith, R.L.Borodychuk, R.S.Swanson, A.Georgiadis, C.Holzwarth, E.Rabung, G.Huell, G.Schwarz, H.Dewald, H.Frank, M.Rubio-Sanchez, R.Gerth, R.Kliche, W.Andres, W.Ficht, M.L.Garcia, A.J.Vanover, C.C.Jones, S.Djurdjevic, T.T.Reis, D.L.Rucker, D.M.Heim, J.C.Brown, K.K.Beardsley, K.M.Greensides, S.W.Cary, J.Kappes, M.Kleine, M.Timmler, J.P.Wolvaardt, B.W.Garland, C.W.Narup, D.M.Moeller, D.Ruccolo, W.H.Schott, W.R.Lewis, J.D.Pickett, F.A.Hernández , B.S.Underwood, D.J.Goodman, D.W.Pfeiffer, M.T.Mickelson, M.T.Miller, Q.W.Saye, R.R.Reeg, S.M.Carlson, T.L.Goodnight, W.G.Carney, S.R.Schutjer, R.Bruchmann, R.F.Percy, F.Lopez, J.R.Santos , F.Torres, V.M.Hernandez, P.Rimlinger, D.J.Bishop, J.A.Daley, J.P.Noonan-Day, M.D.Krueger, M.J.Creegan, M.R.De Blois Jr., S.M.Bolden, S.M.Rindfleisch, P.Keller, A.W.Lyles, C.M.Grainger, J.L.Tellez, J.L.S.Logemann, J.H.Valdez, J.Salazar, A.Schneider, E.Freytag, E.Pitz, G.Roeller, H.Klett, H.Lorenzen, H.Rohwedder, P.Boettcher, P.Kretschmer, S.Gaona-Sanchez, V.Aulock-Von, W.Heid, W.Mueller, B.K.Miller, D.J.Kettler, J.J.Cinnamon, J.S.Wigdahl, K.A.Larson, K.D.Johnson, K.E.Macaulay, M.K.Pasui, R.A.Mc Millan, R.E.Benway, A.N.Greenwood, G.Zago, H.Treloar, S.L.Rehbein, J.Benz, A.T.Benko, D.M.Kerr, E.J.Grant, G.M.Wolfe, H.L.Robinson, J.T.Noonan, N.S.Crowley, R.D.Graff, R.E.Larson, S.D.Stagg, S.L.O Brien, W.K.Warren, S.Merino, E.Landeros, A.Morales, A.J.Nodorft, A.J.Novak, A.W.Nations, D.W.Smith, K.C.Stickler, K.K.Chapin, L.D.Schmidt, M.M.Betts, P.G.Carper, C.Coeuret, A.Eichhorn, B.Huebert, D.Waliczek, J.Rozmiarek, S.R.McGeehon, I.Robledo, A.J.Stanton, C.M.Arnold, H.M.Ramey, L.L.Howard, T.J.Forbes, A.Leitner, R.Lozano , E.Bodmann, E.Moeser, E.Montag, F.Calusic, G.Brueckmann, G.Donaldson, G.Kapuschinski, H.Singer, L.Bugert, R.Franke, V.Braun, W.Biedermann, B.Mc Daniel, D.B.Dubose, K.E.Waddell, P.J.Rippel, R.R.Flanery, S.M.Ford, C.Batel, K.Gaa, T.Schwebler, V.Eberhard, J.N.Galecki, L.J.Clemen, M.K.Baker, N.V.Francis-Pham, S.D.Breon, J.K.White, C.P.Martini, K.I.Bosse, K.J.Thedens, L.J.Mann, S.A.Hudson, F.Sperotto, M.Moore, D.Culpin, J.Pinto, G.L.Livingston, J.Aiken, S.L.Carpenter, S.L.Maynard, R.Chudy, L.R.Cline, S.K.Hostetler, G.P.Edwards, D.M.Jones, L.M.Minnaert, R.J.Eichner, C.Amanatidis, G.Guetzlaff, H.Ligl, H.Limbeck, L.Schodt, R.Goerlitz, R.Greda, U.Braun, W.Beck, W.Jung, W.Laquai, W.Tropf, W.Weick, D.C.Grafft, F.D.Vick, G.J.Treichel, J.K.Hill, S.L.Flynn, S.R.Timm, P.Palacios, R.Manzo , J.Marscholek, J.C.Dejonge, T.R.Toal, C.L.Mason, D.A.Davis, D.C.Gilmore, D.L.Moore, H.J.Booth, K.J.Kaliban, K.L.Ramp, L.M.O Toole, M.A.McCracken, E.J.Gelatti, P.Eich, B.L.Houtakker, K.J.Prowant, K.M.Reynolds, L.C.Dolleman, L.K.Thompson, M.Blandl, R.Ernst, H.Uz, J.Kolb, K.Fendel, M.Markmann, N.Ceri, O.Seibert, T.Reiter, D.W.Williams, S.R.Whiteman, T.J.Fernholz, M. von Pentz, H.C.Olson, S.G.Fernández, M.Turbe-Bion, A.Homberg, F.Kabasakal, G.Brueggemann, G.Gaa, G.Schuppel, J.Pascual-Moran, M.Kuhn, M.Winkler, R.Bernhard, R.Mueller, T.Voigt, V.Emekci, W.Bauer, W.Ernst, J.F.Plunkett, P.G.Slatter, A.S.Ortega , M.Richard, E.Winkler, H.Kaltenbach, J.Hertweck, S.L.Matthews, T.E.Stidom, W.J.Klutho, S.R.Lovelace, L.L.Quillen, R.J.White, J.T.Miller III, K.J.Wild, P.J.De Maine, G.D.Taylor, J.L.Mayer, E.M.B.Vintacourt, T.J.Slinger, C.S.Zabel, J.R.Dunn, R.M.Schiller, R.N.Leeper, S.P.Wagner, T.S.Reasoner, W.J.Dukes, J.J.Meléndez , T.R.Montemayor, F.Carteret, J.Marmier, D.Kamuff, D.Stratmann, E.Feik, E.Salgado-Bernadez, H.Weisbrod, I.Niebler, J.Janas, K.Hoert, O.Gilbert, W.Czech, W.Ruh, S.J.Greyling, E.G.Jones, E.J.Holmstrom, T.Pach, W.Seboek, W.W.Murray, M.R.Hurley Jr., G.Gasnet, D.E.Flack, J.Rosales, D.G.Fehrman, R.S.Cox, A.B.Dickson Jr., D.R.Murphy, J.R.Salazar, P.J.De Grasse, C.A.Schultz, D.L.Pflieger, D.P.Williams, D.S.Anderson, J.M.Stromberg, D.M.Park, A.Muhs, C.Root, F.Heid, K.Maier, R.Hofmann, R.Merkel, W.Krauss, F.Weber, J.H.Ruff, M.K.Ashurst, D.Lange, J.Michel, K.Bold, S.E.Chafe, C.L.Tyler, E.A.Collins, S.K.Hitz, T.A.Budimir, D.F.Ruff, D.K.Bright, J.García , C.Paim, I.Celik, K.Burkhardt, M.Karavdic, B.G.Dickhout, L.E.Kraske, R.J.Dexter, R.Hanot, I.Dumortier, G.L.Johanson, L.J.Hofer, C.M.Rwaai, M.P.Hlatshwayo, S.C.Malape, S.Phadime, T.B.Mndau, W.E.Southon, D.K.Logan, G.F.Graham, J.A.Summers, P.K.Egger, J.M.Cruz, T.Paczkowski, R.F.Medina, **1991** K.E.Christensen, C.R.Buck, F.Siegl, G.Werner, H.Kunze, H.Placzek, I.Gray, P.Frets, S.Hilbert, S.Schend, U.Joest, K.K.Franzen, M.E.Etheridge, S.F.Stueck, T.B.French, W.G.Alexander, G.R.Kinney, A.R.Tsotetsi, J.Hlatshwayo, M.J.Hlanga, M.J.Motsele, M.M.Nama, M.P.Mjoli, R.Olifant, S.S.Mkhwanazi, S.T.Moloja, S.W.Tshabalala, T.E.Rossouw, V.V.Mpinga, D.F.Estep, D.L.Bohm, R.W.Potts, R.W.Williams, W.D.Spain, D.B.Pauli, J.B.Nordhus, T.L.Ryan, R.Charleton, K.Oberst, K.C.Peterson, J.Ellis, J.G.Ramirez, S.Delgado, S.C.Steege, P.S.McCorkle, S.Macias, J.C.Laite, B.J.Jones, D.B.Foss, M.R.Karam, H.Huerta , A.Eitel, A.Novak, A.Schwind, G.Prahs, G.Wigger, J.Garcia-Guereno, K.Konrath, M.Wild, O.Mueller, P.Maletzko, W.Heilmann, A.Gelbhar, J.L.Perales, A.S.McCrary, F.F.Parrish Jr., J.K.Westerlund, A.F.D.Souza, C.Lipke, C.M.Link, F.Johann, G.C.D.Silva, J.A.Fagundes, J.D.A.D.Rosa, L.C.Cichowicz, V.L.Pedo, E.A.Franklin, S.A.Devriese, W.M.Walter Jr., K.W.Maphiliphili, M.D.Fowler, P.S.Miller, S.L.Baker, C.R.Dean, E.W.Canfield, K.M.Gilbert, K.W.Rodgers, M.A.Vanspeybroeck, M.E.Stochl, F.Adler, F.Walter, K.Ries, L.Orth, T.Navas-San-Segundo, W.Lutz, B.A.Japink, J.A.De Jong, J.W.Assen, W.F.Van Alstede, I.M.Brinker, F.Van Dam, T.H.J.Semmekrot, H.Pruim, W.G.J.Tempelman, G.J.H.Ten Cate, D.G.Nix, F.Scheffer, J.G.Geerdink, A.H.Ankone, K.Hofmann, R.Ten Lande, E.B.Rijkschroeff, A.Dubbelman, A.H.Baas, J.Agerbeek, H.H.Klasens, B.R.Von Stockhausen, M.Reuvers, R.J.Keizers, W.Obermeijer, W.N.Van De Horst, T.Van Dyk, I.B.H.Snoeyink, J.M.Breukers, J.Hein, W.Nijkrake, M.Lagmich, J.Oosterhof, J.Van Dykhuizen, M.A.G.Bergers, G.J.Peterinck, G.Oostindie, R.L.Vastrick, H.Post, H.Van Buiten, E.H.J.Swennenhuis, J.H.Holshof, C.Jongedijk, J.A.N.Krijgsman, G.J.J.M.Meekes, R.B.L.Nijland, J.Otten, R.J.Geurts, M.J.H.Evertman, A.J.Liefers, J.A.Kerkhoff-Groot, F.H.Gerritsen, Van J.Ek, H.Rademaker, Jg.Jg Wyering, J.Ireij, A.T.Timmers, F.Laurenssen, J.Meijer, H.F.M.Rouing, H.Van Der Meulen, W.H.Achterbosch, T.J.Manbodh, C.A.Stucky, J.H.Brailsford, K.L.Gladwin, L.A.Hamke, M.A.Vaz, T.R.Dowd, G.D.Wilcox, R.A.Kaminski, C.Maldonado, A.R.Roman, E.A.Lampe, G.M.Heintz, N.D.Muntzing, T.M.Post, W.E.McCoy, S.L.Colvin, P.M.Wynthein, C.A.Peck, G.M.Keyes, L.D.Jurgensen, S.K.Miller, M.Coeur, A.Hemmerich, A.Ramadani, E.Aefelein, E.Schoell, E.Schuetz, H.Fontagnier, H.Muench, H.Steitz, H.Tiebler, J.Pestana-Fernandez, K.Adler, K.Metzger, K.Papadimitriou, L.Noheimer, R.Braun, R.Reischmann, S.Lattuca-Bonamico, W.Sausbier, W.Stauch, J.W.McLean, D.J.Hayes, D.T.Miller, M.A.Heaton, P.G.Jarvis, W.S.Moloi, D.R.Mc Neill, M.A.Danielsen, S.Jugovic, D.S.Gallagher, A.M.Ayala-Garcia, I.R.Thornberry III, M.L.Jones, M.L.Strine, L.Choate, G.C.Campbell, A.Weigel, F.Greco, H.Klinger, H.Maass, H.Wieder, J.Hafner, K.Diefenbach, W.Mandel, Ter H.J.Horst, C.Jillings, E.Elskamp, S.Kuehn, M.Engel, M.L.Wilkerson, R.J.Gitter, V.Wolfe, P.Lipiceanu, B.M.Whisman, M.J.Alvin, S.M.Hawkins, S.P.Carter, J.L.Preston, B.J.Maas, L.J.Lescantz, S.W.Gellner, A.L.Kilworth, A.Y.Chow, B.A.Ullmark, B.R.Matson, B.W.Lovaas, R.C.Blad, R.E.Schmidt, S.L.Peace, A.J.Christopher, G.S.Hinch, S.E.Anderson, T.J.Merrett, A.R.Wolfe, J.E.McConkey, A.M.Keilman-Loding, B.D.Seegert, D.D.Renze, J.C.Schick, K.L.Jernigan, P.D.Cox, T.P.Zellmer, V.Davis, M.M.Bries, P.O.Swenson, A.Zintel, C.Wigger, D.Jueptner, E.Hochlehnert, F.Bollmann, G.Berger, H.Alscher, H.Dewald, H.Gross, J.Dressel, K.Lauffer, L.Koch, O.Neumann, P.Wolf, S.Clauss, W.Guenderoth, W.Haas, W.Thullen, K.Dax, H.Weller, G.Reinelt, A.Becher, H.Brenner, E.Löffler, H.Siebert, W.Seinsche, K.Klein, J.Dzierzewski, P.Prinz, W.Eiffert, M.Müller, B.Heiderich, D.Heiden, R.Pitters, L.Walther , S.Benth, S.Tinnirello, C.Lo Grasso, H.Hahn, D.Hartmann, M.Budig, G.Foti, K.Dehl, B.Schneider, U.Hensel, M.Plank, J.von Scheidt, R.Tinnirello, R.Fleischhauer, C.van der Werf, S.Krause, S.Schenker, K.Pollmann, K.Faldey, H.Jepp, H.von der Wehl, M.Zorn, G.Karpa, F.Schäfer, C.Wallefeld, H.Ostermeier, R.Funke, I.Hielscher, T.Göttfert, K.Schreuer, A.Bloz, B.Schöfer, C.Judaschke, A.Rüdiger, S.Gaadt, T.Lüthy, D.Erckens, M.Schmittseifer, G.Puzzo, S.Zintz, K.Franzkowiak, A.Klein, E.Fischer, K.Morgenstern, M.Seifer, D.Kleischmann, J.Löffler, M.Meckel, G.Gran, D.Steinhoff, H.Odenthal, K.Köp, R.Gräfer, F.Joseph, F.Kölsche , S.Puzzo, G.Eggers, E.Rautenberg, T.Haibel, S.van der Schaaf, U.Lang, C.Mertens, H.Stumpe, J.J.Fernandez , V.Llobera, D.L.Fegter, D.L.Roth, D.S.Miller, K.M.Soltwedel, M.A.Barnes, M.L.Stivers, F.Gernet, H.Butteweg, J.K.Tiedt, C.J.Houtakker, W.D.Smith, J.Albaugh, J.R.Potter, K.G.Whitfield, L.A.Potter, S.M.Klabunde, T.P.Brown Jr., M.D.Mazibuko, F.Rodewies, A.J.Igou, C.H.Carda, J.D.Mc Glaughlin, L.E.Fuller, D.Beckefeld, T.Schuster, K.A.Solomon, K.S.Summers-Day, C.S.Lacy, K.S.Hughes, M.M.Vozikis, S.A.Schrock, A.M.Riechers, L.K.Klassy, C.M.Whitacre, M.W.Freudenberg, J.Castañeda , A.Hartkorn, A.Seeburger, B.Eberle, E.Seitz, K.Wick, J.Weiner, K.Hartmann, K.Heylmann, L.Klamm, O.Erkmen, P.D'Agro, R.Schuhmacher, W.Rothaar, H.Scheel, O.J.Miller, A.Wagner, S.P.G.Glenton, M.D.Pitzer, D.L.Youngers, J.A.Niebergall, H.Seidel, M.Rivera, C.N.Hunt, D.G.Tebbe, E.R.Curtis, J.L.Bess, M.K.Beaderstadt, S.J.Steffensmeier, T.H.Dunn, L.T.B.Kotz, J.L.Raymond, S.D.Iglesias, M.Dalfert, J.Gomez, A.Mueller, B.Leljak, H.Schmitt, K.Fischer, M.Herrmann, M.Tremmel, R.Wagner, S.Koehler, S.Leitz, C.A.Foster, K.G.Sevigny, R.C.Parker, R.D.Birch, K.M.Ridel, S.L.Brown, E.Wesling, M.Ellis, S.Hoffmann, D.M.Ryans, S.S.Hendron, J.Rossi, C.I.Farias, G.W.Murdock, J.A.Williams, J.M.Zipp, M.J.Laughters, R.J.Wilwert, S.G.Johnson, M.Schwarz, K.S.Wright, M.Botella, R.Velazquez, A.Curry, J.W.Smith, G.J.Zamora, J.L.Cruz, E.Hanis, K.Blasius, E.Debruyn, G.V.Ulzen-Noordenbos, E.Ramirez, G.Mendez-Vaquero, M.Goeller, B.N.Lockett, P.Gamboa, D.M.Vonnahme, C.Harris, J.A.Van Acker, T.R.Eckert, F.Cardona, A.Mares, F.Vazquez, J.Loera, B.E.Dybevick, B.S.Shipley, N.C.Foxx, J.V.Fronza, P.D.Kampstra, F.L.Saling, C.S.Gurley, S.Allen, M.M.D.Farias, B.W.Davis, D.N.Buchanan, R.D.Vaughn, T.A.Porter, E.E.Hansen, G.M.Toth, J.V.Mullin, R.A.Atwood, S.J.Denning, J.Picard, J.Conard, A.Deberle, A.Niemiec, A.Oezdemir, C.Sigmund, D.Wagner, H.Meschutt, H.Zoeller, J.Weber, K.Bernstein, K.Moell, K.Scherer, R.Rihl, U.Crews, H.Budde, I.Rocha, E.Hansen-Taylor, S.E.Twito, J.Gauna, E.Akyuez, F.Sihorsch, E.C.Gaona, E.Diaz, J.Ramos, O.Morales, R.Diverres, F.Carrizales, G.Mata, J.M.Rodriguez, P.Gaytan, S.Saucedo, C.Armbruster, C.Surowiec, P.Nowak, J.R.De la Cruz, J.D.Hernandez, R.W.McDonald, J.J.Sams Jr., L.C.Milburn, J.Redondo A., A.M.Keller, B.D.Bannister, R.A.Salazar , M.Cormon, A.Adamietz, H.Nomine, H.Weis, J.Hauk, J.Pueyo-Duarte, L.Henk, S.Zohar, W.Burkart, W.Hamm, W.Marschall, W.Meisinger, W.Rohde, W.Stachnik, K.E.Steer, J.L.Gibbs, E.Schaeffer, L.A.Clausen, C.A.Martinez, J.Zorn, P.Haaf, R.Hirsch, A.S.Williams, I.J.Starr, M.J.Kahl, R.Caillet Bois, A.Darmstaedter, E.Roczniok, E.Woitynek, G.Kuhn, H.Abel, J.Perez-Gomes, K.Peikert, W.Koester, L.C.De Jager, D.A.Drescher, M.A.Oliver, N.M.Karriker, R.C.Brophy, G.H.Garcia, A.Henner, C.Gack, R.Mueller, I.Lobs, S.K.Ndumo, V.T.Masemola, C.E.Ehlers, D.Martinez, E.O.Kraus, R.G.J.Kokje, R.I.Purnell, E.Rodríguez, S.M.Hlatshwayo, **1992** A.Gutierrez-Cejudo, B.Grabovica, C.Michel, G.Heid, G.Riegel, G.Schoenenberger, H.Schaefer, J.Diessner, P.Sczyrba, R.Scherer, S.R.Olson, S.D.Prendergast, A.Banks, B.E.Davis, C.L.Riemenschneider, D.E.Connor, D.G.Stewart, D.J.Kastner, D.R.Percival, H.J.Sills, J.V.Davis, J.W.Harris, K.A.Eilers, K.J.Wilson, L.B.Schwalbauch, L.J.King, L.L.Kaney, L.T.Welch, M.R.Taylor, N.L.Price Jr., P.J.Mallon, R.W.Kershner, S.E.Patterson, A.Cruz, A.S.Santos, J.A.Navarro, J.A.Reyna, J.C.Cepeda, J.J.Magallanes,

Davenport, Iowa, employees with 25th anniversary 690E Excavator, 1994

J.R.Lopez, R.Esquivel, E.Calley, H.Scheuer, S.Talas, E.E.Larsen, A.Tavernari, M.C.Thomsen, R.J.Weems, J.G.Carlin, W.Amaya , S.L.Walker, B.K.Dudley, R.C.Laies, A.Hardt, A.T.Arenhardt, J.E.Cerda, J.M.Duncan, M.T.Finley, P.H.Roberts, B.R.Rodrigues, C.A.Neuhaus, C.E.L.D.Oliveira, C.J.Pohl, D.Bonette, E.C.B.Andrejeski, E.C.Franck, G.Schive, I.D.Santos, J.D.S.Silveira, J.S.T.Kamphorst, M.C.Vallerius, M.D.S.Rosa, M.J.Rodrigues, M.R.Ribeiro, M.Schweig, O.S.D.Rosa, P.C.Gasperin, R.A.Hoffmann, R.K.D.Santos, R.M.Bender, R.R.Hallmann, R.Roberti, S.D.Souza, T.L.Boeno, B.J.Loftis, K.G.Hoehn, B.Urlaub, E.Endres, G.Fuchs, G.Kolb, G.Meneges, G.Schuhmacher, H.Kerner, J.Cebulla, K.Becker, K.Hoehn, M.Wacker, S.Aydemir, T.Diesler, U.Baeurer, V.Caracousi, D.D.Radke, K.G.Hoch, M.P.Medina, L.Mohamed, C.Cantú , P.Soubiran, A.N.Pavon, C.A.Allen, C.S.Bulow, J.R.S.Schneider, P.C.Rodrigues, U.Metz, D.M.Junge, W.K.Wells, C.Alvarado, M.Ayala, S.Mendoza, G.Redemann, P.Kahl, C.L.Ladika, C.S.Dougherty, K.A.Adams, D.J.Duranti, J.C.Cardona, J.G.Escobedo, S.L.Dodds, A.Fath, E.Schneider, G.Becker, H.Glaeser, H.Zeh, J.Klotz, K.Gorsler, K.Gutperle, L.Broeckel, R.Gibtner, R.Juling, R.Schwarz, W.Ringhof, K.Kramer, C.B.Jordan, D.L.Meyer, J.R.Walter, M.K.Conway, R.L.Bartsh MD, E.E.Reis, G.E.Casas, M.Resendez, C.A.Wilkening, A.Tovar, F.A.Vazquez, C.M.Pierce, D.C.Watson, E.M.Brown, K.L.Glassinger, J.G.Balderas, O.Duault, D.Margetic, I.Solonik, J.Forsch, R.Scheller, C.Tillay, C.E.Moye, R.D.Hannon, R.N.Swanson, J.C.Vega, W.Blattner, J.Kakungulu, W.H.Thomas, B.J.Lingner, B.M.Tomlin, F.I.Rabinovich, J.R.Kimball, J.R.Vernon, R.N.Barrett, S.Ovalle, A.Lenz, B.Fischer, B.Hennrich, E.Bittlingmaier, E.Kalus, E.Pelka, G.Brzoska, G.Kowol, G.Krupp, H.Braun, H.Hurka, K.Mayer, M.Zeller, R.Boerschinger, R.Mucha, S.Lichter, U.Schulz, W.Bruck, Y.Celik, H.J.Olde Riekerink, S.M.Bartz, S.T.Kennedy, G.Scocco, G.Bonilla, C.Jenek, J.Heiduczek, J.Kaltbach, N.Tuerk, L.Sanguel, H.A.Carr, B.G.Lopas, G.W.Wurtz, M.Dolejsi, M.E.Finnell, J.R.Cabañas, R.Mendez, B.D.Opsal, B.F.Kalscheur, T.J.Taucher, G.Soto, Y.Fontaine, J.Ellwardt, G.L.Wegner, F.G.Sullivan, J.B.Burnside, R.Gundt, A.Gotha, E.Helfert, E.Hess, J.Pflug, J.Smith, L.Svoboda, W.Wiege, J.M.Gunhus, M.D.Wiklund, W.T.Murray, A.Garcia, M.Reyna, H.Adler, J.Beck, M.Ekspenszid, P.A.Lively, S.B.Hisaw, J.G.Garcia, R.Perez, C.A.Ter Beek, E.Moncivaiz, A.K.Grau, J.A.Pauwels, J.H.Pierce, K.K.Oetker, R.D.Jerauld, J.C.Carmona, J.R.Saucedo, E.R.Smith, L.A.Evert, M.A.Majeed, M.R.Reinert, R.Garza, A.K.Watters-Moeller, B.J.Kruse, C.L.Johnson, J.E.Holl, K.O.Halmstad, L.D.Jones I, M.J.Tallman, R.A.Guinn, W.J.Williams, A.Zuñiga, H.M.Garcia, J.L.Rivera, **1993** A.Broedel, B.Fell, C.Sobotzik, H.Heilmann, I.Zdunic, J.Rehberger, J.Wloka, M.Jiricek, W.Lahm, K.S.Krizek, D.L.Clarke Jr., C.A.Marten, L.E.Salmond, R.Bunce, W.Wilmoth Jr., C.Barreau, M.D.Pflieger, J.L.Medrano, S.R.Silva, G.Elizondo, J.C.Garcia, F.I.Jones, J.L.Murrey, T.Willitts, A.Russillo, M.C.Rediger, T.L.Stanek, A.A.Cruz, B.Dumortier, A.Althapp, A.Harter, B.Wochnik, E.Hottmann, E.Winkler, F.Movatz, H.Hardtmann, H.Leiner, J.Quintans-Rodriguez, M.Oezer, O.Walter, R.Herm, R.Tresser, W.Wrba, V.Lepperhoff, G.Otte, R.R.Rose, B.Isci, R.E.Carbiener, B.Frank, M.Sanders, A.H.Levy, G.R.Knight, P.K.Jennings, S.J.Smith, J.Morales, V.Lara , O.Sonnet, M.Pehlivan, J.A.Trahan, B.Greda, E.Albrecht, E.Mueller, E.Schramm, E.Stein, F.Lauer, G.Mueller, I.Sahin, L.Spacke, R.Hauser, W.Lindenau, S.Schneider, J.A.Wilke, W.T.Mullis, R.Chambard, A.Hoffmann, D.Kirschniok, S.Steeb, J.B.Harbin, K.L.Garrow, J.L.Fuentes, M.K.Wall, P.M.Harris, G.Martinez, D.Seboek, T.Otten, A.J.Dunne, A.Franov-Jurin, C.Busch, H.Erdogan, J.Foeller, J.Topic, M.Kohl, S.Weber, Y.Turhal, A.D.Celotto, W.C.Vila, D.A.Turner, D.J.Hilgemann, J.H.Abraham, R.Y.Hahm, R.S.Underhill, P.Montreuil, M.Sauer, J.F.C.Hospers, B.A.Birchmier, D.G.Tian, K.M.Moore, T.M.Brill, P.R.Grigg, C.C.Stroud, D.Burrell, S.D.Spencer, D.Thary, M.M.Delaney, D.O.Romero, A.Hatzipanagioutou, B.Proebsting, C.Voultzios, E.Brauch, F.Wagner, G.Floris, H.Hanf, H.Schmidt, J.Orlik, K.Heid, M.Mueller, N.Schenk, O.Aydemir, S.Duic, T.Buehrer, T.Herlitzius, T.Steck, W.Folwarczny, B.Patacini, R.S.Crabtree, P.Comas, G.Roland, D.G.Meyer, M.D.Yates, C.A.Weynand, D.S.Koranek, K.S.Hamborg, C.F.Toms, C.Osborn, T.T.Ammons III, T.J.Kraus, A.Amos, A.Richter, B.Wieczorek, N.Coroian, J.M.Miller, C.G.Martinez, F.Voitl, R.M.Ramakers, J.D.Johnson, C.E.Weber, M.L.Lacerda, A.Eustachi, A.Weis, E.Dieter, F.Kopmus, H.Hussong, H.Mandel, H.Walter, J.Eberle, J.Stanossek, M.Baysal, M.Sernikli, M.Zivkovic, S.Demir, W.Mayer, W.Veith, D.Potter, G.Armel, K.D.Funke, D.L.D.Bianco, P.Pelaud, I.Dirik, J.Pawlas, J.Sterzer, M.Kubitschek, N.Sterzer, V.Freiberg, D.L.Katrynuk, A.Roether, G.Kleinpeter, M.Tessitore, C.S.McDonald, S.E.Ramsey, L.Eon, W.Nelson, S.G.Lucas, B.Georget, A.Marschall, D.Tsapanidis, E.Jung, E.Neuwirth, F.Lausecker, G.Weber, H.Bender, I.Mueller, S.Trummer, W.Woelfl, D.M.Brockway, E.Demolombe, A.Kornek, F.Seitz, K.Koehler, C.A.Hunden, G.E.Prevenas, P.T.Schaffer, R.A.Buss, A.E.Collier, B.Cox, K.E.Hall, M.I.Kistner, G.A.Fava, J.A.Fernández, L.A.Clutterbuck, R.A.Roby, S.A.Friend, S.P.Chetcuti, A.R.Llorens, C.J.Lesso, D.L.Mack, M.G.Travis, J.A.Bray, B.G.Trudel, L.W.Duncan, B.A.Keating, M.Segatto, M.V.Pias, A.Keller, A.Martinan-Racero, F.Jacob, G.Bohn, G.Faber, G.Gusinski, J.Heier, J.Passon, K.Mohr, P.Dell'Orto, B.R.Williams, J.E.Vaughn, I.Söhn, K.M.Lewis, B.Spivey, J.Absher, K.K.Mason, M.Phillips, P.L.Tate, R.K.Nicholas, T.M.McMahan, F.M.Ombrello, L.Polk, H.Chow, A.Broedel, B.Bruenneck, B.Kissel, B.Mueller, B.Schreiber, E.Laensitalo, F.Keller, G.Krimitsos, H.Alter, H.Burger, H.Stay, H.Watzel, I.Zezula, K.Feix, M.Mai, R.Kalemba, V.Radivojevic, W.Egner, E.Kugland, D.L.Priest, J.C.Richards, P.J.Shelton, F.B.Nunes, R.K.Harrison, S.C.Pix, M.D.Howard, R.S.Vannorsdel, A.N.Reberger, E.L.Wagner, N.P.Diesel, M.F.Falls, P.D.Coon, S.K.Burton, D.Duncombe, K.A.Poulton, L.E.L.Ramos, A.Kreisel, M.M.De Maine, C.A.Wells, K.E.Knox, L.S.Ledford, Y.E.Sturgeon, D.W.Anderson, J.P.Brantley, M.B.Campbell, M.R.Anderson, S.L.Tasinazzo, R.D.Tiyce, M.Carranza, A.Schraml, H.Konrad, I.Yoeruek, J.Gonzales-Rogelio, L.Rueckert, M.Heinold, M.Nigar, R.Spies, R.Spindler, W.Fess, W.Mueller, W.Stibbe, P.E.Bauer, A.L.Heck, C.Pires, G.Weber, H.J.Peiter, J.Bonazza, J.Sieben, M.L.Hoffmann, M.Lehmen, R.A.Tiecher, R.Tibola, D.D.Clark, J.D.Reimers, R.J.Bunnell, D.A.Peiter, M.A.Vazquez, B.A.Ballew, B.D.Liegel, C.F.Givins, J.R.Zachmeyer, M.J.Hannig, W.M.Hershman, H.F.Ramaglia, M.R.Carnevali, A.K.Dokolas, J.B.Dingler, J.K.Utter, J.M.Robinson, S.J.Bright, R.L.Weber, E.K.Adcock, J.A.Giordano, A.U.Butzke, D.Gerhardt, A.Mitov, G.Georgiadis, G.Hauck, G.Warzecha, H.Akilli, H.Brugger, H.Meissner, J.Turner, K.Geiss, K.Petrich, L.Greulich, P.Berger, R.Gehrig, T.Haussmann, E.Márquez , J.C.Benítez, P.G.Ricker, W.G.Mitchell, H.M.Jones, J.L.Brown, S.M.Kinder, T.L.Boettner, N.R.B.D.Motta, M.W.Waldvogel, M.J.Johnson, B.P.Dunne, D.J.Handford, R.G.Trevisan, T.L.Schindler, J.M.Mbatha, A.Becker, A.Kajzar, A.Schnueckel, D.Baloui, D.Kanauf, E.Stauch, E.Stock, F.Ballweber, F.Canadas-Coleto, F.Gerlach, F.Mayer, G.Gund, G.Schrank, G.Weinmann, H.Bildstein, H.Geiser, H.Haber, H.Kivimaa, H.Lutz, H.Schneider, H.Sprengard, H.Tuerk, H.Wolff, J.Anich, J.Meszaros, J.Saller, J.Trummer, K.Hauswirth, K.Nuesgen, K.Reinemuth, K.Sturm, K.Weik, L.Jentner, M.Demele, M.Fernandez Cisneros, M.Keul, M.Torucuoglu, N.May, N.Trauth, P.Schneider, R.Fontagnier, W.Klein, W.Pfeifer, W.Simon, W.Trunk, P.Mashaba, R.A.Lockhart, R.L.Cothran, A.S.Centeno, B.J.Farmer Jr., C.Schenk, E.M.Moloi, O.A.Ramírez, M.Jones, D.A.Waymack, B.Heidemann, D.Osthaus, D.Szabo, E.Horlaender, E.Maurer, F.Groschopp, F.Horlacher, F.Kowitzke, J.Bielak, J.Bognar, K.Schoenherr, M.Bildersheim, M.Boch, M.Laengle, T.Meng, J.W.M.Pretorius, D.E.Schoenmaker, J.M.Cantin, N.B.Wilson, E.D.Anderson, J.J.Raya, A.M.Jordan, J.J.Timmons, M.B.Boddicker, M.J.Ryken, B.K.Culberson, B.A.Engelkes, G.L.Turner Sr., J.A.Flood, J.K.Bay, J.L.Sturmer, M.S.Earley, R.R.Doerrfeld, D.L.Olson, D.P.Boudreau, G.L.Floyd, J.A.Rieger, J.L.Reynolds, S.H.Wilson, A.Spiller, D.Wehner, E.Gaa, E.Mauss, H.Fanese, H.Haas, J.Behr, J.Pruhs, K.Bacher, K.Ohl, L.Menges, L.Schmid, O.Duerr, T.Poloczek, W.Berger, W.Krings, W.Schroeder, D.A.White, P.A.Ketron, J.Domínguez, C.C.Sala, J.A.Van Vooren, L.F.Ashley, P.K.Westemeier, A.W.Gross, E.R.Jackson, K.L.Wilson, A.Plei, A.Tabar, A.Wagner, C.Bonin-Von, D.Siracusa, E.Langer, E.Malek, E.Medek, E.Richter, E.Riess, E.Senger, E.Zollonds, G.Oberascher, G.Utzinger, H.Behr, H.Ebner, H.Heb, H.Korn, H.Krippleben, H.Lang, H.Nicolaus, H.Treptow, H.Wind, I.Kern, K.Loeser, K.Wilms, L.Ruberto, L.Willits, O.Altemocs, T.Bagirici, W.Krocker, Y.Karakaya, F.Guenther, B.J.Salasek, J.Henry, A.M.Jones, K.R.Mc Amis, R.W.Ellenburg, C.D.McBeth, K.D.Knight, T.L.Burchett, J.Karsburg, M.Hammes, S.G.Massuda, V.Correa, V.O.Tura, A.Puhl, L.F.Nass, L.E.Rivers Jr., A.Renkait, B.Ewald, C.Kunath, E.Lotter, E.Wandura, F.Odenthal, G.Capraro, G.Kansy, H.Grub, H.Schwaab, H.Spiess, H.Ziegler, K.Restemeyer, M.Cakir, M.Oezhan, S.Halagic, S.Schenk, T.Ciatipis, J.D.Hassman, A.E.Tavella, F.A.Piccolo, G.Di Pangrazio, M.H.Domínguez, A.M.Gabe, C.A.Binsfeld, C.C.M.Rohde, E.L.Niesciur, L.A.Richter, M.J.Bechaire, M.J.Soares, M.R.Bonmann, P.R.D.O.D.Moura, R.B.Minetto, E.A.Torres, M.M.Campbell, G.N.Mac Kay, S.Moos, S.Zelmer, A.Gomez Garcia, A.Hick, B.Koca, C.Damm, D.Dietrich, G.Stumpf, I.Oguzhan, J.Huber, M.Menches, O.Tiktas, P.Dressel, S.Ficarra, S.Lissek, G.C.Veidel, J.C.Yattoni, C.M.Casanova, R.O.Pérez, C.M.Tidwell, G.E.Jerome, G.W.Lannan, J.H.Weaver, S.H.Wegman, L.B.J.Groenewald, D.M.Piquet, A.H.Gobbi, J.E.Gallino, C.Lenz, C.Weber, D.Fagundes, D.Sartori, E.Hoesel, J.C.Bender, N.Kahlbann, P.J.Cavalini, R.A.Fritzen, J.A.Garcia, A.Huremovic, A.Marzenell, B.Escrig-Badenes, E.Haas, E.Koziol, E.Weiss, F.Hemlein, F.Klever, G.Lukoschek, H.Feuchtmeyer, H.Schubart, H.Wagner, I.Thielen, K.Peifer, K.Strauss, M.Egea-Marin, M.Gahlich, M.Sahan, R.Wolter, R.Zylka, S.Wolter, T.Schmid, L.J.Brand, V.L.Zago, A.Galan, C.W.Erickson, J.D.Gregory, C.R.Loffland, G.A.Hasenmiller, G.R.Robins, M.A.Muileboom, W.E.Matthis, S.S.Conner, S.L.Peck, D.R.Lascurain, G.C.Blanco, C.A.Sidwell, W.L.Hartman, A.Bender, A.Ringle, E.Morawietz, E.Reblin, G.Daub, G.Kreiser, H.Goetz, H.Hunsicker, H.Schumm, J.Kobas, J.Soria-Fernandez, K.Tarkan, L.Tolic, N.Vassos, O.Yavuz, P.Roswora, R.Forster, S.Bodmann, W.Heb, W.Keller, W.Mueller, W.Stein, B.Carroll, A.F.Molinelli, P.H.Vega, H.O.Vila, A.Appelt, A.L.Franken, A.L.Fydriszewski, C.Weiss, D.D.Moraes, G.C.Rex, M.A.Webler, M.E.Costa, M.G.Massirer, M.R.Decker, P.C.Smaniotto, V.R.Arend, V.Weiss, D.A.Johnson, G.D.Clampitt, F.Molina, A.L.Machado, D.G.Schmitt, G.Boldrin, M.J.S.pech, R.A.Hengen, A.V.Schumann, C.L.Weber, I.Boaski, J.R.Gerhardt, M.J.Hoffmann, N.D.V.Ebrin, U.C.Luiz, V.Bender, B.J.Dierdorff, B.L.Sehen, D.Paraiba, F.Marchalek, J.M.D.Santos, J.O.F.D.Rosa, M.J.Scherer, R.R.Rutsatz, A.L.Ackerman, J.L.Clarke, C.A.R.Silva, A.Huet, A.Steinacker, E.Heider, H.Karakaya, H.Martin, J.Christ, J.Nowak, L.Frueauf, M.Pojatic, P.Moles-Gimenez, W.Bletzer, W.Neumann, A.D.Schmidt, A.E.Cornelius, E.L.Tafarel, J.D.D.Nascimento, M.S.Soares, A.Rivas, B.E.Hawkins, G.R.Noe, E.R.Blanco, M.S.Zamora, D.R.Graveline, K.E.Poppe, W.M.Warner, D.F.Rindfleisch, C.A.Wills, R.P.Walczak, M.J.Reid, C.Fouillot, A.A.Kostiuk, G.S.Hopkins, L.C.Wilfer, L.D.Mullen, M.R.Cormier, N.L.Livergood, P.S.Buchholtz, R.M.Thomas, T.L.Bedtka, N.L.Winter, P.C.Bremm, A.Pawleczko, B.Blietschau, E.Kiss, E.Plickat, I.Bozic, K.Link, K.Tzoutzomitros, L.Bremer, M.Pavlicic, P.Sako, W.Neu, D.L.Treptow, D.M.McReynolds, L.A.Edmondson, M.J.Ballina, M.M.Starkey, P.E.McNeill Jr., R.L.Cole, M.Fiez, A.A.Tormes, C.R.D.Souza, J.L.Duarte, O.Griesang, C.E.Wineland, K.A.Hauschildt, R.W.Degrow, D.S.Murphy, J.R.Allen, D.Martinez, J.G.Torres, J.S.Coronado, R.Martinez, C.S.Guest, J.R.Norman Jr., P.C.Brummitt, **1994** C.Burger, D.Bodenstein, F.Fett, G.Berg, G.Kandzorra, G.Radtke, G.Saitta, G.Schwab, H.Schobel, H.Weimar, J.Adametz, K.Russ, K.Wetzel, L.Spagnolo, M.Djoric, P.Schulz, R.Satzke, R.Schimmelpfennig, W.Heim, W.Speckert, W.Stoever, J.Brouwer, A.M.Henderson, B.K.Johnson, C.E.Braden, C.T.Krantz, G.L.Acton, L.B.Sarratt, M.D.Farage, M.S.Land, S.B.Schroeder, S.C.Holomego, T.W.Clayton, C.H.A.D.Veiga, L.M.Arnold, S.Venier, D.R.Lampe, E.W.Holstein, K.L.Mayhorn, S.A.Kupferschmidt, M.A.Grech, H.M.Adams, E.V.Junior, C.N.Ochoa, B.J.Lindeman, J.D.Leasure, E.S.Wyzykowski, B.J.Rauch, C.D.Wemhoff, C.R.Rickey, J.M.Holmes, F.J.Garibaldi, G.J.Pinales, H.V.Zamarron, J.A.Guerra, J.D.Martinez, J.J.Gauna, M.S.Tirado, A.Barnard, T.M.Motloung, H.Arboe, L.R.Simpson, M.J.Pipho, A.J.Dengo, C.J.Mann, C.Y.Au, F.R.Ibeas, G.D.Smith, J.P.Priebe, L.M.Law, M.McMurtry, M.Phu, P.A.Achim, R.A.McLaughlin, S.Haniff, S.Pullin, V.R.Lynch, C.M.Speroni, H.A.Montivero, A.Ledda, E.Endres, G.Saatcioglu, H.Kilic, H.Kuebler, H.Rudolf, H.Schubert, J.Becker, K.Schaefer, L.Sieg, M.Helwig, M.Wiehn, P.Honczia, S.Karoglu, S.Licina, W.Diehl, W.Krafcyk, P.Y.Jackson, C.A.Darvin, F.D.Revels, J.J.Good, L.E.Walsh, L.R.Kite, P.J.Porter, S.T.Hamborg, K.A.Cilauro, J.Smith, A.Cronst, C.A.Nuske, C.Gerhardt, E.B.Belarmino, P.C.Saquete, H.S.Bredensteiner, J.L.Magee, R.C.Henderson, T.A.Reddish, W.H.Ballew, P.Fumagalli, P.K.McManamy, I.Strapasson, P.N.R.M.Camargo, C.P.Begin, D.L.Goodrich, A.F.Alarcón, C.A.Padilha, C.A.Pedo, C.R.Weber, E.C.Rosso, E.R.Rossato, F.D.A.Martins, F.R.Lang, L.D.Burghausen, M.A.Borgmann, M.Brandenburg, M.C.Stein, M.J.Ostapiuk, M.M.Hirt, M.R.Carlin, M.R.Scherer, M.Wandscheer, O.Fenner, O.J.Carvalho, R.A.Bremm, V.D.Bottega, J.A.Olivares, I.S.Cruz, J.A.Quezada, D.P.Lipischak, D.S.Golden, S.D.Ochsner, A.Nerio, E.Guzman, J.P.Ruiz, M.A.Castillo, V.M.Gonzalez, D.W.Passmore, M.B.Timke, T.P.Solis, G.D.Benincasa, E.Radoske, F.Hess, G.Janisch, H.Stoetzel, H.Wagner, I.Maretic, M.Blazanovic, M.Brunetti, R.Duchauffour, U.Hornung-Morgenthaler, W.Graf von Schwerin, W.Zuther, E.Moloi, H.B.Mokoena, J.G.Ramirez, J.J.Gonzalez, L.A.Pruneda, M.Fraire, C.R.Armstrong, J.D.Volkert, S.A.Grimm, T.D.Wodrich, V.D.Wade, A.P.D.Moraes, C.L.Marx, C.Wendpap, E.Griesang, E.Weiss, J.A.Kinalski, J.L.Hoffmann, L.F.Tartarotti, M.V.Hirt, R.D.Abreu, S.D.Fagundes, S.Zimmermann, V.J.Mattes, E.M.Gilmore, A.J.Leal, J.A.Chavez, J.L.Gauna, G.D.Lollis, J.S.Hickman, P.N.Doherty, R.I.Van Roekel, R.W.Wybrow, S.M.Bronn, O.Jallet, A.E.Torres, L.J.Weegenaar, B.J.Sherer, C.A.Dunning, D.Avolio, E.C.Slinger, J.J.Jongebloed, J.P.Schultz, L.J.Steinich, M.A.Schneider, M.D.Henning, M.L.Thompson, R.C.Ahorner, R.L.Wolter, S.A.Polakowski, T.G.Shookman, T.J.McCormack, G.A.Kuhn, I.I.D.Quadros, J.L.Muller, J.L.Petenon, M.M.M.lenz, P.A.Jehn, V.E.D.S.Salgadinho, J.F.Martinez, O.Torres, R.Medina, R.Reyna, O.Satabin, D.H.Hoesly, L.W.Bergquist, A.Casas, H.Soto, S.Luna, A.L.Young, D.P.Chevalier, M.A.O'Connor, D.Clements, T.P.Pailane, A.Huell, D.La Viola, E.Spitzer, G.Krauss, G.Mperkoutis, G.Slabon, H.Eppel, H.Herbel, H.Huether, J.Hirsch, K.Holzwarth, K.Karakaris, M.Say, V.Derbuc, V.Doubek, A.K.Kallhoff, B.Johnson, E.M.Clark Jr., J.J.Rocco, L.A.Geuna, A.Feuerharmel, L.A.Cepeda, R.A.Guerrero, R.Arguijo, R.C.Zofoli, A.Zimmer, M.Wilhelm, A.F.Bade, D.Muller, J.R.D.Lima, L.P.N.Eckert, M.Balsan, M.V.Weirich, V.Busanello, B.A.Iafrate, B.C.Suen, C.S.Holloway, D.R.Wagner, D.S.Warren, M.R.Meeks, P.J.Brooks, P.J.Duffy, P.J.Sijm, A.Santana, D.E.Galvan, H.M.Moreno, J.J.Rodriguez, R.Zamarripa, B.G.Verstraete, B.Vander Molen, C.M.Pauletti, D.P.Baerg, E.J.Ogle, J.M.Field, R.A.Gordon, V.D'Addario, A.C.Bender, C.J.Seifert, C.Radieske, C.Steffens, E.O.Mohr, J.A.Fank, M.Alves, M.L.Schast, P.R.F.Masera, V.Kalschne, H.M.Rodriguez, J.Olguin, M.Aguirre, O.Gack, R.A.Holt, G.Marmolejo, J.A.Veloz, A.L.Dismuke, A.Monsivais, A.S.Hartwig, W.F.Connolly, A.Fleck, A.Staudt, E.Jakob, E.Staschek, H.Schmidt, I.Eris, K.Stieler, R.Sulger, R.Watzullik, U.Zachmann, C.T.Sr.ajer, D.R.Elg, J.J.Corbin, K.M.Akins, L.R.Duhr, M.J.Kieffer, E.C.Crucillo, M.L.Jackson, J.C.Schutz, D.M.Hagen, N.Bourguigneau, P.M.Pease, S.H.Willis, E.Ganty, A.Garcia, J.C.Hernandez, D.Gardavaud, A.T.Ericsson, A.M.Vespestad, C.G.Munro, D.L.Dufner, J.P.Carlson, K.A.Gruber, K.J.Goering, K.N.Jagerson, M.A.Madetzke, M.J.Driscoll, M.S.Volkstorf, R.D.Frost, S.R.Cauwels, T.J.Dingman, W.I.Feren, G.P.Clark, R.Tew, L.Schwingel, L.Beauhaire, A.Corpus, J.Gallegos, J.J.Vazquez, R.Gallegos, P.Troupet, A.S.Deweerdt, B.E.Black, D.C.O'Connor, G.E.Tice, J.D.Burger, J.E.White, J.L.Gosse, L.D.Raya, M.R.Tyler, D.T.Scott, W.C.Taylor, A.Bonette, A.Lui, C.T.M.Goncalves, J.Hermel, M.J.Lucas, N.Bonette, R.Hammes, V.Bieger, C.V.Longshore, J.P.Marin, M.A.Guzman, U.Torres, J.M.Rivera, P.Ramos, R.M.Vargas, B.D.Pyle, C.D.Jensenius, J.E.Floersch, R.L.Faber, T.M.Wubben, S.A.Lopez, F.A.Hodge, L.A.Johnson, L.R.Erickson, M.R.Eldridge, R.L.Gauvreau, S.W.Poggemiller, A.Marquez, J.A.Mendoza, A.Yildirim, B.Ziegler, E.Boden, G.Labisch, G.Schmitt, G.Volenik, G.Weick, H.Klotz, H.Krueger, H.Lehmann, H.Riesch, H.Schwalm, I.Eisenmann, J.Sandhoefner, K.Dreher, K.Ritzert, K.Weber, M.Bechtel, M.Celebi, M.Kokott, M.Osterroth, M.Pigulla, O.Bifferoni, O.Brandl, R.Seebald, S.Domski, W.Van.Ofwegen, I.Khan, A.L.Groenenboom, M.A.Ruedy, M.B.Refugio, M.S.Egenes, J.Dent, A.Martinez, J.O.Montiel, M.Garza, E.L.Blevins, J.W.Miller, R.Loera, A.Oliphant, G.B.Nkosi, B.J.Potter, B.R.Hueser, C.R.Reiser, G.A.Kern Jr., J.K.Ferry, L.A.Williams, M.J.Thieme, R.A.Humpal, S.A.Priebe, J.O.Fagundes, M.B.D.Lima, R.Lubschinski, V.Bienert, V.Fagundes, E.Gonzalez, E.Lopez, H.J.Morales, T.Davey, R.Rocha, C.A.S.Trevizan, L.G.D.Costa, V.R.Massirer, F.J.Ferrero, B.Klabunde, G.E.Trifilio, J.Cardenas, J.E.Torres, T.Chestier, B-G.Bengtsson, D.L.Krause, J.P.Mann, J.J.Torres, L.A.Cuevas, R.Arellano, R.Carrillo, T.Puente, J.A.Tilvitz, C.W.Foster, A.M.Paulson, A.M.Popescu-Gatlan, C.A.Hoffman, K.J.Banowetz, K.R.Berning, C.Geslin, M.K.Farr, E.Le Monnier, T.Cerda, T.J.Gibson, K.J.Pease, M.Rojas, A.Harder, A.Mueller, A.Plevnali, B.Kopf, C.Linares-Vargas, E.Ohnsmann, H.Steinbach, I.Orbay, J.Carrion, J.Heiler, K.Arndt, K.Huettenberger, K.Schlosser, L.Gogolock, M.Zimmer, N.Polizoidis, P.Soto-Osorio, R.Baermann, S.Schaefer, W.Greulich, W.Ziegler, P.Delacroix, P.Goussay, C.W.Lohmann, M.L.Miller, R.L.Thompson, A.J.Sapiesinscki, C.Gerhardt, M.R.Sartori, V.L.Bieger, J.M.Villela, A.B.Williams, D.A.Bemus, E.L.Tiller, J.B.Riley, J.R.Berckart, J.R.Wasson, M.Abdul-Ali, M.G.Holston, S.L.Banning, T.L.Hunt, W.G.Stapleton, C.V.Fonseca, J.Q.M.D.Santos, C.K.Moore, J.J.Johnson, J.L.Thompson, J.Poole, M.J.Key, D.E.Haaland, H.H.Verastegui, C.J.Hammes, K.J.Morelock, K.L.Dietz, T.J.Epping, N.L.Wolf, J.N.Funderburk, J.R.Fox, L.E.McNair, M.S.Behrens, A.Rosch, E.D.Silva, J.Severo, M.A.Henke, M.P.S.Klassen, P.C.Corso, V.D.Silva, V.Dannenhauer, B.Baratin, E.Bonhomme, A.Lecanis, G.Kessel, G.Seibel, H.Hoffmann, H.Metzger, H.Nickel, H.Oberdoerfer, H.Schmidt, H.Wendel, I.Orsolic, K.Barschel, L.Kunz, M.Astor, M.Ekincioglu, M.Moritz, O.Spatz, R.Ohl, S.Giannuzzi, W.Wuest, T.Minier, D.S.Almond, J.Monreal, A.Schellenberg, A.Schneller, A.Yaman, D.Mehr, F.Rausch, H.Altundag, M.Genova, M.Karolus, M.Madel, O.Baumann, P.Springer, T.Koelsch, T.Rudolph, T.Zobel, J.C.Casas, B.E.Hagar, C.A.Russell, C.F.Verschoore, J.P.Fons, K.A.George, K.J.Brachtel, K.L.Vossoughi, L.A.Dodd, M.A.Cohen, N.L.Wilson, R.D.Durrett, R.S.Stoneking, W.L.Johnson, A.D.S.Marmitt, F.Dietrich, J.A.B.D.Rosa, J.A.D.S.Viana, J.R.Stefanello, L.F.D.Santos, M.R.Pohl, J.Buckmaier, T.Kuehn, E.Binder, R.Schenn, G.Gulam, S.K.Dorreboom, L.Hurault, L.Palmer, R.A.Schindler, J.L.Bagwell, R.D.Golden, D.C.Herbert, G.C.Dani, Z.M.M.Centeno, K.B.De Vries, G.Backes, C.A.Johnson, C.A.Cline, J.G.Mijares, K.A.Smith, L.A.Ferro, C.Altissimo, A.Aslan, A.Engelhardt, A.Sonnenschein, B.Kern, B.Nutz, C.Fuchs, C.Hofer, D.Petrovic, G.Caruana, G.Graeber, H.Kemper, J.Aguilera-Esteban, K.Doll, M.Ekincioglu, M.Elsner, M.Wild, O.Keim, S.Bachmann, T.Hammerschmidt, T.Klein, U.Bachmann, D.Chesneau, D.Pinto, B.Machon, D.K.Hays, E.L.Burris, J.C.Walters, L.S.Simpson, S.Napier, O.T.Cook III, B.J.Jensen, H.Jaramillo, C.Z.Ferreira, D.Graham, H.M.Gibson, J.F.Vanlandeghem Jr., G.J.Clark, W.Mijares , C.A.Arend, E.Brandenburg, I.Christ, P.C.Rosin, J.Martinez, O.L.Dotto, M.Edmondson, R.L.Stanley, T.S.Robins, L.Treviño, C.B.Kikia, M.Castillo, R.Almaguer, P.Cisneros, S.Portet, P.Louet, B.Bialas, D.Draganis, D.Goeksal, D.Utzinger, E.Balk, F.Kaltenbach, H.Eisenmann, H.Hufnagel, H.Jendritza, H.Klenner, H.Mauss, H.Scholl, K.Biber, K.Ruffra, M.Carnerero, M.Dayak, M.Hackray, N.Lulay, N.Tarasinski, R.Burkholder, R.Lahm, R.Schaefer, W.Ochs, D.P.Stern, G.J.Hellwarth, J.C.Medema, N.K.Foch, S.D.Kuhl, J.A.Jaramillo, D.Pluot, R.W.Olecka, H.L.D.P.Junior, M.Adamy, G.Seelinger, S.B.Lees, V.Coulon, C.A.Bald, C.R.Devolder, M.L.Temple, W.A.Rodríguez, M.R.Martini, M.J.Brown, H.Altmeyer, A.L.Garcia, B.J.Brath, B.J.Schwertz, B.R.Pulford, C.J.Jacak, C.O.Rantzow, C.S.Steele, D.C.Wolc Jr., D.D.Terlinden, D.E.Kirkland, D.F.Muench, D.J.Berkevich, D.J.Kuechler, D.J.Kuhaupt, D.J.Stone, D.K.Deibert, D.L.Miller, D.R.Beck, D.W.Krause, D.W.Otte, G.C.Koch, G.E.Neuman, J.A.Erickson, J.A.Krueger, J.A.Lentz, J.A.Netzer, J.J.Klatt, J.Meyer, J.T.Marks, J.T.Schwoch, K.D.Fauser, K.J.Thompson, K.K.Heckman, K.M.Beers, K.M.Farrell, K.R.Vinz, L.D.Last, L.J.Langkau, L.J.Scharrer, M.G.Pilsner, M.J.Kollath, M.L.Amerling, M.L.Frentzel, M.L.Schwarzenbacher, M.L.Stofflet, M.R.Bauernfeind, M.R.Price, M.S.Mecklenberg, N.J.Kronschnabel, Q.C.Vanness, R.D.Vinz, R.E.Meyer, R.F.Hartwig, S.A.Kirchoff, T.A.Kirchoff, T.A.Weisensel, T.D.Uelmen, T.J.Garczynski, T.J.Opperman, W.C.Geier, W.E.Resch, W.J.Snell, W.M.Schmidt, A.A.Schaidt, A.Heissler, J.Norenberg, L.M.Ferreira, P.Jambut, A.J.Wolf, J.K.Thornton, J.M.Blanchette, B.R.Ryan, N.J.Zemanchik, S.J.Grywacheski, L.Guiet, F.Perrotin, A.Braun, A.Fabian, A.Wuellner, B.Malkoc, C.Castillo-Sanchez, G.Maurer, H.Koehler, J.Fischer, K.Lillie, K.Wiegand, M.Katzenmaier, M.Serrano-Jimenez, P.Weihrauch, R.May, W.Schmadtke, G.Grimault, D.E.Biller, D.W.Bode, M.E.Lamb, D.J.Send, I.C.Flores, M.A.Glidewell, W.D.Yur, V.Weiss, S.J.Rébori, D.Nelson, J.M.Farr, G.F.Martina, G.C.D.Santos, G.D.M.Fernandes, O.A.Knebelkamp, M.L.Gohlke, B.C.Prye, M.C.Gordon, M.L.Jorgensen, M.W.Alberts, N.R.Ruhf, J.J.Joubert, J.H.Ross, R.L.Volkweis, L.Hernández , A.Beklevic, A.Klein, D.Mehlhase, H.Griessmer, H.Grohmueller, H.Thur, K.Gerlinger, K.Gross, M.Hanke, L.J.Turpin, F.M.Zabala, J.S.P.D.Silva, V.A.Tolfo, B.A.Longnecker, D.Rehm, M.B.Ballou, U.H.Wasner, L.Janelle, B.A.Gustavson, K.F.Wigginton, M.B.Wigginton, W.J.Cotton, B.Lundberg, M.O.Musillo, D.L.Briggs, P.M.Moreno, S.Sleger, B.Hardouin, **1995** A.Lortz, A.Sefrin, C.Sylla, D.Grasme, G.Kadilar, H.Born, H.Mueller, I.Naujock, J.Hotopp, J.Smolik, M.Goenan, O.Kaestner, O.Soysal, P.Glotzbach, R.Cleemann, R.Hudalla, R.Panic, R.Salzgeber, R.Teister, S.Mueller, W.Buechner, W.Daub, W.Gierstorfer, W.Schuhmacher, E.Stranich, W.J.Nijhuis, S.Malamud, C.Heiermann, B.D.Franke, C.C.Lauersdorf, C.L.Bailey, C.L.Hanni, C.M.Adelmeyer, C.R.Kapral, C.W.Kuhl, D.L.Nies, D.L.Schwandt, G.L.Culver, G.L.Ronning, J.A.Malec, J.C.Feggestad, J.E.Terlisner, J.F.Fehl, J.Orlich, J.W.Pankratz, L.A.Dwyer, L.J.Kranz, L.V.Deets, M.A.Grabarkiewicz, M.A.Plummer, M.C.Smith, M.J.Hocker, P.O.Baker, P.R.Rosenthal, W.R.Hemling, W.W.Koenitzer Sr., D.B.Thiemke, P.A.Henneke, P.E.Olsen, R.A.Laurin, R.M.Friestad, R.Petty Jr., S.J.Brueggen, M.Bauer, M.G.Gouws, R.Hill, C.J.Kuehl, R.D.Vance, J.J.Cunningham, J.L.Farr, J.T.Morris Jr., R.R.Bartell, T.A.Hawk, I.Martin M., K.D.Reynolds, K.S.Christensen, M.B.Jones,

German employees at Grand Detour, Illinois, bike ride, 1996

P.S.Page, R.Sun, R.M.Sartori, C.M.Klimes, J.F.Early, K.D.Ripley, L.G.Overton, S.G.Nash, C.V.Schwengber, C.S.Sloan, J.G.Stabenow, G.F.López, C.M.Owens, J.A.Breunig, R.E.Meadows, S.A.Norman, P.J.Herring, H.Bøgelund , B.E.Branham, B.E.Kolling, J.C.Roo Ortiz, K.F.Ross, E.C.Andrades, F.Ramos, L.P.D.Lima, R.B.Hermann, B.Gradoz, H.Tepe, D.Berber, G.Hahn, G.Mauss, J.Hafner, K.Celik, K.Kartop, K.Kempf, K.Obierai, M.Bachmann, R.Knapp, S.Wohlgemuth, T.Anderje, U.Hainke, W.Hauk, L.Joye, P.Burgos, C.A.Bradley, J.T.Jackson, K.M.Dewitte, L.A.Glascock, P.L.Welch, R.F.Carmack, R.A.K.Iacovenko, I.Viveros, D.Elmas, J.E.Carter, B.K.Anderson, C.K.May, C.L.Houston, C.W.Googe, D.E.Frazer, G.L.Galloway, J.A.Jump, J.L.Doolittle, J.P.Harris, K.A.Behrens, M.B.Pustejovsky, M.C.Armour Jr., M.S.Colquitt, R.B.Griffin, S.A.Tucker, V.F.Herbert, A.Sehn, C.A.Stefanello, C.H.D.Melo, C.R.Freddo, C.Schmitt, D.B.Berger, D.C.Weiss, E.A.D.Rocha, E.A.Pilz, E.E.B.Boeno, E.G.Franck, E.L.Hettwer, E.L.Puhl, E.L.Rutsatz, G.R.Link, I.M.Todeschini, L.L.Londro, M.F.Jablonski, M.J.Lucas, M.J.Soares, M.L.Rosso, M.R.Tusset, O.J.Govaski, P.F.Gollmann, R.D.Garbrecht, R.L.Boeno, S.Tenedini, T.Hirt, V.Q.D.Silva, V.R.Pedo, V.Segato, J.Debiere, H.Oetkuer, J.Petela, D.Bednarz, S.Jahier, C.P.Cathcart, D.J.Smith, J.Bryson, J.Qian, K.C.Kurgan, K.J.Mysinger, K.L.Klauer, L.L.Boyer, M.Curic, M.E.Osterberger, N.M.Kelsall, S.M.Crumbley, S.W.Czyzewski, A.Dudel, G.Kreulich, J.D.Hammes, L.D.L.Silveira, L.Raupp, O.Wagner, S.R.Baungarten, J.Hilt, E.S.Jetter, J.A.Baker, R.N.Thayer, A.L.Henderson, M.J.Henry, C.R.Brotherson, L.J.Luke, S.K.Drum, J.González , A.Cakici, A.Ignjic, A.Piontek, B.Karayel, D.Gonzalez Gargantilla, J.Mrochen, L.Bischoff, L.Schmeiss, P.Spohn, R.Ludwig, R.L.Solessio, A.J.Cunningham, D.J.Karl, J.R.Peterson, M.L.Walsh, S.M.Duster, S.M.Schiereck, T.W.Wagner, R.Rockenbach, A.Herdt, Egil.Walda, V.J.Arthur, B.T.Eastman, D.R.Flatau, W.L.Taylor, M.Keller, Z.Ju, J.A.Krafka, J.B.Chaffee-Morton, J.W.Bookout, P.A.Bennett, R.J.Bailey, S.M.Kaiser, E.T.D.Oliveira, B.Cole, H.H.Strait, M.F.Benson, P.Hess, R.M.Sparks, G.Marino, K.Ernst, C.M.Horrell, B.A.Hoffman, B.L.Thibaut, D.R.Falk, G.D.Goslowsky, J.L.Zamirowski, K.A.Goeller, L.B.Prest, M.A.Wakeland, P.A.Garcia, R.M.White, R.R.Frank, R.T.Bourland, S.Bate , H.C.Hart, P.L.Messick, R.M.McClure, E.Knudsen, H.A.Valdes, J.Harang, B.Gedik, E.Ofenloch, E.Poetschke, E.Ventura, G.Hoffmann, H.Martini, H.Sommer, H.Tonk, I.Boljesic, J.Rekowski, M.Baeuerle, P.Siefert, P.Walder, R.Zimmermann, S.Bohrer, K.Schaefer, R.Wolin, P.Marais, C.M.Harmon, J.C.Johns, L.M.Toney, S.A.Johnson, T.J.Vonnahme, J.M.Flores, E.Muller, I.L.Rodrigues, J.L.E.S.Adriano, T.Lambrecht, V.C.D.Santos, W.Degel, M.C.Edwards Smith, B.E.Ramp, J.Monchicourt, A.R.Laughlin, B.F.Bleacher III, F.C.Gahlman, G.A.Huggins, J.A.Crist, J.A.Moore, J.W.Devries, L.M.Hodge, P.J.Schaub, H.H.Grice, J.Schutz, P.Ghio, C.H.Volquardsen Jr., D.C.Vinson, D.J.Carter, J.Bonanno, K.J.Little, L.K.Klostermann, M.S.Linak, S.E.McClain, S.L.Nass, L.García , C.L.Slaughter, G.C.Alvarado, P.L.Carroll, G.Tarrius, A.K.Ashta, D.L.Smith, J.M.Cammack, K.L.Krieg, M.R.Jones, R.D.Strehlow, R.L.Koepke, D.M.Villán, J.A.Rider, P.A.Boruff, P.J.Vanwaus, C.A.David, C.W.Rampton, D.K.Ditch, E.J.Ekstam, J.A.Ritterbusch, J.Blake, J.J.Mc Caskey, J.P.Sauceman, K.M.Ebalo, S.C.Boser, E.Behr, E.Przybilla, E.Zahn, G.Niestroj, H.Groel, H.Kegel, J.Schmidt, K.Ullrich, M.Zipse, R.Burger, W.Trzaska, J.Doornenbal, P.D'Hoine, G.Bienioschek, M.Temiz, G.Boniperti, H.Chaptas, P.Fretti, F.Hombourger, E.Gormus, J.B.Finn, L.M.Anseeuw, L.W.Burken, R.R.Greenwood, G.D.Montes, N.Demirkol, B.J.Bartscher, D.W.Harbach, E.L.Hamer, G.D.Schonhoff, K.L.Dunkin, K.R.Curran, M.Q.Whan, P.L.Batcheler, R.C.Horst, R.L.Ray, T.J.Cady, T.S.Lee, T.Haeseker, J.A.A.Teggeler, G.Jin, P.S.Schmidt, D.W.Havens, J.Braz, C.J.Groene, C.J.Hanesworth, C.L.Edmondson, G.A.Van Bladel, J.T.Bruchmann, K.J.Baumgard, K.J.Tingle, M.J.Aden, S.M.Fitzer, T.J.Hall, T.L.Johnson, V.L.Berryman, M.B.Passos, M.D.Murphy, A.R.P.Zimmermann, M.Ross, B.J.Soyke, C.A.Grabau, G.R.Lane, M.C.De Poorter, M.M.Passe, M.R.McClain, M.Rukashaza, N.E.Post, P.D.Post, R.E.Lorentzen, S.D.Haack, S.M.Bonny, J.P.Latusek, C.Storgaard, H.J.Jensen, J.B.Andersen, G.R.Milstead, H.Hobby, K.M.Cavill, M.Hein, P.T.Bruss, R.C.Blades, T.E.Morgan, R.J.Chiatti, D.Labrinoudakis, G.Sabia, H.Dupre, J.Glaeser, K.Krauss, M.Greulich, M.Jaersch, N.Linke, P.Favache, P.Mandalka, S.Botic, S.Mai, M.Hein , L.P.Zapata , E.S.Kerger, G.J.Culp, G.J.Raymond, H.A.Mouser, M.C.Holes, R.J.Loehr, S.D.Homan, S.L.Cruise, T.T.Pham, L.Mijares , D.L.Lantau, G.L.Goins, J.J.Wittenburg, J.M.Straub, J.T.Porter, K.F.Lavallee, K.M.December, M.L.Vaughn, T.K.Cheng, B.J.White, C.M.Wilkens, D.A.Smith, D.J.Keehner, E.Barnes, S.R.Risgaard, T.D.Andersen, T.L.Volk, V.B.Mills, M.M.Griffis, A.L.Keller, B.T.Totten, C.C.Huang, C.K.Steinmetz, J.D.Coffey III, J.Lara, R.Alvarez, J.D.Kovalaske, D.J.Haugen, H.L.Clausen, L.L.Walters, E.A.Campbell, J.C.Kim, J.M.Shoemaker, K.C.Newton, S.G.Antes, M.Ragonnet, A.Scheuermann, A.Schneider, C.Stuewe, E.Graf, G.Hoenninger, H.Beck, J.Martinez, K.Neidhart, R.Boehmer, R.Mueller, U.Ates, W.Biehl, P.C.Meijer, A.Ambriz, F.Gauna, G.Hiracheta, H.Ibarra, I.Treviño, J.A.Hernandez, J.C.Diaz, M.A.Hernandez, M.Martinez, R.Valdez, L.Lepoivre, D.Oney, M.D.Bramley, M.D.Schultz, M.J.Keith, G.W.Goepferich, A.M.Welch, D.J.Frederickson, G.T.Derrick, M.H.Porter, M.J.Thomas, P.J.Morton, R.Cisek, S.L.Rule, S.J.Sutterer, D.E.Derscheid, T.E.Iles, L.I.Mondragón, E.C.Wright, A.M.Tyler, G.A.Coulter, L.A.Blake, A.S.Scott, P.Mota De Andrade, B.C.Kelly, J.A.Tofteberg, K.A.Blackert, G.Cortez, J.H.Garcia, J.L.Cura, R.Lopez, C.A.Alderson, R.E.Delo, T.J.Kochuyt, G.Silva , D.Dussud, F.Alexandre, G.Huguenard, J.Ramiro, C.Burgun, H.Endress, H.Hemmerich, H.Huber, H.Schmitt, I.Katic, K.Lauer, L.Bytici, M.Erbektas, W.Spatz, I.Hoppe, A.F.Jurach, C.R.Posselt, D.J.Maia, F.Peiter, G.A.Klinger, J.A.F.D.Passos, J.A.Reisner, J.Benatti, J.L.Gass, J.P.Martins, M.R.Werle, R.D.Meller, S.A.Feix, A.Hernandez, J.G.Rodriguez, P.R.Gutierrez, L.Auriant, A.M.Porter, C.F.Allen, M.J.Mentzer, S.Labuschagne, J.A.Alvarado, B.L.Singer, D.D.Cary, D.J.Boehmer, D.W.Gregor, M.A.Hart, M.L.Atchison, S.I.Mistry, G.Paredes, C.Butz, H.A.Warren, J.J.Girard, C.M.Petersen, J.L.Ose, M.J.Scott, M.L.Gause, R.G.Strike, S.C.Keen, S.K.Geary, W.K.Crocker Jr., Y.Yang, C.Beisel, E.Basson, M.J.Smith, S.Burch, L.D.Baker, S.H.Bacon, A.J.Dockery, G.L.Keys, G.S.Keys II, K.A.Duff-Morgan, M.C.Roberts, M.P.Schemelin, M.R.Strong, N.D.Ariano, E.Porto, V.L.Banning, J.A.Escareño, J.A.Mendoza, J.L.Aguiñaga, J.R.Silva, J.A.Thompson, A.Bub, A.Hock, A.Magnus, A.Mausolf, A.Moritz, D.Betz, D.Mitsch, D.Voigtlaender, F.Schneider, H.Kolm, H.Scholler, J.Metzmann, K.Baier, K.Huether, K.Schneider, K.Sirbu, M.Donath, M.Muensterberg, M.Scherer, M.Wissing, M.Zivkovic, P.Keller, P.Ringhof, R.Bas, R.Rude, S.Haaf, S.Wilhelm, T.Roth, T.Sinner, T.Skupnjak, V.Brunner, W.Wolfsturm, Y.Goekmen, Y.Moos, N.Nöldner, A.L.Rupnow Thole, C.B.Riddle, C.C.Roberts, C.E.Ervin, C.E.Thompson, C.M.Freeman, C.M.Morgan Jr., D.G.Brown, D.L.Douthat, D.R.Bugaresti, D.S.Gardner, E.A.Rosa-Gastaldo, F.R.Sauceman, G.L.Franklin, G.S.Feltman, G.S.Susong, I.V.De Vera Jr., J.E.Oaks, J.L.Morgan, J.W.Hux, K.A.Shipley, L.G.Gregory, M.E.Kirk, M.E.Short, M.K.Jinks, M.W.Brown, P.C.Looney, P.L.Horne, P.M.Sigman, R.E.Jones, R.J.Denney, R.K.Carson, S.A.Weems, S.K.Good, S.M.Meek, S.R.Blake, T.L.Francis, M.C.Negri, B.J.Rathjen, B.K.Corbett, C.L.Johnson, G.D.Simonson, J.W.Riesterer, K.E.Olson, P.J.Senechal, S.L.Northrup, S.L.Spurgetis, V.F.Beecham, C.A.Jagger, D.I.Hecker, C.Dignat, M.J.W.Smit, M.D.Gatlan, E.Lozano , M.C.Ramirez, A.B.Malone, A.L.Buck, B.A.Adams, B.J.Rybacki, C.A.Reddeman, C.Myrick, E.A.Johnson, G.J.Reckentine, J.M.Davies, J.M.Strangstalien, J.Thomas, K.R.Buller, M.E.Hannans, T.R.Wheeler, V.B.Hart, Y.Hou, A.B.Vieira, P.G.McCullough, A.Ancer , E.Martinez, F.Alvarado, H.Parra, J.D.Martinez, J.J.Contreras, J.P.Marquez, L.F.Lopez, L.H.Ovalle, M.A.Cuevas, M.Cruz, R.Porto, J.H.H.Lippinkhof, S.K.Sharpe, D.W.Bailey, C.L.Kimley, G.A.Dickinson, M.B.Kindred, T.Rong, B.Akbinar, E.Garcia Vega, F.Reingruber, G.Jung, H.Dopf, H.Engelhardt, H.Lichy, H.Wack, J.Wagner, M.Leimbach, P.Beck, V.Seitz, W.Bellaire, Z.Milenkovic, A.S.Moon, B.K.Gosnell, B.W.Tillson, C.A.Foley, C.J.Fry, C.M.McCrea, D.A.Jones, D.M.Aldrich, D.Obregon, D.S.Fuqua, F.J.Erickson, F.R.Souza, G.E.Rains, G.W.Hoover, J.E.Morrow, J.E.Murr, J.G.Edwards, J.L.Jones, J.L.Townsell, J.T.Borrall, K.J.Kirkpatrick, K.Kasper, K.W.Vickery, L.A.Macon, L.L.Beahr, M.A.Coates, M.R.Hamilton, M.S.Feekes, M.T.Thorne, N.T.Ackerman, P.S.Collins, R.A.Loney, R.C.Gass, R.D.Harris, R.E.Daniels, R.K.Wyant, R.L.Ritz, R.P.Hill, R.S.Wedding, S.A.Clark, S.L.Greenwood, S.R.Lang, T.A.Wheeler, T.A.Wilhite, T.J.Armstrong, T.L.Davis, T.L.Gardner, T.L.Kight, W.E.Kahler, W.E.Shelton, T.F.Cassie, J.Roy, A.Kerner, S.M.Sousa, K.Saiyed, L.I.Hill, M.A.Officer, R.R.Javellana, R.T.Johnson, S.L.Vandervelde, S.B.Buttress, R.I.Fernandez, K.E.Elsam, D.L.Cervenka, C.T.Klatt, D.M.Baier, J.H.Lenkerd, J.Norwood, P.E.Ferree, W.A.Holmes, S.Doenmez, A.J.Regier, A.D.Frey, B.J.Gaddis, C.L.King, D.D.Glubrecht, D.L.Sweeney, J.A.Hoffman, J.R.Merkle, J.R.Smith, M.L.Puls, M.M.Wittman, S.E.Williams, O.G.Zavala, S.Mastrangelo, B.A.Turnroth, B.K.Daniel, C.T.Smith, D.R.Schmidt II, K.A.Kelchen, K.A.Murphy, P.D.Egel, P.E.Lovelace, R.O.Gatlin, T.V.Seshadri, K.S.Moser, M.W.Alexander, F.Holm, M.E.Miskie, S.M.Hackley, A.Vazzanino, D.Andrae, E.Fiszl, E.Lang, E.Menrad, H.Hamel, J.Peric, K.Holaus, K.Sorg, M.Mikic, R.Karch, R.Lautenschlaeger, R.Moreno-Armayones, R.Obenauer, R.Pinatel-Parada, T.Cvitkovic, T.Kempf, J.C.Pinehiro, J.Oliveira, B.T.Mosdal, J.R.Bowen, L.A.Brewer Jr., R.J.Fagan, S.Slobert, T.G.Ulschmid, E.Rodriguez, M.A.Tamez, A.Moutarde, J.Bragado, L.L.Gerrard, J.D.Klopfenstein, F.A.Banda, J.Rodriguez, L.C.Garcia, J.E.Sabelka, J.R.Chestnut, K.L.Asher, S.E.Reid, S.M.Bergfeld, B.F.Poore, P.D.Marvin, R.J.Ori, F.Fitch, A.Beltran, C.Guzman, D.Nunez, M.E.Jordan, T.L.Lager, A.Sanchez, F.A.Villarreal, F.Romero, H.E.Barajas, N.Gomez, N.R.Aplin, I.Dominguez, E.Casas, O.Silva, D.D.Clark, R.E.Winsor, P.Kristensen, A.Napravnik, A.Reckinger, E.Lenz, F.Menges, H.Kubitza, H.Scheller, I.Idzan, J.Castellano-Iglesias, J.Kubitschek, L.Thomann, R.Biedermann, W.Dreissigacker, W.Endrehs, W.Strobel, C.J.Otto, B.S.Kistner, D.E.McCrea, D.M.Beach, M.C.Saad, M.J.Muscovalley, P.J.Beattie, S.N.Owenson, S.Escobedo, X.Godart, A.Grande, J.J.Cepeda, C.Lacombe, T.Tang, G.W.Watson, J.Morrical, D.Kumar, C.C.Hefel, C.P.Pizaña, C.L.McCord, G.A.Nessa, J.M.McCabe, J.D.Sivina, B.S.Magerkurth, A.Rivera, M.J.Espinoza, R.M.Tague, D.Gonget, **1996** B.Daiger, B.Linke, C.Lejko, C.Reuter, E.Meier, E.Mueller, F.Lehner, G.Giagidou, G.Klocker-Braeuer, G.Ragan, H.Heger, H.Ruf, H.Zeren, K.Lang, M.Gasafi, M.Geiler, M.Konradt, R.Borde, R.Passauer, V.Mankovjanovic, W.Klose, W.Koch, W.Stein, T.Klappert, A.A.Bau, B.J.Scannell, C.A.Levis, C.Ewert, C.J.Palzewicz, D.A.Brauer, D.L.Hofmeister, D.L.Martin, D.M.Tobak, E.A.Rossing, G.O.Hereid, G.Wolff, J.A.Gregory, J.A.Hammer, J.Claypool, J.E.Nie, J.G.Cooper, J.K.Miller, J.V.Propst, J.W.Hafemeister, K.A.Patenaude, K.A.Sandrock, K.A.Sapp, K.P.Danielson, L.L.Anderson, M.A.Miller, M.Canfield, M.J.Brown Jr., M.J.Bruxvoort, M.J.Greshay, N.A.Bensley, P.A.Gornjak, R.A.Ives, R.A.Zarczynski, R.L.Mallon, R.S.Backes, S.A.Behm, S.A.Kaiser, S.A.Wampole, S.F.Henning, S.J.Elder, S.J.Gubine, S.M.Juhasz, S.S.Huck, S.W.Yeomans, T.A.Kelm, T.E.Farr, T.P.Jenkins, T.Snyder, R.G.Farrell, C.G.Tillison, B.J.Perry, B.J.Riesenberg, B.L.Williams, C.F.Cochran, C.R.Graf, D.R.Anderson, J.A.Westhoff, J.C.Kline, J.D.Dahl, J.J.Hindman, J.Morrissey, K.E.Kleman, K.H.Thompson, L.A.Heggen, M.C.Wickman, M.D.Clark, N.D.Block, P.A.Watt, S.B.Woeckener, S.G.Callahan, S.R.McMullen, T.T.Tyler, P.B.D'Angelo, A.Acuña, M.Sanchez, O.Morales, R.Buscholl, C.Van Der Merwe, H.C.Du Plessis, M.Miguel De, J.J.Kinsey, K.A.Pearson, K.J.Crowhurst, L.Smith-Sandrock, M.F.Sprecher, R.W.Harn, C.Gossard, J.Sourdoire, H.Gustavson, B.K.Jensen, B.E.Myers, B.J.Hitt, J.C.Hamlett, K.K.Thompson, M.A.Johnson, M.K.Bush, M.P.Ciesielski, R.A.Rippchen, S.A.Tebbe, S.D.Snyder, S.E.Dietrich, T.I.Burenga III, A.Lopez, D.M.White, M.V.Lauck, A.J.Spagnolo, J.A.Spitler, L.A.McCraw, M.S.Despain, M.V.Neal, T.J.Hedgren, W.Holloway, E.Robin, H.Loeber, A.J.Devrieze, B.A.Merrill, B.J.Merrington, D.J.Evans, D.J.Israel, J.T.Anderson, L.E.Anderson, L.L.Kinzalow, L.Murzinski, S.R.Volkman, S.T.Bergland, T.T.Becton, W.D.Zopf, C.Peter, P.Pis, J.M.Woods, J.P.Meany, L.Fry, G.Velazquez, J.M.Ramirez, J.P.Almanza, R.Pedraza, G.G.Scott III, J.Stachowski, W.Zou, B.L.Preston, G.Schreier , B.Vanpeperstraete, A.Huver, B.Bolies, H.Berlinghof, H.Fuhrmann, J.Gajarszki, M.Mikulasch, O.Ruf, R.Huber, W.Buehrer, W.Quick, W.Schultze, R.Manzanares, G.P.Warwick, K.R.Peterson, S.C.Sundberg, M.Rennhack, C.A.Stephens, L.J.Jensen, C.W.Wright, A.Bach, A.Bonazza, C.D.Lima, C.G.Fernandes, C.M.D.Silva, D.A.Bau, D.Binicheski, D.L.Weiss, D.V.Schroer, E.C.Zawacki, E.L.Marin, E.M.D.Silva, E.R.Mildner, E.T.Niesciur, F.J.Luckemeyer, H.Volz, J.C.Reghelin, J.J.Dahlem, J.W.Bau, M.E.Vintacourt, M.L.Christmann, M.R.Fritzen, M.R.Kuhnel, P.G.Martens, P.J.Petenon, P.J.Widz, R.Canal, R.M.P.Gerhardt, R.Wunsch, J.B.Botti, J.G.Matamoros, M.J.Albaugh, M.M.Thomas, D.C.Whan, N.M.Christensen, B.A.Rauenbuehler, B.J.Segerstrom, D.J.Bensley, G.L.Chrusciel, J.A.Steinhart, J.A.Wilson, J.D.Burns, J.E.Griffin, J.L.Deblare, J.S.Dady, J.T.Whalen, K.J.Reed, S.L.Suelflow, W.H.Smith, J.J.Carrillo, S.J.Rodriguez, D.Southerland, J.E.Monsivais, D.J.Northrup, J.F.Klages, J.M.Declerck, J.Pereyra, J.G.Christiansen, C.L.Britts, D.R.Wright, G.D.Hutchens, L.M.Lynott, F.A.R.Ludvich, A.R.Fernández , L.G.Colunga, A.Waibel, D.Heiss, D.Kretschmar, E.Kobal, E.Kuhn, F.Fraser, G.Gallo, H.Piontek, I.Mujakovic, J.Peikert, J.Stein, J.Zoretic, K.Langlotz, K.Maechtel, L.Ringhof, O.Muenzer, P.Meyer, W.Tacke, C.M.Veldscholten, J.J.Klinker, M.M.Tiernan, M.Flores, G.Trousselle , J.Goeritz, A.D.Wikner, M.J.Mellin, S.J.Garry, A.O.Mendoza, R.Reyna, F.Davoust, H.Kecanovic, J.Peter, G.T.Gray, R.O.Weathers Jr., S.R.Hermanus, S.M.Moloi, D.Fourot, B.D.Jones, C.A.Halsema, C.D.Carlson, C.E.Hoerrmann, C.J.Holdaway, D.A.Lueth, J.A.Kiss, J.L.Rivera, L.H.Ruby, M.A.Weinheimer, N.J.Highly, P.L.Doyle, V.Heckman, X.Hua, J.J.Saldivar, P.Ruff, J.Pendelin, W.Stumpf, E.A.Streicher, J.A.Romo, R.I.De la Garza, V.F.Jimenez, B.C.Ford, B.J.Watts, E.Carrillo, A.Deschatre, R.D.Anderson, H.Leclerc, G.Mackenrot, M.L.Saathoff, R.S.Tyler, T.M.Hall, W.K.Griffin, J.J.Montemayor, C.Loiseau, N.Ashman, S.L.Cockin, G.Douglas, A.Basso, R.L.Campbell, A.Bøgelund, C.Greiffenberg, B.R.Banzet, C.E.Fisher, C.L.Brown, D.D.Fish, J.B.Rafert, J.R.Teeple, R.D.Stafford, R.D.Tracy Jr., R.E.Ray, R.K.Hamaker, S.L.Frederick, S.D.Wilson, C.M.Wu, L.Long, A.Ballesteros-Asenio, E.Kotelmann, G.Boehnke, G.Gauter, G.Lehmann, H.Beikert, H.Huhn, H.Temiz, I.Diemer, J.Kilian, K.Knopf, K.Semar, M.Djelic, N.Ulutas, P.Foerster, S.Habich,

Langar, England, employees celebrate ISO 9002 certification, 1997

W.Geisinger, W.Hussong, W.J.H.Eykelkamp, Th.M.Van Sprang, W.C.Oosthuizen, A.M.Geilhausen, C.A.Williams, D.R.Begger, G.V.Baker, J.D.Lowrey, J.L.Quam, M.R.Viccaro, S.L.Erbe, C.A.López, M.Villarreal, P.A.Tank, J.P.Galloway, M.L.Puente De La, B.L.Cronin, J.J.Johnson, M.J.Glancy, N.K.Hampton, R.L.Gillespie, S.J.Hunzeker, A.A.Estrada, C.R.Gutierrez, F.J.Tamayo, N.Martinez, B.E.Woolfolk, B.P.Blaes, D.P.Hodges, K.C.Peel, K.L.Kirkland, M.R.Hill, R.A.Palmer, D.J.Plummer, A.Luna, A.Martinez, C.A.Mata, J.A.Leal, J.I.Morales, L.A.Cepeda, O.Gonzalez, V.H.Gonzalez, C.J.Sobolik, G.L.Pyle, J.H.McNeese, J.K.House, J.W.Salak, K.R.Clarke, S.L.Hendricks, J.G.Reyes, T.C.Brockmann, K.R.Voss, C.Aleman, H.Sifuentes, D.C.Larson, D.J.Fuqua, D.M.Brija-Towery, J.D.Carroll, K.R.Ver Straete, T.J.Murphy, W.J.Draper, J.Bregent, R.G.Frederick, J.H.Gao, D.Schuele, H.Friedmann, H.Grauwickel, H.Gund, H.Ziegler, J.Roemer, J.Zarallo Nunez, S.Kilic, U.Cimalla, W.Thibaut, A.Cumming, F.Mohd, H.Mayer, M.Petersen, M.Todorovic, V.Pickhardt, L.Chardin, A.D.Halloran, D.L.Yenner, D.R.Chipak, P.D.Melton, R.N.Kilcoin, S.A.Leinhauser, S.E.Terrio, S.J.Mierau, T.M.Pugh, V.L.Nolden, D.Monsivais, E.N.Rodriguez, G.Ledezma, H.Agacyontar, S.Agacyontar, J.M.Barman, K.Jackson, M.A.Quaranta, R.M.Trotter, A.M.Senneff, D.M.Bomleny, E.A.Youngwirth, G.L.Dautermann, J.T.Daly, K.J.Ku, K.M.Haines, L.M.Clewell, L.S.Niemann, M.M.Ward, N.J.Therrien, P.E.Hemmingson, R.D.Adams, S.D.Ellison, S.L.Whitehall, S.N.Mikkelsen, T.M.Griggs, B.A.King, D.R.Fischer, K.C.Gruman, K.L.Taylor, S.J.Ricklefs, A.B.Hendryx, C.R.Jensen, M.A.Davey, T.J.Huegerich, E.De Leon, M.Porto, R.Marois, S.Segelle, R.O.Carranza, A.D.Kershner, A.D.Zunker, A.J.Dobbels, A.L.Lovig, A.Sayago, B.G.Keys, C.E.Hensley, C.L.Maricle, D.E.Lins, D.J.Selle, D.R.Ahlstrand, D.R.Hershey, J.C.Chesterman, J.C.Sabol, J.F.Pearson, J.G.Winkler, J.M.White, J.R.Vande Kemp, K.A.Cook, K.J.Carlson, K.V.Gilchrist, L.M.Stockhecke Lynn, N.A.Mariman, R.R.Lund, S.A.Mezvinsky, S.L.Wilson, T.A.Buhr, T.P.Arp, A.Calahorra, G.Ramirez, L.Hesliere, P.J.Duhaime, C.G.Janasek, D.J.Johannsen, S.J.Szopski, F.A.Gamez, J.A.Mendoza, J.G.Basilio, B.W.Kolls, J.E.Chesser, J.L.Hecht, J.L.Kremer, J.M.Riedl, J.W.Haxton, K.A.Chipperfield, K.G.Wenzel, K.M.Knigge, M.D.Henning, R.C.Iverson, S.H.Buss, T.E.Vanhal, W.A.Ratzburg, H.H.Castañeda, J.H.Schneider, N.V.Harber, J.M.Tapia, R.C.Salinas, M.Camacho, D.Qiu, E.Deffner, G.Blosczyk, G.Spath, J.Rothe, J.Schick, K.Auer, K.Riegler, M.Jekl, P.Lohmann, R.Sass, R.Trautmann, W.Jung, W.Mueller, A.P.Stoltz, B.A.Ketelaar III, B.R.Woodside, B.S.Fife, D.A.Acheson, D.C.Green, D.I.Wiese, E.M.Ellison, J.A.Bauer, J.A.Wilkerson, J.C.Rush, J.Demott, J.R.Knuth, J.S.Dobbins, M.D.Greenwood, M.K.Forbeck, M.Kimberly Eisenzimmer, T.D.Niemann, T.J.Thirtyacre, T.S.Joyce, Y.F.Sherley, S.D.MacDonald, A.A.Fernández , C.Loaiza , J.P.Garcia, A.Kraemer, K.Pelit, M.Koehler, S.Keskin, H.Ogbourne, F.Martinez, G.Espinoza, M.A.Guzman, M.F.Atilano, R.Perales, J.S.Martinez, M.M.Ruiz, R.Kalathur, D.D.Watson, D.Graham-Allen, J.B.Juel, J.S.Allen, M.D.Fugate, M.D.McDowell, M.P.Moeller, M.T.Brewer, P.I.Graham, P.W.Spoehr, R.B.Boysen, R.J.Buller, R.W.Wittich Jr., T.Knode, C.C.M.Schmidt, D.Costa, S.L.Butzke, W.F.Xing, J.F.Fraga, M.A.Arredondo, J.M.Miller, J.F.Garcia, O.Gonzalez, C.A.Kasprzak, D.L.Puhrmann, D.R.Dyer, G.E.Mc Dowell, G.H.Huston, H.M.Millard, J.C.Shaw, K.K.Walgren, L.D.Hurt, M.R.Murphy, R.R.Nieman, T.M.Sr.ajer, T.W.Swegle, C.Marchal, B.Harris, K.M.Weiler, J.A.Ibarra, L.A.Z.Calçada, S.A.Hernandez, C.S.Pashan, D.E.Peth, D.L.Lyman, G.E.Miller, J.C.Waldrop, J.R.Lynch, P.S.Nickles, R.M.Dunn, S.A.Gudenkauf, T.L.Smith, M.L.Del Bosque, L.M.Torres, S.Larroux, A.Haner , K.J.Taylor, J.Fuentes, B.E.Biles, M.A.Halupnik, R.J.Mullen, H.A.Hepner, B.G.Larsen, C.L.Gillitzer, D.M.Boyle, J.B.Hunt, J.E.Falk, J.McGrath, L.E.Anderson, P.A.Cruse, A.Villanueva, J.F.Ortega, R.Garcia, O.Gutierrez, A.Ahmetagic, G.Huver, H.Hoeh, I.Eraslan, J.Bubel, J.Mueller, K.Samstag, K.Wein, N.Domberger, R.Koch, S.Sefrin, W.Helfinger, M.Gallo, R.Castro, X.Del Frate, B.J.Meahan, G.R.Korb, S.F.Forbes, S.H.Jenkins, D.C.Henn, D.S.Jagnow, E.Levandoski, J.D.L.Rosa, J.P.Tormes, M.D.Almeida, M.Saraiva, P.S.D.Almeida, P.Spaniol, V.D.S.Ramos, V.L.Maliszevski, P.Garcia, S.A.Narvaez, J.Ashworth, A.Belter, G.Reyes, J.R.Sanchez, M.de la Cueva, B.Marmier, C.D.Finck, D.J.Ploessl, D.J.Van Dorn, J.Sumrow, K.P.Pfeifer, M.E.May, M.M.Sheehy, R.M.Scheuermann, S.L.Morton, S.R.Plumb, V.L.Johnson, F.Peralta, J.A.Torres, S.Kleingeld, E.L.Jeffers, J.D.Rinkenbaugh, J.W.Parker, T.M.Conlan, A.Karsburg, A.R.Feix, A.R.Lenz, C.Jung, C.R.Savicki, E.D.Matos, E.J.Mohr, E.L.Aisemberg, E.Zappe, M.A.Chmiel, M.C.Koehler, M.V.Conrad, N.Zang, P.R.Rodrigues, R.Rogerio, V.Kaufmann, C.M.Sanchez, C.M.Dochterman, E.Leal, F.L.Koger, H.L.Brandle, N.P.Gresele, R.Valero, C.A.Webb, R.Reyes, M.K.Johnson, J.J.Saucedo, A.E.Modzik, B.G.Rinholm, D.L.Baker, H.J.Davis, J.P.McCarron, J.W.Whitington, K.J.Hermiston, K.R.Kirkman, K.St Clair, L.J.Breitzke, L.K.Lewis, M.L.Herring, M.W.Corrigan, P.F.Quinn, S.D.Lloyd, S.E.Besse, S.L.Johnson, T.C.Cotton, T.E.Edwards, T.L.Fratzke, S.A.Onocko, J.E.Foreman, T.O.Magee, G.Kreulich, G.L.Conrad, J.C.D.S.Brasil, J.L.Bohrer, L.C.D.Lima, V.A.Matter, J.E.Aguillon, R.L.Beam, S.M.Weatherly, J.F.Ponce, A.T.Sims, D.E.Rafferty, M.Stokowski, P.O.Vega, F.Wedemeier, G.Blatt, G.Schittko, H.Fischer, H.Kienert, W.Werner, B.L.Gerloff, C.E.Hill, C.L.Gray, D.C.Wymore, D.J.Crow, D.M.Goodsmith, D.W.Franzen, G.D.Moeller, G.Rodriguez, J.J.Hemer, K.E.Jordan, K.M.Gaul, K.M.Green, K.S.Davis, K.S.Hambly, K.T.Nolan, L.J.Perkins, L.L.Cone, M.D.Fauser, M.D.Sweeney, R.A.Kidd, R.A.Matthews Jr., R.G.Schark, R.R.Heidemann, S.D.Mathis, S.M.Bethune, S.Moses, T.A.Mc Dowell, T.J.Matthews, W.L.Carr, R.W.H.Sanderson, E.A.Veit, D.Fuentes, L.E.Avila, o.Dávila , G.L.Arrambide, G.F.Lai, R.Lee, E.Muñiz, E.Valerio, G.J.Gallegos, H.Flores, J.A.Gonzalez, J.L.Oyervides, J.P.Martinez, M.A.Garcia, A.J.Gorham, A.K.Heller, G.I.Fischer, J.B.Frazier, R.W.Bono, J.Dean, W.Seeto, D.A.Osvald, E.C.Johann, G.L.Sartor, L.C.D.Silva, R.P.Hanauer, V.Franco, V.P.Muller, A.T.Golightly, C.J.Scott, S.A.Hilyard, W.R.Cramer, A.Olivares, C.Quiroz, E.E.Salazar, E.Valdes, J.F.Medrano, L.M.Nieto, D.C.Eckman, D.E.Downs, D.L.Reuter, J.A.Bowers, J.J.Jackson, J.L.Simpson, J.L.Williams, J.T.Riley, K.J.Britt, L.C.Tady, L.H.Mills, L.M.Tichy, M.S.Johnson, P.Heiderscheit, S.E.Geweke, S.J.Hix, S.P.Kolthoff, T.R.Ingles, G.L.Long, M.G.Chadwick, R.J.Mosetter, R.W.Frye Sr., A.P.Chism, C.D.Andrews, T.O.Ehart, G.Lovato, G.R.Garcia, M.A.Kipper, M.L.Bones, P.C.R.Franco, V.J.Neuhaus, V.Radieske, I.J.Andrade, R.M.Manfield, C.Rogers, D.J.Dilenbeck-Brophy, E.R.Harlan, G.S.Messere, H.J.Montgomery, J.J.Schuch, J.V.Minor, M.B.Varner, N.L.Spoljoric, T.L.Smith, P.Huchet, A.J.Bialas, A.R.Wegner, A.Tolfo, C.E.Fagundes, C.V.Jacobi, J.M.Schast, L.A.D.Costa, L.F.D.D.Souza, M.D.S.Marmitt, O.J.Martins, R.L.D.Carli, V.A.D.Souza, T.L.Cannatelli, J.P.Renneker, X.Zhang, J.Balsells, E.J.Nowell, L.L.Knowlton, S.Rodriguez, A.Kirsch, A.Weis, D.Hammerschmidt, E.Nitz, G.Ehmann, G.Heidenreich, H.Beicht, H.Mueller, H.Willenbacher, I.Trauthwein, J.Kurtz, K.Eberwein, K.Haas, K.Hammerschmid, M.Dahlhauser, M.Schliessmeyer, P.Brandt, R.Huber, R.Sevinc, S.Becker, S.Conzelmann, S.Stroeker, T.Schaefer, U.Stenzel, W.Herweck, W.Weber, G.Lavesa, P.Pialorsi, B.D.Hejlesen, P.J.Chapman, E.J.Fischer, J.Espinoza, L.A.Gallegos, A.Birkle, A.De Filippi, A.Hilgert, C.Erkuran, C.Firat, C.Mueller, D.Kleine, D.Sekulovic, E.Guerek, H.Rabold, J.Richert, K.Karabulut, M.Schmitt, P.Martin Marteles, P.Strohscher, R.Berwanger, S.Baur, S.Berbner, S.Kleber, J.C.Kaed, S.Sousa, C.A.Milke, D.A.Doering, F.A.Remmert, M.J.Foran, P.J.Snyder, T.L.Sheldon-Davis, F.D.Guerra, C.L.Steward, J.A.Lytton, M.J.Tobey, G.Garcia, D.Vergara, A.J.Tafolla, B.C.Hardy, B.K.Lopez, C.J.Pauley, D.A.Burrell, D.L.Stuart, D.L.Van Brocklin, J.F.Croom, K.J.Heath, L.A.Vanlanduit, L.D.Zeutenhorst, L.M.Trujillo, M.A.Lynch, M.E.Black, M.J.Gerken, P.C.Tolley, S.A.Glogowski, S.F.Lindner, T.L.Bonertz, P.R.Ely, R.A.Portillo, R.Rocha, J.Dupire, B.D.Johnson, A.E.Debald, A.L.Tilvitz, A.Matter, A.Steil, C.C.Matter, C.Kucner, C.L.Deves, C.M.Wurfel, C.V.Rehbein, F.Weber, G.Borges, G.Costa, G.J.Koglin, G.J.Sartor, G.Kusiak, I.A.B.Muller, J.A.Budske, J.Lopes, J.Martins, L.R.C.D.Freitas, M.J.Soares, M.L.Rex, M.S.Leyedecker, M.V.Koglin, M.V.Rex, N.M.Kleinpaul, N.Rosch, O.D.Lima, R.G.Schmidt, R.Mazurkewicz, R.Parkert, R.R.Stewens, S.L.Haezel, S.O.Jagnow, S.R.Sartor, V.A.Dente, V.C.Gerhardt, V.Hickmann, V.J.Belter, S.A.Picazo, M.G.Massei, A.E.Guiter, D.R.Jablonski, E.A.Zarate, E.M.Nixon, K.W.Miller, L.S.Reiley, M.W.Taylor, P.E.Winter, P.Whitehead, R.E.Vanhyfte, S.A.Bierstedt,

S.L.Hoppes, W.S.Kramer, J.Ksionsek, L.A.Rogerio, A.Rodriguez, F.J.Elorza, C.A.Marshall, C.D.Youngerman, F.L.Frederick, K.L.Buchser, L.C.Miller, M.R.Harper, W.I.Edwards, A.Monachesi, C.R.Valle, G.D.Murúa, H.H.Fernández, J.D.Rosso, J.N.Córdoba, J.A.Zidman, J.R.Deyoung-Prins, B.A.George, B.J.Hoffman, C.L.Nichols, D.D.Goebel, J.M.Ensminger, J.M.Sabel, M.G.Fryer, M.L.Frank, P.L.Buffaloe, S.W.Rorison, C.D.Gobbi, D.E.Zucca, F.A.Bianchi, F.C.Fiorilla, L.M.Fernandez, M.A.Valdez, A.P.Sylvain, B.R.Paterson, R.M.Gainey, S.D.Dunbar, W.R.Ashenberg, A.Kamuf, A.Pieper-Heyne, A.Tekin, A.Tinter, D.Hartmann, E.Hambsch, E.Ludwig, F.Koehler, G.Schober, H.Bayer, H.Busch, H.Schalk, H.Schwab, I.Jung, J.Eustachi, J.Scheller, L.Braune, R.Adrian, R.Guenzel, R.Walter, S.Inan, T.Oppermann, U.Schneider, W.Hessler, W.Loeser, A.D.Baird, C.M.Coene, D.P.Donner, A.F.Hageman, B.A.Fulton, B.C.Cozart, B.C.Stahl, B.W.Kimpton, C.A.Trebon, D.C.Sheeley, D.J.Kerkove, D.R.West, G.P.O Loughlin, J.B.Deboef, J.B.Sullivan, J.K.Hoppenworth, K.M.Barron, M.J.Loveless, N.Boike, N.E.Wurzer, P.J.Simpson, R.J.Mathews, S.D.Meyer, T.J.Stanbrough, T.L.Schroeder, C.Reyes, F.Gabaldon, S.Dramard, S.Ferguson, S.J.Nessa, M.Morales, B.A.Superlano, B.D.Smoldt, B.W.Stock, D.A.Chevalier, D.S.Hodgerson, E.D.Corwin, E.L.Larson, E.M.Orman, J.R.Reardon Jr., L.E.Apling Jr., L.E.Botts, M.W.Feeney, N.L.Folkerts, R.C.Sienknecht, R.E.Erwin, T.E.Saumier, T.L.Nations, A.Aslan, H.Mittelstaedt, S.Guertler, S.Utecht, D.P.Ruczay, J.Stienstra, S.H.Philip, T.R.Douglas, J.M.Ladwig, S.B.Reeder, S.L.Norwood, A.Segovia, D.Flores, D.Valdes, E.Garcia, E.Sanchez, H.Carreon, J.A.Hernandez, J.C.Segovia, L.A.Bedair, O.Alvarado, R.Delgado, S.Martinez, S.Ramos, C.A.Vázquez, R.F.Barrios, A.J.Escareño, V.G.Aguilar, B.E.Schroeder, C.J.Frail, C.W.Battersby, D.C.Jones, D.J.Laufenberg, D.M.Roberson, D.W.Vickers Jr., E.C.Garrett Jr., F.D.Nelson, F.F.Koss, K.J.Anderson, L.N.Young, M.S.Killinger, P.A.Bates, P.B.Hagner, R.A.Urbanowicz, R.B.Woods, R.L.Clevenger, R.N.Collinson, R.P.Mackin, R.Vandekerckhove Jr., T.D.Fellenz, T.P.Houston, W.C.Henry Jr., J.A.Cordero, J.M.Celario, K.J.Oxenham, R.F.Dold, R.W.Sanders, A.K.Klockenga, B.C.Schafer, D.A.Brus, D.C.Bouck, D.F.Maude, D.J.McQuarrie, D.L.Tychsen, D.P.Trabold, D.T.Jones, J.J.Bjorheim, J.Lawrence, J.N.Britt, K.P.Lund, L.R.Lange, P.W.Grummett, R.R.Saland, S.M.Barber, S.M.Westervelt, S.R.Bowers, S.R.Kaluzny, S.R.Schmitt, T.M.Manders, C.A.Lagos, S.Sosa, R.W.Lloyd, V.M.Yepiz, F.Perez, F.R.Gonzalez, J.Urbornyi, E.J.Smith, C.M.Sullivan, L.J.Merritt, R.L.Hutchinson, T.C.Hill, D.Robles, J.L.Perez, R.Saldivar, R.Torres, E.P.Norwood, G.Sandi, J.A.Leos, J.F.Obregon, M.D.Laudick, S.M.Swanson, W.H.Hurst, R.A.Alvarez, B.Weigand, E.Schlosser, G.Schmidt, H.Arlt, H.Gruczka, K.Hollinderbaeumer, K.Muench, M.Wolter, P.Vrionakis, W.Hass, A.Bagus, A.Brillert , A.Laurich, A.Mauritz, A.Resing, A.Ricker, A.Röring, A.Rudde , A.Schmitt, A.Tenspolde, A.Teuber, A.Trombello, A.Waanders, A.Willemsen, B.Bönning, B.Espelkott, B.Hildering, B.Niemeier, B.Nienhaus, B.Rickert, B.Tübing, B.Winkelhaus, B.Wörmer, C.Dapper, C.Göknur, C.Schriewersmann, C.Weitenberg, C.Wenning, D.Bönning, D.Harks, D.Hemsing , D.Hoge, D.Kemper, D.Nordkamp, D.Rickert, D.Wolters, E.Leuker, E.Niehues, E.Niehus, E.Pieper, E.Schneider, E.Südhoff, E.Upgang, F.Boccuto, F.Decking, F.Kemper, F.Schulten, F.Steggemann, G.Cirtaut , G.Hornig, G.Kahla, G.Lansing, G.Mühlenkamp, G.Sommer, G.Tenbusch, G.Vöcker, G.Voigt, GP.Lubberink, H.Abbing, H.Ahlers, H.Bone, H.Bücker, H.Busen, H.Cynapolt, H.Emmerich, H.Fleer, H.Garthaus, H.Hackfort, H.Herker-Orthaus, H.Hettmer, H.Hoge, H.Höing, H.Holtrup, H.Honvehlmann, H.Kappelhoff, H.Kröger, H.Küster, H.Mesken, H.Paskert, H.Scheitelhut, H.Schulz, H.Szilinski, H.Teriet, H.vanNuland, H.Volmer, H.Waltermann, H.Wewers, HJ.Goller, I.Cilas, I.Fellerhoff, J.Banken, J.Beier, J.Brandt, J.Dapper, J.Elsing, J.Everding, J.Fieber, J.Honvehlmann, J.Hovestadt, J.Kerkhoff, J.Middelick, J.Miesing, J.Mol, J.Orthaus, J.Parschert, J.Röring, J.Schuller, J.Schulten, J.Schwering, J.Sibbing, J.Tappe, J.Tendahl, J.Tenostendarp, J.Upgang, J.Volmer, J.Wilhelm, K.Bergmann, K.Brinkmann, K.Weber, K.Wewers, K.Wissing, KH.Schmidt, KH.Schücker, L.Beuker, L.Bußhaus, L.Friede, L.Heumer, L.Ostendarp, L.Schlüter, L.Schulze-Hockenbeck, L.Wenning, M.Ahlers, M.Böckers, M.Dücker, M.Geling, M.Hettmer, M.Kappelhoff, M.Lensker, M.Linfert, M.Löwemann, M.Nolte, M.Rörick, M.Simon-van Bömmel, M.Steppat, M.von dem Berge, M.Wehrmann, N.Keizers, N.Wolters, O.Bengfort, O.Hessing, O.Nordkamp, O.Te Vrugt, O.Tendahl, P.Graffe, P.Koeman, P.Rudde , P.Terlohr, R.Bröker, R.Els, R.Eynck , R.Harker, R.Hemker, R.Paschert, R.Tippke, R.Vens, R.Wiggenbrock, R.Wübbels , S.Hessing, T.Dünne, T.Geling, T.Habel, T.Hericks, T.Kremer, T.Meß, T.Südhoff, T.Wentzek, U.Brüning, U.Demmer, U.Geissler , U.Jödden, U.Räwer, U.Sauerbier, V.Wexler, W.Beuting, W.Brüning, W.Heuer, W.Hoge, W.Mensing, W.Möllers, W.Niehues, W.Schöning, W.Schürmann, W.Ter Haar, W.Terwey, W.Tippke, D.G.Borglin, E.Carr, H.Smith, J.Swan, P.White, B.K.Baur, D.J.Berger, D.S.Faber, G.L.Herrera, K.D.Garrett, K.L.Rice, R.W.Burcher, S.D.Elliott, S.G.Morelock, S.H.Clausen, T.J.Dolan, W.Janssen Jr., D.A.Andreolla, D.J.Wurfel, E.J.Schardong, G.Donat, G.P.R.D.Moura, J.P.D.Silva, M.R.Massirer, P.R.Guerreiro, R.A.Golin, R.Heissler, R.Schulz, T.R.Bender, V.D.Halmann, P.Pegon, H.Juhnke, J.Garcia Magallon, O.Berger, P.Stohner, M.Sanchez, H.Kaiser, R.M.Hitzel, U.Dominguez, J.M.Obermiller, L.A.Friedman, P.J.Pyc, R.C.Laughlin Jr., M.M.Galvan, M.Eichelsbach, D.M.Sebatana, C.H.Rosales, F.Muñoz, E.Eguia, J.A.Lopez, J.Aldape, J.Enriquez, J.R.Ibarra, J.Sarreon, L.G.Perez, M.G.Botello, M.O.Ruiz, R.Lopez, R.Rivera, M.T.Luebke, A.M.Shader, D.L.Quinn, D.M.Owens, F.K.Diecke, G.A.Boshell, H.S.Rettig Jolliff, J.E.Fleming, M.B.Wegmann, R.G.Formas, R.L.Darr, S.L.Johnson, J.F.Strehlow, Y.Lozano, C.Blisson, S.W.Siebert, J.Da Cruz, E.E.Castañeda, D.C.Roach Lindeman, D.L.Darnick, K.A.Eilers, K.M.Heiderscheit, M.A.Rodems, M.T.Schmidt, P.G.Collins Jr., S.A.Harbert, W.E.Behm II, W.L.McWilliam, N.A.Sipple, B.M.Martinez, C.A.Saldivar, C.O.Gutierrez, E.Mendez, J.A.Pinon, V.H.Martinez, S.Huet, S.A.Rourke, T.Hust, J.C.Torres, A.Herguedas, L.S.King, A.L.Rodriguez, M.A.Delgado, A.Kurz, C.Gut, D.Mayer, F.Ficht, G.Bickel, G.Wittmann, H.Litters, H.Wester, J.Krusch, M.Hoffmann, M.Schiebur, M.Thomas, M.Walter, O.Stibitz, W.Ofenloch, W.Spitzfaden, B.J.King, C.M.Savener, C.R.Zelnio, D.W.Bolin, E.L.Fisher, J.L.Stanley, K.D.Shellenberger, R.W.Streicher, S.P.Whites, J.C.Blando, F.Schwarz, H.Werner, J.Hunsicker, M.A.Jacobs, H.L.Dávila, J.C.Casillas, O.Motomochi, R.Guzman, A.De la Torre, A.O.Gamez, I.Rios, J.A.Martinez, J.C.Cantu, J.V.Esquivel, O.Quezada, R.Garcia, R.Mendoza, A.R.Swartz, B.G.Glick, B.L.Destival, C.A.O Loughlin, C.E.Cline, D.J.Hellman, E.E.Geiger, G.L.Steffeney, J.L.Hess, K.H.Brush, K.N.Hager, L.D.Spears, L.E.Lopez, L.E.Morris, P.L.Graf, S.A.White, W.S.Leishman, O.García, D.L.Dotto, E.C.D.S.Ribeiro, E.L.Knop, F.A.H.Pinheiro, G.A.Piccinin, O.L.Gehrke, E.Schneider, S.K.Lewis, D.R.Carter, D.D.Soultz, K.W.Smith, M.R.Groom, N.O.Pinkston, S.S.Morrison, L.J.Robinson, G.Mendoza, A.Nielsen, C.Guerra, E.G.Mendez, F.Cadena, F.Reyna, J.A.Monjaraz, J.L.Salazar, M.A.Garcia, N.Coronado, P.Martinez, R.Diaz, R.Gonzalez, J.Pecina, J.López , D.W.Sill, D.Feldmann, C.S.Kubly, D.J.Kelly, R.J.Anderson, 1997 F.M.Heimberger, I.Wendling, J.L.Leach, K.W.Shire, M.S.Kostka, A.Triana, E.A.Zarate, G.Gardea, K.Martinez, M.Camacho, M.M.Fernandez, O.I.Santana, R.Romo, F.Favreau, A.Leclerc, A.Bredologos, A.Depta, A.Gezen, B.Rausch, E.Schlachter, H.Teufel, J.Wink, K.Weber, K.Weis, L.Edel, M.Bellanca, M.Oemeroglu, M.Schaeff, O.Schneider, R.Klingel, D.Meij, G.Mathee, A.M.Riggins, D.D.Hessell, D.F.Smydra, D.K.Regehr, D.M.Anderson, G.L.Parker, J.H.Plymale, J.M.Binzley, J.R.Heyer, M.A.Gleason, M.D.Nolte, M.W.Elliott Jr., M.W.Farber, P.V.Hulshof, R.F.Spielvogel, R.S.Coates, S.C.Clausen, S.C.Young, S.J.Mc Donald, S.M.Smith, T.D.Heath, T.L.Denys, T.S.Davis, A.Berger, C.D.Silva, L.J.Manteufel, M.L.Immich, R.L.Pascoal, V.C.Junior, L.G.Saldaña, G.Baj, A.D.Dancer, A.L.King, A.M.Snider, A.R.Fleming, B.A.Merrick, B.A.Sweeney, B.C.Allen, B.D.Rooff, B.G.Coplea, B.L.Ollinger, B.L.Sienknecht, C.J.Romani Jr., C.M.Cook, D.A.Adams, D.E.Villarreal, D.K.Parks, D.L.Debarre, D.L.Stuber, D.P.Koster, D.R.Swetalla, D.T.Wersinger, D.W.Brown, D.W.Surratt, F.B.Knecht, F.Sandoval, G.E.Brady, G.J.Karbacka, G.W.Johnson, H.A.Knebel, H.F.Brown, H.L.Schwan, I.L.McCarthy, J.C.Frerichs, J.F.Dunn, J.J.Foxen, J.J.Scharpman, J.L.Brody, J.L.Finley, J.M.Goulet, J.M.Hug, J.M.Mc Coneghy, J.M.Watson, J.R.Lambertsen, J.V.Cybulski, K.B.Kress, K.L.Senechek, K.M.Harmon, L.A.Siebel, L.J.Lloyd, M.A.Wosepka, M.C.Fluegel, M.D.Renner, M.J.Berberich, M.J.Kane, M.L.Meether, P.A.Perkins, R.G.Martin, S.D.Neil, S.E.Henderson, S.G.Kalkbrenner, S.L.Powers, S.P.Edwards, S.W.Hunt, T.A.Willers, T.D.Johnson, T.G.Good, T.G.Poppe, T.P.Mikulecky, T.W.Armbrecht, V.J.Wellman, W.A.Freeman, W.D.Mullis, W.J.Schrage, L.S.Turra, C.E.Herrera, M.Garza, R.Alvarado, E.Ramirez, S.Furlan, Y.Treuillet, A.Herbert, H.Koerner, J.Hess, T.Frevel, M.Boger, P.Köhler, R.Milizia, S.G.Pagliarulo, R.Epton, A.R.Lohmann, B.E.Jebe, B.L.Diercks, B.R.Vierow, C.J.Cannon, C.J.Wilson, C.M.Clausman, C.Z.Hines, D.L.Pfadenhauer, D.L.Stock, D.R.Mulder, D.S.Holven, E.J.Youngblut, E.T.Loeffler, J.W.Kerns, M.D.Mc Laren, M.E.Hagen, N.J.Lane, R.A.Pearce, R.A.Prose, R.A.Riley, R.C.Case, R.C.Worrell, R.J.Bauler, R.J.Shock, R.K.Junkins, S.A.Klingfuss, S.R.Norem, T.E.Watts, T.J.Klingfus, W.C.Anderson, W.J.Riley, C.L.Widz, C.Stumm, E.S.D.Queiroz, E.Turra, T.H.Drescher, D.Avila, J.E.Solano, I.Balderas, H.Schmidt, J.Payer, E.R.Anderson, J.D.Gartner, J.P.Dreger, C.A.Mulé, M.B.Brincks, B.Estrada, C.A.Garcia, G.Guzman, J.R.Adame, N.C.Garcia, H.Chavez, A.D.Marlow, A.E.Graber, A.R.Nolte, B.K.Combs, B.K.Shoesmith, C.E.Finney, C.L.Benda, C.L.Holdsworth, C.L.Krusemark, C.S.Stegh, C.T.Cornwell, D.A.Anderson, D.E.Sturtz, D.J.Praska, D.J.Vannoster, D.L.Morgan, D.L.Pulfrey, D.L.Williams, E.K.Terashima, G.G.Krop, G.J.Rosauer, G.L.Gebel, G.L.Heit, J.E.Read, J.J.Azbill, J.J.Rochford, J.P.Gorman, J.P.Jensen, L.D.Blaine, M.J.Mc Nulty, M.S.Dunnwald, N.J.Rubino, P.R.Nedved, R.A.Westendorf, R.C.Gibson, R.D.Siam, R.E.Watts, R.J.Caldwell, R.L.Schlung, S.A.Reimensnyder, S.A.Schellhorn, S.J.Delagardelle, S.K.Rigdon, S.R.Sass, S.W.Bross, T.E.Dohlman, W.C.Russell, W.H.Ackerman, B.D.Reid, A.Wieschollek, J.Kraus, D.L.Schnuelle, K.W.Peters, R.D.Cramer, J.C.Vargas, J.H.Peña, J.Vazquez, B.O.Ramirez, C.J.Maifield, J.E.Smith, J.M.Wittgreve, J.P.Gartland, T.S.Gill, E.T.Kashambuzi, J.S.Fox, K.M.Allen, M.A.Douthat, N.L.Mc Coneghy, R.E.Crowe, S.M.Maxwell, T.J.Immel, E.I.Gonzalez, A.Vargas, L.F.Morales, M.Meza, M.Herzog, M.Vogtt, C.Williamson, A.A.Spooner, B.K.Churchill, B.M.Frenell, B.V.Gronemeyer, D.E.Mitchell, D.L.Cheeney II, G.W.Mathena, H.C.Carden, J.A.Szymborski, J.G.Pope, J.V.Kent, K.E.Foster, L.L.Walters, M.C.Harting, M.J.Fay, P.J.Weber, P.R.Lair, R.Creighton Jr., R.Garkow Jr., R.L.Samuelson, S.Glenn, S.L.Wessel, M.Bernau, C.D.Hoyt, M.D.Beaudoin, P.J.McCredie, R.K.Elsbury, S.L.Stelk, T.E.White Jr., T.R.McMillan, J.A.Esquivel, J.H.Juarez, S.Gonzalez, L.E.Tellez, D.Henault, A.K.Fleming, B.A.Chamberlin, R.E.Shafer, F.J.Salas, S.A.Alvarado, A.L.Dzubak, G.S.Cable, T.N.Yanowsky, R.L.Butler Jr., J.M.Menchaca, M.Y.Abdel-Fattah, C.C.Flores, O.Gonzalez, S.De , A.Andres, F.Mulone, G.Muehlbeier, G.Schynol, J.Ehlers, J.Oczko, J.Pflug, K.Bentzinger, K.Mayfahrt, K.Peier, N.Karahan, S.Stojic, V.Grounis, W.Franke, W.Schwinn, I.Fuehrer, A.A.Rampersad, C.O.Vest II, C.S.McClure, D.G.Jones, D.S.Lindquist, E.L.Bollinger, G.R.McMains, G.S.Patterson, J.B.Fuller, J.H.Williams, K.S.Logli, L.M.Krugler, M.C.Box, M.L.Rumfelt, M.M.Honeycutt, P.A.Lampman, P.W.Falls, R.C.Dunigan, R.J.McMullen, S.A.Grenier, S.G.Swoik, S.J.Miller, S.V.Elder, T.M.Gregory, A.A.Borgmann, D.D.F.Rezende, J.N.Kollmann, O.Weber, M.V.Ponce, A.Neira, R.A.Menendez, R.López , J.M.Villaseñor, J.Wolk, S.Tressi, D.Büscher, H.Schröer, T.Klöpper, T.Eck, J.R.Taylor, C.A.Colunga, L.A.Martinez, R.Prado, L.A.Gonzalez, A.C.Christopher, J.J.Tyree, L.M.Vanvelsor, M.J.Kromer, P.D.Maldonado, S.W.Parker, N.J.Powell, A.Adiers, C.Z.Perinazzo, E.C.Ribeiro, E.M.Husak, G.D.D.Almeida, G.L.Bastian, H.T.D.Almeida, J.D.Maronez, J.J.Dieckow, J.N.Karsburg, L.C.Dinarte, L.V.S.Correa, L.Mendoza, I.Vetter, D.A.Schinstock, S.A.Dutler, A.Rincon, D.Capistran, J.G.Vazquez, M.J.Alvarado, S.Kan, B.King, J.Bernal, S.A.Engelmohr, K.E.Roberts, C.T.Bebout, D.A.Keller, D.A.McPherson, E.J.Hinshaw, J.A.Devries, J.W.McGinnis, K.A.Bocek, K.B.Britton, L.C.Thompson, L.McCain, M.A.Wortel, M.C.Bote, M.D.Wagner, M.J.Mc Eniry, R.G.Van Vark, T.A.Nelson, T.A.Pustelnik, W.C.Brooks, N.K.Krasilnikow, A.L.Franz, A.Mittelstaedt, C.B.Krewer, C.Decker, C.Petermann, C.R.Steffens, D.A.Franken, D.C.Luiz, D.F.Link, D.S.Haacke, D.V.Telles, E.Gerhardt, E.L.Wunsch, E.R.Burghausen, E.S.Crestani, F.A.Decker, F.E.A.D.S.Bender, F.Tusset, G.Lorenzao, J.C.Rebelo, J.Hoffmann, J.J.Dreher, J.Polla, J.Sturmer, L.D.Weiss, M.A.Manteufel, M.A.Schacht, M.D.Sasso, M.L.Pauli, M.Nass, M.R.Pedo, P.M.D.Moura, R.C.Albrecht, R.D.Feix, R.Rodrigues, R.Zemolin, S.A.A.D.Carvalho, T.L.Cantarelli, V.B.Barbosa, V.L.Krauspenhar, M.A.Sandi, W.G.Contreras, P.Kleemann, D.Delgado, J.S.Ostrander, A.D.A.Moura, D.A.Schweig, E.R.Carlin, E.V.Mattjie, G.N.Chmiel, J.Desbessel, O.A.Alberti, V.J.Bozzetto, J.C.Marino, M.L.Parkison, C.A.Rodriguez, G.Rodriguez, J.J.Laureano, S.Schoen, B.J.Wipperfurth, D.J.Begyn, E.R.Evans, G.D.Krafka, G.T.Dyson, J.E.Short, J.W.Soseman, N.M.Leden, R.B.Mills, R.J.Towndrow, V.Jones, W.J.Dickau, W.W.White, R.C.Moran, M.C.Silva, M.J.Guerra, N.Valdez, O.Garcia, R.Lopez, H.Derbas, M.P.Zahradnik, L.J.Zimmerman, A.B.Jones, L.A.Camp, D.A.Burns, J.I.Wellman, S.R.Garwood, T.L.Pfannenstiel, W.R.Schaeffer, J.Jensen, R.W.Park, M.Ploué, A.Bucher, A.Conticello, A.Dabic, A.Houterman, A.Parisi, B.Pasagic, E.Niestroj, G.Marschall, G.Wengrzik, H.Lober, H.Voit, K.Virag, M.Decker, N.Jaeger, R.Siegert, S.Sariguel, G.Dellert, P.Roux, M.Sørensen, A.R.Andrae, B.L.Dolan, B.L.Walker, C.E.Jennings, C.H.Knary, C.L.Burton, D.Hobbins, D.M.Zigrossi, D.O'Malley, D.S.Mulnix, E.A.Foy, E.A.McLeish, E.F.Skoff, F.H.Crichton, G.L.Hill, J.C.Green, K.S.Harris, M.A.Lindquist, M.H.Moor Jr., M.Judie, N.Sherrod, P.J.Thelen, R.E.Vanwassenhove, R.J.Trahan, R.M.Dereu, R.S.Glassgow, S.E.Klundt, T.W.Bolton, A.L.Tynan, G.Vazquez, J.A.Gonzalez, J.M.Gallegos, J.Torres, H.Nuñez, J.C.Mayagoitia, L.G.Coronado, P.Ostermann, A.Totterer, C.Streib, H.Schweizer, M.Gallo, M.Meier, P.Schulz, H.Hasenkamp, W.E.Hermsen, D.D.Lehman, D.D.Prins, A.Niemiec, E.Garcia, L.C.Cazares, J.C.Jensen, G.A.Wadle, G.M.Labelle, J.D.Munson, J.H.Wheeler, J.K.Baum, J.R.Simpson, J.S.Swaim, J.T.Elder III, L.R.Good, M.A.Cracraft, S.D.Burtney, S.J.Sanner, W.J.Shepherd, C.A.Montani, D.R.Zappalá, F.O.Ferreyra, R.D.Chiodín, F.E.Hahn, Z.D.C.P.Junior, J.Alfaro, L.A.Islas, J.F.Medina,

Dubuque, Iowa "Team Power" team, 1997

M.Campisi, J.Lefkate, J.M.Oña, J.C.Peña, A.A.Tomassini, A.R.Vega, F.Santoro, G.E.Chiodín, O.A.Dimarco, R.Avalos, B.A.Burris, B.Rocha, J.G.Rodriguez, M.A.Acuña, J.Madonia, A.Lee, B.L.Richard, C.C.Vanderpol, C.G.Tekippe, D.D.Banes, D.M.Gibbons, H.K.Nguyen, J.B.Knotts, J.C.May, J.D.Breister, J.J.Johns, J.R.Stawicki, K.J.Haucke, L.E.Black, M.J.Rugeroni, M.J.Zimmer, M.P.Gueller, S.D.McDaniel, S.K.Bunce, S.L.Porter Sheehan, T.E.Bower, E.Landry, F.Lorenzo, L.A.González, M.A.Cordo, S.R.Salina, D.A.Spackman, J.L.Eske, R.I.Wichrowski, O.G.Marquez, R.Dominguez, J.J.Valdez, S.Angel, A.Perales, F.Paillet, A.Brammert-Schroeder, R.B.Sanford, J.L.Cook, R.M.Schaefer, R.A.Ramirez, G.Jimenez, M.D.Costner, E.E.Rodriguez, C.E.Haines, C.S.Scott III, M.Adkins, R.H.Jefferson, R.L.Earnest, S.M.Blair, A.Calvo, C.Peciulewicz, F.A.Vila, G.C.Szittyay, G.H.Villalba, J.A.Pagano, M.R.Ferrari, M.J.L.Lang, C.A.Chimenti, A.D.Buckman, D.A.Blankenship, D.G.Voth, D.M.Mace, J.C.Eddins, J.M.Jutting, K.F.Kutmas, K.M.Laughlin, K.M.Mondeau, M.L.Higgins, S.J.Cappelletti, S.R.Eubanks, T.E.Schick, V.S.McNalley, W.T.Smith, D.J.Gallagher, J.R.Tena, E.Kristensen, E.Lundgaard, S.K.Hansen, B.D.Roschen, B.D.Sibthorp, D.Mercado, G.M.Ito, K.J.Holevoet, K.L.Stayzer, P.J.Gibbons, T.J.Frandsen, A.G.Setzu, C.A.Laies, R.J.Lacona, C.A.Cazares, D.A.Gordillo, I.Carrillo, J.Martinez, L.G.Lopez, O.Hernandez, V.G.Cantu, C.Urbina, F.J.Frias, S.J.Garrido, S.R.Jaramillo, B.Kubach, D.Berning, D.Miskovic, D.Stoeckler, E.Gundacker, E.Welsch, G.Larscheid, H.Novak, J.Tochtermann, K.Meyer, L.Ballandies, M.Neumann, R.Essert, S.Avramovic, S.Martin-Iglesias, U.Lhotsky, W.Quittkat, Z.Djuric, P.Abbing, C.Postma, B.Kühl, C.D.Brewer, M.R.Loechler, M.A.Vazquez, M.A.Vazquez, A.M.Buss, A.M.Lee, B.P.Boberg, C.G.Evershed, C.K.Barfels, C.P.Mott, D.J.Genac, D.L.Hoerschelmann, D.Ruzanske, E.D.Lange, E.E.McColley, G.C.Snider Jr., J.J.Gorman, K.C.Hall, L.Beauregard, L.K.Maxwell, M.D.Smith, P.J.Cavanaugh, R.Johnson, R.L.Brath, R.L.Morris, R.R.Kohrt, R.W.Gonzales, S.R.Hess, T.A.Meeks, T.D.Armitage, A.A.Cauce, M.A.Garcia, R.Avila, S.Chazaro, A.Ramirez, K.Haines, C.J.Reavis, G.E.Battocchio, R.D.Pozo, S.Muñiz, S.Mueller, A.C.Kurth, N.D.Cicao, J.Rangel, B.A.Vanderweele, D.L.Sprinkle, G.W.Herbst, K.L.Rowell, L.M.Wood, M.M.Lamontagne, M.W.Kennett, P.D.Hancock, R.D.Moller II, E.Rasia, Y.Olger, J.S.Platte, J.W.Marquardt, C.M.Lien, K.A.David, L.J.Blasberg, R.S.Iliff, R.W.McQuitty, G.E.Rébori, G.R.Merlo, R.Castro, J.I.Halliwell, J.F.Dotson, J.L.Bash, L.Basilico, L.J.Witwer, L.Michaels, L.R.Istok, M.G.Niemann, N.P.Geary II, R.S.Kaufmann, S.R.Feddersen, V.D.Sanchez Dickson, P.F.Cerda, H.Pflueger, R.Weinkoetz, M.J.Mhlambi, L.M.Narcisse, A.A.Wiskow, R.A.Carrillo, C.K.Cowan, J.A.Medrano, J.F.Landeros, N.Marie, J.A.Lujan, M.Sanchez, N.F.Tarango, C.W.Leland, D.A.Collins, D.R.Wilson, E.A.Hardcastle, J.A.Botkin, J.A.Klitzkie, J.G.Petersen, J.J.Ranum, J.K.Johnson, M.D.Ervin, R.M.Manikkam, R.P.Fuchs, S.A.McDonald, S.Santiago, T.J.Van Camp, A.A.López, M.F.Roffey, J.A.Alvarado, F.Martin, J.T.Guthrie, G.Cerda, J.A.Mercado, A.L.Strickland, A.M.Godwin, A.R.Miller, D.G.Black, D.J.Minkus, E.R.West, F.D.Page, G.A.Beaune, G.C.Van De Kraats, G.D.Chapman Jr., H.L.Brown Jr., J.A.Brown-Page, J.A.Hubbard, J.D.Gallant Jr., J.D.Lucas, J.L.Nance, J.R.Beasley, L.A.Smith Jr., M.J.Cash, M.P.Adams, R.A.Richardson, R.G.Tart, R.H.West, R.S.Longoria, R.W.Boger, S.A.Fenn, H.T.Kristoffersen, E.J.Smith, L.A.Mizaur, M.L.Miller, B.Frangos, E.Schoenborn, G.Bramstedt, G.Gaeckle, G.Karch, G.Wittmann, H.Bauer, H.Fleig, H.Herrmann, H.Korthoeber, H.Leutz, J.Kurth, K.Daub, K.Matzen, K.Zapf, L.Radowsky, M.Dautner, M.Tiletzek, R.Pogrell, R.Wegh, U.Hofer, V.Krneta, W.Willer, A.A.Joyner, O.Bertheau, A.L.Bates, A.Olsson, C.A.McKeag, C.J.Steed, C.M.Borduzak, D.L.Harris, D.V.Shafer, G.F.Davis, J.C.Journey, K.C.Keeler, K.L.Shearer, K.R.Haezebroeck, K.V.Patterson, L.J.Loewen, L.L.Larson, M.R.Williams, S.I.Dhabalt, S.J.Fladhammer, S.K.Crissey-Williams, S.K.Martin, T.A.Menke, T.C.Payne, T.L.Sheffey, T.P.Pratt, V.D.Foster, V.M.Barber, W.D.Webb, M.S.Cogo, J.J.Fabila, A.Laratta, F.Odriozola, H.Campos, O.Nieto, X.Merlin, M.Handschick, N.Schmitt, H.Padilla, F.J.Huerta, M.Valenzuela, A.L.Hurd, R.Estrada, J.M.Tolbert, J.O.Cabrera, M.F.Pellegrini, A.Seville, A.C.Seibert, A.E.Boes, A.S.Ridgeway, B.J.Hitchler, B.R.Barnes, D.E.Chamberlain, D.E.Smith, D.R.Perry, D.W.Zahn, K.E.Eipers, R.C.McMahon, T.H.Krutz, T.Leonard, T.N.Geltz, W.R.Allison, M.A.Vlieg, B.E.Rodriguez, C.A.Maciel, J.E.Aldana, G.Campos, C.Cozzo, G.Tortorici, P.Berg, N.Maraha, J.M.Siebert, M.A.Montivero, J.M.Nkonyane, D.C.Balcom, J.B.Sivertson, J.E.Malone, K.A.Price, M.G.Lamb, T.Sihm, A.M.Geisinger, B.L.Swanson, D.R.Ortiz, J.A.Renteria, J.Galicia, E.P.Mc Cann, A.S.Ehm, A.W.Kelly, B.A.Beaudry-Rouse, B.E.Thurber, B.M.Errthum, B.M.Poletti, C.A.Sutton, C.C.Bruggemann, C.C.O Donnell, C.D.Snyder, C.E.Plattner, C.E.Rehmert, C.M.Eisele, C.M.Stein, D.M.Meade, D.R.Christensen, D.T.Leibfried, E.J.Dorn, H.I.Stecher, J.D.Geiger, J.D.Krantz, J.E.Kiesey, J.Herrmann, J.L.Magera, J.M.Christy, J.M.Davis, J.M.Smith, J.M.Verwers, J.P.Rogers, J.R.Starr, K.D.Bishop, K.R.Corrigan, K.S.Howard, K.Y.West, L.K.Conlan, L.Z.Powell, M.D.Anderson, M.W.Thompson, P.A.Garcia, R.A.Bruck, R.L.Caruso, R.L.Walker, S.L.Adams, V.Gambleton, W.A.Brockmann, W.A.Hansen, A.P.Pitt, H.E.Wilson, H.E.Gonzalez, I.N.Infante, J.G.Martinez, S.Guillemot, B.K.Wilson, L.Leishman, M.Y.Steele, P.Kung, S.J.Anger, T.R.Young, A.F.Jek, C.L.D.Carli, C.R.Massmann, I.R.Sormani, M.A.Stringari, M.E.Bones, M.R.Berger, M.R.Maliszewski, M.Visentini, O.M.Bau, P.F.Unfer, P.J.D.C.Spengler, R.Flesch, S.J.Fagundes, V.M.Brauwers, J.P.Hernandez, M.A.Vazquez, R.Zielonkowski, S.Evans, B.A.Fabin, D.L.Marchese, J.G.Pelton, R.J.Victor, R.Gonzalez, A.G.Dailey, D.J.Huegerich, J.Bjorlo, K.D.Kellogg, N.R.Ebbens, T.R.Ancelet, C.Castañeda, E.O.Lara, E.Yague, J.C.Landeros, F.Pascaire, M.B.McAvella, C.E.Mauri, H.Martinez, L.Aguirre, G.Neumann, W.Braun, A.J.Peterson, A.R.Freeseman, B.C.Crockett, B.D.Gunst, B.E.Holthaus, B.P.Jost, C.D.Setser, C.J.Nesset, C.M.Baughman, C.S.McGathy, D.A.Baum, D.D.Gaede, D.M.Reilly, E.C.Wobig, G.G.Jahnke, J.B.Baumeister, J.C.McClurg, J.M.Mc Avoy, J.M.Steining, K.D.Monk, K.L.Fuller, L.A.Barnes, L.M.Huston, M.D.Sallis, M.M.Chaney, M.P.Leone, P.S.Lee, R.L.Hoyt, R.L.Neitzel, S.B.Ramsey, S.J.Schuttloffel, T.J.Sutter, R.M.Stines, S.A.Carpenter, S.M.West, W.A.Wells, A.J.Birk, G.S.McCunn, H.Jayaraman, J.C.Goodwin, J.W.Schulz, S.D.Kolterman, T.L.Crumley, W.A.Hornung, W.S.Wilfert, J.A.Resendiz, T.K.Christensen, J.Gauvin, E.Klemm, G.Cheret, G.Mistler, H.Nissen, H.Wack, K.Gohde, L.Ludwig, M.Richter, O.Kinay, R.Strasser, D.Ottmann, A.J.Mudderman, A.L.Jensen, A.L.Tisdale, B.P.Perles, C.A.Wall, C.E.Jennings, C.F.Eastman, C.G.Norton, C.J.Fuhrmann, C.L.Sehmann, C.R.Stoffregen, D.D.Caldwell, D.G.Bishop, D.P.Hoese, D.P.Sabatos, D.R.Porter, D.R.Shelton, E.A.Keen, E.K.Williams, E.R.Walker, E.T.Cufr, E.T.Green, J.A.Stott, J.M.Dohrmann, J.M.Ellsworth, J.Pasui, J.R.Hoke, J.W.Panning, K.M.Diesburg, K.M.Schwartz, M.A.McDougall, M.A.Voors, M.D.Newton, M.J.Ehr, M.M.Haas, M.R.Grimson, M.R.Tigges, M.V.Carnes, N.A.Granaman, N.C.Heinrich, N.J.Phillips, P.M.Wilcek, R.D.Speirs, R.S.Bowman, S.D.Heller, S.E.Aegerter, S.H.Crawford, S.J.Mai, T.C.Masker, T.C.McWhirt, T.J.Boekhoff, T.L.Arp, T.R.Deeds, T.W.Lowrance, D.R.Peralta, J.L.Ferrer, E.M.Link, F.V.Tusset, J.A.D.S.Ramos, L.M.Dias, C.Valero , G.Castañeda, H.Rios, J.J.Hernandez, D.Denis, D.Steinhoff, M.Mehrer, N.Massoth, R.Mueller, R.Zaun, A.Hüttermann, J.Zergiebel, P.B.Roos, C.J.Campbell, F.Peña, N.L.Crary, M.A.Gutierrez, U.Strasser, J.D.Nolting, V.P.Buttice, J.A.Urbina, R.Rojas, M.Piechotta, D.Arellano, A.P.Wiens, A.R.Kennedy, B.G.Couch, C.P.Smyser, D.Henley, E.B.Garner, G.D.Tillman, J.A.Jordan-Ramaraju, J.D.Farlow, J.E.Dobson, J.F.Boyd, J.M.Jongebloed, K.M.Harrington, L.McCord, M.H.Whitaker, R.C.Ferland Jr., R.D.Oliver, R.H.Page, T.E.Davidson, W.I.McKelvey, D.O.Garcia, J.M.Rivas, L.R.Leal, J.R.Ibarra, M.C.Lira, J.Lizinski, A.Costa, W.P.McNamara, S.R.Ibarra, A.L.Peterson, B.K.Lock, B.M.Broemmer, C.R.Reynolds, C.T.Law, D.A.Burchfield, D.A.Ernst, D.J.Haworth, D.L.Stirling, D.M.Stanton, D.R.Fabin, D.S.Thornton, G.D.Digout, I.Medina, J.M.Hill, L.Berei III, M.A.Hann, M.I.Norfolk, M.Meier, P.R.Thompson, R.B.Perkins, R.M.Roark, R.R.Rederus, R.W.Whittington, S.E.Duelberg, T.E.Hughes, T.H.Castor, T.L.Erickson, T.M.Walke, T.W.Jeffries, Y.A.Rashada, H.R.Carrizales, M.A.Limon, C.L.Wilson, M.W.Jones, J.A.Blázquez, C.L.Gamez, E.Luna, J.J.Arellano, L.F.Saucedo, A.Ehret, F.Wedekind, G.Messerschmidt, J.J.Renteria, J.F.Jimenez, D.C.Gallagher, P.J.Mulligan, T.J.Webb, A.A.Brizola, L.R.Maliszewski, D.Lopez,

A.A.Shelton, A.R.Brunson, B.J.Reidy, B.P.Jacobsen, C.A.Krienert, C.J.Brackin, C.L.Morrison, C.R.Bremner, D.B.Kletzli, D.E.Overmann, D.G.Evans, D.K.Aschbrenner, D.M.Langel, D.R.Tenge, E.N.Pearson, H.N.Clark, J.A.Blasberg, J.Deguire, J.L.Bahlmann, J.W.Bauler, K.B.Rauch, K.L.Sisco, M.A.Avis, M.J.Degroote, M.K.Selesky, M.L.Carpenter, M.S.Bealer, M.S.Newell, P.N.Destival, R.C.Jenkins, R.C.Knight, R.M.Peterson, R.P.Youngblut, R.R.Ragsdale, S.A.Schaefer, T.Reid, L.Amparan, J.J.Espinoza, J.L.Aguillon, M.A.Campos, N.Rodriguez, P.A.Gonzalez, R.Hernandez, N.Rasilier, S.Lozano, G.M.Machetta, M.L.Jeffries, A.S.Tomkins, A.Esparza, J.P.Hernandez, A.B.Appleton, B.D.Boraas, B.Herting, C.J.Fox, G.A.Cobb, J.F.Barrett, J.P.Powell, J.Wang, M.D.Messman, R.D.Stone, D.Casillas, I.Martinez, O.M.Perales, J.Pasaye, P.P.J.Botha, R.Alexander, D.R.Schafer, M.A.Buttschau, P.J.Capos, R.E.Broderick, W.Du, G.R.Tello, C.Loureiro, J.L.Peiter, M.R.D.Vargas, R.Orzechoski, V.Eggers, J.G.Torres, A.Rivas, G.Guillen, H.Lizarraga, J.M.Vaquero, L.Pellerin, P.Solano, A.Kunz, A.Nedic, A.Rottlaender, A.Rutz, A.Thomann, B.Hoess, C.Keskin, G.Brizzi, G.Wieland, H.Greving, H.Staffen, J.Fauer, J.Huether, L.Bartha, M.Kraus, M.Patino, M.Rupp, M.Vidic, P.Sanchez Cofrades, R.Adak, R.Jochem, R.Yavuz, S.Koszowski, V.Karnatz, B.W.Lerwick, D.S.Lombard, E.Guerrero, J.C.Velez, R.A.Rodriguez, P.Ey, A.L.Bridges, E.Ovalle, J.A.Johnson, J.C.Osborne, J.G.Gause, J.R.Wickabrod, J.W.Grosso, L.K.Arensdorf, R.E.Prater, T.C.Hedden, T.F.Hutchings, A.Guevara, J.Keller, S.Brown, B.D.Klinge, C.B.Osofsky, C.R.Kronberg, D.E.Lick Sr., H.A.Mason, J.L.O'Donnell, J.T.Vaaler, J.W.Kellett, M.W.Griebel, T.Gok, T.H.Alderson Jr., T.R.Fullerton, J.H.Munoz, J.L.Banfield, R.Alday, J.L.Gutierrez, J.Martinez, M.Lenz, A.J.Markwart, B.C.Proeber, C.M.Smith, E.B.Smith, E.J.Wessels, G.A.Perman, J.A.White, J.J.Baker, J.L.Helgeson, L.D.Bunch, L.M.Hoerner, M.L.Schryer, N.D.Miller, N.N.Fredricksen, T.D.Owen, S.J.Redfern, A.L.Hermes, C.R.Knuppe, M.V.Ribeiro, D.Jimenez, H.Martinez, M.I.Tamez, O.Delgado, S.Urreta, D.Hailstone, B.O.Tshabalala, A.Soriano, B.E.Berghoefer, E.G.Aguirre, O.P.Santana, P.P.Ramirez, J.Wardrop, S.K.Rusk, T.A.Cardeal, J.L.Hoste, A.Carrillo, C.F.Salas, J.A.Romero, J.C.Rodriguez, J.E.Reyna, J.H.Estrello, A.Escamilla, C.A.Soto, D.Gonzalez, E.Romero, F.De Santiago, G.Guzman, G.I.Picazo, G.Salinas, H.Saenz, I.Ramirez, J.A.Adame, J.A.Velazquez, J.C.Santillano, J.D.De la Cruz, J.J.Nuñez, J.P.Camacho, J.R.Perez, L.G.Mares, L.G.Puentes, L.P.Jacquez, M.A.Diaz, O.E.Aguilera, R.Esparza, A.J.Schmitt, B.C.Young, B.D.Lehman, B.S.Cue, C.A.Gardner, C.H.Hicks, C.S.Perry, D.K.Mc Clintic, D.L.Danielson, D.R.Harp Jr., E.R.Stephens, F.A.Graves, G.A.Shirley, G.R.Bragg, J.M.Blanchard, J.McQuerry, J.T.Callahan, L.E.Rion, L.J.Caloud, L.W.Albertson, M.A.Brown, M.J.Leahy, M.W.Lundy, R.A.Voelzke, R.F.Zmolek, S.D.Lucier, S.L.Hopkins, T.C.Tierney, T.J.Anderson, W.J.Kinard, W.K.Harding, L.G.K.Drews, M.Bierhals, F.J.Rivas, J.M.Anchondo, R.Rivera, F.Sanchez, I.Reyes, J.R.Aguirre, S.A.Gonzalez, A.Mejia, R.Paredes, D.S.Weber, M.A.Martinez, J.M.Lewis, E.Castillo, J.A.Reyna, C.H.Holler III, C.J.De Vries, C.R.Thomson, C.S.Fawcett, D.L.Wintjen, D.S.Jaggers, H.A.Morris, K.Watkins, L.M.Farley, M.D.Godmaire, P.D.Bauer, S.L.Tope, A.E.Arredondo, F.J.Padilla, P.Loera, R.S.Leal, J.Ferree, A.Ramirez, F.J.Rojas, H.Hernandez, M.A.Ramos, R.G.Castro, J.P.Jackson, R.P.Holland, S.A.Jarman, A.J.Bonde, D.Gomez, G.M.Ouellet, K.S.Hauer, S.L.Besler, S.M.McNally, S.Reich, A.R.Mattjie, E.Staffen, G.D.C.Esteves, G.R.D.Almeida, H.S.Lorenzzon, I.D.S.Ribas, J.A.Nagel, J.B.Rodrigues, J.J.Garbrecht, J.M.Pires, L.A.D.Motta, M.D.S.Viana, M.F.Daniel, R.F.Bauerfeld, V.H.Menin, M.Lorré, M.Lowinski, A.Kubina, A.Rabung, G.Kahmann, H.Voegele, J.Borchert, J.Dillmann, J.Kandiros, J.Wosiek, K.Boehler, K.Stankic, L.Reiss, M.Kaiser, N.Lautenschlaeger, R.Mayer, R.Semenic, V.Grimm, J.Grobmeier, M.Robert, R.Robert, T.Krieger, T.Müller , C.J.Fetes, D.L.Feaster, D.M.Butler, D.R.Westerlund, J.K.Dolash, M.G.Marty, P.A.Schmitt, R.A.Troutman, R.T.Peterman, T.E.Clarke, W.D.Tadlock, W.E.Woods Jr., R.P.Torrisi, A.B.Rozin, A.J.Saueressig, A.L.Fockink, C.M.Mattjie, C.M.Schroder, C.Ribeiro, E.L.Conti, F.C.Zirbes, G.F.Boiaski, J.J.D.Cunha, J.L.Kristensen, L.E.Mazurkiewicz, L.R.Pereira, M.A.Kuhnel, M.J.Bortoli, R.C.Amaral, S.O.Coitinho, J.B.Medrano, J.D.Amaya, M.Reyes, R.Diaz, M.T.Reyes, P.F.Reece, P.G.Desy, J.M.Estrada, F.J.Huerta, J.C.Garcia, I.G.Oliveira, J.B.M.Rebequi, A.Hernandez, C.Cruz, G.Hernandez, A.E.Joyner, B.T.Halleck, C.A.Peak, C.D.Harness, D.B.McBain, D.D.Mc Donald, D.E.Stephens, D.J.Welcher, D.S.Jans, E.C.Mixdorf, G.D.Hughes, G.L.Johnson, G.M.Burke, J.D.Bouldin Jr., J.D.Weidman, J.S.Walter, K.A.Bacon, K.K.Kelchen, L.A.Moss, L.A.Randecker, M.A.Schreiber, M.A.Webber, M.D.Small, M.L.Balvanz, M.L.Sanders, M.W.Johnson, R.A.Mericle, R.C.Benson, R.C.Tomkins, R.K.Popoola, R.M.McKelvey, R.M.Place, R.P.Ladeburg, S.A.Clarke, S.A.Lampe, S.J.Quam, S.M.Whiteman, T.A.Harn, T.A.Holmes, T.E.Carroll, T.H.Reagan, W.A.Brown, W.G.Seals, W.Jones Jr., A.Saldaña, C.Varela, M.C.Villarreal, D.Kutchoukov, D.X.Zhang, H.Li, H.P.Shao, J.B.Wang, S.Gao, S.H.Zhang, W.X.Bao, W.X.Li, Y.G.Tang, A.Rodriguez, L.E.Sanchez, C.M.Scarcella, A.Lopez, M.A.Pinto, O.Martinez, J.L.Senter, R.B.Smith, C.Neal, C.S.Thomas, C.W.Doolittle, D.A.Vanderbilt, E.L.Wade, J.A.Matthews, J.T.Downard, P.A.Gainer, R.A.Gerdes, R.Wells, S.K.Dickey, A.Ochoa, E.A.Ponce, H.A.Portillo, S.Perez, L.F.Garcia, A.E.Perez, A.Tovar, D.Gomez, E.Sanchez, F.Casas, F.J.Rivas, G.De Leon, G.Luna, H.Rojas, J.A.Espinoza, J.A.Olguin, J.A.Rocha, J.C.Luna, J.F.Benitez, J.F.Gonzalez, J.G.Cuan, J.G.Delgado, J.M.Cardenas, M.G.Barron, M.P.Elizondo, R.Lopez, R.Mena, R.Ramos, S.A.Garcia, T.Rodriguez, M.Toebes, H.M.Johnson, E.R.Gonzalez, J.A.Contreras, J.C.Olvera, M.R.Kline, A.D.Rodriguez, J.Cepeda, J.M.Nogay, M.Montañez, A.B.Boddicker, A.Dail, K.D.Kuznia, M.K.Spivey, M.T.Broadway, M.T.Malone, M.W.Tribble, R.A.Henson, A.Acevedo, R.Tochetto, I.S.Bazaldua, J.A.Velazquez, L.F.Garcia, D.S.Hawkins, M.Bajc, S.H.Skidmore, C.M.Kirby, C.T.Randolph, D.A.Bayless, J.D.Hudson, J.G.Ingram, K.A.Hora, K.K.Flaherty-Grampp, R.A.Turner, R.K.Wiggins, R.S.Webb, T.L.Gilmore, B.L.Tarter, J.A.Brown, M.K.Graf, R.Hansens, R.L.Maitland, V.L.Chinchankar, A.D.V.Ebrin, D.Tauchen, L.D.Godoy, J.Cantisany , G.Cordova, E.Josset, B.Lamberti, E.Vernoux, A.Hofer, A.Schmidt, B.Passauer, C.Lillig, D.Foerch, G.Pernek, H.Bertram, H.Bienek, H.Mader, H.Markert, H.Ohlemeyer, H.Pilger, I.Korn, J.Insua-Santos, K.Berni, K.Blasius, K.Kaminski, K.Lange, K.Schmidt, L.Schueppenhauer, M.Alganatay, M.Horoz, M.Lukic, M.Markovic, M.Scherer, M.Schirrmann, M.Zimmermann, P.Rakocevic, P.Schoenenberg, R.Bayer, R.Geier, S.Bauer, S.Wieczorek, T.Barnetz, T.Dahl, T.Stalter, U.Hoefgen, V.Knickel, V.Schmidt, W.Friess, A.A.J.Gering, B.W.Heetbrink, A.J.Byleveldt, D.Kelder, E.A.Dunn, G.Nortje', B.S.Buchholz, D.F.Thorne, J.R.Richter, L.A.Devries, M.K.Lear, R.M.Campbell, T.R.Petrusyk, A.Poblano, J.G.Hernandez, J.G.Nolasco, J.I.Alvarado, J.L.Cruz, P.C.Recio, R.Rodriguez, S.Perrin, A.Haas, A.Nirenberg, B.Mueller, C.Haas, D.Weber, J.Pilat-Luber, K.Russ, K.Wedel, L.Vitello, M.Bauer, M.Lueck, M.Poetzsch, M.Rausch, S.Gieser, S.Huebner, S.Jeckel, S.Weinelt, T.Baum, T.Kuntz, T.Seefeldt, U.Sahan, V.Ghorbani, H.N.Schroeder, R.P.Fisher, J.C.Abundis, V.Garcia, C.Peinado, R.G.Lyons, D.E.Little, A.De la Cruz, J.C.Borda, A.J.Wolf, B.K.Mc Elhose, C.L.Shindelar, D.D.Webb, D.G.Meguffy, D.L.Weis, D.M.Lockhart, D.W.Halverson, E.L.Allen, E.M.Williams, G.G.Brinker, G.I.Mighall, J.D.Twitchell, J.J.Menuey, J.L.Puls, J.N.Krutsinger, J.R.Callahan, K.D.Bate, K.S.Nedved, L.D.Good, L.K.Goldsberry, M.A.Crowder, M.L.Uhlenhopp, P.M.Whitley, R.A.Cole, R.A.Norton, R.J.Rand, S.J.Roloson, S.P.Rannells, T.E.Rettig, W.J.Lampe, I.Vazquez, J.A.Garcia, J.A.Guillen, L.Paz, O.J.Lopez, R.Bautista, S.Cazares, J.J.S.Pienaar, E.J.Jevcak, K.H.Ho, C.P.Holst, D.Vollmar, J.A.Santana, J.G.Hernandez, J.N.Ortega, M.A.Hernandez, R.A.Ramirez, S.Shi, R.Chmura, B.K.Hibbert, B.W.Heinen, C.McGuire, D.Yao, G.K.Henry Jr., J.A.Ford, J.M.Bush, J.R.Subbert, M.A.Scaletta, M.W.Therrien, P.F.Dcamp, R.A.Thomas, T.S.Halstead, K.H.Davison, A.Pott, J.L.D.Oliveira, A.Aguilera, A.M.Carrera, A.Rincón, C.Gutiérrez, E.Cardona, E.Lopez, F.Olivas, H.Lira, J.P.Guerra, J.Quiroz, J.Rodriguez, L.S.Martinez, P.C.Diaz, R.Ayala, R.E.Cervantes, R.Martinez, R.Rios, V.H.Castro, V.M.De la Rosa, B.Dezenter, V.Graeff, A.Bussmann, J.H.Heyneman, C.W.Neely, S.C.Hoyle, T.L.Neely, O.J.Diaz, F.Blot, R.Wexler, K.M.Leith, S.A.Reinke, M.A.Gutierrez, S.Ortega, E.D.Dalton, G.Ramos, G.Robledo, P.E.Flores, T.A.Cordero, A.J.Dewitte, B.J.Nelson, D.B.Newton, J.A.Dodson, J.E.Hilton, K.A.McCulley, K.A.Tatum, K.M.Watters, M.J.Cartmell, R.A.Maynard II, R.E.Pippin, S.D.Paris, T.A.Bell, T.A.Kuban, P.E.Clarke, P.A.Villa, M.Fernández, U.Ranchod, M.L.Arthur, T.J.Williams, A.Rodriguez, D.R.Castillo, I.De la Pena, R.Sanchez, B.J.Ferstl, J.A.Tucker, J.L.Alvarez, M.Schostag, A.Orozco, J.J.Lopez, O.Renteria, A.R.Hazen, B.D.Thome, C.E.Rich, C.K.Mehmen, C.L.Gilfillan, C.L.Larson, D.A.Larson, D.D.Greer, D.R.Krueger, D.R.Power, E.J.Hau, G.A.Mc Gee, G.D.Atkins, G.L.Barkow, G.R.Madden, G.S.Weich, J.E.White, J.L.McMeekan, J.M.Lauth, J.M.Wolking-Tharp, J.R.Melzer, K.A.Davis, K.M.Byrd, K.M.Shaw, K.M.Stover, L.D.Atkin, L.J.Granato Jr., M.E.Severson, M.J.Barnes, M.J.Hovey, M.P.Freemon, P.E.Jungen II, R.L.Van Riper, R.S.Allen, S.M.Stone, S.R.Oberbroeckling, S.S.Rice, T.J.Lawrence, T.May, V.C.Crow Sr., W.J.Dixon, A.Mendoza, B.Maltos, C.A.Sanchez, F.J.Martinez, F.J.Silva, H.A.Loredo, H.Torres, J.Adame, J.F.Castillo, J.G.Castillo, J.G.Esparza, J.G.Sanchez, J.J.Oviedo, L.A.Aviles, D.Beaufort, G.Sirop, S.Creuzet, A.Cochran, H.L.Chrysler, J.G.Hill, O.Fiallos, T.E.Baker, C.A.Ackerman, M.C.Harrington, M.D.Dittmer, M.H.Haynes, P.A.Mc Clain, R.W.Hewlitt Jr., V.K.Cox,

Commercial & Consumer Equipment employees, Raleigh, North Carolina, 1997

F.V.D.Silva, D.Cruz, J.R.Macias, M.Carrizales, M.Pardo, E.Pantoustier, C.Luengo, F.Behr, H.Graf, H.Neumann, H.Volenik, J.Muehlbeier, K.Korfhage, K.Probst, M.Benz, M.Kaeufl, M.Lamers, N.Ofenloch, P.Muench, S.Freund, S.Porst, W.Klein, W.Stark, W.Woelfel, A.D.Bailey, B.A.Jennings, B.L.Holt, B.R.Igl, B.S.Fraser, C.M.Castle, C.S.Daugherty, C.W.Smith, D.E.Brown, F.J.Hicks, J.B.Fraser, J.E.Hill, J.G.Brehm MD, J.H.Trent, J.L.Thomae, J.M.Welch, J.T.Henry, K.H.Torborg, K.M.Meadows, K.W.Murr, L.S.Holt, L.W.Hamlin, L.W.Hogan, L.Waddle, M.D.Jarnagin, M.L.Norton, P.A.Murr, P.E.Garritt, P.R.Bowers, R.D.Fogg, R.L.Tank, S.C.Bacon, T.E.Massey, T.F.Hopson, T.L.Myers, W.C.Davis, J.E.Uribarri, D.M.Venables, E.A.Figueroa, J.A.Hernandez, J.C.Tapia, M.I.Quintana, R.Lugo, S.Montelongo, M.C.Hewlett, R.Rivera, L.A.Snow, B.De la Pena, J.M.Rodriguez, J.M.Kessens, A.Anguiano, J.C.Gaytan, N.Ayala, B.A.Isle, B.J.Goodhart, B.W.Ketner, C.R.Cornell, D.J.Lane, D.J.Olson, D.P.Henry, I.Pietrantoni, J.E.Rathburn Jr., K.A.Budreau, K.D.Moon, L.A.Debaillie, L.S.Fey, L.Zhang, M.C.McBride, M.E.Thoren, M.J.Day, M.J.Livermore, M.L.Hungate, O.E.Scott Jr., P.E.Kirlin, P.J.Bultynck, R.W.Krapp, R.W.Morris, S.O.Krantz, T.M.Hanrahan, T.M.Heusinkveld, V.C.Bailey, C.C.T.Saldanha, C.A.Avila, M.Ovalle, O.Delgado, S.Camisan, A.Astorga, A.Islas, A.Moreno, C.A.Arambula, C.Cazares, E.R.Morales, H.Reyes, J.C.Macias, J.C.Soto, J.G.Villagrana, J.J.Diaz, J.L.Rios, J.L.Santos, J.O.Gonzales, J.Rocha, L.A.Rodriguez, M.A.Favela, P.Rodriguez, R.C.Martinez, A.Porthault, C.A.Jones, F.J.McGowan, J.P.Gagnon, J.P.Harlan, T.Iapicco, M.Blockhaus, D.Lopez B., J.G.Taylor, M.G.Mezvinsky, R.A.Edwards, S.Kilbreath, M.Quintana, H.A.Brown, J.S.Abbott, T.M.Lee, S.De Saeger, R.Mairien, A.J.Garcia, J.C.Lona, J.L.Palomares, J.R.Ferrer, J.Zapata, M.A.Olivares, S.Muñoz, V.H.Cepeda, A.A.Lowe, A.J.Johnson, A.S.Parton, B.A.Loveless, B.B.Cashman, B.J.Heck, B.L.Retherford, C.L.Taylor, C.S.Delotto, C.W.Grimm, D.E.Secrist II, D.G.Reiter, D.J.Buls, D.J.Burkhardt, D.L.Benson, D.L.Hellman, D.M.Dalke, D.M.Jahn, D.S.Schmelzer, D.W.Irvine, F.C.Buck, G.D.Palmer, G.E.Fobert, J.A.Cross, J.A.Wilson, J.E.Van Schie, J.F.Eberhart Wilson, J.J.Stewart, J.K.Utt, J.P.Barnett, J.P.Manning Jr., J.S.Murphy, J.T.Myers, K.A.Steimel, K.Bench, K.D.Erdmann, K.S.Skaggs, L.A.Skillman, L.E.Bolduc, L.M.Greer, M.A.Hollister, M.A.Ottinger, M.D.Peterson, M.F.Schreder, P.C.Spore, P.Combs, P.G.Britton, R.G.Dawson, R.M.Clark, R.R.Crevier, S.A.McKeen, S.A.Soldwisch, S.C.Meier, S.J.Rolison, S.K.Nagel, T.A.Freeman, T.A.Oesterle, T.A.Wilson, T.C.Curran, T.L.Hougen, T.Tiller, W.E.Harney, W.F.Boyle, W.J.Hunt, W.J.Parry, W.L.Tullos, A.Talbot, R.Cooper, L.Li, A.A.Serna, J.R.Lopez, N.Coudert, J.J.Ripslinger, S.J.Quick, S.A.Litchfield, D.Faivre, M.Richter, A.F.Catalfano, A.L.Dark, B.D.Morgan, B.J.Orand, E.W.King, H.D.Ferguson, I.D.Sane, J.F.Rossi, J.L.White, J.P.Buckley, L.A.Dunbar, M.Leatherman, M.R.Palmer, M.S.Campbell, M.W.Burse, P.A.Gilbert, P.J.Ellis, P.M.Thomsen, R.A.Williford, R.D.Ervin, R.D.Slemp, R.M.Murr, S.A.Harris, S.E.Herrera, S.L.Nyenhuis, S.Ok, B.W.Smith, E.A.Almaguer, S.A.Carrazco, J.R.Oldham, F.B.Jackson, R.F.Cervantes, A.K.McDermott, M.R.Garratt, T.J.Shinners, W.V.James, A.Rivera , B.Baumann, C.Hemme, D.Drexler, E.Freudensprung, H.Kapp, H.Lurg, J.Rieth, J.Styletz, K.Kauther, M.Dursun, O.Moch, R.Dufner, W.Schwitzke, A.Milizia, D.Pacey, A.J.Wuebben, A.R.Torres, B.D.Kreiner, C.L.Stufflebeem Jr., C.R.Corbisier, D.C.Keeney, D.E.Webb, D.L.Bureau, D.L.Ford, D.W.Miller, E.A.Yenner, E.Mannapso, G.D.Terronez, G.M.Fritch, G.M.Seaman, J.A.Buckwalter, J.A.Smith, J.B.Blumenstein, J.C.Sandoval, J.N.Parsons, J.Sonheim, J.W.Guzzo, K.A.Peterson, K.M.Noel, L.A.Dryoel, L.C.Wilson, L.J.Peters, M.A.Searie, M.Jobin, M.S.King, N.Smith, R.A.Behnken, R.A.Creager, R.G.Exbom, R.L.Corder Jr., R.R.Lafountaine, S.A.Michael, S.C.White, T.J.McConnell, T.J.Splear, T.R.Foglesong, K.M.McMaster, R.Lubbers, A.Kehrwald, C.Bencke, D.D.Almeida, F.C.Schmidt, P.A.Huttmann, A.Torres, R.Garza, F.Boutillier, C.Joseph, J.Dempzin, A.Camilleri, L.Reynoso , M.L.Gardner, J.J.Gonzalez, M.A.Ramirez, J.Buchs, J.R.Arthur, C.Gutierrez, C.H.Lamm, C.R.Williams, D.F.Hastings, D.K.Schluetter, D.W.Crosiar Jr., D.W.Lawrence, E.G.Johnston, E.J.Young, E.K.Schreiber, F.M.Morrow, G.L.Collett Jr., G.U.Patterson, G.W.Bever Jr., I.L.Sykes, J.A.Nelson, J.J.Pajor, J.N.Evans, J.T.Baker, J.W.Mefford, J.W.Overton, K.D.Eckel, K.E.Woodall, L.J.Glick, L.J.Reimann, L.L.Ritz, L.S.Holzhauser, M.A.Fenton, M.K.Mc Elhose, M.L.Bowen, M.L.Faison, M.V.Guiter, N.J.Klein, N.M.Berg, P.E.Klosler, R.B.Morgan, R.W.Rich, R.Y.Dunn, S.A.Thomas, S.L.Hoenicke, S.L.Nielsen, T.D.Allen, T.J.Anderson, T.L.Pilcher, T.M.Bennett, T.P.Anderson, T.W.Martin, Z.J.Barnes, M.A.D.Silva, A.Santos, D.M.Jones, D.Macomson, H.A.Mitchem, J.Angi, R.E.Nze, R.W.Bomar, T.A.Mitchell, B.A.Zavala, C.A.Galindo, J.A.Rodriguez, J.Alvarado, J.G.Zurita, R.Aguillon, S.A.Aguirre, C.Guillon, A.Mueller, N.E.Schott, H.Tinggaard, A.L.Seemann, A.Taylor, B.K.Williams, B.R.Kelly, C.R.Richardson, D.A.Showen, D.L.Kirkland, D.L.Paulos, E.B.Gehle, G.Dell'Unto, J.E.Warren Jr., J.L.Brown, K.M.Chapman, L.A.Lukehart, L.H.Martin, M.A.Rysdam, M.D.Haynes, M.L.Rysdam, M.T.Parkins, M.W.Reece, O.R.Frederic, R.A.Dunbar, R.A.Hazelwood, R.L.Spurlock, S.D.Harris, S.L.Wright, S.M.Kruse, T.W.Woods, W.A.Byrd, E.Garcia, J.A.Banda, J.Esquivel, J.Gutierrez, A.Ceniceros, A.Hernandez, D.Hernandez, F.J.De la Rosa, J.M.Barrera, J.M.Delgado, J.O.Chavez, L.Esquivel, M.A.Flores, M.Armendariz, O.Ibarra, O.Muñoz, R.Valero, S.Sosa, V.H.Alvarado, V.M.Valero, J.A.Sanchez, A.V.Chirackal, M.L.Johnson, A.Gladin, G.Bañuelos, A.C.Knoll, B.K.Van Engelenhoven, C.D.Barnes, C.E.Linder, D.L.Sherwood Jr., H.Attouchi, J.E.Roe, J.M.Callas, K.L.Hannigan, M.E.Cutler, M.G.Den Hartog, M.J.Cline, M.J.Workman, M.T.Sales, T.R.Buffington, T.W.Mays, V.M.Jordan, V.Z.Coker, W.F.Cormier, L.Lechuga, J.A.Ramos, J.Gongora, C.Herzog, K.J.Piber, F.A.Rodriguez, Y.Lamerant, R.O.Y.Keizers, A.A.Metcalf, A.J.Bertolozzi, A.L.Williford, A.R.McNeill, A.S.Gregory, B.C.Cutler, B.J.Doty, B.L.Hauglie, B.M.Werley, C.D.Hackett, C.G.Linke, C.L.Schrader, C.R.Douglas, D.A.Pringle, D.G.Kinzler, D.J.Haynes, D.Watson, G.E.O'Bryant Jr., J.A.Borelli, J.A.Macklin, J.D.Garrison, J.E.Williams Sr., J.H.Cassity, J.S.Halamaj, J.V.Miller, K.A.Carlough, K.J.Cooper, K.K.Klein, K.L.Crawford-Haney, K.M.Donlon, L.A.Jenison, L.C.Dennis, L.L.Payne, L.S.Silvers, M.A.Elliott, M.L.Meeker, R.D.Freeman, R.J.Olmstead, R.Nelson, S.A.Knight, S.A.Novak, S.L.Young, T.D.Skelton, T.Groulx, T.J.Mills, T.J.Nemmers, W.B.Kitterman, M.L.Cereceres, A.Castillo, C.M.Cota, F.C.Barragan, J.E.Thomae, C.A.Castillo, F.Anaya, A.Rutz, D.Waibel, D.Yilmaz, G.Kurz, H.Baumbach, H.Froehlich, H.Graetsch, H.Huegel, J.Kaiser, K.Gredel, M.Herceg, M.Safar, T.Jann, V.Reis, W.Kisling, O.Sánchez, C.M.Garza, S.M.Simmons, F.M.Orozco, S.E.Hernandez, H.R.Burkett, A.Gonzalez, E.F.Viera, A.A.Navia, B.N.Culp, C.D.Parkhurst, C.E.Elkins, C.K.Chidley, D.A.Nitschke, D.C.Allen, D.C.Ryan, E.L.Griffith, G.L.Pyles, J.J.Perkins, J.J.Spitzer, J.T.Stone, K.J.Scott, L.A.West, M.A.Cothron, M.D.Jones, M.J.De La Rosa, O.F.Ewumi, R.A.Miller, T.J.Simpson, T.L.Bickford, T.S.Flickinger, T.W.Johnson, V.L.Stephens, W.L.Sharp, J.Wang, G.Lara, G.Obregon, J.P.Barragan, M.Gonzalez, A.Streck, C.Barber, A.J.Zeglin III, A.P.Paquin, B.M.Alexia, B.N.Doy, C.F.Dutton, C.L.Coffman, C.L.Mc Kittrick, D.D.Weller, D.E.Lampe, D.F.Ingalls, D.J.Burkholder, D.R.Mc Ie, D.R.Tarrant, D.W.Bodlak, E.L.Hayek, E.N.Young, G.T.Thompson, J.C.Mays, J.M.Hegarty, J.M.Schweitzer, L.M.Vandevoord, M.F.Gan Jr., M.H.Johnson, M.J.Ford, M.L.Valentine, M.V.Richards, R.L.Petersen Jr., R.R.Covert, S.C.Long, S.L.Stage, T.A.Averkamp, T.A.Johnson, D.H.Maghenzani, G.A.Messina, A.Rodriguez, B.Saucedo, S.A.Villarreal, A.Freyler, H.Barthel, K.Blatt, C.M.Schroeder, G.H.Choi, R.M.Fitzpatrick, A.R.Roe, T.E.Kluver, E.P.Olson, C.L.Spears, G.S.Davis, D.L.Wilhoit, C.A.Conner, B.S.Jolliff, A.E.Amprimo, **1998** L.B.Julsgaard, R.Christiansen, T.Schrøder, J.Jin, R.Hu, A.Mann, A.Turner, D.Peric, F.Ried, G.Boegem, G.Hamm, G.Hendriks, G.Roumeliotis, H.Conrad, H.Weidner, J.Lebek, K.Hauk, K.Karmann, K.Mueller, T.Wagner, W.Elsner, M.Pellegriti, S.A.Valderrabano, A.L.Kolb, A.L.Sullivan, A.P.Allen, A.S.Pollock, B.D.Ray, B.D.Thiese, B.E.Douglas, B.J.Fillard, B.J.Ivey, B.L.Higgins, B.L.Krupa, B.L.Laneville, B.L.Raasch, B.R.Jillson, B.S.Horvatin, C.A.Demmel, C.B.Adams, C.M.Drouin, C.M.Gormley, C.N.Anderson, C.S.Gehrke, C.W.Seuser, C.Yanak, D.Arbour, D.B.Elgersma, D.D.Harrington, D.J.Schmidt, D.McLean, D.N.Austin, D.R.Leytem, E.A.Schoonover, E.J.Keup, E.L.Eddy, E.N.Cunningham, E.S.Lopshire, G.E.Leese, G.J.Biles, G.J.Lems, G.J.Shipshock, G.R.Larson, H.D.Hopkins Jr., H.J.Behnke, H.R.Saunchegrow, J.A.Sturch, J.D.Hopkins, J.E.Meister, J.F.Puetz, J.Green, J.J.Dudzik, J.K.Kirchoff, J.L.Wagner, J.M.Dodd, J.M.Healy, J.M.Williams, J.S.Knickerbocker, J.S.Knutsen, J.S.Underwood, J.W.Reimann, K.A.Coleman, K.A.Prunty, K.D.Johnson, K.D.Kirchhoff, K.D.Stancil, K.J.Williams, K.L.Rudd, K.M.Rankin, K.M.Smith, K.S.Campbell, K.S.Tigges, K.W.Gatling, L.D.Doss, L.G.Melssen, L.H.Daniel, L.H.Schwoch, L.J.Spellious, L.L.Kiser, L.S.Nedelcoff, L.T.Riley, M.A.Frye, M.A.La Coste, M.A.Vevera, M.D.Heft, M.D.Sille, M.E.Morley, M.J.Jurgella, M.J.Peters, M.J.Shabley, M.L.Prieve, M.L.Wise, M.R.Schroeder, N.J.Bednarek, P.J.Swick, P.M.Horton, P.W.Apfelbeck, R.A.Hodges, R.D.Haun, R.D.St Aubin, R.F.Beason, R.J.Glaser, R.J.Kollmann, R.L.Hessling, R.L.Marschke, R.L.Weatherby, R.M.Bindl, R.M.Feckers, R.R.O'Donnell, S.A.Lloyd, S.E.Reitz, S.J.Coleman, S.M.Boden, S.M.Mann, S.M.Schaub, S.M.Schulz, S.M.Stanic, S.M.Teasley, S.M.Zubke, S.R.Adams, S.R.Petter, S.W.Koppmann, T.A.Nevitt, T.J.Gronau, T.L.Nitschke, T.M.Wokasch, T.P.Smith, T.R.Paulson, V.T.Swartz, W.A.Jacobs, W.A.Wolf, W.B.Shockley, W.H.Bomberry Jr., W.T.Mischler Jr., M.A.Smalley, A.A.Bravo, A.A.Ramirez, A.Adame, B.Ortiz, E.A.Serrano, F.Gonzalez, F.Jasso, F.Medina, H.E.Longoria, H.O.Martinez, J.A.Sanchez, J.Alvarado, J.B.Gonzalez, J.C.Gaytan, J.G.Presas, L.Perez, M.Obaya , R.Martinez, S.Mendoza, V.H.Garcia, O.Rodriguez, Y.Garnery, Y.Guerret, S.Ollu, D.Obligis, K.Guerin, P.Sandmayer, B.F.Adams, D.M.Metzger, J.E.Roe, J.T.Bircher, M.J.Hooten, M.J.Mitchell, M.M.Dalbey, S.D.Anton, S.J.Heller, S.L.Seifert, T.H.Laumeyer, A.De la Rosa, A.Obregon, J.G.Ramos, J.J.Cepeda, B.Greer, S.Gepp, D.Pfleghaar, G.Hartmann, H.Struve, N.Selmani, S.Schubert, J.H.Leinart IV, R.D.Cork, A.Torres, C.M.Jensen, S.Rasmussen, A.S.Devrieze, B.D.Davison, B.J.Harrington, B.J.Mahoney, B.Q.Dixon, C.J.Belser, C.R.Timmerman, D.H.Bradford, D.J.Straley, D.L.Steinlage, D.M.Steele, D.N.Lindell, G.D.Radke, H.D.Ramey, J.E.Ditzman, J.J.Engelbrecht, J.J.Wagner, J.L.Burns, J.P.Buck, J.R.Mason, J.T.Dalton, J.T.Gilbert, J.W.Gradert, K.E.Griffin, K.E.Harrington, K.M.Artz, L.H.Isbill, L.J.Boyd, L.R.Sanford, L.R.Telleen, M.A.Czerwinski Jr., M.A.Thonn, M.D.Dudley, M.D.Olson, M.J.Willcox, M.R.Foley, N.J.Cole, P.R.Moorman, R.L.Houk, R.L.Tarrant, R.P.Pedersen, R.W.Dotson, S.K.Todd, S.W.Wilks, T.E.Aring, T.E.Peters, T.G.Funseth, T.J.Bulten, T.J.Rock, T.L.Johnston, W.D.Gibbs, J.N.Palma, H.V.Hernandez, J.F.Alanis, R.Gonzalez, R.Rivera, D.Crevel, H.Roth, T.Weirich, E.A.Shindelar, F.J.Roth, C.P.Cardoso, D.R.Pohlmann, I.Rysdyk, J.D.Oliveira, J.D.S.Santos, J.H.Wagner, M.A.Lopes, M.Mattes, M.R.Wilke, V.O.Schweig, B.G.Guajardo, A.K.East, B.A.Chouinard, L.A.Caballero, D.L.White, L.Evans, B.F.Xu, R.Lozano, E.Bebber, J.Dieter, G.C.Reese, J.Whittle, L.M.Paterson, M.J.Cocayne, M.P.Drescher, A.A.Maruzin, B.J.Baker, B.R.Dodd, C.M.Rush, D.D.Hofmeister, W.J.Harvey, E.J.Aguilar, B.Deschamps, P.Dethune, C.Boulestin, I.Peic, A.E.Dobbs, B.E.Ratledge, B.J.Phillips, B.W.Manske, C.E.Brown, C.J.Goodman, C.K.Eifler, C.L.Bird, C.R.Davis, D.C.Hasken, D.F.Stoker, D.L.Gales, D.Ross, G.A.Cagle, J.B.Watts, J.D.Rottinghaus, J.D.Townsend, J.L.Piasecki, J.R.Eddy, K.D.Grider, K.K.Hardy, L.A.Coleman, L.L.Yarborough, M.W.Freshour, N.P.Julien, R.A.Breeden, R.G.Tipton, S.Diaz, S.L.Nance, T.D.Hudson, T.F.Best II, W.K.Dyer, C.G.Rosales, C.E.Altamirano, F.Cuellar, J.D.Luevanos, J.L.Rodriguez, R.Almanza, R.Jimenez, C.Gwiazdowski, A.E.Jones, A.N.Groat, B.D.Johnson, C.A.Happel, C.J.Gruss, C.R.Jex, D.J.Docherty, D.J.Schaefer, D.J.Wells, D.McDonald, E.J.Edwards, G.A.Gomez, J.C.Collis, J.D.Hedley, J.D.Ploessl, J.F.Balister, J.L.Barman, J.L.Coyle, J.L.Heyman, J.L.Jackson, J.M.Swan, J.S.Hunter, K.D.Alexander, K.E.Larson Jr., L.A.Morgan, L.L.Collins Jr., L.L.Holldorf Jr., M.A.Brand, M.R.Riegler, R.D.Abel, R.J.Koetz, R.M.Fettig, T.Barton, T.E.Dohrmann, T.J.O Brien, T.L.Kirkland, T.W.Neer, L.R.Bowman, A.Benavides, I.Garcia, G.Leichtnam, H.J.Jensen, R.K.Young, Q.Dong, M.Stemmle, J.M.Rawson Balaski, J.E.Cantu, F.J.Guzman, I.Arguello, J.C.Vazquez, J.F.Reyes, J.Herrera, J.M.Alejandro, M.Garcia, R.Rangel, B.J.Nichols, N.Dybro, M.Höglmaier, N.J.Shire, P.Chont, C.Vittet, A.Hoechel, A.Maestre-Villalon, G.Rebmann, H.Kiefer, H.Kurz, K.Knittel, M.Lieber, M.Yilmaz, P.Novak, W.Loch, G.J.L.Van Der Hoeven, M.E.Van Der Velde, A.Koch-Schulte, A.M.Arnold, B.T.Madsen, C.M.Arndt, E.R.Robertson, F.M.Amato, H.C.Freimann, J.A.Hart, J.B.Chapin, J.M.Hummel, J.R.Martin, J.T.White, K.J.Delles, K.J.Schwarzkopf, L.J.Veale, R.A.Williams, R.R.Ruland, S.M.Hetzel, T.L.Burens, T.L.Staten, T.V.Manuel, W.R.Jones, A.O.Faccio, S.H.Doffo, I.J.Manjabosco, V.Meneghini, R.Cruz, G.A.Gutierrez, M.Uriarte , A.V.Gonzalez, J.R.Verastegui, R.Galarza, D.Przybyl, E.Gountenidis, H.Al-Osman, H.Egner, J.Graf, J.Storzum, K.Rheinheimer, M.Braun, O.Saf, R.Lecei, R.Wuerges, S.Huether, W.Kindler, S.R.Dunn, T.A.Myers, J.L.Navarro, A.R.Blanco, A.J.Moore, A.A.Kurylo, A.H.D.Reis, A.I.Link, A.Kaim, A.L.Hammann, A.R.Bonmann, A.R.Dreissig, A.S.Leonhardt, B.L.D.Luz, C.A.Brauer, C.A.Ferreira, C.E.Rugerio, C.Engelmann, C.Kochhann, C.R.Ziebert, D.D.Bottega, D.D.S.D.Santos, D.Knorst, D.Liebert, D.S.D.Silva, E.Fuchs,

E.L.Frese, E.R.Fernandes, E.Rodrigues, F.Colling, F.H.Horst, F.R.Giordani, F.Tibola, F.Wildner, G.M.M.Lenz, G.V.Kuhn, H.M.J.Bastian, I.C.Borgmann, J.Fernandes, J.M.D.Souza, J.S.Aosani, L.C.D.Rosario, L.J.Schmidt, M.A.Belarmino, M.A.Losekann, M.C.S.Bohrer, M.G.Hirt, M.Ioris, M.R.Bender, M.R.Hirt, N.J.Muller, N.R.Bencke, P.P.Wesling, P.R.Hoffmann, P.R.Klein, R.F.Missio, R.R.D.Silva, R.T.A.D.S.Bender, S.Wander, T.A.Lorenzet, T.H.Dickel, V.Vargas, W.G.Minini, J.E.Vidaurri, R.Montemayor, J.C.Alaniz, R.E.Mendoza, L.J.McSoling, A.M.Lauersdorf, A.M.Ormord, B.R.Grady, C.A.Voshell, C.P.Reiter, D.E.Orona, D.G.Gallacher, D.G.Workman, G.A.Ingersoll, J.A.Flockhart, J.A.Pedrotty, K.J.Thompson, L.L.Kaster IV, M.Gutang, N.A.Rudolph, P.J.Uhl, P.M.Zuccolo, P.R.Hutchinson, R.E.Cline II, R.J.Mc Daniel, R.J.Shadle, R.L.Day, R.S.Dejonge, R.S.Folkerts, R.S.McCarty, S.C.Shumaker, S.L.Brown, T.A.Coleman, T.D.Kasemeier, T.E.Kay, T.G.Kimberley, T.L.Gilfillan, W.H.Adams, E.A.Isolabella, W.J.Mathews, C.N.D.Agnol, A.Gaytan, J.R.Arizpe, S.Biziorek, H.Kuzu, S.Brizzi, T.Goebel, V.Baj, G.L.Davidson, R.M.Lutze, T.Eicher, A.O.Adams, B.C.Steffens, I.Nøhr, F.V.D'Auria, F.H.Poulsen, M.Delach, T.A.Tallman, E.Boisot, A.A.Schneider, A.M.Hilgendorf, A.Reyes, B.Bolet, B.J.Tank, B.J.Weber, C.A.Gee, C.D.Bernier, C.H.Calfee, C.L.Johnson, D.C.Christensen, D.J.Moon, E.A.Winterhalter, E.J.Pettigrew, E.W.Cooper, G.B.Moses, J.A.Lagaisse, J.C.Ward, J.Christianson, J.L.Beeth, J.L.Bein, J.P.Mason, J.R.Figueroa, J.R.Hayes, J.R.Samples, K.B.Winfield, K.D.Little, L.L.Knutson, M.E.Fritts, M.J.Lauritzen, M.R.Eldridge, M.R.Johnson, N.C.Horst, N.K.Inman, N.S.Erickson, P.A.Jorgensen, P.A.Smith, P.J.Ahlf, P.L.Carroll, R.D.Schluenz, R.J.Gonzalez, R.Juarez, R.L.Peterson, S.J.Bealer, S.M.Kohr, S.T.O'Brien, T.L.Predmore, T.M.Wilson, C.A.Talamantes, G.J.Garcia, L.G.Garcia, M.A.Hernandez, D.Retana, D.Rodriguez, E.Montoya, F.Del Real, G.De Anda, F.Holdrinet, A.Zakel, G.Becker, S.Sabotic, S.M.Makulubete, C.A.Brown, P.Gansera, D.G.Park, F.J.Kraftt, A.P.Hagler, J.D.Ferguson, S.E.Newman, A.L.Young, B.W.Cormaney, C.C.Sayers Jr., C.M.Potts, C.R.Tobin, D.A.Bonzer, D.E.Reisner, D.M.Mc Broom, E.A.Carinder, F.A.Passig, G.A.Felderman, H.A.Perez, J.A.Lentz, J.C.Pesek, J.P.Dunakey, J.S.Wyant, J.T.Brammann, K.A.Claeys, K.F.Jagers, K.K.Heckman, K.S.Graham, K.T.Krueger, L.A.Mc Cool, L.A.Starman, L.Howard, L.J.Ludwig, M.A.Judge, M.E.Akers, M.J.Haugen, M.J.Thacker, R.A.Meirick, R.C.Merkin, R.D.Eisenmenger, R.H.Beck, R.J.Larson, R.J.Pierce, R.L.Van Arsdale, R.S.Leisinger, S.C.Deitrick, S.S.Zilke, T.D.Hanrahan, T.M.Havill, T.N.Signer, T.S.Bulver, W.C.Miller, W.J.Lillis, G.D.Piro, P.T.Murray, B.Juarez, E.A.Herrera, E.Zuñiga, G.Flores, R.Rodriguez, R.Treviño, A.Sander, H.Huth, K.Yologlu, W.Fink, L.D.Claussen, T.L.Wallace, O.A.Martinez, J.M.Dilks, W.D.Robinson, M.M.Cheung, N.S.Cowan, S.C.Foley, K.A.Bottomley, B.K.Pearson, D.V.Parekh, M.A.Durnell, T.J.Roszhart, O.Sørensen, A.Bildersheim, A.Dick, A.Weigand, A.Willinger, B.Gorini, E.Gantelas, E.Lahm, E.Reinys, H.Jost, I.Halilovic, K.Acar, K.Feldt, L.Kokas, M.Acikgoez, M.Knerr, M.Zeiter, N.Ziegler, R.Schlemmer, S.Akkaya, P.M.Blixt, A.L.Thomas, B.Foster, D.E.Matthews, D.L.Spybey, D.R.Slavish, E.Harpole Jr., F.A.Ford, F.M.Allen, F.W.Hadley Jr., G.A.Clear, G.P.Holland, J.L.Erschen, J.L.Vander Meersch, J.R.Lawrence, J.R.Whitney, K.J.Boyd, K.J.Hinkle, K.J.Lamphere, K.Lischka, K.S.Kasten, K.W.Green, M.A.Dierickx, M.J.Pipho, M.L.Williams, M.R.Masters, M.T.McCarthy, M.W.Lopez, R.E.Meuse, R.J.Johnson, R.V.Blackman, R.V.Keith, S.C.Rhodes, S.C.Spors, S.M.Riley, T.Jorgenson, A.M.Lanzarin, J.A.Lopez, P.Lucand, B.Schiesser, R.Windstein, A.Gutfreund, A.Jastrow, A.Kurtaran, A.Teutsch, I.Arslan, S.Gruenblatt, H.W.Lapole, A.Braunagel, H.Biedron, C.Haas, D.Jakubith, W.Dippel, A.H.Wilkerson, A.M.Price, A.S.Turner, C.M.King, D.P.Holst, E.L.Huger, G.J.Mc Millan, J.B.Knight, J.L.Kehoe, J.N.Troxel, J.T.Andringa, K.L.Hansen, K.L.Lewis, K.M.Hunter, P.A.Van Ess, R.C.Lambi, R.G.Simmons, R.H.Marringa, R.M.Digman, R.R.Reed, S.A.Mason, S.Horianopoulos, S.Schmitt, T.M.Campbell, W.D.Pope, W.M.Stidham, E.E.Sherman, C.A.Schere, C.A.Schutz, C.G.Kamm, C.Lipke, C.R.Ritter, C.R.Spanhol, C.Tusset, D.L.Winter, L.C.S.D.Silva, M.Arbter, M.Kretschmer, M.L.Arend, M.R.Dutra, O.Buligon, S.D.Moura, V.D.L.Rosa, A.Martinez, A.Bobrow, B.Eker, F.Uffelmann, G.Zewoldy, R.Stein, S.Lazar, S.Oezdemir, W.Kampf, W.Kaucher, Y.Sorma, Z.Markovic, C.E.Sandoval, E.A.Perkins, R.S.Dougherty, A.K.Lauer, R.J.Zabor, E.Bieber, V.Rink, V.Kershaw, M.T.Newman, T.R.Hoeg, F.Flores, G.H.Ambrosius, V.A.M.Arts, J.A.R.Audenaert, J.M.H.Beeren, G.Clephas-Aerts, A.C.W.M.van Doremaele, F.P.Douven, R.G.F.Douven, T.H.A.Douven, L.J.A.Driessen, M.H.G.A.Driessen, A.G.J.Duijkers, P.J.J.Geerarts, P.J.C.van de Goor, J.P.M.Gubbels, J.G.T.Hagens, W.J.Hesen, H.P.M.Hesen, J.H.C.Hofmans, T.P.W.Holtermans, L.J.J.Huijs, H.J.G.Jacobs, W.H.J.Jans, G.W.J.Janssen, J.M.C.M.Jenneskens, J.T.M.van Kempen, G.J.C.van Kempen, H.P.W.Kessels, F.K.G.Krah, H.M.A.Laemers, W.L.M.Manders, K.P.M.van den Munckhof, G.L.P.van den Munckhof-Stappers, R.P.A.Nefkens, M.P.T.van Ooyen, W.J.C.M.Peeters, M.J.Peeters, J.H.G.Peeters, E.H.M.Peys, G.H.A.Roodbeen, M.H.L.Schreurs, H.H.P.Smetsers, G.W.Smits, L.A.G.Sternheim, E.T.L.J.Teuwsen, G.M.Tonnissen, P.A.W.van Vegchel, R.A.J.G.Verbruggen, L.W.Verhaegh, J.C.T.Verlinden, A.F.J.Verstralen, J.G.M.Vervuurt, G.L.P.Weijs, J.Wilting, J.M.H.Wismans-Luypers, A.C.Widish, A.D.Bly, A.L.Schares, A.Ramani, B.C.Chaney, B.K.Hammond, B.M.Heath, C.A.Hodgin, C.E.Strubel, C.Plouffe, D.E.Schmitz, D.G.Toppert, D.L.Douglas, D.L.Woolam, D.W.Smith, E.E.Russell, G.Bagou, H.L.Hayes, H.P.Gagne, H.R.Bradford, J.A.Lundeen, J.A.Sorenson, J.B.Pace, J.C.Steen, J.D.Meier, J.G.Bodensteiner, J.J.Hahn, J.L.Miller, K.D.Garrison, K.D.White Jr., K.J.Hawley, K.L.Richardson, K.M.McMurray, L.P.Pauling, M.A.Elliott, M.B.Albright, M.G.Mc Elmurray, M.J.Cherney, M.R.Thibodeaux, M.W.George, N.W.Sealman, P.P.Blunt, R.G.Roberts, R.W.Brandhorst, S.B.Ryman, S.J.Breiner, S.R.Bradley, T.A.Underwood, T.P.Jones, X.Wang, J.A.Vela, A.Hernández , J.D.Cabrera, A.J.Aguilera, E.Chapon, M.Grangeret, A.Ruediger, J.Lupic, L.Orschulko, M.Felker, M.Merkel, R.Wiltschek, T.Isik, B.D.Rudin, C.R.F.Tronco, A.Bozan, A.Strzys, A.Walter, G.John, H.Goesch, M.Berksoy, M.Celikkanat, M.Kizilirmak, N.Peter, O.Duranidis, T.Jakob, U.Kizilkaya, C.L.Tormes, F.D.S.Alves, V.Pinheiro, H.Oberlaender, I.Zekri, M.Pezzetti, A.M.Prenevost, C.A.Barker, C.A.Kavonius, C.E.Harvey, C.L.Wilson, C.M.Haase, C.M.Hager, C.S.Rush, D.B.Dexter, D.J.Batchelor, D.J.Janz, D.J.Roach, D.L.Peterson, D.M.Chambers, D.M.Halterman, D.R.Bischoff, D.R.Hansen, E.R.Bilby, F.Ariganello, H.C.Olsen, H.W.Pfister, J.A.Hupf, J.J.Braun, J.K.Vosekuil, J.L.Abresch, J.L.Rataczak, J.L.Werner, J.R.Warner, J.S.Schumacher, K.A.Moreland, K.L.Meighan, L.A.Sobrilsky, L.M.Toivonen, M.E.Putz, M.J.Walker, M.K.Meyer, M.L.Mack, M.L.Nash, M.M.Dougherty, N.R.King, R.A.Kramer, R.J.Shaw, R.R.Smith, R.W.Sommercorn, S.Echols Jr., S.F.Bell, S.K.Grantham, T.A.Knight, T.D.Harvey, T.M.Vlasic, T.N.Beasley, T.R.Smith, T.S.Smit, W.S.Wolfenbarger, W.W.Hamm, S.G.Gomez, S.S.Silva, H.Lai, T.Klinke, F.J.Mendez, J.A.Gephart, J.L.Noriega, A.Garcia, A.K.Zimmerman, A.L.Reeves, A.M.Doornenbal, A.T.Roper, D.E.Koranda, D.R.Dodd, D.R.Shininger, D.R.Smith, D.S.Parnell, G.C.Thomas, G.W.West, J.D.Sprague, J.F.Cerda, J.L.Place, J.Nocero, J.Witmer, K.A.Dotts, K.L.Carpenter, L.C.Zaft, L.E.Wilcox, L.K.Kinn, L.P.Ferguson, M.E.Bowles, M.J.Bredar, M.M.Dale, M.R.Merims, M.V.Lebeck, N.E.Medrano, N.J.Graf, P.C.Gratton, P.L.Huss, S.A.Hollis, S.D.Pollock, S.R.Yarbrough, S.S.Linderbaum, S.Hernandez, A.Lopez, A.Ramos, F.J.Aparicio, F.J.Hermosillo, F.J.Pantoja, H.A.Covarrubias, H.H.Menchaca, H.Martinez, I.Gallegos, I.Moreno, J.Davila, J.L.Garcia, J.L.Martinez, J.L.Mireles, J.Mireles, L.E.Rangel, M.A.Rivas, M.A.Sanchez, O.C.Hernandez, R.Aguilera, R.Ramirez, V.M.Muñoz, E.Jansen, A.B.Wiskel, C.Cerminara, C.M.Brosmer, D.F.Nelson, D.M.White, G.W.Ashby Jr., J.B.McEwan, J.B.Morrison, J.R.Hurdis, K.J.Thornell, R.C.Garman, R.J.Douglas, R.L.Wilson, P.M.D.Rosa, R.A.Rost, R.Dietrich, L.G.Cazarin, B.Blandin, D.Demesmay, S.Girod, H.Gomes-Duarte-Alves, J.Simon, E.Vicariot, A.Kerbs, D.Elfner, E.Fuchs, E.Hasenfratz, E.Jekic, E.Klein, F.Kardes, F.Rohrbacher, F.Schenkel, F.Toth, G.Kormann, H.Hartmann, H.Schmidt, H.Schnetzer, J.Jochim, K.Ludwig, M.Arns, M.Beck, M.Fritz, M.Kandora, M.Sabon, P.Wilhelm, R.Preiss, R.Roehm, S.Helmeck, S.Zimmermann, T.Lenz, W.Goebel, R.Judith, J.J.Du Toit, S.A.Lacroix, A.Kulpinski, R.B.Nielsen, A.S.Lucas, C.A.Kirschbaum, C.W.Schmidt, D.L.Abbas, D.L.Dewitt, D.M.Dolin, D.M.Tuller, D.W.Martin II, E.M.Johnson, G.E.Baxter, J.S.Mysak, M.L.Dolan, P.D.Vyncke, R.D.Dabney, R.J.Devine, R.J.Petty, R.L.Hubbartt Jr., T.D.Wynn, T.G.Miller, R.M.Kelly, R.D.Francescatto, R.F.Mulder, A.Penner, D.Kubis, G.Fink, M.Schickendantz, R.Froehlich, S.Yavuz, T.Doerr, T.Moeller, T.Rudolph, W.Herbert, V.P.Schonarth, G.E.Dickerson, E.Buck, A.D.Grau, A.D.Youngberg, A.M.Mosley, B.J.Pearson, B.T.Becker, C.Gomez Jr., C.L.Wirth, D.J.Orme, D.L.Borrison, D.M.March, D.R.McLean, D.W.Trees, F.Knechel Jr., G.M.Miller Jr., G.R.Barefoot, G.R.Ely, J.A.Hagge, J.A.Smith Jr., J.E.Hillyer, J.L.Baker, L.J.Schwab, M.G.Kennedy, M.L.Shivers, R.D.Juhl, R.L.Howard-Wright, S.N.Rieber, T.B.Thorson, T.C.Wise, W.J.Haertjens, M.F.Wening, A.Fonseca, E.Sanchez, M.J.Cross, M.Mc Glinchey, A.Penner, F.Spataro, S.Becar, S.Paglino, W.Bitsch, B.W.Shelton, G.E.Vanderheyden, G.R.Nelson, G.T.Tome, J.W.Gowan, L.J.Charley, M.P.Nowels, C.B.Christensen, K.E.Sørensen, J.A.Palmer, J.D.Hepola, K.L.Udelhofen, L.K.Schnackel, L.Y.Cooke, M.J.Buchheit, M.J.White, M.L.McKellar, R.D.Pippin, S.F.Mellick, S.K.Blanton, H.C.Boyland, L.C.Zibart, J.C.Ponce, A.Gamez, A.Gonzalez, C.Morales, D.Ontiveros, E.M.Esquivel, E.Villarreal, G.Rojas, H.Rodriguez, J.A.Herrera, J.Anguiano, J.E.Arellano, J.Rubio, M.A.Ortiz, M.F.Hadad, M.Rodriguez, M.Villalobos, O.Argomaniz, O.G.Alonzo, C.Limberger, E.Anders, M.Duendar, A.P.Brent, C.A.Hanson, M.S.Swift, C.J.Zamin, E.Rinsche, I.Shehata, A.C.Hetzel, A.C.Wright, A.G.Duhaime, B.E.Wood, B.K.Dobbratz, B.L.Chestnut, B.T.Werner, C.B.Price, C.E.Bonilla, C.H.Blundy, C.L.Cooley, C.M.Ealy, C.M.Mixdorf, C.S.Zoellick, D.D.Weikert, D.K.Williams, D.R.Bransted, D.R.Froemming, D.S.McGee, E.M.Scott, G.A.Karnes, G.W.Sponable, H.A.Smit, H.L.Reeves, J.A.Pitzlin, J.E.Lang, J.F.Hardin, J.J.Weber, J.L.Schmidt, J.L.Swenson, J.Sanchez, K.L.Kinkead, K.M.Teletzke, L.Green, L.L.Zeidler, L.S.Lloyd, M.A.Dickson, M.A.Steger, M.E.Powell, M.L.Adkins, M.T.Grafton, M.Wolthuis, N.M.Schlagel, P.D.Fuller, R.A.Gorman, R.S.Jurek, S.B.Kopp, S.R.Lepple, S.W.Schmidt, T.J.Collins, T.L.Thomas, W.D.Byrne, E.L.Lewis, J.K.Platt, C.D.S.Pinto, R.A.Cabral, J.R.Salazar, J.U.Trejo, L.Klamm, H.Herz, C.N.Fisher, D.C.Kuykendall, J.A.Walling, L.C.Blue, M.A.Egger, M.E.Havey, R.L.Davis, S.L.Tucker-Stanbro, S.P.Peters, C.Brindley, C.A.Maclean, C.M.Puryk, I.A.Lang, J.J.Peterson, J.K.Chahal, K.F.Knueppel, M.J.Treiber, M.Nalecz, R.A.Goris, T.D.Rice, D.A.Swanson, F.Lopez, K.L.Richard, K.R.Yarosh, C.Espanel, L.Perrin, A.Van Scoter, F.Pakura, F.Peseke, F.Santamaria-Barbero, H.Billik, H.Born, H.Rothe, H.Thornton, J.Prudlik, K.Pajonk, M.Schleier, N.Leimbach, O.Schmidt, S.Kolb, F.Morandi, B.A.Monday, B.K.Smith, C.J.Garrett, D.C.Harberts, D.G.McCabe, D.M.O'Brien, J.R.Mills, K.L.Oleszkiewicz, M.M.Voss, M.S.Schillinger, P.C.Dougherty, P.S.Wallace, R.G.Fawson, R.G.Oneill, R.L.Wilmoth, R.M.Etnier, R.T.Rosario, S.A.Kilmer, T.D.Jordan, D.J.Magill, I.Govaski, M.T.Veber, J.M.Vazquez, L.M.Nava, B.Chavetnoir, Y.Magnaguagno, A.Gorecki, A.Janitzki, B.Cetin, F.Rushiti, G.Kilic, I.Hofmann, J.Toledo-Delgado, M.Boffo, M.Yapici, P.Kroeneck, P.Seim, R.Huether, W.Borzucki, W.Rudzki, W.Weinbender, J.M.Dean, C.L.Vanham, P.J.Stanley, L.M.Wilson, M.S.Johnson, T.R.Herzog, G.Jaquez, A.A.Hopkins, A.J.Delisi, A.J.Taszreak, C.F.McCullen, C.J.Spore, D.A.Plathe, D.J.McWilliams, D.L.Miller, D.M.Betcher, F.L.Hunt, H.Zhang-Freking, J.D.Peters, J.L.Oelke, J.M.Chesterman, J.M.Edgin, J.M.Norman, J.S.Krosch, J.W.Caldwell, K.K.Montgomery, M.J.Theis, M.M.King, M.N.Schallhorn, P.J.Begyn, R.E.Frerichs, R.J.Peters, R.L.Fixen Jr., S.Aljabari, S.D.Williamson, T.R.Schueller, T.W.Christensen, T.W.Tillery, V.K.Lem, C.M.Davis, T.S.C.Goncalves, R.McCall, A.Muñiz, G.A.Benavides, J.Aguirre, J.G.Berlanga, L.Alvarez, M.I.Cortinas, O.Sanchez, P.Contault, A.Schaefer, S.Bluemmel, J.L.Woolley, C.Eulenberger, S.Pop, V.Muljanow, A.J.Anderson, C.R.Schluter, L.E.McKeever, M.J.Ackerman, M.J.O'Brien, P.C.Gratton, R.D.Bruflat, R.J.O'Flanagan, T.C.Pool, G.Hernandez, B.Lutolli, M.Kremer, M.Tuku, J.A.Flick, M.R.Lastrapes, R.D.Lynch, A.A.Elsawy, A.J.Steenblock, A.M.Beardsley, A.S.Watts, B.A.Thomsen, B.R.Mahalko, B.W.Van Zante, C.A.Lindquist, C.J.Baughman, C.M.Leis, C.M.Tannahill, D.J.Blint, D.M.Detloff, D.R.Jacobs, E.B.Page, E.M.Fontenoy, G.R.Machetta, G.W.Johnson, H.L.Bernhardt, H.L.Snyder, J.A.Dyson, J.D.Esche, J.E.Cushing Jr., J.K.Alexander, J.K.Hendrix, J.K.Humphreys, J.L.Bruhn, J.M.Galloway, J.M.Westerman, J.M.Whedbee, J.M.York, J.R.Moeller, K.H.Burns, K.J.Lindsay, K.J.Schmitz, K.L.Veasman, L.A.McNaught, L.A.Snider, L.L.Carrell, L.Washington III, M.J.Marriott, M.J.Martin, M.L.Gleason, M.M.Anderson, M.Saskowski, N.J.Taiber, P.J.Michels, R.A.Sommer, R.D.Mathus, R.E.Armbrister, R.K.Johnson, S.A.Seavert, S.A.Wolf, S.D.Jurgemeyer, S.G.Blohowiak, S.M.Kruse, S.M.Zumdahl, S.T.Maher, T.B.Wilson, T.H.Daniels, T.L.Cherrier, V.D.Ngo, V.P.Khare, V.Rengasamy, D.J.Burghardt, E.A.Kohls, V.Schurer, L.M.Luna, J.Kapp, A.Herwig, B.D.Lees, J.A.Allen, J.P.Bradley, P.N.Davis, R.J.Rodeffer, A.D.Kimball, C.Cash, D.K.Di Santo, S.J.Roberts, Z.I.Knutson, M.B.Crowley, M.K.Nguyen, A.M.Leal, J.Hennig, P.Wong, H.Richter, O.Ayaztepe, F.Lopez B., A.J.Berret, A.J.McCallister, B.J.Pelisek, B.K.Marovets, C.D.Cosby, C.J.Hanna, C.R.Demeester, D.G.Surridge, D.I.Feig, D.L.Miller, E.J.Stachowski, G.F.Sierens, H.L.Bell, H.M.Arthofer, J.C.Freeman, J.J.Young, K.D.Ehlers, L.F.Rudolph, M.C.Wikstrom, M.J.Arino, M.T.Bergfeld, N.J.Zietlow, P.D.Diemer, R.E.Osborn, R.J.Tornquist, R.L.Hudachek, R.L.Salvador, S.I.Drissel, T.A.Davis, T.J.Livingstone, T.M.Charlson, W.Cole IV, L.Dupre La Tour, K.A.Normoyle, M.J.Helmich, R.W.Burjes, C.W.Chong, S.M.Braemer, A.L.Baldwin, C.A.Bubla, C.A.Coble, D.J.Wilhelm, E.A.Hill, J.A.Brown, J.M.Smith, M.L.Duffin, R.W.Rose, S.P.Kipp, R.Andersen, A.D.Hill, A.J.Manternach, A.L.Galvan, B.A.Bowlyou, B.G.Cash, B.K.Haddock, B.S.Wohlgemuth, B.Segebart, B.T.Lightner, B.W.Dohrmann, C.A.Tipton, C.D.Dietrich-Miller, C.D.Turner, C.K.Brown, C.S.Hayes, D.C.Johnson, D.J.O Keeffe, D.M.Manternach, D.W.Stockel, E.F.Wright, E.L.Callahan, H.A.Cooley, J.A.Morgan, J.D.Haecker, J.H.Degabriele, J.L.Doyle, J.L.Pfohl, J.M.Elkins, J.Swain, J.W.Beneke, J.W.Harris, K.D.Oard, K.L.Ewing, K.L.Horn, L.A.Franklin, L.R.Rients, M.A.Arends, M.A.Neil, M.A.Saffold, M.A.Schenk, M.C.Hurst,

Langar, England, employees commemorating new training center, 1998

M.D.Theuerkauf, M.S.Grau, N.E.Duquette, P.F.Stern, R.A.Myers, R.J.Blodig, R.M.Bares, R.R.Goeders, R.W.Schildroth, S.A.Lesh, S.C.Thomas, S.E.Stover, S.J.Dasso, S.M.Wyatt, S.O.Roy, T.A.Ricchio, T.L.Reiman, T.M.Nelson, V.L.Saxton, V.S.Arumugam, W.A.Beams, W.C.Christensen, W.D.Echols, Y.Alemu, Y.Xu, J.H.Cabral, B.Cross, A.E.Bonmann, A.Johann, A.Wachtmann, C.C.Pearson, C.D.Gross, C.E.Lukarsewski, C.I.Krauspenhar, D.L.Kowalski, E.C.Fagundes, G.Fagundes, J.W.Hansen, L.A.Goelzer, L.R.Franken, M.A.Schmitt, M.A.Schwingel, M.Correa, M.D.Fritsch, M.Levandovski, N.Backes, O.J.Smaniotto, S.M.Schuh, S.Stumpf, T.H.Stein, A.B.Mizuta, C.O.Newlands, M.J.Kerber, A.Castillo, F.Tamez, H.Berlanga, L.R.Paez, C.Valdez, G.Rosas, K.Hernandez, M.A.Vargas, L.T.Vergeldt, A.Bernhard, E.Ries, G.Dietrich, H.Kocer, H.Kremer, H.Roloff, J.Heldt, J.Zuell, L.Benoit, M.Wegerle, N.Nicklis, U.Beicht, Y.Fidan, D.L.Slaikeu, J.C.Garner, J.R.Williams, L.A.Holdorf, D.Dole, C.Yerli, D.Maksimovic, I.Hillenbrand, J.Musiol, M.Savic, M.Schaefer, E.J.Miller, J.K.Swiencki, S.C.Davison, C.J.Nelsen, J.Renner, A.L.Wagner, B.S.Knepper, C.A.Trapkus, C.D.Leja, C.E.Taylor IV, C.L.Hosfield, D.A.Covert, D.A.Scott, D.M.Johnson, E.B.Hillary, H.J.Ennis Jr., J.E.Lynch, J.E.Preszler, J.J.Ruplinger, J.K.Chui, J.M.Strief, J.R.Kreiling, K.K.Svendsen, L.P.Hushak, M.J.Dammeier, M.R.Oliver, P.J.Mayer, P.R.Pearson, R.C.Rump, S.D.Lodico, S.M.Wilhelmi, T.A.Davis, T.A.Reynolds, V.M.White, M.Mu, A.Kungel, A.Scheibel, A.Schlindwein, J.Hoffart, M.Supper, M.J.Gonzales, E.M.Peterson, M.Valdez, A.L.Carr, A.R.Abbring, A.S.Guttmann, B.K.Lynch, B.P.Tabor, C.J.Koglin, C.J.Reed, C.M.Jones, D.L.Asheim, D.M.Patten, D.M.Sims, E.L.Butler, G.S.Fetner, J.B.Maclay, J.D.Rodriguez, J.D.Schuette, J.H.Whitman, J.Hosty, J.L.McKoy, K.B.Bell, L.C.Trier, L.D.Jones, L.E.Hart, L.Withner, M.A.Smith, M.L.Hernandez, M.W.Gwin, P.L.Geswein, R.A.Horton, R.E.Robinson, R.L.Dukes, R.M.Petrosino, R.O.Young, R.R.McCabe, S.D.Harmon, S.E.Brinkley, S.J.McComb, S.L.Snyder, S.Lynn, S.W.Addison, K.Foran, D.Vazquez, J.Noriega, E.Espanel, A.Oberle, D.Schroeder, J.Gilles, M.Hadji, M.Herguedas Werner, R.Keyzer, A.C.Moelker, B.N.Wesselink, A.P.De Rusha, B.J.Kurt, C.A.Cauthen, D.J.Hutton, D.S.Becker, J.D.Webber, B.Chanthavong, H.Seber, S.Fell, W.Catsimpas, R.G.Moore, V.R.Anderson, W.A.Clevenger, A.E.Guimaraes, A.Koehler, A.L.Binsfeld, A.L.Schuh, A.Schmitt, C.L.Keller, C.R.Felten, C.R.Pinheiro, C.V.Bornholdt, E.L.Dehgen, M.A.Bamberg, M.Keller, P.C.L.Pavan, P.J.Tilvitz, R.A.Gerhardt, S.Minuzi, V.D.Barella, H.Aydin, A.C.Espiritu, A.D.Tillman, A.J.Forero, A.L.Green, B.C.Roesti, B.E.Farris, B.K.Kellogg, B.L.Mann, B.L.Van Dyne, C.M.Cook, D.A.Bebber, D.A.Kabele, D.A.Truman, D.D.Lively, D.E.Jackson, D.G.Gregory, D.Gardner, D.P.Macdonald, E.L.Eisele, G.L.Mueller, H.L.Ciha, J.D.Thur, J.D.Tilden, J.K.Miller, L.L.Beeler, L.N.Strong, M.D.Moran, M.H.Hadwin, M.L.Cousins, N.J.Baxter, P.J.Hines, R.B.Whited, R.E.Alexander, R.E.Banks, R.L.Lawson, R.S.Pattillo, S.B.Waldroup, T.L.Garrett, T.L.Hennings, T.L.Johnson, V.L.Howard, W.E.McBride, E.Weber, R.Alcorta, W.Rheinfels, C.M.Racht, S.J.McLaughlin, S.Pastor, J.R.Stegner, B.Girola, J.Wang, M.B.Moreno M., A.A.Anderson, C.B.Jackson, C.L.Tart, D.E.Meyer, D.S.Kuehn, G.L.Breuer, H.S.Smeaton, J.D.Pope Sr., J.E.Meyer, J.M.Bethea, J.P.Chenevert, K.L.Neibergall, L.L.Carney, L.M.Mendoza, L.S.Fay, M.G.Housel, M.L.Meyer, M.L.Mills, M.M.Geyer, M.P.Hanna, M.R.Perry, N.J.Chupka, N.L.Souza, P.W.Doyle, R.S.Smith, S.D.Reinart, D.Rodriguez, A.Murillo, B.Diaz, F.Acosta, H.A.Mesta, H.Villalba, J.R.Valdez, L.A.Rodriguez, L.Sanchez, M.A.Verdal, O.Del Toro, O.Tabares, R.A.Mendoza, R.Garcia, S.Favela, V.Rios, D.Karibo, J.C.Van Fossen, K.P.Tew, N.S.Elkhatib, R.S.Eck, T.J.Carrey, B.J.Gilmore, E.M.Grobarcik, J.A.Francque, J.J.Heldt, M.M.August, R.J.Dieckman, S.Fronczek, V.R.Dumoulin, B.G.Payró, D.J.Bucci, M.D.A.Canabarro, J.Oviedo, L.E.Nohemi, L.P.Huerta, R.Alonzo, S.R.Thelen, J.André, E.Catto, A.Braun, A.Klingshirn, A.Mueller, B.Klein, D.Kauer, F.Keil, G.Gross, G.Plomer, H.Burger, H.Kluetzing, H.Nieschulze, H.Schmitt, H.Sen, I.Baklan, J.Couade, J.Klassen, M.Mastranestis, N.Marks, O.Lutz, P.Michel, R.Akcoep, R.Fester, R.Heimlich, R.Loch, S.Kljajic, U.Buss, U.Gueven, W.May, W.Paprotny, G.Bosch, M.Borchmann, L.Geisen, I.Gradillas, A.J.Lange, A.M.Holt, A.R.Barnes, B.A.Karaus, B.M.Baldwin, B.R.Cochran, C.D.Lewis, C.E.Rios-Meyer, C.J.Coleman Jr., C.J.Muino, C.Verheij, D.B.Leslie, D.D.Dinnon, D.J.Jarchow, D.L.Bard, D.L.Richardson, D.R.Klein, E.C.Chambers, H.M.Schenkelberg, J.G.Thibault, J.J.Smith, J.M.Gilbert, J.R.Gibbons, J.S.Difederico, K.H.Smith, K.N.Beauman, M.B.Downey, M.D.Witwer, M.E.Robinson, M.M.Boddorf, M.P.Tubb, R.D.Roberts, R.J.Leslie, R.W.Mays, S.A.Gulley, S.L.Lloyd, T.L.Duke, P.W.Welsh, A.J.Schreiber, A.K.Lanza, A.Schubert, C.C.Kappaun, C.Cassol, E.P.D.Lima, F.J.H.Ferri, G.J.Sartor, I.L.Schaedler, J.A.Wendpap, J.L.Lehner, J.L.Ramos, J.M.L.Bade, A.Lucot, A.Schann, R.Gropp, V.Beifuss, C.D.Garrett, D.M.Demaray, D.O.Smith, T.D.Schatz, T.J.Cole, D.M.Ellis, J.D.Dixon, K.M.Entsminger, M.A.Bartee, A.Michel, B.C.Southworth, R.Hermida, A.M.Girard, B.E.Garretson, C.J.Adams, D.E.Isaac, D.G.Wisner, D.W.Sims, G.H.Schwab, J.Cowal, K.L.Merritt, M.A.Jenkins, M.A.Larue, M.E.Winkers, P.A.Bolduc, S.J.Lybeck, S.J.Schulze, S.L.Goody, A.J.Brown, E.Rodriguez, M.Pimentel, G.Turturiello, A.Ritter, I.Simeone, J.Bleiholder, T.Nagy, T.Nischwitz, V.Schulze, M.Mozo, A.G.Miller, M.A.Onderick, N.Cooke, C.Tareau, J.L.Beavers, J.L.Nichols, S.M.H.Verheijen, M.Fallon, H.Gomez, B.C.Allen, D.K.Ticku, D.M.Stephens, E.J.Rasgorshek, G.A.Fields, G.L.Formanek, G.L.Waters, H.R.Shadof, J.A.Kronlage, J.J.Humphreys, J.R.Scott, K.A.Whitted, K.Uno, M.E.Freeman, M.G.Farrell, M.R.Keaton, P.N.Peiffer, R.A.Atkins, S.D.Garrison, S.J.Murray, S.R.Fox, T.L.Johnson, T.M.Bodoh, T.M.Greene, F.Madden, A.D.D.Araujo, C.Baungarten, C.Dalcin, C.M.D.Porciuncula, C.R.Wengrat, E.D.Kirchhof, F.B.Barz, J.D.S.Guioti, M.Zvoboter, N.J.Kohler, V.Dallagnese, P.A.Perea, C.Ruiz, A.Knoll, E.Boettcher, E.Tulic, F.Wayss, R.Weinhold, C.A.Dow, A.A.Deangelis, A.L.Hamlyn, D.A.Balcom, D.E.Wuenne, E.C.Von Gries, E.R.Maine, J.A.Zarczynski, J.D.Burnham, J.H.Millard Jr., J.L.McMullen, J.M.Capaul, J.M.Kearney-Wheeler, J.M.Lang, J.S.McGee, K.D.Gerein, K.H.Diehlmann, L.T.Pope Jr., M.D.Robinson, M.G.Rabe, M.J.Brown, M.L.Neevel, M.S.Jones, N.R.Thomas, P.F.Rabe, R.D.Morris, R.J.Stam, R.S.Lundgren, S.A.Hartwick, S.A.Nunneley, S.C.Heath, S.L.Sawyer, S.M.Lucero, S.P.Stafford, S.P.Tyndall, T.A.Beers, T.L.Bennett, T.L.Smith, A.H.Ruiz, C.R.Villasana, E.M.Cervantes, E.Valadez, H.Martinez, I.Reyna, J.L.Perez, J.M.Medrano, J.S.Rodriguez, L.E.Gonzalez, L.J.Alba, M.A.Rodriguez, M.Guardado, O.Castillo, R.Martinez, S.Arriaga, V.Moreno, T.N.Togias, R.Rojas, B.D.Brown, B.K.Duggins, C.H.Armstrong Jr., D.S.Cline, G.A.Weber, J.C.Maxwell, J.C.Monger, J.H.Crisp, J.S.Mason, J.W.Lee, K.G.Tipton, R.A.Gladson, S.M.Powell, V.M.McDougald, B.L.Burns, B.R.Koesters, C.Supra, D.M.Chrestman, D.M.Heathcoat, F.C.Pruitt, K.D.Desmet, K.D.Stovall, K.M.Timm, M.A.Perez De Tejada, M.S.Chu, O.P.Harshaw, R.S.Park, S.A.Simmering, S.D.Clair, T.J.Stewart, V.M.Johnson, A.J.Weber, J.D.Cothren, M.P.McGrew, F.Roger, A.Rembert, D.Price, D.Scheib, E.Hoffmann, F.Steib, G.Kelch, H.Boeke, H.Krohn, J.Eichhorn, J.Martin, J.Streckenbach, K.Trier, M.Frank, M.Guthmann, R.Calama Luis, R.Tudor, R.Wolss, T.Goerguelue, T.Vogel, W.Fleck, W.Huether, A.Voß, B.Busen, F.Rose, T.Seggewiß, N.Hube, M.Jung, T.Schmidt, D.M.Ingram, J.J.Kemmerer, J.M.Mahoney II, K.J.Harris, T.J.Bowker, T.L.Foster, N.G.Johnson, E.Schmitz, L.C.Wachholz, J.M.Moreno, J.Ibarra, A.Kinderknecht, C.Hauck, G.Stefanidis, N.Omlor, T.Cuda, W.W.Jones, B.M.Tolley, M.A.Berlanga, K.Lockart, W.A.Andersen, B.H.Brahm, C.A.Engelke, C.L.Schlichte, D.C.Queal, D.F.Olson, G.S.Zupancic, J.D.Hergenreter, J.K.Klein, J.M.Shallow, M.A.Brannum, M.A.Verbeke, N.M.Green, P.Esparza, R.J.Fontes Jr., S.J.Edwards, S.J.Sablan, T.A.Snell, T.E.Schutte, T.J.Meiners, T.J.Pals, T.J.Tielbur, W.J.Wilson, W.R.Henson II, Z.W.Yohannes, J.S.Hulm, V.Beltran, M.Leszczynski, R.Rauer, V.Spasojevic, A.G.Handbury, G.M.Volcko, J.P.Delaney, T.A.Bayles, E.F.Leza, I.Gonzalez, J.A.Lomas, J.A.Ramirez, J.C.Ramos, J.J.Lopez, M.A.Zamora, S.A.Luna, S.Reut, M.T.Portman, M.D.Mildner, J.Nielsen, A.B.Sulak, A.C.Dewar, A.F.Otts, A.J.Armstrong, A.L.Stahl, B.K.Pearman, C.A.Lohse, C.D.Jones, F.L.Andreassen, H.Foster, H.Yu, J.D.Kalyanapu, J.M.Bonner, J.T.Sutherlin, J.W.Kenyon, K.A.Bolte, M.C.Klossner, M.L.Desmond, M.L.Mourning, M.L.Olive, R.Romero Alvarez, R.W.Martin, S.J.Rogers, W.M.Stephany, W.P.Blakely Jr., R.Kerber, A.A.Perez, E.E.Reyes, E.G.Cardenas, E.Melendez, E.Mendez,

F.F.Aviles, G.A.Calvillo, G.Ramirez, H.Vazquez, J.A.Alba, J.A.Romero, J.Cepeda, J.E.Hernandez, J.M.Gamez, J.Martinez, J.Orozco, J.P.Rodriguez, J.P.Villarreal, L.F.Almaguer, M.A.Villela, M.Esquivel, R.A.Tello, R.Maldonado, S.Baena, S.Facundo, S.Ruiz, R.Castillo, P.Thil, M.Bitter, P.Leathem, N.K.Yarbrough, J.Rong, D.E.Gutierrez, A.L.Dall, B.G.Cobble, B.J.Bolton, B.J.Wedding, B.L.Modena, B.L.Sauceman, B.S.Stevens, C.E.Gregg, C.J.Starnes, C.Y.Barnette, D.W.Hopson, E.J.Dobson, E.J.Duckworth, G.K.Hill, H.N.Dobson, H.Sellers, J.B.Howlett, J.R.House, J.T.Bowman, L.A.Foshie, L.E.Gonce, L.H.Hux, L.S.Ramirez, M.Ball, M.N.Tolley, P.A.Monk, P.E.Johnson, P.L.Grooms, R.A.Martino, R.Early, R.H.Moore, R.R.Ward, T.A.Foshie, T.J.Asselin, W.E.Early, A.Didier, S.C.Pegg, A.D.Shobert, A.J.Gemrich, C.A.Dykes, C.B.Stephens, C.C.Boyd, C.M.Crahen, C.M.Gibson, D.R.Wahlert, E.E.Halfman, J.B.Flynn, K.R.McElmeel, M.L.Armstrong, M.W.Stender, P.M.McLintock, T.A.Stewart, T.D.Howard, W.D.Boozer, W.F.Vanderhoff, F.J.Marchetti, J.Briones, J.O.Gomez, O.G.Vazquez, R.J.Sanchez, R.R.Ruiseñor, S.Valdez, A.Cruz, C.A.Villa, E.Gonzalez, F.R.Rojas, H.H.Galindo, J.A.Castillo, J.Arriaga, J.Coronado, J.G.Gonzalez, M.A.Talamantes, N.I.Dominguez, O.Galindo, R.Santana, U.Sanchez, Y.A.Lara, D.L.Tozier, E.A.Boog, M.D.Talbott, R.R.Rizzo, E.B.Fuentes, N.R.Cuevas, J.A.Mackey, B.D.Wehr, B.J.Reid, B.L.Witkowski, C.A.Amerling, C.D.Ayers, C.D.Lowman, C.L.Siefers, D.M.McMurrin, E.E.Entwistle, F.P.Lewis, G.T.Freadhoff, J.A.Van Der Lee, J.D.Harrington, J.E.Luckenbihl, J.M.Beals, J.P.Olson, J.R.Fullmer, J.T.Quiggle, J.W.Sheptenko, K.G.Nordkap, K.P.Kusznir, L.A.Shafer, L.D.Cade, M.A.Duncan, M.K.Hawkins, M.O.Miller, M.P.Becker, M.W.Cumings, P.A.Madden, R.F.Williams, R.F.Young, S.P.Dobrot, T.B.Niemann, T.L.Harriettha Jr., T.L.Polfliet, W.B.Lambeth, M.B.Hansen, A.C.Loyd, A.C.Morrison, B.A.Penn, D.L.Roberts, D.S.Moline, J.L.Dickson, K.B.Backmeyer, M.Gheissari, V.L.Bulkley, A.L.Boggino, C.I.Sansone, R.D.O.S.Bertrand, J.H.da Silva, A.L.Valdes, L.Garcia, G.Santibañez, M.G.Fierro, G.H.J.Cremers, L.Barrot, A.Julien, J.Claus, X.Poulain, A.Cezik, A.Ghiani, A.Gross, A.Hoffmann, A.Radke, B.Rohrbacher, B.Weis, E.Bussek, E.Rippberger, G.Mikosch, G.Reinig, H.Beckenbach, H.Stauner, J.Klein, J.Seebode, M.Billhardt, M.Diaz, M.Fornaci, M.Gebhard, M.Hoeh, M.Rabung, M.Rottlaender, M.Stock, N.Drach, N.Ettgen, P.Weiss, R.Gruenke, R.Marschalk, S.Jaeger, S.Ratsch, S.Zimmermann, T.Bausch, T.Breyer, W.Kokott, W.Michel, S.Gonzalez C., J.Smith, A.R.Hundley, B.M.Haberer, D.M.Werkmeister, J.L.Gomez, J.J.Mota, J.Padilla, B.Pfirrmann, B.Stricker, C.Benz, C.Knapp, C.Stuermer, D.Scheffner, D.Will, H.Braunert, M.Holler, M.Tolvig, M.Zimmermann, N.Bajramovic, O.Bilgic, P.Klingmann, P.Locke, S.Balogh, S.Bradneck, S.Gomolla, S.Heendorf, S.Klein, S.Vogel, T.Hans, T.Seitz, T.Weber, S.L.Clutterbuck, J.R.Paulsen, J.R.De Leon, L.Fuentes, L.P.Vazquez, C.Rubio, J.Gonzalez, M.Alvarado, U.Solis, A.Atienza , A.J.Steidl, B.W.Wilbanks, M.A.Muehlhausen, M.R.Jensen, P.K.Powers, R.Bourgault, S.P.Mueller, T.A.Chavis, T.P.Poff, A.F.Liska, C.E.Goelzer, F.R.D.Silva, P.R.Herbstrith, S.A.Tischler, J.A.Perez, R.Uros, B.J.Meeker, J.K.Rosenthal, A.L.Nelson, S.S.Gollin, A.Ellis, B.M.Russell, C.A.Beckwith, C.P.Mulkey, C.T.Knable, D.E.Vavricek, H.B.Cornelius, K.F.Beaulieu, L.L.Ferry, M.L.Warrelman, M.P.Shannon, N.Dakua, P.G.Daughtry, R.N.Vormelker, T.G.Ament, V.Pande, P.H.D.Silva, H.A.Galindo, J.L.Aguilar, M.Gallardo, J.Chassiboud, B.Pierrefiche, A.Kagan, M.Lorusso, M.W.Jahnke, R.G.Leone, S.Mata, L.C.Van Leeuwen, G.Strik, E.J.Beauregard, J.B.Dahlstrom, S.J.Hartley, W.H.Jacobs, L.R.Duret, R.J.Bacola, A.D.Rodriguez, B.A.Colville, C.J.Isle, C.S.Fenton, D.A.Kolodziej, J.F.Degele, J.S.Deloose, K.J.King, M.S.Bascom, T.G.Chancey, T.K.McGrath, A.B.Ferreira, D.J.Wilke, G.Pistore, J.G.Tesche, V.B.Silva, V.Hamm, R.Treviño, J.M.Perez, I.L.Collins, S.A.Klein, E.A.Ramirez, G.Cervantes, J.C.Azpilcueta, J.C.Saucedo, J.G.Hernandez, J.L.Santellano, R.Avalos, A.Salazar, A.C.Traeger, A.L.Miller, B.A.Morrissey, C.G.Myers, D.J.Klas, D.M.Walton, E.B.Houser, F.M.Blake, J.M.Shively, L.R.Seals, M.B.Palmer, M.J.Petersen, M.P.Erwin, P.E.Moore, R.C.Tew, R.D.Lavelle, S.F.Zubak, T.A.Rippe, T.J.Francis, Y.D.Morgan, A.G.Olmos, A.G.Ortega, I.Varela, J.F.Hernandez, M.Hernandez, R.Sierra, D.R.Bouder, J.G.Thomason, P.A.Johnson, T.T.Dolan, A.A.Aucoin, A.A.Clement, A.B.Lorio, A.B.Strausser, A.Becnel, A.Breaux, A.C.Weaver, A.E.Oncale, A.E.Thibodaux, A.Goudeau, A.Hebert, A.J.Adams, A.J.Badeau Jr., A.J.Bourg, A.J.David, A.J.Fletcher, A.J.Folse, A.J.Ledet, A.L.Breaux, A.L.Oncale, A.L.Pennington Jr., A.M.Jupiter, A.M.Thibodeaux, A.P.Louque, A.Percle, A.R.Mays, A.Ricouard, A.Rose, A.S.Webre, A.Savoie, A.T.Medhus, B.A.Cancienne, B.A.Hebert, B.A.Roussel, B.B.Thibodeaux, B.Bourgeois, B.C.Aucoin, B.C.Naquin, B.Chiasson, B.Creech, B.E.Dugas, B.E.Percle, B.G.Leblanc, B.J.Bellanger, B.J.Benoit, B.J.Blanchard, B.J.Carrier, B.J.Carrier Jr., B.J.Chiasson, B.J.Daigle, B.J.Fields, B.J.Himel, B.J.Rodrigue, B.J.Thiac, B.L.Martinez, B.Naquin Sr., B.Nora, B.P.Adams, B.P.Hotard, B.P.Landry, B.P.Leblanc, B.P.Zeringue, B.Richard, B.Rodrigue, B.T.Chiasson, C.A.Bergeron, C.A.Boudreaux, C.A.Thibodaux, C.B.Clement, C.C.Chiasson, C.C.Ferreira, C.C.Spears, C.Castano, C.D.Jorgensen, C.D.Thomas, C.F.Larose, C.Frye Jr., C.G.Bourgeois, C.J.Babin, C.J.Burke, C.J.Cortez, C.J.Gauthier Jr., C.J.Lagarde Jr., C.J.Landry, C.J.Spears, C.K.Adams, C.K.Fruchey, C.Knobloch, C.L.Caballero Jr., C.L.Ordoyne, C.M.Arceneaux, C.M.Bourgeois, C.M.Chiasson, C.M.Daigle, C.M.Dansereau, C.M.Ordoyne, C.Miller, C.Morvant, C.N.Leonard Jr., C.Naquin Jr., C.P.Andras, C.P.Breaux, C.P.Clement, C.P.Fazzio, C.P.Lebouef, C.P.Morvant, C.P.Rodrigue, C.Richard, C.S.Green, C.S.Gros Jr., C.Verdin, D.A.Ledet Jr., D.A.Ordoyne, D.A.Torres, D.A.Zeringue, D.Alexander, D.Andras, D.B.Albares, D.Barthel, D.Bogen, D.Bolotte, D.Burke, D.C.Toups, D.Cavalier, D.Chadwick, D.E.Kellar, D.E.Lebouef, D.F.Guidry, D.G.Andras, D.G.McMillan, D.G.Roger, D.Gravois, D.Guillot, D.J.Acosta, D.J.Barrios Jr., D.J.Bonvillain Jr., D.J.Cancienne, D.J.Champagne, D.J.Corbett, D.J.Giroir, D.J.Guidry Jr., D.J.Knight, D.J.Lasseigne, D.J.Ledet, D.J.Pitre, D.J.Richard, D.J.Rome, D.J.Sciortino Jr., D.J.Tabor, D.L.Conrad Jr., D.L.Sanders, D.Lecompte, D.Ledet, D.M.Boudreaux, D.M.Gros, D.M.Molliere, D.M.Thibodaux, D.M.Trosclair, D.P.Ferreira, D.P.Kern, D.P.Martin, D.P.Morvant, D.P.Morvant Jr., D.P.Naquin, D.P.Pitre, D.P.Richard Jr., D.P.Rodrigue, D.P.Zeringue, D.Prejean, D.S.Allen, D.Sagona, D.T.Boudreaux, D.W.Giardina Jr., E.A.Clement, E.Alexander, E.C.Aysen, E.Glaxner, E.J.Bourgeois, E.J.Chiasson, E.J.Duet, E.J.Louviere Jr., E.J.Pogue, E.J.Simmons Jr., E.J.Trosclair Jr., E.L.Edwards, E.L.Redmon, E.L.Studer Jr., E.M.Filce, E.M.Torres, E.P.Thibodaux, E.R.Gaubert, E.Triggs, E.Velasco, F.A.Cortez, F.A.Hebert, F.A.Lebouef, F.B.Billizon, F.B.Pierce III, F.Benoit, F.H.Adams III, F.P.Kraemer, F.P.Lecompte, F.P.Oncale, F.Richard, F.W.Flanagan, G.A.Cheramie, G.A.Dronet, G.A.Folse, G.A.Jones, G.A.Thomassie Jr., G.Bilbo, G.Blanchard, G.Boudreaux, G.D.Wilson, G.E.Cullett, G.J.Breaux Jr., G.J.Landry, G.J.Morvant, G.J.Pertuit, G.J.Thibodaux Jr., G.L.Knight, G.M.Dufrene, G.M.Simoneaux, G.P.Clement, G.P.Trosclair, G.R.Lorio, G.R.Simmons, G.R.Simoneaux, G.T.Kraemer, G.W.Moore Jr., G.W.Webber Sr., H.A.Griggs, H.C.Molaison, H.D.Portier, H.F.Luwisch, H.H.Adams Jr., H.H.Lewis, H.J.Bourg, H.J.Cortez Jr., H.K.Nguyen, H.Lafont, H.T.Stein, I.A.Boudreaux, I.Gomez, I.J.Ordoyne, J.A.Boudreaux, J.A.Devillier, J.A.Giardina, J.A.Gros Jr., J.A.Himel, J.A.Klingman, J.A.Leray, J.A.Naquin, J.Allen, J.B.Dupre, J.B.Fabregas, J.C.Brown Jr., J.C.Chiasson, J.C.Graham, J.C.Richard Jr., J.Chiasson, J.D.Carlisle, J.E.Bogle, J.E.Gil, J.E.Melancon, J.E.Naquin, J.E.Plaisance, J.E.Sirois, J.E.Thibodaux, J.E.Yeates, J.F.Gravois, J.Freyou, J.G.Himel, J.G.Ledet, J.G.Tuleu, J.Granier, J.Gros, J.H.Boudreaux, J.H.Constant, J.H.Goodroe, J.Himel, J.J.Andras, J.J.Arceneaux III, J.J.Benoit, J.J.Bonvillain, J.J.Granier, J.J.Guidry, J.J.Knight, J.J.Ordoyne, J.J.Robichaux, J.J.Simoneaux, J.J.Thibodaux, J.J.Tregre, J.Joseph, J.K.Baugh Jr., J.Krieg, J.L.Bonvillain Jr., J.L.Cavalier, J.L.Jumonville, J.L.Legendre, J.L.Oldham, J.L.Riche, J.L.Roberts, J.M.Adams, J.M.Cedotal, J.M.Chiasson, J.M.Credeur, J.Naquin, J.P.Aizen, J.P.Benoit, J.P.Blanchard, J.P.Boudreaux, J.P.Breaux, J.P.Breaux Jr., J.P.Eschete, J.P.Folse, J.P.Krieg, J.P.Lasseigne, J.P.Lester, J.P.Pertuit, J.P.Richard, J.P.Rome, J.P.Scrivner, J.S.Danos, J.Sherman, J.T.Michel, J.Thibodaux, J.W.Davis III, K.A.Babin, K.A.Benoit, K.A.Guidry, K.A.Triggs, K.E.Aucoin, K.E.Babin, K.E.Johnson, K.Hamilton, K.J.Babin, K.J.Bonvillain, K.J.Cortez, K.J.Ledet, K.J.Morvant, K.J.Richard, K.J.Rodrigue, K.L.Jenkins, K.M.Ledet, K.M.Naquin, K.Mayeux, K.Naquin, K.P.Benoit, K.P.Fangue Jr., K.P.Ordoyne, K.P.Pitre, K.P.Ponvelle, K.R.Richard, K.Richard Jr., K.T.Barrilleaux, K.Thibodaux, K.Uzee, K.W.Bergeron, K.W.Dolen, L.A.Cavalier, L.A.Himel III, L.A.Himel IV, L.A.Triche, L.C.Ledet, L.C.Ponvelle, L.Chiasson, L.Duet, L.E.Rodriguez, L.Folse, L.I.Triche, L.J.Aucoin, L.J.Breaux, L.J.Gilmer, L.J.Landry, L.J.Traigle Jr., L.Kraemer, L.L.Landry, L.M.Jones, L.P.Andras, L.P.Himel, L.P.Ledet Jr., L.P.Lirette, L.P.Naquin, L.T.Williams, L.U.Danos, M.A.Amedee, M.A.Blanco, M.A.Boudreaux, M.A.Clifton, M.A.Lebrun, M.A.Matherne, M.A.Thibodeaux Jr., M.Andras, M.Benoit, M.C.Chiasson, M.C.Kellar, M.D.Davenport, M.Driest, M.E.Billizon, M.Ferreira Jr., M.G.Capps, M.Gauthreaux, M.George III, M.H.Lasseigne, M.Hymel, M.J.Benoit, M.J.Bergeron, M.J.Boudreaux, M.J.Cancienne, M.J.Conrad Jr., M.J.Labue, M.J.Ordoyne, M.J.Robertson, M.J.Robichaux III, M.J.Rodriguez, M.J.Zeringue, M.K.Weller, M.L.Dupre, M.L.Hinds, M.Landry, M.P.Arcement, M.P.Duplantis, M.P.Gaubert, M.P.Stripling,

Waterloo, Iowa, 9000 Series Tractor line, BPE team, 1999

M.S.Louviere, M.S.Walters, M.Thibodeaux Jr., M.W.Spears, N.A.Folse Jr., N.A.Thibodeaux, N.E.Folse, N.E.Hebert, N.Gros Jr., N.J.Foret Jr., N.J.Gros, N.J.Guillot, N.J.Peltier, N.K.Chiasson, N.M.Gravois, N.P.Boudreaux, O.J.Folse, O.P.Benoit, O.S.Norman, P.Benoit, P.Bourgeois, P.Daigle, P.E.Reed, P.F.Cortez, P.G.Adams, P.Gaudet, P.H.Hebert, P.I.Milazzo Jr., P.J.Chiasson, P.J.Daigle, P.J.Gros, P.J.Sylvest, P.Lagraize III, P.M.Falcon, P.P.Knight, P.P.Plaisance, R.A.Boudreaux, R.A.Boul Jr., R.A.Pitre, R.Acosta, R.Arabie, R.Aysen Jr., R.C.Molaison Jr., R.C.Thompson, R.Clement, R.H.Porche, R.Hebert, R.J.Babin, R.J.Billiot, R.J.Boudreaux, R.J.Bourgeois III, R.J.Chiasson, R.J.Cortez, R.J.David, R.J.Duet, R.J.Hebert, R.J.Lirette III, R.J.Ordoyne, R.J.Pate, R.J.Pitre, R.J.Riche, R.J.Robichaux, R.L.Breaux, R.L.Breaux Jr., R.L.Plasket Jr., R.L.Rumore, R.Lawson Jr., R.M.Leblanc, R.P.Chiasson, R.P.Ferreira, R.P.Folse, R.P.Gautreaux, R.P.Landry, R.P.Sanchez, R.P.Templet, R.P.Thibodeaux, R.P.Zeringue, R.S.Acosta, R.S.Rivault Jr., R.S.Weimer, R.T.Simon, R.Toups, R.Vedros Jr., S.A.Bourgeois, S.A.Guillot, S.A.Tabor, S.A.Thibodaux, S.A.Toups, S.Ferreira, S.G.Uzee, S.Hebert, S.J.Babin, S.J.Badeaux, S.J.Fields, S.J.Guidry, S.J.Hebert, S.J.Thibodeaux, S.J.Zenthoefer, S.K.Thomas, S.M.Andras, S.M.Clement, S.M.Gauthreaux, S.M.McDonough, S.M.Melancon, S.M.Pellegrin, S.M.Richard, S.M.Thibodaux Jr., S.N.Clause, S.Naquin, S.P.Boudreaux, S.P.Naquin Jr., S.P.Rodrigue, S.P.Sanders, S.Pitre, S.Robichaux, S.Rutter, S.S.Acosta, S.T.Bourgeois, S.T.Thibodeaux, T.A.Clement, T.A.Daigle, T.A.Pierce, T.Adams, T.Bergeron, T.G.Landry, T.H.Ordoyne, T.J.Boudreaux, T.J.Bourgeois, T.J.Breaux, T.J.Clement, T.J.Daigle, T.J.Dardar, T.J.Knight, T.J.Legendre, T.J.Morvant, T.J.Naquin, T.J.Reckert, T.J.Rodrigue, T.J.Savoie, T.J.Thibodeaux, T.J.Use, T.L.Choate, T.M.Adams, T.M.Braud, T.M.Gautreaux, T.M.Landry, T.N.Legendre, T.P.Adams, T.P.Boudreaux, T.P.Boudreaux Jr., T.P.Clement, T.P.Landry, T.P.Ledet, T.R.Thibodeaux, T.T.Callahan, T.T.Rodrigue, T.Thibodaux, T.W.Schifferns, T.W.Tamplain, V.J.Molaison Jr., W.Aucoin, W.Broomfield, W.E.Andras Jr., W.J.Cancienne, W.J.Chiasson, W.J.Duet, W.J.Himel, W.J.Kraemer, W.J.Landry, W.J.Larose, W.Melancon, W.P.Chiasson, W.P.Duet, W.P.Rodriguez, W.P.Thibodaux, W.R.Coleman, W.R.Lyles, W.Ridgway, W.Simoneaux, A.A.Aucoin, A.A.Clement, A.B.Lorio, A.B.Strausser, A.Becnel, A.Breaux, A.C.Weaver, A.E.Oncale, A.E.Thibodaux, A.Goudeau, A.Hebert, A.J.Adams, A.J.Badeau Jr, A.J.Bourg, A.J.David, A.J.Fletcher, A.J.Folse, A.J.Ledet, A.L.Breaux, A.L.Oncale, A.L.Pennington Jr, A.M.Jupiter, A.M.Thibodeaux, A.P.Louque, A.Percle, A.R.Mays, A.Ricouard, A.Rose, A.S.Webre, A.Savoie, B.A.Cancienne, B.A.Hebert, B.A.Roussel, B.B.Thibodeaux, B.Bourgeois, B.C.Aucoin, B.C.Naquin, B.Chiasson, B.Creech, B.E.Dugas, B.E.Percle, B.G.Leblanc, B.J.Bellanger, B.J.Benoit, B.J.Blanchard, B.J.Carrier, B.J.Carrier Jr, B.J.Chiasson, B.J.Daigle, B.J.Fields, B.J.Himel, B.J.Rodrigue, B.J.Thiac, B.L.Martinez, B.Naquin Jr, B.Nora, B.P.Adams, B.P.Hotard, B.P.Landry, B.P.Leblanc, B.P.Zeringue, B.Richard, B.Rodrigue, B.T.Chiasson, C.A.Bergeron, C.A.Boudreaux, C.A.Thibodaux, C.B.Clement, C.C.Chiasson, C.C.Ferreira, C.C.Spears, C.D.Jorgensen, C.D.Thomas, C.F.Larose, C.Frye Jr, C.G.Bourgeois, C.J.Babin, C.J.Burke, C.J.Cortez, C.J.Gauthier Jr, C.J.Lagarde Jr, C.J.Landry, C.J.Spears, C.K.Adams, C.K.Fruchey, C.Knobloch, C.L.Caballero Jr, C.L.Ordoyne, C.M.Arceneaux, C.M.Bourgeois, C.M.Chiasson, C.M.Daigle, C.M.Dansereau, C.M.Ordoyne, C.Miller, C.Morvant, C.N.Leonard Jr, C.Naquin Jr, C.P.Andras, C.P.Breaux, C.P.Clement, C.P.Fazzio, C.P.Lebouef, C.P.Morvant, C.P.Rodrigue, C.Richard, C.S.Green, C.S.Gros Jr, C.Verdin, D.A.Knight, D.A.Ledet Jr, D.A.Ordoyne, D.A.Torres, D.A.Zeringue, D.Alexander, D.Andras, D.B.Albares, D.Barthel, D.Bogen, D.Bolotte, D.Burke, D.C.Toups, D.Cavalier, D.Chadwick, D.E.Kellar, D.E.Lebouef, D.F.Guidry, D.G.Andras, D.G.Mcmillan, D.G.Roger, D.Gravois, D.Guillot, D.J.Acosta, D.J.Barrios Jr, D.J.Bonvillain Jr, D.J.Boudreaux, D.J.Cancienne, D.J.Champagne, D.J.Corbett, D.J.Giroir, D.J.Guidry Jr, D.J.Lasseigne, D.J.Ledet, D.J.Pitre, D.J.Richard, D.J.Rome, D.J.Sciortino Jr, D.J.Tabor, D.L.Conrad Jr, D.L.Sanders, D.Lecompte, D.Ledet, D.M.Gros, D.M.Molliere, D.M.Thibodaux, D.M.Trosclair, D.P.Ferreira, D.P.Kern, D.P.Martin, D.P.Morvant, D.P.Morvant Jr, D.P.Naquin, D.P.Pitre, D.P.Richard Jr, D.P.Rodrigue, D.P.Zeringue, D.Prejean, D.S.Allen, D.Sagona, D.T. Boudreaux, D.W.Giardina Jr, E. Alexander, E.A.Clement, E.C.Aysen, E.Glaxner, E.J.Bourgeois, E.J.Chiasson, E.J.Duet, E.J.Louviere Jr, E.J.Simmons Jr, E.J.Trosclair Jr, E.L.Edwards, E.L.Redmon, E.L.Studer Jr, E.M.Filce, E.M.Torres, E.P.Thibodaux, E.R.Diaz, E.R.Gaubert, E.Triggs, E.Velasco, F.A.Cortez, F.A.Hebert, F.A.Lebouef, F.B.Billizon, F.B.Pierce III, F.Benoit, F.H.Adams III, F.P.Kraemer, F.P.Lecompte, F.P.Oncale, F.Richard, F.W.Flanagan, G.A.Cheramie, G.A.Dronet, G.A.Folse, G.A.Jones, G.A.Thomassie Jr, G.B.Boudreaux, G.Bilbo, G.Blanchard, G.D.Wilson, G.E.Cullett, G.J.Breaux Jr, G.J.Landry, G.J.Morvant, G.J.Pertuit, G.J.Thibodaux Jr, G.L.Knight, G.M.Dufrene, G.M.Simoneaux, G.P.Clement, G.P.Trosclair, G.R.Lorio, G.R.Simmons, G.R.Simoneaux, G.T.Kraemer, G.W.Moore Jr, G.W.Webber Sr, H.A.Griggs, H.C.Molaison, H.D.Portier, H.F.Luwisch, H.H.Adams Jr, H.H.Lewis, H.J.Bourg, H.J.Cortez Jr, H.Lafont, H.T.Stein, I.A.Boudreaux, I.Gomez, I.J.Ordoyne, J.A.Boudreaux, J.A.Devillier, J.A.Giardina, J.A.Gros Jr, J.A.Himel, J.A.Klingman, J.A.Leray, J.Allen, J.B.Dupre, J.B.Fabregas, J.C.Brown Jr, J.C.Chiasson, J.C.Graham, J.C.Richard Jr, J.Chiasson, J.D.Carlisle, J.E.Bogle, J.E.Gil, J.E.Melancon, J.E.Naquin, J.E.Naquin Sr, J.E.Plaisance, J.E.Sirois, J.E.Thibodaux, J.E.Yeates, J.F.Gravois, J.Freyou, J.G.Ledet, J.G.Tuleu, J.Granier, J.Gros, J.H.Boudreaux, J.H.Constant, J.H.Goodroe, J.Himel, J.J.Andras, J.J.Arceneaux III, J.J.Benoit, J.J.Bonvillain, J.J.Granier, J.J.Guidry, J.J.Knight, J.J.Ordoyne, J.J.Robichaux, J.J.Simoneaux, J.J.Thibodaux, J.J.Tregre, J.Joseph, J.K.Baugh Jr, J.Krieg, J.L.Bonvillain Jr, J.L.Cavalier, J.L.Himel, J.L.Jumonville, J.L.Legendre, J.L.Oldham, J.L.Riche, J.L.Roberts, J.M.Adams, J.M.Cedotal, J.M.Chiasson, J.M.Credeur, J.Naquin, J.P.Aizen, J.P.Blanchard, J.P.Boudreaux, J.P.Breaux, J.P.Breaux Jr, J.P.Eschete, J.P.Folse, J.P.Krieg, J.P.Landry, J.P.Lasseigne, J.P.Lester, J.P.Pertuit, J.P.Richard, J.P.Rome, J.P.Scrivner, J.S.Danos, J.Sherman, J.T.Michel, J.Thibodaux, J.W.Davis III, K. Mayeux, K.A.Babin, K.A.Benoit, K.A.Guidry, K.A.Triggs, K.D.Bergeron, K.E.Aucoin, K.E.Babin, K.E.Johnson, K.Hamilton, K.J.Babin, K.J.Bonvillain, K.J.Cortez, K.J.Ledet, K.J.Morvant, K.J.Pitre, K.J.Richard, K.J.Rodrigue, K.L.Jenkins, K.M.Ledet, K.M.Naquin, K.Naquin, K.P.Benoit, K.P.Fangue Jr, K.P.Ordoyne, K.P.Pitre, K.P.Ponvelle, K.P.Uzee, K.R.Richard, K.Richard Jr., K.T.Barrilleaux, K.Thibodaux, K.W.Dolen, L.A.Cavalier, L.A.Himel III, L.A.Himel IV, L.A.Triche, L.C.Ledet, L.C.Ponvelle, L.Duet, L.E.Rodriguez, L.Folse, L.I.Triche, L.J.Aucoin, L.J.Breaux, L.J.Gilmer, L.J.Landry, L.J.Traigle Jr, L.Kraemer, L.L.Landry, L.P.Andras, L.P.Chiasson, L.P.Himel, L.P.Ledet Jr., L.P.Lirette, L.P.Naquin, L.T.Williams, L.U.Danos, M.A.Amedee, M.A.Blanco, M.A.Boudreaux, M.A.Clifton, M.A.Lebrun, M.A.Matherne, M.A.Thibodeaux Jr, M.Andras, M.Benoit, M.C.Chiasson, M.C.Kellar, M.D.Davenport, M.Driest, M.E.Billizon, M.Ferreira Jr, M.G.Capps, M.Gauthreaux, M.George III, M.H.Lasseigne, M.Hymel, M.J.Benoit, M.J.Bergeron, M.J.Boudreaux, M.J.Cancienne, M.J.Conrad Jr, M.J.Labue, M.J.Robertson, M.J.Robichaux III, M.J.Rodriguez, M.J.Zeringue, M.K.Weller, M.L.Dupre, M.L.Hinds, M.Landry, M.M.Ordoyne, M.P.Arcement, M.P.Duplantis, M.P.Gaubert, M.P.Stripling, M.S.Louviere, M.S.Walters, M.Thibodeaux Jr, M.W.Spears, N.A.Folse Jr, N.A.Thibodeaux, N.E.Folse, N.E.Hebert, N.Gros Jr, N.J.Foret Jr, N.J.Gros, N.J.Guillot, N.J.Peltier, N.K.Chiasson, N.M.Boudreaux, N.M.Gravois, O.J.Folse, O.P.Benoit, O.S.Norman, P.Benoit, P.Bourgeois, P.Daigle, P.E.Reed, P.F.Cortez, P.G.Adams, P.Gaudet, P.H.Hebert, P.I.Milazzo Jr, P.J.Chiasson, P.J.Daigle, P.J.Gros, P.J.Sylvest, P.Lagraize III, P.M.Falcon, P.P.Knight, P.P.Plaisance, R.A.Boudreaux, R.A.Boul Jr, R.A.Pitre, R.Acosta, R.Arabie, R.Aysen Jr, R.C.Molaison Jr, R.C.Thompson, R.Clement, R.H.Porche, R.Hebert, R.J.Babin, R.J.Billiot, R.J.Boudreaux, R.J.Bourgeois III, R.J.Chiasson, R.J.Cortez, R.J.David, R.J.Duet, R.J.Hebert, R.J.Lirette III, R.J.Ordoyne, R.J.Pate, R.J.Pitre, R.J.Riche, R.J.Robichaux, R.L.Breaux, R.L.Breaux Jr, R.L.Rumore, R.Lawson Jr, R.M.Leblanc, R.P.Chiasson, R.P.Ferreira, R.P.Folse, R.P.Gautreaux, R.P.Landry, R.P.Sanchez, R.P.Templet, R.P.Thibodeaux, R.P.Zeringue, R.S.Acosta, R.S.Rivault Jr, R.S.Weimer, R.T.Simon, R.Toups, R.Vedros Jr, S.A.Bourgeois, S.A.Guillot, S.A.Tabor, S.A.Thibodaux, S.A.Toups, S.C.Willett, S.Ferreira, S.G.Uzee, S.Hebert, S.J.Babin, S.J.Badeaux, S.J.Fields, S.J.Guidry, S.J.Hebert, S.J.Thibodeaux, S.J.Zenthoefer, S.K.Thomas, S.M.Andras, S.M.Clement, S.M.Gauthreaux, S.M.Mcdonough, S.M.Melancon, S.M.Pellegrin, S.M.Richard, S.M.Thibodaux Jr, S.N.Clause, S.N.Naquin, S.Naquin, S.P.Boudreaux, S.P.Naquin Jr, S.P.Rodrigue, S.P.Sanders, S.Pitre, S.R.Rutter, S.Robichaux, S.S.Acosta, S.T.Bourgeois, S.T.Thibodeaux, T.A.Adams, T.A.Clement, T.A.Daigle, T.A.Herrington, T.A.Pierce, T.Adams, T.Bergeron, T.G.Landry, T.H.Ordoyne, T.J.Boudreaux, T.J.Bourgeois, T.J.Breaux, T.J.Clement, T.J.Daigle, T.J.Dardar, T.J.Knight, T.J.Legendre, T.J.Morvant, T.J.Naquin, T.J.Reckert, T.J.Rodrigue, T.J.Savoie, T.J.Thibodeaux, T.J.Use, T.L.Choate, T.M.Adams, T.M.Braud, T.M.Gautreaux, T.M.Landry, T.M.Rodrigue, T.N.Legendre, T.P.Boudreaux, T.P.Boudreaux Jr, T.P.Clement, T.P.Landry, T.P.Ledet, T.R.Thibodeaux, T.T.Callahan, T.Thibodaux, T.W.Schifferns, T.W.Tamplain, V.J.Molaison Jr, W.Aucoin, W.Broomfield, W.E.Andras Jr, W.J.Cancienne, W.J.Chiasson, W.J.Duet, W.J.Himel, W.J.Kraemer, W.J.Landry, W.J.Larose, W.Melancon, W.P.Chiasson, W.P.Duet, W.P.Rodriguez, W.P.Thibodaux, W.R.Coleman, W.R.Lyles, W.Ridgway, W.Simoneaux, C.Albrechtsen, J.A.Søndergaard, B.K.Woodburn, D.A.Groff, D.D.Piro, J.K.Albers, J.L.Andes, K.L.Fields, T.J.Harvey, A.G.Ciambotti, A.M.Colaneri, A.Hunsicker, C.Linke, C.Schroeder, C.Stuecker, C.Unser, D.Dietrich, D.Kuna, D.Moos, D.Zelkjovic, E.Vogelbacher, F.Vazquez-Cervelo, G.Ackermann, H.Hajrulahi, H.Schwab, I.Duran, I.Mulasmajic, J.Cordero-Fernandez, M.Kovanci, M.Puettmann, M.Sardatzki, M.Schuster, M.Walzer, P.Degen, P.Seboek, R.Wolf, S.Graef, T.Haag, T.Schaefer, W.Flohr, W.Schneider, W.Stellberger, M.Lang, E.F.Stephenson, D.Alscher, A.A.Knopp, A.D.Dent, A.L.Koss, A.L.Stinemates, A.M.Kitchen, A.M.Lookman, A.M.Wirtz, A.W.Hoekstra, B.C.Butler, B.F.Skyles, B.J.Bradley, B.J.Howland, B.L.Cunningham, B.L.Rake, B.M.Schepp, B.P.Coffey, B.S.Arndt, B.S.Harter, B.W.Clemens, B.W.Hampton, C.A.Gloede, C.A.McCann, C.A.McDonald, C.D.Bramhall, C.J.Plasky, C.J.White, C.L.Grimm, C.L.Reifsnider, C.M.Adelmeyer, C.M.Paul, C.M.Zielinski, C.Tanner, D.A.Dionysius II, D.A.Mueller, D.B.Bogus, D.D.Adelmeyer, D.E.Fredenburg, D.J.Champeau, D.J.Poetter, D.J.Stippich, D.J.Trejo, D.L.Clevenger, D.L.Koss, D.L.Kruse, D.L.Yundt, D.Puente, D.S.Kranz, D.S.Yerian, D.V.Lopez, D.W.Peters, E.A.Loth, E.K.Krettler, E.L.Yerian, E.M.Augustyn, E.M.Hudson, E.M.Reinwald, F.J.Chenevare, G.D.Ladwig, G.D.Wianecki, G.H.Gensch, G.Loving, G.M.Lucero, J.A.Erbacher, J.A.Graff, J.A.Knasinski, J.A.Steinhoff, J.C.Spangler, J.D.Wittchow, J.E.Garcia, J.G.Burgart, J.G.Bushaw, J.J.Morse, J.J.Sabish, J.J.Vinz, J.L.Lemke, J.L.Sellnow, J.M.Aguilera, J.M.Clemens, J.M.Ertel, J.M.Neuman, J.N.Helbing, J.P.Monaghan, J.R.Sydney, J.R.Weissmann, J.R.White, J.S.Bittner, J.W.Connell Jr., J.W.Schaad, K.A.Grabowski, K.C.Lenhardt, K.D.Friday, K.J.Clemens, K.J.Kuhn, K.J.Stinemates, K.K.Zweig, K.R.Walker, K.S.Holman, L.A.Cherti, L.A.Stewart, L.B.Legate, L.H.Miller, L.M.Biggs, L.M.Hammer, L.M.Loehning, L.M.Posthuma, L.M.Roedl, L.R.Smith, L.Veiga, M.A.Haessly, M.A.Hartley, M.A.Kapfenstein, M.A.Krummel, M.A.Martinez, M.A.Wuensch, M.C.Boots, M.D.Watts, M.J.Cronlotac, M.J.Kaiser, M.J.Werner, M.K.Hoefs, M.K.Hultquist, M.L.Jacobson, M.L.Miller, M.L.Schepp, M.M.Bernhard, M.M.Martino, M.P.Taffe, M.R.Bosek, M.S.Osborne, M.T.Marcoux, M.W.Aguilera, N.A.Schuster, N.C.Anderson, N.F.Bedker, N.L.Neuber, N.Parrilla, P.A.Gregory, P.C.Drinkwine, P.C.Williams, P.J.Black, P.J.McNicol, P.R.Back, R.A.Gray, R.A.Lettau, R.C.Moldenhauer, R.C.Sommers, R.D.Slager, R.H.Krause, R.J.Latendresse, R.L.Burwitz, R.L.Fude, R.S.Clemens, R.S.Goes, R.S.Steiner, R.S.Wells, R.T.Stephens, R.V.Koch, S.A.Fesmire, S.A.Fritze, S.A.Kutzke, S.C.Payne, S.L.Lepple, S.L.Ritter, S.L.Rohn, S.L.Salzman, S.L.Schwebke, S.L.Vierck, S.M.Bogus, S.M.Murphy-Fredenburg, S.R.Dins, S.Sanchez, T.A.Gladson, T.D.Garriety, T.G.Hummelmeier, T.H.Weiss, T.J.McGowan, T.K.Landsee, T.L.Frakes, T.L.McLain, T.L.Wells, T.M.Abbott, T.R.Atkins, T.R.Rawson, T.R.Ziebell, V.J.Loomans, V.L.Kelley, V.L.Kelm, W.A.Shaver, W.G.Bradbury, W.M.Muhek, W.T.Fecke, W.W.Nagle, W.W.Staidl, Y.Pillsbury, I.Ribeiro, J.L.S.Pech, E.Ewald, M.Guenther, P.Gdynia, R.Jennrich, S.Wietstock, J.Fdz.-Pello, I.J.Booth, J.A.Rixton, C.E.Behn, D.D.Askew, D.L.Knight, J.R.Sharpe Jr., R.F.Cobble, S.D.Smith, J.W.Grills, C.M.Disch, D.M.Baxter, G.P.Steffen, H.D.Logan, J.A.Sandy, J.C.Cogil, J.E.Switzer Jr., J.L.Persinger, P.E.Lucado, F.J.Sifuentes, E.Camcaz, J.Laukert, M.Foerderer, S.Granzin, L.D.Merk, E.J.Dejoode, B.Duccini, B.J.Dewall, D.M.Terry, L.A.Precourt, L.Beck, N.L.Lentz, R.M.Barkau, S.M.Demeo, A.L.James, A.L.Williams, A.R.Alvarez, A.S.Lane, B.L.Ackerley, D.G.Reed, D.K.Dodson, D.L.Green, D.M.Fuller, D.M.Williams, E.R.Perkins, F.C.Williams, H.C.Grine, J.A.Peters, J.C.Large, J.D.Dixon, J.F.Daniel, J.M.Nagle, J.R.Driver, J.S.Lawson, K.L.Swanson, K.M.Bloodsworth,

K.M.Mirimanian, L.L.Wooff, L.M.Kelley, M.S.Loughridge, R.L.Burke, S.A.Knoll, S.M.Renick, S.W.Johnson, S.W.Kendall, T.A.Vanlengen, T.L.Rideaux, T.L.Wickline, T.R.McTigue, T.R.Swalley, V.A.Swift, P.Guyot, E.Feldbusch, H.Heinze, M.Potyka, M.J.Kingdom, R.Hebert, H.Juarez, D.M.Sadler, L.E.Hunt,
P.C.Fischer, W.J.Williams, J.A.Perez, C.A.Schmitt, D.A.Wirth, D.L.Robinson, E.P.Krueger, F.J.Nesom, J.E.Davis, J.K.Hanson, J.S.Dunlop, K.D.Straw, M.W.Dunnington, N.E.Jacobs, R.A.Lawler, S.M.Faulkner, N.J.Clement, O.Pantoja, S.Hel, M.Rieger, R.Mandel, D.D.Carter, A.C.Severt, A.D.Scott, A.H.Babe,
A.N.Fillers, B.J.Palczak, B.L.Perry, B.R.Campbell, B.S.Carter, C.L.Crisp Jr., C.P.Powers, C.R.Hawk, D.Harrison, D.Honeycutt, D.L.Coakley, D.R.Woolsey, E.L.Tipton, E.M.Sutherland, G.M.Horton, J.L.Moore, J.M.Collins, J.M.Hanks, J.W.Stills, M.D.Kinnick, M.N.Weems, M.R.Jinks, P.A.Shelton,
P.B.Johnson, P.D.Compton, R.D.Farmer Jr., R.K.Seals, S.A.Thompson, S.B.Madden, S.K.Sampson, S.L.Culver, S.L.Talley, T.C.Campbell, T.F.Childress, V.J.Corso II, Z.M.Holt, R.G.Graves, T.R.Leitch, F.S.Jensen, A.Reder, A.Strobel, E.Karakaya, G.Birkenbach, G.Danner, K.Kuznik, K.Rutz, L.Baumhauer,
L.Christmann, L.Fischer, R.Akkanat, S.Dopf, T.Mayer, W.Schobel, U.Hänsch, U.Keßler, M.Köster-Bonrath, A.Mancarella, A.N.Fitzpatrick, A.R.Gellings, A.S.Neuy, A.Vanhoose, B.A.Weiland, B.J.Bentz, B.S.Harkins, C.A.Weber, C.Earwood, C.L.Moore, C.L.Morrison, C.Nowak, D.H.Petri Jr., D.J.Murra,
D.L.Dykstra, D.L.Vujnovich, D.Murphy, D.R.Mohr, F.L.Babcock, F.N.Persong, G.L.Reschke, J.A.Zimmerman, J.B.Tomesch, J.E.Roy, J.J.Liebenow, J.J.Thrall, J.L.Terlisner, J.L.Zander, J.P.Ziolkowski, K.H.Weiss, K.J.Knoll, K.J.Werner, K.K.Steinbarth, K.M.Schraufnagel, K.O.Wilcox, K.O'Reilly, K.R.Bohle,
L.L.Galligan, L.M.Freimann, M.E.Fleming, M.J.Begg, M.J.Moroney, M.K.Hopstetter, M.R.Sales, P.A.Guerry, P.J.Sykes, P.N.Ellis, R.A.Boer, R.A.Stutzman, R.B.Lahmann, R.H.Henning, R.M.Janzen, S.D.Wallestad, S.G.Kaemmerer, S.R.Vree, T.D.Backen, T.J.Wiskow, T.L.Lockard, T.R.Barker, T.R.Salyer,
W.J.Wallace, W.L.Stielow, A.Contreras, A.I.Morales, C.A.Martinez, F.Wong, L.M.Calleros, M.A.Mota, M.Gonzalez, R.Arechiga, S.L.Ibarra, G.Le Roux, B.Polèse, C.Bastian, C.Wolf, G.Blanco Martinez, P.Wojcik, R.Gedik, S.Finocchiaro, T.Cakmak, R.R.J.Ter Haar, R.A.Clark, F.L.Manjabosco, O.Smaneoto,
A.Quirasco, J.A.Gomez, F.G.Esquivel, J.F.Reynolds, J.A.Gutierrez, G.F.Hautly, A.T.Anderson, D.J.Ploessl, D.K.Feld, D.L.Brooks, D.R.Jaeger, D.R.Pierce, E.K.Valentino, F.P.Ruck, G.A.Wessel, H.D.Wolfe, J.E.Hays, J.E.Mitchell, J.J.Hogan, J.J.Wolter, J.Lamberty, J.S.Tudor, K.J.Andresen, K.L.Metzdorf,
K.W.Ludovissy, K.W.Orth, L.J.Gradecki, L.Taylor, M.R.Grimes, P.C.Hamilton, P.L.Frasher, R.K.Hiley, R.L.Weitz, S.A.Masengarb, S.L.Hadley, S.Vinson, T.R.Olig, V.S.Corder, J.Iadroxitz, I.C.S.Mattos, J.J.Ledet, C.Arana, L.R.Melendez, F.J.Valdez, E.De la Rosa, H.Finkbeiner, P.Koehler, J.A.Ver Ploeg,
M.K.Driscoll, M.Guevara, A.K.Rodgers, G.C.Leif, I.R.Johnson, J.A.Eng, J.B.Amidon, J.C.Gillfillan, J.D.Collins, J.E.Adams, J.E.Reed, J.L.Seehusen, J.W.Reep, J.Y.Steele, K.A.Fitzgeralds, K.A.Miller, K.L.McCalmon, L.L.Kistner, L.M.Click, M.C.Wooley, M.J.Ridenour, M.Krasic, M.Saleem, N.E.Bollweg,
R.L.Overy, R.S.Reierson, S.E.Marcel, S.K.Bell, S.M.Schultz, S.S.Conway, S.S.Witter, T.C.Sheley, T.D.Uphoff, W.H.Lemke, M.Ibarra, A .R.Silva, E.Urquiza, F.J.De La Cruz, J.A.Arizmendi, J.C.Ramirez, N.Acosta, P.A.Romero, P.Carrera, R.A.Meza, R.Alvarado, S.Lopez, T.S.Olmos, J.G.Carreon, S.Valenzuela,
G.Hampel, A.Miller, A.R.Krause, B.H.Williams, M.L.Coffman, A.L.Norton, G.A.Koele, R.Pinedo, G.W.Guimaraes, J.A.Allen, S.R.Hotwick, J.Gadens, A.L.Gohlke, C.L.Dunn, C.M.Gardner, K.M.Beck, M.A.Rebilas, M.M.Lashmett, R.W.Schmidt, T.D.Hardesty, A.L.Calzadillas, J.C.Diaz, L.R.Olivas,
M.A.Gonzalez, O.O.Orozco, V.M.Baquera, C.Almaraz, D.Ballet, P.Guarnaccia, B.A.Wells-Vonderheide, C.R.Van Dike, C.V.Rothermich, D.A.Gall, D.J.Dewitt, D.R.White, H.K.Varshney, L.L.Tilley, M.B.Haer, P.B.Porter, P.D.Maloney, R.L.Weires, W.F.Gavin, G.C.Petry, F.A.Gonzalez, J.Carmona, J.J.A.Moreno,
R.Simental, A.Ramos, C.A.Escobedo, E.R.Contreras, G.E.Aguilera, J.A.Ordaz, J.C.Rosales, J.Esquivel, J.G.Pacheco, J.L.Delgado, J.Ojeda, L.E.Loya, L.Garcia, M.T.Mayorga, R.Alvarado, R.Ambriz, R.Gomez, R.Rivas, A.E.Humphries, A.L.Geist, B.A.Reis, C.L.Rozenboom, D.P.Ellert-Beck, G.D.Houghton,
K.N.Frankovic, R.L.Vanderheiden, S.T.Tzintzum, T.J.Burkle, T.R.Fitzgerald, A.Barcena, M.J.Keltjens, B.Le Caer, A.Bruenesholz, A.Jasari, B.Schopf, C.Eichholtz, C.Fischer, D.Berger, E.Freyer, E.Mathes, F.Jungmann, F.Linsbauer, F.Wittenmaier, G.Scherer, H.Bilgin, H.Jacob, I.Greiderer, J.Monot, K.Kessler,
K.Sebald, L.Schulyk, M.Baumann, M.Ordon, P.Zuparic, R.Felix, T.Bormann, T.Rueck, J.Kempers, C.M.McHenry, J.A.Cherevko, M.T.Clark, A.C.Galera, P.Gilles, E.Holguin, J.A.Rodriguez, L.D.Palma, M.E.Magallanes, M.Mancinas, O.Caballero, A.Castillo, A.Jimenez M., B.A.Bedard, C.D.Washburn,
C.L.Borwig, D.E.Blume-Woock, D.S.Mercer, E.A.Meyer, J.J.Hockaday, K.S.Schroeder, M.E.Marquess, M.R.Cornett, M.R.Jessen, P.S.Spencer, R.A.Hansen, R.A.Leemans, R.J.Cawelti, S.E.Frizzell, J.A.Cuevas , E.A.Lampson, M.J.Johnson, C.B.Clark, C.C.Dupree, D.L.Laumeier, J.A.Inhelder,
K.A.Bloodgood, M.A.Bazely, M.L.Harper, P.G.Detemple, P.J.Roberts, R.B.Batts, S.E.Schaefer, S.P.Metcalf, T.M.Beyer, T.C.Conrad, R.R.Richard, A.O.Ochoa, G.Montana, R.M.Vargas, A.K.Fuentes, H.J.Muller, P.T.Riffel, W.D.Taylor, D.A.Lang, J.A.Schrier, R.W.Miksa, T.J.Gass, A.Armendariz, J.I.Lopez,
C.E.Beck, C.J.Essert, D.L.Goad Jr., J.L.Jaramillo, M.D.Griffin, O.A.Wright, S.H.Queen, S.J.Weber, J.A.Berlanga, D.A.Mortarotti, E.C.Madden, C.L.Bearden, F.Zampiero, R.Constante, **1999** C.P.Niehaus, J.G.Krestic, R.L.Edochie, R.L.Scala, R.P.Smead, S.A.St-Gelais, P.Wang, R.H.G.M.Litjens, A.Bambakas,
B.Lambacher, B.Winkler, C.Kufner, D.Mihajlovic, D.Tacke, E.Diez Aguilar, E.Exler, E.Reek, G.Johne, H.Fuchs, H.Huether, H.Rode, J.Frangart, K.Hofmann, K.Kuerschner, K.Lambropoulos, K.Schmidt, L.Heissler, M.Ascic, O.Brehmer, O.Uenver, P.Schoening, R.Kutzner, S.Holst, S.Mehl, HP.Frick,
W.J.Kunkeler, B.Kratz, C.Sikorra, S.Sivalingam, E.Guillen, H.Steffens, A.D.Dockery Jr., B.D.Daniel, B.D.Sulzer, B.G.Toppert, B.J.Goedken, B.R.Nash, C.A.Williams, C.M.Fuston, C.R.Gradert, D.L.Dennis, F.M.Snyder, G.A.Zokal, G.K.Sams, H.L.Peters, J.A.Hansen, J.A.Martinov, J.B.Kelley, J.B.Weaver,
J.D.Goebel, J.F.Cantrill, J.L.Osborne, J.L.Teague, J.L.Ziemba, J.M.Swanson, J.P.Dagenhart, J.R.Marthaler, J.R.Rucinski, J.S.Myska, J.T.Hoffman, J.W.Dutemple, K.A.Gero Molumby, K.B.Daane, L.G.Stanley, L.J.Kurth, L.W.Herriman, M.A.Holzrichter, M.D.Sealey, M.L.Peters, O.A.De Jesus, R.A.Lopez,
R.D.Brown, R.J.Wille, S.A.Schaalma, S.E.Schadler, S.L.Fort, S.L.Steffey, S.S.Seedorff, T.D.Maertens, T.J.Schreier, T.T.Chuich, T.T.Coleman, K.J.Paolini, L.Fulton, M.J.Gardarsson, L.V.S.Carvalho, A.Pena, A.Rubio, B.E.Toquinto, C.A.Hernandez, D.O.Ordonez, E.A.Marquez, E.A.Valles, E.Garcia, F.J.Tamez,
G.Sanchez, H.R.Herrera, J.A.Ramirez, J.A.Realvazquez, J.Aragon, J.Lopez, J.R.Rodriguez, L.A.Reza, N.A.Silveyra, N.Leon, R.A.Llanes, R.A.Renteria, R.A.Talavera, R.Amezcua, R.Ballesteros, R.Cardona, R.Gomez, B.C.Enriquez, E.G.Guerrero, M.R.Banda, B.Leroy, S.Chauvet, E.Schuller, A.J.Loop,
G.K.Mewhirter, H.K.Voelp, J.A.Reinke, J.A.Schaefer, K.J.Downey, L.L.Burens, L.V.Bozzer, M.M.Brogan, M.R.Fisher, P.E.Boring, S.Saucedo, T.E.Schlotman, T.S.Cipressi, T.W.Schwickerath, A.Lurka, T.Bryant, T.J.Sparks, P.Winter, A.J.Alexander, A.L.Bickett, B.E.Thorpe, B.F.Burris, B.J.Fagerholt,
C.A.Carlstrom, C.B.Hodge, C.Orr, D.A.Gigandet, E.A.Howard, G.D.Finnes, G.K.Fosu, J.A.Nicholson, J.J.Geistkemper, J.L.Schultz, J.L.Torresin, J.M.Austin, J.N.Adams, J.O.Steed III, J.T.Adamson, J.W.French, K.A.Harmon, K.F.Humiston, M.A.Brown, M.A.Harris, M.F.Ruppert Jr., P.D.Thole, P.J.Parks,
R.J.Huntley, R.S.Binder, S.C.Thornton, S.K.Nell, T.G.Phillips, T.L.Thiede, T.M.Hartwig, T.P.Murphy, W.R.Heiser, J.Cullen, K.C.Bourgeois Jr, R.Bates, A.Corona, A.Garcia, A.Gonzalez, A.Marquez, D.A.Cadena, F.Gonzalez, G.I.Ramirez, I.G.Tena, J.F.Valles, J.M.Lopez, L.A.Gonzalez, L.M.Amador, N.I.Morales,
O.I.Munoz, O.I.Sanchez, R.C.Acosta, R.E.Ramirez, R.G.Mendoza, R.Ramirez, S.Macias, M.E.Hernandez, R.A.Gonzalez, O.Doll, U.Oberst, J.Meter, A.K.Raveling, T.L.Wegmann, R.A.Young, R.R.Schultz, R.W.Koster, C.L.Prokopiec, N.J.Emmelhainz, B.J.Henniges, B.Jennings, B.L.Kolb, D.C.Diederich,
E.L.Maxwell, H.M.Moritz, J.M.Cooper, K.L.Ewald, L.M.Mattson, R.Daigle, R.L.Cason, S.C.Fegenbush, T.R.Helin, C.A.P.Pretorius, M.J.Selvakumar, G.L.R.Pilla, J.A.Schneider, D.Jennings, R.D.Daigle, T.A.Borne, A.Beltran, A.Rangel, E.L.Rivas, E.Valverde, E.Venegas, F.G.Coronado, G.Martinez, G.Poblano,
J.A.Chacon, J.Beltran, J.Gonzalez, J.M.Rios, M.A Olivas, O.M.Venegas, P.Calderon, R.H.Leon, S.Deras, J.Lopez, A.Vogel, J.Gunst, R.Hotz, R.Ulrich, A.D.Harrison, B.J.Crist, E.J.Brashear, J.G.Merten, J.L.Schlutt, J.R.Johnson, J.T.Nelson, K.A.Wilson, K.D.Collins Jr., L.K.Easterberg, Q.D.Echols,
R.L.Jungwirth, S.L.Bratcher, T.D.Hessel, T.H.Wilson, K.S.Bucholz, R.Merlo, P.H.G.Titulaer, C.D.Do, J.L.Coppock, S.Lawrence, A.K.Khanna, R.D.N.Simonen, J.Weissig, S.V.Arteaga, A.K.Murjani, C.L.Legrand, C.M.Arnett, C.R.Showalter, C.S.Hobart, G.S.Francis, J.J.Brcek, J.P.Kempel, K.C.Chritton,
K.K.Lott, L.A.Behnke, L.M.Heckroth, M.A.Lycan, M.Neis, P.A.Reihbandt, P.D.Priewe, R.A.Bollman, R.D.Zahn, T.L.Dyer, V.E.Stewart, G.L.Autrey, A.A.Hernandez, A.E.Delgado, A.R.Avila, C.A.Medellin, C.I.Parra, E.Jacquez, F.V.Perea, G.I.Cobos, G.Lara, G.R.Rodriguez, L.Parra, L.R.Tovar, M.E.Jimenez,
M.G.Zapata, M.M.Ruiz, M.J.T.Pouwels, O.Wehling, C.A.Parrish, J.P.Edwards, E.Orozco, D.A.Kemp, E.J.Schmadeke, L.R.Sherlock, R.E.Chopp, R.D.Thompson, A.D.Stuber, A.L.Ochsner, A.N.Galanek, B.J.Oppelt, D.A.Johnson, D.J.Rowan, D.L.Bert, H.L.Waldmann, H.M.Harrison, J.A.Freking, J.D.Carson,

Company-wide "Team Power" participants, Moline, Illinois, 1999

J.J.Zmolek, J.K.Resch, J.M.Gipple, J.R.Payne, K.A.Sprossel, K.L.Sniadach, K.Schwerdtfeger, M.A.Schmidt, M.H.Clark, P.L.Van Gundy, P.R.Bradley, R.J.Barton Jr., T.G.Meyers, W.V.Curlee Jr., Z.Polak,
P.J.Missio, J.B.Talbot, K.J.Trosclair, A.Valadez, C.Hernandez, C.M.Luna, E.E.Gonzalez, F.J.Munoz, G.I.Orona, G.M.Hernandez, G.Martinez, J.G.Armendariz, J.L.Figueroa, J.Ugarte, L.A.Tarin, L.Cera,
L.J.Aguirre, LI.B.Holguin, M.Grijalva, M.Torres, O.A.Peralta, O.Ramirez, P.Flores, R.C.Franco, R.Chacon, R.G.Serrano, R.Terron, R.Toquinto, T.D.J.Armendariz, G.Duran, J.O.Mora, A.Medina, A.Rios,
B.Ramirez, C.De Santiago, C.E.Alcantara, E.F.Trujillo, F.Carrillo, F.Rivera, H.U.Diaz, I.Rangel, J.A.Mireles, J.Hernandez, R.Capuchino, S.A.Sleiman, V.M.Garcia, J.J.López , J.L.Thijssen, J.Delmas,
C.Saint-Dizier, A.Mehmeti, B.Kuntz, C.Horak, D.Eckstein, D.Heiler, D.Stanisic, E.Bischoff, F.Doser, G.Kuehne, H.Bender, H.Erdogan, H.Fettel, H.Kolb, H.Schwitalla, H.Weiss, J.Schankula, J.Wieczorek,
K.Roeckl, K.Zimmermann, M.Broll, M.Busch, M.Greulich, M.Knobloch, M.Rust, S.Eresin, S.Krajina, S.Stanic, S.Westphal, T.Trapp, U.Sprengelmeyer, W.Dalheimer, W.Klimm, W.Schuhmann,
S.Podßun, A.C.Watts, A.E.Draper, A.J.Fisher, A.Stevens, A.W.M.Jones, B.G.Phelps, B.T.Thomas, C.A.Chalcraft, C.A.Sheldon, C.Broadhurst, C.H.Renwick, C.J.Beech, C.J.Smith, C.M.Cockerill,
C.R.Hutchinson, D.A.Hall, D.A.Naylor, D.C.Longville, D.C.Rogers, D.Dodsworth, D.J.West, D.J.Williams, D.L.Gage, D.Meeks, D.W.Green, E.C.J.Nicholls, E.J.Ashmead, E.J.Wilkins, E.S.Bond,
G.A.Croly, G.E.Bell, G.K.Ford, G.M.Eales, H.Musgrave, I.Humphreys, I.P.McTaggart, J.A.Riley, J.A.Wilks, J.C.Williams, J.E.Lenczuk, J.E.Spayne, J.G.C.Rawlings, J.H.Lord, J.M.Boothroyd, J.Nicholls,
K.I.Broadhurst, K.L.Lacey, K.L.Stephens, K.M.Patel, K.Swift, L.J.Smith, L.M.Fletcher, L.M.Trott, M.A.Callaghan, M.A.D.Hardiman, M.J.Smith, M.J.Sparey, P.E.Taylor, P.J.Guy, P.J.Morgan, P.M.Ryan,
P.S.Beech, P.S.Taylor, P.Yeates, R.J.Payne, R.Kinsey, R.N.Hellewell, S.A.Trotman, S.G.Chilman, S.G.Crichton, S.J.Hunt, S.J.Uzzell, S.L.Chubb, S.L.Jones, S.M.Barson, S.M.Rodway, S.P.Joslyn,
S.W.Parkes, S.Wontumi, T.C.Dunne, T.G.Williams, T.J.Nicholls, T.Woodman, J.L.Decherd, P.V.Manukonda, R.N.Nelms, T.B.M.Pinheiro, E.R.Barkley, A.S.Stewart, B.M.Evers, B.W.Shaffer Jr.,
D.A.Marlow, E.A.Staab, G.K.Joines, J.M.Kohlhase, J.M.Peterson, J.S.Chambers, K.E.Shultz, K.J.Nehmer, L.H.Garris, L.R.Skala, M.R.Hoover Jr., P.J.Said, P.L.Hammonds, R.J.Wyrick,
S.C.Bredenberg, S.R.Uecker, T.D.Thomason, J.I.Bianco, A.D.Nascimento, A.J.Quitaiski, A.M.D.Santos, A.R.Borges, A.R.Schmidt, A.Rossi, C.D.Pinheiro, C.E.Kalchner, C.M.Messer, C.Marin,
C.R.Garcia, C.W.Junior, D.A.Hensen, D.A.Steffens, D.J.Schulz, D.R.Ziebert, E.R.Feix, E.R.Vianna, F.Halmann, F.Tratsch, G.M.D.Oliveira, J.C.Schakofski, J.D.S.Paraiba, J.J.Boeno, J.L.Marciniak,
J.L.Sartori, J.L.Vogt, J.R.Berger, J.R.Scherer, L.C.Strehlow, L.J.Fischer, L.Kissmann, M.Koehler, M.L.Beilke, M.L.Immich, M.L.Losekann, M.V.Rathke, N.S.Maronez, O.J.Luckemeyer, P.C.Schmidt,
P.D.Marciniak, P.F.Schneider, S.M.Sarassa, T.Scheid, V.J.Almeida, L.M.Hahn, A.Ma, Z.W.Tian, A.Delgado, A.G.Gutierrez, A.I.Parra, A.Rodriguez, C.Baez, C.I.Carrasco, C.Salazar, D.E.Fierro, D.G.Rios,
E.Ceballos, I.Flores, J.G.Serrata, J.G.Villa, J.Lzermeno, J.Martinez, J.R.Mota, L.R.Erives, M.A.Gardea, M.D.J.Alejo, M.D.L.Chavez, M.I.Gonzalez, M.Mendez, O.F.Sanchez, O.G.Solis, S.A.Acosta,
V.S.Martinez, W.Ortega, A.De Leon, E.H.Nuñez, M.T.Perez, A.Laug, S.Simon, M.D.Moroney, A.L.Breitweiser, C.A.Cox, C.L.Ragsdale, D.E.Fenske, D.J.Hutzler, D.L.Sievers, E.A.Rogers, F.A.Wolfrom,
G.D.Ellis III, J.C.Gonzalez, J.K.Brown, J.L.Rothbardt, J.M.Gamba, J.R.Dressler, J.W.Farber, K.A.Krause, K.L.Reamy, K.P.Kane, L.K.Benson, M.A.Alexander, M.A.Ruby, M.E.Lacross, M.F.Judd,
M.R.Jackson, N.J.Scott, T.A.Khan, T.A.Leeper, T.E.Burchill, W.G.Harding, E.V.W.Rohde, A.E.Moreno, A.M.Robles, A.M.Villa, A.Quintana, C.G.Sanchez, C.H.Payan, C.I.Ortega, C.Martinez, C.R.Nieto,
E.E.Cardenas, E.Tinoco, H.Holguin, J.A.Gonzalez, J.A.Navarro, J.Frausto, J.G.Martinez, J.I.Reza, J.M.Melendez, J.M.Salinas, L.C.Mendez, L.H.Ramos, M.D.C.Rubio, M.Ibuado, M.L.Montelongo,
M.P.Ponce, N.E.Reyes, O.I.Gutierrez, R.Garcia, R.Ledezma, S.Villela, V.Alfaro, V.H.Salcedo, V.M.Vergara, V.Pulido, A.Alvarez, A.Esquivel, D.Montoya, F.Avalos, F.Centeno, J.E.Zamora, J.O.Olivas,
J.Rodarte, L.G.Barcena, L.Marquez, R.C.Martinez, R.Hernandez, R.Morales, R.O.Nava, S.Medina, S.Sanchez, V.E.Rios, N.Dubois, S.Jacquierre, A.Altiparmak, S.Schlaefer, U.Weber, M.H.Kuipers,
K.Schwarz, A.Soares, C.P.Golon, D.J.Reznicek, D.Torchia, J.D.Lally, P.D.Collins, R.L.Brault, S.L.Fearman, A.T.Keitt, S.D.Bateman, J.E.Myers, S.D.Allen Jr., W.A.Barnes, J.A.Cerda, B.L.Weisensel,
B.S.Eljawhari, C.L.Ambrose, D.J.Sommerfeld, D.S.Umstead, G.Subramani, J.S.Brooks, K.Franck, K.I.Roberts, K.J.Herrick, K.M.Lovelace, K.McLean, L.S.Baker, M.A.Pavcik, N.J.Baier, R.E.Lipka,
R.G.Voy, R.W.Beyer, T.A.Smith, T.D.Tuten, T.E.McGuire, T.J.Bishop, V.A.Walz, W.B.Reynolds, W.J.Pickart, A.Larios, D.Davila, E.Diaz, I.Gomez, J.I.Sotelo, J.L.Caballero, J.L.Salazar, J.R.Valerio,
N.A.De La Rocha, S.Vazquez, V.H.Holguin, L.Lopez, A.L.Castillo, C.P.Railton, R.M.Hoy, R.W.Sprinkle, W.C.Brennan, C.F.Schaefer, J.J.Dudney, J.T.Ford, R.M.Connelly, S.L.Dunbar, T.Y.Miller, S.C.Sieber, D.K.Fischels, G.B.Farmer, G.M.Prakash, G.R.Ehrke Jr., G.W.Thompson, J.P.Schmitz, M.S.Ege,
S.Duckworth, S.L.Hahn, T.V.Clark, M.S.Jensen, A.L.Lewis, B.J.Sweeney, C.A.Chesmore, C.L.Geist, C.L.La Vanway, C.L.Santilli, C.T.Graham, D.J.Wilken, D.R.Croegaert, E.G.Miller, E.L.Williams, G.F.Gaddis, G.Matthews, L.C.Alvarado, M.J.Sproston, M.M.Marnholtz, N.J.Pilgrim, R.A.Lee, R.C.Conley,
R.F.McElveen, R.Kaseman, S.J.Lynch, S.S.Bush, T.G.Clearman, T.H.Faria, T.L.Friday, T.W.Flach, V.J.Clark, D.C.Hicks, P.Wanckel, I.Grabin, A.Gallegos, B.A.Renteria, D.A.De Luna, E.Delgado, F.Coronado, F.J.Manjarrez, L.Ortega, L.Rascon, M.A.Vallejo, M.C.Marentes, M.Chavez, R.Holguin, R.Yanez,
S.E.Gonzalez, A.Rodriguez, C.V.Chavez, F.E.Gutierrez, J.D.Alvarez, J.Favela, J.Hernandez, J.J.Espinoza, J.Zuñiga, R.Hurtado, S.Uribe, S.Vazquez, V.Arreola, V.Reyes, M.Hoeijmakers, A.Argento, A.Brunn, A.Fillinger, A.Kuecuek, B.Fluhrer, C.Dingler, C.Schaumburger, D.Bowyer, D.Gregor,
E.Schuhmacher, F.Beck, G.Flicker, G.Mastio, H.Danner, H.Ringle, J.Harsdorf, J.Kreienbaum, J.Tsobanis, K.Abolouh, K.Pauli, K.Seemuth, L.Baab, M.Schuetz, O.Burry, O.Poebl, P.Greif, S.Baba, S.Kircheis, S.Sertel, W.Friedrichsen, W.Gralla, W.Schwarz, R.Schöneborn, E.J.Saldaña, T.A.Clifton,
T.R.Thomas, G.R.Warren, G.Fosado, A.Derksen, T.A.Kempf, M.Wunsch, J.G.Paul, J.N.Newton, R.Van Wouw, A.Hadziahmetovic, B.A.King, B.I.Simpson, B.P.Rogers, C.R.Moeller, D.A.Martin, D.W.Ertmer, E.N.Allbritton, F.D.Hopkins, G.L.Petty Jr., H.L.Duckett, J.A.Giese, J.C.Reed Jr., J.L.Sliter,
K.A.Kuhl, L.D.Brecheisen, L.O.Crumley, M.A.Whitehead, M.D.Ladd, M.M.Malinowski, M.S.Despain, R.A.Harmon, S.V.Keeling, T.J.Martin, W.M.Eriksen, Y.D.Gallman, D.C.R.Reynolds, J.M.Jackson, F.M.Dotto, L.T.Borges, A.Frescas, A.Torres, C.H.Martinez, E.E.Grado, E.L.Saenz, F.A.Reyes,
F.De La Rosa, F.J.Gaytan, F.Lomas, G.J.De Luna Montes, J.A.Martinez, J.A.Sanchez, J.J.Holguin, J.M.Corona, J.M.Veldenea, J.Nava, M.Sosa, V.A.Beltran, M.Stollhof, M.Bischl, A.J.Clemons, C.L.McGinn, R.D.Werden, S.F.Sun, J.O.Quintana, P.K.Madsen, A.Furney, A.H.Arnold, A.Hess, A.J.Dondero,
A.L.Bowers, A.M.Ernst, A.Mueller, A.Norris, A.Youngberg, A.Zetterbaum, B.A.Boswell, B.Cox, B.E.Beisner, B.Hatch, B.J.Bowers, B.L.McCoy, B.L.Reimnitz, B.L.Schulz, B.Lichty, B.N.Binnix, B.Norton, B.Perkins, B.Sealls, B.Stockinger, B.T.Ballard, B.W.Brown, C.A.Hulsey, C.A.Rinauro, C.Benevides,
C.Chen, C.Christenson, C.Davis, C.Jerome, C.Jones, C.L.Pond, C.M.Dunning, C.Monson, C.Olson, C.Simonsen, C.Wallentine, C.Zimmerman, D.A.Finecy, D.A.Hearn, D.B.Glaeser, D.Becker, D.Berg, D.Chambers, D.Cloninger, D.D.Dowers, D.D.Muellenberg, D.D.Witham, D.DeLong, D.E.Hansen,
D.E.Martin, D.E.Weimer, D.F.Ernst, D.Friesen, D.G.Mowat, D.J.Andres, D.J.White, D.Laboy, D.M.Blau, D.M.Everson, D.M.Gilbertson, D.M.Lardy, D.M.Linskens, D.McBee, D.O.Edmondson, D.Peterson, D.R.Pate, D.Regier, D.S.Zepernick, D.Sudduth, D.Thackery, D.W.Doyle, D.W.Krekel, D.Wood,
E.A.Johnson, E.J.Kozak, E.J.O'Neil, E.M.Korbel, E.M.Rueles Jr., E.W.Golden, E.W.McCoy, G.A.Sanders, G.Karger, G.L.McKay, G.M.Farrell, G.N.Barnes, H.Abraham, H.S.Kinsler, J.Astorga, J.B.Clark, J.Bain, J.C.Fisher, J.C.Gotti, J.C.Thompson, J.Eagleton, J.F.Garcia, J.F.Pickett, J.Fitzsimmons,
J.Franco, J.Freeman, J.Fruetel, J.G.Atilano, J.Gehring, J.Hanson, J.J.Lueger, J.Jackson, J.K.Willett, J.L.Lenherr, J.L.Marcks, J.L.N.Perez, J.Larsen, J.Lichty, J.Liu, J.M.Coats, J.M.Delaney, J.M.Papineau, J.M.Prehm, J.Peters, J.Purser, J.R.Mishler, J.S.Kimes, J.S.Tomlinson, J.Sanders, J.Soderholm,
K.A.Davis, K.A.McCaffery, K.Asleson, K.Bangasser, K.Engelstad, K.Fountain, K.G.LeShure, K.Haynes, K.J.Meyer, K.Klenke, K.Kohls, K.M.Collins, K.M.Drais, K.M.Schrader, K.M.Stinson, K.Payne, K.R.Benedict, K.Sandberg, K.Tucker, K.Wenzel, L.A.Crawford, L.A.Stone, L.E.Karraker, L.H.Falling,
L.M.Cosyns, L.M.Unruh, L.Moll, L.Pankratz, L.Pownell, L.R.Henricksen, L.Thorne, L.Wagner, M.A.Campos, M.A.Creaghe, M.A.Lange, M.A.Moore, M.Allen, M.B.Miller, M.B.Zepernick, M.Colvard, M.E.Brown, M.Fuglie, M.G.Moore, M.Gehres, M.Hoffke, M.J.Ketchum, M.K.Schabel, M.K.Wheeler,
M.Pankratz, M.Porter, M.R.Lemen, M.R.Smith, M.Senn, M.Sotomayor, M.Spain, N.D.Luoma, N.M.Urban, P.C.Steele, P.E.Lehnhausen, P.Knutson, P.L.Fallis, P.Whitman, R.Allen, R.Conrad, R.D.Graham, R.F.LeVine, R.F.Raeth, R.Falconer, R.Grams, R.J.Blackburn, R.J.Greiving, R.J.Ownbey,
R.L.Gardner, R.L.Leiker, R.R.Castor, R.Riffey, R.W.Jones III, S.A.Rippie, S.Boesker, S.Holler, S.J.Harty, S.J.Koehn, S.J.Thomas Roberson , S.K.Wienhold, S.Lindblad, S.M.Day, S.M.Drais, S.Pautzke, S.R.Shirley, S.S.Tucker, S.Stoecklein, S.Turner, S.Webber-Peterson, S.Zimmerman, T.Braun,
T.Curtis, T.D.Taylor, T.D.Vaughn, T.Galyon, T.J.Guettler, T.J.Jerke, T.L.Glaum, T.M.Michael, T.Marxhausen, T.Molitor, T.Moreno, T.Murphy, T.Noyce, T.Paulsen, T.R.Burgey, T.R.Horsley, T.R.Martin, T.R.Taylor, T.Renner, T.S.Rickets, T.Wenger, U.Bauer, W.Iliff, W.Liming, Y.M.Yearout, C.R.Stamp Jr.,
K.A.Hancock, N.E.DeVane, M.H.Ford, J.E.Heerin Jr., A.A.Moerke, A.D.Burns, A.D.Hagelmeier, A.D.Siewert, A.D.Wieland, A.Deckard, A.Diaz, A.F.Avart III, A.F.Lemke, A.J.Luick, A.J.Norby, A.Kallis, A.Kozievsky, A.M.Arnold, A.M.Haugen, A.Mahinfallah, A.Meuchel, A.R.Bjerke, A.R.Poitra, A.R.Wright,
A.Shlyak, A.Swartwood, A.Tweed, A.W.Fleeker, B.A.Barnick, B.A.Wehri, B.B.Bossert, B.Basiewicz, B.Bortell, B.D.Dehn, B.D.Haugen, B.D.Jeffers, B.D.Revering, B.Dennis, B.F.Harrison, B.Hyde, B.J.Haugen, B.J.Kringen, B.K.Lankford, B.Klinnert, B.L.Jacobsen, B.L.Neale, B.L.Thomson, B.L.Webster,
B.M.Keafer, B.McCrary, B.Meade, B.P.Jamison, B.P.Wutzke, B.R.Kensok, B.R.Viken, B.S.Wood, B.Smith, B.W.Thorvilson, C.A.Anderson, C.A.Lien, C.A.Prante, C.A.Snyder, C.Broaddus, C.Camille, C.Clary, C.D.Jenkins, C.D.Livdahl, C.D.Reedy, C.Dyer, C.Eberhart, C.J.Olson, C.J.Stanton, C.Johnson,
C.Kunz, C.L.Schmitt, C.L.Straube, C.L.Watt, C.L.Young, C.M.Pederson, C.Meyer, C.N.Greicar, C.Nance, C.Needham, C.Paine, C.R.Johnson, C.R.Specht, C.R.Wiebusch, C.S.Jacobs, C.W.Ophoven, C.Young, D.A.Anderson, D.A.Beierle, D.A.Cossette, D.A.Hoffman, D.A.Johnson, D.A.Ramey,
D.A.Reynolds, D.Aceituna, D.Baker, D.C.Collins, D.C.Gira, D.C.Willett, D.D.Janssen, D.D.Shanle, D.Ewen, D.F.Nelson, D.Gaddie, D.H.Ehlers, D.I.Kornack, D.Ihlenfeldt, D.J.Bjerke, D.J.Coleman, D.J.Gaskins, D.J.Gerdes, D.J.Halvorson, D.J.Johnson, D.J.King, D.J.Wald, D.J.Wanzek, D.K.Jensen,
D.K.Lomelino, D.K.Siverson, D.L.Kasowski, D.L.Nation II, D.L.Stephenson, D.L.Thompson, D.L.Usher, D.Luparell, D.M.Bates, D.M.C.Lee, D.M.Markel, D.M.Munter-Murray, D.M.Pope, D.M.Thompson, D.M.White Bear, D.M.Yost, D.Miraldi, D.N.Roehrich, D.Oliver, D.P.Tommerson, D.R.Franssen,
D.R.Hagen, D.R.Kelley, D.R.Smith, D.Runsvold, D.S.Gordon, D.Stade, D.Strack, D.T.Grant, D.W.Herman, E.A.Crissey, E.A.Fuglstad, E.A.Joplin, E.Conkle, E.D.Frank, E.E.Milliron, E.H.Beauchesne, E.Hoerner, E.J.Mc Canna, E.J.Stalemo, E.Kamer, E.Martinez, E.Moltumyr, E.S.Martinez, E.Titsworth,
G.A.Kunz, G.A.Miller, G.B.Ward, G.C.Paulson, G.D.Mitzel, G.Hagen, G.Higgins, G.Howard, G.J.Drake, G.J.Tillman, G.K.Harmelink, G.L.Bricker, G.L.Newbury, G.L.Webster, G.M.Moroff, G.O.Bowhall, G.R.Hjertaas, G.Schmitt, G.Sprinkel, G.W.Hagen, G.W.Meyer, H.K.Saar, H.L.Barnes, H.Olson,
H.R.Ballenger, H.Rudnick, H.Schleder, I.A.Sturm, I.P.Kahl, J.A.Cody, J.A.Jelinek, J.A.Mulder, J.A.Sauvageau, J.A.Springer, J.A.Stromme, J.Ashcraft, J.Blanchard, J.C.Herdt, J.C.Thomas, J.Camille, J.Carter, J.Comerford, J.Cunningham, J.D.Flatt, J.D.Paulson, J.D.Vandrovec, J.E.Anderson,
J.E.Johnson, J.E.Rasmussen, J.E.Sterling, J.E.Thomas, J.F.Hanson, J.G.Johnson, J.Goodson, J.Halerewicz, J.Hopman, J.J.Gravelle, J.J.Miraldi, J.J.Wanner, J.K.Propp, J.L.Coltom, J.M.Carpenter, J.M.Fahey, J.M.Liddle, J.M.Livermont, J.M.Martinez, J.M.Olsen, J.M.Ryan, J.M.Schlitt, J.M.Tharp,
J.McCoy, J.Molohon, J.Morin, J.N.Mercier, J.P.Beeter, J.P.Tomlinson, J.R.Goldade, J.R.Neisen, J.R.Weishaar, J.S.Martin, J.S.Munighan, J.S.Puhalla, J.S.Westphal, J.Stein, J.T.Jacobson, J.Tolstedt, J.Vaneman, J.W.Bailey, K.A.Donaldson, K.A.Jandt, K.A.Kelly, K.A.McIntyre, K.A.Mortensen,
K.A.Pulicicchio, K.A.Spelhaug, K.Aghai-Tabriz, K.B.Larsen, K.Bullock, K.C.Bartz, K.D.Fordyce, K.D.Wanner, K.E.Johnson, K.E.Morman, K.F.Miller, K.G.Andres, K.Guidinger, K.Hingle, K.J.Bricker, K.J.Voegele, K.K.Kevorkian, K.Karna, K.L.Bodin, K.L.Brekkestran, K.L.Johnson, K.L.Schumacher,

K.M.Frank, K.M.Jorgensen, K.M.Schwartz, K.Maguire, K.Malone, K.McElroy, K.N.Eisenbeis, K.O.Hagel, K.O.Mertins, K.P.Cowles, K.R.Kirkeby, K.W.Tasset, K.Whitworth, L.A.Hammann, L.A.Kjelland, L.A.Miller, L.A.Pfannsmith, L.A.Sundquist, L.D.Bergeron, L.D.Petersen, L.Eldred, L.Foley, L.G.Tofte, L.J.Braaten, L.J.Patterson, L.J.Pulst, L.Jasken, L.L.Gaffney, L.L.Kalb, L.M.Brooks, L.M.Olson, L.P.Morrison, L.Pederson, M.A.Dehaan, M.A.Dodd, M.A.Hajicek, M.A.Humann, M.A.Khan, M.A.Pruitt, M.A.Smith, M.A.Tuchscherer, M.A.Wallis, M.A.Wolfe, M.B.Guttormson, M.B.Kelley, M.B.Walters, M.Belcourt, M.Bonn, M.C.Blacknik, M.C.O'Keefe, M.Ceynar, M.D.Carpenter, M.D.Krueger, M.D.Oshesky, M.D.Schmaltz, M.D.Strand, M.D.Whelan, M.E.Kellus, M.E.Sullivan, M.E.Uggerud, M.H.Nyland, M.I.Olstad, M.J.Aaser, M.J.Frueh, M.J.Jones, M.J.Lemmon, M.J.Melton, M.J.Zurn, M.Karrick, M.L.Burgard, M.L.Dooley, M.L.Lester, M.L.Miller, M.L.Valnes, M.M.Cordray, M.M.Thorstad, M.McCracken, M.Meloy, M.Muldrow, M.Nyland, M.Prose, M.Q.Hackmann, M.R.Birdsall, M.R.Franz, M.R.Karnopp, M.R.Speaks, M.R.W.Bond, M.Reich, M.S.Dahlvang, M.Schlichtmann, M.W.Beshear, M.Wilson, N.D.Stetz, N.J.Kinnaman, N.P.Neighbors, N.R.Larson, N.S.Warren, P.A.Mortenson, P.A.Nystuen, P.A.Stanius, P.Cabler, P.E.Ames, P.F.Gray, P.J.Kruger, P.M.Hager, P.T.Weisenburger, R.A.Berg, R.A.Bleibaum, R.A.Hall, R.A.Levos, R.A.Mallett, R.Askew, R.B.Cruff Jr, R.B.Ochoa, R.C.Eubank, R.E.Carlson, R.G.Landman, R.H.Barnwell, R.J.Browning, R.J.Kind, R.J.Krause, R.J.Livdahl, R.J.Mastel, R.J.Miesen, R.J.White Owl, R.L.Applegate, R.L.Jensen, R.L.Prososki, R.L.Sanders, R.M.Kirkeby, R.O.Perry, R.O.Zacher, R.R.Doeden, R.Rositas, R.S.Kean, R.Shaw, R.Vernon, R.W.Kvalvog, R.Young, S.A.Darden, S.A.Gurule', S.A.Hagen, S.A.Reule, S.A.Richmond, S.A.Shoemaker, S.A.Wohl, S.Aper, S.Carr, S.Davis, S.Defraties, S.Eggleston, S.G.Stone, S.Harrison, S.I.Gulland, S.Irving, S.J.Amundson, S.J.Bosh, S.J.Gothe, S.J.Kees, S.J.Sutton, S.J.White, S.K.Bolgrean, S.K.Erickson, S.K.Flem, S.K.Rodacker, S.L.Kelly, S.Lind, S.M.Kennelly, S.M.Knapp, S.N.White, S.Nalluri, S.Ohl, S.P.Greelis, S.R.Ringgenberg, S.S.Bell, S.Schinzler, S.Stanton, S.Taylor, S.W.Erickson, S.W.Peterson, S.W.Smith, S.W.Wicks, S.Walker, T.A.Braun, T.A.Fryman, T.A.Gerdon, T.A.Hughes, T.A.Weatherly, T.D.Bowen, T.D.Fuss, T.E.Laurent, T.E.Scott, T.F.Sparks Jr, T.Gasen, T.J.Brumfield, T.J.Frank, T.L.Austif, T.L.Hunt-Kaeding, T.L.Johnston, T.L.Reither, T.L.Tasset, T.M.Perry, T.P.Kaeding, T.P.McDonough, T.Payne, T.R.Gilles, T.T.Nguyen, T.W.Phillips, T.W.Turley, T.Wilson, V.Barkus, V.G.Segal, V.J.Brodsky, V.J.Louden, V.J.Osborn, V.L.Hughes, V.L.Rossman, V.L.Wilkie, V.Peterson, V.Tremain, W.Eden, W.F.Cooper, W.F.Paul, W.J.Hrdlicka, W.Kelly, W.M.Johnson, W.McGuire, X.Ma, Y.Barwari, Y.C.Schulz, A.M.Brown, B.D.Batcheller, B.M.Bassier, B.R.Shriver, C.D.Maxwell, C.M.Brooks, C.R.Stamp Jr., D.C.Williams, D.D.McGregor, D.K.Mrvan, E.L.Boulet, F.J.Wooten, F.M.Knary, G.S.Roman, J.A.O Leary, J.C.Anderson, J.M.Fryer, J.M.Yanek, K.L.Copley, K.M.Jahns, L.C.Anderson, L.K.Shaw, L.L.Balsar, M.A.Neuman, M.K.Swartz, M.T.Deutmeyer, R.A.Thompson, S.K.Beard, S.K.Bernstine, S.L.Wallace, T.L.Lemons, Y.M.Bigras, S.Y.Younger, P.C.Hickmann, A.G.Saenz, B.V.Reyes, C.Cortez, C.E.Quinonez, C.Gomez, C.Molina, D.H.Martinez, E.Montanez, H.D.Gutierrez, I.Lozoya, L.A.Armendariz, L.C.Lira, M.Acosta, M.Becerra, M.Chalaca, M.E.Velazco, M.G.Ponce, M.M.Sigala, P.Castaneda, R.E.Reyes, R.Garcia, E.Magallanes, E.Reyna, F.J.Morales, F.Lopez, G.Chavez, J.E.De Hoyos, J.M.Chong, J.P.Carrillo, J.Y.Castañeda, R.Bañuelos, R.I.Urquizu, R.Martinez, S.E.Palacios, U.Castillo, G.W.C.Litjens, C.Kleine, M.Hubrich, R.Leis, C.L.C.Webb, L.B.Sørensen, A.L.Assink, A.Z.Thomas, D.E.Macdougall, D.J.Hawkins, K.M.Thorne, M.T.Armes, N.A.Falcone, R.D.Jones, S.A.Lukens, V.R.Shank, R.Balboa, A.M.Owens, J.N.Vogel, M.G.Buehler, S.P.Holmgren, J.Vazquez, L.G.Alcaraz, A.K.Gilman, A.C.Lacewell, A.K.Stolley, A.R.Hagen, B.J.Bourke, B.K.Durrell, D.J.Britz, D.P.Reiter, E.T.Spurgeon, J.M.Kelly, J.M.Stoller, K.L.Harmsen, M.A.Rahim, M.B.Westrum, M.L.Brown, M.L.Burr, M.M.Baker, V.C.Devenney, J.A.Williamson, L.J.Lowe, M.J.Dunne, M.M.B.Mussoi, A.Rivera, E.Martinez, F.Y.Ochoa, G.Ponce, G.Sias, G.Vallejo, H.F.Santana, J.M.Lopez, J.R.Olague, M.H.Martinez, S.Lira, A.Becerra, R.Gonzalez, S.S.Lima, A.C.Johnson, R.H.Bushby, R.Miller, R.Nelson, N.L.Morkve, A.J.Gardner, A.K.Gregory, A.L.Barker, B.D.Hunter, B.Langston, C.A.Nipstad, C.M.Rodriguez, D.A.Hubbs, D.E.O'Keeffe, D.M.Pope, J.D.Boyd, J.E.Fortenberry, J.H.Rookwood, J.M.Nass, K.A.Currence, K.S.Chupp, K.S.Robbins, K.S.Slavish, L.J.Knebel, L.J.Newsome, L.M.Loete, M.A.Ellison, M.K.Vayding, M.W.Falusi, P.A.Sparks, P.E.Gibson, P.J.Pangallo, R.A.Loy, R.E.Brown, S.A.Gonzalez, S.J.Ditzler, S.K.Collins, S.L.Jones, S.M.Phillips, T.C.Thomasson, T.M.Goss, T.M.Hansel, T.P.Aller, D.F.Landry, T.P.Delatte, E.Urrutia, F.J.Martinez, J.C.Perez, J.L.Garcia, M.A.Monarrez, M.O.Vega, R.A.Ramos, L.G.Lindsey, A.Arguijo, G.Lavin, D.L.Lucas, J.B.Engelby, J.L.Morrill, L.S.Kellner, D.S.Krantz, E.L.Drescher, J.A.Gunn, L.A.Fox, E.J.M.Sijbers, A.Kizilkaya, D.Giro, D.Piontek, G.Langenbahn, G.Neumann, H.Benke, H.Huebner, H.Karakas, H.Laier, H.Mundry, H.Tillack, H.Volb, I.Caner, I.Les, J.Klenert, J.Walle, K.Limbeck, K.Schleef, M.Alganatay, M.Boegem, M.Maass, M.Mende, M.Schneider, M.Wabro, P.Hehn, P.Kahler, R.Graf Zu Lynar, S.Tsoumbas, T.Schwab, V.Stratigis, W.Buchmann, W.Mueller, W.Schmidt, S.C.Bloemhof, V.J.W.H.Vosmer, A.G.Slade, C.R.Kelly-Elkins, D.G.Lewis, S.Jarman, W.Delonais, A.A.Snyder, B.A.Love, B.D.Gallagher, B.J.Hager, B.K.Baxter, C.D.Brown, C.L.Ostertag, C.W.Polley, D.E.Jewell, D.G.Bolch, D.J.Barnes, D.W.Cole, E.W.Townsend, F.E.Drew, G.C.Wallace, J.A.Hayes, J.D.Chisholm, J.D.Cook, J.M.Campbell, K.W.Isbill, L.R.Giannetto, M.A.Brown, M.L.Craig, M.M.Coffman, N.J.Hand, P.M.Adams, R.D.Shaw, R.W.McKay, S.L.Jobman, S.P.Murdock, T.C.Henderson, T.J.Brown, T.L.Hammerich, T.R.Pennisi, T.R.Robinson, W.M.O'Connor, G.Dentee, C.Ruiz, D.A.Granados, G.Vela, L.A.Gardea, L.E.Sanchez, M.A.Contreras, O.A.Montes, V.Wolf, E.Martinez, A.P.Ellis, B.C.Burckhalter, D.B.Drake, D.R.Trahan, E.R.Lowe, E.W.Cerniansky, J.D.Cunningham, J.E.Montgomery, M.G.Sonksen, R.K.Galloway, R.T.Carmain, T.D.White, T.H.Hamlet, T.T.Rabun, A.Wojcik, B.Seljmani, K.Willmann, M.Hoffmann, M.Stam, T.Müller, D.W.Peters, J.Schrank, K.L.Fischer, A.E.Krick, A.E.Tippitt, B.C.Nanjappa, B.D.Ruppert, C.M.Bigger, D.A.Collins, D.B.Butler, D.I.Hintermeister, D.L.Reyes, D.R.Moritz, D.Y.Gentry, J.M.Gaba, K.L.Smith, L.A.Westimayer, M.D.Shrieves, M.E.Gwinn, P.M.Barry, R.W.Hicks, S.J.Keller, S.M.Hubb, S.M.Kohlrausch, T.M.Hopkins, W.G.Barefoot, B.Rodriguez, H.A.Apodaca, I.I.Antonio, J.M.Rivera, L.M.Hernandez, S.Saucedo, E.I.Mendoza, I.Guerrero, L.A.Ortiz, L.E.Verastegui, R.H.Castro, G.Bittner, G.Mulas, J.Strunk, M.Lambert, M.Mueller, W.Stryczek, B.E.Thomas, B.W.Charroux, J.A.Degenfelder, A.L.West, S.Subramani, G.R.Mostiack, J.M.Pina, A.C.Myers, B.E.Melton, C.A.Bailey, C.A.Kincaid, C.E.Davis, C.M.Lane, D.C.Walton, G.G.Miller, J.D.Lavin, M.A.Oody, M.M.Miller, R.L.Tate Jr., R.W.Blankenship, S.R.Birchfield, R.Hering, R.Kratz, M.Persson, N.G.Pommainville, P.J.Falconi, S.J.Swegle, G.A.Ruiz, L.Burdett, A.D.Lee, B.T.Galvin, C.Galligan, C.J.Pesant, C.M.Todd, D.C.Fairgrieves, D.W.Perkins, D.W.Smith, E.F.Kulka, E.V.Crawford, J.D.Jasmin, J.D.Scott, K.C.Petersen, L.J.Smith, M.A.Gault, M.D.Carter, M.M.Stevens, M.X.Hill, P.J.Jensen, P.J.Osborn, R.D.Harrington, R.S.Homolka, R.W.Davis, S.A.McClure, S.C.Blake, S.W.McCoy, T.L.Stoelk, W.G.Wise, E.Alderete, R.Torres, N.J.Hall, J.S.Clymer, S.M.Lathrop, K.E.Toups, L.A.Phillips, M.Park, A.C.Whitmore, A.M.Montgomery, C.A.Dowe, C.A.Webb, C.J.Holliday, C.L.Pope, D.G.Halfmann, E.E.Jones-Willis, G.L.Alt, H.J.Nelson, J.D.Hollenback, J.J.Sneath, L.B.Griffith, L.K.Hofmann, M.J.White, M.R.Lena, S.J.Michel, S.M.Balsom, S.Mast, S.O.Hammersley, S.J.Cooley, J.A.Rivas, J.C.Moreno, L.Gonzalez, M.R.Enriquez, T.R.Burzynski, D.C.McCormick, F.Richter, A.L.Vandeest, S.A.O'Brien, R.M.Wehr, G.P.Augspurger, R.W.Fleming, T.N.Trone, J.D.Parish, P.V.Møller, P.J.B.M.Hermans, A.Gonzalez-Lopez, A.Kirsch, A.Roemer, A.Strauf, B.Agne, C.Jimeno-Gracia, D.Wentz, E.Etsch, F.Freyler, F.Maier, F.Von Dallwitz, F.Zander, G.Batke, H.Knapp, H.Strauss, J.Podhajsky, K.Moos, M.Erbay, M.Peric, N.Kamberi, O.Beikert, S.Korica, S.Tasdemir, U.Seibold, W.Schmidt, B.J.Hulsman, D.Van Raalte, I.Maartensson, L.Mederos, V.Holland, A.Muto, B.L.Lockhart, B.M.Brown, C.A.Carlson, C.A.Darnielle, D.F.Ottavianelli, D.G.Fleming, D.L.Purvis, E.G.Pederson, J.D.Goodwin, J.L.Chase, K.M.Sanders, L.A.Seiler, M.L.Gremmels, M.L.Lentzkow, M.V.Porter, N.D.Contonis, S.M.Stocchiero, S.S.Mackenzie, W.O.Ifode, C.Jariz, R.I.Sarmiento, H.Caballero, A.C.Vega, F.M.Gutierrez, M.G.Elias, O.Ortiz, R.A.Hernandez, C.Ponet, A.Hoering, A.Schlatter, C.Sica, I.Sánchez , A.J.Bruggeman, S.J.Headley, E.Y.Choi, A.Gracia, D.B.Spears, M.W.Toyne, B.S.Gelinske, C.L.Giese, N.L.Butts, A.D.Schwickerath, A.T.Mims, A.Z.Clark, B.J.Honsey, B.S.Mayer, B.W.Duggins Jr., C.A.Franklin, C.B.Smith, C.D.Ford Jr., C.D.Timmer, C.J.Bakotic, C.S.Christ, D.D.Suleski, D.E.Moore, D.G.Steele Jr., D.H.Roy, D.J.McCombs, D.L.Wollenburg, D.M.Zurn, D.O.Knighten, D.R.Jackson, E.T.Matteson, G.L.Hearon, J.Bell, J.E.Drury, J.G.White, J.H.Oody, J.M.Beam, J.P.Ehrhardt, J.W.Bradsher, K.A.Brackin, K.J.Schmidt, L.A.Miller, L.L.Lee, L.W.Norgate, M.K.Shuker, M.L.Mitchell, M.R.Hamm, N.L.McLean, P.J.Heil, R.A.McCauley Jr., R.J.Ruden, R.L.Brown, R.L.Laney, S.A.Sparks, S.H.Hairston, S.S.Greywall, T.A.Pace, T.A.Rogers, T.J.Manton, T.S.Sadowski, V.A.Knox, W.T.Rodems, M.A.Cupples, B.Reza,

John Deere Credit employees, Porto Alegre, Brazil, 1999

J.Ramos, M.A.Martinez, H.E.Musa, G.E.Gonzalez, M.G.Aguilar, A.Adam, E.L.Randon, K.R.Miller Jr., P.D.French, A.D.McGregor, B.L.Leistikow, C.J.Ficzere, G.Shantz, J.C.Sastre, K.A.Sarbaugh, L.S.Bobyk, S.J.Wirth, D.J.Kapparos, B.Johnson, D.D.Sand, S.A.Wahl, A.C.Kunz, A.C.Terrell, A.K.Knudson, A.K.Schmidt, A.L.Biermann, B.A.Berns, B.A.Plummer, B.A.Zehring, B.M.Miller, B.M.Windmeyer, B.Poutre, B.R.Wage, B.T.Petersen, C.C.Chilcutt, C.E.Green-Santa Rita, C.L.Dexter, C.L.Gill-Van Blair, C.R.Benson, D.A.Branscomb, D.J.Stonier, D.M.Van Utrecht, E.J.Goulet, E.J.Ward, E.Little, E.M.Fox, E.M.Walters, F.A.Manning, H.K.Beck, J.A.Abogunrin, J.A.Arrowood, J.A.Jepsen, J.A.Schultz, J.C.Keele, J.C.Pillitteri, J.D.Forster, J.D.Graeve, J.L.Guan, J.P.Stone, J.R.Jobes, K.A.Musgrave, K.E.Evans, K.J.Roth, K.K.Sewell, K.M.Carda, K.W.Sulzberger, L.B.Johnson, L.J.Myers, L.L.Glenzer, M.A.Majewski, M.B.Martens, M.D.Hamilton, M.F.Collins, M.Guinn, M.J.Hohnecker, M.L.Arrington, M.L.Fiscus, M.Mannoochahr, M.R.Aufdermauer, M.R.Harbin, M.R.Theisen, M.S.Reglin, N.A.Kidd, N.D.Owenson, N.J.Hackenmiller, N.J.Horstman, P.J.Crane, R.F.Bennett, R.M.Riewerts, R.R.Jerome, R.T.Rasmer, S.A.Greene, S.A.Webster, S.E.Scheiber, S.J.Boyer, S.R.Noffsinger, S.T.Patton, T.D.Cowger, T.F.Leconte, T.L.Decker, T.L.Velnosky, T.M.Alsdorf, T.S.Fulton, T.S.Simpson, V.M.Demean, W.C.Ziegler, W.D.Rose, W.G.Wulf, W.J.Goebel, A.Ashner, A.M.Temple, A.Annoni, R.Malecki, S.Eisleb, J.A.Nash, B.S.Wilson, D.H.Dougherty, E.Solomon, I.Rush, J.A.Clare, K.D.Funches, K.E.Bowen, Z.C.Wenzel, Z.W.Slavens, J.L.Stern, K.W.Eckel, A.M.Pitre, L.F.Franzen, T.Enander, D.E.Krueger, M.D.Bartelson, M.Snopko, V.C.Truong, A.J.Jamerson, A.K.Baker, A.M.Patton, B.H.Masters, B.M.Schult, C.A.Blazicek, C.J.Hoden, C.L.Welp, C.T.Cooper, D.A.Gilley, D.L.Briggs, D.M.Ecker, D.M.Handley, D.N.Pluto, D.R.Marotz, D.W.Bergin, E.A.Marvin, E.J.Fisher, E.J.Wipperfurth, E.M.Haney, E.S.Katz, G.A.Dickinson, G.E.Thrasher, G.J.Walton, G.M.Frodsham, H.K.Miller, H.L.Bozek, H.M.Gray, H.M.Slominski, I.A.Obleton, J.A.Dean, J.B.Grafft, J.C.Gilbeck, J.D.Fielding, J.E.Boyles, J.E.Stesney, J.L.Moser, J.L.Steffens, J.L.Walters, J.M.Walker, J.O.Levister, J.R.Tickner, K.K.Vander Linden, K.M.Perry, L.A.Grubb, L.L.Burch, L.L.Simmons, M.A.Priest, M.D.Van Roosendaal, M.K.Maedke, M.R.Dietsche, M.R.Helling, M.S.Cox, M.S.Murr, M.S.Turner, N.J.Phelan, O.A.Vasilyeva, P.E.Palmer, R.L.Gray, R.M.Budden, S.A.Carothers, S.A.Franklin, S.J.Eisenhauer, T.G.Didelot, T.K.Miller, T.L.Harland, T.T.Miller, T.Y.Coneway, V.P.Jones, W.B.Kosanke, W.M.Ellis, L.Clark, A.M.Gallegos, A.Ruiz, M.Salas, S.E.Hernandez, D.A.Clarke, K.K.Kischer, L.J.Gant, R.A.Stankus, T.D.Beckey, M.L.Davila, K.Ryman, A.L.Schaffter, G.F.Saloky, G.T.Vu, K.A.Luke, J.A.Boone, A.Anzola, J.B.Aubin, L.W.Gakstatter, M.A.Roman, M.J.Cliff, M.Conti, D.G.Desjardins, J.P.Sprinkle, R.K.Dwyer, S.M.Piunno, W.J.Gennings, L.Finau, I.Hernandez, J.G.Ramirez, L.Rosales, M.D.L.Aguilera, R.Lara, O.Enriquez, S.Rabier, B.F.Boeshans, E.A.Timmerman, R.C.Mitra, A.George, A.H.Petra, A.J.Schulz, A.M.Porter, B.D.Newman, B.D.Showalter, B.M.Brinkema, B.Miller, C.A.Haben, C.J.Petra, C.L.Hultgren, C.M.Volkert, C.W.Norris, D.C.Dick, D.M.Leinen, E.C.Harms, E.E.Eberts, G.J.Gillespie, H.A.Carey, J.D.Spooner, J.E.Crosheck, J.G.Peters, J.H.Buchs, J.R.Waits, J.W.Boyes, K.A.Nesmith, K.C.Johnson, K.D.Allen, K.K.Cushman, K.L.Deblieck, K.L.Devogel, K.M.Yu, K.P.Colville, L.C.Gagnon, L.J.Hausner, M.A.Benson, M.D.Moberg, M.J.Pellett, M.L.Allen, M.T.Davison, N.R.Nichols, P.L.Tuning, P.S.Shearer, R.D.Trujillo, R.Narayan, R.R.Edmunds, R.W.Long, S.E.Gannon, S.M.Luoma, S.S.Chan, T.M.Brooks, V.R.Cunningham, W.L.Gerk, W.R.Hough, D.M.Perks, R.Ayers, C.Reyes , P.H.W.H.Billekens, P.G.J.Vullings, A.Ott, A.Poehlmann, C.Aronica, D.Weidner, E.Boehmer, E.Bohnert, E.Wedel, G.Altmann, G.Martos, H.Faber, H.Lahm, H.Schuemann, I.Coban, K.Prowald, M.Wosnitzka, O.Oster, T.Kersten, J.A.Avci, E.T.H.Hartendorp, C.J.Heuvel, D.Dörschel, J.Höschler, K.Korte, T.Sedlaczek, P.Freer, S.A.Cross, C.B.Shope, C.J.Bobbitt, C.S.McCulloch, E.A.Johnson, E.R.Vander Woude, E.S.Dougherty, I.E.Johnson, J.Dicenso, J.N.Riter, J.R.Newman, K.L.Mann, N.P.McClellan, R.E.Boyd, R.K.Smith, R.L.Handley, S.L.Yates, W.E.Tate, W.M.Bennett, A.R.Crandell, A.D.Greenlee, A.E.Stotlar, A.M.Schafer, B.E.Wren, B.J.Didelot, B.R.Booth, C.Reed, D.De Bastiani, D.G.Beauchamp, D.J.Burke, J.E.Goldschmidt Jr., J.E.Mahan, K.A.Williams, K.E.Enstrom, K.L.Klosak, K.Teh, K.W.Patton, M.M.Patterson, R.C.Mehaffey, R.Froemming, R.Irwin, R.W.Egleston, S.L.Foster, S.M.Hill, T.A.Gunn, T.J.Hahm, T.J.Schieltz, T.L.Pearson, T.W.Kiddoo, E.Lechuga, M.Jardon, M.Pinon, R.Amaya, B.Chanthalangsy, E.Heinze, E.Rauleder, G.Kaltwasser, K.Fojcik, P.Betzga, W.Opelender, C.D.Wells, H.Miller, J.A.Midbo, P.P.Le Floch, A.L.Hickey, B.B.Powell, D.B.Dodson, D.E.Coada, F.R.Davis, G.W.Freeland, J.A.Brown, J.C.Teague, J.L.Wilburn, K.L.Cash, P.D.Cusick, R.B.Harvey, S.G.Ruff, S.M.Haynes, T.H.Stinnett, B.Weets, A.J.Skeel, C.J.Hauser, G.M.Smith, M.R.Navarro, A.A.Svoboda, A.B.Cook, A.M.Schelling, B.J.Keen, B.J.Rea, B.M.Ryser, B.R.Sponseller, C.A.Casteel, C.A.Conrad, C.A.McCray, C.C.Krapfl, C.D.Fox, D.A.Hartschuh, D.D.Peters, D.R.Jones, D.S.Berg, H.S.Gilson, J.B.Kelly, J.C.Denson, J.K.Cuvelier, K.E.Moldt, L.M.Betsworth, M.E.Payne, M.L.Sileo, M.R.Oliver, R.L.Henson, S.M.Diddy, S.V.Price, T.A.Leith, T.E.Lunnie, T.E.Ressel, T.V.Calloway Jr., V.K.Henson, W.K.Borrenpohl, W.P.Barklay, Z.L.Lee, J.C.Ortiz, R.Rivera, R.Tarango, S.L.Reynoso, J.L.Rivas, B.Cengiz, J.Romano, J.Sommer, V.Levun, G.E.Brown, J.L.Moceri, J.P.McAlister, J.W.Eiler, K.M.Amann, P.R.Morris, S.J.Keithley, T.D.Hagen, M.K.Chase, N.M.Byres, F. Every, J.M.Mcalister, P.Xiao, R.J.T.A.Hendrikx, C.Henninger, C.Voelker, W.Schmitz, S.Gonzalez L., A.M.Stone, J.F.Valenzuela, K.H.Phillips, L.A.Herrig, M.J.Helms, M.P.Jacobs, Q.S.Early, S.L.Smith, N.K.Smith, S.Bisson-Ellefson, L.L.Belgarde, P.M.Wollan, S.K.Rindy, A.C.Herrmann, A.G.Henn, A.J.Sanville, B.S.Atkins, C.P.Lamarque, D.F.Schmidt, D.H.Rodgers, D.M.Curtis, D.S.Zellmer, G.C.Koutroulakis, G.S.Shirton, J.K.Clum, J.L.Mullins, J.T.Chial, K.M.Keltner, K.Pointer, L.T.Jackson, M.A.Cook, M.D.Pollard, M.J.Snelling, M.J.Waddick, N.Dey, P.A.Mayo, P.R.Heide, R.E.Pommer, R.Jeffcoat, S.J.Miller, S.J.Pettis, S.R.Siasoco, S.R.Sparrow, V.R.Boyd, G.Payne, C.L.Loff, W.P.Simoneaux Jr, C.A.Calleros, A.Jaramillo, A.Ramirez, A.Towns, D.J.Hidrogo, F.G.Estrada, H.Favela, J.C.Ontiveros, J.E.Fernandez, J.F.Muñiz, J.Galindo, J.R.Cruz, J.R.Martinez, L.A.Rojas, M.De la Rosa, M.E.Medina, M.G.Monreal, S.A.Rodriguez, S.S.Andrade, S.Velazquez, V.E.Avila, L.Fester, W.Gujo, J.R.Ibbotson, J.Zarich, D.J.Matherne, F.S.Jones, T.J.Risinger, R.A.Martinolich, V.Liebert, J.H.Aguilera, J.R.Jasper, M.Lodzinski, B.B.Duffy, M.H.Peasley, A.L.Momon, A.L.Sheets, A.M.Gosnell, A.M.Saxonmeyer, B.A.Cobble, B.D.Hilton, B.D.Unglesbee, B.S.Harvey, C.E.Sexton, C.L.Godfrey, C.R.Neumann, C.T.Evers, D.A.Long, D.D.Holt, D.M.Tipton, D.S.States, D.W.Kimbrough, D.W.Stepp, F.D.Ganter, G.Francis III, G.Joanis, G.W.Hensley, J.B.Warner, J.G.Ricker, J.J.Sims, J.M.Duyck, K.D.Starnes, K.L.Sheffler, K.M.Cone, L.L.Hensley, L.R.Lacy, M.A.White, M.W.Peterson, R.Bischof, R.D.Lambert, R.P.Madden, S.A.Jones, S.J.Schultz, S.T.Zupan, S.Wales, T.L.Caron, T.L.Young, T.M.Johnson, V.Sr.iram, W.G.Morris, V.M.Calvert, C.A.Boudreaux, R.K.Dufrene, G.Lopez, H.E.Arias, J.A.Lechuga, V.M.Badillo, A.Torres, C.A.Morales, F.Cervantes, F.Martinez, G.Perez, H.A.Rodriguez, H.Romero, J.E.Hernandez, L.A.Alvarado, M.Saldaña, O.M.Morales, P.M.Pichardo, R.Martinez, W.I.Morales, R.Jackson, C.M.Neis, R.L.Glass Jr., D.J.Boudreaux, D.M.Schalk, G.J.Schwickerath, K.R.Braadt, P.D.Holst, T.M.Burnett, D.M.Boudreaux, C.D.Newton, J.P.Bremser, L.T.Hartz, T.P.Weiler, P.R.Herrmann, T.B.Stein, J.H.Liu, J.Si, L.Xu, Z.B.Deng, J.M.Valdez, M.A.Nava, T.Eberl, S.P.A.Boers, O.Leveque, A.Bosnjak, A.Goere, C.Herden, E.Buning, F.Suessdorf, G.Balk, H.Luebbers, H.Sorg, J.Krebs, J.Rutz, J.Scherer, K.Heiser, K.Kinzel, M.Schmahl, M.Weise, R.Schuero, R.Viola, S.Burckhardt, S.Koenig, S.Koessler, S.Koskeridou, S.Mustafa, V.Laufer, W.Kickertz, G.Compagni, S.Ferrerio, P.M.Koger, R.Nijenhuis, H.Van Vliet, R.Wachtmeester, G.Van De Worp, H.Hemmert, U.Hüskens, K.M.Urbanek, J.L.Alves, J.L.Himel, M.V.Nasonov, R.Sperotto, J.G.Himel, C.Xing, V.Qu, A.Montoya, C.Chavarria, C.L.Lujan, E.Gutierrez, H.R.Aguilar, J.L.Valencia, L.A.Perez, L.E.Nieto, M.Olivas, M.T.Tarango, O.A.Trevizo, S.G.Reyes, S.Lopez, E.Ramos, F.Flores, D.Weichholdt, F.Vogelgesang, D.M.Brunton, S.E.Westman, A.H.Heitman Keefe, B.E.Lanfair, C.A.Burmania, C.L.Caruso, C.L.Colas, D.R.Dietz, J.B.Ramos, J.L.Huff, J.L.White, J.M.Lobaito, P.J.Montgomery, R.A.Crowe, R.L.Hudachek, S.B.Herring, S.L.Cahalan, T.R.Kiely, P.G.Brock, A.L.Hardin, C.C.Spittel, J.D.Johnson, M.W.Naylor, F.D.Gros, J.P.Moore, M.J.Thibodaux Jr, S.M.Miracle, A.Cao, M.A.Hernandez, F.Roth, M.D.Nicholas, R.M.Bea, A.M.Eckhart, A.O.Oyaide, D.A.Knight, D.E.Culp, I.C.Carreno, J.B.Zoet, J.Campbell, J.J.Lichtenberg, J.M.Sloan, K.A.Bouchard, K.P.Matthews, N.B.Offerdahl, R.J.Smith, S.C.Holmgren, S.D.Fulton, T.G.Barnfield, T.M.Rodrigue, W.A.French, I.F.Vasques, D.J.Knight, D.P.Gros, K.Landry, M.E.Tabor Jr, R.R.Breaux, T.T.Rodrigue, A.Gomez, A.S.Espino, C.M.Ramirez, E.Garcia, M.J.Gutierrez, N.Espino, O.A.Rascon, V.M.Franco, V.Villa, M.P.Saracho, B.Rodique, W.D.Howe, C.Williams, A.J.Currie, M.D.Wolf, R.D.Hiss, R.E.Mikruta, C.Kutsch, S.A.Schulz, J.J.Garcia, V.H.Udave, A.E.Huebner, A.E.Swenson, A.R.Ariano, B.Mattei, C.R.Fredricksen, C.R.Place, C.T.Welch, D.Carr, D.G.Wiederin, E.K.Jones, G.A.Rupp, G.G.Boisvert, J.K.Phillips, J.P.Landry, K.A.Minck, M.E.Vandevoorde, M.L.Samuelson, M.V.Salz, R.K.Hopkins, R.McClain, S.A.Fuller, T.Robinson, C.R.Honnef, L.F.Bartz, L.Wolfart, S.S.Kretschmer, B.G.Knight, J.J.Tabor, P.C.Rogers, A.P.Gonzalez, B.A.Flores, B.Olivas, C.A.Lopez, C.J.Villa, E.Hernandez, E.Soto, F.J.Calderon, J.Hernandez, J.Valenzuela, L.Torres, M.D.C.Aguilera, M.Madrid, O.Gardea, R.A.Maldonado, R.Morales, S.R.Macias, V.Alvarez, C.Robles, F.Sturm, A.M.Keefe, J.D.McClanahan, J.K.Engstrom, M.M.Winchek, D.Wang, J.D.Dupuis, J.Ho, A.E.Bushong, B.A.Brinson, C.A.Sanders, C.M.Slavich, C.R.White, D.B.Hamby, D.J.Young, E.A.Butler Jr., E.F.McCall, E.G.Walker, G.F.Clinton, J.B.Solberg, J.D.Whitney, J.F.Palmer, J.M.Basinger, J.R.Benoit, J.W.Shirley, K.C.Crumb, M.D.Cole, M.D.McLean, M.L.Holland, M.W.Ellis, N.E.McQuade, N.Milot, P.J.Richter, P.L.Steen, P.L.Thomas, R.D.Cable, R.G.Schackow, R.L.Self, S.A.Rhynehart, S.E.Sallows, S.L.Caudy, S.L.Ethridge, T.D.Johnson, T.P.Marchese, R.I.Cloake, E.Boudreaux, J.Daggs, R.J.Gros, A.Flores, B.Simental, C.R.Jaramillo, E.Alvarado, G.Alvarez, J.A.Lozoya , J.Lara, L.T.Lara, M.D.J.Gallegos, M.R.Rmairez, R.A.Vazquez, R.D.Vazquez, R.Vargas, T.D.J.Banda, T.D.J.Gonzalez, S.Lagaude, A.Warren, C.J.Ryner, K.M.Huffman, Z.S.Fleming, J.P.Rodriguez, A.L.Langfrey, C.J.Herron, J.A.Winchester, B.F.Becker, T.A.Link, C.I.Gonzalez, C.Moreno, C.O.Avena, J.E.Ramirez, M.D.J.Hinojos, N.Enriquez, O.H.Holguin, S.Palma, A.C.Legott, C.L.Leacox, D.J.Carroll, E.M.Wong, H.V.Kavalier, P.Pathak, R.L.Biddle, W.P.Richardson, J.Kopic, F.L.Gregory, G.L.Melton, J.M.Franklin, C.A.M.Engels-Nabben, A.P.J.Hiernard, A.Roth, A.Eis, A.Goenan, A.Meller, A.Sahin, D.Eckfelder, D.Scheich, D.Toson, E.Torschmied, H.Dirscherl, H.Laun, H.Roth, J.Winkler, L.Mueller, M.Fabello-Agromayor, M.Gammella, M.Garcia-Martin, M.Myers, P.Schmidt, S.Ninnsger, S.Voellmer, T.Emser, B.Gevers, C.Gräwers , H.Lucaßen, M.Pennekamp, A.E.J.Spoelstra, T.Bubenzer, B.Cox, J.Smee, A.A.Hill, A.D.Bahr, A.I.Schwartz, A.J.Miller, A.K.Webber, A.M.Erlandson Brown, A.M.Esquivel, A.V.Diew, B.A.Blum, B.E.Fisher, B.H.Clark, B.H.Walker, B.J.Stroede, B.L.Zillmer, C.D.Laver, D.A.Kuhn, D.D.Bednarek, D.G.Sitzman, D.L.Imel, D.L.Wilkinson, D.M.Sanchez, E.E.White, E.W.Klintworth, G.J.Malson Jr., H.L.Hunsucker, J.A.Lenhardt, J.D.Herringa, J.J.Bohnert, J.M.Roque, J.R.Jahnke, J.S.Martinez, J.V.Terlisner, J.W.Forster, K.A.Rettschlag, K.K.Tetzlaff, K.L.Rueckert, K.L.Ruff, L.A.Gross, L.A.Livingston, L.D.Sullivan, L.E.Zumm, L.J.Finn Jr., L.L.Dahl, L.R.Lettau, L.S.Erber, M.J.Oft, M.J.Pennekamp, M.M.Moritz, M.O.Stoner, M.S.Wimberly, P.B.Robson, P.J.Wash, P.R.Rank, P.S.Moodey, R.B.Hill, R.C.Williamson, R.L.Schroeder, R.L.Williamson, R.R.Sheely, S.C.Kastenmeier, S.J.Rourke, S.L.Goodall, S.M.Schellin, S.R.Reynolds, T.K.Murphy, T.M.Neuman, T.R.Lookman, W.J.Schweiger, A.D.Rossarola, A.G.Jung, C.Hammes, D.J.Butzke, E.J.Pinheiro, F.C.Hilgemann, F.J.Marx, F.S.Haezel, G.Rodrigues, J.A.Rupp, J.J.D.Cunha, J.L.Schneider, M.J.Rodrigues, R.P.Klein, S.L.Mallmann, C.H.I Issa, F.Daigle, W.B.Billiot, W.T.Lawson, M.I.Perea, S.Baumgart, S.Suess, T.Ehresmann, T.Schmidt, M.Zanini, A.Enns, S.Goodbourn, P.Martin, S.Lee, A.T.Lounsbury, B.M.Dreyer, C.D.Fredrich, G.G.Horton, J.A.Foster, M.L.Patenaude, C.L.Myers, G.Washington, S.P.O'Hanlon, A.R.Melendez, A.R.Sandoval, A.Rodriguez, E.Andrew, G.Dominguez, M.H.Ceballos, M.R.Gamboa, N.L.Rivera, R.G.Gamez, R.Gaspar, K.C.Lyon, J.O.Erickson, B.A.Butler, B.J.McLemore, B.S.Andric, C.A.Wilson, C.G.Martin III, C.N.Willis, D.L.Klostermann, E.W.Lambert, G.F.Frederick, I.S.Gatewood, J.A.Smith, J.H.Numberger, J.I.Ramsey, J.R.Boling, J.W.Runyon, K.J.Saxon, K.L.Gordinier, L.F.Klemm, M.A.Boone, M.Butler, M.J.Frank, M.J.Smith, M.L.Merritt, P.A.Clark, P.J.Henderson, R.J.Seymour, R.Robles Jr., S.D.Mizer, S.M.Edwards, V.M.Robinson, J.L.Correa, A.Holguin, A.M.Rodarte, A.Perez, B.M.Torres, C.Guerrero, C.P.Corral, C.Perez, D.S.Salinas, E.Cruz, E.Martell, J.A.Alarcon, J.A.Valles, J.Guzman, J.L.Garibay, J.P.Cinco, L.Anchondo, L.S.Garcia, M.Diaz, M.I.Rodriguez, M.S.Gutierrez,

M.Tarango, O.Venegas, R.Molina, S.Ceballos, S.M.Arevalo, S.Mancinas, S.Soto, V.Calzadillas, T.B.Bachand, B.K.Berry, K.P.McGinty, J.D.Gonzalez, C.F.Cue, D.S.Jones, R.J.Stevenson, J.Villarreal, J.L.Sublett, L.Mertins, S.L.Paulson, T.R.Bodvig, A.B.Gallagher, A.J.Cusmano, B.A.Hans, B.J.Green, D.L.Schroeder, D.S.Lickness, E.B.Robertson, E.J.Patterson, F.A.Hartwell, G.J.Hildebrandt, J.A.Mahoney-Hansen, J.E.Dominic, J.E.Loudon, K.J.Christensen, K.K.Stanze, L.N.Lyons, M.D.Steger, M.E.Goodson, M.L.Browning, M.R.Cooke, S.E.Ellis, S.J.Foss, T.A.Farkas, T.L.Franklin, T.P.Chaires, V.Shepard, W.McKirdy, P.E.Gwynne, S.R.Long, K.Neal, K.P.Foret, P.Zhao, A.C.Sosa, A.Chapa, A.G.Cisneros, A.Perales, C.Dominguez, C.Palafox, C.Rodriguez, D.Montana, D.N.Aguirre, E.M.D.J.Monarrez, E.R.Rodriguez, G.E.Sanchez, G.Tarango, J.A.Tena, M.A.Ochoa, M.C.Tinoco, M.D.C.Chavez, M.Hernandez, M.I.Terrazas, M.J.Burciaga, M.M.Rodriguez, M.Macias, M.T.Hernandez, R.A.Meza, R.M.Diaz, V.Estrada, Z.R.Garay, O.Mora, H.V.Juarez, A.Ehmann, A.Mainz, A.Mairle, C.Augustin, C.Wassner, D.Goubet, H.Bruns, J.Lubianka, M.Rennies, M.Weinberger, R.Schubach, S.Kardumovic, S.Svrga, T.Bourdon, T.Eren, U.Laak, W.Hein, W.Schaefer, W.Wegfahrt, J.S.Langness, C.R.Travis, K.J.Menke, J.Brown, C.A.Ornelas, C.Arias, D.A.Torres, E.I.Guajardo, E.N.Espinoza, F.Nunez, G.E.Escarcega, H.Flores, H.Rascon, I.V.Espinoza, J.A.Arroyo, J.J.Espinoza, J.J.Holguin, J.L.Cruz, J.M.Alvidrez, L.E.Vazquez, M.L.Chavez, M.R.Reyes, M.T.Diaz, O.R.Chavez, A.A.Libio, J.T.Allman, J.V.Patterson, T.K.Osei, R.Nixon, J.D.Malarkey, M.M.Gerdon, A.Awhaitey, A.L.Vonnahme, A.N.Choudhry, A.T.Ninyeh, A.Y.Ninyeh, B.J.Bauer, C.L.Weber, C.Lovell, C.W.Leach, D.Perry, G.A.Benns, G.N.Lamptey, J.Hill-West, J.Mazzei, J.McGee Jr., K.L.Lundahl, M.A.McFeders, M.P.Speak, R.I.Vrbanac, R.L.McClain, R.P.Hansen, S.Zornes, T.A.Loes, T.E.Golladay Jr., T.L.Farmer, T.M.Cook, W.E.Lance, A.A.Parella, A.G.Trajtenberg, F.A.Luis López, M.J.Gibbs, R.A.Parnis, A.C.Sato, D.D.Dal Pizol, F.A.C.Moraes, B.A.Guerrero, E.Estrada, H.M.Miramontes, L.Mendoza, L.R.Lara, M.Hernandez, M.Lamas, M.Mandoza, N.I.Guerra, R.C.Lira, R.Garcia, R.Torres, S.Burchett, M.J.Branham, J.R.Rubick, R.K.Mooney, S.B.Watts, K.J.Svensson, A.L.Smith, L.M.Parks, W.W.Christopher, F.Jennngs, P.Lamoreau, D.M.Anderson, R.R.Krause, B.J.Hibberts, B.J.Stevens, B.W.Banks, C.A.Berg, C.A.Caruso, C.A.Meeske, C.M.Duea, C.W.Julian, D.C.Coates, D.Goel, D.K.Jackson, D.L.Freeman, J.J.Neal, J.M.Barber, J.M.McGriff, J.M.Thompson, J.W.Cook II, K.A.Olerich, K.A.Sedam, K.J.O'Donnell, K.L.Lane Jr., L.L.Buhr, M.K.Iseminger, M.K.Leidel, M.R.Evers, M.T.Shields, M.Trinidad, R.A.Deblaey Jr., R.G.Kucharski, R.J.Carpenter, S.E.Faulkner, S.M.Boyd, S.T.Johnson, T.E.Sherer, T.S.Mateer, A.S.Murdoch, A.Holguin, A.L.Caraveo, A.L.Rivera, A.Mendoza, A.Ontiveros, B.Gaytan, C.Montes, E.S.Vega, E.Varela, G.Gutierrez, H.Martinez, I.Lozano, J.A.Caro, J.A.Rodarte, J.G.Munoz, J.L.Rivera, J.Ochoa, J.Salazar, J.Saucedo, L.L.Galvan, M.Carrillo, M.D.C.Luna, M.Gardea, M.I.Guaderrama, N.I.Avila, N.I.Quinonez, N.R.Lopez, R.Cano, S.Ramirez, B.C.Hooten, G.E.Ratchford, J.P.Gilbreath, L.R.Felice, R.S.Wilharm, T.Q.Le, W.O.Warthen, G.Martinez, C.Stiggins, A.W.Verstraete, C.A.Alanis, C.G.Cobb, G.R.Talkington, J.W.Holladay, K.G.Johnston, K.M.Hill, M.L.Perkins, M.R.Reynolds, N.B.Watts, P.V.Lillis, C.S.D.Moura, G.G.Radmann, I.C.Stefanello, L.B.Creasso, L.C.H.Bohlke, M.L.Domanski, D.M.Oubre, J.A.Cervantes, J.L.G.Bertrams, R.C.D.Verhaegh, C.Lebon, J.Creissel, A.Celebi, A.Erdle, A.Flaig, A.Hofer, A.Laubenthal, A.Lindenau, A.Maier, A.Nickel, A.Sage, A.Spacke, A.Swaydan, A.Top, A.Veith, A.Vunic, A.Weinheimer, B.Bubel, B.Ickhorn, B.Roll, C.Bas, C.Doerr, C.Stasch, C.Thoenes, D.Hasenfratz, D.Szarzynski, E.Simon, F.Barth, G.Field, G.Freyer, G.Schilha, G.Seyler, I.Ordel, J.Nowak, J.Pelczer, J.Strischakov, K.Bleifuss, K.Gerwig, K.Goerguelue, K.Klinner, L.Jaenicke, M.Brand, M.Calik, M.Firat, M.Harbauer, M.Krause, M.Moellendick, M.Neumann, M.Opazo Bustamente, M.Pytel, M.Ratano, M.Richter, N.Bruch, O.Sandhas, P.Cnota, R.Jungblut, S.Bley, S.Gegenwarth, S.Glowatsch, S.Knapp, S.Kron, S.Metzler, S.Scholler, S.Vanselow, S.Vural, T.Fuchs, T.Gola, T.Weber, T.Zoller, U.Scheff, W.Drachenberg, W.Lampe, W.Moch, W.Oesterreicher, Z.Kopic, B.M.J.Ensink, A.Koenders, M.Razzaki, P.Thio, C.Miller, A.B.Roberson, P.A.Heyman, J.R.Putnam, B.S.Smith, F.F.Vave, A.A.Almeida, A.Bustillos, A.P.Zuniga, C.A.Gonzalez, C.V.Gonzalez, D.Pallares, D.V.Chavez, E.A.Lozoya, E.Cornejo, E.R.Soto, F.J.Torres, G.Barradas, H.A.Borunda, J.L.Holguin, J.R.Tarango, K.A.Simental, K.E.Mejia, L.Hernandez, M.C.Contreras, M.D.Miranda, M.E.Solis, M.Gallegos, M.L.Bonilla, M.Martinez, M.Y.Aguirre, R.C.Martinez, R.Chavarria, S.C.Inzunza, Y.Franco, H.Weinland, S.Frank, M.A.C.B.Schaepman, S.A.Cound, D.Gillmore, E.S.Reeves, H.D.Lyons, J.D.Haskins, J.L.Schreier, J.M.Wyns, J.N.Djorgee, K.Gracey, L.J.Walker, L.S.Iliff, M.S.Sowers, M.Wieschkowski, N.M.Chemerika, P.M.Baldwin, P.R.Seberger, S.G.Pacyna, S.R.Bowlin, T.Carter, T.V.Watson, M.L.Derma, D.Ata, F.Eira Da, J.Jagemann, K.Wagner, T.Spann, C.L.Determan, D.Spiers, K.E.Zazula, T.R.Owens, C.F.Pinto, L.V.Bastianelli, K.G.Perez, W.E.Bergen, R.Mahoney, P.Nielsen, J.Autowski, J.P.Lackman, N.Hawk, R.A.Poitra, S.A.Kitsmiller, S.A.Westman, B.L.Waterman, C.E.Stanley, C.S.Johnson, D.J.Bland, D.P.McCoy, F.S.Bolton, G.W.Halcro, K.C.Duax, K.T.Wood, L.G.Hall, L.S.McDougald, M.D.Colville, M.W.Grothusen, P.A.Strohmeyer, P.J.Kenkel, R.D.Gossett, R.L.Horn, S.Rimmington, T.B.Maynor, T.M.Genter, V.E.Williams, H.S.Scheid, D.M.Folse, A.A.Cano, A.Hernandez, A.Loya, A.M.Rodriguez, A.R.Ramos, D.E.Carbajal, D.Molina, E.I.Espinoza, F.O.Davila, G.Balderrama, G.Samaniego, J.A.Reyna, J.F.Rosales, J.G.Soto, J.L.Perez, J.Tarango, L.A.Soto, L.P.Moya, M.C.Valdez, M.D.Arreola, M.Gonzalez, M.S.Chavira, R.Baez, R.F.Dominguez, Y.B.Enriquez, E.Mena, P.J.M.Groenen, H.T.M.Joosten, N.Claudel, A.Ort, N.Fritz, Y.Demir, A.Valdivia Jr., R.P.Gates, F.Ibarra, A.A.Griffin, B.E.Janita, K.Y.Countryman, T.M.Zeringue, J.Schmitt, T.Zgaljic, M.J.Hamilton, P.J.Kiernan, C.V.Torres, D.Trevizo, G.Lugo, J.A.Tovali, L.M.Saenz, O.R.Madero, S.E.Flores, D.M.Vuiyale, C.I.Bullington, J.Fletcher, J.L.Krueger, A.L.Stombaugh, A.M.Scott, A.Renzi, B.C.Alwin, B.M.Thompson, C.A.Allie, D.A.Hodges, D.Lett, H.H.Burke Jr., K.W.Trumbull, M.M.Grubbs, M.S.Lucas, N.Jones III, N.V.Morrow, P.A.Kulas, P.Bray, P.G.Herstedt, P.S.Brewer, R.R.Farrell, S.D.Newman, S.E.Montgomery, S.H.Plunkett, S.L.Maxwell, S.P.Eppel, T.R.Rice Jr., M.D.Lewis, C.Armendariz, E.Duran, S.A.Rivera, A.Cardoza, A.F.Vital, A.Ledezma, C.A.Estrada, C.A.Palacios, E.Ramirez, H.U.Hernandez, J.A.Rojas, J.A.Sanchez, J.C.Martinez, J.G.Lara, J.G.Salas, J.L.Madrid, M.A.Davila, M.A.Lopez, M.M.Mora, O.G.Esquivel, O.Hernandez, O.Ramirez, R.Serrano, S.Gonzalez, E.Karahan, M.Eigenmann, T.Oran, W.Renner, A.L.Izzo, A.M.Renfro, J.H.Braun, S.K.Backen, F.A.Munaro, C.J.Silva, J.F.Butler, M.C.Kittleson, R.D.Brewer Jr., R.D.Feeney, K.A.Kronafel, E.Dedaj, M.Jarosch, A.P.Pottebaum, V.Nikola, D.L.Briggs, K.J.Zimbelman, K.L.Klocke, N.B.Christoferson, V.E.Sonju, A.E.Stone Jr., A.Vann Jr., C.L.Goeller, C.M.Henson, C.M.Stephenson, C.P.Bryant, C.T.Norton, C.W.Bau, D.J.Kimble, D.S.Baker, E.R.Orcutt, E.W.Ivey Jr., H.M.Jennings, J.A.Schlautman, J.J.Reische, J.R.Jurgensen, J.R.Shukla, J.T.Lashley, J.W.Mason, J.W.Morissette, K.S.Daugherty, L.E.Spain, L.L.Cofield, L.R.Blumberg, M.A.Ventresca, M.C.Noel, M.J.Handley, M.L.Jones, M.M.Francisco, M.S.Dawson, N.A.Himes, N.R.Johnson, P.B.Hill, P.Fourn, R.R.Scarf, R.R.Thompson, R.S.Fazekas, S.A.Rathje, S.R.Bentz, T.C.Reid, T.L.Cyrus, T.R.Self, T.S.Nelson, W.A.Larsen, A.Hernandez, B.G.Chavez, C.A.Zermeno, D.P.Rodriguez, E.Contreras, F.Y.Gaspar, G.Chavez, G.Murillo, I.Chavez, K.A.Gonzalez, M.G.Jasso, M.Mata, M.S.Portillo, P.C.Rodriguez, R.I.Garibay, R.Larios, S.E.Espinoza, S.L.Chacon, G.A.Quintero, T.N.Bazzle, D.Bertolo, S.M.Chitko, A.L.Moose, C.D.Hanley, C.J.Jonas, C.S.Wells, D.A.Norenberg, D.K.Schmidt, D.M.Liske, D.W.Cox, H.L.Kay, J.E.Rafter, J.J.Hinds, K.J.Tucker, K.R.Landen, L.G.Hofmann Jr., M.J.Brahs, M.W.Shook, R.A.James, R.D.Rodgers, R.J.Mason Jr., R.L.Lamb, T.A.Wolos, W.P.Kostrewski, C.A.Quintana, E.E.Chavez, E.Gutierrez, E.Prieto, E.Ramirez, H.Armendariz, I.Varela, J.A.Adame, J.A.Herrera, J.A.Zapien, J.A.Zubiate, J.E.Alvarez, M.Lopez, M.P.Torres, O.M.Alanis, S.P.Cervantes, S.Portillo, T.A.Chavez, V.J.Contreras, V.Murillo, D.G.Holtz, G.A.Searl, J.I.Lynch, J.T.Upmeyer, R.E.McBride, S.J.Macdonald Graves, P.Duquennoy, C.Bourcier, A.Cakir, A.Huver, A.Maier, B.Brill, C.Bauer, C.Fieber, D.Leisse, D.Schoenborn, D.Vucenovic, E.Manser, G.Sucietto, H.Dietrich, H.Frank, H.Reinwald, H.Sauer, I.Bilac, J.Wind, K.Dobert, L.Brandenburger, L.Henschke, L.Stripf, M.Caliskan, M.Gehm, M.Lambert, N.Oppermann, R.Bognar, R.Martin, T.Donner, T.Fickus, T.Metzger, T.Mueller, W.Anacker, W.Koellner, F.Ayuso , H.Li, C.W.Duke, G.P.Rogers, K.K.Kapp, K.R.Wagner, R.Worrel, T.A.Cromwell, B.S.Brown, C.L.James, C.L.Simmons, C.R.Lewis, C.R.Sikkenga, D.L.Murphy, J.W.Lerdal, K.A.White, M.J.Hayes, M.L.Swain, R.F.Szymusiak, S.C.Albright, S.C.McCartney, S.J.Spence, S.R.Godwin, S.W.Philbrick, Y.Hayslett, B.P.Vicknair, H.Baron, A.Rascon, C.A.Sigala, C.D.Arzate, D.Amaya, E.Casas, J.Molinar, L.A.Marrufo, L.G.Gutierrez, M.A.Avila, O.Gonzalez, O.V.Aragon, S.E.Hidalgo, D.Pfab, S.Baron, P.J.G.Everloo, A.E.Fragola, M.L.Riedesel, T.Y.Maddox, V.L.Dean, N.H.Jorgensen, K.Jones, C.W.Southall, C.A.Phelps, C.Hernandez, D.A.Martinez, G.Ochoa, J.D.Diaz, J.Garcia, L.E.Beltran, M.Diaz, M.J.Ramos, M.Mendoza, M.Ruiz, M.Tellez, R.A.Aguirre, R.L.Gomez, R.M.Rico, R.V.Marquez, S.O.Carrillo, S.P.Lechuga, T.E.Diaz, T.V.Reynoso, C.Herden, A.R.Marshall, D.J.Black, J.Bartodziej, M.Henry, M.J.Olson, B.R.Waugh, C.A.Knupp, C.E.Jones, C.L.Yeater, C.M.Sivertsen, C.R.Lohr, C.S.Pates, D.A.Knopf, D.A.Quam, D.D.Willis, D.J.Brockington, E.L.Gregory, G.Wienke, J.A.Morehead, J.B.Vann, J.Cox, L.D.McCaw, M.D.Stubblefield Jr., P.S.Huntley, S.M.Terry, T.J.Baer, T.L.Washington, V.E.Nottingham, I.Lopez, C.Alvarez, J.A.Martinez, A.Demirtas, A.Zaper, C.Kraechan, P.Vigni, H.Lashon, A.Puscher, L.A.Sebastian, J.M.Montalto, K.M.Swiderski, M.J.Azotini, R.J.Tyminski, S.Vezeau, S.W.Bassette, W.J.Infantino, M.S.West, M.Y.Gray, R.A.Hanson, T.M.Ward, C.S.Bennetts, A.Valerio, E.P.Maldonado, F.M.Lopez, G.F.Y.Diaz, J.L.Castanon, J.L.Hernandez, J.L.Rojo, J.R.Reyes, N.Rodriguez, O.I.Ponce, R.Hernandez, V.H.Paez, Y.Hernandez, M.M.Becker, N.Cosby, A.Wanless, C.M.Grover, E.R.Sorrell, E.S.Donahue, M.G.McAdam, N.J.Stower, R.G.Thackray, B.S.Battistelli, C.L.Denning, C.T.McCord, D.D.Morris, D.R.Dussault, J.D.Ringer, J.L.Rosenow, K.J.Karow, M.Robinson, N.E.Blank, R.C.Knudsen, T.H.Wurm, T.M.Tatum, K.A.Jones, A.M.Chatagnier, M.J.Benoit, D.R.Acuna, C.A.Sandoval, A.Carrasco, V.Lopez, C.Karch, C.Maciej, K.Steiner, R.Dechant, Y.Salman, A.J.Cole, C.L.Minor, D.J.Bucher, E.G.Noll, T.W.Ewanochko, L.J.Gray, P.Fenton, I.Brodsky, B.L.Foster, D.L.Waldschmitt, D.M.Frields, L.M.Morris, P.R.Zen, E.Nolan, T.Heib, S.J.Arnold, T.M.Elliott, D.Cannon, K.Engweiler, G.W.Sayers, J.F.Henning, J.J.Rogahn, M.J.Daum, M.R.Jensen, R.D.Paulson, A.A.Yeater, A.Able, A.R.Buescher, B.A.Currie, B.D.Birckett, D.M.Shragal, E.K.Williams, J.A.Land, J.D.Vaughn, J.E.Young, J.L.Harris, J.L.Vesey, J.N.Adam, J.S.Magnuson, K.Clark, K.J.Devries, K.J.Pitre, K.L.Aschbrenner, K.M.Feuerbach, K.R.Raber, L.A.Gomez, L.A.Lainberger, L.M.Murray, L.W.Sidwell, M.A.Dodd, P.C.Mayes, R.L.Ingram, S.A.Charles, S.A.Evenson, S.A.Harbar, S.C.Barker, S.L.Gordy, S.Mani, S.R.Barton, T.S.Jankowski, W.K.Ripberger, W.L.Sutton Jr., J.E.Daigle, J.M.Becnel, K.P.Pitre, A.Juarez, A.Milburn, C.Gutierrez, C.Rodriguez, E.Garcia, F.J.Miranda, G.Cereceres, J.Basaldua, J.C.Zamarron, J.L.Alcantar, J.Nevarez, L.Hernandez, M.Ortiz, P.A.Chavira, R.L.Martinez, S.A.Santos, D.Baez, E.A.Tovar, E.E.Maldonado, E.J.Rocha, E.Liceaga, F.A.Barrera, F.A.Escalante, F.A.Villanueva, F.J.Alday, F.Lopez, H.A.Rivas, I.Camarillo, I.E.Padilla, J.D.Esquivel, J.De Leon, J.J.Guerrero, L.A.Garcia, M.A.Lopez, M.Mendoza, P.Perez, R.A.Zavala, R.Gomez, R.Leyva, U.E.Montiel, J.Rudolph, J.A.Mixdorf, J.C.Hutter, J.S.Way, C.D.Brinkley, A.P.Miller, J.E.Hanson, J.L.Turner, L.J.Lirette, S.M.Lirette, T.J.Martin, M.A.Thimmesch, H.R.Deen, J.M.Nation, P.J.Neuwohner, P.Ramanathan, R.J.Peterson, R.M.Beardsley, T.L.Irwin, T.L.Rademacher, V.S.Sierra, S.Schmalz, R.D.Sagvold, S.E.Olstad, S.L.Bredeson, J.K.Iverson, D.E.Johnson, D.M.Roberg, P.L.Weshnevski, M.J.Knight, C.A.Lambrecht, J.L.Schmaltz, D.E.Haugen, S.D.Berntson, M.Petrowitz, K.E.Getzlaff, K.R.Shape, C.W.Wieck, T.L.Moser, G.J.Gregoryk, C.O.Spitzer, D.E.Nilsen, D.L.Lysne, R.S.Roberg, J.C.Manstrom, D.L.Scheen, J.L.Gerhardt, L.S.Jacobson, E.G.Jewett, J.A.Smedshammer, J.Volk, B.Nelson, F.Schroeder, J.D.Martin, C.Mooridian, T.Roaldson, S.A.Anderson, D.A.Veselka, R.Knight, D.F.Breuer, J.Greenley, L.J.Nishek, C.A.Tangen, E.C.Horsager, J.D.Lindgren, J.H.McAllister, D.J.Smith, J.M.Haugen, C.Duffy, D.L.Peter, T.D.Burchill, K.E.Hovland, G.Reed, M.L.Olstad, T.A.Broberg, B.Lechtenberg, R.Petrie, A.Grantham, K.R.Ceynar Jr., L.R.Dickelman, L.R.Miller, T.D.Krueger, B.F.Yakimetz, B.M.Weeks, B.V.Azzoto, C.D.Stout, D.A.Rocha, D.Baier, D.C.Labus, D.D.Dicken, D.L.Ambort, E.S.Bradford, G.A.Refbord, J.E.Sloggy, J.J.Martin, K.A.Robertson, K.D.Goedken, K.L.Jones, K.T.Bartee, M.C.Bertlshofer, M.L.Yates, M.P.Gannon, M.P.Olsen, P.L.Fenwick, P.L.Krenz, R.J.Heller, R.J.Young, R.P.Ferguson, R.R.Thibert, T.M.Arnold, T.W.Schoonbaert, W.T.Needler, F.Marinelli, M.M.Eddison, R.B.Alves, A.J.Vicknair, C.A.Cox, J.A.Pitre, J.C.Martin, L.A.Jimenez, L.P.Wells, M.J.Acosta, M.J.Rodrigue, M.P.Richard, Z.J.Adams, C.A.Lopez, C.L.Grado, E.A.Castellanos, E.Balderrama, G.Rangel, H.Naca, J.A.Acosta, J.A.Rivera, J.L.Torres, J.O.Espinoza, L.Molina, L.Y.Rivera, M.C.Payan, M.D.L.L.Torres, M.E.Reyes, M.G.Catano, Mmm.G.Espinosa, R.Gil, W.Grado, A.Saldaña, C.A.Rodriguez, J.H.Rodriguez, S.Fernandez, H.Jakupovic, A.Leibfahrt, D.Martin, E.Wittmann, G.Cammilleri, G.Leeb, H.Preisendanz, H.Weber, K.Dietrich, K.Schwind, K.Waibel, K.Wenz, M.Bruestle, M.Falkenstein, P.Schwab, R.Daub, R.Haas, R.Loesch, T.Frosch, U.Wolk, W.Bohn, W.Bolhuis, W.Rendgen, M.H.Ter Weele, M.Yilmaz, D.Claxton, T.Beall, B.L.Martin, J.C.Kritchman, J.J.Fox, K.K.Kuhle, K.P.Alsteen, S.A.Apfelbeck, S.E.Eagle, A.G.Saucedo, A.Gonzalez, A.Lizcano, B.Acuña, E.Ponce, F.Guerra, H.E.Jaramillo, J.M.Marin, J.M.Martinez, L.A.Acuña, L.A.Araujo, L.A.Garcia, M.A.Covarrubias, M.A.Martinez, M.A.Perez, O.Maldonado, R.O.Lopez, V.A.Mata, V.Peña, D.Brochet, A.Michalski, A.Odoj, C.Steinert, G.Fassoth, I.Colletti, M.Lahm, M.Richter, M.Thiele, U.Gerlach, U.Grobe, U.Hamman, F.Santopolo, S.Pattberg, A.K.Diorio, J.J.Benoit, J.L.Hoefler, G.S.Hocking, E.Medeiros, J.M.Good, J.P.Benoit, J.E.Sanchez, J.Albert, D.Alexander, J.Alisobhani, J.Beck, J.Dragovich, T.Durand, J.Friese, P.Galyean, J.Genta, V.Hartung, M.Hashimoto, R.D.Hatch, R.Hatch, J.Huang, M.Kaplan, S.Kim, H.Kunze, C.Lai, R.Le, G.Lesperance, D.Li, J.C.Litton, J.D.Litton, M.Masui, J.Mayo, B.Miller, J.Moore, C.Morton, T.Newman, L.J.Palmer, J.Quan, M.Rentz, P.Rosenboom, A.Serna, T.Sharpe, P.Smotrys, G.Stout, J.Taylor, R.Thrasher, P.Williams, K.T.Woo, R.Young, M.Zeitzew, D.J.Vignaroli, C.P.White, D.R.Neal, K.M.Anderson, L.L.Schmidt, R.C.Cruff, A.S.Frederick, B.H.Appelgate, B.R.Smith, D.A.Jordan, D.B.Walker, D.E.Day, D.E.Izzo, D.L.Gillins, D.M.Fournier, G.W.Charette, J.S.Dmytrow, M.D.Levis, M.G.Schlender, P.Walker, R.M.Huggins, G.P.Castilho, B.J.Marcel, B.M.Marcy, C.J.Orgeron, C.M.Hue, D.J.Foret, F.J.Fields, J.A.Leblanc, J.G.Lagarde, L.A.Benoit, L.B.Ponvelle, L.J.Cooley, M.H.Guillot, R.J.Boudreaux Jr, R.J.Chiasson, L.Ye, C.F.Fierro, E.Flores, E.Saldivar, I.N.Juarez, J.A.Flores, J.R.Ponce, L.E.Alanis, L.F.Castro, M.E.Mina, M.J.Hernandez, P.Y.Alvarez, R.Garcia, R.M.Maldonado, R.Padilla, V.M.Morales, L.H.Olivares, A.Cordova, A.G.Ramirez, H.Rivas, J.A.Cedillo, J.C.Hernandez, J.C.Mejia, J.Chavarria, J.M.Ramirez, M.A.Vazquez, S.Medina, S.Moreno, S.Segura, J.Fries, M.Dietz, M.L.Richter, J.Carmona, L.W.Hancock, M.Sonokawa, C.C.Dugas, T.K.Brien, F.Fettig, J.Kosumi, M.Aslan, S.Krause, Z.Liu, D.J.Smith, J.A.Urbanek, L.O'Donnell, C.Welch, J.Hyde, K.M.Klatt, L.M.Jelinek, M.L.Tedford, W.N.Schulz, A.K.Rasmussen, B.A.Vernon, B.G.Turner, B.Porpealia, C.A.Peters, D.J.Thielen, D.J.Vrbicek, D.L.Peterson, D.S.White, G.V.Stevenson, J.A.Lawson, J.A.Riggle, J.A.Robb, J.L.Bartels, J.R.Humphrey, K.D.Bergeron, K.J.Leblanc Sr., K.T.Folkerts, L.A.Roan, L.E.Larocque, L.G.Courteau, M.A.Eley, M.B.Dailey, M.W.Anton, M.W.Rogers, P.S.Murnane, R.D.Goodrich, R.M.Burnett, S.L.Spry, T.D.Christopher, T.G.Tuttle, T.W.Werley, M.L.Wilkins, V.A.Beckett, B.J.Triche, B.M.Olsen Jr, C.A.Ordoyne, D.A.Thibodeaux, J.P.Danos, K.L.Adams, K.W.Bergeron, L.A.Brown, L.R.Reulet, M.G.Tardo, M.H.Williams, R.P.Adams III, R.P.Burgo, W.Johnson, B.Moreno, E.Y.Alvarez, G.Ceballos, G.H.Fernandez , G.Ocon, J.M.Chavez, L.Huerta, L.Monreal, M.D.Cardona, M.Reyes, S.A.Santos, C.A.Lopez, C.A.Ramos, D.H.Ledezma, F.Nuñez, G.Garcia, H.J.Alton, J.A.Monsivais, J.J.Gallegos, J.L.Perez, J.R.Hernandez, O.Linares, T.Urbina, A.A.Gamez, C.Zamora, E.Perez, F.G.Barraza, G.Cortinas, G.Herrera, H.F.Delgado, H.R.Alvarez, I.Talamantes, J.C.Vazquez, J.D.Garcia, J.G.Contreras, J.L.Becerra, J.M.Sanchez, L.A.Garcia, M.Lopez, N.Arguijo, V.Martinez, A.Aab, A.Caliskan, D.Rubcic, H.Deutsch, Z.Maranic, G.Gentry, T.A.Hendrickson, K.D.Qualls, A.R.Lean, A.H.Garza, R.Van Wouw, K.M.O'Brien, A.Maders, L.J.Zeringue, R.C.Brown, J.S.Hunter Jr., L.A.Vaughn, R.A.Cantu, B.Nguyen, J.A.Greer, N.R.Warburton, A.R.Clarkson, D.M.Reynolds, J.Divra, J.L.Guerra, L.A.Uttech, N.K.Kesselring, S.M.Fury, S.M.Sincennes, D.A.Bennetts, J.T.Mussared, K.L.George, K.R.Burgess, L.T.Higham, J.K.Lapeyrouse, J.L.Strother, F.Q.Chang, E.Guerrero, F.D.Ponce, G.Sepulveda, J.G.Herrera, N.E.Rascon, R.Murillo, T.M.Lucero, R.Buettner, K.Bo, D.Ehlers, E.E.Rydell, R.Marchetti, S.A.Hanson, A.A.Meisner, A.L.Laud, A.M.Roberts, B.L.Partin, B.M.Schmitz, C.I.Johnston, C.K.Rodriguez, C.L.Lawson, C.L.Zimmerman, D.D.Wright, D.E.Whisnant, D.I.Mason, D.L.Brown, D.S.Kunst, E.J.Rechtenbach, E.L.Buwalda, G.D.Bracht, H.F.McLean, J.A.Bartz, J.E.Borne, J.L.Shores, J.W.Hogue, K.L.Tuper, K.M.Johnson, K.N.Falardeau, K.Shen, L.A.Pritchard, L.J.Epperson, L.M.Cohen, M.P.Vanalstine, N.K.Schultz, N.M.Boudreaux, P.May, R.M.Hunt, S.C.Eybel, S.D.Barefoot, S.K.Wallace, T.C.Crouch, T.H.Stringer III, W.A.Snook, B.M.Baye, G.M.Pitre, G.P.Bergeron Jr, J.E.Walker Jr, N.P.Boudreaux, P.P.Adams, S.A.Babin, S.J.Dufrene, J.E.Ortega, J.L.Escobedo, L.Ramirez, M.Chavez, M.G.Rodriguez, P.Alvarez, M.R.Zamarron, D.F.Chan, M.B.Sullivan, M.E.Fox, Z.Udovicic, C.Viney, R.Boomer, K.A.Pedersen, S.Rupp, A.D.Welch, A.E.Smith, A.M.Ripley, A.R.Johanningmeier, B.J.Crum Jr., B.M.Buchanan, C.A.Campbell, C.E.Gullatta, C.E.Lawson, C.L.Slattery-Werthmann, C.W.Coakley Jr., D.A.Demick, D.D.Paithane, D.R.Davis, D.W.Patrick, E.D.Tolley Jr., E.S.Seaton, G.J.Oliver, G.J.Schiltz, G.R.Andersen, J.A.Ledford, J.D.Moncier, J.L.Earl, J.P.Goforth, J.R.Whitson, K.R.Moore, L.K.Darnell, L.M.Coleman, M.H.Partin Jr., M.L.Hicks, P.D.Brown, P.D.Taylor, P.L.Foley, R.A.Compton, R.D.Waye, R.G.Norton, R.K.West, R.M.Eberhardt Jr., R.M.Gillian, R.S.Couch, R.S.Peterson, S.A.Kelley, S.D.Butler, S.E.Smith, S.J.Murchison, S.J.Schuck, S.Murray, S.R.Kilby, T.K.Ripley, T.M.Banks, T.M.Harrison Jr., T.M.Mayhew, W.B.Johnson, W.E.Riddle, J.P.G.Soro, E.Riojas, C.T.E.J.Coppus, H.M.T.Litjens, F.Crochard, S.Le Boursicaud, A.Abbas-Mohammad, A.Orlando, D.Uhlendorff, E.Barta, E.Loch, G.Schoerry, G.Suetlue, G.Wiesinger, H.Schulz, H.Weggert, L.Schneble, M.Haass, M.Rosenkranz, P.Wallach, R.Pfisterer, W.Heid, W.Musialla, J.W.Brinkhuis, J.H.Kampherbeek, B.Martron, A.M.Jensen, M.Coulter, F.M.Jones, D.J.Meinders, D.L.Wieland, F.P.Windsor, G.M.Rupchan, G.R.Tolentino, J.G.Langille, J.L.Smith, J.Podence, K.S.Sales, L.F.McBride, M.C.Cleator, M.E.Fairfax, M.J.Lemieux, M.J.Smith, M.J.Stroud, M.S.Earl, N.C.Gibson, P.Beaudry, P.J.Samuelson, R.T.Davies, S.B.Perez, S.S.Khatri, T.V.Haight, W.A.Sherrod, W.A.Slaughter, M.E.Cillero, B.J.Healy, A.J.Bruno, C.Collins, G.W.Webber Jr, J.A.Pitre III, J.J.Hubbell, L.Jack Jr., M.A.Bourgeois, M.B.Stewart, M.L.Fuller, R.T.Borne, S.M.Arceneaux, A.Aro, A.O.Pinela, C.A.Martinez, C.Garcia, J.G.Murillo, L.Torres, M.D.J.Olivas, M.I.Hernandez, M.O.Espinoza, M.R.Rangel, A.Rocha, A.Rodriguez, L.L.Ledet, W.G.Qu, M.Lindenberger, J.S.Millick, C.G.Keplinger III, M.H.Legendre, J.A.Garza, A.C.Scott, A.M.Brown, B.N.Crum, C.M.McAmis, D.E.Castor, E.D.Cobbs, H.A.Rust, J.E.Ricker, J.J.Bowers, K.A.Brown, K.J.Evans, L.M.Fuller, L.N.Waddell, M.G.Dobson, M.P.McMahon, O.Stewart Jr., P.A.Wilkerson, R.A.Spillman, R.G.McEwen, R.R.Carmack, S.C.Roberts, S.D.Franklin, S.R.Cooper, T.A.Lamb, T.C.Freeman, T.E.Mathis, T.L.Sams, T.M.Johnson, V.C.Stanton, V.L.Tignor, J.Coultas, S.M.Sheffler, A.D.Narveson, M.A.Razzaque, R.W.Crowell, A.J.Schneider, A.M.Bridgeman, H.D.Dunwoody, J.L.Newkirk, J.M.Frazier, K.B.Shuler, T.C.Cooper, V.H.Helvey, W.L.McDonald, D.R.Basham, J.G.Roddy, P.C.Strausser, D.L.Garcia, M.V.Paez, J.G.Rios, D.Ngo, R.J.Bartlett, N.A.Acosta, W.G.Ciupka, B.Fiffe, J.Holihan, R.Bridgeman, E.C.Lowell, J.A.Nazzaro, J.C.Martin, J.J.Jacobs, L.C.Olson, S.C.Koziatek, J.H.Ahlf, J.J.Martin, S.Rodas, S.Ponce, J.H.Morales, T.Dang, B.P.Lewman, C.R.Grabatin, D.M.Celetti, J.A.Martin, M.M.Dickson-Schmidt, S.L.Blalock, V.R.Swarts, M.L.Garcia, R.Caldera, A.R.Winter, A.L.Geary, C.C.Knebusch, C.J.Valentine, D.J.Fox, J.D.McCloud, J.H.Owens Jr., M.M.Ordoyne, M.W.Lee, N.C.Young, R.H.Fender, T.J.Goerdt, Y.Pierre-Louis, C.E.Á.Cesar, R.S.Moura, M.J.Ordoyne, C.A.Sabka, E.Li, E.Zhou, F.Tian, O.Salazar, C.R.Atkins, D.H.Buchanan, D.R.Reed Jr., G.M.Williams, H.Schide, J.R.Fowler, K.T.Green, L.M.Taylor, L.S.Mills, M.J.White, R.W.Shaffer Jr., T.E.Walton, T.H.Campbell, T.L.Ward, N.H.Gilardoni, C.M.Williams, D.Pasch

MRP-9000 software installation team, Jiamusi, China, 1999

John Deere At a Glance

Scope: John Deere is one of the world's oldest and most respected enterprises. The company does business in more than 160 countries, manufactures products in 10 countries, and employs more than 38,000 people worldwide.

Longevity: John Deere is one of the five oldest companies in the U.S. (Only DuPont, Colgate-Palmolive, Cooper Industries, and Phelps Dodge are older, according to Moody's Manuals and the Fortune 500 listing.)

Operations: John Deere has been the free world's largest producer of agricultural equipment since 1963 and is a leading producer of construction and forestry equipment. The company markets North America's broadest line of commercial and consumer grounds-care equipment for homeowners and commercial users. Its power systems division is a major producer of diesel engines for off-highway use and builds various powertrain components for Original Equipment Manufacturers.

John Deere is also a significant supplier of parts for its own products as well as those of other manufacturers. John Deere Credit is among the United States' 25 largest sources of retail and lease financing, providing credit financing for agricultural, industrial, lawn and grounds care, and recreational equipment, and revolving credit for agricultural-input purchases. John Deere Health Care subsidiaries provide health-care benefit-management services to more than 1,100 client companies.

Dealer Network: The company has nearly 5,000 dealers worldwide, including approximately 1,600 agricultural equipment dealer locations in the United States and Canada, and about 2,800 worldwide when including industrial (construction and forestry equipment, and engines) and lawn and grounds care equipment dealers.

Corporate Headquarters:
Completed in 1964, the Deere & Company Administrative Center on the outskirts of Moline, Illinois, was designed by the renowned architect, Eero Saarinen. The building has received many architectural awards, including the Gold Medal of the American Institute of Architects in 1965.

Worldwide Customers

Agricultural Equipment

World's premier producer of agricultural equipment.

Major customers: farmers around the world, including commercial, or custom harvesting and baling operations.

Key products: full line of farm machinery, including 4-wheel-drive, row-crop, and utility tractors; combine and sugarcane harvesters; cotton pickers; tillage, seeding, and hay equipment.

Construction Equipment

Leader in forestry equipment; among leaders in many types of construction equipment.

Major customers: utility, underground, and earth moving contractors—both large and small—as well as rental companies, municipalities, loggers, and other forestry specialists.

Key products: construction and forestry equipment such as backhoes, crawler dozers, four-wheel-drive loaders, excavators, and log skidders.

Commercial and Consumer Equipment

World leader in premium turf-care equipment and work vehicles.

Major customers: homeowners, commercial-mowing and grounds-care operations, golf courses, farmers and motor home owners.

Key products: lawn and garden tractors, commercial and homeowner mowing equipment, utility tractors and vehicles, skid-steer loaders, golf and turf equipment, handheld power products.

Credit

Major provider of financing and leasing to agricultural, construction and grounds-care customers.

Major customers: on retail level, owners of agricultural, construction, and grounds-care equipment, as well as motor homes. At wholesale, dealers of agricultural and construction machinery, engines, manufactured housing, and recreational vehicles.

Key products: retail and wholesale financing, leasing, revolving credit, and crop-production loans.

Health Care

Health-benefits provider that plays key role in containing John Deere health-care expenses.

Major customers: John Deere employees, as well as employees of some 1,600 other companies and government agencies in four states.

Key products: managed health-care services, including John Deere Health Plan, Inc., a health-maintenance organization, and John Deere Health Care, Inc., a manager of health-benefit services.

Parts

Major provider of repair parts, accessories and aftermarket support.

Major customers: owners/operators of John Deere and other makes of farm, construction, and lawn-care equipment.

Key products: warehouses and distributes more than 350,000 different parts for John Deere and other makes of equipment.

Power Systems

Leading manufacturer of off-highway, diesel engines for internal use; growing presence in original equipment manufacturer markets.

Major customers: John Deere equipment divisions, other OEMs, and makers of stationary equipment such as irrigation pumps and generator sets.

Key products: diesel and natural-gas engines, transmissions, and powertrain components.

Special Technologies

Five operating units, providing range of electronics-related products and services.

Major customers: John Deere equipment divisions, other equipment and vehicle manufacturers.

Key products: agribusiness information-management systems, mobile equipment control and monitoring devices, Internet-based agribusiness data collector, and vehicle-tracking systems.

Worldwide Locations

Agricultural Equipment

Factories and Engineering Centers

Arc-les-Gray, France
*balers, forage equipment,
material-handling equipment*

Bruchsal, Germany
tractor and combine cabs

Catalao, Brazil
sugarcane harvesters

Des Moines, Iowa
*cotton harvesting, tillage,
and planting equipment*

East Moline and Silvis, Illinois
combine harvesters and engineering center

Horizontina, Brazil
*agricultural tractors, combine
harvesters, planting equipment*

Horst, Netherlands
spraying equipment

Jiamusi, China*
combine harvesters

Madrid, Spain
components

Mannheim, Germany
agricultural tractors

Moline, Illinois
*planting equipment and
hydraulic cylinders*

Monterrey, Mexico
tillage tools, cultivating equipment

Nigel, South Africa
tillage and planting equipment

Ottumwa, Iowa
hay and forage equipment

Pune, India*
tractors and engines

Rosario, Argentina
seed equipment and components

Saltillo, Mexico
agricultural tractors

Stadtlohn, Germany
headers for self-propelled forage harvesters

Thibodaux, Louisiana
sugarcane harvesters, spraying equipment

Valley City, North Dakota
air seeding equipment

Waterloo, Iowa
*agricultural tractors and major components;
engineering center; foundry*

Welland, Ontario, Canada
material-handling equipment, rotary cutters

Zweibrücken, Germany
combine harvesters, forage equipment

Sales and Administration Offices

North America:
Atlanta, Georgia
Columbus, Ohio
Dallas, Texas
Davenport, Iowa
Grimsby, Ontario, Canada
Kansas City, Missouri
Lenexa, Kansas
Minneapolis, Minnesota
Moline, Illinois
Monterrey, Mexico
Reno, Nevada

Outside North America:
Beijing, China
Brisbane, Australia
Madrid, Spain
Mannheim, Germany
Milan, Italy
Montevideo, Uruguay
Nigel, South Africa
Nottingham, England
Ormes, France
Rosario, Argentina

Construction Equipment

Factories and Engineering Centers

Davenport, Iowa
construction and forestry equipment

Dubuque, Iowa
construction equipment

Edmonton, Alberta, Canada
remanufactured components

Kernersville, North Carolina
Deere-Hitachi Construction Machinery Corporation**
excavators

Richards Bay, South Africa*
articulated dump trucks

Saltillo, Mexico
excavators

Vancouver, British Columbia, Canada*
hydraulic excavators

Sales and Administration Offices

Atlanta, Georgia
Baltimore, Maryland
Dallas, Texas
Denver, Colorado
Grimsby, Ontario, Canada
Moline and Vernon Hills, Illinois
Phoenix, Arizona
Seattle, Washington

Commercial & Consumer Equipment

Factories and Engineering Centers

Augusta, Georgia
commercial utility tractors

Chihuahua, Mexico
handheld power products

Columbia, South Carolina
saw chain

Enschede, Netherlands
commercial riding mowers

Greeneville, Tennessee
walk-behind mowers and lawn tractors

Greer, South Carolina
handheld power products

Gummersbach, Germany
walk-behind mowers

Horicon, Wisconsin
lawn and garden equipment

Knoxville, Tennessee
commercial products

Raleigh, North Carolina
commercial and golf and turf mowers

Welland, Ontario, Canada
utility vehicles

Williamsburg, Virginia
utility vehicles

Sales and Administration Offices

Charlotte and Raleigh, North Carolina
Knoxville, Tennessee

Deere Power Systems Group

Factories and Engineering Centers

Coffeyville, Kansas
power transmission equipment

Dubuque, Iowa
engines

Rosario, Argentina
engines

Saran, France
engines

Springfield, Missouri*
engines, remanufactured engines

Torreon, Mexico
engines and axles

Waterloo, Iowa
engines

Sales and Administration Offices

Saran, France
Waterloo, Iowa

Special Technologies Group

Factories and Engineering Centers

John Deere Special Technologies Group, Inc.
Atlanta, Georgia

AGRIS Corporation
Atlanta, Georgia

John Deere Information Systems (JDIS)
Moline, Illinois

Navcom Technology, Inc.
Redondo Beach, California

Phoenix International Corporation
Fargo, North Dakota

VantagePoint Network
Fort Collins, Colorado

Parts Distribution Centers

Bruchsal, Germany
Indianapolis, Indiana
Milan, Illinois

Export Sales Branches

Mannheim, Germany
Moline, Illinois

John Deere Credit

John Deere Credit Company
Moline, Illinois; West Des Moines, Iowa

John Deere Capital Corporation
Reno, Nevada

Deere Credit Services, Inc.
Madison, Wisconsin; West Des Moines, Iowa

Farm Plan Corporation
Madison, Wisconsin

Deere Credit, Inc.
Bloomington, Illinois; Manasquan, New Jersey;
West Des Moines, Iowa

John Deere Credit Inc.
Burlington, Ontario and Edmonton, Alberta, Canada

Arrendadora John Deere S.A. de C.V.
Monterrey, Nuevo Leon, Mexico

John Deere Credit Limited
Brisbane, Australia

John Deere Credit Limited
Gloucester, England

John Deere Credit Group PLC
Gloucester, England

John Deere Credit S.A.S.
Ormes, France

John Deere Credit – Germany***
Frankfurt, Germany

John Deere Funding Corporation
Reno, Nevada

John Deere Receivables, Inc.
Reno, Nevada

Senstar Capital Corporation
Pittsburgh, Pennsylvania

John Deere Health

John Deere Health Care, Inc.
Moline, Illinois

John Deere Family Healthplan Inc.

John Deere Health Plan, Inc.

Corporate Headquaters

Deere & Company
One John Deere Place
Moline, IL 61265-8098
Phone: (309) 765-8000

www.johndeere.com

* owned by joint venture or affiliate
** joint venture
*** partnership

Selected Bibliography

Books

General Company History

Inside John Deere: A Factory History
(Rod Beemer and Chester Peterson Jr.,
Motorbooks, 1999)

John Deere's Company: A History
of Deere & Company And Its Times
(Wayne G. Broehl, Doubleday, 1984)

Products

Designing the New Generation John Deere Tractors
(Merle L. Miller, ASAE, 1999)

The Big Book of John Deere Tractors
(Don Macmillan, Voyageur Press, 1999)

John Deere New Generation Tractors
(Rod Beemer and Chester Peterson,
Motorbooks, 1998)

John Deere Tractor Data Book
(Lorry Dunning, Motorbooks, 1998 revision)

Deere & Company's Early Tractor Development
(Theo Brown, Two-Cylinder Club, 1997)

The John Deere Styled Letter Series 1939-1952
(J.R. Hobbs, Green Magazine, 1997)

A Specialized Look Into The Unstyled Model A:
The Handbook of the John Deere Model A, 1934-1938
(Wesley W. Malcolm, Malcolm & Malcolm, 1996)

Combines and Harvesters Photographic History
(Jeff Creighton, Motorbooks, 1996)

John Deere Tractors: First Numbered Series,
Models 40, 50, 60, 70, 80 (J.R. Hobbs,
Green Magazine, 1996)

The John Deere 20 Series
(J.R. Hobbs, Green Magazine, 1996)

Farm Tractors 1975-1995 (Larry Gay, ASAE, 1995)

John Deere Buggies and Wagons
(Ralph C. Hughes, ASAE, 1995)

John Deere Model B Restoration Guide
(Robert N. Pripps, Motorbooks, 1995)

John Deere Photographic History
(Robert N. Pripps, Motorbooks, 1995)

Big Green John Deere GP Tractors
(Robert N. Pripps and Andrew Morland,
Motorbooks, 1994)

John Deere 30 Series Photo Archive
(Peter Letourneau, Iconografix, 1994)

John Deere Limited-Production & Experimental Tractors
(Peter Letourneau, Motorbooks, 1994)

John Deere Model A Photo Archive
(Peter Letourneau, Iconografix, 1994)

John Deere Tractors 1918-1994
(Ralph C. Hughes, ASAE, 1994)

John Deere Tractors Worldwide: A Century
of Progress 1893-1993 (Don Macmillan, ASAE, 1994)

The John Deere 30 Series: End of the Two-Cylinder Era
(J.R. Hobbs, Green Magazine, 1994)

The Little Giants: John Deere Dubuque Works Tractors
1947-1960 (J.R. Hobbs, Green Magazine, 1994)

John Deere Farm Tractors: A History of the
John Deere Tractor (Randy Leffingwell,
Motorbooks, 1993)

John Deere General-Purpose Tractors 1928-1953
(Peter Letourneau, Motorbooks, 1993)

John Deere Model B Photo Archive
(Peter Letourneau, Iconografix, 1992)

John Deere Model D Photo Archive
(Peter Letourneau, Iconografix, 1992)

John Deere Two-Cylinder Tractor Buyer's Guide
(Robert N. Pripps, Motorbooks, 1992)

John Deere Tractors and Equipment 1960-1990
(Don Macmillan and Roy Harrington, ASAE, 1991)

John Deere Tractors and Equipment 1837-1959
(Don Macmillan and Russell Jones, ASAE, 1988)

How Johnny Popper Replaced the Horse
(Donald S. Huber and Ralph C. Hughes,
Deere & Company, 1988)

Management, Operation & Service Books

For a complete list, contact a John Deere dealer,
or call 1-800-522-7448, or visit the Web site:
http://www.johndeere.com/about us/pub/jdpub

Children's

How John Deere Tractors and Implements Work
(Roy Harrington, ASAE, 1997)

Grandpa's John Deere Tractors
(Roy Harrington, ASAE, 1996)

A Tractor Goes Farming
(Roy Harrington, ASAE, 1995)

Centennial Surprise
(Lois Hobbs, Deere & Company, 1991)

Pioneer Plowmaker: A Story About John Deere
(David R. Collins, Carolrhoda Books, 1990)

Family Reunion (Lois Hobbs, J.R. Hobbs,
Kris Carr, Deere & Company, 1989)

Johnny Tractor and His Pals
(Louise Price Bell, Deere & Company, 1988)

Corny Corn Picker Finds A Home
(Lois Hobbs, Deere & Company, 1988)

Toys

International Directory of Model Farm Tractors
and Implements (Raymond Crilley Sr. and
Charles Burkholder; Onsted, Michigan, 1993)

The Toy and the Real McCoy (Ralph C. Hughes; ASAE, 1990)

A Guide to Collecting Farm Toys
(Robert Zarse and Eldon Trumm; Worthington, Iowa, 1989)

Evolution of the John Deere Toy
(Eldon Trumm; Worthington, Iowa, 1982)

Dick's Farm Toy Price Guide and Checklist
(Richard Sonnek; Mapleton, Minnesota)

Ertl and Toy Tractors
(Robert Zarse and Eldon Trumm; Worthington, Iowa)

Magazines

Green Magazine, (Bee, Nebraska)

The Toy Farmer, (Claire D. Scheibe; LaMoure, North Dakota)

The Toy Tractor Times, (Rick and Linda Larsen; Osage, Iowa)

Two Cylinder, (Grundy Center, Iowa)

Web sites

http://www.genuinevalue.com

http://www.johndeere.com

Index

quality innovation integrity commitment ubuHle umKhuba ubuQo
integriteit verbintenis स्तरीयता नवीनता सत्यनिष्ठा प्रतिपदता qualidade inovação integridade
dání kvalitet nyhed hederlighed engagement laatu uudistus kokonaisuus sit
tion integrität verpflichtung качество иновация интегритет ангажимент in
novazione onestà impegno ryo-shitsu shinkijiku seijitsu yakusoku pumjil
質 創新 誠實 求信 kwaliteit innovatie integriteit verplichting 품질 혁신 성실
qualidade inovação integridade compromisso calitate inovatie integritate
kovost inovacija neoporecnost obveza calidad innovación integridad con
ність иновация честність рішучість quality innovation integrity commit
обязательство kwaliteit innovasie integriteit verbintenis स्तरीयता नवीनता सत्यनिष्ठा प्रतिपदता
alita inovace celistvost odevzdání kvalitet nyhed hederlighed engagement la
gagement qualität innovation integrität verpflichtung качество иновация in
s komitmen qualità innovazione onestà impegno ryo-shitsu shinkijiku sei
النوعية الابداع الریادة التكـ kwaliteit innovatie integriteit verplichting 품질 혁신 성실
ie qualidade inovação integridade compromisso calitate inovatie integritate
neoporecnost obveza איכות חידוש שלמות התחייבות calidad innovación in
ahhüt quality innovation integrity commitment ubuHle umKhuba ubuQo
rbintenis स्तरीयता नवीनता सत्यनिष्ठा प्रतिपदता qualidade inovação integridade compromis
hed hederlighed engagement качество иновация честность обязательс